Jews in Israel

Jews in Israel
Contemporary Social and Cultural Patterns

Uzi Rebhun and Chaim I. Waxman

Editors

BRANDEIS UNIVERSITY PRESS
PUBLISHED BY UNIVERSITY PRESS OF NEW ENGLAND
HANOVER AND LONDON

Brandeis University Press

Published by University Press of New England,
One Court Street, Lebanon, NH 03766
www.upne.com

© 2004 by Brandeis University Press

Published with the support of the Jacob and Libby Goodman Institute
for the Study of Zionism and Israel.

Designed by Dean Bornstein

Printed in the United States of America
5 4 3 2

ISBN–13: 978–1–58465–327–1
ISBN–10: 1–58465–327–2

Library of Congress Cataloging-in-Publication Data
Jews in Israel : contemporary social and cultural patterns / Uzi Rebhun
and Chaim I. Waxman, editors.
p. cm.
Includes bibliographical references and index.
ISBN 1-58465-327-2
1. Israel—Social conditions. 2. Jews—Israel—Social conditions. 3. Immigrants—Israel—Social conditions. 4. Social integration—Israel. 5. Israel—Civilization.
I. Rebhun, Uzi. II. Waxman, Chaim Isaac.
DS126.5.J43 2003
956.9405—dc22
2003018716

The Tauber Institute for the Study
of European Jewry Series

Jehuda Reinharz, General Editor
Sylvia Fuks Fried, Associate Editor

The Tauber Institute for the Study of European Jewry, established by a gift to Brandeis University from Dr. Laszlo N. Tauber, is dedicated to the memory of the victims of Nazi persecutions between 1933 and 1945. The Institute seeks to study the history and culture of European Jewry in the modern period. The Institute has a special interest in studying the causes, nature, and consequences of the European Jewish catastrophe within the contexts of modern European diplomatic, intellectual, political, and social history.

The Jacob and Libby Goodman Institute for the Study of Zionism and Israel was founded through a gift to Brandeis University by Mrs. Libby Goodman and is organized under the auspices of the Tauber Institute. The Goodman Institute seeks to promote an understanding of the historical and ideological development of the Zionist movement, and the history, society, and culture of the State of Israel.

Gerhard L. Weinberg, 1981
World in the Balance: Behind the Scenes of World War II

Richard Cobb, 1983
French and Germans, Germans and French: A Personal Interpretation of France under Two Occupations, 1914–1918/1940–1944

Eberhard Jäckel, 1984
Hitler in History

Frances Malino and Bernard Wasserstein, editors, 1985
The Jews in Modern France

Jehuda Reinharz and Walter Schatzberg, editors, 1985
The Jewish Response to German Culture: From the Enlightenment to the Second World War

Jacob Katz, 1986
The Darker Side of Genius: Richard Wagner's Anti-Semitism

Jehuda Reinharz, editor, 1987
Living with Antisemitism: Modern Jewish Responses

Michael R. Marrus, 1987
The Holocaust in History

Paul Mendes-Flohr, editor, 1987
The Philosophy of Franz Rosenzweig

Joan G. Roland, 1989
Jews in British India: Identity in a Colonial Era

Yisrael Gutman, Ezra Mendelsohn, Jehuda Reinharz, and Chone Shmeruk,
    editors, 1989
The Jews of Poland Between Two World Wars

Avraham Barkai, 1989
From Boycott to Annihilation: The Economic Struggle of German Jews, 1933–1943

Alexander Altmann, 1991
The Meaning of Jewish Existence: Theological Essays 1930–1939

Magdalena Opalski and Israel Bartal, 1992
Poles and Jews: A Failed Brotherhood

Richard Breitman, 1992
The Architect of Genocide: Himmler and the Final Solution

George L. Mosse, 1993
Confronting the Nation: Jewish and Western Nationalism

Daniel Carpi, 1994
*Between Mussolini and Hitler: The Jews and the Italian Authorities in France
    and Tunisia*

Walter Laqueur and Richard Breitman, 1994
Breaking the Silence: The German Who Exposed the Final Solution

Ismar Schorsch, 1994
From Text to Context: The Turn to History in Modern Judaism

Jacob Katz, 1995
With My Own Eyes: The Autobiography of an Historian

Gideon Shimoni, 1995
The Zionist Ideology

Moshe Prywes and Haim Chertok, 1996
Prisoner of Hope

János Nyiri, 1997
Battlefields and Playgrounds

Alan Mintz, editor, 1997
The Boom in Contemporary Israeli Fiction

Samuel Bak, paintings
Lawrence L. Langer, essay and commentary, 1997
Landscapes of Jewish Experience

Jeffrey Shandler and Beth S. Wenger, editors, 1997
*Encounters with the "Holy Land": Place, Past and Future in American
   Jewish Culture*

Simon Rawidowicz, 1998
State of Israel, Diaspora, and Jewish Continuity: Essays on the "Ever-Dying People"

Jacob Katz, 1998
*A House Divided: Orthodoxy and Schism in Nineteenth-Century
Central European Jewry*

Elisheva Carlebach, John M. Efron, and David N. Myers, editors, 1998
Jewish History and Jewish Memory: Essays in Honor of Yosef Hayim Yerushalmi

Shmuel Almog, Jehuda Reinharz, and Anita Shapira, editors, 1998
Zionism and Religion

Ben Halpern and Jehuda Reinharz, 2000
Zionism and the Creation of a New Society

Walter Laqueur, 2001
Generation Exodus: The Fate of Young Jewish Refugees from Nazi Germany

Yigal Schwartz, 2001
Aharon Appelfeld: From Individual Lament to Tribal Eternity

Renée Poznanski, 2001
Jews in France during World War II

Jehuda Reinharz, 2001
Chaim Weizmann: The Making of a Zionist Leader

Jehuda Reinharz, 2001
Chaim Weizmann: The Making of a Statesman

ChaeRan Y. Freeze, 2002
Jewish Marriage and Divorce in Imperial Russia

Contents

Part VI: Israel and Diaspora Jews

Part VII: Conclusion

For the future
of our children and grandchildren
in Israel's multicultural society

☙

Introduction

It is now more than fifty years since the State of Israel was established. It has passed the initial stages of nation building and is today, in many respects, a Western, technological society. It was never, however, a "new nation," created ex nihilo. It was built, in large measure, on the experience of ideologically driven Jewish settlement in Eretz Israel (Palestine), which began in the nineteenth century. It also had as its background the Holocaust and its tragic results for the Jewish people; war and an ongoing military struggle with neighboring countries; and the necessity of absorbing unprecedented numbers of new immigrants from very different backgrounds. It has a multiethnic population, comprising groups that vary widely in their degree of Jewish cultural traditionalism as well as their level of modernization. While the challenges of immigration, absorption, and the external threat of war served as unifying factors for Jewish society in Israel for much of Israel's history, the situation has shifted in recent years.

Partly as a result of the establishment of formal relations with a number of major Arab neighboring states and the ongoing search for reconciliation with the Palestinian Arabs—a relationship which again flared up and doused aspirations for a speedy accord—the strengthened self-assurance of Israel's long-term existence shifted the focus of Israeli public discourse to domestic matters. In addition, Israel has experienced significant socioeconomic development and, along with it, the emergence of a pattern of individualism characteristic of other advanced Western societies. Additional Western, mainly American, cultural influences, particularly in the area of consumerism, have also, through rapid growth in electronic communication, increasingly penetrated, inter alia, into Israel's social structure. Israel of today is thus a society in transition where different sets of values occasionally increase intergroup tensions and challenge social cohesion. The rhythm of events, trends, and innovation in various areas is intense. Israel continues to be a living laboratory for social research.

This book consists primarily of new articles, as well as a few that are expansions and elaborations of previous work, by foremost specialists on the central issues of contemporary Israeli Jewish society. Our approach to understanding Jewish life in Israel is largely interdisciplinary but with an overriding sociological perspective. We focus on the behaviors of people, rather than institutions or organizations, within the many social, cultural, and political realms. We begin with a social history of Jews in Israel over the last century (Rebhun), to provide background for the rest of the volume. This is followed by a detailed analysis by

Sergio DellaPergola of the major demographic trends among Israeli Jews during the 1990s, including immigration, residential mobility and dispersal, ethnic composition, socioeconomic stratification, family patterns, and population projections.

Absorption processes and integration of new immigrants, including ethnic differences and relations, will be discussed in depth in part II. Sammy Smooha opens the section with an analysis of the two major Jewish ethnic groups, the Ashkenazim and the Sephardim. He reviews the two major theoretical perspectives, conflict and consensus, and provides arguments for an alternative perspective that looks at the persistence of Jewish ethnicity in a series of social and cultural domains. The following two essays analyze the sociodemographic characteristics and absorption processes of the two major recent Jewish immigrant groups. Elazar Leshem and Moshe Sicron focus on Russian immigrants, and Steven Kaplan and Hagar Salamon analyze the Ethiopian Jewish community—Beta Israel—in Israel.

Part III focuses attention on major contemporary social and political patterns. The kibbutz, which was the symbol of the pioneering spirit of the Zionist idea, has undergone revolutionary transformations as part of broader socioeconomic and cultural changes in Israeli society, and this transformation is examined in detail by Eliezer Ben-Rafael and Menachem Topel. The multicultural character of Israeli society manifests itself in significant ways in the political sphere. Asher Arian analyzes the twists and turns in Israeli voting patterns that which have shaped the character of political party strength and governmental coalitions. Hanna Herzog analyzes the significance of gender in various realms as well as the struggles of women in Israeli society. Her analysis is especially revealing, given the symbolically egalitarian role of women in much of classical Zionist ideology. Israel's political structure is unusual in the Western world in that it includes religious political parties that play major roles. This section, accordingly, concludes with a discussion by Chaim I. Waxman of the differential rises and declines of influence by the major religious political parties.

Part IV is devoted to analyses of paradigms of Jewish identity and identification. Eliezer Schweid analyzes the types of Jewish culture created in Israeli society and their manifestations in such central issues as education, national ideology, and literature. Using the latest survey data, Shlomit Levy, Hanna Levinsohn, and Elihu Katz analyze religious beliefs and observances among Israeli Jews, suggesting that they are considerably more entrenched and reflect deeper religious traditionalism than is widely perceived. Although the Orthodox dominate the Israeli religious establishment and Orthodoxy is widely perceived to be the authentic manner of Jewish religiosity, there are non-Orthodox religious movements, Reform and Conservative in particular, and they strive to gain footholds of religious and religio-political legitimacy in Israeli society. These are an-alyzed by Ephraim Tabory. Another alternative to Orthodoxy is the growing movement toward Jewish spirituality associated with secular Israelis searching for Jewish knowledge, a relatively new phenomenon that is examined by Elan Ezrachi.

The realities of geopolitics in the Middle East, with its inherent insecurities, along with the travails of the majority of Israel's Jewish immigrants concerning their countries of origin, play important roles in the civil commitments and col-lective memories of Israelis (part V). Military service has not only a defense di-mension but an important social one as well. The nature of one's military ser-vice and attitudes toward those who do not serve reflect changing social values and commitments in the broader society (Gabriel Ben-Dor and Ami Pedahzur). Ephraim Yuchtman-Yaar and Zeev Shavit discuss Israel's self-definition in the context of Arab-Jewish relationships, as well as the role of Arabs as a minority within Israeli society.

The place of Israel as "The Holy Land" (Eretz Israel) is deeply rooted in Jewish culture. As Yoram Bilu suggests, however, it is not only the land, per se, but specific places that become sanctified within both folk and civil religion. How the process takes place and with what ramifications are the subject of his essay. The Holocaust is also deeply rooted in Israeli consciousness and culture. As Dalia Ofer indicates, it has created an ongoing dialogue between "different voices" that is constantly striving to understand the meaning of the Holocaust as well as to incorporate its lessons into the collective memory of Israel.

The overwhelming majority of world Jewry lives in countries other than Israel. The relationships, both institutional and interpersonal, between Israelis and Diaspora Jews (part VI) have undergone significant change in recent dec-ades, which Gabriel Sheffer analyzes. Despite the ideology of immigration, *aliya,* within Zionism and Israeli culture, there has always been emigration as well. Steven Gold analyzes the patterns of Israeli emigration to Western countries, as well as the emigrants' patterns of adaptation to their new surroundings, con-cluding with their implications for one's identity as a Jew and as an Israeli.

In the "Conclusion," the editors discuss the implications of the various trends and changes for Jewish life in Israel and suggest a number of additional challenges facing Israeli Jewry in the twenty-first century. They especially em-phasize the tension between two conflicting desires: to maintain the unique character of a Jewish state on the one hand, and to embrace the cultural plural-ism and individualism of a modern democratic society on the other.

PART I

Establishing the Framework for
Contemporary Jewish Life in Israel

CHAPTER ONE

Major Trends in the Development of Israeli Jews: A Synthesis of the Last Century

ↄ

Uzi Rebhun

The Ideological Background of Immigration and Settlement in Palestine

Throughout the generations, notwithstanding periods of conquest and violence, the strong ties between the Jewish people and their historical homeland served as a stimulus for the continuous residence of Jews in Palestine. There was always a small group of Jews, often dependent on financial support from the Diaspora, who, impelled by religious or messianic motivations, fulfilled the precept of settling the land. Thus, the difference between modern times and the past does not lie in the existence of settlement per se; the change—toward the end of the nineteenth century—lies rather in the characteristics of the Jewish migrants. Those who came during this period were moved by a nationalist ideology, and aspired to found agricultural settlements, to work the land, and to establish a Hebrew culture in a modern, predominantly secular, atmosphere. Gradually the number of these pioneers increased and Jewish settlements based on the norms of independent labor and production were set up in various parts of the country. These served as an important factor when it came to international recognition of the rights of Jews in Palestine, and they become the central social and political power laying the foundations for the State of Israel (Eliav 1978).

The earliest modern immigrants, influenced by the forerunners of the Zionist nationalist movement, rejected the premise that a Jewish minority can sustain authentic religious life and tradition in a modern, largely non-Jewish society. While the movements of Emancipation and Enlightenment had indeed created a greater measure of tolerance toward Jews, providing them with legal ways to participate in the social and intellectual mainstream of Europe, at the same time they confronted them with novel hardships and dilemmas. Jews were now forced to face the challenges of either merging into the general, mostly Christian society, whose norms were a threat to the traditional Jewish way of life, or maintaining their religious group identification (Avineri 1981). This change in their status gave Jews the choice between social and economic destruction if

3

they did not accept the challenges of liberalization, or spiritual-cultural obliteration by the broad exposure to modern society (Eisenstadt 1967). These were the days of rising nationalism in Europe, which strengthened the awareness of the particularities of each distinct nation. Coming to grips with both emancipation and Nationalism, both of which developments were unique to the late nineteenth century, became the basis of modern Jewish nationalism (Avineri 1981). The ancient bond with Zion made it the natural site for the liberation and new self-definition of the Jewish nation.

With the increase of antisemitism and pogroms in Eastern Europe, and the economic hardships suffered by the Jews, limiting them in their choice of residential areas and discriminating against them in occupational opportunities, many Jews living in the Czarist empire left for the United States or (in much smaller numbers) other countries such as Argentina, South Africa, and Western Europe), exchanging one Diaspora for another. In this same hope for a better life, some tens of thousands of Jews, mostly from the middle classes and intellectual circles, were driven by strong nationalistic motivations to emigrate to and settle in the land of Palestine. The Zionist movement was multifaceted, comprising various philosophies and attitudes. It encompassed: religious Zionists, for whom the rebuilding of Eretz Israel was a religious act and part of a messianic process, and who thus sought to establish a state based on the principles of traditional Judaism; revisionist Zionists, who emphasized the need for Jewish military might and acquisition of territory; and cultural Zionists, who were less interested in Jewish sovereignty than in the cultural-intellectual character of the Jewish community (the Yishuv) (Medoff and Waxman 2000). One of the earliest and largest of these groups was the socialist Zionists. They saw the collective settlement, later to be known as the kibbutz, as the most appropriate form of building the new Jewish society. Its basic principles were those of equality and common possessions: the kibbutz was to meet the needs of all its members, and there was strong emphasis on social justice and security, pitting the principle of social solidarity against economic forces (Eisenstadt 1967). All worked in and for the kibbutz, and all tasks were considered of equal status.

Socialist Zionism was the strongest socioeconomic and political force in the pre-state days. Those who immigrated as *halutzim*, pioneering settlers, were pre-eminent in the various elites of the social construct taking shape in Eretz Israel. Their ideology, which was institutionalized within the frameworks of the Labor parties and the Histadrut—the Federation of Jewish Laborers of Eretz Israel— was the starting point of the infrastructure of the settlements. The leaders of the pioneering immigrations, alongside world Zionist leadership, were largely responsible for the character of the activities and development of the future Jewish society in Israel.

4

The identification of the Zionist revolution in Eretz Israel with socialist ideology was not dictated by the number of land-working pioneers. During the period between 1881—the onset of ideological immigration—and the outbreak of World War I in 1914, the total number of Jewish settlers in Palestine grew from 24,000 to 94,000 (Shavit 1983; Bachi 1974). Yet only 15 percent of these lived in agricultural settlements, and even fewer in collective settlements. However, these settlements were founded in different areas of the country. They widened the territorial expansion of the Jewish population and strengthened the urban centers and were major incentives in the development of Israel's main thoroughfares. Extensive cooperation existed among the various agricultural settlements themselves, as well as between them and the urban centers; there was constant movement of workmen, artisans, merchandise, and services (Shavit 1983). The ideology of the new Jewish settlers viewed the redemption and cultivation of the land as a central social and national value; urban settlement, preferred by the majority of the immigrants, received far less attention and support from the Zionist movement.

The Social and Political Frameworks of the Jewish Community

Following World War I and the establishment of the British Mandate in Palestine, Zionism turned from an ideology into a practical reality. The political basis was laid by the British Empire, which, in the declaration known by the name of Foreign Minister Lord Balfour, stated its explicit approval and support for the founding of a national homeland for the Jewish people in Eretz Israel and assented to facilitating the achievement of this goal. Although the institutional structure of the Jewish population developed under the administration of the British Mandate government, in social and physical surroundings composed mainly of Arabs, the Jews, reflecting a basic wish to create a separate Jewish body, never fully integrated into the British system. The social, cultural, and political structures of the Jewish population were thus not only adapted to its needs at the time, but also symbolized the desire on the part of Jewish society to be a modern Jewish entity (Eisenstadt 1967).

The political and public organization of the Jewish community revolved around two main axes: the World Zionist Organization (and later the Jewish Agency); and the institutions of the Yishuv (lit., settlement), the pre-state Jewish community—the Elected Assembly and the National Council (Rubinstein 1976). The former constituted the dominant bulk and was responsible for Zionist politics and international affairs, whereas the latter, characterized by democratic vote, albeit on a voluntary basis, took care of such internal matters as education, health, culture, and current public affairs. Within the framework of the

World Zionist Organization, decisions were made at two administrative centers: that in London and that in Jerusalem. Though constitutionally speaking both administrations were elected by the Zionist Congress and had equal status, until the mid-thirties London was the site of most of the important political decisions; from then on, Eretz Israel took the lead. This transition was due, among other reasons, to the election of central figures to key positions in the Zionist administration in Jerusalem, chosen from the dominant Labor Party of Eretz Israel—specifically, the election of David Ben-Gurion as head of the Zionist administration in Palestine. This election ended the basically nonparty leadership in Eretz Israel and marked the beginning of Labor Party hegemony. At this point the relations between the Zionist administration and the Yishuv institutions, which were also dominated by members of the Labor Party, deepened. It should be noted that there was cooperation between Labor and smaller parties within the Zionist administration, and coalitions were formed, inter alia, with the religious Zionist parties. The only exception to this coalition building was the Revisionist Party, which was in constant and bitter conflict with the Labor movement.

The active participation of the religious Zionist parties, both in the Zionist administration and in the political and organizational bodies leading the Yishuv, reflects a process of institutionalization that, even though led by secular groups, was by no means militantly anti-religious (Eisenstadt 1967). The secular inclinations of the great majority of the Zionist parties were not as yet formalized in their contention with Jewish religious traditions. Thus the authority of the Chief Rabbinate concerning religious affairs, such as the supervision of ritual slaughter, the kashrut of food, and provision of religious services, was legally established, whereas compromises regarding the religious character of various activities in public life in general were agreed upon. A complementary aspect of the ingathering of population was the revival of the Hebrew language. Within a relatively short period of time Hebrew became the common language of public life in the Yishuv; it not only facilitated communication among all parts of the population, but as a major common cultural component the language served to diminish intergroup tensions between traditional and modern Jews, between religious and secular, between Ashkenazim and Oriental Jews, and among the various socioeconomic strata.

Hebrew became the official language of the educational system developed in Eretz Israel. By teaching various subjects in Hebrew, including the Bible, as central components of the curriculum, the schools helped fashion a new Eretz-Israel human type, which was to become one of the outstanding manifestations of the cultural-national development in the days prior to the establishment of the State of Israel (Rubinstein 1976). Among the prominent features of the elementary educational system was its division into ideologically based sectors. This was due to the segmentation of the Jewish population: the general sector, which stressed nationalist education with its liberal tendencies; the religious sector, which emphasized the study of Judaism and its rituals (*mitzvot*); and the socialist sector, which, in addition to nationalist values, introduced its own ideology. In addition to these groups, which adapted themselves to the national educational system, another quarter of the Jewish pupils studied in the ultra-Orthodox (*haredi*) schools. Elementary schooling was free or cost very little, whereas secondary schools were mostly in private hands and required tuition fees; these prepared pupils for matriculation exams recognized by the Hebrew University (although not by the Mandatory government or by British universities). As a matter of ideology, schools in the agricultural settlements did not expect their pupils to sit for matriculation exams, claiming that education should be for its own sake.

A further expression of the aspiration toward Jewish independence in the Land of Israel was economic. The establishment of an independent Jewish economy comprising various sectors created dependence on the size of immigration and the resulting increase in the Jewish population, as well as on the receipt of funds from abroad (Giladi and Avitzur 1982). The association of the Jewish economy with nationalist goals and the general political struggle of the Yishuv influenced the lines along which the economy expanded, giving top priority to agricultural development, with industry and commerce taking second place. On the whole, the occupational structure of the population was similar to that of the developed countries, and the demographic increase of the Jewish settlers brought about a relative growth in the internal market. Nevertheless, demand did not exceed supply, and during most of the period between the two World Wars the rate of inflation was negative.

In fact, both the political struggle and the development of Jewish society in Palestine were motivated by the constant arrival of immigrants, the development of settlements, and growth in the number of Jewish inhabitants in the cities and villages alike. Ultimately, these were the major factors in the decision to establish a Jewish state. In those days, the arrival of Jews in Palestine was not a given. Until 1936 the immigration policy of the British Mandatory government was selective, based upon economic criteria: the number of immigrants was to be no larger than the ability of the economy to absorb them, as assessed by the British. It seems, however, that various developments abroad greatly influenced the pace and extent of immigration to Palestine. Not least among these were the limits imposed by the United States on immigration to that country; political upheavals in Eastern Europe and later in central Europe; and of course the economic crisis there. In other words, the greater the need of the Jews to leave their countries of residence, the fewer were the options, and settling in the once most desired countries, mainly the United States, became ever more difficult. Thus, for an increasing proportion of Jewish immigrants, Eretz Israel became an alternative destination. After 1937, the restrictions on migration into Palestine became even more stringent, being now based on demographic and political criteria aimed at maintaining a balance between the Jewish and Arab populations. Now, and particularly after World War II, this policy prevented access to Jews who wanted to settle in Eretz Israel, in particular refugees and Holocaust survivors. Toward the end of the British Mandate, many of the Jews who wished to enter Palestine did so illegally, thus becoming an important symbol in the struggle for Jewish national independence (Goldscheider 2002).

The Foundation of the Jewish State

On the eve of the foundation of the State of Israel in 1948, the Jewish population in Palestine was estimated at 650,000. Over 110,000 lived in agricultural settlements all over the country, including kibbutzim, collective settlements, and *moshavot*. The overwhelming majority of the population (85 percent) was Ashkenazic, coming from Europe (and a few from America), with only a small percentage from the Oriental countries. This lack of ethnic balance was also obvious from the settlement patterns of the two groups: most of the settlers who turned to (mostly collective) agricultural settlements were Eastern Europeans, whereas the Oriental Jews tended to settle in the cities, particularly in "holy cities" such as Jerusalem and Safed. This tendency reflects, inter alia, their diverse reasons for immigration: Zionist ideology on the one hand, religious-messianic on the other. The Oriental Jews had been less exposed to modernization processes in their countries of origin, making their social and cultural adaptation on arrival in Eretz Israel more difficult. A large percentage of these Jews retained a lower socioeconomic status, and were concentrated within the frameworks of institutions and political parties based on ethnic consciousness (Eisenstadt 1967).

The United Nations (U.N.) decision of November 29, 1947, granting the Jewish people a Jewish state in parts of Palestine, served as the international pledge for the establishment of the state of Israel. This decision demanded termination of the British Mandatory rule in Palestine. The political solution of the territorial question entailed a division into two states, one Jewish and one Arab. Jerusalem and its surroundings were to become a separate entity, "*corpus separatum*," under international dominion, administered by the U.N. Many factors made the U.N. decision feasible—above all the need for a solution of the problem of the Jewish people, particularly after the events of World War II. However, there can be no doubt that the readiness of the Jewish population in

Palestine in terms of numbers, economic situation, and military force, as well as the experience in self-rule accumulated by the political governing bodies, all pushed in the direction of the acceptance of the rule over a new sovereign state.

The proclamation of the State of Israel on May 14, 1948, found the new state in a cruel military struggle. This began in the summer of 1947, with local Arab forces bringing the long-standing Jewish-Arab conflict to a breaking point. This conflict had already been going on in varying degrees during the period of the British Mandate, and continued when the armies of four Arab states invaded the territory of Israel the day after the declaration of the state. This war, known in Israeli historiography as the "War of Independence," is important for an understanding of the Israel-Arab struggle, which has continued to this day. It is also a decisive factor in the understanding of specific internal processes in the Jewish society living in Israel. The outcome of the war drastically changed the geopolitical division of Israel, as well as the demographic composition of its parts. Israel's territory extended over larger tracts than those allotted her by the U.N. plan, to the north, east, and south. It also included the western part of Jerusalem. However, dominion over Judaea and Samaria and the eastern part of Jerusalem remained in the hands of the Hashemite Kingdom of Jordan; a strip of land to the Southwest—the Gaza Strip—was under Egyptian military rule. The Palestinians were left without a state of their own, and hundreds of thousands of refugees were scattered throughout the Arab world.

Shortly after the founding of the state, the Israeli Defense Forces (IDF) were officially established; this army was to replace the Hagana, the independent Jewish defense force, which had been active in the days of the British Mandate. The transition from an organization such as the Hagana, which functioned on a voluntary basis, to a regular state army under a constant, tangible security threat demanded, first of all, an increase in manpower. There was no escaping the need for compulsory service of both men and women. Additional manpower was drafted from among the new immigrants who reached Israel's shores from refugee camps in Europe, as well as from North Africa and the Middle East. While enlisting people for the war effort, it was nevertheless essential to maintain the country's economy, toward which end people had to be held back in industrial plants, harbors, agriculture, and vital public services (Pa'il 1983).

The War of Independence officially ended in July 1949 with the signing of armistice agreements, but without a peace agreement between Israel and the Arab states. The first years of Israeli statehood evinced the problems and challenges which were to accompany Israeli society in the future, even to the present: the necessity for a strong military force for self-defense, absorption of immigration, and the building of an economy that balances the wish to develop a free modern economy with the constant need to maintain Israel's security. These circumstances no doubt influenced political behavior, the social cohesion of the Jewish population, the country's cultural penchant, and the nature of Jewish and Israeli identity in both private and public life. The interaction among these aspects is a dynamic one, with each of them experiencing ups and downs, periods of ebb and flow, and in turn influencing prospects in other realms. In addition, Israel is open to outside modernizing and Westernizing influences as well as the phenomenon of globalization, all of which factors may explain the directions of some of the changes taking place.

The Jewish community made the transition from an autonomous political organization within the framework of the British Mandate to a functioning sovereign state without major internal crises. The declaration of the state in turn gave new status to the existing organizations and governing bodies. These required various technical and administrative preparations, mainly, the transformation of certain political structures from one level of institutionalization to another (Horowitz and Lissak 1978); a number of temporary governing appointments, such as a parliament to serve until the first elections, were imperative, and several committees to prepare ministries of economy, foreign affairs, and municipalities were nominated. The constitution of these bodies reflected the balance of the political powers within the Yishuv on the eve of the establishment of the state, reflecting the democratic character of the sovereign Jewish society. According to the constitutional structure, the head of state is a president elected by the Knesset, whose functions are mainly ceremonial and representative. The governing institutions consist of the legislative authorities, that is, the Knesset elected by secret ballot on the basis of proportional representation from party lists for a period of four years; executive authorities, that is, the government, whose members are nominated by a prime minister apparent who, having been appointed to this function by the president of the state, must form a government approved by the Knesset; and judicial authorities, including civil and rabbinic courts.

Even though Israeli governments have always been made up of coalitions comprising several parties (as there was never any one party large enough to have an absolute majority in the Knesset), for the first thirty years of statehood all governments were formed and led by the Labor Party. This reflected the continuation of the ideological preference of the Yishuv from the days preceding the founding of the state. The boundaries of the various coalitions highlighted the exclusion of the Revisionist Party on the one hand, and the Communists on the other. Even a non-Zionist, ultra-Orthodox party (Agudat Israel) joined the first temporary government, as did several others later on. Because of the political hegemony of the Labor Party, a number of central ministries were in the hands of members of this party, imbuing them with a socialistic influence. They stressed the fusion of tradition with modernism, as was felt in many spheres of life starting with security and foreign affairs, through the structure of the Israeli economy, and even in cultural and welfare services (Eisenstadt 1967).

The Ingathering of Exiles

The establishment of the state signaled the opening of the gates for mass immigration of Jews. Immigration and the ingathering of Jews from the various diasporas were foremost on the ideological agenda of Zionism and of the sovereign Israeli society. As stated in the Declaration of Independence, "the State of Israel will be open to Jewish immigration." This was reinforced by the Law of Return of 1950, which declares the right of every Jew to come and settle in Israel as an immigrant, immediately receiving full rights of citizenship upon arrival. This was also the time to legitimize the status of those who had entered the country illegally in the days of the British Mandate. During the first three and a half years after the establishment of the state, until the end of 1951, about 680,000 Jews immigrated to Israel. The original population doubled itself and now numbered about 1.4 million. In those days immigration was unrestricted and for the greater part unselective. The first to come were Jews from Europe, uprooted Jews and concentration camp survivors. These were followed by Jews from Asia and later from Africa. One of the impressive phenomena of those days was the uprooting of entire Jewish communities, such as those of Iraq, Yemen, Bulgaria, and Libya, and their transplantation to Israel. By the end of 1951 hardly any Jews were left in the Arabic-speaking countries of Asia.

These special circumstances, involving the doubling of the population within a very few years and the need to absorb all the newcomers, greatly challenged the entire population and put a heavy burden on the local economy. Most of the immigrants were economically weak, many had little education and meager vocational skills, and they did not speak Hebrew. They needed to be supplied with food, clothing, housing, and some kind of work. The state took this obligation upon itself at a time when funds were low, as a result of the military effort that accompanied the establishment of the state.

The situation called for austerity. Prices were strictly controlled and, more significant, food supplies and other basic commodities were rationed and could only be bought by means of special coupons distributed by the government; the entire system was called *Tzena* (austerity). Despite certain criticism, on the whole this regime went hand in hand with a more general attitude in favor of governmental involvement and supervision over the economy, especially in times of crisis.

After a relative lull between the years 1952 and 1954 another, far more modest, wave of immigration arrived. This flow was more planned and regulated by the government. In general, Jewish immigration to Israel presents a wavelike pattern: there are years with large numbers of immigrants and others with fewer. The waves remain heterogeneous, however, consisting of Jews from both Europe and Africa. By 1965, over half a million additional immigrants had reached the country. The mid-sixties is an important point in the history of immigration to Israel: it marks the termination of Jewish immigration from Asia and Africa (except for Ethiopia), after which only very small numbers of Jews remained in these countries.

A few years later, between 1968 and 1973, immigration was again on the rise. The two main sources were the Soviet Union and its neighboring states, satellites of the Soviet Union in Eastern Europe; small groups received permission to leave for the first time after more than forty years. Jews also came from North and South America and from Western Europe, all of them attracted to Israel by the optimism and euphoria that followed in the wake of the Six Day War, specifically after the reunification of Jerusalem. From then until the late 1980s, the number of immigrants was small and on the whole showed a continuous tendency toward decline (DellaPergola 1986, 1999).

One of the outstanding features of immigration to Israel is its heterogeneous nature. During the first five decades of Israel's statehood, the country absorbed immigrants from over forty different countries, all over the globe. The ratio between the European and American Jews, on the one hand, and Asian and African Jews, on the other, changed dramatically, owing at least in part to their different patterns of fertility: the pronounced majority enjoyed by Ashkenazic Jews in 1948 was balanced over the years. But in addition to the numerical aspect there were obvious social and cultural differences between the sectors, which came to be a central domestic problem with which Israeli society would grapple for many years to come. The encounter between the immigrants and the process of their absorption and integration into established Jewish society were conducted according to the Zionist way of thinking. This ideology stressed such ideas as "ingathering of exiles" and "fusion of exiles," implying homogeneity and equality within the new Israeli society. The "melting-pot"—the creation of patterns of behavior that would mix and unify the multiform cultures and values of the heterogeneous groups of immigrants so as to absorb them into the existing society—seemed the ideal model to the Zionist vision. Nonetheless, there was a preference, even if latent, for Western European patterns of behavior. This may have something to do with the origin of the leading figures of the country at that time, or with the aspiration to build a nation that would soon become one of the leading nations of the world (Schmelz, DellaPergola, and Avner

1991). Hence, the meeting between the Oriental immigrants and the existing Israeli social and cultural structures was highly traumatic.

The normative and cultural differences came to light in many fields. These comprise, among others, the nature of the Hebrew spoken in Israel and the disparate nature of Oriental and European religiosity; family patterns and division of functions between the sexes and generations; consumption patterns; entertainment and dress codes. On the ideological-political level, the intellectual discourse of the Ashkenazic veterans or European immigrants involved such notions as socialism, modernism, and pioneering, all of which were foreign to most of the Oriental immigrants (Lissak 1998).

The two ethnic groups also differed significantly in their structural characteristics. The level of education of immigrants from Asian or African countries was, on the whole, lower than that of European immigrants; they lacked skills in "modern" occupations, and stayed at the lower levels of the economic ladder, earning little (Sicron 1986). Whether as a result of social and cultural characteristics, or because of availability of housing and the policy of population dispersion, physical distance was created between the ethnic groups, augmenting the basic social polarization (Lissak 1998). The European immigrants found houses and unpopulated areas in the more central and urban regions of the country. In those cases in which they were housed in temporary dwellings (*ma'abarot*), they managed to leave quickly, thanks to a certain amount of money available to them, to their professional skills, or connections with veteran Israelis or with the housing authorities. By contrast, immigrants from Asia and Africa were settled in semiperipheral spots around the larger cities or in outlying regions of the country, far from the major centers of economic, cultural, and political activity (Schmelz, DellaPergola, and Avner 1991).

Toward Social and Cultural Polarization

With time, certain geographical and social changes in the situation of the Oriental immigrants started to take place: there began to be upward mobility and an increasing measure of integration in various social fields. The geographical distribution of these immigrants and their children—second generation in Israel—became better balanced in all parts of the country; there was an overall increase in the number of those who graduated high school and received higher education; interethnic marriages became more common, until today they represent about a quarter of all newlyweds. Nevertheless, some of the gaps between Sephardim and Ashkenazim in certain vital spheres are still significant, creating the ongoing feeling among large parts of Israeli society of an overlap between ethnic origin and social status.

Moreover, there was a feeling among the Oriental Jews of not belonging to the social mainstream, and particularly of not taking part in political life in Israel. This and other factors led this sector—toward the end of the 1970s—to turn their feelings of deprivation into political protest; in large numbers, they gave their vote to the Revisionist Party (Herut-Likud), in the opposition since the foundation of the state, a move that greatly contributed to the political turn-around of 1977 (Eisenstadt 1984). At this stage some Oriental Jews began to protest against the existing system; others entered the social-political core by becoming part of the existing parties and influencing then from within. A few years later this process caused a situation in which they separated and formed a party of their own (Shas), which, notwithstanding the fact that its leaders and ideology are Orthodox (and even ultra-Orthodox), enjoys massive support among (non-Orthodox) traditional Oriental Jews, who regard this party as representing their interests as the socially and economically weaker population.

The political protest of the Oriental Jews was one of the first signs of a broader transformation from the ideal of Israel as a "melting-pot" to that of a pluralistic, multicultural society in which individualism is respected and each community is free to adhere to and express its own values and traditions. This change took place after a long period of internal cohesion and common responsibility in facing the challenges of nation building, absorption of immigration, and economic development, all of which were accomplished while simultaneously meeting military threats and other emergencies. After the consolidation of the institutional frameworks, a certain feeling of security and economic well-being prevailed. Subsequent to the peace agreement with Egypt and the onset of apparent reconciliation with the Arab world, which began in 1979 and led to the Oslo agreements with the Palestinian authorities and the peace treaty with Jordan, some effort was turned inward to shaping the lifestyle and character of the Jewish nation in its country. The aims were to achieve more individual freedom and independence and less religious coercion. The growing strength of ethnically oriented political parties, first of the Oriental Jews and then of the immigrants from the USSR who began arriving in large numbers at the end of the 1980s, is a political reflection of this tendency. The same disposition is seen in cultural areas, such as the decline in the status of the youth movements and what they stood for—simplicity, the value of working for the good of others, and collectivity—in favor of Western forms of entertainment stressing materialism and individualism. Another facet of these changes is the increase in the number of those who shirk draft to the Israel Defense Force (IDF) and subsequent reserve duties, and a general decline in concern for duties and commitments toward the country as a whole; the weakened status of the kibbutz; the efforts of nonreligious factions to change the status quo pertaining to religious affairs; and an overall attempt to lessen the influence of religion on public life in Israel.

This last point, the strife between the religious and the nonreligious, is the locus of increasingly acrimonious cultural polarization. Religious disputes always existed between these two sectors of the Israeli public. During the early days of statehood the Jewish character of Israeli society was defined by several compromises on major issues, and the religious identity of the state was agreed upon. A major point of agreement was the nondivision between state and religion. These compromises had far-reaching consequences for central public issues: rabbinical courts were given the authority to deal with all matters of personal and family law; the character of the Sabbath and of Jewish holidays was to be preserved; and food in official places would be kosher (Etzioni-Halevy 2002). The status quo, requiring freedom of religion in private life and a traditional Jewish character to public life, has lately been under much fire. Resulting to a large extent from modernization and progress in technology and from a much greater emphasis on materialism and individualism, consumption and entertainment patterns have changed, as has the quality of life. Today, many nonreligious Israelis are demanding that shops and malls be open on the Sabbath; they want all places of entertainment to be open seven days a week; they consume fast food in international (mostly American) restaurants, which often means nonkosher food, and in general their tastes have become more Epicurean. They learn about new dress and language styles through television and the Internet, and have on the whole become more permissive in sexual matters as well. At the same time, there is a tendency within religious circles toward stricter adherence to the *mitzvot,* and the younger generation of today is more observant than were their parents (Etzioni-Halevy 2002). These circumstances have made it very hard to find a middle-of-the-road sense of identity to please all tastes and beliefs.

Among the questions relating to religious issues, the legal definition of "Who is a Jew?" is the most central. The pluralistic attitude expressed by the leftist leaders holds that any person who declares himself to be Jewish is a Jew and should be legally considered as such without any need for further proof. This is opposed to the demand of the religious parties that in order to be considered a Jew a person must present evidence that his or her mother was Jewish or that he or she converted to Judaism according to Jewish law (Eisenstadt 1967). Eventually, after years during which the nonreligious attitude had prevailed, it was ruled at the end of the 1950s that conversion should be in accordance with *halakha,* traditional Jewish religious law. The entire issue, which comes up again and again, is strongly associated with the ties between Israel and Diaspora Jewry, mainly that of the United States. Not only does the largest Jewish community live there, but most American Jews identify with either Conservative or Reform Judaism, both of which aspire, each in its own way (the first less, the second more so), to adapt *halakha* to the present-day realities of a pluralistic, modern society. Despite great efforts by both the Conservative and the Reform movements to achieve official recognition in Israel of conversions conducted by their rabbis, up to now they have failed. This is also the case in the question of recognition of these two communities and their rabbis on issues of family law and their representation in the official religious councils in Israel. All this means that conversions—the need for which has increased in Israel of the late 1990s with the massive immigration from the former USSR, among whom there are many mixed marriages—are strictly supervised and must follow the principles of Orthodox Judaism. More generally speaking, the lack of official acceptance of non-Orthodox rabbis in Israel, particularly restrictions barring them from officiating in various religious life-cycle events, is one of the topics, and probably the most crucial one, discouraging American Jewry from making strong bonds with Israel (American Jewish Committee 1995).

The rift between the religious and nonreligious in Israel parallels the political controversy between these two camps on the question of the state's borders and the peace process. Though traditionally the ideological split between Left and Right reflected support of socialist as against nonsocialist Zionism, with Israel's rapid progress toward a capitalistic economy this difference now reflects mainly political opinion, particularly concerning the future of the territories Israel has held since the Six Day War and peace with the neighboring Arab countries. After the signing of peace agreements with Egypt and Jordan, the controversy now concerns the Golan Heights on the Syrian border, Judea and Samaria, and East Jerusalem, all of which for many religious Jews are part of the God-given promise of a homeland for the people of Israel. This dispute has intensified over the past decade, in light of the change in relations with the Palestinians, leading to a rift whose climax was the assassination of Prime Minister Yitzhak Rabin in 1995.

Complexities and Uncertainties at the Turn of the Twenty-First Century

These controversies does not necessarily point to well-defined, clear-cut divisions between Ashkenazim and Sephardim within Israeli society, nor between religious and nonreligious, nor even between leftists and rightists. With the growing rate of interethnic marriages and the increasing number of second- and third-generation Israelis, ethnic identity receives a new meaning without much relation to personal experience or any explicit feeling of group belonging. There is no clear dichotomy between the religious and nonreligious, since the majority of Israeli society has some affinity with Jewish tradition and its customs. The same is true of the political constellation, in which there is no reliable congruence between political and religious stances. For example, while there are many religious Israelis who object to a political compromise, and many nonreligious who find themselves at the left end of the political spectrum, the convergence of the religious organizations with parties who agree to territorial concessions in Eretz Israel carries great weight; and there are parties headed by nonreligious leaders that are adamant regarding any territorial modifications. Oriental Jews can be found in both leftist and rightist parties. Ethnic origins are no indication of religious ties, so that Ashkenazic Jews are found both in ultra-Orthodox parties and in parties fighting religious coercion. It stands to reason that, if there is a correlation at all between any two features, it will be between Oriental background and a relatively greater valuing of religious traditions.

Moreover, it may well be, though it is too early yet to fully evaluate the situation, that the violence that erupted in the fall of 2000 between Israel and the Palestinians, known as "Intifida El-Aqza," has caused many of those who hitherto held moderate political views to rethink their position. This violence has deeply wounded any emergent feelings of mutual trust, as a result of which a greater number of Israelis today are skeptical as to the possibility of attaining a stable peace agreement. At the beginning of the outbreak of this violence and unrest, Israeli Arabs who identified with the Palestinian cause also rebelled, shattering the laboriously built bridges of good will between the Jewish and Arab populations in Israel. These last developments have in many ways reunited the various factions in Israeli society, overriding internal strife and disputes.

About five million Jews live in Israel today. The social, cultural, and political developments in the country during the course of the first five decades of its existence as an independent state have been influenced by three separate but interdependent circles. Of major impact on the outer global circle was the wish to fashion a modern, developed society in line with the most progressive countries in the world. The second, the regional circle, comprising the Mediterranean area, is dominated by the external threat of the political struggle with the Arab states, which dictates the country's priorities as to the distribution of economic and human resources. The local circle evinces a constant groping for basic common denominators that will, within the framework of a Jewish state, satisfy the needs of a people with divergent religious ties and political opinions, gathered together from various places and cultures. The dynamics of these diversified aspects and their subdivisions have never been static and have experienced some interesting shifts, which together provide insights into Jewish life in contemporary Israel.

REFERENCES

American Jewish Committee. 1995. *American-Jewish Relations: Continuity and Change.* Jerusalem: American Jewish Committee.

Avineri, Shlomo. 1981. *The Making of Modern Zionism: The Intellectual Origins of the Jewish State.* New York: Basic Books.

Bachi, Roberto. 1974. *The Population of Israel.* Jerusalem: Jewish Population Studies, The Institute of Contemporary Jewry, The Hebrew University.

DellaPergola, Sergio. 1986. "Aliya and Other Jewish Migrations: Toward an Integrated Perspective." In *Studies in the Population of Israel (In Honor of Roberto Bachi),* ed. Uziel O. Schmelz and Gad Nathan, 172–209. Jerusalem: Scripta Hierosolymitana.

———. 1999. *World Jewry Beyond 2000: The Demographic Prospects.* Occasional Papers 2. The Third Frank Green Lecture. Oxford: Oxford Center for Hebrew and Jewish Studies.

Eisenstadt, Shmuel N. 1967. *Israeli Society.* London: Weinfeld and Nicolson.

———. 1984. "Some Reflections on the Ethnic Problem in Israel." *Megamot: Behavioral Sciences Quarterly* 28 (2/3): 159–68 (Hebrew).

Eliav, Mordechai. 1978. *Eretz Israel and Its Yishuv in the Nineteenth Century, 1777–1917.* Jerusalem: Keter Publishing House (Hebrew).

Etzioni-Halevy, Eva. 2002. *The Divided People: Can Israel's Breakup Be Stopped.* Lanham, Md: Lexington Books.

Giladi, Dan, and Shmuel Avitzur. 1982. "The Growth and Consolidation of the Jewish Economy." In *The History of Eretz Israel, The British Mandate and the Jewish National Home,* ed. Yehoshua Porat and Ya'akov Shavit, 193–202. Jerusalem: Keter Publishing House and Yad Itzhak Ben-Zvi (Hebrew).

Goldscheider, Calvin. 2002. *Israel's Changing Society: Population, Ethnicity, and Development.* 2nd ed. Boulder, CO: Westview Press.

Horowitz, Dan, and Moshe Lissak. 1978. *Origins of the Israeli Polity: Palestine Under the Mandate.* Chicago: University of Chicago Press.

Lissak, Moshe. 1998. "The Social-Demographic in the 1950s: The Absorption of the Mass Immigration." In *Independence: The First Fifty Years,* ed. Anita Shapira, 13–55. Jerusalem: The Zalman Shazar Center (Hebrew).

Medoff, Rafael, and Chaim I. Waxman. 2000. *Historical Dictionary of Zionism.* Lanham, Maryland, and London: Scarecrow Press.

Pa'il, Meir. 1983. "The Fighting Forces." In *The History of Eretz Israel, The War of Independence (1947–1949),* ed. Yehoshua Ben-Arie, 107–50. Jerusalem: Keter Publishing House and Yad Yitzhak Ben-Zvi (Hebrew).

Rubinstein, Eliakim. 1976. "From Yishuv to State: Institutions and Parties." In *The Jewish National Home: From the Balfour Declaration to Independence,* ed. Binyamin Eliav, 129–284. Jerusalem: Keter Publishing House (Hebrew).

Schmelz, Uziel O., Sergio DellaPergola, and Uri Avner. 1991. *Ethnic Differences Among Israeli*

Jews: A New Look. Jewish Population Studies, no. 22. Jerusalem: The Institute of Contemporary Jewry, The Hebrew University.

Shavit, Ya'akov. 1983. "The Old Yishuv (1882–1917): The Historical Framework and Base Lines." In *The History of Eretz Israel, The Last Phase of Ottoman Rule (1799–1917),* ed. Yehushua Ben-Arie and Israel Bartal, 257–74. Jerusalem: Keter Publishing House and Yad Itzhak Ben-Zvi (Hebrew).

Sicron, Moshe. 1986. "The 'Mass Immigration': Its Size, Characteristics and Influences." In *Immigrants and Transit Camps,* ed. Mordechai Naor, 31–52. Jerusalem: Yad Izhak Ben Zvi (Hebrew).

CHAPTER TWO

Demography in Israel at the Dawn of the Twenty-First Century

&

SERGIO DELLAPERGOLA

A Population Laboratory

Israel is a small country. Its elongated north-south shape covers a surface similar to that of the North American state of Massachusetts. Population size and average density per square mile are about the same in the two states but, with more than half of its territory nearly empty in the southern Negev desert, Israel's effective population density is actually far greater. In addition to its internationally (at least de facto) recognized borders, since the June 1967 war Israel has held military control over East Jerusalem, the West Bank, Gaza strip, and Golan heights, whose combined surface roughly corresponds to that of the State of Delaware—with four times as many inhabitants.

Since Israel's independence in May 1948 as the successor of the Jewish State envisaged by the United Nations partition plan of Palestine of November 1947, a unique human and social laboratory emerged within this tiny geographical space (Bachi 1977; Goldscheider 1996). Under the impact of powerful Jewish immigration streams, Israel's total population (without the post-1967 territories) grew by eight times, from about 800,000 in May 1948 to about 6.5 million at the end of 2000. The large and heterogeneous stream of newcomers from scores of countries in five continents featured a whole gamut of cultural modernization, demographic patterns, economic development, and political emancipation. Their absorption deeply affected the character and structure of Israeli society and its institutions. The nature of demographic, social, economic, and cultural transformations among Jews in Israel reflected both their passage from a Diaspora of minorities to majority status in a sovereign state, and adaptation to a Middle Eastern regional context already imbued with social diversity and conflict. Conceivably, the various immigrant groups in Israel could either remain segregated following distinct evolutionary paths, or develop over time new, original demographic and socioeconomic models. To what extent, then, were Zionism's ideal programs of the *ingathering of the exiles* and the *fusion of the diasporas* practically achieved?

The complexity of Israeli society evidently extends beyond its Jewish component and involves the presence of and constant interaction with important non-Jewish communities. At the end of 2000, Israel's population comprised nearly five million Jews, a million Muslims, over 100,000 Christians belonging to various denominations (especially Greek Orthodox), 100,000 Druzes, and over 200,000 immigrants from the former Soviet Union (FSU) included in the Law of Return whose religion was other than Jewish, or unclassified. Moreover, about 200,000 non-Jewish foreign workers recently joined as temporary residents, mostly from developing countries in the Balkans, East Asia, and Africa. In the West Bank and Gaza, over three million Palestinians lived the predicament of an as yet unsolved conflict that crucially impinges on the State of Israel's experience and very existence. How do the demographic trends and prospects look in this unique societal complex inclusive of Israel and the Palestinian Territories?

Israel's rapid population increase and demographic transformation occurred along with a steady process of societal growth that led the country up the ladder of the world system of nations. Around the year 2000 Israel ranked twenty-third out of 190 nations regarding national income per capita, and a similar rank obtained concerning several other indicators of human and socioeconomic development. At the same time, Israel has not yet attained a definitive status among more developed societies, as significant social inequalities still operate in its midst. Recent and prospective sociodemographic trends are plausibly associated with cultural differences between Israel's main ethnic and cultural groups. Comparative analysis needs to focus at least selectively on three main axes of population differentiation:

- between Jews and Arabs in Israel, with an eye to changes in the Palestinian Territories;
- between the Asian-African and the European-American origin groups within the Jewish population. Such an admittedly oversimplified dichotomy misses many significant nuances across individual countries of origin, but it catches the essence of various, partly overlapping criteria for classifying countries of origin:
     (a) comparatively less vs. more developed countries
     (b) predominantly Christian vs. Muslim societies
     (c) Ashkenazi vs. Sephardi-Oriental Jewish communities;
- between the more and the least religious components of Jewish population.

The expected course of evolution of such a multicultural society following Jewish immigrant absorption and interaction of Jews with Arabs and others cannot be reduced to the mere adoption by one subordinate group of the characteristics of another dominant one. This is only one of several possible models of integration, both theoretical and empirical, that is, based on Israel's actual experience. Several possible scenarios for the experience of people with different initial characteristics encountering Israeli society include convergence (widespread adoption of intermediate patterns relative to those originally displayed by various groups), catching up (gap reduction on the part of those with initially less favorable data), divergence (enhancing polarization), and sharing of similar trends though at unequal rates. Gender differences constitute a further important factor to be considered, cutting across the several other analytic dimensions (DellaPergola 2000).

One central aspect in the analysis of Israel's demography is the complex relationship between local society and Diaspora. Israel's Jewish population has been continuously affected by trends and developments initiated elsewhere—directly through immigration, and indirectly through historical and unequal processes of modernization and acculturation that affected Jewish communities in their countries of residence. At the beginning of 2001 Israel's Jewish population had grown to constitute 37 percent of a total world Jewish population estimated at 13.2 million (by the core definition, excluding non-Jewish members in Jewish households). By converse, Israeli Arabs and the Palestinians in the West Bank and Gaza represented together 48 percent of a global Palestinian population very roughly estimated at 8.5 million (DellaPergola 2001a). Both diasporas constitute relevant frames of reference as sources of potential future immigration and of economic and political support for the respective populations in Israel. In this chapter we review international migration, marriage and fertility patterns, socioeconomic stratification, and population prospects in Israel.

Population Size and Components of Demographic Change

Israel's population passed the 1,000,000 mark in 1949. The 2, 3, 4, 5, and 6 million barriers were crossed in 1958, 1970, 1982, 1991, and 1998 respectively. The renewal of rapid population growth in Israel followed the immigration wave that began in late 1989, chiefly from the former Soviet Union (FSU) and, on a smaller scale, from Ethiopia and several other countries. Mass immigration has been part and parcel of the demographic growth model that has prevailed in Israel since its establishment—in fact, since the second half of the nineteenth century—alternating periods of very fast and slower growth.

Population growth rates in the early post-independence years exceeded 20 percent per year. In 1990–91, the annual growth rate was more than 5 percent—remarkable when contrasted with the relatively moderate growth of the preceding period (an annual average of 1.8 percent in 1983–89) but rather similar to the mid-1950s situation. Since 1992 population growth rates in Israel have ranged around 2.5 percent, quite above the current world population average of 1.3 percent. The importance of international migration balance (immigration minus emigration) tended to decline over time, from 87 percent of total population growth in 1948–51 to 6 percent in 1983–89. In 1990–91, the migration balance accounted again for roughly 70 percent of total population growth (78 percent among the Jewish population alone). Overall, between 1948 and 2000 immigration accounted for 42 percent of total population growth in Israel, and 50 percent of Jewish population growth.

The other major factor in population growth, the balance of births and deaths, or natural increase, was relatively stable. Natural increase per thousand of population in Israel diminished slowly from 21–22 in the late 1950s to 15–16 in the 1980s and 1990s. For the Jewish population alone, the rate of natural increase fell from 20 to 12 per thousand, respectively. These changes are quite moderate when compared with the steep decline in natural increase in most developed countries over the same period. Natural increase among Israeli Muslims raised from 38 per thousand in the late 1950s to 45 in the 1960s and declined to 32 per thousand in the late 1990s.

A third component of population change is the balance between conversions to and from Judaism. In the unique conditions of a Jewish majority, the stream of accessions may be estimated to be the larger, though of minor import in the overall demographic equation. Since the late 1990s the number of converts in Israel increased significantly, following the growth in the number of non-Jewish immigrants.

The Role of Immigration in Israel's Population Development

The resumption of large-scale immigration to Israel is one of the factors that most strongly influenced demographic change in past years. Immigration directly affected the growth rates and composition of the population in several respects, such as the absolute and relative share of population groups according to religion and ethnic affiliation, country of origin, and duration of stay in Israel. However, immigration also affected other sociodemographic variables such as the geographic distribution of the population and its composition by age groups and marital status.

Immigration (in Hebrew *aliya,* "ascent") reached Israel at a very unsteady pace, in the shape of subsequent waves. Early immigration played an important role in establishing the primary cultural, political, and institutional infrastructure of Palestine and, later, in the Jewish state. Roughly 60–70,000 Jews immigrated to Palestine toward the end of Ottoman rule (1880–1918), and about 483,000 arrived during the years of the British Mandate (1919–48). Until 1948 official immigration policies restricted the size of Jewish immigration and directly or indirectly stimulated selectivity of immigration by countries of origin and the sociodemographic profile of migrants (Friedlander and Goldscheider 1979). Migration opportunities radically changed with Israel's independence in May 1948 and its adoption of nearly unrestricted admission policies for Jewish immigrants epitomized by the 1950 Law of Return. Between 1948 and 2000, over 2.9 million people immigrated to Israel, mostly Jews but also their non-Jewish family members included in the framework of the Law of Return. The initial immigration wave of 1948–51 comprised 688,000 people. In subsequent years the intensity of immigration waves, each covering 5–10 years, weakened significantly. The most recent influx from the FSU brought immigration back to its historical maximum levels, with 385,000 immigrants in 1990–91, followed by 55,000–75,000 arrivals yearly through 2000. Relative to the size of the recipient population in Israel, the initial three and a half years of mass immigration produced a doubling of population and required an absorption effort practically unequaled in recent world demographic history. The most recent immigration, while similar to the formative initial wave in absolute numbers, was obviously much less onerous in the context of a larger and economically strengthened absorbing population.

Since 1948, the rhythm of immigration from the various countries was quite different. Four principal models provide a basic typology that can be extended to all possible countries of origin of immigrants:

- total transfer to Israel between 1949 and 1951 of a country's existing Jewish population—as in the cases of Iraq, Yemen, Bulgaria, and to a lesser extent several other countries in the Middle East and the Balkans area;
- large-scale and rather unselective migration spread over longer time spans of the absolute majority of preexisting Jewish population, the pace of migration being mostly determined by the shifting opportunities to leave the country of origin. These, in turn, largely reflected changing migration policies of the respective governments—typically in the FSU, but also in Romania and most other countries in Eastern Europe, Morocco, and Ethiopia;
- more selective Jewish emigration, uninterrupted over time but of variable intensity, reflecting periodical economic and political crises and their consequences for the Jewish community in the respective countries of origin—as in Argentina and most other Latin American countries, as well as South Africa;
- comparatively scant and highly selective Jewish emigration, with the exception of a more intense period following the 1967 Six Day War—as in the United States and most Western developed countries.

24

These different models clearly indicate that the principal determinants of the timing and volume of migration to Israel reflected changing and often negative situations in the countries of origin more than Israel's "pull." At the same time, the role of cultural-ideological determinants in migration decisions among Diaspora Jews cannot be dismissed. The influence of Zionism and of a broader Jewish identity significantly determined choosing Israel over alternative targets such as the United States, Canada, Australia, or France, once "push" factors emerged in the countries of origin.

As immigration to Israel reflected all possible stages of demographic, socioeconomic, and cultural modernization attained in Diaspora communities, many of the typical global East-West or North-South cleavages were introduced through immigration into the Israeli context. In sweeping generalization, immigrants from Muslim countries constituted a comparatively more traditional population in terms of cultural orientation and socioeconomic development, relative to immigrants from European countries and the relatively small component of American origin. This implied among the former:

- demographically, higher levels of mortality and fertility, and an overall younger age composition aggravated by heavier dependency ratios;
- socioeconomically, lower average levels of educational attainment, especially among women, and very low frequencies of people with experience in the liberal professions and management;
- culturally, greater frequencies of attitudes and behaviors inspired by religious or other traditional norms.

Incidentally, concomitantly large Jewish migration streams from the same countries of origin to Western countries—particularly from North Africa to France and from Eastern Europe to the United States—comprised smaller proportions of children and elders relative to migrants to Israel and featured better levels of socioeconomic training and specialization. In other terms, Israel had to absorb and integrate a Jewish population with unusually onerous initial demographic and socioeconomic profiles, which was all the more frustrating because of the integration elsewhere of a large share of the respective social and intellectual elites. In this context, it is worth noting that out-migration (emigration, also called *yeridah*) from Israel was a comparatively far lesser factor. Emigration was comparatively stable over time. Excluding occasional fluctuations, the number of Israeli residents who left Israel and spent more than four years abroad usually ranged between 10,000 and 20,000 per year, and these numbers declined as a percentage of Israel's total population.

Structural Changes

Age Composition

The resumption of large-scale immigration in the 1990s brought about significant changes not only in the size of the Israeli population but also in its socio-demographic characteristics. These changes reflect both the specific profile of immigrants and entrenched trends several decades old. Indeed, since the 1950s interplay between the main factors affecting age composition (fertility and birth rates, mortality, and migration) resulted in only moderate changes in age distribution. The percentage of children under age fifteen remained quite stable. The share of young adults (15–44) grew, that of mature adults (45–65) dropped slightly, and that of the elderly (65+) increased steadily. It is worth noting that the age pyramid of Israeli population is characterized by several major "steps," which reflect historical developments connected with immigration and other demographic changes both in the Diaspora and in Israel. The substantial disparities between contiguous age groups across the age ladder create very powerful and somewhat cyclical fluctuations in the social systems functionally connected with these age groups.

One major reason for age stability is the long-term persistence of rather stable and relatively high fertility rates, reflected in a steady "supply" of infants at the bottom of the age pyramid. Indeed, in international comparison with OECD countries Israel has long been the country with the youngest age composition. In 1970, children (0–14) constituted 33 percent of the population, as against a median of 25 percent in the 22 OECD countries. The figures were 33 percent and 22 percent in 1980, and 31 percent and 19 percent in the 1990s. Rapid growth of the child population (0–14) in the 1970s placed Israel's education system under considerable pressure, forcing it to cope with demand that was growing by 4 percent per year. In the 1980s, pressure from the youngest sector of the child population (0–9) eased but that of the 10–19 age group continued, with significant effects on post-primary education and the military.

At the older end of the age spectrum, in 1970, seniors (65+) accounted for 7 percent of the population in Israel as against a median of 11 percent in the OECD countries; in 2000 the figures were 10 versus 15 percent. In other words, population structure in Israel only moderately reflects the marked aging process that characterizes nearly all developed countries, although in Israel, too, the numbers and share of the elderly have increased—especially the "old-old" (aged 75+). Similar conclusions, although of lesser variance from the OECD figures, apply to Israel's Jewish population alone.

The effects of immigration on demographic structure are evident in all sectors of the population, but are most marked at specific junctures that correspond to the particular makeup of the immigrants. The immigrants' demographic make-up, as expected, reflects the population structure of the community of origin, but the characteristics of immigrants to Israel were quite selective in comparison to members of the same communities who remained in their country of origin, or to migrants who preferred countries other than Israel. A unique contribution came from Ethiopian immigrants, more than half of whom were children aged 0 to 14. Immigrants from the FSU who had the strongest impact were collectively older than the host Jewish population, although not dramatically so in view of the extreme age of the Jewish population at origin. Equally significant was the difference between the immigrants' age structure and that of Jews in the FSU, whereas immigrants to Israel included a comparatively high share of young adults. However, the longer the same immigration wave continues, the more representative of the source population it becomes, resulting in greater aging of immigrants and their families.

At least in the immediate future, the decisive long-term factor affecting the age composition of the Israeli population is the fertility rate. Reflecting high fertility and birth rates, age compositions of Israeli Arabs and of the more strictly religious sectors of Israeli Jews continued to include very high shares of children and younger adults. Apart from their direct effects on social structure, changes in the age composition of a population play an important mediating role in demographic dynamics. The number of marriages, births, deaths, and, to some extent, emigrants, correlates with the size of the age groups from which these events typically stem. Salient differences in the age composition of groups within the Israeli population, such as Jews and Muslims, are not just the results of past demographic processes; they also determine differences that will persist long into the future. Even if fertility and mortality rates of Jews and non-Jews converge, the latter's younger age structure leads to much faster growth rates than those of the Jewish population for years ahead.

Geographic Distribution

The population in Israel is chiefly urban—at least under current definitions that do not necessarily reflect changes in lifestyle or in the social makeup of localities. In Israel all localities with more than 2,000 residents are defined as urban. Among Jews, the share of town dwellers exceeded 90 percent since the early 1970s, and was 90.2 percent in 2000. The Arab population, too, was been characterized by a gradual transition to a large urban majority, from 63 percent in 1961 to 92 percent in 2000.

An element important to the appraisal of the process of immigrants absorption relates to the preoccupation of Israeli governments with strategic population dispersal over the national territory. Despite its small size, Israel features significant regional climatic and socioeconomic differences. The incoming population naturally tended to concentrate in the more developed and geographically more accessible areas. The veteran population, mostly of European origin, thus tended to occupy geographical locations closer to the central areas in the country, in and around the Tel Aviv metropolitan area. Subsequent immigration waves were largely settled in northern and southern areas that, besides being more peripheral, were also less economically established and more often affected by security problems. Similar mechanisms operated regarding the settling of veterans and of new immigrants at the center and periphery of major urban areas, and similar patterns reemerged with the more recent large-scale immigration from the FSU.

In the context of wave-like immigration, with each wave dominated by a different set of countries of origin, the early environments of newcomers tended to be quite homogeneous. Many new immigrants were directed to small rural localities (especially *moshav*-type cooperative villages, known as *moshavim)*, to newly built development towns, or to developing residential quarters in older cities where new housing blocks (known in Hebrew as *shikunim*) were built. While these policies produced reasonably quick and extensive solutions to the main impelling problems of housing in a situation of unusually rapid population growth, the resulting geographic and social distribution of Jewish population in Israel could well be described during the late 1960s as a mosaic of segregated groups.

Gradually, however, while the share of people born in the country increased ceaselessly, powerful streams of internal geographical mobility worked to narrow residential gaps both between the different administrative divisions at the country level and within individual localities. The enhanced social intermingling and integration occurred particularly in newly developed urban areas that tended to attract residents from a great variety of geographical origins who were compatible with the socioeconomic characteristics of each new neighborhood. In terms of geographical origins, a more heterogeneous profile tended to develop within each residential area, while the differences between the various areas tended to diminish. These transformations affecting population distribution were to some extent the consequence and to a large extent the premise for the development of several other trends toward greater integration among the different origin groups within the Jewish component of Israeli society. At the same time, high residential segregation continued to prevail between Israeli Jews and Arabs.

Taking an overview of the past thirty years, these trends largely leveled off and no great changes emerged in Israel's population distribution by main geographic divisions. The share of the Jerusalem District out of the total population grew from 11 percent in 1972 to 12 percent in 2000, the Haifa and Northern Districts together remained around 30 percent, the Tel Aviv and Central Districts combined dropped from 47 percent to 41 percent, the Southern District grew from

II percent to 14 percent, and the Jewish population of Judea-Samaria and the Gaza District rose from 0.1 to 3 percent. In terms of internal population distribution, recent immigration helped to temporarily restore a Jewish majority in the Northern District, after more than a decade in which Jews were in the minority there. In 2000, however, the Northern district again had an Arab majority. Concurrently, the trend toward consolidation of the Central District has come mainly at the expense of the Tel Aviv District. Much of the Jewish population's increase in Judea-Samaria is functionally connected with the Central and Jerusalem Districts and reflects lower costs of housing as well as ideological motives.

The distribution of immigrants by first places of residence was quite different from that of the veteran Jewish population. Immigrants showed a greater preference for the Northern, Haifa, and Southern Districts, relative to the local population. Nearly one-third of the immigrants settled in Israel's development areas, the Northern and Southern Districts, while quite a few settled in Judea-Samaria and Gaza. Housing incentives in the peripheral areas attracted significant numbers of immigrants even after their first settling in the country. Some of the least socially mobile among the recent immigrants were steered to the peripheral districts and tended to stay there rather than flowing to the suburban belts around the central metropolitan areas. Thus immigration played an important role in shaping the geographic balance between center and periphery. However, it also tended to concentrate weaker population groups (in terms of integration) in the very regions where opportunities and channels of mobility, for oldtimers and immigrants alike, are scantier.

Geographic Origins

The Jewish population of Israel is composed almost entirely of immigrants and descendants of immigrants. In 1951, after the mass immigration following Israel's independence, three-quarters of the Jewish population were foreign-born, and about half of all Israelis had lived in the country for five years or less. Over the years, the share of Israeli-born in the Jewish population rose from 47 percent in 1972 to 63 percent in 1988. The recent immigration wave only lowered this percentage to 62 percent in 2000. The median years that the foreign-born had lived in the country rose to over twenty.

Following an early numerical predominance of the European group, in the course of time the share of the Asian-African-born as a percentage of all foreign-born Israelis rose markedly, though the European-American-born remained the larger group. The children's generation shows a different trend: since the early 1970s, Israeli-born Jews of Asian-African extraction outnumbered those of European-American extraction. Overall, the division between the two main origin groups (comprising foreign- and Israeli-born nationals, including members of the third generation) was quite close. In 1988, the percentage of Israeli Jews of Asian-African extraction stood at 52 percent of all Jews in the country. This percentage would have been slightly higher if it included Soviet immigrants from the Caucasian and Central Asian republics, who, like all Soviet immigrants, were customarily classified as European-born. With the large immigration of recent years, the number of Israelis of European origin rose again. By 2000, 39 percent of all Jews were of European-American origin, 32 percent were of Asian-African origin, and 29 percent were Israelis of the third and subsequent generations.

Clearly, the concentration of large numbers of newly landed immigrants of fairly similar origin may hinder, at least temporarily, the process of integration of immigrants of different origins. The ability of Israeli society to continue absorbing the newcomers without disrupting processes and policies meant to integrate existing population groups is now being seriously tested.

Family Processes and Natural Increase

Marriage, Marital Status, and Families

Family patterns are reflected in several indices: changes in marriage trends, population composition by marital status, and composition of families by number of persons and degree of kinship. Family patterns, even if they do not directly affect the size of the population, importantly affect long-term demographic processes. Israelis generally displayed a strong propensity to marry, expressed by relatively young ages at marriage and low percentages of single adults. A marked exception to this pattern are some of the Christian communities, in which the proportion of never-married is two to three times higher than among the Israeli population as a whole.

The model of nearly universal marriage that prevailed in Israel eroded somewhat in recent years. In the Jewish sector in particular, the trend toward early marriage slackened. The percentage of never-married in the 25–29 age group rose from 27 percent among men and 12 percent among women in 1970 to 50 percent and 27 percent, respectively, in 1995. In the 45–49 age group, the small share of Jewish men never married (about 3 percent) hardly changed, but the share of never-married Jewish women rose from 2 percent in 1970 to 5 percent in 1995. Among the non-Jewish population, which includes an array of groups with different marriage customs, the proportion of never-married remained stable or even dropped. We may conclude that whereas in the 1970s there were no great differences between Jews and non-Jews in the share of the never-married in the aforementioned age groups, by the 1990s the percentage of Jewish never-married was considerably higher.

To fine-tune our appraisal of family trends in recent years, we may examine period indices of the propensity to marry, which point to results that would be achieved were the age-specific trends observed in a specific year to continue indefinitely. The current behaviors of younger Jewish adults, and of adults in general, indicate a much lower propensity to marry than that obtained from a cohort measurement that describes the actual results for mature adults, say at fifty. In other words, if current trends continue, the share of the never-married may become much higher than its actual incidence today. Among the non-Jewish population, the marriage propensity reached a peak in the early 1970s, ebbed perceptibly later in the 1970s, and again tended to rise strongly in recent years.

Israeli marriage trends still differ vastly from the situation that characterizes most developed countries today, where marriage propensity has plummeted in unprecedented fashion since the 1970s to rates that fail to reach 60 percent of the adult cohort. Such low rates clearly indicate a downturn in the normative centrality of the conventional nuclear family in Western countries. Concurrently, the incidence of cohabitation among the unmarried grew significantly. The latter trend also appeared in Israel, though not as much as in other places.

The impact of various explanatory factors of marriage in Israel varied over time and within different sectors of the population. Among these were economic circumstances that fell short of expectations and needs, a preference for individual independence, a weakening of the traditional allegiance to familism, and an imbalance between the number of women and men of marriageable age. The last factor in particular reduced Jewish women's chances of finding spouses of suitable age. The postponement of marriage may cause important changes in consumption patterns. High costs of housing in Israel may impair marriage feasibility, but the reverse relationship may be true too. With low marriage rates, fewer young couples wish to purchase housing and more young singles seek to rent, either by themselves or with roommates. In the longer term, the entrenchment of these new patterns may erode more significantly and permanently the traditional family model, as has happened in other countries.

Among non-Jewish Israelis, improvements in economic conditions presumably enhanced marriage rates, relative to the expectations of this population group, which do not necessarily coincide with those of the Jewish sector. Cultural norms affecting the family seemed to reflect an intensification of religious traditionalism, especially in the Muslim sector of the population, and both factors together overcame constraints caused by the age composition of the marriageable population.

Concerning the choice of spouse, a significant indicator of mutual integration of immigrants is the frequency of marriages between people belonging to different origin groups. During Israel's early years and under the impact of mass *aliya,* marriages mostly occurred within the respective communities of origin. Measures of homogamy (within-community attraction) computed on the basis of the usual dichotomy Asia-Africa vs. Europe-America reached quite high levels and tended to increase. Evidently during the initial period of acquaintance of the mass of new immigrants with their new country, a shared geographical origin, language, and to a large extent social class offered a buffer to early absorption difficulties. At one time, a person's own origin group was a natural frame of reference for establishing social relations and, eventually, marriage. Later on, a clear trend toward declining geographical homogamy emerged. By the mid-1990s, more than half the distance between full homogamy and partnering that is totally random with respect to geographical origin had been completed.

The same tendency toward diminishing homogamy appeared for each individual origin group separately. In general, immigrants from more modernized countries (e.g., Germany) displayed less homogamy than immigrants from more traditional societies (e.g., Yemen). A temporary increase in homogamy appeared soon after the increased immigration from the FSU in the 1970s, and, after the major immigration of the 1990s, another increase may have taken place for specific countries (the FSU, Ethiopia). One can reasonably expect, however, that beyond these temporary effects the predominant trend toward increasing group integration will continue. Evidence has indeed accumulated showing that the social environment of spouses plays a far more significant role than geographic origin as a determinant of marital partner selection.

Another aspect of family life and changes in family status is illustrated by changing propensities to divorce. Here, too, as with marriage, Israeli society is rather conservative. The divorce rate among different cohorts of couples that married in Israel over the past three decades has shown rather moderate and slow change. The total divorce rate among Jewish couples relative to a follow-up of twenty years of marriage is 15 percent, against much higher divorce rates in most developed countries. Nevertheless, a comparison of couples who married in different years does show a steady rise in the divorce rate. Three years after marriage, couples married in the 1990s, compared with those that married in the 1970s, experienced divorce rates 60 percent higher; after seven years of marriage divorce rates were 46 percent higher. In this respect, too, the Jewish population of Israel is following in the footsteps of Western developed countries, though at a more cautious pace.

The foregoing trends affect the composition of Israeli families. The percentage of single-parent families rose significantly. This feature is quite frequent among FSU immigrants, as clearly shown by the family composition of this group. The influence of immigration in this respect reinforces an existing Israeli trend. The share of divorcing couples with children rose from 47 percent in 1970 to 66 percent in 1990. The proportion of households with children up to age seventeen and with a lone parent (or adult caregiver) increased from 7.5 percent in 1980 to 10.3 percent in 2000—a relative growth of 37 percent.

Fertility

Fertility rates are higher in Israel than in other developed countries; they vary among religious and national population groups. The Total Fertility Rate (TFR, a measure of the number of children who would be born if age-specific fertility rates observed during a given period of time remained unchanged) dropped slightly from 3.9 in 1955–59, to 3.5 in 1970–1974, 3.0 in 1990, and 2.95 in 2000. Jewish fertility passed from 3.6 children in the late 1950s to 2.7 in 2000.

A major feature in Israeli Jewish fertility was the converging trend of the main origin groups—Asia-Africa and Europe-America—reflecting at least partly the marital convergence just outlined. The fertility of the Asian-African origin group was moderately high in Israel's early years and actually increased to about 6.5 during the early 1950s following mass immigration, because of rapid improvements in health and mortality and a consequent rise in the duration of marital cohabitation. Since the 1960s, declining fertility has mirrored modernization, vastly improved education, and greater birth control among women in this group, among other things through the intervention of mechanisms of radical innovation such as the enlisting of young women in the Israeli army.

The fertility of women of European-American origin started out lower but remained fairly stable. A lengthy period of low fertility, lasting until the mid-1960s, was followed by a significant upturn that persisted into the early 1980s at a level above 2.5 children. The latter, while not very high in absolute terms, was by far higher than that of Jewish communities and of total populations in the respective countries of origin. The gap between fertility rates of women born *abroad* in the two major origin groups narrowed from 113 percent (more than double) in 1955–59 to a mere 12 percent in 1980–84. The fertility rates of Israeli-born women fell somewhere in between the rates for women of different ethnic origin born abroad, reflecting a relatively uniform Israeli Jewish fertility pattern.

Since the beginning of the 1990s large-scale immigration affected fertility levels. Immigrant women from the FSU brought to Israel a TFR of roughly 1.5, which caused a decline in the fertility level of the whole European-American group born abroad. In 1991, for the first time, the TFR of this group dropped below 2.1—the intergenerational replacement rate under conditions of low mortality. During the second half of the 1990s this trend was reversed, evidently depending on the nature of the immigrants' absorption. A relatively successful economic and cultural integration of women immigrants into Israeli society probably elicited an increase in fertility, as had previously happened with women immigrants from other low-fertility countries. The reverse happened among women of Asian-African origin following the Ethiopian immigration. The traditional fertility patterns of Ethiopian women temporarily restored the disparity between the fertility rates of the Asian-African and the European-American origin groups. That gap stood at roughly 60 percent in 1991 but had again dropped to 40 percent in 2000.

The stability and convergence of Israeli family patterns is confirmed by the data for the Israel-born women, which appear to be intermediate between those for immigrant women from different continents. This strengthens the argument for progressive amalgamation of the demographic behaviors of the various Jewish origin-groups. Around 2000, Jewish women in Israel with a TFR of 2.6–2.7 had the highest fertility among developed countries, which were characterized since the end of World War II by two salient processes: enhanced fertility rates during the "baby-boom" period (which lasted in the United States until the late 1950s, while in Western Europe sustained fertility lasted until the mid-1960s); and rapid decline since the mid-1970s. No developed country currently displays fertility levels above the level of generational replacement, which implies population decline in those societies in the longer run—besides the possible effects of international migration.

Interestingly, the evolution of TFR among Jewish women who left the same countries in Europe, Asia and, Africa and migrated to Israel and various western countries was largely determined by the different demographic models of the receiving countries. Jewish fertility levels in France and the United States equals about half that in Israel. A clear split between a Diaspora demographic model, characterized by insufficient Jewish reproduction, and an Israeli model with sufficient demographic replacement emerged.

Among non-Jewish women, Muslim women had the highest fertility, followed by Druze women and Christian women. The total fertility rate of Muslim women has at times been one of the world's highest with an average of about 10 children per woman in the early 1960s, followed by an impressive drop in total fertility to roughly 4.7 in the mid-1980s. This process of modernization has since stopped and has actually reversed direction, although minimally. The trend toward lower fertility rates in the Muslim sector was contrasted by a combination of economic (relative prosperity) and socioreligious factors that tend to strengthen traditional family structures.

Fertility rates among Christians in Israel decreased quickly and reached lower levels than those of the Jewish sector. Druze total fertility rates, too, have fallen rapidly after having long resembled those of the Muslims. The integration of the Druze into various areas of Israeli-Jewish society has expedited the modernization of demographic patterns in the Druze community and resulted in nearly full convergence with Jewish fertility levels.

The explanatory factors of changing fertility levels are intriguing and differ from one population group to the next. Based on a major survey of the late 1980s (Peritz and Baras 1992), the major finding points to the influence of cultural and ideological variables within the larger array of family-building processes in a context of family planning. Available data on the preferred number of children revealed that in Israel potential growth was greater than actual growth. At the end of the 1980s, ideal family size among Jewish women in Israel was about 3.5–4 children on the average—about one child more than currently born on average—versus a preference for around two children in the majority of developed countries.

Among Jewish women, the best predictors of the number of children (desired or actual) were the mother's degree of religious observance, the number of siblings she herself had (positive correlation), and her educational level (negative correlation). With respect to the latter factor, it should be noted that a level of twelve years' schooling is now so common in Israeli society that the education gap between women of different ethnic origin, and the consequent gap in fertility rates, was minimized. The greatly increased participation of Jewish women in the labor force had only minor effects on fertility. The role of socioeconomic status was then minor, and that of geographical origin was not significant.

Among Muslims, a strong (negative) correlation still prevailed between a woman's level of education and fertility. Another factor that had a bearing on fertility in this population sector was the type of marriage—whether or not it included a *mohar,* a bridal payment—since this is an indication of how traditional the woman's family environment is. Woman's participation in the labor force was related to fertility.

Mortality

Steady reduction in mortality levels is a paramount indicator of the improvement in Israel's standard of living and health services. While life expectancy in Israel is on the rise, the trend differs from that of other developed countries in its gender variation. In men's longevity, Israel in 1999, with a life expectancy of 77.1 years, ranked sixth best country in the world. For women, with a life expectancy of 80.7, Israel ranked twenty-second. Among Israeli Arabs, too, the difference between the life expectancies of men and women is less than that in developed countries.

The gap between longevity of Jews and Arabs in Israel, once large, narrowed over time, and the pace of this narrowing accelerated in the past few years. The life expectancy of Israeli Arabs increased to more than 74.9 years for men and 78.1 for women in 1999, and in the Palestinian Territories it reached 70 for men and 73 for women.

Educational Attainment and Occupational Stratification

Another set of variables central to the study of the processes of integration in Israeli society concerns socioeconomic achievements of different origin groups. A first important aspect concerns the functioning of the public education system in the formation of a substantially homogeneous population in terms of educational attainment and training toward possible occupations. The level of education of immigrants, especially during the initial period of mass immigration, displayed a sharp disadvantage among those coming from the Middle East and North Africa. This reflected high proportions with low or no education, and low proportions of people with academic training. The Israeli education system aimed at equalizing the level of education attained by its citizens of different origins within a reasonable frame of time. We may try to reconstruct the size of educational gaps observed between the two main origin groups throughout the various stages of the standard course of education, from the entrance to the system at age six to a college degree. For the 1970s, 1980s, and 1990s, we compared the degree of achievement among Jews originating from Asia-Africa relative to the achievement of Jews originating from Europe-America. After attributing to the latter group a standard level of 100 regarding each of the main steps in the educational course, we obtained an index of relative disadvantage for the former group.

During the years of mass immigration, the educational attainment of immigrants from Asia and Africa was comparatively low: 50–60 percent of men aged seventy-five and over were illiterate, versus about 15 percent among immigrants from Europe and America. Among women, illiteracy was more widespread. Illiteracy rates were practically reduced to zero among the young generation raised and educated in Israel, thanks to the general enforcement of compulsory education. The low educational level of up to eight years of study gradually disappeared, too. Thanks to the efforts of the public education system, the proportion of youth dropping out of school before completing secondary studies tended to decline significantly from its rather high levels in the 1950s and 1960s. With a median level of education of twelve years, the vast majority of the younger generations raised in Israel completed a course of secondary studies or its equivalent. At these levels of schooling, the reforms introduced by the educational administration in Israel reduced the gaps between the major origin groups.

By the mid-1990s, educational lags at the initial stages of the educational life-course were sharply reduced if not eliminated. The gap in school attendance at age seventeen of pupils of Asian-African versus European-American origin had narrowed from 38 percent fewer in the 1970s to 11 percent fewer in the 1990s. Convergence of levels of educational attainment, however, was not completed in at least two respects. The first was the greater tendency of youngsters of Asian-African origin to be enrolled in secondary schools of a technical rather than humanistic orientation. The corollary was a lesser tendency to successfully pass matriculation (*bagrut*) exams—the fundamental prerequisite for admission at Israeli universities. The lag of youngsters of Asian-African origin versus their peers of European-American origin was in the range of 70 percent fewer in the 1970s and had risen to 30 percent fewer in the 1990s. The second aspect related to the underrepresentation of those of Asian-African origin among university students and, at the end of their course of studies, among college graduates. In the 1990s the percentage of graduates among those of Asian-African origin was still 70 percent lower than for those of European-American origin, still very significant yet better than in the 1970s when that same lag reached 83 percent fewer. It should be noted, at the same time, that the spread of higher education had significantly increased among all origin groups, with total exposure rates of 55 percent among Jews aged 25–34, versus 27 percent among those aged 65 and over in the year 2000, and rates of 26 percent and 11 percent, respectively, among Israeli Arabs. Women were rapidly closing the preexisting educational gap versus men. By the 1990s, the exposure of Jewish women to higher education was already significantly higher than that of men, announcing further improvements in future socioeconomic status and decisional power.

The spread of higher education was greatly enhanced over the 1990s with the significant expansion of the Israeli higher education network, in particular the opening of numerous new colleges whose criteria for admission were less selective than the ones adopted by major universities, but which nonetheless allowed for further expansion of the population with higher education. Indeed, according to data for the late 1990s, the origin-related gap in university enrollment had narrowed to −35 percent, anticipating a substantial reduction in the gap of college graduates in future years.

Another significant aspect of integration and equalization trends among origin groups appears from data that summarize the socioeconomic stratification of Jews of the two main origin groups in Israel in 1966 and in 1996. Both in 1966 and in 1996, the percentages of academic and associate professionals, and of managers and clerical personnel were higher among those of European-American origin (38 percent and 56 percent, respectively) than among those of Asian-African origin (16 percent and 45 percent, respectively). This was counterbalanced by higher proportions of workers employed in industry, construction, transport, and agriculture among the Asian-African origin group (60 percent and 35 percent, respectively) than among the European-American origin group (40 percent and 29 percent, respectively). The general direction of change in the social stratification of the Israeli labor force over time clearly points to a growing predominance of white-collar over blue-collar occupations. The state as an nondiscriminating employer obviously contributed to the large-scale access to the lower echelons of white-collar jobs—an opportunity largely utilized by persons of Asian-African origin. Overall, similar mobility trends involved the Israeli Arab citizens, though at a lower average socioeconomic status. It must be remembered, on the other hand, that much of the upward mobility of Jews was enhanced by the availability after 1967 of a large pool of Palestinian labor from the West Bank and Gaza, which substituted for Jewish employees at the lower levels of occupational stratification. Since the 1990s, these same tasks were taken up to a large extent by non-Jewish foreign workers.

With regard to socioeconomic status, too, we computed an index of relative disadvantage of the Asian-African origin group versus its European-American counterpart, based on the index of dissimilarity relative to major occupational categories. The latter measures the percentage of persons belonging to a less favored group who ought to change their occupation in order to achieve a distribution identical to that of a more favored group. Such a gap diminished between 1966 and 1996, from −22 percent to −15 percent, thus showing that the Asian-African origin group had experienced comparatively more rapid occupational improvements within the general Israeli context of significant upward mobility. In 1996, the occupational profile of the Asia-Africa origin group actually closely resembled the profile of the Europe-America group in 1966, and was indeed slightly better (index of dissimilarity-relative advantage: +7%).

In the light of these data, the persisting gap between major origin groups in the Jewish population can be described mostly as transitional rather than as the product of insurmountable obstacles inherent in the social structure of Israeli society and its attitudes toward Jewish ethnocultural divisions. The outstanding issue is the *speed* of the trend toward closing the gaps rather than its *pattern*. The fact that, as documented here, social gaps continue to be significant at the higher levels of the Israeli social ladder, implies that the production of leading cadres provided with a higher level of training continues to be affected by the imbalances between the social profiles of the respective origin groups in a more distant past. At the same time, the seriousness of the problem is to some extent mitigated by the fact that the group provided with less formal education has often been able to develop alternative channels of upward social mobility independently of the conventional paths of education.

The Twenty-First Century: Scenarios and Challenges

Jews, Arabs, and Others

Population projections that consider various scenarios for the Arab and other minorities in the State of Israel generally point to a continuation of rapid demographic growth (DellaPergola, Rebhun, and Tolts 2000). Recessive demographic trends in the Jewish Diaspora, and the overwhelming concentration of Jews in relatively stable and affluent Western countries, foreshadow a likely decline in the future volume of immigration. The main factor at work in Israel's future population is the continuing gap in fertility between Muslims, with a TFR of 4.6, versus Jews (and Christians), with a TFR of 2.5–2.7. These Muslim traditionalist family patterns, notwithstanding significant modernization and improvements in educational attainment, employment status, and standards of living, point to the contemporary vigorous action of more traditional forces within the community. The question of demographic interest is whether and when the higher fertility of Israeli Muslims will converge toward that of the Jews, as has already happened among the Israeli Christian Arabs and Druze. Demographic scenarios basically vary according to the timetable for such possible reduction of existing gaps. In the 1990s the Palestinians' TFR was estimated at 5.7 in the West Bank and 7.4 in Gaza, significantly higher than in most Arab countries.

Reflecting assumptions about possible slight increases (to 2.9 children) or decreases (to 2.1 children) in current fertility levels, Israel's Jewish population was projected at a range of 6.1–6.5 million in 2020. By 2050, the Jewish population would range between 6.9 and 9.7 million. One further aspect relates to the patterns of absorption of non-Jewish members of households who recently immigrated in the framework of the Law of Return. These persons often have Jewish ancestors and some of them might in the course of time apply for formal adoption of a Jewish identification. Their number, above 200,000 in 2000, might increase to 200–400,000 in 2020 and to 450–650,000 in 2050 as a product of continuing immigration and some natural increase in Israel, providing a further potential source of growth for the Jewish population in Israel. On the other hand, temporary foreign workers in Israel, roughly estimated at 200,000 in 2000, may become permanent residents, thus further augmenting Israel's total and non-Jewish population. These workers were excluded from our projections.

Israel's Arab population of 1.2 million in the year 2000, in the case of gradual convergence to current levels of Jewish fertility, would grow to 2.0 million in 2020 and to 3.1 million in 2050. Were Israeli Arab TFRs to remain at present levels, the respective population would reach 2.1 million in 2020 and 4.4 million in 2050. In the most unlikely eventuality of immediate adoption of Jewish TFRs, the Arab population would be 1.9 million in 2020 and 2.1 in 2050. Summing these figures to the estimated higher and lower Jewish population projections, Israel's total population of 6.3 million in the year 2000 would grow to a range between 8.2 and 9.0 million in 2020, and between 9.4 and 14.8 million in 2050.

The imponderables of demographic mechanisms are further illustrated by the expected development among the total Palestinian population of the West Bank and Gaza, roughly approaching 3 million in 2000. If fertility were to decline gradually to levels similar to those of Israel's Jews, that population would grow to 5.7 million in 2020, and 11.6 million in 2050; at unchanged current fertility levels it would grow to 6.6 million in 2020 and to 21.7 million in 2050; at (unlikely) instant Jewish fertility levels, it would grow to 4 million in 2020 and 6 million in 2050. The total inhabitants in the whole piece of land extending between the Mediterranean sea and the Jordan river including Israel's Jews, Arabs, and others, and the Palestinians would then grow from 9.3 million in 2000 to a total of 12.1 to 15.6 million in 2020, and 15.4 to 36.5 million in 2050. Some of these figures admittedly defy imagination and cannot be taken as actually expected scenarios. Feedback mechanisms of one kind or another may be expected to intervene to modify the current trends. The high population densities implicit in these projections, however, unveil a course of demographic development bound to seriously problematic consequences for the land's "carrying capacity" and for the optimal equilibrium between human, economic, and environmental resources. It stands to reason that these concepts imply an upper boundary, even if not easily quantifiable. Implications of expected population trends foreshadow complicated social and political circumstances for the State of Israel and the Palestinian Authority.

Religious, Traditional, and Secular

A further question concerns the future of Israel's population according to degrees of religious identification. It is not easy to provide a clear estimate of the size of different segments of Jewish population in Israel by the respective degree of religious observance. Jewish ideological-cultural differences operate more as a nuanced continuum than as one sharp cleavage between the religious and nonreligious. One indirect way to estimate the size of different groups is by looking at the number of pupils enrolled in the different educational networks that officially operate in the Israeli educational system—State, State religious, and Independent religious or *haredi*. In 2000–01, the following distribution of total pupils obtained: State 66 percent, State religious 18 percent, Independent religious 16 percent (Israel CBS Statistical Abstract 2001: 8–30). Considering the larger family size of the more religious population segments, their share of total population is actually smaller. Indeed in a national survey of religious attitudes in Israel in

1991 and 1993, 14 percent self-defined their religiosity as strictly observant, 24 percent reported to be observant to a great extent, 41 percent somewhat observant, and 21 percent totally nonobservant (Levy, Levinsohn, and Katz 1993). Another national survey conducted in 1991–92 revealed a somewhat different Jewish population distribution in relation to a question on subjective religious attitudes: 15 percent religious (including *haredi*), 11 percent traditional-religious, 34 percent traditional-not so religious, and 40 percent not religious (Israel CBS 1995). By taking together these various indications, one can roughly estimate the more religious part of Jewish population at about 25 percent—about 7 percent *haredi* or "segregated religious," and 18 percent "national religious"—and the majority, ranging from moderately traditional to very secular, at about 75 percent.

Keeping in mind the limited accuracy of these estimates, we can attempt evaluate the prospective demographic change of different ideological-cultural segments of Jewish population. One in-depth study of the demography of Jerusalem in 1995 estimated the average number of children born to the inhabitants of various types of neighborhoods representing good proxies for the underlying Jewish population sectors (DellaPergola 2001a). The respective TFRs were 6.4 children in areas where 70 percent or more of residents voted for religious parties—a proxy for the "segregated religious"; 4.4 in areas with a religious vote of 40–70 percent—a proxy for the "national religious"; and 2.4 in areas with a religious vote below 40 percent—a proxy for a range of moderately traditional to very secular. The ensuing annual rates of Jewish population growth resulting from natural increase only were, respectively, 3.6 percent, 2.3 percent, and 1 percent. The same rates of growth can be applied to the countrywide distribution of Jewish population sectors by religiosity, keeping in mind that Israel's countrywide distribution is markedly different from Jerusalem's.

Under these assumptions, the share of the "segregated religious" would grow from 7 percent in 2000 to 11 percent in 2020 and 17 percent in 2050, the "national religious" would grow from 18 percent to 21 percent in 2020 and 24 percent in 2050, and the moderately traditional to secular majority would pass from 75 percent to 68 percent in 2020 and 59 percent in 2050. Such estimates operate within the constraints of the grand totals for Israel's medium population projection mentioned above and obtained independently of ideological divisions. Since separate projections for each population sector would generate higher totals, this constraint implies a gradual slowing down in the current rates of demographic growth for each sector. Alternatively, the projection implies continuation of past trends that resulted in a net transfer from the more to the less religious sectors of Jewish population in Israel. Under these assumptions, a significant—yet not truly revolutionary—change would obtain in the relative share of different Jewish identificational groups by the mid-twenty-first century.

Concluding Remarks

A demographic snapshot of Israel at the dawn of the twenty-first century reveals a very complex picture of past trends as well as rather blurred prospects regarding the amount of continuity and change to be expected. True, the very complexity of the human makeup of Israeli society plays as a determinant of continuity in known patterns, since at least some sectors of society are characterized by very slow change and therefore function as an anchor to prevailing trends. Since the continuing influx of immigrants was inextricably connected with the demographic and historical development of Israeli population and society, an expected reduction in the inflow of immigrants may be a prelude to stronger processes of sociodemographic convergence among a population that becomes more veteran. On the other hand, a continuation of conflict—political and military between Jews and Palestinians, and cultural between different sectors of the Israeli public—would lead to resilient differences in the mode and pace of demographic behaviors. The broad range of trends implicit in these assumptions argues against dramatic changes of known demographic patterns.

Cultural and ideological factors in Israeli society combine with economic and social variables to create a sociodemographic fabric quite unlike that found in other developed or developing countries. Israeli demographics reflect a special combination of rational economic sociodemographic and traditional values and norms. Planners and politicians should always bear this particular blend in mind if and when they attempt to construct a social-policy system based on reasonable forecasting of future demographic processes.

As a conclusion to this overview, several major mechanisms of social and demographic change in Israel may be mentioned to highlight the thrust of past trends, and to provide a possible guideline for the future:

- *Compositional changes,* such as variations in the size of successive birth cohorts, the size and composition of immigration waves, the size of promotions joining the educational system and the labor force, and the like. By affecting the basic size and composition of the population, and the environments within which each specific process occurred, these changes powerfully determined the constraints and opportunities that were available periodically to individuals and to society in general.
- *Behavioral changes,* namely diffuse transformations in the attitudes of or opportunities available to the public at large. Changes in Israel's economic position—whether because of its intrinsic productive capacity, foreign help, or other factors—led to sharp and widespread changes in income and consumption patterns and in standards of living. Changes in educational attain-

ment, namely the general diffusion of secondary and tertiary schooling, fundamentally affected the training of younger generations toward meeting the manpower needs of a modernizing nation. Continued exposure to mass communication channels and more frequent contacts abroad, among other factors, stimulated large-scale changes in the population's values and norms. These individual, yet quite diffuse changes in the perception of self in society affected a full array of variables, such as preferred family size, school enrollment propensities at various educational levels, occupational preferences reflecting the evolving prestige of different occupations, individual attitudes toward religion, political behaviors, etc.

- *Institutional interventions,* particularly the introduction of laws and regulations affecting the whole of Israel's population or very large sections of it. Relevant examples were the introduction of compulsory education or the lengthening of its duration; regulations establishing the basic approach and technical standards concerning the absorption of new immigrants; regulations affecting the labor market and the main patterns of economic activity; compulsory national insurance and transfer payments; compulsory military service; official recognition of the role of religion in society; and other broad interventions of the institutional system in the life of families and individuals. Similar effects were obtained for specific and quite large communities within the total population, through sectorial exemptions and incentives.

A further significant factor of sociodemographic change, whose impact went beyond its basically compositional nature, was the role of non-Jews—mostly Palestinians—on Israeli processes of societal development such as Jewish immigrant absorption, ethnic integration, and socioeconomic stratification. The presence of important Arab minorities within the State of Israel inside the pre-1967 "green line," and, even more significant, the contiguity with and access to a large Palestinian population in the areas administered since 1967, deeply impinged on socioeconomic and political processes among the Jewish population. For about a quarter of a century, the major effect probably was the easy availability of a relatively large and unsophisticated labor force that could fulfill roles at the bottom of the social ladder, thus enabling the lower sectors of the Jewish labor force (mostly of Asian and African origin) to move toward other endeavors. Further important effects touched upon the corporate patterns of Jewish group identity and political behaviors—and, not less important, upon the fundamentals of Palestinian identity. At the dawn of the twenty-first century, however, the main gist of demographic processes in Israel shifted to the basics of the changing quantitative balance between Jews and Arabs, and to its implications for the deepest foundations of Israel's existence.

REFERENCES AND FURTHER READING

Bachi, Roberto 1977. *The Population of Israel.* Jerusalem: The Hebrew University of Jerusalem and Prime Minister's Office.

DellaPergola, Sergio 1993. "Demographic Changes in Israel in the Early 1990s." In *Israel Social Services 1992–93,* ed. Jacob Kop, 57–115. Jerusalem: The Center for Social Policy Studies in Israel.

———. 1998. "The Global Context of Migration to Israel." In *Immigration to Israel: Sociological Perspectives,* ed. Elazar Leshem and Judith Shuval, 51–92. New Brunswick and London: Transaction.

———. 1999. *World Jewry Beyond 2000: The Demographic Prospects.* Oxford: Oxford Centre for Hebrew and Jewish Studies.

———. 2000. "Jewish Women in Transition: A Comparative Sociodemographic Perspective." In *Jews and Gender: The Challenge to Hierarchy. Studies in Contemporary Jewry, An Annual,* no. 16, ed. Jonathan Frankel, 209–42.

———. 2001a. "Jerusalem's Population, 1995–2020: Demography, Multiculturalism and Urban Policies." *European Journal of Population* 17: 165–99.

———. 2001b. "Demography in Israel-Palestine: Trends, Prospects, Policy Implications." Paper presented at XXIX General Population Conference. Salvador de Bahia: International Union for the Scientific Study of Population.

DellaPergola, Sergio, and Leah Cohen, eds. 1992. *World Jewish Population: Trends and Policies.* Jerusalem: The Hebrew University of Jerusalem.

DellaPergola, Sergio, Uzi Rebhun, and Mark Tolts. 2000. "Prospecting the Jewish Future: Population Projections, 2000–2008." *American Jewish Year Book* 100: 103–46.

Friedlander, Dov, and Calvin Goldscheider. 1979. *The Population of Israel.* New York: Columbia University Press.

Goldscheider, Calvin, ed. 1992. *Population and Social Change in Israel.* Boulder, Co.: Westview Press.

———. 1996. *Israel's Changing Society: Population, Ethnicity, and Development.* Boulder, Co.: Westview Press.

Israel Central Bureau of Statistics (ICBS). Yearly. *Statistical Abstract of Israel.* Jerusalem.

———. 1995. *Time Use in Israel: Time Budget Survey 1991–92.* Jerusalem.

Levy, Shlomit, Hanna Levinsohn, and Elihu Katz. 1993. *Beliefs, Observances and Social Interaction Among Israeli Jews.* Jerusalem: The Louis Guttman Israel Institute of Applied Social Research.

Peritz, Eric and Mario Baras. 1992. *Studies in the Fertility of Israel.* Jerusalem: The Hebrew University of Jerusalem.

Schmelz, Uziel O., Sergio DellaPergola, and Uri Avner. 1991. *Ethnic Differences Among Israeli Jews: A New Look.* Jerusalem: The Hebrew University of Jerusalem and The American Jewish Committee.

PART II

Immigration and Social Adaptation

CHAPTER THREE

Jewish Ethnicity in Israel: Symbolic or Real?[1]

SAMMY SMOOHA

Introduction

Israel belongs to a large category of societies built by European settlers and immigrants during the modern era. In this respect it is essentially similar to immigrant countries such as the United States, Canada, Mexico, Brazil, South Africa, Australia, and New Zealand and markedly different from nonimmigrant countries like the United Kingdom, France, Germany, India, China, and Japan. Immigration and internal migration resulting from economic and social dislocations have become universal, however, and are prevalent even among traditionally nonimmigrant societies. What is the long-term impact of large-scale movements of population—heterogeneity and conflict, or amalgamation and tranquillity?

The fate of immigrants depends on many factors. Their chances to adjust, to reach equality, and to integrate are better when the newcomers come in small and unthreatening numbers, scatter all over the country, arrive voluntarily and can leave at will, possess good skills and resources, resemble the resident population in language, culture, and appearance, and enjoy the assistance and goodwill of relatives, acquaintances, oldtimers, and the government.[2]

For a long time successful absorption, adjustment, and integration of immigrants has been associated with assimilation. The newcomers are expected to discard their cultural heritage and ties with their country of origin and to completely assimilate into their new society. It is assumed that both immigrants and established residents share the goal of mutual assimilation and that societal cohesion is based on cultural homogeneity. Disillusionment with assimilation has, nevertheless, become evident since the late 1960s. It was found that assimilation is far from complete and immigrants form new ethnic groups instead of melting into the society at large. The ethos of assimilation has gradually been replaced by the new ideology of multiculturalism, according to which societies can function well with and even benefit from cultural diversity (Parekh 2000).

The United States is the best-known case and leading model of immigrant society. It was formed by the WASPs (White Anglo-Saxon Protestants) who established themselves during the first two centuries of settlement as a charter group and fully absorbed newcomers from northern and western Europe. The mass immigration of non-WASPs from Catholic Ireland and eastern and southern Europe arriving in the nineteenth century and later disrupted the pattern of full assimilation ("Anglo conformity") and changed it to "cultural pluralism." The Irish, Italians, Polish, Jews, and other European immigrants became "white ethnics," a middle group distinguished from the founding and dominant group. The lower stratum in American society is composed of descendants of Natives, Hispanics, and Africans.

The controversy over assimilation versus multiculturalism can be aired by the American experience. Despite its huge territory and population, the United States has a distinct culture consisting of the English language, the British legal tradition, the American way of life, individualism, civic nationalism, liberal democracy, and other patterns. Almost all population groups currently share this WASP culture. The fusion of the population is enormous, registering high intermarriage rates averaging 15 percent among African-Americans, 35 percent among Natives and Mexican-Americans, and over 50 percent among white ethnics. Gans (1979) argues that the ethnicity of the white ethnics has become symbolic rather than real. Symbolic ethnicity is expressed in symbols like folklore and self-identity but not in fateful life choices like where to live, which occupation to choose, whom to befriend and whom to marry. When ethnicity becomes symbolic it is diminished considerably, but its soft forms may persist for generations. On the other hand, the ethnicity of African-Americans is real, still determining their life situations. They challenge American society to recognize their different heritage and to have it represented in the national culture.

The persistence of symbolic ethnicity of the white ethnics and of the real ethnicity of the African-Americans makes a case for multiculturalism. The extent to which the United States is a multicultural or assimilating society is ambiguous and contentious on both the empirical and normative level. Multiculturalism has become a rallying cry of minorities to obtain equality while keeping their separate culture and identity. Its precise meaning varies from one society to another (Joppke 1996, 1999). It presents a special challenge to Western liberal democracies that are based on the principle of individual rights and freedoms, deny collective rights, privatize ethnicity, and encourage assimilation (Kymlicka 1995). It challenges the United States to face its heritage of white superiority and racism and to provide full racial equality and collective rights to African-Americans. It challenges the United Kingdom to face its heritage as an ex-Empire and to treat equally its former subjects who moved to the British Isles. It challenges Germany to redefine its ethnic nation in civic terms and to extend citizenship and full membership to its non-German denizens (guest workers and asylum seekers). These challenges have in common the need to reconcile collective rights with individual liberalism, to move away from the model of a single culture to cultural pluralism, to recast the nation and national identity in a way that would include minorities, and to achieve solidarity and unity amid persistent ethnic diversity and separation.

The question of assimilation versus multiculturalism in Israel varies with the type of internal division. As a whole Israel is a tricultural society without multiculturalist ethos. In addition to the majority's predominantly secular Jewish culture, there is an Arab minority culture and an ultra-Orthodox minority culture. The State aspires to cultural homogeneity but reluctantly recognizes the right of these nonassimilating minorities to separate existence and equips them with the necessary institutional arrangements to preserve their genuine cultures. Israel is an officially Jewish state in its language, majority, institutions, goals, symbols, and policies. The Arab minority, one million (16 percent of the total population of 6.2 million in 2001)[3] enjoys civil rights but is excluded from the national core. The Arab citizens deny the legitimacy of Israel as a Jewish-Zionist state and wish to turn it into a binational state. Arab culture is well protected but not respected by the Jewish majority and is kept off limits of the national culture. Multiculturalism is rejected by the ultra-Orthodox minority (about 7 percent of the total population). It does not make do with full cultural autonomy and assured self-preservation, and attempts to impose its halakhic culture on the entire country.

While these tensions divide three permanent and distinct cultures, the division between Jews hailing from different countries hinges on issues of assimilation and multiculturalism. The cleavage between Ashkenazim (mostly East-European Jews, 55 percent of the Jewish population) and Mizrahim (Jews originating from the Middle East, 45 percent) is widely seen as transitional, superficial, and to a large extent even illegitimate. The doctrine of assimilation applies strongly to this division between Jewish immigrants. It is in this respect that the divide between Mizrahim and Ashkenazim in Israel is similar to the divide between the WASPs and the white ethnics in the United States. The main questions are the following: Is Jewish ethnicity in Israel in fact diminishing into symbolic ethnicity like the white ethnicity in the United States? Can it really be preserved in the name of multiculturalism, and if so, in what form?

The Assimilationist Model

The dominant theme in the public thinking and social science approach to Jewish ethnicity in Israel is assimilation (Eisenstadt 1985; Ben-Rafael 1982; Lissak 1999).[4] It is presumed that Israel as an immigrant society has successfully absorbed Jews from over one hundred countries thanks to the prevalence of several favorable conditions. These circumstances include the preexisting Jewish

49

identity and solidarity, the Zionist ideology of creating a single Jewish nation-state, assimilationist state policies, the great flow of capital from abroad that enables allocation of large sums for immigrant absorption without hurting the oldtimers, and the unifying factor of an external common enemy. Some elaboration on these factors is in order.

Israel essentially differs from other new states in the West and developing world that lack preexisting nationhood. European settlers who did not share a common peoplehood, culture, and identity formed states such as the United States. They had to create these commonalties anew on the basis of living together for two or more centuries. In many developing countries, such as Nigeria, the artificial state boundaries put together ethnic groups that have little in common and the state has to forge a common nation from scratch. On the other hand, Israel greatly benefits from preexisting common Jewish nationhood. Although the Jews live in the Diaspora as minorities that appreciably differ in their daily language, culture, and appearance, they believe in sharing a common ethnic descent (being descendants of the biblical Jacob), a common membership in one Jewish people, a common single religion (Judaism), a common ancient language (Hebrew), a common history, and a common homeland (Eretz Israel). These essential components of a modern nation predated Zionism. They provide strong common bonds of brotherhood and interdependence of fate among the dispersed Jewish communities all over the world in general, and between Mizrahim and Ashkenazim in Israel in particular.

Zionism as an ideology and movement accepted the idea and historical reality that Jews constitute one people and aimed to turn them into a modern nation-state in Eretz Israel. Central to Zionism is the tenet of the ingathering and amalgamation of exiles. All the Jews are urged to return to their historical homeland and to merge into one nation, shading off their Diaspora heritage and ethnic division. Jewish settlers and newcomers are not considered as immigrants but rather as "returnees," namely, people who were "temporarily" and forcibly absent from their homeland and returning to it with devotion and full rights. Zionism aspires to fashion in the ancestral homeland a new Jewish society, a modern Jewish nation, a modern Jewish culture, a modern Hebrew language, and a new modern Jew (without a minority mentality, economically productive, assertive, fighting, patriotic, and generally devoid of the Galuth ills). Classical Zionism is strongly assimilationist and uniculturalist in its orientation toward Jewish ethnicity in Israel. It delegitimizes ethnic differences and seeks to base national unity on uniformity. In view of the preexisting nature of the Jewish people and the nation-building project of Zionism, it is no wonder that assimilationist policies and practices have predominated in the Yishuv (the modern Jewish community in Palestine before 1948) and Israel. The Law of Return grants every Jew the right to free immigration to the country and to instant, automatic, full, and equal citizenship. New arrivals are accorded a package of aids designed to facilitate their absorption. As a Jewish state Israel grants Jews a favored status and a series of entitlements denied to Arabs. The state encourages the ethnic mixing of the Jewish population. Special programs, such as compensatory education and urban renewal, are launched to help Jews from deprived areas to achieve social mobility and full integration. Mixed marriage among Jews is considered as a fully legitimate and even desirable option. Jews from Moslem countries are not provided with any means, such as separate schools and separate communities, to preserve their heritage and to foster a distinct identity. Separate ethnic institutions are usually frowned upon as divisive. Only folkloristic patterns are tolerated as items for preservation by ethnic groups.

Since proclamation in 1948, Israel has enjoyed ample foreign aid and a continued rise in living standards.[5] Israel's new frontiers after 1967 have also contributed to the steady enlargement of its opportunity structure. The structural discrimination against Arab citizens has diverted some resources for investment in the Jewish sector. The expansion of Israeli resources by external sources has enabled the government to invest in immigrant absorption, to extend welfare services, to improve living conditions, and to furnish opportunities for social mobility for the Jews without depriving the oldtimers. The oldtimers have not suffered and have not had to make sacrifices in order to absorb the newcomers. The assimilationist model emphasizes that Israelis blessed with a noncompeti- *really?* tive situation (a nonzero-sum game) that vastly contributes to harmonious relations between current and previous waves of immigrants.

Finally, the incessant Israeli-Arab conflict creates strong solidarity between all Jews in Israel. The resident Jewish population is dependent on continued immigration in order to fulfill the causes of Zionism, to reinforce Israel's viability and deterrence potential, to reduce the per capita security burden, and to fight the fateful wars.

Although the assimilation of the non-European immigration in the 1950s presented special difficulties due to its large size and lack of modernism, it is argued that the ethnic problem has been moderated considerably over the first fifty years of statehood.[6] This is shown in the emergence of a common Israeli culture, the universal use of Hebrew, the high rate of mixed marriages, widespread social mobility, the coming of Mizrahim to power, and the virtual lack of ethnic conflict (personal discrimination, separate identity, ideological dispute, unrest, and violence). The ethnic problem has persisted, however, in certain pockets that are hard to tackle (mostly poor and working-class Moroccan Jews in the development towns and urban centers).[7] Jewish ethnicity has become more symbolic than real, as is the case with European ethnicity in the

United States. It will endure for generations to come but in progressively milder forms. Israel has actually moved over the years from the ideology and policy of complete fusion of exiles to cultural pluralism. Mizrahim and later immigrants, like Russian and Ethiopian newcomers, are no longer expected to fully dispose of their cultural heritage and are allowed instead to keep their particularity while integrating into the wider society. According to this neo-assimilationist approach, Israel has become increasingly multicultural and tolerant of ethnic differences. Cultural pluralism has grown to a counterproductive degree, encouraging sectorial interests and harming national unity.[8]

The Critical Model

The predominant assimilationist perspective on Israeli Jewish ethnicity is challenged by critical social scientists (Smooha 1978, 1986; Swirski 1989; Yiftachel 2000) and by social critics (Meir 1998; Chetrit 1999; Alternative Information Center 1999).[9] They attribute special significance to certain factors that tend to sustain ethnicity. These factors include the strong gross power asymmetry between newcomers and veterans, tendency of established groups to keep their dominance, the reproduction of ethnic disparities through class inequalities, and the contribution of the core-periphery split to the perpetuation of the ethnic division and state discriminatory policies. The main thesis of these critical scholars and social critics is that Jewish ethnicity is potent and persistent and not just symbolic. These critical ideas need some clarification.

The point of departure of the critical model is the simple fact that European Jews had already established themselves as a founding core group by the time of the mass immigration of Jews from Moslem states to Israel during the 1950s. Zionism originated in Europe at the end of the nineteenth century in response to the "Jewish question" there. Jewish life was precarious and unsettling. In the authoritarian, backward, and nationalist Eastern Europe, the Jews did not enjoy civil rights and suffered from exclusion, while in the progressive central and Western Europe Jews continued to suffer from gross discrimination despite emancipation, social mobility, and assimilation. Zionism emerged, therefore, as one solution to the Jewish predicament, copying the rise of ethno-nationalist movements in Europe at the time. European Jews immigrated to Palestine and formed the new Yishuv and then the State of Israel. Since no similar crisis in Jewish life under Islam took place until the 1940s, Jews from the Middle East constituted only 12 percent of the immigrants before 1948.[10] When they were forced to leave Islamic countries because of the Arab-Jewish confrontation in Palestine and to come en masse to Israel in the 1950s, they found Ashkenazim well entrenched in the core institutions of society.

While preexisting Jewish identity made the immigration of Mizrahim to Israel possible and provided a common feeling of brotherhood and peoplehood, it did not and could not counteract the well-established Ashkenazi dominance. Three factors combined to streamline the Mizrahi newcomers to the lower echelons of society: Mizrahim's weaknesses, the state's dire needs, and institutional discrimination.

Mizrahim came without capital and adequate education, their families were very large, and they had few relatives and acquaintances among the oldtimers to draw on. As a result of the Jewish-Arab dispute, Mizrahim became de facto refugees, forcibly driven out of their countries of origin, had no other place to go but Israel, and after arrival could not leave the country. Israel in the 1950s urgently needed to settle the lands occupied during the 1948 war beyond those allocated by the United Nations, to strengthen the army, to expand the economy, to widen the middle class, and to increase the state administration and welfare services. To meet these exigencies, a large population amenable to mobilization and to manipulation was required.

The targeting of the Mizrahi immigrants for meeting the state's urgent needs was due not only to their inherent vulnerability but also and mostly to the preconceptions of the Ashkenazi establishment. In the eyes of the state and the Ashkenazi charter group, the Jews from Arab countries were backward and latecomers who should modernize, improve greatly, and prove themselves before aspiring to influence and privilege. In the eyes of the Labor establishment and veteran Ashkenazim, Mizrahi immigrants were the mirror opposite of themselves and of what the new society should be: Mizrahim represented the most despised Arab or Levantine backwardness (Rejwan 1998) and Galuth mentality (Diaspora heritage) (Raz-Krakotzkin 1994). They were perceived as "the other," the opposite of the new Jew and Israeli (the *Tzabar*)

Ashkenazi rejection and maltreatment of Mizrahim were driven by colonial spirit and insecure Western identity. As Europeans, Ashkenazim saw Jews from Moslem lands as Arabized Jews infected with inherent mental inferiority and underdevelopment (Tzur 1997). This view was reinforced by a sense of insecurity as Westerners. East European Jews who immigrated to central-Western Europe were seen by local fellow Jews as inferior and were pressured to Westernize quickly. Originating mostly from Eastern Europe, Israeli Ashkenazim did to Mizrahim what Western Jews did to them: Identifying themselves as Westerners, they felt ashamed of Mizrahim, "Orientalized" them (i.e., stigmatized them as culturally inferior) and conditioned their acceptance of them on fundamental cultural transformation (Khazzoom 1999). These Ashkenazi ill-feelings toward Mizrahim were, however, moderated by strong nationalism that underscores Jewish unity and equality and the Mizrahi ability to change and Westernize.

Ashkenazim feared that the primitive Mizrahi mass immigration might undermine the new, secular, modern culture and the young and fragile Israeli democracy.[11] This paternalistic view drove the government to forestall these dangers by controlling the immigrants and benefiting from them at the same time. The assailable Mizrahi immigrants were enlisted to relieve the immediate state problems. They were culturally despised and repressed, discriminated against in the allocation of services and resources (employment, positions of power, and settlement in the urban centers), and exploited as a channel for the collective social mobility of both the Ashkenazi oldtimers and newcomers (Bernstein 1989).

This combination of forces formed ethnic stratification during the 1950s. Ashkenazim moved en masse to the middle class and higher while the majority of Mizrahim found themselves in the working class and lower (Bernstein and Swirski 1982). The critical model posits that, once a system of ethnic stratification was established, it is predisposed to self-reproduction by the normal mechanisms of class self-reproduction in capitalist societies. Ethnic class perpetuation can, however, be moderated or even eliminated by government intervention or large-scale societal changes in favor of the lower rungs of society.

The core-periphery split also facilitates ethno-class reproduction. A disproportional part of Mizrahim were dispatched by the government in the 1950s and 1960s to development towns and agricultural settlements in the periphery of the country, and many had no choice but to stay there. Since the standards of development and services in the periphery were and still are much lower than in the urban centers, the chances of the deprived Mizrahim in the periphery to enter the middle class were and are slim. Hence the core-periphery divide indirectly consolidates ethnic inequality. Rather than being symbolic and transient, critics claim, the division between Ashkenazim and Mizrahim is real and pervasive. Neither government intervention nor structural transformation has been undertaken to phase it out.

Areas of Persistent Ethnicity

The indications for the persistent significance of Jewish ethnicity are various and numerous. The following are the most important manifestations of ethnicity among Jews in Israel in the early 2000s.

Collective Memory

There is a sharp contrast in the collective memory of the two ethnic groups, especially of the 1950s as a formative decade. In the collective memory of most Mizrahim, including the second and third generations, these were years of deep distress, degeneration in the transit camps and development towns, destruction of tradition and religion, cultural repression, degradation, blatant ethnic discrimination, condescending establishment, profound disillusionment, alienation, and marginality. The sense of injustice and trauma can account for the rejection that most Mizrahim feel toward the left, the ruling establishment at the time, and for their support of the right.

The collective memory of most Ashkenazim and their descendants is totally different. As far as they are concerned, during the 1950s the newcomers and old-timers suffered alike from deprivation; the oldtimers consented to mass immigration although it far exceeded the absorbing capability of the new and poor state; the Mizrahi immigrants came without education and assets; an attempt was made to replace their backward culture with the modern Israeli culture; the ruling establishment acted in good faith; the errors that were occasionally committed were unavoidable; Mizrahim should feel grateful for what was done for them; and the grand project of the mass immigration and absorption was overall a great success. This Ashkenazi narrative is inherently quasi-colonialist and Orientalist (Peterburg 1995), dating back to the beginning of the twentieth century (Shafir 1990).[12] It leaves no room for Mizrahi grievances, there is nobody to blame, and there is no injustice to remedy. In the Ashkenazi historical consciousness, Mizrahi feelings of deprivation are recognized but not justified. Irrationality is attributed to the Mizrahim for acting according to an unjustified sense of inequity and vengeance.

After its defeat in the 1996 elections, the Labor Party under the fresh leadership of Barak feels politically obliged to correct its historical image among Mizrahim. Barak, its new leader argued that bitter collective memory blocks Mizrahim from voting for the party in spite of its policies in favor of the lower strata and ethnic integration. Only admission of wrongdoing in the past and request of forgiveness by the party, Barak maintained, can overcome the mental block Mizrahim feel about the party. Barak managed to persuade the Labor Party to officially ask Mizrahim for pardon for its wrongdoing in the 1950s, mostly for not respecting the Mizrahi immigrants and for not recognizing their contribution to the country (*Ha'aretz,* September 29, 1997). This step should be understood against the foil of forgiveness and reconciliation pursued in the West (including South Africa and Japan) by charter groups. It was also prompted by Labor dependence on gaining further votes from Mizrahim in order to win the national elections.

Whatever its causes, the pardon initiative is quite significant. It is doubtful, however, that Ashkenazim in general, including Ashkenazi supporters of Labor in particular, have changed their mind and feel remorse. Barak's request of pardon was rejected by a large number of top politicians and intellectuals in the Labor Party and the Left. To name just a few, Shimon Peres, a former Prime Minister, and Yitzhak Navon, a former President of the state, and Teddy Koleg, a former Mayor of Jerusalem, opposed the move. It is argued that no wrongdoing was committed, immigrant absorption was a great success and Mizrahim were not the only group that suffered at the time.[13] Anita Shapira, a mainstream historian, identified with the Labor Party and Director of the Rabin Center for Israel Studies, also took exception to the resolution. She declared: "I can understand Japanese apologizing to the Koreans. I cannot understand for what is to apologize to Mizrahim" (interview in *Ha'aretz* Weekly Supplement, October 10, 1997).

Cultural Hegemony

Inspired by Zionism to create a new Jewish culture and a new Jew, the Ashkenazi charter group formed before 1948 a new indigenous culture that later became the Israeli culture. It is a national culture, shared by all except the ultra-Orthodox and Arab minorities who hold distinct cultures of their own. Underpinning Israeli culture is Hebrew as a modern language for daily thinking and functioning and for accessing a rich Jewish heritage. The modern Israeli culture favors change, espouses the Protestant ethics, and values education and exposure to mass media. Its values also include informal interpersonal relations, bad manners, aggressiveness, disrespect of privacy, and the view of law as a bending and negotiable norm. Israeli culture is familistic, nationalistic, and materialistic. Although formed by Ashkenazim, this culture is a new product that does not resemble Ashkenazi or Mizrahi cultures of the Diaspora. Neither is it Western despite its Western orientation and pretension to be Western.

Israeli culture is hegemonic.[14] As an ideology multiculturalism provides for the recognition of the right of the ultra-Orthodox Jews and Arabs, to be different and separate. This recognition does not, however, protect these against minority cultures disdain, and it falls short of treating them as integral and equal parts of the national culture. At the same time, the original cultures of the immigrants in general, and of the Judeo-Arab cultures of the Mizrahim in particular, were repressed and shattered, not just adapted to Israeli life. To begin with these uprooted cultures had little chance of surviving in the new modern Israeli environment, and in the face of the harsh policies of cultural repression, and having severed ties with their life source (the degraded, failing, and demonized Arab world).

Some cultural openness developed in the 1970s, however, when it became evident that the Israeli culture is strong and the fears of Levantization were over-exaggerated. Cultural expressions compatible with the core Israeli culture were permitted and even encouraged. A component known as "Mizrahi Heritage" was added to the school curriculum. It included folkloristic elements and chapters in the history and literature of Mizrahim. Viable ethnic subcultures, held by Anglo-Saxons, Russians, Moroccans, Yemenites, Iraqis, Ethiopians, and others, have flourished. Such optional, minor ethnic subcultures enrich and refresh, rather than weaken and displace, the core culture. They are found in all Western settler-immigrant societies and liberal democracies. The original Mizrahi cultures were partially retained, hybridized and Israelized (Shokeid and Deshen 1999; Lewis 1984). They were transformed into Israeli Mizrahi subcultures. Some of them contain folk patterns, particularly components of "folk religion" (inconsistent observance of Orthodox religion, pilgrimages, cults of saints, healing services, rabbinical blessings and magic).[15]

Three features characterize the Israeli cultural scene in the early 2000s. First, Ashkenazim enjoy cultural hegemony because the culture they formed has become the Israeli dominant culture and they do not need to make any cultural adaptation. This Israeli culture is not Western, Ashkenazi, or Mizrahi, but rather a new, locally made culture, containing diverse elements. Second, ultra-Orthodox Jews and Arabs maintain separate cultures but are denied tolerance and acceptance. And third, immigrant groups cling to ethnic subcultures in addition to acquiring Israeli core culture. Cultural alienation has declined as a result of the incorporation of certain patterns from the ethnic subcultures into the national culture. Mizrahim still suffer however from cultural stigma, and their subcultures are still held in low regard corresponding to their proletarian and lower-class positions. This ambiguity is evident, for instance, in music. Mizrahi musicians who manage to adapt their work to the "high Western standards" are accepted nationally, while common Mizrahi music is considered to be low in quality and is not allowed to compete freely despite its popularity among Mizrahim (Regev 1997).[16]

like Adalusion Orchestra

Social Separation

Contrary to the Zionist ideal of free mixing of Jews regardless of ethnic origin, most Israeli Jews still live with members of their own ethnic group as friends, next door neighbors, classmates and marriage partners. Most striking is the separation in residential quarters. Most Mizrahim live in development towns, in Moshavim that were established after 1948, and in working-class and poor neighborhoods in the urban centers, whereas Ashkenazim are concentrated in middle-class and well-off neighborhoods in big cities, in Moshavim that were established before 1948, and in the privileged "communal villages" (*yishuvim kehilatyim*). As a result of the increasing stability of the population in these areas, ethnic communities have crystallized.

Residential isolation brings about separation in education, which is very high in kindergartens and primary schools. The policy of ethnic integration formally applies to seventh to ninth graders only and it actually includes only half of them. Tracking in high schools and the underrepresentation of Mizrahim in the universities further contribute to educational separation.

Religion is the only area in which ethnic separation is institutionalized. Israeli law provides for two chief rabbis and two local rabbis in localities in which each ethnic group constitutes at least one-third of the population. Synagogues, the cornerstones of religious life in Judaism, are highly ethnic. Ethnic separation is largest among the ultra-Orthodox and substantial among the national religious.

The rate of mixed marriages is significant but not sufficiently high to blur ethnic boundaries. On the one hand, about one-quarter of the newlywed each year are ethnically mixed, and the bulk of them comes from the middle class. These intermarriages increase interethnic contacts, tolerance, and equality not only for the couples involved but also for a larger circle of relatives and friends. On the other hand, the rate of marriages within the same ethnic group (i.e., among Ashkenazim from different countries of origin and among Mizrahim from different countries of origin) is over 50 percent. It makes for internal homogeneity of the two ethnic groups and for sharpening of the boundaries between them. Contrary to preconceptions, education has not replaced ethnicity as the prime factor in the selection of marriage partners (Shavit and Stier 1997).

Politics

Israeli politics since the early 1980s has been polarized into two political camps. The right-wing camp is headed by the Likud Party and includes the religious parties and the Radical Right. It officially stands for Greater Israel, negotiates toughly before making territorial concessions in exchange for peace, protects Jewish interests more than universal rights, and treats religion favorably. On the other hand, the Left camp is led by the Labor Party and contains the Zionist Left (Meretz) and Arab parties. Its prime movers are the partition of Eretz Israel in order to keep Israel Jewish, the defense of general values, and the restriction of the role of religion in public life. There is, nevertheless, no difference between the two camps on social issues since both support privatization, a predominantly market economy, and a welfare state and globalization.

This division into two political camps is ethnically marked and reinforced. Most Ashkenazim support the Labor camp whereas most Mizrahim back the Likud camp. Mizrahim prefer the Likud because of their deep resentment toward Labor for past injustices, anti-Arab sentiment, attachment to traditional religion, competition in the labor market with Arabs (Lewin-Epstein 1989), and vital gains derived from being Jews in a Jewish state. For these reasons the shift in voting of Mizrahim is by and large within the camp rather than toward the Labor camp.

Mizrahim enjoy nearly equal representation in Israeli politics. Nearly half of the Jewish members of the Knesset and government ministers in 1998–2001 were of Mizrahi origin. In 2001 the head of the Histadrut (Federation of Labor) and the chief of staff of the army, The Minister of Defense, the Minister of Treasury, and the State's President were Mizrahi as well. Mizrahim also filled the posts of a defense minister and a foreign affairs minister and contested the top positions of the prime minister and the State's president. In addition, two parties are identified with Mizrahim. Gesher is a splinter party from the Likud, led by Knesset member Levy, who failed to secure the leadership of the Likud. It leads the social lobby. The other Sephardic party is Shas, a breakaway from the ultra-Orthodox party Agudat Israel, and is led by Rabbi Ovadia Yosef. Its strategy is to build a new Sephardic sector as the Ashkenazi Aguda has done.

Despite the Mizrahim's impressive political representation and their two ethnic parties, they do not have an equal share of power. Ashkenazim control the two major political parties and the two political camps. They set the political agenda as the peace process rather than pressing internal issues. They decide that the economy should be privatized and restructured in order to compete in the world market. They determine Israel's orientation toward the West rather than integration into the region. All the social movements that have come with a new political message and gathered political clout, of which Peace Now and Gush Emunim are the most important, are Ashkenazi movements. Since most Mizrahi politicians are and see themselves as representatives of their parties rather than their ethnic groups, they do not try to articulate and serve Mizrahi interests and outlooks.

Class

Israel is a middle-class society, but the gaps between the higher and lower classes are substantial and growing. For instance, the income differential between the lowest and highest paid employee in industry and banking is enormous. However, destitution can hardly be found in Israel because of the provision of universal services and transfer payments to the poor. Thanks to the expansion of the economy and society in Israel's first fifty years, Israelis irrespective of social class and ethnic origin have enjoyed rising educational and living standards and high rates of social mobility (Smooha 1993).

Inequality in the distribution of resources is the most central component in ethnic relations in Israel. Its disappearance is a national goal and its continuity is a source of feelings of deprivation and severe tensions. Educational inequality is considered the key to the ethnic problem. While inequality in school attendance through the end of high school is small and declining, Mizrahim receive education of much lower quality (Swirski 1995). Their high school education is more vocational than academic, leading less often to matriculation diplomas (Shavit 1990; Dar and Resh 1990; Swirski 1990). The real bottleneck is higher education, where for every Mizrahi student there are two to three Ashkenazim.[17] The ratio of ethnic inequality among persons with a university degree in the general population is even greater—1 to 3–4. The ethnic disparities in education are associated with similar inequalities in employment, income, and standard of living. To illustrate, Ashkenazim are overrepresented as much as four times among persons employed in the professions and scientific occupations. The overwhelming majority of the Jewish and nonimmigrant poor are Mizrahi. Family capital accumulation is much greater among Ashkenazim because they have higher incomes, live in better-off neighborhoods, and inherit much more per capita (Lewin-Epstein, Elmelech, and Semyonov 1997).

As a result, the class structure of Israeli-Jewish society is ethnically distinct. The marginal, unemployed stratum of those living on welfare, criminals, the disabled, and the nonworking and nonstudying youths, etc., is nearly all Mizrahi. The stratum of production and service workers, who earn low wages and of whom many border on poverty, is predominantly Mizrahi. The middle class is ethnically mixed with a disadvantage to Mizrahim. Ashkenazim enjoy a marked lead in the upper-middle class of professionals, managers, and the petit-bourgeois. They staff and control the new high-technology economy. The elite in all areas of life, with the exception of politics and the army is by and large Ashkenazi.

Two serious manifestations accompany this ethnic stratification. The substantial representation of Mizrahim in politics has not brought about similar penetration into the elite of the economy, bureaucracy, law, professions, management, science, universities, mass media, the intellectuals, and social movements.[18] The strong tendency to recruit people to the elite from among relatives, acquaintances, and persons already in another elite position blocks the mobility of Mizrahi high achievers (Etzioni-Halevy 1993). The meager representation in nonpolitical and nonmilitary elites restricts the Mizrahim's effective power and perpetuates popular doubts concerning their competence.

Even graver is the fact that ethnic socioeconomic discrepancies persist in spite of cultural convergence (Benski 1994). They are passed on to the local-born generation, which shares Israeli culture. The ethnic gap in earnings, education, and occupational standards among the Israeli-born is as high as or even higher than among the foreign-born (Nahon 1987; Eisenstadt, Lissak, and Nahon 1993; Cohen and Haberfeld 1998).[19] This persistence of ethnic stratification is due not only to normal processes of class reproduction but also to the exceptional accomplishments of the Ashkenazi Israeli-born, who are socialized for achievement and success and enjoy a high investment in formal and informal education, a positive self-image, a small-family milieu, and a transfer of substantial assets from the older generation of founders and oldtimers.

The overlap between class and ethnicity renders ethnicity real. Ethnicity appreciably determines, through social class, the life chances and lifestyles of Israeli Jews.

Conflict

Ethnic conflict in Israel is not intensive. The low intensity of ethnic conflict is evident in several areas. The blatant manifestations of ideological rejection of the regime, biological racism, legal discrimination, violent disturbances, and severe alienation, which are common in deeply divided societies, are absent in Jewish ethnicity in Israel. There is, also cross-ethnic Jewish consensus on basic issues—the hegemony of Zionism, Israel as a Jewish state, the "Arabs as aggressors" narrative of the Arab-Jewish conflict, orientation toward the West, the distinctiveness of the Israeli culture, and assimilation as the main means to resolve the ethnic problem. Attitudinal surveys of Mizrahim and Ashkenazim show that ethnic identity, feeling of distance, desire of avoidance and perception of ethnic discrimination are weak and have declined over the years, and, most importantly, are the lowest compared to parallel attitudes dividing newcomers and oldtimers, religious and secular, right and left supporters, and Arabs and Jews (Peres, Ben-Rafael and Fishler 2001).[20]

While Jewish ethnicity does not make Israel a deeply divided society, there is a wide range of relatively moderate expressions of ethnic tension that testify to the significant repercussions of the Mizrahi-Ashkenazi division. Beyond the national Jewish consensus on fundamental values and orientations, significant disagreements prevail. Mizrahim are more predisposed than Ashkenazim to give more weight to religion and to national interest in individual and public life, to support affirmative action for achieving ethnic equality and integration, to favor an increase in Mizrahi influence on the national culture, and to blame Ashkenazim, the State, and the Labor Party for their predicament. These ethnic discords are reinforced by the overlap between ethnicity, class, and politics. To be sure, Mizrahim demand greater cultural and political influence and greater integration, not multiculturalism and separation.

The dominant Israeli culture has an attitude of superiority and contempt toward the Orient, viewing Mizrahim as afflicted with the backwardness of the underdeveloped world. Many of the Israeli leaders have expressed such views and warned against Levantization. Although such pronouncements have become less frequent and more subtle over the years, an ethnocentric element continues to characterize the thinking of the elite, of Hebrew literature, of the mass media (Shohat 1987), and of the general public. The Mizrahi Jew is perceived unfavorably as less Israeli. Both Ashkenazim and Mizrahim regard the Mizrahi as less intelligent, more primitive, more vocal, more irrational, and more extreme than the Ashkenazi, but also warmer and more sociable. This stereotype is common even among educated Ashkenazim, the Israeli-born, and teachers (Stahl 1991), and since it is internalized by the Mizrahim themselves, it generates among them a basic feeling of incompetence and low self-esteem. Besides, Ashkenazim feel more reserved about having a Mizrahi as a friend, a next-door neighbor, or a marriage partner. Such ethnic stereotyping and rejection are intertwined with class deprivation. The image of Mizrahim cannot be positive as long as they predominate among the working and lower classes, are identified with the poor and criminal, and are virtually absent from the nonpolitical and nonmilitary elites.

Ethnic discrimination largely takes institutional forms and is only partly personal and intentional. As such it is latent, effective, and acceptable. Social institutions, such as the economy and education, are set up in a way that favors Ashkenazim in fulfilling self-potential and in competing for resources. This widespread, "normal," and institutional kind of discrimination is reflected in keeping lower the minimum wage and the wages of production workers, in offering mostly dead-end jobs to residents of development towns, in designing the educational system to fit the life experiences of the Ashkenazi middle class, and in centralizing political power. These practices hurt more Mizrahim since they are concentrated in the lower classes and on the periphery. At the same time Israel has not taken steps toward affirmative action, common in North America, in favor of deprived groups. The programs of compensatory education fall much short of counterbalancing the definite advantages enjoyed by Ashkenazi children. Urban renewal and subsidized mortgages hardly equalize the tremendous ethnic gap in housing whose cost in Israel is one of the highest in the world. In the absence of a crash program to bring Mizrahim to a par with Ashkenazim, normal processes of ethnic and class reproduction predominate.

Land allocation can well illustrate the intricacies of institutional discrimination and the intermediary position that Mizrahim occupy in Israeli society. Around 93 percent of the land in Israel is owned by the state or the Jewish National Fund. A substantial portion of the land is leased to Moshavim and Kibbutzim for agricultural use. Driven by the need to help this rural sector, which endured financial crisis, and by liberalization and privatization policies, the government planned to privatize these public lands and to award Moshavim and Kibbutzim about one-quarter of their land-holdings. The core of the scheme is re-zoning, which would increase the value of the land many-fold. The beneficiaries of the program are mostly veteran Ashkenazim who hold the bulk of these lands. Yet some Mizrahi members of Moshavim are bound to benefit, too, though to a smaller degree. While the program was stalled during the 1990s by various protest groups led by the Keshet Hademocratit Hamizrahit, another program was undertaken to assist poor Mizrahim by privatizing at subsidized rates publicly owned apartments in poor neighborhoods. Another program was launched during the 1980s, which established about 160 "communal villages," mostly in the Galilee and Northern Negev. These are Jewish settlements in Arab areas in Israel proper designed to break down Arab territorial contiguity. The owners of the private houses in these new and state-subsidized communities are mostly middle-class Ashkenazim, but some of them are Mizrahim too. Taken together these programs of land allocation (Yiftachel and Kedar 2000), while appearing universal and color-blind, reinforce ethno-national stratification in which Arab citizens are at the bottom, Ashkenazim at the top, and Mizrahim in between.

In view of the persistence of inequalities and lack of equal opportunity, the low level of ethnic protest is striking. Ethnic violence and unrest is lacking. Ethnic protest is sidetracked by voting for the Likud bloc and Shas and by hate of the Left and Arabs. It is softened by continuing improvement in living standards and by sustained belief in social mobility. Cooptation of political leaders and ongoing assimilation steadily diminish the protest potential. Yet sporadic eruptions of ethnic protest deeply irritate public opinion and serve as a reminder that there is at a deeper level a dormant reservoir of intense feelings of deprivation, bitterness, envy, and hatred among wide strata of Mizrahim. These genuine, pent-up emotions do not surface in daily consciousness and behavior but erupt occasionally.

The support of Shas is the most important indicator of Mizrahi discontent and protest. One third of all Mizrahi voters and a half of North African voters voted for Shas in the 1999 Knesset elections. Shas won 17 seats in the Knesset and emerged as the third largest political party. The majority of these voters are religious or traditional, neither ultra-Orthodox nor secular. Shas is no doubt an enigma, a complex phenomenon, combining diverse and conflicting tendencies (Willis 1995; Peled 2001; Pedahzur 2000). Yet its non-mainstream character is widely evident. It aims to bring Mizrahim back to religion and to replace the secular nature of Israeli society with the Sephardic version of Orthodoxy. It accuses Zionism of cultural repression, secularization, pauperization and marginalization of Sephardim in Israel. It fights for religious legislation and for the retention and augmentation of special privileges for the Haredim. It also displays certain properties of the radical right, including attacks against the Supreme Court, hate of Arabs, animosity toward the left, and exclusionary measures against foreign workers. By supporting Shas, Mizrahim express protest and disaffection.

To illustrate the sporadic surge of ethnicity, a brief mention of several occurrences in the late 1990s would suffice. A militant protest group, headed by Rabbi Meshulam, demanded the appointment of a state inquiry commission to investigate allegations that during the early 1950s hundreds of babies of Yemenite immigrants were kidnapped for adoption by "better qualified," childless Ashkenazim in Israel and abroad. The protest turned highly violent. The leader of

Shas, Dar'i, was tried for personal corruption. He and his supporters accused the police, the justice department, and the Supreme Court of ethnic discrimination and inability to tolerate a successful Sephardic party and a rising Moroccan leader. David Levi, the leader of the Gesher Party, accused Natanyahu, before breaking away with Likud, of treating him and his supporters as a bunch of criminals and primitive monkeys. Immediately after taking office in mid-1998, Yitzhak Levi, the new Sephardic minister of education and culture, initiated a policy of giving higher priority to Mizrahi culture by increasing the funding to Mizrahi arts, music, dance, theatre, and the like. The Ashkenazi cultural elite reacted with shock, dismay, and harsh opposition for fear of losing vested privilege. Two candidates ran for the post of State president in 1998—the incumbent Weitzman and Amor, a Moroccan Knesset member who played the ethnic card ("I will be the first President from Second Israel") with the blessing of the Likud political bloc.[21] The ethnic overtones coloring the contest were disturbing to many. The minister of defense, Mordechai, born in Kurdistan, decided to choose Mufaz, of Iranian origin, as the army's chief of staff. He was accused of personal revenge and ethnic favoritism against General Vilnai, the Ashkenazi contender and the favorite of the establishment.

Most telling was the Or Affair. Knesset member Or is an ex-general, a top Labor leader and a person of integrity. In a press interview drawing a lesson from the Labor Party's appeal to Mizrahim for forgiveness, Or expressed disappointment. "I feel sad because the request of pardon has not helped. It must be clear: I am accusing Mizrahim, not Barak." He blamed Mizrahi political leaders, his fellows in the party in particular, of oversensitivity, honor complex ("Defense Minister, Yitzhak Mordechai, is the champion of [honor] complexes"), and insusceptibility for rational discussion. They feel deprived, get insulted quickly, shy away from self-criticism, misinterpret any criticism as an ethnic attack, and manipulate their ethnicity for political gains. "The problem is that I cannot talk to them as I talk to others who are *more Israeli in their character*." Or continued: "When I say Mizrahim, I mean Moroccans in particular. This is the largest and most problematic ethnic group. I feel sad because these strata *lack curiosity* to know what is surrounding them and why is it so. When I appear before them, I see their lack of interest in listening, understanding and recognizing life in order to know what is right and wrong. This troubles me because it hurts not only them but also the entire Israeli society" (Ben-Simon 1998).

Or's pronouncements stirred a public storm. He was accused of racism, the Labor Party decided to deprive him of any representative role, and some of his fellow Knesset members demanded his resignation from the Knesset and party. Of highest concern was the potential electoral damage to the party. Or made vague apology and declined to resign from the Knesset. He explained that he had the good intention of raising the neglected ethnic problem and excising it from politics. He insisted on having wide popular support and initiated a series of meetings with Moroccan Jews who were Labor supporters and residents of development towns. He succeeded in engaging in "a genuine dialog on the ethnic issue" and was well received.

The Or Affair confirmed that statements that are seen as racist or quasi-racist are not politically correct in Israel of the 2000s, that Mizrahim have accumulated enough power to retaliate against such statements, that subtle and covert racism and paternalism still lurk in the minds of many Ashkenazim, and that the ethnic problem has remained an open wound in Israeli society despite all efforts to negate its existence and to deny it legitimacy. A Moroccan journalist and entertainer wrote in reaction to Or's interview: "From Golda's 'they [the Black Panthers in 1971] are not nice' to Or's 'they [the Moroccans] lack curiosity,' this country was founded by such people. Their racism is most difficult to eradicate because it is, as it were, buried under tons of goodwill. It is hardest to fight their racism because it extends a helping hand and smiles. But make no mistake, in Israel of 1998, this is the most problematic and degrading racism" (Levi 1998).[22]

Implications of Historical Developments

Three great historical developments are reshaping Israeli society in the nineties and 2000s. These are mass immigration from the former Soviet Union, advancing globalization, and transition to peace. What are the implications of these grand forces for the ethnic division? It is expected that they are going to strengthen Jewish ethnicity rather than blur it.

Continuing immigration will hurt Mizrahim. Since Israel is a society of Jewish immigration and since over 85 percent of Diaspora Jewry is Ashkenazi, it is inevitable that immigration will reduce the weight of Mizrahim in the total Israeli population and deflect attention from the Mizrahi question. In fact, the advent of close to one million Russian-speaking immigrants to Israel in 1989–2001 has already transformed the Mizrahi status from that of a numerical majority to that of a numerical minority. The Russian immigrants have undermined the Mizrahim's majority even in their traditional strongholds—development towns and working-class communities. They decided the Knesset elections by voting for the Labor bloc in 1992 and switching to the Likud bloc in 1996, and supporting the Labor bloc in 1999. In 2001 they had three ethnic parties: Israel BeAliya (established in 1996), Israel Betenu (1999) and Habehira Hademokratit (2000), 9 Knesset seats and two government ministries.

The impact of the Russian mass immigration on Mizrahim is expected to be even greater in the socioeconomic sphere than in politics. New Russian immigrants have definite advantages over most Mizrahi oldtimers, who are concentrated in the working and lower classes. They come to Israel with higher education and technological skills, have extremely small families, espouse a strong achievement drive and high aspirations, feel culturally superior to the Israeli population, and help each other. In view of these assets, the Russian immigrants successfully compete with Mizrahim in the labor market and for social mobility into the middle class. It is estimated that they will enter the middle class en masse after a transition period of 5–10 years of adjustment.[23] Advancing globalization has a similar adverse impact on Jewish ethnicity. From its inception, Israeli society has been open to the influence of global forces. Immediately after the proclamation of the state, Israel shifted from a subsistence to a market economy, joined the West in science and technology, allied itself with the West in the Cold War, and adopted a strong Western orientation in law, criminal justice, culture, mass media, leisure, and sports. Globalization took off in the 1980s. The Israeli economy approached the world capitalist core through an increase in competition, in its share of multinationals, in privatization, in the collapse of the Histadrut industrial complex, in the gradual disappearance of labor-intensive jobs, and in the phenomenal growth of high technology industries (communications, electronics, software, medical equipment, missiles, and other cutting-edge technologies). Israel became part of the world media network through a new telephone system, cable television, and the Internet. Israelis broke records in the volume of tourism to other countries.

The effects of growing globalization are diverse and divisive. Globalization increases Western influences on Israel, making it more materialistic, consumerist, individualistic, secular, and pragmatic. It decreases social solidarity and exacerbates class inequality. Globalization fits the outlooks and serves the interests of the higher strata, resonating with and reinforcing their more cosmopolitan views. It multiplies the opportunities for people with know-how, initiative, and connections. On the other hand, the lower strata are hard hit by globalization. Their jobs and wages are threatened and depressed by automation and cheap labor,[24] and their life conditions are made worse by the erosion of the welfare state as a result of diminishing solidarity. The implications of globalization for the ethnic scene are evident. Ashkenazim, who tend to be more secular and better off, are bound to benefit from it, while Mizrahim, more traditional and worse off, are liable to get hurt. Globalization widens social and ethnic inequalities.

Paradoxically the peace process operates like globalization (Smooha 1998). Israel was born and has lived in a hostile environment during the entire twentieth century. It built a formidable war machine, highly mobilized the Jewish population, and fostered a sense of threat and a sort of militaristic ethos in order to survive. It will continue to maintain a strong army because the region will re-

main unstable and unfriendly. Authoritarian regimes, class polarization, population explosion, Islamic fundamentalism, border disputes, competition for regional hegemony, terrorism, and the threat of long-range missiles will continue
to haunt the Middle East long after the Israeli-Arab conflict subsides. Relations
with other states in the region will continue to be overburdened with tensions,
envy, and disagreements. Furthermore, the settlement of the Palestinian question will leave many other issues unsettled and a considerable grudge in both
sides. While the Middle East is not developing the way western and central Europe did after 1945, the Israeli-Arab conflict is on a diminishing trend with
painful setbacks. The Oslo accords provide for mutual recognition between the
Jewish and Palestinian peoples, the settlement of their disagreements through
negotiation, and the acceptance of territorial partition as the chief means for
conflict regulation. The peace process is backed by the superpowers and the
public opinion of both Israelis and Palestinians. Since this process began to un-
fold, when Israel and Egypt signed a peace treaty in 1979, Israel has increasingly
become a nonwarfare society. The political discourse hinges on peace, the belief
in peaceful options is spreading out, the militaristic ethos is eroding, and the
willingness to make sacrifices is weakening.

The Al-Aqtza Intifada that erupted in late September 2000 is a grave setback
in the settlement of the Palestinian question. The Labor government under
Barak made very significant concessions to the Palestinians in exchange for "the
end of the conflict." The Palestinian administration under Arafat rejected the
offer because it fell short of Israel's retreat to the pre-1967 borders and acknowl-
edgement of the Palestinian refugees' right of return to Israel proper. As the
Palestinians and Israelis approach the end of the conflict, the core issues and
stumbling blocks surface. Palestinian violence and terrorism and Israeli reactive
repression distance the two sides form each other.

The winding transition to the non-warfare era has affected the ethnic cleavage in a mostly adverse way. By expediting the pace of globalization, it widens
class disparities, inflicts unemployment, hurts the lower strata, and encroaches
on traditional values, thereby indirectly hurting Mizrahim. With the withering
away of the common enemy, social solidarity weakens and the willingness of the
higher strata to support welfare services and redistribution declines. Mizrahim
are hardly likely to recoup the losses caused by these adversities. Peace dividends
are not likely to do them any good because the defense budget must remain
large. The settlement of the Palestinian question will not compensate Mizrahim
for their property losses in Arab countries. If Arabic speakers are needed to fulfill intermediary positions between Israel and the Arab world, it is more appropriate to recruit bilingual and bicultural Arab citizens than Mizrahim, whose
Judeo-Arabic languages and cultures are phasing out.

Triple Melting Pots

An intensive process of cultural and social assimilation has reduced the dimensions of Jewish ethnicity. But instead of a single ethnic melting pot fusing all exiles into one unified nation, three melting pots have been evident in Israeli society. These have abolished the Galuth ethnicity and created a new Israeli ethnicity, dividing the Jewish population into Israelis of Ashkenazi origin (nicknamed "Ashkenazim"), Israelis of Mizrahi origin (nicknamed "Mizrahim"), and Israelis of mixed origin. The differences among these three kinds of Israelis were fashioned by the interethnic encounters and life situations in Israel during the first fifty years of statehood, and only partly by the Diaspora heritage.

The group of Israelis of Ashkenazi descent was formed as a result of the amalgamation of Jews originating from Russia, Poland, Rumania, Hungary, Czechoslovakia, and other countries in Europe and America. The differences dividing them were made indistinct in the face of the striking discrepancies between them and the Mizrahi immigrants. Their common East-European background, their fast modernization in Palestine and Israel, and their en masse mobility into the higher classes from the working class eased the assimilation of the Ashkenazi oldtimers and newcomers to the extent that marriage among them has become a standard, devoid of any connotation of intermarriage. Ashkenazim share a common fate and status as a dominant group, and most of them are aligned politically with the Labor bloc and the Left.

Less advanced is the process of assimilation among Israelis of Mizrahi descent. For them country of origin still carries a significant impact on their identity, social relations, and cultural heritage. They are also divided by social class, scattering along the entire socioeconomic scale and experiencing a wide gap between the two-fifths in the middle and upper strata and the three-fifths in the working and lower strata. The better-off Mizrahim also enjoy opportunities for integration and assimilation into the Ashkenazim. Mizrahim are also split between the one-third who support Shas and the two-thirds who do not support Shas. Despite these internal differences, Mizrahim share a common ill-feeling about Ashkenazi hegemony, attribution of blame to Labor for the ethnic gap, and support of the Likud bloc as a political means for improving their lot.

Israelis of mixed origin, who are descendants of mixed marriages, lack clear ethnic membership and tend to see themselves as all-out Israelis. To this category belongs also a third or later generation of Israeli-born who tend to ignore any ethnic attachment. All these ethnically mixed Israelis are close in culture and class to Ashkenazim and strongly predisposed to assimilate with them.

According to the Zionist vision of fusion of exiles, it should be expected that the melting pot of Israelis of mixed origin and of Israelis indifferent to ethnicity would be the most dynamic and inclusive while the other two melting pots would not be in existence at all. But this is not the case. This genuine Israeli group is actually the smallest and least distinctive (in a representative opinion survey conducted in 1995 only 11 percent of Israeli Jews defined themselves as of ethnically mixed origin). In contrast, most Israelis of Mizrahi origin are crystallizing as a distinct group and developing an identity of their own, although not intentionally isolating themselves and not aspiring to ethnic separation. On the other hand, Israelis of Ashkenazi origin, who have achieved full ethnic assimilation, as a dominant group do not see themselves as a separate ethnic group with an Ashkenazi identity.

The triple melting pot in the ethnic sphere is in line with the growing division of Israeli society into corporate sectors. The Russian immigrants are differentiating themselves from the wider society as a separate linguistic, cultural, and social sector, with their own neighborhoods, mass media, voluntary associations, and political parties. The Ashkenazi ultra-Orthodox maintain autonomous communities and institutions. The national-religious Jews also have their institutions and neighborhoods, and the settlers from among them even live in separate settlements. The Sephardic party Shas is building a separate sector for working-class, traditional Mizrahim. The Kibbutzim constitute an autonomous sector. The Arab minority has separate localities and institutions and demands institutional autonomy.[25]

Conclusions

The ethnic division among the Jewish people emerged during two millennia of exile. Despite the commonalties of descent, religion, peoplehood, ancient language, preexilic history, and experience of being a persecuted minority, Jews in Christian areas and Jews in Moslem lands differed appreciably in language, culture, and level of development and felt estranged from each other. These divergences predated their encounter in Palestine and then in Israel, but were considered irrelevant, counterproductive, and illegitimate in Israeli society. The ideal was a melting pot corresponding to the official ideology of Zionism, which viewed all Jews as one people and sought to bring them back to their ancient homeland, to forge them into a modern nation, to build a Jewish state, and to create a new Jew.

The dominant approach in Israeli social sciences and public opinion is assimilationist. It presumes that an attitude of mutual acceptance, the free circulation of people, uniform public education, shared experience in the army, the welfare state, and political democracy will eventually blur and abolish ethnic differences. Advancing assimilation is evident in the spread of the Hebrew language, Israeli culture, and mixed marriages on the one hand, and in the weak ethnic consciousness and identity and low intensity of ethnic conflict on the other. According to this interpretation, ethnicity has become symbolic, relegated to optional and relatively insignificant spheres of life, such as pastime, foods, festivities, religious rituals, and daily manners.

In contrast, the critical approach sees Jewish ethnicity as tenacious and real. It emphasizes the simple fact that Ashkenazim constitute a charter group in Israeli society. They established the new Jewish society, dominated it from the very beginning, and tailored it to their views and needs. The mass immigration of Mizrahim in the 1950s provided the state with a human reservoir able to meet the urgent State needs of projecting to the world an image of a viable Jewish state, settling the remote and frontier areas, expanding the army, and widening and modernizing the economy. The accomplishment of these vital tasks was facilitated by the Mizrahi weaknesses: lower education, large families, lack of connections, and absence of alternative destinations for immigration. At the end of the 1950s Mizrahim found themselves in the lower echelons of society, pushing Ashkenazim upward.

While assimilation is indeed a strong force that mixes and equalizes Jews, ethnic barriers remain quite significant. They include a sharp contrast in the collective memory of the two ethnic groups, Ashkenazi cultural hegemony, considerable ethnic separation, overlap between the ethnic and political cleavages, substantial socioeconomic gaps across generations, gross underrepresentation of Mizrahim in the political and nonpolitical elites, and the fact that Mizrahim are still suffering from negative stereotyping, low self-image, and institutional discrimination. As a result, Jewish ethnicity in Israel is real rather than apparent and is and will be solidified for the foreseeable future. The three potent historical developments that have been reshaping Israeli society since the 1980s, that is, continued mass immigration, globalization, and transition to a nonwarfare society, have adversely affected ethnic equality and assimilation, hurting Mizrahim and keeping them apart from and unequal to Ashkenazim.

Improvement in ethnic relations took place during the first generation after 1948, especially against the foil of the troublesome 1950s. But the ethnic problem at the beginning of the third millennium has remained fairly intractable. Conflicting forces of continuity and change are underway, reflecting two general patterns—ethnic assimilation and ethnic dominance.

Instead of amalgamating the Jewish population into a single, unifying and homogenizing melting pot, three melting pots have been in operation in Israel in its first three years. One contains Israelis of Mizrahi origin (Yemenites, Iraqis, Moroccans, and other Jews originating from Moslem lands), another Israelis of

Ashkenazi origin (Polish, Russians, Romanians, and other Jews originating from Christian regions), while the third melting pot contains Israelis of ethnically mixed or detached origin. While the third, the "fully Israeli" group, is expected by Zionism to be the largest and most significant in Israel, it is in fact the smallest and least significant.

The split of the Jewish population into Mizrahim, Ashkenazim, and "non-ethnic" Israelis and the further diversification into countries of origin (Russians, Ethiopians, Anglo-Saxons, Moroccans, and others) correspond to the strengthening of the sectorial nature of Israeli democracy. The Ashkenazi ultra-Orthodox under Agudat Israel, the Sephardic ultra-Orthodox and traditional under Shas, the national-religious under Mafdal and Gush Emunim, the Arabs, the Kibbutzim, and others—each group maintains its own sector.

This reality of multiplicity of cultures, subcultures, and sectors creates a false impression of Israel as a multicultural democracy. The barriers to making Israel multicultural on the normative plane are both ideological and practical. Zionism as a hegemonic ideology frowns upon multiculturalism. It aspires to have a single, modern culture among the Jews and to combine secular Jewish heritage with Western culture, and it rejects Arab and Judeo-Arab culture. It views multiculturalism among Jews as a product of the Diaspora and dispersion and as a sign of weakness. Facing the stark reality of persistent cultural differences, however, Zionism and the Jewish population have been forced over the years to develop a certain tolerance toward them. Not less inhibitory is the structure of dominance. When culture overlaps with class, cultural diversity inevitably turns into cultural hierarchy. The culture or subculture of the lower classes, namely, Arabs and Mizrahim, will continue to be considered as inferior, a hindrance to social mobility, and a recipe for failure. As long as the culture of the better-off who are predominantly Ashkenazi continues to be dominant, anyone who does not espouse it is understandably bound to fail.

The full and genuine Israeli will remain the successful, secular Ashkenazi man for many years to come. Despite the growing tolerance of other kinds of Israelis—a Mizrahi, an ultra-Orthodox Jew, an Arab, a Russian immigrant, an Ethiopian Jew—they will be perceived as less Israeli, subject to negative stereotyping and more prone to failure.

True multiculturalism in the wider Israeli context would mean a social and ideological revolution. For this end Israel will have to abandon its grand Zionist mission of building a homogeneous, secular, Jewish, Western society and shift to an open, multicultural, and non-Zionist state. Groups must give up dominance they enjoy or aspire to. The full shift to multiculturalism requires that mutual tolerance achieve currency. Tolerance may be built on "the agreement to disagree," and not necessarily on liberal values (respect for personal autonomy, cultural relativism). The formation of a meaningful, overarching, civic community and a common minimum value core uniting the particular ethnic and religious communities and sectors is necessary.

Such multicultural transformation of Israel would have different gains and losses for different groups. For Mizrahim it would mean greater integration—incorporation of their cultural expressions into the national culture, socioeconomic equality, and treatment as equals. But it would also require certain losses for them qua Jews and religious. For secular Jews, multiculturalism would mean less religious coercion and more freedom from religion where religion uses the State for crafting the public domain and penetrating individual life. But they will lose dominance and the ability to shape the entire society according to their ideals and images. For Orthodox Jews multiculturalism would provide a shield against intervention in their separate institutions and a vehicle for preserving their own way of life. But they would lose their disproportionate power and influence and would have to forgo their expansionist goal of making Israel a halakhic state. For Israeli Arabs multiculturalism would bring about equal treatment, institutional autonomy, power-sharing, and the transformation of the Jewish-Zionist state into a binational state. Yet it would increase for them the real danger of high rates of assimilation.

Multicultural democracy stands a slim chance in Israel because all groups will refuse to make the necessary painful concessions and transformations (Yona 1998). Furthermore, in a broader perspective, it is a mixed blessing. Multicultural democracy will moderate some of the conflicts but exacerbate others. It will bring justice to some groups and injustice to others (the Arab *minority* would be happy with a binational state while the Jewish *majority* would feel miserable). It will cause both unity and disunity. Its emphasis on the right to be different distracts from the struggle for socioeconomic equality and social rights. It is, therefore, not clear whether the balance sheet of multicultural democracy will be positive or negative.

At the beginning of the third millennium, Israel has remained a society with cultural diversity or multiplicity of cultures but without multiculturalism (Kimmerling 1998). Its brand of multiculturalism is primarily dominative, inegalitarian, and intolerant in nature, facing no solid multiculturalist ideology or movement. It is solidified by an ethnic-class structure that is not effectively constrained by any serious social-democratic ideology or movement.

Multiculturalism in Israel is, however, incrementally and slowly becoming more egalitarian and tolerant as a result of the growing democratization of society, erosion of Ashkenazi hegemony, increasing realization that certain cultural differences are tenacious, spread of adverse social problems, and empowerment of deprived groups. Since ethnic "multi-sub-culturalism" (the flourishing of ethnic subcultures) is already an established fact, it could gradually expand to a mild form of ethnic multiculturalism.[26]

NOTES

1. A draft of this paper was presented in the international conference on "Islam in the Middle Eastern Studies: Muslims and Minorities," National Museum of Ethnology, Osaka, Japan, January 1998.

2. For a review of factors facilitating the assimilation of immigrants, see Marger, 1994, pp. 125–29.

3. These figures exclude about a quarter of a million of non-citizen residents of East Jerusalem and Golan Heights and another quarter of a million of foreign workers.

4. For an opposite view that, by the 1970s, Israeli sociology of migration had become differentiated and the assimilationist model had lost its dominance, see Shuval and Leshem 1998.

5. The annual rate of economic growth averaged 5 percent during the 1950s and 1960s, dropped to 2.5 percent in the 1970s, and declined further to 1.5 percent in the 1980s and 1990s. Despite the low rate of economic growth since the 1973 war, living standards in Israel continued to rise. According to the United Nations figures, in 1997 Israel ranked 23 out of 174 countries on the human development index (UNDP 1999: 143–44).

6. Assimilationist historians and social scientists depict the fifties in uncritical terms, subtly blaming the Mizrahi immigrants for their predicament. See Fisher 1991; Hacohen 1994, 1998; Ofer 1996; Tzur 1997.

7. For a quantitative study, based on official statistics, and showing integrative and assimilative processes, see Schmelz, DellaPergola, and Avner 1991.

8. Moshe Lissak, a leading Israeli sociologist, maintains that Israeli society has fractured into diverse sectors, such as Russian immigrants, the ultra-Orthodox, and Arabs, who seek self-interest and autonomy. Ethnicity naturally thrives in such a society. For his critical view of the separatist tendencies among the new Russian immigrants, see Lissak 1995.

9. For a background survey of Sephardic communities in Israel and the Diaspora, see Elazar 1989. For a defense of the assimilationist approach and a critique of the critical approach, see Shokeid 2000.

10. Since non-Ashkenazi Jews constituted only 8 percent of the Jewish people before World War II, their rate of immigration was higher than that of Ashkenazim even before 1948. But the fact that they were a minority in the Yishuv was fateful for subsequent developments.

11. For numerous quotations of Ashkenazi leaders and press reports depicting Mizrahim in very negative terms, see Smooha 1978; Segev 1985; and Meir 1998. A study of the Mizrahi image in history textbooks for junior high schools during the 1948–67 period reveals the at-

tribution of the following traits to Mizrahim: "apathy, impotence, primitiveness, stagnancy and backwardness. Mizrahim were portrayed as poor, dirty, physically degenerated, sickness-stricken, inferior and devoid of love of work" (Firer 1985, p. 38).

12. The wholesale negative stereotyping of Mizrahim during the fifties is a common knowledge that even mainstream sociologists, like Lissak (1987), are ready to concede. However, they do not trace it to the quasi-colonialist and Orientalist thinking that critical scholars attribute to Ashkenazim as Europeans.

13. Peres decided not to confront Barak on the question of pardon in order not to "undermine the effort to return to power." Instead of apologizing, he declared: "Mistakes were made, yes! But my heart is full of true pride of the pioneering, Zionist enterprise, that does not have any parallel in this century." Navon said that by asking for pardon, Barak gave "retroactive confirmation to a set of false charges and smears against the Labor Party. The undertaking of immigration was a wonderful chapter, though painful, in the history of Zionism. When 250,000 come in four years, of course there are big difficulties and suffering. It is possible to express sorrow for the suffering and to identify with the pain, but not to ask for forgiveness. Pardon means that we are regretting, while the Labor Party of all generations has nothing to regret." Kolek labeled the charge that the Labor Party hurt Mizrahim as "unjustifiable invention.... There is nobody from whom I should ask pardon. I personally did my utmost for immigrant absorption" (*Ha'aretz*, September 29, 1997). Even the Iraqi-born writer Amir, whose novels focus on the absorption of Mizrahim in Israel, opposed Barak's gesture. He speaks of "the myth of deprivation," universality of immigration hardships, and Israel's great success (Amir 1998).

14. In contrast, Kimmerling (2001a, 2001b) holds that (Ashkenazi) cultural hegemony in Israel has come to an end, and that the founding group (secular, Zionist and veteran Ashkenazim) has become only one of seven groups vying for attention, acceptance and dominance. The other six groups are the national-religious, the ultra-orthodox, traditional Mizrahim, Russian immigrants, Ethiopian immigrants, and Israeli Arabs.

15. Many of these practices constitute clear deviations from Orthodox religion, such as Sabbath observance that includes watching television and going to the beach, or folk belief in talismans.

16. Yehoshua (1998), who justifies the request of the Labor Party for pardon, sees the policy to take away the Mizrahi music as the harshest step in the effort to eradicate the Galut and Mizrahi culture from the Mizrahi immigrants. This is because music is the intimate code through which an individual is connected to his culture. It was better to conduct a dialog than to repress Mizrahi culture.

17. The ethnic gap in higher education has not consistently declined over the years and has remained substantial (see Shavit, Cohen et. al. 2000; Kraus and Yonay 2000). On the other hand, Fridlander, Eisenbach et al. (2000) reach an opposite conclusion based on a study of persons born in 1950–1980 with cumulated records from the 1995 and previous censuses. They show reduction in the ethnic gap in educational attainments at various levels, though they show less reduction in ethnic gap in acquiring matriculation diplomas and entering post-secondary institutions. Most critical is the finding that the ethnic gaps almost disappeared in the third generation, a finding pointing to the gradual phasing out of ethnic inequality in edu-

cation as the weight of third and later generation Israeli Jews increases in the veteran population. According to Fridlander and his associates, with transition to the next generation, Mizrahim (and especially those originating from Asia) are expected to close the gap with Ashkenazim in educational standards because of their shift from vocational to academic tracks in high schools, the rise in their parents' educational level, and the decrease in their family size to that of the Ashkenazi. These future projections can further be supported by the ongoing revolution in the system of higher education: the proliferation of undergraduate colleges is making the attainment of B.A. degrees universal. The belief that the ethnic gap in access to universities lies at the heart of ethnic inequality propelled the crusade in the 1990s of Silvan Shalom, the Minister of Treasury in 2001, to fight for open admission to the universities (only a matriculation diploma is required regardless of the grade-point average), a policy approved by the Israeli government in August 2001. See also: Council on Higher Education 2001.

18. Levy (1998) maintains that the Israeli army up to the end of the 1970s reproduced and legitimized the inferior position of Mizrahim, while later on they achieved more mobility and equality within the army. Yet they could only partially convert their military attainments into civilian social mobility because of the decline in the centrality of the army, that is, in militarism and in the role of the "fighter." Discharged soldiers are also less rewarded; because they are under represented among "manager officers" and highly technical staffers in the army, positions that are highly transferable to the civilian labor market.

19. This generalization is controversial. For instance, Razel (1997) argues that cumulative evidence shows that the ethnic gap in scholastic achievements is declining steadily to the extent that it will vanish completely by the year 2012. For a critique of Razel and the view that the gap remains substantial and stable, see Dahan, Yonah, et al. 1998.

20. Another opinion survey of Mizrahi residents of development towns, conducted in 1998, shows not only that they accept these stratifications within Israeli society, but that this is even more true among the second generation (Yiftachel and Tzfadia 1999).

21. Minister Sharon set the slogan for Amor's campaign: "First President from Second Israel" (*Yediot Aharonot*, February 11, 1998).

22. The censure of Or's statement was far from unanimous. Many said that it was inappropriate and pointless to speak this way, but did not condemn the statement as racist. The social advocate and historian Gorny, for instance, expressed the view of many in this regard. He wrote that the concept "racism" should be kept to denote extreme cases like apartheid in South Africa, white supremacy in the Deep South, and Nazism. According to Gorny, Or expressed only prejudice that characterized many groups in the history of the Jewish settlement before and after 1948. Since the treatment of Mizrahim in the fifties fell into the same pattern, Barak's apology was neither necessary nor justified (Gorny 1998).

23. For studies of the Russian mass-immigration to Israel, its high human capital and its emergence as an empowered community, see Sicron and Leshem 1998; Lissak and Leshem 2001.

24. It is estimated that Israel had about 250,000 foreign workers in 2000. They replaced most of the Palestinian workers from the West Bank and Gaza Strip who became high-security risks after 1996. The importation of foreign workers is an integral part of globalization. For-

eign workers compete with members of the lower classes in the labor market, increase unemployment and reduce wages in the low-technological economy.

25. For an empirical study that tested and confirmed the triple melting pot thesis, see Benski 1994.

26. Certain leftist elite groups in Israel, influenced by the spread of multiculturalist ideology and movement in the West, endorse multicultural or even consociational democracy for Israel. Multiculturalism is the leitmotiv in the recommendations of the state-appointed Committee on Public Broadcasting (2000). Kimmerling (2001a) and Yonah (1999) advocate the transformation of Israel from a Jewish and democratic state to a binational state (consociational democracy).

REFERENCES

Alternative Information Center. 1999. *The Mizrahi Revolution: Three Essays on Zionism and Mizrahim.* Jerusalem: Alternative Information Center (Hebrew).

Amir, Eli. 1998. "The Pardon and the Thanks." *Alpayim* 16: 186–91 (Hebrew).

Ben-Rafael, Eliezer. 1982. *The Emergence of Ethnicity: Cultural Groups and Social Conflict in Israel.* Westport, Conn.: Greenwood.

Ben-Simon, Daniel. 1998. "What Pardon, Which Pardon." *Ha'aretz,* July 29.

Benski, Tova. 1994. "Ethnic Convergence Processes under Conditions of Persisting Socioeconomic–Decreasing Cultural Differences: The Case of Israeli Society." *International Migration Review* 28(2): 256–80.

Bernstein, Deborah. 1989. "The Mass-Immigration of the 1950s and Its Implications." *Skira Hodshit* 36(3): 24–36 (Hebrew).

Bernstein, Deborah, and Shlomo Swirski. 1982. "The Rapid Economic Development of Israel and the Emergence of the Ethnic Division of Labour." *British Journal of Sociology* 33(1) (March): 64–85.

Chetrit, Sami Shalom. 1999. *The Ashkenazi Revolution Is Dead: Reflections on Israel from a Dark Angle.* Tel Aviv: Kedem Publishing (Hebrew).

Cohen, Yinon, and Yitchak Haberfeld. 1998. "Second-Generation Jewish Immigrants in Israel: Have the Ethnic Gaps in Schooling and Earnings Declined?" *Ethnic and Racial Studies* 21(3) (May): 507–28.

Committee on Public Broadcasting. 2000. *Report of the Committee on Public Broadcasting, Submitted to the Minister Matan Vilnaie.* Jerusalem: Ministry of Science, Culture and Sports (Hebrew).

Council on Higher Education. 2001. *Who Benefits from Higher Education? Proceedings of a Study Day, June 13, 2000.* Jerusalem: Council on Higher Education (Hebrew).

Dahan, Yossi, Yossi Yonah, Izhak Sporta, Yehuda Shenhav. 1998. "Closure of Scholastic Gaps between Mizrahi and Ashkenazi Students: A Meta-Analysis and Its Misuse." *Megamot* 39 (3): 320–25 (Hebrew).

Dar, Yehezkel, and Nura Resh. 1990. "Socioeconomic and Ethnic Gaps in Academic Achievement in Israeli High Schools." In *Contemporary Issues in Cross-Cultural Psychology*, ed. N. Bleichrodt and P.J.P. Drenth, 322–33. Amsterdam: Suets and Zeitlinger.

Eisenstadt, S. N. 1985. *The Transformation of Israeli Society*. London: Weidenfeld and Nicolson.

Eisenstadt, S. N., Moshe Lissak, and Yaacov Nahon. 1993. *Ethnic Groups in Israel and Their Social Location*. Jerusalem: Jerusalem Institute for Israel Studies (Hebrew).

Elazar, Daniel J. 1989. *The Other Jews: The Sephardim Today*. New York: Basic Books.

Etzioni-Halevy, Eva. 1993. *The Elites' Connection and Israeli Democracy*. Tel Aviv: Sifriat Paoalim (Hebrew).

Firer, R. 1985. *Agents of the Zionist Education*. Tel Aviv: Afik (Hebrew).

Fisher, Shlomo. 1991. "Two Patterns of Modernization: Analysis of the Ethnic Problem in Israel." *Teoria Vebikoret* 1: 57–82 (Hebrew).

Friedlander, Dov, Zvi Eisenbach, Eliyahu Ben Moshe, Dan ben-Hur, Shlomit Leunievski, Ahmad Hleihel, Lilach Lion Elmakias. 2000. *Religion, Ethnicity, Type of Locality and Educational Attainments among Israel's Population: An Analysis of Change over Time. Part 2. Working Paper Series*. Jerusalem: Department of Population Studies, the Hebrew University.

Gans, Herbert J. 1979. "Symbolic Ethnicity: The Future of Ethnic Groups and Cultures in America." *Ethnic and Racial Studies* 2 (1) (January): 1–20.

Gorny, Yosef. 1998. "In the Racist Devil's Circle." *Ha'aretz*, August 14.

Hacohen, Dvora. 1994. *Immigrants in Storm: The Big Immigration and Its Absorption in Israel, 1948–1953*. Jerusalem: Yad Ben-Zvi (Hebrew).

———. 2001. "Immigration and Absorption." In *Trends in Israeli Society*, ed. Ephraim Yaar and Zeev Shavit, 365–486. Tel Aviv: Open University (Hebrew).

———. 1998. *Ingathering of the Exiles: Immigration to Eretz Isrtael—Myth and Reality*. Jerusalem: Zalman Shazar Center (Hebrew).

Joppke, Christian. 1996. "Multiculturalism and Immigration: A Comparison of the United States, Germany and Great Britain." *Theory and Society* 25: 449–500.

Joppke, Christian. 1999. *Immigration and the Nation-State: The United States, Germany, and Great Britain*. Oxford: Oxford University Press.

Khazzoom, Aziza. 1999. "Western Culture, Stigma, and Social Closure: The Origins of Ethnic Inequality among Jews in Israel." *Sociologia Israelit* 1 (2): 385–428.

Kimmerling, Baruch. 1998. "The New Israelis—Multiplicity of Cultures without Multiculturalism." *Alpayim* 16: 264–308.

———. 2001a. *The End of Ashkenazi Hegemony*. Jerusalem: Keter (Hebrew).

———. 2001b. *The Invention and Decline of Israeliness: State, Society an the Military*. Berkeley and Los Angeles: University of California Press.

Kraus, Vered and Yuval Yonay. 2000. "The Power and Limits of Ethnonationalism: Palestinians and Eastern Jews in Israel, 1974–1991." *British Journal of Sociology* 51 (3): 525–51.

Kymlicka, Will. 1995. *Multicultural Citizenship*. Oxford: Oxford University Press.

Levi, Amnon. 1998. "Face of Racism." *Ma'ariv*, July 31.

Levy, Yagil. 1998. "Militarizing Inequality: A Conceptual Framework." *Theory and Society* 27: 873–904.

Lewin-Epstein, Noah. 1989. "Labor Market Position and Antagonism toward Arabs in Israel." *Research in Inequality and Social Conflict* 1: 165–91.

Lewin-Epstein, Noah, Yuval Elmelech, and Moshe Semyonov. 1997. "Ethnic Inequality in Home Ownership and the Value of Housing: The Case of Immigrants in Israel." *Social Forces* 75 (4): 1439–62.

Lewis, Herbert. 1984. "Yemenite Ethnicity in Israel." *Jewish Journal of Sociology* 26 (1) June: 5–24.

Lissak, Moshe. 1987. "Immigrants' Images: Stereotypes and Labeling during the Mass-Immigration in the 1950s." *Cathedra* 43: 125–44 (Hebrew).

———. 1995. "The Immigrants from the Commonwealth of Independent States between Separation and Integration." In *Allocation of Resources for Social Services 1994–95,* ed. Yaacov Kop, 167–74 Jerusalem: Center for the Study of Social Policy in Israel (Hebrew).

———. 1999. *The Great Aliya of the 1950s: The Failure of the Melting Pot.* Jerusalem: Mossad Bialik (Hebrew).

Lissak, Moshe and Elazar Leshem, eds. 2001. *From Russia to Israel: Identity and Culture in Transition.* Tel Aviv: Hakibbutz Hameuchad (Hebrew).

Marger, Martin N. 1994. *Race and Ethnic Relations: American and Global Perspectives.* Third ed. Belmont, Calif.: Wadsworth.

Meir, Yosef. 1998. *Babylon and Catrealivka: Birth of Oriental Political Zionism.* Tel Aviv: Yaron Golan Publishing (Hebrew).

Nahon, Yacov. 1987. *Patterns of Educational Expansion and the Occupational Opportunity Structure: The Ethnic Dimension.* Jerusalem: Jerusalem Institute for Israel Studies (Hebrew).

Ofer, Dalia, ed. 1996. *Between Immigrants and Oldtimers: Israel during the Mass-Immigration, 1948–1953.* Jerusalem: Yad Ben-Zvi (Hebrew).

Parekh, Bhikhu. 2000. *Rethinking Multiculturalism: Cultural Diversity and Political Theory.* London: Macmillan.

Pedahzur, Ami. 2000. *The Extreme Right-Wing Parties in Israel: Emergence and Decline?* Tel Aviv: Ramot–Tel Aviv University (Hebrew).

Peled, Yoav, ed. 2001. *Shas—The Challenge of Israeliness.* Tel Aviv: Miskal–Yedioth Ahronoth Books and Chemed Books (Hebrew).

Peres, Yochanan, Eliezer Ben-Rafael and Avital Fishler. 2001. *The Interethnic Cleavage in Israel. A Research Report.* Tel Aviv: Yitzhak Rabin Center for Israel Studies.

Peterburg, Gabriel. 1995. "The Nation and Its Story-Tellers: National Historiography and Orientalism." *Teoria Vebikoret* 6: 81–130 (Hebrew).

Raz-Krakotzkin, Amnon. 1994. "Galuth within Sovereignty: A Critique of 'The Negation of the Galuth' in Israeli Culture (Part Two)." *Teoria Vebikoret* 5: 113–32 (Hebrew).

Razel, Micha. 1997. The Closure of Scholastic Gaps between Mizrahi and Ashkenazi Students: A Meta-Analysis. *Megamot* 38 (3): 349–66 (Hebrew).

Regev, Motti. 1997. "Fluent or Stammered: Organizational Skills and Cultural Salience in the Music Industry in Israel." *Teoria Vebikoret* 10: 115–32 (Hebrew).

Rejwan, Nissim. 1998. *Israel's Place in the Middle East: A Pluralist Perspective.* Gainesville, FL: University Press of Florida.

Schmelz, U. O., S. DellaPergola, and Uri Avner. 1991. *Ethnic Differences among Israeli Jews: A New Look.* Jerusalem: Institute of Contemporary Jewry.

Segev, Tom. 1985. *1949—The First Israelis.* London: Collier Macmillan.

Shafir, Gershon. 1990. "The Meeting of Eastern Europe and Yemen: 'Idealistic Workers' and 'Natural Workers' in Early Zionist Settlement in Palestine." *Ethnic and Racial Studies* 13 (2) (April): 172–97.

Shavit, Yossi. 1990. "Segregation, Tracking and Educational Attainment of Minorities: Arabs and Oriental Jews in Israel." *American Sociological Review* 55 (1) (February): 115–26.

Shavit, Yossi, and Haya Stier. 1997. "Ethnicity and Education in the Marriage Patterns in Israel: Changes over Time." *Megamot* 38 (2): 207–21 (Hebrew).

Shavit, Yossi, Yinon Cohen, Haya Stier, and Svetlana Bolotin. 2000. "Ethnic Inequality in University Education in Israel." In *Distributive Justice in Israel,* ed. Menachem Mautner, 391–403. Tel Aviv: Ramot Publishing (Hebrew).

Shohat, Ella. 1987. *Israeli Cinema: East/West and the Politics of Representation.* Austin, Texas: Texas University Press.

Shokeid, Moshe. 2000. "On the Sin We Have Not So Much Sinned in the Study of Near Eastern Jews." *Mekarov* 3: 79–89 (Hebrew).

Shokeid, Moshe and Shlomo Deshen. 1999. *The Generation of Transition: Continuity and Change among North African Immigrants to Israel.* Jerusalem: Yad Izhak Ben-Zvi (Hebrew).

Shuval, Judith T. and Elazar Leshem. 1998. The Sociology of Migration in Israel: A Critical View. In *Immigration to Israel: Sociological Perspectives,* vol. 8, ed. Judith T. Shuval and Elazar Leshem, 3–50. New Brunswick, N.J.: Transaction.

Sicron, Moshe and Elazar Leshem, eds. 1998. *A Profile of Immigration: Absorption Processes of Immigrants from the Former Soviet Union, 1990–1995.* Jerusalem: Magnes (Hebrew).

Smooha, Sammy. 1978. *Israel: Pluralism and Conflict.* London: Routledge and Kegan Paul.

———. 1986. "Three Approaches to the Sociology of Ethnic Relations in Israel." *Jerusalem Quarterly* 40: 31–61.

———. 1993. "Class, Ethnic, and National Cleavages and Democracy in Israel." In *Israeli Democracy under Stress,* ed. Ehud Sprinzak and Larry Diamond, 309–42. Boulder and London: Lynne Rienner Publishers.

———. 1998. "The Implications of the Transition to Peace for Israeli Society." *The Annals of the American Academy of Political and Social Science* 555 (January): 26–45.

Stahl, Abraham. 1991. "Teachers' Prejudices: A Perennial Problem in Israeli Education." *Urban Education* 25 (4) (Spring): 440–53.

Swirski, Shlomo. 1989. *Israel: The Oriental Majority.* London: Zed Books.

———. 1990. *Education in Israel: The Area of Separate Tracks.* Tel Aviv: Brerot (Hebrew).

———. 1995. *Seeds of Inequality.* Tel Aviv: Brerot (Hebrew).

Tzur, Yaron. 1997. "The Immigration from Moslem Countries." In *The First Decade: 1948–1958,* ed. Zvi Tzameret and Hannah Yablonka, 57–2. Jerusalem: Yad Ben-Zvi (Hebrew).

UNDP. 1999. *Human Development Report 1999.* New York: Oxford University Press.

Willis, Aaron P. 1995. "Shas—The Sephardic Torah Guardians: Religious 'Movement' and Political Power." In *The Elections in Israel 1992,* ed. Asher Arian and Michal Shamir, 121–39. Albany, State University of New York Press.

Yiftachel, Oren. 2000. "Ethnocracy and Its Discontent: Minorities, Protest, and the Israeli Policy." *Critical Inquiry* 26 (4): 725–56.

Yiftachel, Oren and Erez Tzfadia. 1999. *Policy and Identity in the Development Towns: The Case of North-African Immigrants, 1952–1998.* Beer Sheva: Negev Center for Regional Development, Ben-Gurion University of the Negev (Hebrew).

Yiftachel, Oren and Alexander Kedar. 2000. "On Power and Land: The Israeli Land Regime." *Teoriya Vebikoret* 16: 67–100 (Hebrew).

Yehoshua, A. B. 1998. "Pardon." *Alpayim* 16: 178–85 (Hebrew).

Yonah, Yossi. 1999. "Fifty Years Later: The Scope and Limits of Liberal Democracy in Israel." *Constellations* 6 (3) (September): 411–28.

CHAPTER FOUR

The Soviet Immigrant Community in Israel

Elazar Leshem and Moshe Sicron

Dimensions of the Community

The Soviet immigrant group is the largest of the immigrant groups in Israel, comprising the immigrants who entered Israel from the former Soviet Union (FSU) in the various immigration waves. It includes Jews and non-Jews and their first-generation children born to them in Israel. This group was estimated at the beginning of the year 2000 to be about 1.1 million persons and it constituted 18 percent of the total population of Israel. The majority of this community comprises the immigrants who arrived since the end of 1989 as part of a large exodus from the FSU. The number of these living in Israel at the beginning of 2000 was 800,000 (including their children). It is estimated that, in the decade 1990–99, approximately 1.3 million left the various republics of the FSU: 800,000 immigrated to Israel, 300,000 to the United States, 100,000 to Germany, 50,000 to Canada, and smaller numbers to other countries (estimates based chiefly on DellaPergola 1999). The influx was especially massive in the years 1990 and 1991, when 330,000 immigrants arrived in Israel. In the previous wave of the 1970s, a total of 150,000 immigrants arrived. In the FSU, the 1990s emigration decreased the size of the Jewish community from an estimated 2.5 million in 1989 to an estimated 1 million in 1999. Defined as the "enlarged" Jewish community, it includes the "core" Jewish population (i.e., those declaring themselves Jews) together with their non-Jewish spouses, children, and grandchildren, and others entitled to enter Israel under the Law of Return enacted in 1950 (Tolts 1998).

As a result of the continuing immigration to Israel from the FSU (50,000–60,000 per year), and despite its low natural increase, this community grew at a faster rate than did the Israeli population. In 1998–99 it grew annually by 5–6 percent (double the rate of the total population—2.5 percent). Emigration *from* Israel by those who arrived in the 1990s, at least in the first years of their stay in the country, was much lower than that of the previous waves. Some 10 percent of immigrants in previous waves emigrated from Israel.

Crude projections, prepared by the Israeli Central Bureau of Statistics (CBS), show that the segment of the community that immigrated to Israel after 1990 will grow to 1.1 million by the year 2020 (based on "medium projections" that assume an immigration of half a million from the FSU in the period 2000–20). They will constitute (including their children born in Israel) some 13 percent of the total population, or 15–16 percent of the total Jewish population (CBS unpublished data).

Table 1. Immigrants Born in the FSU by Period of Immigration to Israel (Numbers in thousands)

1919–1948	1948–1951	1952–1960	1961–1964	1965–1971	1972–1979	1980–1984	1985–1989	1990–1991	1992–1995	1996–1999
52	8	14	5	25	137	12	18	332	264	226

Source: CBS 2000a.

Subcommunities

The Soviet immigrants are not a monolithic community. They arrived from various republics that were previously within the Soviet Union and spoke the Russian language, but differed in many respects (traditions, culture, customs, etc.). A crude distinction (based on geography, rather than ethnicity) is made between those from the European republics and those from the Asian continent.

Eight of every ten immigrants who arrived in the 1990s were from the European republics. Ninety percent of the Jews in the FSU lived in the European republics in 1989; of these, 63 percent lived in the Russian Federation and Ukraine. The remaining 20 percent came from the Asian republics (where only 10 percent of the Jewish community in the FSU lived); this migration brought about two-thirds of this Jewish population to Israel.

And even within these major groups we can find a number of communities, each having its particular character (CBS 2000b). Another distinct community arrived from the Caucasus region, among whom were the Mountain Jews, speaking the Tat language. According to very rough estimates, the number of these immigrants in the 1990s was around 40,000 (Altshuler 1987; King 1998). See Table 2.

Some Demographic Characteristics

RELIGION A special attribute of the FSU community in Israel is its significant proportion of non-Jews. These are mostly spouses of Jewish partners and children or grandchildren of Jews entitled to enter as immigrants under the Law of Return. Some define themselves as Christian, others as having no or undefined

Table 2. Immigrants from the FSU by Last Republic of Residence (1990–1998)
(Numbers in thousands)

Republic	Number	Percent
Russian Federation	227	30.8
Ukraine	239	32.3
Belarus	62	8.4
Moldova	43	5.8
Baltic Republics	18	2.5
European Republics (total)	589	79.8
Georgia	18	2.5
Azerbaijan	30	4.1
Uzbekistan	70	9.5
Kazakhstan	13	1.8
Tajikistan	10	1.4
Other Republics	7	0.9
Asian Republics (total)	149	20.2
Not Known	19	
TOTAL	757	100

Source: CBS 2000b.

religious affiliation. At least 170,000 did not declare themselves as Jews (more than 20 percent of the immigrants from the FSU in the decade of the 1990s). While the percentage of non-Jews was less than 5 percent among those who immigrated in 1990, their proportion was larger among immigrants who arrived later (16 percent in 1992; more than 35 percent in 1996; and close to half of the 1998 immigrants) (CBS 2000b).

AGE STRUCTURE The community is characterized by a low and decreasing proportion of children, and a high and increasing proportion of older persons, compared to the general Israeli population. The low percentage of children is the result of a very low fertility in this community—although the level of fertility has increased slowly as their stay in Israel has lengthened.

The proportion of children (ages 0–14) of this community was 19 percent compared to 29 percent in the total population (26 percent in the Jewish population). The proportion of the older population (65 and over) was 15 percent compared to 10 percent among the total population (or 11 percent among the Jewish population). The proportion of older persons among the immigrants on arrival in Israel was only a little higher than that of the veteran population, but the cohort aged 55–64 was very large, and as they aged they inflated the numbers of those aged 65 and over. By the year 2020, according to the CBS projections, they will constitute 19 percent, as compared to 14 percent within the total population (CBS, unpublished projections).

GENDER The proportion of women in the community is much higher than in the total population (53.4 percent women compared to 50.7 percent). This is partly a result of the older age structure, but in practically all age groups from 25 and over the proportion of women is larger (in ages 65 and over, 63 percent compared to 57.3 percent).

MARITAL STATUS Members of this community marry at a younger age than does the general population of Israel, thus the percentage of single men and women in the younger age groups is smaller, and that of married men and women is larger than that of the total Jewish population (TJP).[1] In addition, the proportion of divorced men and especially that of women, is very high (12.5 percent of all women of the Soviet community 15 and over are divorced, compared to 6.4 percent of the TJP—the proportion of divorced women aged 30–49 approaches 20 percent (data for 1996, CBS 2000e).

NATURAL MOVEMENT As mentioned above, the community has very low fertility (the number of children per woman—"total fertility"—was 1.7 compared to 3 for the total population and 2.7 for Jews). As their stay in the country lengthened, women's fertility in the younger ages did increase slowly.

The community experienced a higher crude death rate, mostly reflecting their older age structure. For those aged 10 and over, male deaths numbered 9.7 per 1,000 in the community as compared to 7.6 among the TJP; for women, these figures were 9.4 and 7.0, respectively. The number of births to this community in 1998 was 9,000 and the number of deaths 6,000, resulting in a natural increase of about 3,000 (0.3 percent, compared to 1.2 percent in the TJP).

HEALTH CONDITIONS In a 1995 survey, a larger proportion (22 percent) of immigrants defined their health status as "not so good" compared to the veteran population (6 percent). Slightly less than half of the Soviet immigrants reported in a 1993 survey that they had a chronic disease, disability, or handicap, compared to 30 percent of the veteran population.

Immigrants use health services less than do veteran Israelis. However, the immigrants' utilization of health services increases with time and becomes increasingly similar to the veteran population. Immigrants were less satisfied than veterans with various aspects of service provision such as communication, instructions, and the ability to navigate the system (Nirel et al. 1998).

HOUSEHOLDS AND FAMILY The Russian community (RC) nuclear family is smaller than that of the veteran Israeli family, generally having one or two children. Most households are composed of a couple with 0–2 children. But in a significant number of households, the nuclear family lives with other family

Table 3. Households of the RC and the JDC by Size (1998) Percent

No. of persons in HH	All Jewish Households	RC Households
1	18.7	14.9
2	24.6	31.2
3	15.7	23.1
4	18.4	19.2
5+	22.6	11.6
Total	100.0	100.0
Average	3.19	2.86

Source: CBS 1999b. Tables 2.29, 2.30.

members, especially parents of one spouse or other related persons, or even another family. This partially reflects the pattern of residence in the FSU, which was advantageous for financing the costs of purchasing an apartment and receiving higher mortgages in Israel.

The average number of persons of the RC household in 1998 was 2.8–2.9 compared with 3.2 in TJP households. This average hides the large differences in the distribution of households by size. The proportion of large households in the RC is much smaller than it is in the TJP: households of 5 or more persons constitute less than 12 percent of RC households as compared with 22.6 percent. See Table 4.

Table 4. Households of the RC and the TJP by Type of Household (1998)
(Numbers in thousands)

Type of HH	TJP	RC	TJP %	RC %
One person HH	267	37	18.7	14.9
One family in HH	1,110	189	100.0	100.0
Couple, no children	261	48	23.5	25.4
Couple, with children	674	77	60.7	40.7
Couple, with or without				
children & others	30	20	2.7	10.6
One parent family	129	38	11.6	20.1
Others	16	6	1.5	3.2
Two families in HH	35	18		
Other	16	2		
ALL HOUSEHOLDS	1,427	246		

Source: CBS 2000a. Tables 2.29, 2.30.

In the RC, the two-person households were composed of 64 percent couples and 34 percent single-parent families with one child as compared with 77 percent and 22 percent respectively in the TJP. Households of single-parent families with children living alone or with other relatives (e.g., older parents) are much more widespread among the RC than in the TJP (20 percent compared with 11 percent of one-family households).

Geographic Distribution

Though members of the RC are found in practically every locality in Israel, we find them concentrated in large numbers in specific places. In some, they constitute 30–50 percent of the whole population, while in many localities their number is very small. They constitute large numbers mostly in some of the "development towns" in the peripheral areas of the country; usually (but not exclusively) in lower sociodemographic localities, and in lower-status neighborhoods in the larger cities. In each of the 10 towns listed, there were at least 25,000 RC persons in 1998.

In ten towns they constitute 30 percent or more of the population (Nazaret Illit—50 percent; Or Aqiva—44 percent; Sederot and Ma'alot—40 percent). The proportion of the RC in the three largest cities is smaller than their share of the total population (CBS 2000e).

The concentration in these development towns, which are located mostly in the Southern and Northern Districts of Israel, results in a distribution of the RC

Table 5. Population of Towns with 25,000 RC Persons or More, 1998
(Numbers in the thousands)

Town	RC Pop.	% of Total Pop.
Haifa	50	22
Ashdod	47	30
Be'er Sheva	42	25
Bat Yam	30	22
Netanya	30	19
Tel-Aviv	28	9
Jerusalem	27	6
Rishon LeZiyyon	26	14
Ashquelon	26	28
Petah Tiqwa	25	15

Source: CBS 2000e.

population that differs from that of the TJP. The share of the RC population is larger in the peripheral areas, in particular in the Southern District (especially in the towns closer to the Tel Aviv metropolis), the Haifa District, and the Central District, and much smaller in the Tel Aviv and Jerusalem Districts. Moreover, the internal migration of this community, after some years in the country, shows a net loss within the Tel Aviv and Jerusalem Districts and a net gain in the Southern and Central Districts (CBS 1999d; 2000f). The population of the RC in the Tel Aviv District was 23.8 percent in 1990, declining to 15.5 percent in 1998; in the Southern District it increased from 11.9 percent to 25.3 percent. Immigrants gravitated toward the fringes of the Tel Aviv metropolis and to the Southern District. This in turn affected the geographic distribution of the total population, increasing the percentage of the TJP in the Southern and Central Districts and decreasing that in the Tel Aviv District.

Under the policy of "direct absorption," immigrants in the 1990s could choose for themselves the place they wanted to live with no formal government intervention. Factors determining these choices were: family members, relatives, and friends already living in a locality; availability of housing (in the beginning of the 1990s in "unoccupied apartments" and later, in areas where government "initiated housing" was built, mostly in the peripheral regions); housing prices in various towns; and at a later stage, the availability of suitable employment.

Since the share of RC immigrants who settled in development towns was large and as they had much more education than did the veteran population, this wave of immigration contributed to the significant increase of human capital in these towns. See Table 6.

Table 6. Distribution of the RC and the TJP by Districts (End of 1998)
(Numbers in thousands)

District	RC.*	TJP	RC%	TJP%	RC%
Jerusalem	33	509	4.8	10.6	6.4
Northern	93	490	13.7	10.2	19.1
Haifa	120	596	17.6	12.5	20.2
Central	145	1224	21.3	25.6	11.8
Tel Aviv	105	1097	15.5	22.9	9.6
Southern	172	701	25.2	14.7	24.5
Judea and Samaria	13	169	1.9	3.5	7.6
TOTAL	681	4786	100.0	100	14.2

*Does not include children born to them in Israel.
Source: CBS 2000e.

Children and Youth

At the beginning of 1999, there were 170,000 children and youth from the FSU in Israel, including those who were born in Israel to mothers who immigrated in the 1990s. One quarter of this group consisted of children up the age of 4, a similar proportion were aged 5–9, approximately one-third were in the age bracket of 10–14, and the smallest group was made up of children between the ages 15 and 17.

Several factors contributed to the absorption of the children and youth immigrants (Horowitz 1998). These relate mainly to the social and cultural conditions in their place of origin, the conditions for integration into the receiving society, and personal factors. More specifically, the social and cultural background of the immigrants entails especially the conceptions of family, parenthood, and the education and culture of the young, given the changes that affected them as a result of the crisis in both Soviet and post-Soviet society. The conditions of absorption depend mainly on the policies of the education system, which are based on ideas of assimilation, monolingualism, and stereotyping, as well as the integration climate of Israeli society in general, and especially of the relevant age group, when among the Israeli-born adolescents there is considerable antipathy toward these immigrants. The personal factors that shape the nature and success of the integration of children and youth are expressed in the individual's confrontation with "culture shock"—the identity crisis and the integration patterns in their respective age group and the education system.

Studies conducted in the first half of the 1990s (Horowitz 1998) revealed many anxieties and considerable distress among a large segment of the younger immigrants, especially the youth. These hardships were reflected in the mental, familial, economic, and social spheres and in social relations in both the formal and informal educational systems, including a significant dropout rate among high school students and an unprecedented rate of juvenile delinquency (Habib 1998). Tracing these phenomena shows certain changes in the areas mentioned as well as the continuing problems (Epstein 2000; Sever 2000). Based on a longitudinal study attempting to explore the distress factors among immigrant pupils in the elementary and high schools, Sever has found an improvement (especially after the third year in Israel) in the areas of home and family, mental and emotional adjustment ("culture shock"), and in the social sphere, which is expressed in the relations with peers from the same age group. Starting from that time, a significant decline in anxiety levels is perceived among children and youth in the areas mentioned, and a further improvement appears at the end of the fifth year, especially in the implications of "culture shock." However there is no such improvement in the feelings of anxiety and distress in the school system. This is evident in both the formal and informal school systems in the relations between the immigrant students and their Israeli-born peers (Sever 1997a; 1997b). The difficulties of social integration in school among the immigrant students do not diminish with time, including their rejection by their Israeli-born counterparts.

There is further evidence that, alongside the excellence demonstrated by a significant portion of the immigrant high school students, the width of the student periphery (the proportion of students with failing grades or no grades at all in a particular subject) is high relative to Israeli-born students. This is true for Hebrew language, mathematics, and English. Nevertheless, the proportion of matriculants among the immigrants who finished twelfth grade is 50 percent, the same as that of the Israeli-born students.

Immigrant students drop out of the educational system at significantly higher rates than other students—particularly at the high school level.

Of the FSU immigrants in grades 9–12, 8.4 percent dropped out from Jewish schools under the auspices of the Ministry of Education in the 1998–99 school year, or between that year and 1999–2000, as compared with 4.8 percent among their Israeli-born peers. The percent of dropouts from grade nine is the highest (10.3 percent of the FSU immigrants vs. 5.2 percent among Israeli-born students). Among the students in grade 9 who arrived in Israel between the years 1990–1995, the dropout rate is 8.5 percent, whereas among those who came between 1996–1999 it is 16.1 percent (CBS, forthcoming). Besides the youth dropouts, there is an additional group of those who are enrolled as students in high school, but are not occupied in actual studies, whether reflected in inconsistent attendance or other shortcomings in their school functioning ("latent dropout"). In five Israeli localities—Carmiel, Rehovot, Netanya, Ramleh, and Ofakim—between 16 percent and 22 percent of immigrant youths were absent for at least one full day of studies each week, exclusive of absences due to illness (Noam, Ellenbogen-Frankovich, and Wolfson 1998). Between 1997–1998 and 1999–2000, the proportion of FSU immigrants among the latent dropouts reached about 14 percent (Sachar 2000).

These trends are even more serious among the children and youth from the Caucasus (Ellenbogen-Frankovich and Noam 1998); only 30 percent of the Caucasus-born immigrants who graduated from twelfth grade in 1998 passed the matriculation exams. A quarter of those aged 14–17 in this population dropped out of school. Among those aged 16 and above, the portion of dropouts is 36 percent. Furthermore, in 1997, 15 percent of the youth reported that they absented themselves from school at least four times a month for reasons other than illness (Lifshitz 2000; Noam, Ellenbogen-Frankovich, and Wolfson 1998).

The hardships of the immigrant children and youth also find expression in the large numbers who are under the care of various welfare agencies. In October

2000, 4,059 children of parents from the FSU were in the care of the Child and Youth Division of the Ministry of Labor and Welfare. The Youth Probation Service, aimed at working with youths subsequent to referrals by the police regarding crimes such as assault, drug- and sex-related crimes, robbery, and burglary, dealt with 3,320 immigrant minors from the FSU (2,200 from the European republics of the FSU, and 1,120 from the Asian parts). Many of these minors have problems of vagrancy and neglect, have run away from home, dropped out of schools and boarding schools, have occasionally used drugs and alcohol. Many come from difficult socioeconomic backgrounds (Lifshitz 2000). The percentage of FSU immigrants among all minor offenders in Israel is consistently on the rise. For ages 12 to 18, the rate grew from 12 percent in 1995 to 15 percent in 1997 and 18 percent in 1999. This proportion reflects an overrepresentation of the immigrants among juvenile delinquents in Israel as compared with their relative weight in the general young population. These delinquents are mostly male (91 percent), and delinquency is most often found among those aged 16–17 (59 percent). The proportion of immigrant youth among all juvenile delinquents in Israel is especially high in crimes related to drugs, property, and sex (Ben Arieh and Tzionit 1999). Data indicative of these problems among immigrant girls from the FSU are available from the Department of Services for Girls in Distress in the Ministry of Labor and Welfare. In October 2000, some 1,400 girls aged 13–21 received care from the department for vagrancy, neglect, running away from home, pregnancy in minors, and dropping out of school and boarding school. Most of the girls were from single-parent families (Lifschitz 2000).

The Human Resources

The immigrants achieved a high level of education and before migrating to Israel were to a large extent employed in scientific, academic, and technical occupations. For immigrants in general, the "economic returns" on their human capital tend to be lower than that of the absorbing population with the same level of human capital. This was manifested in the downgrading of the positions in which immigrants were employed, being the least desirable and lowest paying jobs. The difficulties of entering occupations appropriate to their skills were even more acute, as the labor market was unable to produce enough suitable jobs for the many highly educated RC immigrants. Though with longer stays in the country the "loss" resulting from immigration tended to decrease (Friedberg 1998), it remains pronounced after a decade. The loss of human capital and the cost to the immigrant as a result of immigration have been investigated by, among others, Eckstein and Weiss (1998, 1999) and Semyonov (1997).

The high level of human capital of the RC can be seen by comparing their level of education to that of the general population (Table 7). This is a crude comparison, as the system of education in the FSU and in the different republics is quite different from that of the Israeli population.

Participation in the Labor Force

In 1999, 350,000 members of the FSU community, who arrived in 1990 and afterward, were part of the Israeli labor force. In addition, there were an estimated additional 60,000 immigrants who had arrived prior to 1990 (to this figure one can also add those who were born in Israel to members of this community). Thus, they contributed in total 17–18 percent of the total Israeli labor force in 1999, which is a share larger than their proportion of the TJP.

We shall limit our analysis to the group that arrived in 1990 and afterward, since detailed data are available for them. This group experienced higher rates of participation in the labor force in their country of origin than did the Israeli population; this was especially true of the women: 64 percent of the FSU immigrant women stated that they had been in the labor force before immigrating, compared to 44 percent of the women in Israel in 1989. The entry of these immigrants into the Israeli labor force was a process that took time and was accompanied by problems and difficulties. For younger men, it took up to two years; for women, even three years; for those aged 55–64, the process was longer and more painful; and most of the elderly (65 and over) did not find employment.

The participation rate in Israel in 1999 of all those aged 15 and over who immigrated in 1990 and afterward was 56.5 percent as compared with 55 percent for the TP), while for those who arrived in 1990–91 this rate was even higher (60 percent). The differences in the participation rate of women were even larger than for men (52 percent compared to 48 percent). These differences are found in most

Table 7. Level of Education of Immigrants Who Arrived in the 1990's to Israel, and of the TJP, 1998
(Percent)

Years of Study	15 and Over			Employed		
	All Immig. 1990+	Immig. 1990–91	TJP	All Immig. 1990+	Immig. 1990–91	TJP
0–10	24.9	21.9	24.4	16.0	12.5	13.5
11–12	20.9	19.6	36.6	20.0	17.3	35.8
13–15	34.4	35.2	22.0	38.3	38.4	26.2
16+	19.8	23.3	17.0	25.7	31.8	24.5
TOTAL	100	100	100	100	100	100

Source: CBS 2000d.

Table 8. Participation in the Labor Force, of Those 15 and over, of the 1990 Immigrants and the TP, 1999

	Total			Men			Women		
	TP	Immigrants		TP	Immigrants		TP	Immigrants	
		90+	90–91		90+	90–91		90+	90–91
In the LF									
(,000)	2,320	392.5	166.2	1,268	193.2	84.6	1,052	199.4	81.7
% in the LF	55.1	56.5	59.7	62.4	62.3	66.5	48.2	51.8	54.0
Unemployed									
(,000)	207.5	45.2	14.3	108.4	21.0	6.7	99.1	24.1	7.6
% unemployed	9.0	11.5	8.6	8.6	10.9	7.9	9.4	12.1	9.3

Source: CBS 2001.

age groups for men, but are greater for women. The exception is in ages 55 and over, where the rates for all immigrants (1990+) were lower than those of the Israeli population. Surprisingly, the rates for ages 55–64, of the group that arrived in 1990–1991, was higher than that of the Israeli population but this can be explained both by their longer stay in the country, and by assuming that those in these age groups who entered the Israeli labor force at younger ages continued working while aging. The pattern of participation by education is similar to that

Table 9. Percent in the Labor Force of those 15 and over, of the RC and the 1990 Immigrants, by Age and Sex—1999

Age	Total			Men			Women		
	TP	Immigrants		TP	Immigrants		TP	Immigrants	
		90+	90–91		90+	90–91		90+	90–91
15–17	9.0	11.4	12.3	10.3	12.5	16.7	7.7	10.4	8.3
18–24	45.0	47.0	44.1	43.9	44.8	42.6	46.2	49.0	45.6
25–34	74.1	79.7	83.5	81.9	83.8	85.8	66.3	76.2	81.6
35–44	77.8	86.8	90.9	86.4	90.9	94.7	69.7	83.5	87.5
45–54	78.0	82.0	90.6	87.1	88.5	94.6	69.5	76.4	86.2
55–59	60.8	54.0	62.6	75.0	71.9	82.3	47.8	40.3	45.6
60–64	38.9	31.5	45.8	56.8	46.4	73.3	23.6	20.9	23.7
65+	9.3	4.3	4.9	15.1	7.0	7.7	4.9	2.6	3.1
total 15+	55.1	56.5	59.7	62.4	62.3	66.5	48.2	51.8	54.0

Source: CBS 2001.

found in the general population: the more years of schooling, the higher the participation. This, too, is even more pronounced for women.

It is interesting to follow the labor force participation of those immigrants who arrived in 1990–91 through the period of their stay in the country. See Table 10.

Employed and Unemployed

In 1998, 89 percent of those who were in the labor force were employed—more than 70 percent of them worked full time in the reference week—while 11 percent were unemployed and looking for work. The share of the unemployed in this community was a little higher than in the general population (9 percent). The higher percentage of unemployed can be attributed to the more recent immigrants; the percent of unemployed among the immigrants who arrived in 1990–91 is similar to that of the general population. The same phenomena held for both men and women. See Table 11.

The level and the fluctuations in the unemployment rate of this group depend on the general level of unemployment in the country, but also on the length of their stay in the country. It takes a few years until an immigrant enters stable employment.

The pattern of unemployment of the immigrant community by age is similar to that of the total population; that is, higher rates for the younger age groups (15–24) and lower rates for the main working age groups (25–54), and slightly higher rates for those aged 55 and over.

The employed immigrant worked, on the average, longer hours than the general population (72 percent of the employed immigrants worked full time, compared to 67 percent of the general population), the difference being larger for women.

Table 10. Labor Force Participation Rates in Israel of Immigrants Who Arrived in 1990–1991

Age	1999	1998	1997	1996	1995	1992
18–24*	44.1	43.2	45.4	43.6	43.2	49.4
25–34	83.5	80.0	82.2	82.5	80.7	75.7
35–44	90.9	89.8	90.4	89.2	88.4	81.6
45–54	90.6	86.8	86.2	85.5	84.1	75.8
55–64	53.4	49.3	48.0	49.2	48.0	38.8
Total 15+	59.7	57.2	58.4	57.1	56.9	53.5

*Rates in this age group are influenced by those in military service, who are not counted as part of the civilian labor force.
Source: CBS 2001.

Table 11. Percent Unemployed in 1998

	Total	Men	Women
1990–91	8.7	8.6	8.9
1992–93	10.5	10.5	10.4
1994–98	15.7	13.7	17.9
Total population immigrated	8.6	8.1	9.2

Source: CBS 2000e.

Occupational Composition

As described earlier, the immigrants in this community had a high level of education and had been employed in the FSU in higher-level occupations. Two-thirds of those employed in 1990–99 were in scientific, academic, professional, and technical occupations—85,000 defined themselves as engineers or architects, 18,000 as physicians or dentists, 15,000 as musicians, writers, and other artists. It was evident that so much human capital could not be integrated into the same occupations in Israel. Therefore, the process of their integration into the Israeli labor force not only required successful employment, but necessitated an entry process into a specific job that often required retraining and adjustment to the needs and opportunities in the Israeli labor market. One of the results of the arrival of this immigration was economic growth that increased the demand for various low-level occupations, and the entry of the immigrants into the labor force was marked by their shift to blue-collar and unskilled or semi-skilled occupations. It took some years for only part of the immigrants who had begun their employment in low-level jobs to move back into the occupation they had held in the FSU, or at least closer to it (see also Flug et al. 1992).

When we analyze the occupations of the members of this community in 1999, after a large number had already been in Israel close to 6–10 years, the picture that emerges is the following:

Many from this community were employed in academic, scientific, professional, and technical occupations (23 percent of all the 1990s immigrants and 31 percent of the older cohort who had arrived in 1990–91). At the same time, 65 percent of them were employed as skilled and unskilled workers in manufacturing, construction, etc. They were underrepresented in managerial and administrative occupations (less than 2 percent), and in clerical jobs.

As the immigrants' length of stay in the country increased, a larger proportion moved to higher-level occupations away from blue-collar occupations. Nevertheless, their occupations, even after years in the labor force, were much lower than the ones they held before immigrating.

Table 12. Percent of the Employed Who Worked Full Time 1998

	Total	Men	Women
1990+	72	83	62
1990–91	74	83	64
Total population immigrated	67	79	52

Approximately half of the immigrants who arrived during the 1990s and who had sixteen years or more of schooling, worked in academic, scientific, professional, and managerial occupations, but this was true for 59 percent of those who had arrived in 1990–91 (compared to 76 percent of the TP at this level of education). A large proportion of this group (26 percent) worked in blue-collar jobs (compared with 6 percent of the TP); the rest were clerical, sales, and service workers.

The proportion of the immigrants in the academic, scientific, and professional occupations is similar to that in the TP. The proportion in managerial and clerical occupations is much lower; while in the blue-collar occupations it is much higher than in the TP.

Male immigrants (1990+) in the academic, scientific, and professional occupations constitute a larger proportion of the employed immigrants than their proportion among the TP, and the difference is even larger when we compare the immigrants of 1990–91 to the TP. The proportion of female immigrants who immigrated in 1990–91 in these occupations is similar to their proportion of the TP. Men and women immigrants are represented in much lower proportions than the TP in the clerical and managerial occupations, and in much higher proportions in the blue-collar occupations.

The immigrants are concentrated in a limited number of occupations: half of all employed immigrants are to be found in ten occupations, with 9,000 or more immigrants in each one. These immigrants constitute a large proportion of all those employed in these occupations. See Table 13.

A group that received substantial government assistance (subsidized employment for three and sometimes five years) in its professional absorption was that of "scientists"—13,000 immigrants (mostly from the FSU) were registered as scientists. Three-quarters of them found employment in their fields; some 4,000 were employed in the private sector (mostly in industry), and 2,000 in the academic sector. Only a small proportion of those absorbed in the universities were given tenured positions, but their integration in industry was more rapid (Shai, in Ministry of Immigration Absorption 1999). See Tables 14, 15, and 16.

Table 13. Immigrants in Selected Occupations

Occupation	Number of Immig. Employed in Occupation	% of TP Employed in Occupation
Engineers, architects	14,000	25
Physicians, dentists	11,000	30
Nurses and other paramedical personnel	8,000	17
Personal care workers	35,000	38
Domestic and related helpers, cleaners, and launderers*	34,000	45
Welders, locksmiths, etc.	18,000	30
Electrical and electronic equipment workers	18,000	27

*Percentage of all the employed resident population (not taking into account the large number of foreign workers in these occupations).
Source: CBS 2001.

Wage Earners and Self-Employed

Of the RC employed, 95 percent were wage earners and salaried employees, compared to 85 percent of the TP. A large proportion of these wage earners worked in temporary jobs, even paid by the hour (35 percent were employed on a monthly basis, and only 54 percent had permanent jobs). A large proportion was afraid of being fired (Ministry of Immigration Absorption 1999). Those who were employers or self-employed constituted a very small proportion, although this was slowly increasing. A number of government and public programs were initiated to help immigrants establish their own businesses, but the impact of these measures was very limited.

Low Earnings of the Wage Earners

As mentioned above, a large proportion of wage earners of the RC are employed in the relatively low-wage blue-collar occupations, which brings the average wages of the RC to a figure below that of the TJP. Furthermore, the wages are lower than those of the TP in various other occupation groups as well. This can be explained in part by the entry of RC wage earners into the bottom rungs of each occupation group and by differences in seniority. There may also be some discrimination in wages paid to RC wage earners.

To illustrate: the average gross RC monthly wage in 1998 was 4,012 New Israeli Shekels (NIS) compared to 5,830 for all wage earners, a difference of 30 percent (CBS 2000, and unpublished data). As the number of hours worked was very simi-

Table 14. Occupational Distribution of the Immigrants and the TP.
(1999)—percent

Occupation	Total Population	All Immig. 1990+	Immig. 1990–1991	Immig. as % of Total Population
Academics, professionals	12.5	11.7	15.8	15.5
Associate professionals and technicians	14.7	11.5	15.3	13.1
Managers	6.3	1.4	1.6	3.7
Clerical workers	17.0	8.8	11.6	8.6
Agents, sale and service workers	18.3	20.1	17.9	18.2
Agricultural and skilled workers	1.9	0.9	0.6	7.6
Manufacturing, construction and other skilled workers	21.0	28.0	25.2	22.1
Unskilled workers	8.3	17.6	12.0	35.3
All occupations	100.0	100.0	100.0	16.5

Source: CBS 2001.

lar (41–42 hours per week), the difference in the relative hourly wage was similar (23.5 NIS compared to 34.5). Though wages of RC women were lower than that of men (21.7 NIS compared to 25), the relative difference of wages between RC and TP was around 30 percent for both men and women. The difference in the hourly wage was larger for those with higher education. In fact, there was a difference of 42 percent for those with an education of 16+ years, partly as a result of the fact that a large proportion of these RC members were employed in lower-level occupations. It is interesting to note that these differences are smaller for those employed in unskilled and blue-collar occupations; for women, this difference was only 5 percent. The large number of new immigrants entering the labor force with lower wages could be expected to bring about a general decrease in wages. In 1990–92, real average wages did not increase; they actually changed less than did the cost of labor per unit of production. However, from 1993, wages did rise slowly, but the changes were not uniform. The wages of the veterans in the scientific, academic, professional, and technical occupations (where the number of immigrants was largest), did increase substantially by 10–15 percent, while that of the unskilled workers declined, increasing the wage gap between occupations.

The lower average earnings of immigrants, caused both by higher unemployment and lower earnings in the various occupations, contributed to increase inequality in household income.

*Table 15. The Occupational Distribution in Israel of the Employed 1990+
Immigrants, and of the TP by Sex (1998)*

| | Total pop. | | Immig. 1990+ | | Immig. 1990–91 | |
| | Men | Women | Men | Women | Men | Women |
Occupation	(Percent)					
Academics, professionals	13.7	13.5	14.5	10.1	18.5	13.6
Associate professionals and technicians	11.8	19.5	10.6	16.7	13.2	20.7
Managers	9.3	3.0	1.8	0.7	2.1	0.6
Clerical workers	8.9	29.9	2.9	14.3	3.7	17.4
Agents, sale and service workers	15.5	21.4	8.8	26.6	9.2	23.4
Agricultural workers	2.7	0.5	0.6	0.3	0.6	0.2
Skilled workers in manufacturing, construction, etc.	30.9	4.8	46.2	13.2	41.5	11.9
Unskilled workers	7.2	7.4	14.6	18.1	11.2	12.2
All occupations	100.0	100.0	100.0	100.0	100.0	100.0

Source: CBS 2000e.

Living Conditions

To learn about the economic well-being of the RC in Israel, especially in comparison with that of the veteran population, a number of indicators were studied: the resources available to the RC households, that is, the various sources of income; and the uses of these resources—for consumption and its components, or for saving; the housing conditions of the households, and their ownership of household equipment and other durables.

Resources

The RC households had in 1998 an average gross money income of 6,700 NIS, a gap of 30 percent below the average income of the TP (CBS 2000c). After deducting income tax, health tax, and National Insurance payments, this gap decreased to 24 percent. As RC households are smaller than those in the general population (2.8 persons compared to 3.4), the gap per person shrank to 15 percent. Within the RC households we found that those who immigrated in 1993 and afterward had a gross money income lower by 28 percent than those who arrived in 1990–92, with a difference of 24 percent in net income. The main source of income was wages and salaries as only a very small percent are self-employed. The RC household received 23 percent of its total income from al-

Table 16. Occupations of Those with 16 Years and More of Education (1999)

Occupation	Total Pop.	Immig. 1990+	Immig. 1990–91	Immig. 1990–92
Academic and associate professionals				
Technicians and managers	75.8	52.0	58.8	43.1
Clerks, sales, and service workers	16.4	21.5	20.1	23.4
Skilled workers in agriculture, manufacturing construction, etc.	5.4	17.0	14.5	20.2
Unskilled workers	2.2	9.4	6.5	13.3
All occupations	100.0	100.0	100.0	100.0

Source: CBS 2001.

lowances and assistance (mostly from the National Insurance Institute), compared to 13 percent that the TP received. See Table 17.

Though the RC households had lower incomes than the general population, the percent of households below the "poverty line" (defined as half the net median income of the total population) was 15.3 percent in 1998 compared to 16.6 percent of the TP. This refers to the net money income (after deducting income tax and social security payments and including transfer payments). Transfer payments to a very large extent reduced the proportion of new immigrants to under the poverty line (National Insurance Institute 2000, p. 49).

Consumption Patterns

Consequent to the lower household income of the RC, their total consumption is also lower than that of the TP, though it increased at a higher rate with the length of stay in the country. In 1998, the average consumption of the RC was 5,840 NIS, two-thirds that of the general population. If we take into account the smaller size of the RC households and the distribution of households by size, the difference shrinks: RC household expenditure was 76 percent that of the TP. The immigrant households that arrived in 1990–92 attained a level of 85 percent of that of the TP. The expenditures of the small RC households, especially those of older persons, were even lower.

Expenditures of the RC for most items were, as expected, lower than those of the total population, but by different degrees. The proportion of the total RC expenditure for housing and food was higher than that of the TP: housing constituted 26 percent compared to 23 percent; and food, 21 percent compared to

Table 17. Average Household Monthly Income of RC and the TP (1998)

	Total RC	Immig. 1990–92	Immig. 1993+	Total Population	Total RC as % of TP
Income type:					
gross money income	6,664	7,704	5,594	9,527	70
net money income	5,591	6,302	4,777	7,394	76
net money income per person	1,997			2,175	92
Sources of income:					
from work	4,846	6,048	3,602	7,113	68
from capital	919	1,181	647	2,023	45
pensions, social insurance funds	14	7	20	642	2
allowances and assistance	1,761	1,593	1,934	1,455	
Total gross income	7,539	8,829	6,204	11,232	67

Source: CBS, Household Income Survey and Household Expenditure Survey, 1998. Unpublished data.

18 percent. On some items, the expenditure of the RC households was even higher than that of the TP, that is, alcoholic beverages, cigarettes, tobacco, public transport, and monthly rent. Other expenditures were much lower, such as meals away from home, culture, domestic help, sports and entertainment, education (as a result of smaller numbers of children in the household), travel abroad, private cars, owner-occupied housing (there were relatively fewer owner-occupied apartments and more rented apartments). As the length of stay in the country increases, the pattern of expenditure approaches that of the veteran population.

Housing Conditions

The housing conditions of the RC in Israel are somewhat inferior to those of the TP, but the longer their stay in the country, the better are the conditions. They live in smaller apartments, and though they have smaller households, the number of persons per room is, on the average, a little larger than the TJP. The average density was approximately one person per room in 1998 (compared to 0.94 for the TJP). Only 1.2 percent of the RC households lived in apartments with more than two persons per room. These data do not include those living in absorption centers or institutional dwellings. Some of the elderly of the RC who live alone have poor housing conditions.

Around half of the households of the RC (of those who arrived in 1990–92 more than 60 percent) had succeeded in purchasing their own apartment by 1998, compared to 70–75 percent of the TJP. More of these owner-occupied dwellings were in development towns and small towns (60–70 percent owner-occupied) than in the larger cities (in the three largest cities, only 33–40 percent), where they were in the lower status neighborhoods. (CBS 1999a, 1999b). The apartments rented by the RC were mostly owned by the private sector, but some were government-subsidized housing. The owner-occupied apartments were larger and had lower density than the rented ones.

The estimated average value of the owner-occupied apartments of the RC (owing to their location and size) was only 60 percent of the value of those of the TJP (and 70 percent per room) (CBS 2000g, and unpublished data). Ownership of the dwelling is accompanied by a high monthly payment for mortgage and other loans for housing. Though mortgages for immigrant housing are subsidized, still the household paid 1,350 NIS monthly for these loans—a significant burden on a lower-income household.

The portion of the total expenditure going to housing, including the rent paid and the imputed value of the rent of the owner-occupied apartments, though smaller in absolute terms than that of the TJP, represented 26 percent of the total expenditure of the RC in 1998, compared to 23 percent of the TJP.

The heavy demand for housing to accommodate the large wave of 1990s immigration was filled at the beginning of the 1990s by a large supply of "empty apartments" that were available at that time. Later, caravans and other temporary housing met the need. However, massive housing construction, a large part of it with government initiative and support, was also necessary. In the decade 1990–99 close to half a million apartments were completed, filling the demand of the new immigrants as well as the veteran population.

Household Equipment and Other Durable Goods

In 1998 practically all RC households had a refrigerator and a stove; 90 percent or more had a color television and telephone; and 85 percent had a washing machine. Close to 90 percent were connected to cable TV (more than the TP—62 percent). A lower percent possessed other durable goods: vacuum cleaner and video recorders (around 60 percent—similar to the TJP). For other durables the percent was lower than that of the TJP: microwave (40 percent compared to 58 percent); air conditioner (31 percent compared to 47 percent); personal computer (27 percent and 37 percent). A car was at the disposal of 32 percent of the RC households compared with 53 percent in the TJP (for households with two earners, 64 percent compared to 81 percent). For some goods which are at the disposal of a smaller proportion of the TP (16–26 percent), the proportion of the RC households with these items was negligible (deep-freezer, dishwasher, clothes dryer).

These figures perhaps point to the preferences of the RC for the various items compared to the TJP (figures from the CBS 2000a; 2000g; and unpublished data on the RC).

Social, Cultural, and Political Characteristics

Ten years after the beginning of the mass immigration wave from the FSU, we may describe the immigrant population as a rather cohesive ethnic community on both the local and national levels, which has become a new social segment in the multifaceted structure of Israeli society.

The apparent structural characteristics of the community are:

- A common language: Russian;
- Systems of informal interwoven social networks;
- Groupings of ethnic housing in most urban localities;
- A wide and variegated ethnic market of products and services;
- Ethnic patterns of leisure and entertainment;
- Independent cultural creativity in the fields of theater, film, music, dance, painting, sculpture, literature, and poetry;
- Open cultural borders for the consumption of ethnic cultural products and services from the country of origin, including four television channels that enjoy widespread viewing;
- Russian-language newspapers: dailies, weeklies, local newspapers, and monthlies: more than fifty regularly appearing publications a month, on a profit-making basis;
- National and local networks of cultural centers and services especially for FSU immigrants in most of the urban centers;
- A network of complementary and alternative education on the preschool, elementary, and high school levels;
- The active use of Russian as a second language in private, and even to a certain extent in the public sector, including translation and special Russian language editions in most of the media channels;
- The existence of an official radio station (Reshet REKA) and local television channels in Russian;
- Hundreds of local and national third-sector organizations operating in the areas of society, welfare, health, education, and culture, organized by umbrella organizations, that represent the community in the society at large;
- Local and national ethnic parties that receive significant support in the immigrant community and representation in most of the municipal coalitions (15 percent of the representatives in local governments in the elections of 1998) and on the national level, in Israel's Knesset, beginning with the 1996

elections (10 out of 120 Knesset members in the 1999 elections); this includes representation on a ministerial level in the governments that were established in 1996, 1999, and 2000 in important offices from the point of view of services, opportunities, and financial resources needed by immigrants.

• Ethnic legislation, as seen in the "Veteran's Law," that assures rights to the veterans and disabled of World War II among the immigrants, as well as recognition of a national holiday of the USSR—the Day of Victory over the Nazis—as a national holiday of the State of Israel. In January 2001, the political parties of the immigrants succeeded also in legislating some amendments to social security laws for the benefit of the immigrant population.

These and other characteristics of the FSU community in Israel are to be found in studies on the community's social, cultural, and political spheres.

The Social Sphere

Most of the immigrant population has informal intragroup social networks (Slonim-Nevo, Sharaga, and Abdelgani 1999; Mirsky, Baron-Dreiman, and Kedem 1999; Damian and Rosenbaum-Tamari 1999; Al-Haj and Leshem 2000). Meetings with veteran Israelis are largely limited to the workplace (60 percent meet with Israelis often or very often) or in the residential neighborhood (56 percent meet with Israelis often or very often). In the educational framework, or social and family gatherings, the frequency of meetings with veteran Israelis is very low (19 percent meet with them often or very often in the framework of studies, 18 percent in social meetings, and 11 percent in family gatherings). Of the immigrants aged 18 and over, 71 percent reported toward the end of 1999 that not one of their five best friends in Israel was a veteran Israeli, while 66 percent asserted that all five were from the FSU (Al-Haj and Leshem 2000). This social isolation was even more prevalent among the immigrants from the Caucasus (King 1998).

Despite the relative detachment from the Israeli informal social networks relationships, the immigrants see themselves as being quite close to the secular Ashkenazic segment (of European origin and their descendants), and approximately 9 out of every 10 are willing to have members of this segment as neighbors, as superiors in their place of employment, as friends for their children, and even as spouses. On the other hand, the immigrants express a larger social distance from other sectors of Israeli society, and their order of preference in the areas mentioned above after the secular Ashkenazim, is: Oriental Jews (of Asian or African origin and their offspring), religious Jews, Ethiopian immigrants, and at the bottom of the list the Arab population (Al-Haj and Leshem 2000).

These findings are similar to those of Lissitza and Peres (1999). They found that among the religious groups within the Jewish population, the group closest to the immigrants are the secular Jews, after them the traditional observant group, and the most distant group are the ultra-Orthodox. Examining the distances of the immigrants from the various ethnic groups in the Jewish population shows that the extent of separation from the Ashkenazim is significantly less than the extent of separation from the Oriental Jews. Lissitza and Peres point out that within the veteran Jewish population, all the religious and ethnic groups keep about the same social distance from the FSU immigrants. There is in this regard no real difference between Ashkenazim and Orientals, nor is there between the secular, traditional, and observant Jews. The ultra-religious keep the greatest distance from the FSU immigrants. Researchers note that the reason for this is that the forces that attract or repel the veteran groups to or from the immigrants are rather similar. The repelling forces, according to them, are: (a) the immigrants are seen as strangers and culturally different; (b) the immigrants are seen as competitors for resources; (c) the immigrants retain their independence and refuse to commit themselves to one group or another; (d) the tendency of the immigrants to preserve their culture is sometimes seen as self-aggrandizement. The forces that attract the immigrants to the various veteran Israeli groups are: (a) according both to Zionist ideology and the Nationalist-Israeli idea, the immigrants constitute an addition to the population that strengthens the State; and (b) all the groups see the immigrants as potential allies (precisely because they are not committed to any group in particular).

Culture and Identification

The immigrants, including the young population, tend to maintain the life style, norms, and behavioral patterns that characterized Soviet society and culture (Al-Haj and Leshem 2000). There are differences between veteran Israelis and immigrants in attitudes toward family planning (Amir, Remenick, and Elimelech 1997) as well as significant disparities in conceptions of parenthood. The immigrants' concept of parenthood differs from that of veteran Israelis in its emphasis on developmental expectations, educational methods, the division of labor between the home and the educational framework, and methods of punishment. Immigrant mothers to toddlers (3–4 years old) emphasize development through structured learning, knowledge provision, and teaching functional independence, whereas Israeli-born mothers stress attainment of psychological independence by means of individual experience, free choice, encouragement of decision making, and reaching logical conclusions (Roar-Streir and Rosental 2001). Immigrant parents are also more willing to inflict physical and emotional punishment on their children (Shor 1999). At the same time, the family is seen as the locus of security and commitment in relation to the hostile external environment (Horowitz and Leshem 1998; Al-Haj and Leshem 2000).

As far as interpersonal relations and employment are concerned, the immigrants' decisions and behavior have stressed individualism, rationality, and pragmatism (Horowitz and Leshem 1998). Their attitude toward law and government is ambivalent. This attitude is reflected, on the one hand, by defense of government and law and order at the expense of freedom and individual rights, and, on the other hand, by suspicion and lack of trust in the motives of the government and the establishment, as well as a relatively permissive attitude to white-collar crime. In the defense of strong government, 84 percent of the immigrants maintain that freedom of expression does not need to be protected when there is a breach of security in the state, or when people use terminology that is harmful to state security (83 percent). Seventy-nine percent would not even be willing to give lawful defense, in the name of freedom of expression, to those who publicly burn the flag of the state, and only 42 percent attach great importance to the existence of a free press without government censorship (Al-Haj and Leshem 2000). At the same time, in accordance with the experience of survival in a totalitarian regime, they tend to distrust the social services the government offers its citizens (Sharlin 1998). Actually there is manifest distrust of the whole social environment. The immigrants feel completely free to speak their mind only at home among family members (87 percent), as compared with 39 percent who feel this way at their place of work when with their colleagues; 29 percent in public gatherings; and 26 percent in the presence of the "boss" in their place of employment (Al-Haj and Leshem 2000). Likewise, the immigrants are relatively understanding of white-collar crime. This tolerance is manifested in the relatively low level of willingness among the immigrants, as compared with the Israeli public, to report white-collar crime to the authorities in incidents of string-pulling (*protectzia*), embezzlement, tax evasion, consumer fraud, and receipt of and giving of bribes. For example, 39 percent among the immigrants are unwilling to report bribe-giving to the authorities as compared with only 14 percent of the total Israeli population. Sixty-one percent of the FSU immigrants would not be willing to report an incident of favoritism and string-pulling to the authorities, as compared with 32 percent of the Israelis.

These values of the immigrants as well as other sets of values they brought from their country of origin find expression and are reinforced in the Soviet community media in Israel (Zilberg and Leshem 1999). Moreover, as found by Al-Haj and Leshem (2000), 77 percent of the immigrants aged eighteen and over watch television stations broadcast from Russia daily, as opposed to 25 percent who always watch the local Hebrew TV channels. Among the FSU immigrants, 40 percent listen every day to radio broadcasts in Russian as against 21 percent who listen every day to Hebrew broadcasts. Sixty percent of the immigrants read daily Russian language newspapers published in Israel, compared with 9 percent who read the Hebrew newspapers. The growth in the number of daily and other periodicals that appear in Israel in the Russian language should be noted in view of the immigration from the FSU in the 1990s. In 1985 there were 16 newspapers and periodicals; in 1990, 25; and in 1995, 37 (CBS 1998b). Of the 18 daily newspapers which appeared in Israel in 1995, 7 appeared in Hebrew, and 4 in Russian. At the same time 18 weeklies appeared in Israel in Russian, as opposed to 31 in Hebrew (CBS 1998b).

It should be noted that most of the immigrants do not see the cultural characteristics of the immigrant community as a passing phenomenon of the first years of immigration and sociocultural integration. They stress the unique cultural contribution of the FSU immigrants to Israeli society and strongly support the preservation of cultural heritage and the maintenance of ethnic Russian institutions and organizations (Al-Haj and Leshem 2000). It is important or very important to 91 percent of those surveyed that their children know Russian; to 88 percent that they should be familiar with Russian culture; to 80 percent that institutions of Russian culture in Israel should be preserved; to 66 percent that the continuation of the framework of informal education should be ensured; to 57 percent that the frameworks of formal education in the Russian language be maintained; and to 73 percent that the political parties of immigrants from the FSU should continue.

The demand to preserve Russian culture in Israel is accompanied by a sense of cultural superiority over the local culture in Israel. The FSU immigrants of the 1990s evaluate their own influence on Israeli society as far more positive than that of Israeli society on themselves. They gave the highest scores to their influence in the following fields: Israeli cultural life (88 percent perceive the influence of the immigrants in this area as positive or very positive), science and technology in Israel (86 percent), economic growth (86 percent), political life (75 percent), and even the area of security (64 percent) (Al-Haj and Leshem 2000). According to the findings of Lissitza and Peres (1999) most of the immigrants feel that in the field of science and technology they have nothing to learn from veteran Israelis.

The only area in which the immigrants think that they have more of a negative than a positive influence on Israeli society is that of crime. About half of the immigrants think that in this field the immigration from the FSU had either a negative or a very negative influence on Israeli society (Al-Haj and Leshem 2000). A large majority (87 percent) of the immigrants would like cultural life in Israel to be like that of Western Europe, but only 9 percent think that this is actually the case. Seventy-five percent of the immigrants see the existing culture in Israel as oriental, while only 11 percent of them approve of such culture (Hazz 1999).

Nevertheless, in practice, the leisure-time culture of the FSU immigrants is different from that of Israelis of Western background. Very few immigrants go to the cinema (25 percent, as compared with 40 percent), especially to see Israeli films (9 percent vs. 40 percent). Their share of theatergoers, visitors at museums, and even concerts of classical music is lower than the average among the Western segment of the Israeli population. Their share of persons studying, or in public or voluntary activities is smaller (23 percent and 13 percent vs. 38 percent and 33 percent, respectively). Only their portion of those who read books is a bit higher (95 percent vs. 91 percent). We may assume that at least part of this difference in the leisure patterns of the immigrants as compared with that of the average Jewish population of Western origin is due to economic constraints, a lack of leisure time, or poor command of the Hebrew language. There is great similarity between the indoor leisure activities (over 85 percent of both immigrants and Western-origin Israelis watch television, read newspapers and books, and meet with friends and relatives), although in leisure activities outside the home there is a difference between the two groups, with the immigrants preferring, at least at this stage, activities as delineated above (Hazz 1999).

These differences do not impair the feelings of superiority of the FSU immigrants or their expectations of continuing their unique cultural patterns in the new surroundings. These feelings and expectations are just one of the expressions of group identity, with the Jewish and Russian components being emphasized, and the Israeli—and particularly the Zionist—components being secondary. Lissitza and Peres (1999) note the FSU immigrants stress their Russian and their Jewish identities equally, as these two identities were acceptable to them before their immigration, while just a minority emphasize their Israeli identity.

According to the findings of Al-Haj and Leshem (2000), 78 percent of the immigrants of the 1990s feel themselves to be, to a large or even a very large extent, first and foremost Jews; 66 percent as Jews from the FSU, that is, a unique subgroup defined by their country of origin; 44 percent as Israelis; and 21 percent as Zionists. Low Zionist identification was found also by Hazz (1999).

According to Al-Haj and Leshem (2000), the Jewish component receives more emphasis in the older age groups (55+) while the Israeli component is more important among the young (18–24). It is also interesting to note that the Russian identity is emphasized more among those with high school and academic training than among those with lower levels of education (Hazz 1999).

Stressing the Jewish and Russian components of group identity in Israel raises the question of general solidarity with the receiving society. In fact, only one-third of the immigrants feel themselves to be an inseparable part of Israeli society, as compared with 79 percent of veteran Israelis (Lissitza and Peres 1999; Hazz 1999). Nevertheless, two-thirds of the immigrants who were interviewed by Lissitza and Peres (1999) state that Israel is the country in which they want to live. This attitude was found among 82 percent of the veteran population.

The Political Sphere

In the political sphere, the electoral strength of the 1990s' immigrants was felt in the Knesset elections of 1992. However, in the 1996 elections, the "Russian vote" generated a significant change not only in the political representation of the immigrants, but in the political and cultural structure of Israeli society in general (Horowitz 1994, 2001). Of the Soviet-origin voters in these elections, 42 percent supported an immigrant party.

This success on the national level overflowed to the local level, where the immigrants took advantage of their political weight in the national coalition government to gain support locally. In the local elections of November 1998, 45 percent of the voters supported Russian parties; 44 percent supported mixed immigrant and veteran lists; and only 11 percent voted for parties that had no immigrants (Al-Haj and Leshem 2000). Of the 1,049 mandates to local councils in Israel, FSU immigrants received 162 (15 percent). These achievements on the local level were followed closely by the 1999 Knesset elections where 10 percent of the 120 Knesset mandates went to FSU immigrants, this representation being mainly concentrated in two ethnic parties of FSU immigrants. These elections proved that the results of the 1996 elections were neither accidental nor were they an anomaly.

The large wave of immigration from the FSU came at a time when Israel was in a prolonged political stalemate (Lissitza and Peres 1999); the main segments of the political structure (the religious, the ultra-Orthodox, the Arabs, development towns, oriental population, and the secular upper-middle class) were each committed to a defined political camp, Left or Right, and almost automatically promised that camp the majority of their votes. In every election during the 1990s, the FSU immigrants, as a politically non-committed segment, favored the winning side. As the findings of Al-Haj and Leshem (2000) show, regarding the 1999 Knesset elections, this type of ethnic voting by the immigrants has not been found to be connected to their level of satisfaction with their integration in Israel. Nevertheless, a significant relationship has been found between voting for an immigrant party in support of the FSU immigrant group interests in Israel, and preservation of the ethnic group's identity. These sectoral interests are directed in each election campaign at the political group within the veteran population that will best serve the immigrants' interests.

Factors Facilitating the Development of the Ethnic Community in Israel

Zilberg and Leshem (1999), Leshem and Lissak (2001) and also Al-Haj and Leshem (2000) indicate the factors that brought about the consolidation of a community of immigrants with a manifested ethnic identity and a formal and informal organizational framework on both the local and national levels. The sources of these factors are to be found in the characteristics of the immigrant population as well as in those of the receiving society. The characteristics of the immigrant population that were molded in the immigrants' country of origin as well as in their process of integration in Israel are:

STRENGTH IN QUALITY AND QUANTITY This immigration approaches one million persons and is the largest that ever came to Israel since its establishment. This critical mass, both from the point of view of the development of the internal social activity within the community, and from the point of view of its weight relative to the surrounding society, is felt even more strongly owing to the very significant human capital that it brought (Table 7) as compared with all other origin groups in Israel (Leshem and Lissak 2001).

ECOLOGICAL CONCENTRATIONS Large concentrations of more than 25,000 immigrants are to be found in not a few urban settlements in Israel (Table 5). Eighty-four percent of the immigrants stated that they live in neighborhoods where a third or more of the residents are FSU immigrants from the 1990s (Al-Haj and Leshem 2000).

MIGRATION MAINLY AS A RESULT OF "PUSH" FACTORS Most of those who came were driven by the crisis in their society of origin, especially in regard to the economy and employment; nevertheless, their cultural attachment to their country of origin remains strong.

DOMINANCE OF SLAVIC ELEMENTS Most of the immigration of the 1990s came from states in the Slavic center of the FSU, and from the centers of Soviet education in these areas, which are inextricably joined to Russian-Soviet culture. Most of them never received any Jewish education, and their rate of intermarriage with the dominant ethnic group is quite high (Leshem and Lissak 2001). It should also be noted that most of the immigrants from the peripheral areas of the FSU who were outside the Slavic center also originated in these areas, and on their settlement in the peripheries clearly served as vehicles of Russian culture.

THE PRESENCE OF AN "INTELLIGENTSIA" The population that arrived in Israel during the decade had a relatively high proportion of persons from Moscow, St. Petersburg, and Kiev who had held elite positions in the fields of culture, science, and technology. Not a few of them were representatives and bearers of Russian culture and had influenced the direction of its development. This social stratum commands the deep respect and legitimization of the immigrants for the functions of public leadership it has taken upon itself within the immigrant community (Leshem and Lissak 2001).

RUSSIAN LANGUAGE AS A COMMON DENOMINATOR Russian is the main language of the immigrants, both among the old and young immigrants, with only limited use of Hebrew in daily life, with the exception of the work place. The immigrants' limited knowledge of Hebrew, which is particularly obvious in the older population, prevents meaningful contact with the social and cultural surroundings and preserves both their interrelations within Russian-speaking networks and their dependence on Russian media and cultural products (Leshem and Lissak 2001; Al-Haj and Leshem 2000).

INTENSIVE INTERRELATIONS WITH THE COUNTRY OF ORIGIN AND ITS CULTURE Immigrants of the 1970s from the USSR were cut off from almost all contact with its society and culture after leaving its borders because of the restrictions of the totalitarian regime. Open borders in the 1990s have allowed immigrants to maintain ties on both the personal and sociocultural levels, whether as intensive reciprocal visits or as cultural exchanges in real time via the mass media from cultural and social centers in the land of origin, not to mention economic ties.

THE DEVELOPMENT AND FUNCTIONING OF THE RUSSIAN PRESS IN IS- RAEL The rapid growth of the immigrant population from the FSU in Israel brought with it the development of periodicals in the Russian language. Already by 1993, this wave of publications reached about 50 regularly-appearing periodicals, about half of which were weeklies and dailies. This is the largest and most variegated group of periodicals produced by any language group in Israel, respective of size. This massive commercial immigrant press played a significant role in the crystallization of the heterogeneous immigrant population and its evolution from an imaginary to an actual community. It served not only to supply the immigrants with information they needed, but also to give expression to their social and personal distress, to supply the opportunity to present their problems, to point out those who were to blame for the problematic situation, and to emphasize their common symbols and heritage while at the same time delineating the boundaries of the community and giving its speakers and leaders a platform (Zilberg and Leshem 1999).

SOCIAL AND ECONOMIC DISTRESS The process of migration from the FSU and absorption in Israel exposed quite a few immigrants to distress situations. Among a significant portion of immigrants aged eighteen and over, a feeling of economic deprivation and loss of socioeconomic status are seen as a result of immigration. Thus, two-thirds of the immigrants (age 18+), who came in the last decade, stated in 1999 that either their income did suffice for a small part of their needs, or it was not at all sufficient (24 percent said it was not at all sufficient). Likewise, half of the immigrants perceive themselves as belonging to either the lower-middle class in Israel, or to the lower class (24 percent), while in the FSU only 6 percent of these immigrants had belonged to these classes (4 percent to the lower-middle class, and 2 percent to the lower class) (Al-Haj and Leshem 2000).

The quantitative and qualitative power of the immigrants, their ecological concentrations, their limited ties with the veteran population, the strong connection with their society of origin and its culture, as well as their social and economic distress created the basis for the consolidation of the community, and these basic conditions were taken advantage of by the immigrant press and their leaders to build the community and its organizational and political frameworks. Significant developments within contemporary Israeli society also helped to consolidate the immigrant community (Leshem and Lissak 2001). These developments include:

The Intensification of Cultural Pluralism in Israeli Society and the Lack of a Dominant Cultural Model

Internal cultural and social processes in Israeli society, and interrelations with global cultural centers in the 1990s, have in fact legitimized cultural pluralism in Israel and weakened the demands that in the past were directed at the immigrants to conform, identify with the dominant culture of their new country, and abandon their culture of origin.

Intensification of Sectoralism in Israeli Society

The descent of the dominant cultural model and of the collective identity of Israeli society, mentioned above, and the intensifying pluralism were accompanied by increasing empowerment and consolidation of sociocultural sectors, splitting the society on the basis of religion, ethnicity, or nationality (Yatziv 1999). This schism, which manifested itself clearly in Israeli society just before this wave of immigration, and the political-economic achievements of the new sectors presented a desirable social-cultural-political model of community organization for the new immigrants.

Growing Antagonism against the Immigrants

As the contact of the receiving society with the immigrants increased, so did negative stereotypical attitudes and prejudices against them. Although quite a few in the receiving Jewish community exhibit a positive attitude toward immigration and the immigrants, various surveys show that ever since the beginning of this immigration wave there has been a clear exacerbation of negative attitudes toward the immigrants. These negative attitudes, and the rejection the immigrants subsequently experienced, worsened the culture shock that accompanied their absorption and increased their hostility toward the surrounding society (61 percent of the immigrants aged eighteen and above see the ruling attitude of veteran Israelis toward the immigrants as "exploitation" [Al-Haj and

Leshem 2000]). These feelings deepened the isolation of the immigrants in their social networks, further strengthened their Russian identity, and contributed to the preservation of their culture.

An Absorption Policy with a Low Level of Control over Absorption Processes
The "direct absorption policy" that was applied in the initial stages of this immigration substituted financial assistance for services, and directed the immigrant to the free market rather than answering his needs. This seriously limited the interrelations between the government and the immigrant population as compared with earlier immigrations, and increased the importance of relatives and friends in Israel as the main support system in the integration process. These mutual relations strengthened the social and cultural segregation of the immigrants.

Change of the National Election System in Israel
The separation of the vote for prime minister from the vote for a national party, introduced in the general elections of 1996, enabled the immigrant population, as well as other sectors, to clearly express their particular interests by voting for an immigrant ethnic party, while at the same time their votes for the prime ministerial candidate symbolized their identification with the state in general (Horowitz 2001).

Changes of Government in the Elections of 1992, 1996, and 1999
Beginning with the elections of 1992, the immigrant vote was viewed by the Israeli public, and by the immigrants as well, as the prime cause of the government's turnover. This feeling provided them with a sense of power that has grown with each round of elections and has strengthened group identity and community-sectoral consolidation (Horowitz 2001).

This combination of characteristics of the immigrant population from the FSU with the characteristics of Israeli society in the 1990s developed among the European middle class in Israel the first example of a secular group that attempted to legitimize its unique identity as an ethnic group (Ben Rafael, Olshtain, and Geijst 1994). This level of communal-ethnic consolidation is unique to the FSU immigrants in Israel in the 1990s, and we do not find it among the immigrants of the 1970s in Israel, or in the Jewish migrations from the USSR to the United States or Australia (Leshem and Lissak 2001). At this stage of the integration process, it is difficult to predict whether the consolidation of the Russian community in Israel will become a permanent phenomenon, or whether the second and third generations of this immigration will assimilate into the Ashkenazi Western-origin secular group, which is, in many aspects, culturally and socially quite close to the Russian sector even in the eyes of the immigrants themselves (Al-Haj and Leshem 2000).

There are, however, social mechanisms whose influence on the immigrants may accelerate integration in Israeli society. Among these, we shall mention: IDF service of the community's youth; education together with Israelis in schools at the various levels; the daily meeting with Israelis in the workplace; meetings at cultural gatherings in general (concerts, theater, museums, etc.); and sometimes even marriage to Israeli spouses.

Conclusion and a Look at the Future

More than a decade has passed since the start of the large wave of immigration from the FSU, in the course of which more than 800,000 persons arrived in Israel by the year 2000. This stream continued into 2001 as well. Over this period, a large community (the largest of the Jewish ethnic communities in Israel) with unique characteristics crystallized. A perspective of more than one generation will be needed to assess its integration process into Israeli society.

In this chapter we have assessed the first decade. The assessment has focused on the instrumental aspects including the housing situation, employment, standard of living, and others. Furthermore, the formation of an ethnic community having unique social, cultural, and even political features was observed.

Regarding the future of this community, we shall need to trace processes as they occur under the circumstances of both the FSU and Israeli societies. The main questions for study in the coming years are:

- How many will not find their places in Israel and will emigrate to other destinations or perhaps back to their country of origin?
- Of those who stay, to what extent will the members of this community adapt their demographic behavior (in the fields of marriage and family building, fertility rates, etc.) to that of Israeli society?
- How many will find employment that fits their human capital?
- Will the second generation of this immigration merge into pluralistic Israeli social networks and adopt Israeli lifestyles, or maintain their Russian culture?
- What will be the effect of the compulsory service in the IDF on the future consolidation of the community?
- Will the gap between the income and the standard of living between the immigrants and the Israeli population fade away over time?
- What will be the future of the ethnic organizations of the Russian community on the local and national levels?
- What will be the community leadership commitment to the collective public agenda of the State of Israel?

- Can we see, in the immigrants' interest in preserving the culture of their country of origin and their moral responsibility, a selective preservation of some components along with the abandonment of others?
- What type of communal consolidation will develop among those immigrants from the Asian Republics, especially the Caucasus, Georgia, and Bukhara?

It will be possible to answer these questions and many others in a few years. However, these answers will depend largely on the future immigration trends from the FSU and the pattern of ties with FSU centers of culture and Jewish life. The social, economic, political, and security challenges facing present-day Israel will also affect the outcomes of the integration process, as well as new intervention projects and policy measures that the local or central government will develop to integrate the FSU immigrants into the sociocultural fabric of the general culture and to make use of their unique human capital.

NOTE

1. We denote in this article: RC = Russian Community (arrived 1990 and after); TJP = Total Jewish Population of Israel; TP = Total Population of Israel.

REFERENCES

Al-Haj, Majid, and Elazar Leshem. 2000. *Immigrants from the Former Soviet Union in Israel: Ten Years Later.* Haifa: University of Haifa, Center for Multiculturalism and Educational Research.

Altshuler, Mordechai. 1987. *Soviet Jewry Since the Second World War: Population and Social Structure.* New York: Greenwood Press.

———. 1990. *The Jews of the Eastern Caucasus.* Jerusalem: Ben-Zvi Institute for the Study of Jewish Communities in the East; and the Institute of Contemporary Jewry, Hebrew University.

Amir, Delila, Larissa Remenick, and Yuval Elimelech. 1997. "Educating Lena: Women Immigrants and 'Integration' Policies in Israel—The Politics of Reproduction and Family." In *Russian Jews on Three Continents,* ed. Lewin-Epstein Noah, Yaacov Ro'i, and Paul Ritterband, 495–509. London: Frank Cass.

Ben-Arieh, Asher, and Yaffa Tzionit. 1999. *The State of the Child in Israel—A Statistical Abstract.* Jerusalem: National Council for the Child, Center for Research and Public Education (Hebrew).

Ben Rafael, Eliezer, Elite Olshtain, and Idit Geijst. 1994. *Aspects of Identity and Language Acquisition among Immigrants from the Commonwealth of Independent States.* Jerusalem: Hebrew University, School of Education and NCJW Research Institute for Innovation in Education (Hebrew).

Israel Central Bureau of Statistics (CBS). 1997. *Employment of Immigrants Who Arrived from the Former USSR in October–December 1993, A Follow-Up Survey Two Years after Immigration.* Current Briefing.

———. 1998b. *Daily Newspapers and Periodicals published in Israel, 1995.* Current Briefing 4.

———. 1999a. *Immigrant Population from the Former USSR, Selected Data, 1997.* Current Briefing 5.

———. 1999b. *Household Density and Households in Israel 1997–1998.* Special Publication no. 1122.

———. 1999c. *Pupils in Post-Primary Schools (Grades IX–XII)—Staying on Vs. Dropping Out, 1986/87–1995/96.* Current Briefing in Statistics 1.

———. 1999d. *Immigrants of 1990–1995, Geographical, Demographic and Socio-Economic Characteristics.* 1995 Census of Population and Housing Publications no. 11A.

———. 2000a. *Statistical Abstract of Israel.*

———. 2000b. *Immigration to Israel* (2000) (annual publication, last issue 1998).

———. 2000c. *Income Survey, 1997–1998.* Briefing 8 (Hebrew).

———. 2000d. *Labour Force Survey, 1998.* Special Publication no. 1104.

———. 2000e. *Immigrant Population from USSR, Selected Data, 1998.* Current Briefing 17.

———. 2000f. *Internal Migration in Israel 1997–1998.* Current Briefing in Statistics, 16.

———. 2001. *Labor Force Survey, 1999.* Special Publication no. 1152.

Damian, Natalia, and Yehudit Rosenbaum-Tamari. 1999. "Immigrants from the Former Soviet Union and their Social Integration in Israeli Society: Expectations and Realities." *International Review of Sociology* 9 (2):149–59.

DellaPergola, Sergio. 1999. "World Jewish Population." *American Jewish Yearbook 1999.* Vol. 99. New York: American Jewish Committee.

Eckstein, Zvi, and Yoram Weiss. 1998. *The Absorption of Highly Skilled Immigrants: Israel 1990–1995.* Tel Aviv: Foerder Institute for Economic Research, Working Papers.

———. 1999. *The Integration of Immigrants from the Former Soviet Union in the Israeli Labor Market.* Tel Aviv: Foerder Institute for Economic Research.

Ellenbogen-Frankovich, Sarit, and Gila Noam. 1998. *The Absorption of Immigrant Youth and Children from the Caucasus: Survey Findings.* Jerusalem: JDC–Brookdale Institute.

Epstein, Alek. 2000. "The Excellence Challenge as a Solution for Immigrant Housing Difficulties: Immigrants in the Israeli Educational System." *The Former Soviet Union Jews in Transition* 4 (19): 181–95 (Hebrew).

Flug, Karnit, Nitsa Kasir, and Gur Ofer. 1992. *The Absorption of Soviet Immigrants in the Israeli Labor Market, Occupational Substitution and Retention.* Discussion Paper no. 92.13. Jerusalem: Bank of Israel. Also appears in Carmon Naomi, ed. 1993. *Immigrants: Liability or Asset?* Haifa: Technion and Frank Cass.

Friedberg, Rachel. 1998. *The Impact of Mass Immigration on the Israeli Labor Market*. Discussion Paper no. 98.01. Jerusalem: Maurice Falk Institute for Economic Research in Israel.

Habib, Jack, 1998. "Groups at Risk among the New Immigrants." In *Profile of an Immigration Wave: The Absorption Process of Immigrants from the Former Soviet Union, 1990–1995,* ed. Moshe Sicron and Elazar Leshem. Jerusalem: Magnes Press, Hebrew University (Hebrew with English summary).

Hazz, Hadassa. 1999. "The Leisure Time Culture in Israel, 1998." *Panim—Quarterly for Society, Culture and Education* 10: 106–34 (Hebrew).

Horowitz, Tamar. 1994. "The Influence of Soviet Political Culture on Immigrant Voters in Israel: The Election of 1992." *Jews in Eastern Europe* 1 (23): 5–22.

———. 1998. "Immigrant Children and Adolescents in the Educational System." In *Profile of an Immigration Wave. The Absorption Process of Immigrants from the Former Soviet Union, 1990–1995,* ed. Moshe Sicron and Elazar Leshem, 368–408. Jerusalem: Magnes Press (Hebrew).

———. 2001. "The Political Strengthening of the Immigrants from the FSU in Israel: From Passive Citizenship to Active Citizenship." In *From Russia to Israel—Identity and Culture in Transition,* ed. Moshe Lissak and Elazar Leshem, 100–23. Tel Aviv: Hakibbutz Hameuchad Publishing House (Hebrew).

Horowitz, Tamar, and Elazar Leshem. 1998. "The Immigrants from the FSU in the Israeli Cultural Sphere." In *Profile of an Immigration Wave. The Absorption Process of Immigrants from the Former Soviet Union, 1990–1995,* ed. Moshe Sicron and Elazar Leshem, 291–333. Jerusalem: Magnes Press (Hebrew).

Israel Ministry of Education. 2000. *Working Paper (Shachar 11/12/2000)*. Jerusalem: Ministry of Education, Welfare and Education Services.

King, Judith. 1998. *The Absorption of Immigrants from the Caucasus in the 1990s*. RR-326-98. Jerusalem: JDC–Brookdale Institute.

Leshem, Elazar, and Moshe Lissak. 2001. "The Russian Community Formation in Israel." In *From Russia to Israel—Identity and Culture in Transition,* eds. Moshe Lissak and Elazar Leshem. Tel Aviv: Hakibbutz Hameuchad Publishing House (Hebrew).

Lifshitz, Hen. 2000. *Immigrant Adolescents in Israel—A Report for The Interministry Committee.* Jerusalem: JDC–Brookdale Institute, Ashalim—Association for Design and Development of Community Services for Children and Adolescents, Ministry of Immigration Absorption.

Lissitza, Svetlanna, and Yohanan Peres. 1999. *Immigrants from the Former Soviet Union in Israel—Identity Formation and Integration Procedures.* Tel Aviv: Itzhak Rabin Center.

Ministry of Immigration Absorption. 1999. *Immigration Absorption, 1998.* Jerusalem (Hebrew).

Mirskey, Julia, Judith Baron-Dreiman, and Perry Kedem. 1999. Social Support Networks for Immigrant Students from the Former Soviet Union. *Society and Welfare* 19 (1): 39–52.

National Insurance Institute. 2000. *Annual Survey 1998/1999.* Jerusalem.

Nirel, Nurit, Baruch Rosen, Revital Gross, Ayelet Berg, Dan Yuval, Michal Ivnekovsky 1998. "Immigrants from the Former Soviet Union in the Health System: Selected Findings from National Surveys." *Social Security* 51: 96–115. (Hebrew).

Noam, Gila, Sarit Ellenbogen-Frankovich, and Michal Wolfson. 1998. *The Absorption of Immigrant Youth from the Former Soviet Union: Findings from a Study Conducted in Five Cities.* Jerusalem: JDC–Brookdale Institute.

Roar-Streir, Dorit, and Miriam Rozsental. 2001. "Culture in Transition—Differences in Growth and Socialization of Children: Implication for Society and Education." In *From Russia to Israel—Identity and Culture in Transition,* ed. Moshe Lissak and Elazar Leshem, 149–74. Tel Aviv: Hakibbutz Hameuchad (Hebrew).

Semyonov, Moshe. 1997. "On the Cost of Being an Immigrant in Israel: The Effects of Tenure, Origin and Gender." *Research in Stratification and Mobility* 15: 115–31.

Sever, Rita. 1997a. "Learning from Experience? Israeli Schools and the Task of Immigrant Absorption." In *Russian Jews on Three Continents,* ed. Noah Lewin-Epstein, Yaacov Roi, and Paul Ritterband, 510–40. London: Frank Cass.

———. 1997b. "Immigration and the Education System in Israel." In *The Immigration Influence on Israel,* ed. K. Hershkowitz, 71–86. Jerusalem: Konrad Adenauer Fund.

———. 2000. *Time Heals (not) all Ills. How Does Time in Israel Affect Young Post-Soviet Immigrants?* Paper presented at the International Conference on Post Soviet Youth—A Comparative Study, May 22–23, 2000, at the Hebrew University of Jerusalem.

Sharlin, Shlomo. 1998. "Soviet Immigrants to Israel: Users and Non-users of Social Work Services." *Int. Social Work* 41 (4): 455–69.

Shor, Ron. 1999. "Inappropriate Child Rearing Practices Perceived by Jewish Immigrant Parents from the Former Soviet Union." *Child Abuse and Neglect* 23 (5): 487–99.

Slonim-Nevo, Vered, and Yana Sharaga. 1997. "Social and Psychological Adjustment of Soviet-Born and Israeli-Born Adolescents: The Effect of the Family." *Israel Journal of Psychiatry* 34: 128–38.

Slonim-Nevo, Vered, Yana Sheraga, and Ana Abdelgani. 1999. "Social and Psychological Adjustment of Former Soviet Immigrants and Israeli-Born Adolescents." *Society and Welfare* 19 (1): 81–97. (Hebrew).

Tolts, Mark. 1998. "Recent Jewish Emigration and Population Decline in Russia." *Jews in Eastern Europe* 35 (1): 5–24.

———. 1999. *Demography of the Jews in the Former Soviet Union: Yesterday and Today.* Paper presented at the Conference on Jewish Life after the USSR: A Community in Transition, Harvard University, February 13–15.

Yatziv, Gadi. 1999. *The Sectorial Society.* Jerusalem: Bialik Institute (Hebrew).

Zilberg, Narspy, and Elazar Leshem. 1999. "Imagined Community and Community in Reality: Russian Language Press and Renewal of Community Life among Immigrants from the Former Soviet Union." *Society and Welfare* 19 (1): 9–38. (Hebrew).

CHAPTER FIVE

Ethiopian Jews in Israel: A Part of the People or Apart from the People?

&

STEVEN KAPLAN AND HAGAR SALAMON

Introduction

The Beta Israel (Falasha) of Ethiopia or, as they are more commonly called today, Ethiopian Jews, may be per capita the most talked about and written about group in the world.[1] Each time they have been "discovered" and "rediscovered" a flood of articles and books has ensued. The past decade alone has seen more than a dozen books, hundreds of articles, and several international scientific conferences (Kaplan and Ben-Dor 1988; Salamon and Kaplan 1998). Yet, despite all this attention, many features of the groups' life remain little understood. Nowhere is this truer than with regard to their assimilation to Israeli society.

At the beginning of 1977, fewer than 100 Beta Israel lived in Israel. By the end of 2001 more than 60,000 Ethiopian immigrants had settled in the country (Table 1). When the more than 19,000 children born in Israel are included (and those who have died subtracted), the Ethiopian community of Israel can be said to number over 75,000. Seldom has any community undergone so dramatic, complete, and irreversible a change in so short a period. Moreover, their arrival in Israel has brought to the fore a variety of issues regarding the borders of Judaism and the importance of race in Israeli society.

In this essay we seek to explore the extent to which Ethiopian immigrants have, on the one hand, become part of Israeli society and, on the other, remain a group a part, isolated from its other citizens and residents. We begin, however, with an examination of the events that preceded their arrival in the country.

Historical Background

The history of the Beta Israel did not begin, of course, with their arrival in Israel.[2] Long before their encounter with world Jewry, the Beta Israel worshipped and created, struggled and fought, all within the context of the wider stream of Ethiopian history and society (Shelemay 1989; Quirin 1992; Kaplan 1992; Salamon 1999). Although some aspects of this history, particularly the question of

"Falasha origins," have provoked considerable controversy, events prior to the late nineteenth and early twentieth centuries are of little relevance to the concerns of this article.

More recent events form the starting point for our discussion. For almost a century and a half prior to their *aliyah,* the Beta Israel were exposed to outside influences that slowly altered their religious life, social norms, and self-perception. While none of the changes from this period had as immediate and overwhelming an impact as emigration from Ethiopia and immigration to Israel, neither can they be ignored. It is possible to report the effects of the move to Israel faithfully only if we begin with an accurate picture of what preceded it (Kaplan and Rosen 1994; Summerfield 1997).

The modern history of the Beta Israel can be said to have begun in 1859 with the establishment in their midst of a Protestant mission under the auspices of the London Society for Promoting Christianity amongst the Jews. It was the mission's activities more than anything else in the period before the twentieth century that made these isolated Jews aware of the existence of a more universal form of Jewish identity and brought them to the attention of world Jewry (Kaplan 1992; Quirin 1992; Seeman 1999).

In response to the missionary threat, a number of prominent Jewish leaders began to lobby for aid to be sent to the Beta Israel. In 1867, Joseph Halévy was sent to Ethiopia as a representative of the Alliance Israélite Universelle (Halévy 1877). Despite Halévy's unequivocal confirmation of the Beta Israel's Jewishness, and his enthusiastic support for the establishment of institutions to assist

Table 1. Immigration to Israel from Ethiopia

1948–1971	167
1972–1979	306
1980–1989 (including "Operation Moses")	16,965
1990–1992 (including "Operation Solomon")	27,803
1993	863
1994	1,192
1995	1,312
1996	1,361
1997	1,660
1998	3,105
1999	2,290
2000	2,228
2001	3,274
Total	62,526

Source: Israel Central Bureau of Statistics.

them, no action was taken for almost forty years, when Halévy's pupil Jacques (Ya'acov) Faitlovitch journeyed to Ethiopia in 1904. Faitlovitch, who dedicated his life to the cause of Ethiopian Jewry, was responsible more than any other individual for their entry into Jewish history and consciousness. The common thread that ran through all aspects of his program on their behalf was the attempt to bring them closer to other Jewish communities. To this end, he depicted them as a "lost tribe" essentially different from and foreign to their Ethiopian neighbors. He also sought to raise their standards of education and create a Western-educated elite capable of interacting with their non-Ethiopian Jewish counterparts. Yet another of his initiatives was the reform of Beta Israel religion in an attempt to bring it closer to "normative" Judaism. Among the innovations he introduced were the lighting of Sabbath candles, the recitation of Hebrew prayers, the use of the Star of David, and the observance of holidays such as Simhat Torah. Faitlovitch continued his work on behalf of Ethiopian Jewry until his death in 1955. However, the policies he initiated were to set the tone for relations between world Jewry and the Jews of Ethiopia for the remainder of the twentieth century (Summerfield 1997).

During the years immediately following the establishment of the State of Israel, no attempt was made to bring the Beta Israel on *aliyah*. Lingering doubts concerning their Jewishness, as well as social, medical, and political considerations, all convinced successive Israeli governments to defer any decisive action. Efforts were made, however, by the Jewish Agency and other organizations to strengthen their ties to world Jewry and Israel. From 1953 to 1958, representatives of the Jewish Agency's Department for Torah Education in the Diaspora were active in Ethiopia. Two groups totaling twenty-seven Ethiopian youngsters were also brought to the Kfar Batya Youth Aliyah village in Israel to be trained as teachers and future leaders of their fellow Ethiopians (Kemon 1996). Eventually a network of schools was established throughout the Gondar region, which at its peak served hundreds of students. The impact of their efforts was not felt evenly among all sectors of the population. Some communities, particularly those in remote regions, remained largely unaffected. Others, in or near villages in which schools were established, underwent a dramatic transformation as they were exposed to rabbinic Judaism, Zionism, and modernization. Israel and Jerusalem, which had existed mainly as symbols of a lost biblical period, began to be perceived as living realities and for some a goal to be struggled toward. Not surprisingly, youngsters tended to adopt new ideas more quickly than their elders, and in some cases generational tensions developed.

Such intergenerational tensions were exacerbated following the Ethiopian revolution of 1974, which led to the overthrow of Emperor Haile Selassie and the institution of a military Marxist regime (Sabar-Friedman 1989). Young people exposed to secular education and political indoctrination rejected the ways of their elders as old-fashioned. Contacts with non–Beta Israel increased significantly as young people joined political organizations, were conscripted into the security forces, or simply sought the professional and educational opportunities available in urban areas.

Although promises of land reform and freedom of worship led many to hope that Ethiopia's Marxist rulers would ameliorate the situation of the Beta Israel, this did not prove to be the case. While seldom victims of organized persecution, they suffered all the tribulations afflicted on the general population as well as those reserved for particularly weak and vulnerable minority groups. As conditions in Ethiopia deteriorated, their religious devotion to Jerusalem began to be transformed into an active desire to emigrate.

Despite the speed with which it took place, the Ethiopian immigration was not a single event but a series of waves each with its own special characteristics. Prior to 1980, for example, only about 250 Ethiopian immigrants had come to Israel. Starting in 1980, Jews from the relatively isolated regions of Tigre and Walqayit began to migrate to refugee camps in the Sudan. Although some were to wait there for as long as two or three years, by the end of 1983 the entire population of these regions (over 4,000 people) had been taken to Israel. As word spread of this Sudanese route, Jews from the Gondar region driven by a desire to reach Israel began to migrate as well. As conditions in the Sudan deteriorated, the Israeli government abandoned its policy of gradual immigration. Between mid-November 1984 and early January 1985, 6,700 Ethiopians were taken to Israel in what came to be known as "Operation Moses" (Parfitt 1985; Rapoport 1986; Karadawi 1991).

Following an Israeli press conference confirming the airlift, the Sudanese suspended the operation, stranding hundreds of people. A few months later, the CIA-sponsored "Operation Joshua/Sheba" brought a further 648 Jews to Israel. From August 1985 until the end of 1989 only about 2,500 immigrants reached Israel. The restoration of diplomatic relations between Ethiopia and Israel in the autumn of 1989, however, cleared the way for a renewal of emigration in a manner agreeable to both countries. It also raised expectations among the Beta Israel, and by the summer of 1990 over 20,000 Ethiopian Jews had migrated to Addis Ababa, where they faced disease, malnutrition, and inadequate housing. When Ethiopian leader Mengistu Haile Mariam fled the country in mid-May as rebel forces advanced on the capital, a dramatic rescue effort was executed. During a period of thirty-six hours, between 24 and 25 May, over 14,000 Beta Israel were taken to Israel in "Operation Solomon" (Friedmann 1992; Graebner 1992).

Even after the completion of "Operation Solomon" small groups of Jews remained in remote provinces in Ethiopia, including approximately 2000 in isolated regions of Qwara. Over the course of time most of these were contacted and brought to Israel. More problematic, however, is the issue of Christian Ethiopians of Jewish (Falasha) descent (Kaplan 1993; Seeman 1997; Salamon 1994, 1999). Although it had generally been believed that the Beta Israel community had clearly defined borders separating it from its Christian neighbors, in recent years this picture has been greatly revised. It is now recognized that a large community of converts also existed. Several thousand of these had migrated to Addis Ababa in 1991. Others had remained in their villages.

At the time of "Operation Solomon" it was decided to leave these converts, known as Falas/Faras Mura, in Ethiopia. In recent years the right of these converts to come to Israel has been the subject of fierce controversy. Many have close relatives in Israel and those who have journeyed to Addis Ababa have little possibility of returning to their previous villages or lives. Moreover, those residing either there or in the regional capital of Gondar have been exposed to Israelis and rabbinic Judaism for several years and some have even formally converted (or in the view of some "returned") to Judaism.

In November 1996 the Israeli Chief Rabbinate, which had hitherto been supportive of efforts to cultivate ties with the Falas Mura, withdrew this support, citing doubts about the genuineness of the converts and their connections to Judaism. Several members of the Ethiopian community also questioned the wisdom of bringing former Christians to Israel. Others, noting the high rate of HIV-positive cases (between 5 and 10 per cent) among those in Addis Ababa, have questioned the public health risk of this immigration. The Ethiopian government for its part has objected to what it views as a provocative intervention in its internal affairs and has claimed that the number of potential immigrants willing to identify themselves as converts from Judaism could be in the tens or even hundreds of thousands.

Since 1991 about 11,000 Ethiopians (mainly Falas Mura) have arrived in Israel. While activists on their behalf claim that another 28,000 remain to be brought to Israel (keeping the number flexible and constantly changing), Israeli officials in both Addis Ababa and Jerusalem believe that only several thousand of these have the right to make *aliyah*.

Housing

Household Structure and Size

Several features of the household composition of Ethiopians in Israel are noteworthy and have serious implications for the community's social, and particularly economic, well-being. According to the national data, the number of one-parent families is about 27 percent. This figure (about 50 percent of all households if singles are counted) is consistent with the 24–30 percent found in all the communities surveyed. Second, the national data reveal a high percentage (21.3) of households with six or more members. Indeed, even the Ministry of Absorption's partial data identify almost half of the Ethiopians as living in households with six members or more. Among these large families, moreover, almost 1,000 are headed by individuals aged sixty or older.[3] The large number of one-parent families and the high average household size have important economic implications that in turn are of major consequence for housing (Kaplan and Salamon 1998).

Temporary Housing

Not surprisingly, housing the successive waves of Ethiopian immigrants proved one of the most complex challenges facing the Israeli immigration authorities. While comparatively small numbers of immigrants arriving as part of an orderly process could usually be accommodated in existing absorption centers or even directly settled in apartments, large "surprise" influxes, as in the case of both "Operation Moses" and "Operation Solomon," exceeded the capacity of these resources. In these cases, ad hoc solutions such as housing immigrants in hotels, empty apartment blocks, and mobile homes (*karavanim*) were employed. Each of these "housing solutions" brought with it a variety of problems.

Standard absorption centers appeared to be by far the best of these options. By concentrating immigrants in separate housing, authorities were able to provide services such as Hebrew instruction, job information, and health care more efficiently. On the negative side, such facilities tended to isolate immigrants from society as a whole and foster dependence upon absorption officials and the services they offered (Ashkenazi and Weingrod 1984; Hertzog 1998).

Hotels were not only extraordinarily expensive ($13,500 per year per immigrant), but they also offered families virtually no opportunity for normal family life. Most hotel residents failed to develop even the most basic skills needed for independent living, and thus, after a period of several years, were moved not to permanent housing but to another temporary site. In the 1980s this meant a move to absorption centers only recently vacated by other immigrants; in the 1990s it usually meant a move to mobile homes.

At the time of "Operation Moses" several hundred families were placed in previously abandoned mobile homes on the outskirts of small towns and cities. Not only were these sites even more isolated than standard absorption facilities, but their physical condition was often substandard. Despite these difficulties, the expense and disadvantages of hotel accommodations led the absorption authorities to make massive use of mobile homes for "Operation Solomon" immigrants. Huge mobile-home settlements for both Ethiopian and Russian immigrants were erected in isolated open areas far from major concentrations of veteran Israelis. In December 1993 almost one-third of all Ethiopians in the country were living in twenty-one caravan sites, uncannily reminiscent of the tent camps (*maabarot* used to house immigrants from Arab lands in the 1950s (Kaplan and Rosen 1995).

The Move to Permanent Housing

From the outset, absorption officials had a multifaceted agenda in housing Ethiopian immigrants. They sought to limit the immigrants' stay in temporary housing and, at the same time, to avoid their concentration in large numbers in particular buildings, neighborhoods, and, especially, in economically disadvantaged peripheral towns and cities. Often these differing priorities conflicted with each other. For their part, the immigrants often wished to be housed near (extended) family members. Since they arrived in waves over periods of years this frequently meant that recent arrivals asked to be housed near relatives in areas that were already "full" of Ethiopians.

In May 1993 the Ministry of Absorption initiated a special mortgage program for Ethiopian immigrants designed to encourage them to leave temporary housing and purchase apartments in relatively strong settlements in the center of the country. It included a grant equivalent to 90 percent of the price of the apartment, which could be used to acquire housing in fifty-two authorized locations believed to have the social, economic, and educational resources necessary to accommodate the new population. Special outreach and informational programs were designed to encourage immigrants to apply for mortgages.

Although the mortgage program was designed to limit the number of Ethiopian families who settled in sites with weak economies and educational systems, it was not always successful. Not only did many Ethiopians find their way to poorer municipalities, including Kiryat Malachi, Netivot, and Ofaqim, but even within stronger communities they were often settled in undesirable neighborhoods. Educational difficulties and high unemployment among Ethiopians are thus, in part, a consequence of their settlement in these problem-ridden areas.[4]

Education

Providing appropriate educational frameworks for Ethiopian immigrants has always been one of the major challenges facing successive Israeli governments. Not only is this necessary when dealing with a population in which over 50 percent are of school age, it also reflects the general tone of absorption policies that emphasize the transformation of immigrant youth. Yet despite this commitment, educational policies often lagged far behind the sweep of events (Wagaw 1993; Israel Association for Ethiopian Jews 1995). In the 1980s special programs and even teacher-training schemes were generally not developed until after the thousands of Ethiopian students were in the educational system. More recently, a comprehensive plan for improving the educational conditions of Ethiopian children, presented in August 1995 by the Ministry of Education's Center for Ethiopian Immigrants within the Educational System, remained largely unimplemented.

Initially, it was decided that all Ethiopians would attend state religious schools during their first year in Israel. This policy, based both on political considerations and on a desire to avoid the rapid secularization that confronted immigrants in the 1950s, severely limited the options available to educational authorities. At a single stroke, hundreds of schools were excluded from the absorption effort, while others were required to take on full responsibility. Even under the best of circumstances it would have been difficult to find sufficient schools close to immigrant housing to serve the appropriate age groups. While calling for a total of no more than 25 percent immigrant students in any one class, the Education ministry often found itself with schools which were 60 to 70 percent Ethiopian.

While parents were allowed to transfer their children after the first year, few Ethiopian adults were sufficiently familiar with the schools to take such an initiative. Even though this requirement was eventually dropped, the bulk of Ethiopian students remain in the state religious schools. In 1988, 92 percent of Ethiopian students were in the state religious school system and in 1995 this figure had declined only slightly to 86 percent. Overall, they make up about 10 percent of pupils in the state religious system and only about 1 percent of those in secular schools (G'dor 1996).

During the first year of schooling most Ethiopian youngsters were put in special absorption classes. In practice, many remained in such frameworks well behind the first year and thus were effectively isolated from other Israeli students. Yet another factor furthering the isolation of Ethiopian students was a tendency to direct them toward special education classes. Critics argue that cultural misunderstandings, parents' lack of familiarity with the school system, and the school interest in the additional funds available to those in special education have combined to result in a disproportionate number of Ethiopians being sent to special education (*Ma'ariv*, December 29, 1995).

High Schools and Youth Aliyah

During the 1950s numerous immigrant children from the Middle East and North Africa were separated from their parents and educated in Youth Aliyah institutions in the hope of speeding their acculturation.[5] Despite the grave misgivings that developed regarding such policies in the 1980s, over 96 percent of

Ethiopian teenagers were placed in youth villages. What began as a method to care for those who had arrived without parents became a standard track for Ethiopian youths (Amir, Zahavi, and Fargi 1997). Criticisms of Youth Aliyah can be divided into two categories. On the most general level, serious questions exist concerning the long-term effects of removing teenagers from their families and weakening their links to local communities. Educationally, Ethiopian youth often found themselves in classes with other weak students placed in boarding schools or sent to Youth Aliyah classrooms because of family and personal difficulties. Within the boarding schools Ethiopian high school students were overwhelmingly placed on vocational tracks that offered virtually no opportunity for admission to post-secondary education). Indeed, many often trained in vocational courses with only limited practical relevance. Recently Youth Aliyah has revised its policies so that 80 percent of those in boarding schools are now in nonvocational tracks. Few, however, are expected to be able to meet the full matriculation certificate requirements.

Youth at Risk

Perhaps the most troubling phenomenon regarding Ethiopian children is the large number of youths who have either dropped out of school, or whose attendance or other aspects of their behavior have caused them to be defined as "at risk." No exact figures regarding their number exist, but 900 youngsters have been identified and are receiving some sort of attention or treatment. This figure is based on only a portion of the community, and some officials claim that the total number is closer to 2000 (Kaplan and Salamon 1998). Further support for these figures is found in statistics from the Ministry of Education, according to which 1,044 Ethiopians were in twelfth grade in the 1996–67 school year; approximately 55 percent of the Ethiopians were in that age group. According to the Israel State Comptroller, local authorities reach only about half of such youths in the general population (Israel State Comptroller Annual Report 1997: 511–23). Confirmation of this troubling trend, if not of the precise numbers, is found in the dramatic rise in police files opened against Ethiopian youths. Most cases involved either property offenses or public disturbances, and all but a handful of cases (nine during a period of three years) concern young men (State Comptroller 1997).

Higher Education

Only a small percentage of Ethiopian immigrants arrived in Israel after having completed secondary education. Absorption authorities including the Jewish Agency, the Student Authority, and the Ministry of Absorption set up special preparatory courses to give those who seemed qualified for higher education an opportunity to acclimatize and qualify for admission to universities. At the same time, standardized tests, such as the nationally administered psychometric exams, were found to be relatively weak predictors of Ethiopian students' performance and hence given less weight than usual in admission decisions. Such programs and decisions offered access to university training to students who might not normally have qualified.

In recent years, as the number of Ethiopian-educated immigrants has declined, their place has been taken by Ethiopian Jews who have grown up, and been educated, in Israel. As noted above, relatively few of these students qualified for university admission. Only about 19 percent of Ethiopians successfully passed matriculation exams (*bagrut*) at the end of the 1996–97 school year—an improvement over the previous year's 12 percent (and the 7 percent in 1994–95), but still a lower figure than that of any other group other than the Beduin.[6] However, many others have been directed to the pre-academic programs available at different universities. These include a special program for Ethiopians at Haifa University and regular preparatory studies at the country's other campuses.

The encouragement offered Ethiopian students has not been limited to special programs and sensitive admissions conditions. Ethiopian students—both those who came to the country as immigrants and those born in Israel—receive enhanced financial assistance enabling them to pursue higher education. These include grants for tuition, student housing, auxiliary tutoring, and living stipends. The Student Authority, a joint agency of the Ministry of Absorption and Jewish Agency, sponsors all Ethiopian students who study in accredited BA programs (up to the age of thirty and up to six years of study). All of these have resulted in a continuous rise in the number of Ethiopian students studying in colleges and universities. According to the Student Authority (October 2000) there were 687 Ethiopian students registered in regular university studies and 700 in pre-academic studies.

Army

Military service has long been one of the most important symbols of membership in Israeli society. Those who are routinely excluded from such service—most notably Israeli Arabs and the ultra-Orthodox—have to a significant extent opted out of, or been excluded from, the mainstream of Israeli life. In this context the high percentages of Ethiopians serving in the Israeli Defense Forces is particularly noteworthy (Shabtay 1995). In June 1993, 850 Ethiopians were on active duty, including 17 officers. By 1996 these numbers had more than doubled with about 1,750 serving, including 150 women (a rise of over 300 percent over three years earlier). The number of officers had grown, moreover, to 68 in 1997 and 129 by the year 2000 (Ministry of Immigrant Absorption Website). Twenty-three percent of Ethiopian men serve in combat units, compared to 20 percent among the native Israeli population.

This sharp rise in the number of Ethiopians serving in the army results from the fact that 95 percent of Ethiopian boys (compared to 80 percent of native Israelis) eligible for service were inducted in both 1995 and 1996. Indeed, the army routinely waives some of its requirements for Ethiopian inductees. Although generally a successful policy, some feel this generous admissions policy is one of the factors behind a number of suicides among Ethiopian recruits—ten in the past four years, according to the army. Also cited in connection with the suicides are "hazing" (a common experience of recruits) and at times outright racism (on the part of individual soldiers) encountered by Ethiopian soldiers.

Employment

Although issues of religious status and medical treatment have produced the most dramatic eruptions of Ethiopian protest since the Ethiopians' arrival in Israel, most surveys (Benita, Noam, and Levy 1994) indicate that economic concerns are the most common chronic problem for most Ethiopian households.

Ethiopians' problems in finding employment can be divided into two parts: having lived primarily in Ethiopia as subsistence farmers and rural craftsmen, most Ethiopians arrived in Israel with few skills that were marketable in Israel's modern and modernizing economy. In addition, long periods of enforced inactivity, whether in the Sudan or Addis Ababa, fostered dependence on others. This pattern continued in Israel during the stay in hotels, absorption center, and caravan sites. Although programs were developed to occupy immigrants in Addis Ababa and upon their arrival, the move to permanent housing frequently meant leaving one job and beginning the job search yet again (Kaplan and Rosen 1995).

Although in April 1996 the Ministry of Absorption published figures indicating that over 80 percent of Ethiopians in selected towns were employed, these figures must be read with extreme caution. First, all employment figures relate to those between ages 15 and 65 counted as being in the labor force, that is, employed or looking for work. Those who do not work because of illness, age (more than 50 percent of Ethiopians are under age 15 or over age 65), studies (which account for the vast majority of those aged 15–18), or childcare responsibilities are, for example, not counted in the labor force. According to the Central Bureau of Statistics, in the general Israeli public 16 percent of all Jewish men and 34 percent of women were not part of the labor force in 1995. Among Ethiopian immigrants local surveys conducted in 1995 and 1996 reveal a much higher percentage of men (19–31 percent) and women (58–86 percent) who are not part of the labor force. In the former case, this is usually due to illness, while in the latter case either illness or household and childcare responsibilities keep women out of the workforce. Thus, it is probable that close to 50 percent of Ethiopian adults who are not working do not figure in unemployment figures. On the other hand, it should be noted that significant numbers of immigrants, particularly women, work in the informal sector doing household work that is not reported to the authorities in order to avoid paying taxes and jeopardizing their welfare benefits.

In general, unemployment is higher among those aged 40 and above. Indeed, men aged 25–45 are about the only group among Ethiopians whose employment rates are consistently similar to the rest of the Israeli population. Among women of all ages, in contrast, both the percentage of those in the labor force and of those employed is generally much lower than that of their Israeli counterparts. Again it must be remembered that there are women who work in the informal sector cleaning and doing other menial jobs who do not appear in official statistics. Overall, however, Israeli policies intended to encourage women to work outside the household and to find employment in other than menial tasks have not been successful. In part, at least, this represents a continuation of the traditional pattern in which the household was viewed as the woman's sphere and care for the usually large number of children primarily her responsibility. Women in Israel who deviate from this model are often met with disapproval on the part of their family. Nevertheless, social security and other government programs give women a far wider range of options than was the case in Ethiopia and some do take advantage of these, either within the framework of marriage or outside it.

Even when Ethiopian immigrants are employed, many find themselves at the bottom of the economic ladder pursuing unskilled low-paying jobs. Their households are, moreover, usually large, with six or more members. When these are complex households in which there are more than two adults, this may make possible a degree of economic security. More frequently, even when they work extra shifts or long hours, Ethiopian householders have difficulty making ends meet. The growing number of Ethiopian teenagers living in their communities and not at Youth Aliyah boarding schools has, for example, increased their families' economic burdens, because the sums spent on them by the schools are not transferred to the families, who must now meet all their expenses.

Health Issues

In contrast to Russian immigrants, many of whom were older and came to Israel with chronic and even terminal diseases, the Ethiopians were a comparatively young population and generally presented a positive health profile. Nevertheless, the arrival of Ethiopian immigrants confronted the Israeli medical authorities with a variety of challenges (*Israel Journal of Medical Sciences* 1991, 1993). Not only did many arrive with unfamiliar problems, but most had only a limited understanding of the Western biomedical system. Moreover, each wave of immigrants presented a slightly different health profile. Those who survived the journey to, and life-threatening conditions in, the Sudan usually arrived in Israel in poor physical shape. Most suffered from malnutrition and parasites and many had contracted malaria. The medical care offered in the 1990s to those who passed through Addis Abada saved countless lives. Nevertheless, parasitic infections, Hepatitis B, and tuberculosis remained common.

One particularly troubling phenomenon among "Operation Solomon" immigrants was the high rate of exposure to HIV/AIDS. Although HIV was not found among either "Operation Moses" immigrants or those who arrived until 1990, 226 of approximately 10,000 immigrants tested in 1991 were found to be carriers.[7] Health officials tried to find a balance between taking necessary precautions, educating the Ethiopian community, and avoiding stigmatizing the entire community. While medical personnel were warned to treat Ethiopians as a "high-risk group" and sporadic educational programs were begun in the community, public discussion of the problem and related policy decisions were suppressed. While stories occasionally appeared both in Israel and abroad warning of the problem, government officials publicly played down the significance of the issue.

On January 24, 1996 the Hebrew daily *Ma'ariv* ran a story revealing that officials of the Magen David blood bank had for years been routinely (and without notifying the donors) disposing of blood donated by Ethiopians. A few days later several thousand Ethiopians and supporters demonstrated outside the prime minister's office against what they viewed as a racist policy. Unprecedented violence flared as the "blood scandal" proved to be the catalyst for the expression of frustrations over a wide range of topics (Seeman 1997). In response, a commission chaired by the former Israeli President Itzhak Navon was set up. In July 1996 it released its report, which noted that Ethiopians were carriers in 550 of approximately 1,386 HIV-positive cases already identified in Israel.[8] The Navon Commission also reported that the percentage of HIV-positive cases among immigrants from Ethiopia had risen from 3 percent in 1992 to 8 percent among those who arrived during the first three months of 1996. Because of the high rate of HIV-positive immigrants among recent arrivals, Ethiopians accounted for 80 percent of new HIV-positive cases in Israel in 1996. The commission advocated a policy that identified blood donors not on the basis of ethnic origin but on the basis of a series of questions regarding residence in countries where HIV was widespread and sexual contact with residents of such countries. In practice, such questions would identify most Ethiopian immigrants and all those who arrived in Israel after 1991 as being "high risk." The committee also advocated extensive efforts to educate the Ethiopian community concerning the dangers of the disease.

Although far less dramatic than AIDS, a number of other conditions and diseases, including diabetes, tuberculosis, and hepatitis, have posed challenges to the Ethiopian community and Israeli health authorities. Moreover, the growing public perception of Ethiopian immigrants (regardless of their date of arrival) as carriers of infectious diseases threatens their integration into Israeli society.

Religious Status

The Conversion Controversy

Prior to the "blood scandal" of 1996, the most sensitive issues around which Ethiopian immigrants mobilized were generally related to their religious status. Although the Israeli chief rabbis had recognized the "Jewishness" of the Ethiopians as a community, they continued to raise doubts regarding the personal status of individuals. Since the Ethiopians had not been familiar with *halakha* their religious leaders (*qessotch*) could not have performed valid divorces and conversions. Thus, virtually the entire community was suspect of being either (in the former case) illegitimate or (in the latter case) not fully Jewish.

The first Ethiopians who arrived in Israel were required to undergo a modified conversion ceremony, which included ritual immersion, the acceptance of rabbinic law and (in the case of men) symbolic recircumcision. The last of these demands was dropped in late 1984. Initially, most immigrants accepted these ceremonies either because they did not understand them or because they wished to be fully accepted as Jews in Israel. From late 1985, however, opposition to the ritual demands grew. This resistance eventually culminated in a month-long strike opposite the headquarters of the chief rabbis in the autumn of 1985 (Kaplan 1988).

Although an agreement was reached that put an end to this strike, many issues under dispute were not resolved for several years. The Ethiopians' "Jewishness" remains one of the most sensitive issues facing the Ethiopian community. In June 1989 Rabbi David Chelouche, Sephardi Chief Rabbi of Netanya, was appointed marriage registrar for all Ethiopians in the country. Since he did not believe that Ethiopians needed to undergo any form of conversion, those who married under his auspices were exempted from any preconditions not imposed on other Israelis. Eventually, other rabbis under his auspices also agreed to follow suit. While the chief rabbis viewed this as a compromise that protected both their authority and the dignity of the immigrants, many Ethiopians viewed it as a form of discrimination. Some chose to marry through ceremonies conducted by their own priests. Although such marriages were not themselves recognized by the state, when accompanied by registration through a notary public they provided couples with all the rights of a married couple.

The Role of the Qessim

The dispute with the rabbinate over marriages reflected one aspect of the anomalous situation faced by the Ethiopian communities' *qessotch* (priests) or, as they are called in Hebrew, *qessim* (Kaplan and Rosen 1993). In Ethiopia these religious officials led religious services and performed weddings, funerals, divorces, ritual slaughter, and sacrifices. They were usually influential community leaders, with strong ties to their local society and to individual members (Ben-Dor 1990; Salamon 1987). When they arrived in Israel, this community-based pattern of leadership was shattered. Lacking even the most minimal familiarity with rabbinic traditions, they were denied the authority to perform marriages, divorces, funerals, and other rituals for their fellow immigrants. Yet, paradoxically, the Israeli authorities frequently cited their desire to preserve community traditions and often appeared at public ceremonies flanked by large numbers of *qessim*.

In early 1992 a group of young activists organized a series of demonstrations demanding that the Israeli authorities recognize the *qessim* as spiritual-ritual leaders of the Ethiopian community. The chief rabbis refused, noting that to do so would mean granting the Ethiopians status as a separate community like the Karaites and prejudice their status among other Jews. In November 1992 an interministerial committee recommended that all *qessim* be given paid positions on their local religious councils. Not all local councils have been willing to incorporate Ethiopian officials, and in some cases local Ethiopians have objected to the specific *qes* appointed in their community. Nevertheless, bridges are being built and tensions have been reduced in this manner.

Some *qessim* and a number of young Ethiopians have sought to avoid confrontation with the rabbinic authorities by immersing themselves in rabbinic traditions and attempting to close the gap between their community and other Jews. About a dozen have even been ordained as rabbis. Here too training programs, even if completed successfully, have not always resulted in appropriate job placements.

Ethiopian Jews and Israeli Judaisms

The status of the Ethiopians as Jews and the position of their *qessim* have been the most visible issues in the encounter between the Beta Israel and Israeli Orthodoxy. More privately, almost all Ethiopians have had to find some compromise between maintaining their own traditions as practiced in Ethiopia and completely accepting the dictates of the Israeli religious establishment. Since, as we have noted, most of their children attend state religious schools, their daily lives deeply immerse them in a form of Judaism foreign to their parents. While Hebrew prayers, post-exilic holidays, and symbols such as the Star of David had made their way into some villages in Ethiopia, many immigrants had little or no familiarity with "normative" Judaism. Many women found the expectation that they would abandon or radically change their traditional practice of isolation during their menstrual periods and after childbirth particularly stressful (Trevisan Semi 1985; Doleve-Gandelman 1990; Phillips Davids 1999). Other immigrants had trouble adjusting to eating the meat of animals that had not been slaughtered in their presence.

In the past, immigrants to Israel have tended to establish their own synagogues, which preserve their distinctive ethnic practices and forms. Although there are numerous Ethiopian communities in the country, only two have founded their own synagogues. Efforts have also been made to adapt some traditional Beta Israel practices. *Sigd,* a pilgrimage holiday that commemorates the return from the exile as described in the Books of Ezra and Nehemiah, is annually celebrated in Jerusalem (Ben-Dor 1987).

Communal Organization and Political Leadership

Although the Ethiopian reaction to the "blood scandal" was unusual because of its extent and its unprecedented violence, it was only the latest in a series of political initiatives taken by Ethiopian immigrants. Concerns over immigration, religious status, housing, and medical care had all sparked strikes, protests, and marches. Indeed, it is difficult to think of any community in Israel that has demonstrated as great a readiness as the Ethiopians to form organizations and stage protests.

At least in part, the multiplicity of Ethiopian organizations can be traced directly to either patterns in Ethiopia or circumstances related to their arrival in Israel (Kaplan 1987). The Beta Israel community in Ethiopia was actually a loosely defined web of villages and local groupings sharing religious, cultural, and kinship ties. No community-wide institutions existed on the political or social level. Traditional community divisions often followed regional identities found among the general Ethiopian population. In the twentieth century contacts with world Jewry and differing rates of modernization further exacerbated tensions between different regions.

The move to Israel not only accelerated changes that were already taking place in Ethiopia, but also introduced new sources of divisiveness. While Israeli absorption officials had expected to be able to deal with a single, united Ethiopian community, they found themselves confronted by a divided group with numerous claimants to the mantle of leadership. Already in the early 1980s Tigrean Jews clashed with Gondaris, who arrived later but quickly became numerically dominant.[9] For many years family reunification and support for further immigration from Ethiopia were the issues that united virtually all Ethiopians, and even here disagreements existed over tactics.

The willingness of immigration authorities to coopt their most vocal critics by offering them funding for their organizations or employment as advisors encouraged the formation of dozens of pro-Ethiopian groups in the 1980s. Talented individuals often rose to prominence by demonstrating their ability to organize demonstrations, embarrass the government, and present their case to the media. In 1990 the leaders of seven prominent Ethiopian organizations united to form an umbrella group, the United Ethiopian Jewish Organization. This move was strongly encouraged by the Jewish Agency and other absorption authorities, which provided the organization with 1 million shekels in 1996. Using these resources, the umbrella organization has vigorously sought to consolidate its position as the official representative of Ethiopian Jewry. It organizes the largest annual celebration of *Sigd,* a unique Beta Israel festival celebrated in November, and the Memorial ceremony for those who died on the way to Israel. It publishes the country's only monthly magazine in Amharic and Tigrinnya, *Fana* (The Torch), and supports various programs for Ethiopian immigrants both financially and organizationally.

Despite the UEJO's attempt to portray itself as the sole legitimate representative of the Ethiopian community, it has never held community-wide elections to test this claim and has been widely criticized within the Ethiopian community. Critics claim it is unrepresentative and dominated by a small group of immigrants, most of whom reached Israel prior to 1988. Other independent organizations continue to exist, particularly on the local level or focused on specific causes such as the Falas Mura. Relationships between the UEJO and other organizations remain strained.

Elders and Experience

In Ethiopia there were no community-wide institutions and local leaders such as the elders, and the *qessotch* played a major role in daily life (Kaplan 1987; Kaplan and Rosen 1993; Weil 1995). They had, however, only limited power and depended on experience and their skills in achieving a consensus rather than coercion to enforce their dictates. Although it was a strongly patriarchal society, senior women also possessed considerable influence and were widely consulted on issues such as childbirth, illness, and disputes between younger women. However, already in Ethiopia their authority had begun to decline. Modern education, and in later years the Marxist revolution of 1974, were only two of the factors that weakened traditional patterns of communal organization and leadership.

As we have discussed in our consideration of religious organization, the status of the elders and priests deteriorated rapidly when they reached Israel. Faced with unfamiliar challenges in a strange new land, their years of accumulated experience were largely irrelevant. Settled haphazardly around the country, their reputation for shrewdness accumulated on a village level evaporated. The immigration authorities generally saw them not as a resource but as a problematic group that would never fit in in Israel. The marginalization of the elders and clergy was significant, not only for its impact on them but also for its effect on the community at large. At precisely the time when the Ethiopian community was experiencing extreme difficulties, one of its important institutions for dealing with crises was itself in crisis. While some organizations have attempted in recent years to consult and mobilize community elders, most are isolated and ignored.

In their place a generation of young leaders has emerged as the most vocal spokespersons of the Ethiopian community. Valued by Israeli policymakers because of their ability to speak Hebrew, understand Israeli society, and move from confrontation to cooperation, they quickly replaced older immigrants as representatives both of and to the Ethiopian immigrants. Although frequently allied with prominent elders and religious leaders, these young, predominantly male activists have largely dominated the Ethiopian community's dealings with the Israeli authorities (Weil 1995).

Family Organization

The emergence of a young leadership replacing the traditional patriarchs is a reflection in the public arena of one of the major changes occurring in Ethiopian family life. In brief, the changes being experienced by Ethiopian families in Israel can be divided into two types. On the one hand, many of the functions traditionally dealt with by household or family groups are now the responsibility of outside official bodies. These include education, employment, care for the aged, and housing. At the same time, roles within the family have been drastically redefined in relation to the positions of children and women (Westheimer and Kaplan 1992; Phillips Davids 1999).

The first of the changes has been dealt with extensively if obliquely in much of our discussion above. The second needs to be considered more explicitly at this point. Israel is, in contrast to Ethiopia, a highly child- and youth-oriented country. Many of the policies implemented and programs initiated can be attributed both consciously and unconsciously to this emphasis on youth. Although officials were adamant that they did not intend to repeat past mistakes and that adults would not be treated as "a generation of the wilderness," only in rare circumstances were programs designed to strengthen family units or work through (rather than around) them, Even today, it is striking that while nongovernmental organizations (NGOs) decry the poor economic condition of the Ethiopian community, the NGOs have invested most of their own energies and finances in school-age and even preschool children.

Given children's intensive exposure to outside influences in school and after-school programs and, in particular, their greater facility in learning Hebrew, it is little wonder that children have adapted faster than their parents. Often this results in a reversal of roles in which children, acting as "heads of household," represent the family in dealings with outsiders. Parents, many of whom have also lost their economic functions as providers, are left isolated, frustrated, and dependent.

In Israel, Ethiopian women have been encouraged to take a greater role in family decision making and to have more responsibility and autonomy in their dealings with the society around them. Traditional assumptions regarding menstrual purity, premarital behavior, and employment have been challenged. Nevertheless, as we noted in our discussion of employment, women still remain underrepresented in the work force, while government assistance to them and their children has increased their options. Girls and young women, in particular, have been presented with unprecedented choices regarding education, age of marriage, and the number and timing of children. Inevitably these new choices have produced benefits, confusion, and tensions. Few role models exist within the Ethiopian community for women seeking to follow new paths, and many Ethiopian males resent their loss of status and control. Both premarital pregnancies and family violence have been reported as problems among Ethiopian immigrants. The Ethiopians' struggle to redefine their family with regard to both its internal division of labor and its relationship to the outside world will probably continue well into the next generation (Westheimer and Kaplan 1992).

Ethiopian Jewish Culture in Israel: Can It Survive?

The challenges posed to Ethiopian religious practice and family life by the encounter with Israeli religious authorities are part of a larger encounter between Israeli cultural traditions and those brought from Ethiopia. Many accounts of Israeli absorption depict the 1950s as a period when Israeli absorption agencies tended to treat immigrants from North Africa as a *tabula rasa* and aggressively sought to transform them as quickly as possible into (modern, westernized) Israelis as part of a "melting pot" philosophy of absorption. Accordingly, critics today blame many of the problems faced by such communities on the dislocation and culture shock of the prevailing paternalistic policies and practices. In an attempt to avoid repeating what are perceived as the mistakes of that period, Israeli officials charged with assisting Ethiopian immigrants spoke frequently about the need to preserve Ethiopian traditional culture. In practice, such policies of cultural preservation proved to be mainly rhetoric. Most authorities adopted a utilitarian attitude that sought to understand Ethiopian culture only in so far as this was necessary in order to formulate more successful absorption policies and programs in Israel (Kaplan and Rosen 1993).

Since the Ethiopians' arrival in Israel sporadic attempts have been made to record for posterity the oral traditions, literature, and customs of the Ethiopian Jewish community of Israel. Since Ethiopian culture was preserved in Ethiopia primarily through ritual and word of mouth, the death of each elder is similar to the destruction of an entire library. Yet despite the necessity that interviews and other forms of documentation be carried out as soon as possible, only scattered attempts have been made to record this material and these have often been unsystematic and unscientific in nature.

One product of such unscientific attempts at documentation has been the popularization of highly idealized and nostalgia-tinged images in which life in Ethiopia is depicted in a static and ahistorical fashion. In these portrayals an idealized, trouble-free, preemigration existence in which there were no generational conflicts, no psychological problems, no crime, and no inner communal tensions is contrasted to the trouble-plagued life in Israel. By positing a Utopian past, such portrayals not only distort the historical record, but also increase the difficulties inherent in understanding the impact of resettlement on Ethiopian life (Budowski and David 1996). It is not our intention to discount the phenomenon of nostalgia as such. Rather, we wish to emphasize that it is an important topic for analysis, insofar as it is the nostalgia of the immigrants and not a projection of the researchers.

Yet another attitude toward traditional culture is its "folklorization." This term refers to attempts to present elements of Ethiopian culture including dance, folk songs, traditional foods, and crafts such as pottery and weaving outside the context of their conventional social structure. Through the organization of dance troupes and arts cooperatives, small groups of Ethiopians are able to participate in the reenactment of traditional arts and crafts. In most cases, however, the products of such groups, whether they be music, sculptures, dances, or woven materials, differ markedly from what was produced in Ethiopia and often reflect the wider non-Jewish Ethiopian environment or the impact of Israeli life as much as they reproduce works done by Ethiopian Jews in Ethiopia (Shwartz-Beeri 1991; Sarin 1990, 1994; Kaplan and Rosen 1996).

Although Ethiopian Jewish culture cannot be preserved in Israel, it can be documented (examples of such studies are Ben-Dor 1987, 1990; Salamon 1987,

1999). Unless immediate action is taken in this area, when the first generation of Israeli-born Ethiopian Jews begins to search for its roots, they will find only scattered books and unclear memories of their oral traditions, prayers, rituals, and historical records.

Nowhere is the demise of Beta Israel culture clearer than in the area of spoken language. In Ethiopia most Ethiopian Jews spoke the most important "national" language, Amharic; those from the northern provinces spoke Tigrinnya. In addition to both these Semitic languages, the community recited prayers, which were primarily in Ge'ez, an ancient Semitic language, that has not been a spoken tongue for several centuries; or in Agawinnya, a Cushitic language known to only a few community members. Prior to the encounter with world Jewry, the Ethiopian Jews had no working knowledge of Hebrew. Even their Bible and other holy books were in Ge'ez. Most lay community members were illiterate, although religious leaders often could read and some younger members, especially those who moved to cities, had attended school.

Ethiopians in Israel, like other immigrants, have been exposed on a massive scale to Hebrew, not only as a spoken language but also as a language to be written and read. Given the relatively high illiteracy of Ethiopian immigrants and their lack of familiarity with classroom situations, teaching them Hebrew presented special difficulties (Anteby 1996). In fact, few adults mastered Hebrew and most of them remained dependent on their children or other young relatives in encounters with Israeli officials. At the same time, many young people, including those who were born in Israel or arrived in the country at a young age, neither read nor write Amharic or Tigrinnya, although most understand the spoken languages from their homes and speak them to some extent. Only a few programs attempt to teach Amharic to Ethiopian youngsters. The combination of high illiteracy among immigrant adults and the intense exposure of children in Israel to Hebrew rather than Amharic means that already today more Ethiopians read and write Hebrew than Amharic. While government agencies and pro-Ethiopian organizations assiduously print informational material in Amharic, they have little audience.

In contrast, surveys indicate that up to 90 percent of the Ethiopian community listen to broadcasts on Israeli radio in Amharic or Tigrinnya. These include daily news broadcasts and a variety of public service and informational programs, which make the nationwide broadcasts a major vehicle for communication throughout the Ethiopian community. In May 1997 a half-hour weekly television show, primarily in Amharic, was inaugurated. Indeed, one of the striking aspects of the survival of some aspects of Ethiopian culture in Israel is the manner in which new media—radio, video, tapes, and compact disks—have become a major vehicle for traditional song, dance, and stories.

Race and Racism

It is impossible to discuss the situation of Ethiopian Jews in Israel without considering whether they are the subject of racism or racial discrimination.[10] The issue is far more complex than might be expected (Salamon 1998). One of the most unusual aspects of the Ethiopian immigration is that it brought immigrants from sub-Saharan Africa to a country with no resident Black African community. Moreover, they were brought not as refugees or migrant workers, but to be integrated as citizens (Salamon 2001a, 2001b). Expectations among both immigrants and hosts were high and in many cases unrealistically optimistic.

Prior to the arrival of the Ethiopians, race in the sense of skin color and other physical traits was not a major issue in Jewish-Israeli culture. Indeed, the terms "race" and "racism" were usually used only with regard to antisemitism in discussing Jewish-Christian relations and particularly the Holocaust (Salamon 2001a, 2001b). Relations between Jews and Arabs and between Ashkenazi and Sephardi Jews were discussed in terms of discrimination rather than racism. Moreover, the categories Jew/Arab, Jew/Christian, and East European/Middle Eastern were all far more significant distinctions than black/white (Salamon 2001a, 2001b).

For their part, Ethiopian immigrants were confronted for the first time with a situation in which their physical appearance, most notably their skin color, identified them both as a minority and as members of a particular ethnic group. In Ethiopia neither their physical appearance nor their skin color distinguished them from most of their neighbors. Most had had only limited contact with non-Ethiopians and few had ever lived as a racial minority. Indeed, in their indigenous color terminology they did not view themselves as "black" but as "reddish-brown." "Black" was a designation reserved for darker, kinky-haired residents of the southern regions of Ethiopia who were generally considered by northerners, including the Beta Israel, to be racially inferior (Salamon 1995, 1998, 1999).

Israeli absorption authorities, painfully aware of the situation of most African diaspora communities in other Western countries, sought to avoid setting in motion patterns of discrimination and segregation, Housing programs were designed to prevent ghettoization, job programs to avoid Ethiopians being channeled into domestic work, and university requirements adjusted to produce an educated elite as soon as possible. Indeed, affirmative action programs in housing, education, and army recruitment—the subject of much debate elsewhere—were implemented in Israel with only limited discussion. "Affirmative action," "reverse discrimination," "ghettoization" are just a few of the terms borrowed by Israeli authorities to discuss the situation of the Ethiopians. It is our contention that when applied in an attempt to understand the specifics of Ethiopian Jews in Israel these borrowed terms are extremely problematic. (Kaplan 1999)

Nevertheless, racism became a common explanation for policies or programs that did not meet expectations. Thus, in the 1980s and 1990s delays in bringing Ethiopians to Israel were condemned as motivated by racism, as were the rabbinate's demands for special conversions. Special absorption classes for Ethiopian students were condemned by some as segregation, and attempts to exclude Ethiopians from towns with existing economic and social problems were challenged in the Israeli Supreme Court as discriminatory. Indeed, accusations of racism became the standard reaction to any unpopular policy or statement. Thus, an absorption bureaucracy that sought to advance Ethiopians' interests was often saddled with blanket accusations depicting it as inherently anti-Ethiopian.

While it is difficult to make a case for institutionalized racism as a major factor in the Ethiopian encounter with Israeli society, racial prejudice clearly exists on a variety of levels. The Israeli tendency to ascribe to different groups unchanging predetermined "mentalities" has led the Ethiopians to be characterized as a group with ingrained immutable attributes. While in the case of the Ethiopians such generalizations are often "positive"—that is, quiet, polite, gentle (not so with all immigrant groups)—they are inherently dangerous since they encourage stereotyping, neglect the individual, and replace the complex dynamics of cross-cultural communication with an image of an inherently alien "other." A widespread willingness to associate a low level of technology with "primitiveness" has also resulted in the Ethiopians being labeled by many as "backward" and naive (Salamon 2001a, 2001b). Although it is difficult to substantiate claims that there is a clear pattern of racial discrimination against Ethiopians, and officials usually act quickly to punish those guilty of such behavior, many Ethiopians have little confidence in the Israeli authorities they encounter. Thus, individual incidents become widely known throughout the community and, whatever their significance or motivation, are easily interpreted as evidence of widespread racism.

Although few officials will publicly discuss the topic, special problems exist between Ethiopian and Russian immigrants. These can be attributed, at least in part, to the tensions that resulted from placing immigrants from vastly different cultures side by side during the 1990s. Hotels and caravan sites were often the place for the first face-to-face encounters between Ethiopians and Russians. The decision of officials to devote far greater resources per immigrant to the Ethiopians inevitably produced resentment among the Russians.

In the final analysis, situations and policies not perceived by most Israelis as racist may be genuinely understood as such by Ethiopians. Some Ethiopians' hypersensitivity to racial prejudice is no more justified or realistic than some Israelis' blanket denials. Such differing interpretations are almost inevitable in a situation in which neither side has much previous experience with the specific situation and both sides are repeatedly called upon to walk the borderline between cultural sensitivity and color-blindness. Clearly, the publicly stated goal of both Ethiopian spokespersons and Israeli officials is the successful integration of Ethiopian immigrants into the dominant Jewish population of the country. What exactly this means, how this is to be achieved, at what speed and at what price (both economically and culturally) is the subject of much debate.

While some would condemn all policies that treat Ethiopians as a group with special needs, in the short term such programs are probably necessary and helpful. Separate absorption classes for new immigrant youth can, however, easily become segregrated classes. A color-blind policy in army entrance or in the admission of Ethiopians to higher education would doubtless lower their numbers in both frameworks. However, special treatment for all those of Ethiopian descent regardless of their needs, length of time in the country, or even country of birth risks creating the perception of a "right" based on national origin and also risks fomenting the forms of backlash engendered by such programs elsewhere in the world.

Conclusions

Although the primary purpose of this report has been to present an up-to-date summary of the situation of Ethiopian immigrants in Israel, the implications of their experience in Israel can be fully appreciated only if they are considered against the broader background of similar phenomena.[11] To this end, it is useful to place the Ethiopian immigration in context by briefly comparing it both to other waves of immigration to Israel and to the resettlement of recent migrants and particularly refugees in Europe. Perhaps of greatest interest, however, are the questions that arise concerning the phenomenon of migration of a group from Sub-Saharan Africa to a country with no previous experience of residents from that part of the continent.

The absorption of the Ethiopians into Israeli society marks a unique attempt to incorporate a nonwhite group as equal citizens with full rights as part of the dominant population in a Western, predominantly white country. As such it represents an ambitious attempt to deny the significance of race and assert the primacy of national identity and religion (specifically Judaism). Ethiopian immigrants have for the most part accepted this promise of equality in pressing their cause before the Israeli authorities. Their claims for equal treatment with regard to issues such as religious status or health policy are not, for example, voiced in the universalist language of civil or human rights, but in their right to be treated equally as Jews in the Jewish state. Their commitment to this goal, moreover, has defined the nature of their political groupings and activities in Israel. In a manner probably unparalleled among first-generation migrants, Ethiopian Jews in Israel have organized not on the basis of past political allegiances in Ethiopia or with respect to the controversial political issues that divide that country. Rather, all their political groupings in Israel are devoted in one way or another to issues concerned with their lives in the new homeland such as housing, religious status, education, and immigration.

Although in one form or another the absorption of immigrants into the country's dominant Jewish population has been the goal of successive Israeli governments with regard to all waves of immigrants, in no recent case has this demanded so much investment of resources and energy as is required with the Ethiopians. Their appearance, cultural heritage, educational attainments, and occupational skills sharply distinguish them from most of Israel's other Jewish residents. While the first of these is obviously immutable, strenuous efforts have been made to "close the gap" (in the words of absorption officials) in the other three areas and thus position the Ethiopians firmly within the boundaries of Jewish Israeli society. Housing programs, special education opportunities, army service, and even economic opportunities, all serve to separate Ethiopian immigrants from non-Jewish residents of Israel. Indeed, when closures of the occupied territories have created labor shortages, the authorities have responded not by hiring replacements from the large numbers of unemployed Ethiopians but by allowing the entry of foreign workers. Thus Ethiopians have not been given jobs typically reserved for non-Jews in Israel.

Viewed from the perspective of Israel's total history of immigrant absorption, the Ethiopian immigration can be said to have been accorded a significance far beyond that merited by its numbers alone. The close to 60,000 Ethiopian immigrants who have arrived to date are dwarfed, for example, by the North African immigrants of the 1950s and the immigrants from the former Soviet Union who arrived in the 1980s and 1990s. Indeed, the approximately 60,000 immigrants from the Caucasian republics of the former Soviet Union form a community comparable in size to that of the Ethiopians, but have received only a small fraction of the attention.

Although it is not always easy to unravel the connection between cause and effect, several factors would appear to explain the public fascination with the Ethiopians. The dramatic airlifts that brought over half of all Ethiopian immigrants to Israel were the subject of international attention and one of the rare instances in which Israel made headlines outside the context of the Arab-Israeli conflicts. The depictions of these airlifts as the rescue of an embattled lost tribe from a hostile African setting provided most Israelis and many other Jews with a powerful vindication of the Zionist state's role as a nonracist nation that serves as a refuge for Jews in distress. For American Jews in particular the arrival of the Ethiopians seemed to offer the opportunity to both purge their feelings of guilt regarding their inactivity at the time of the Holocaust and rebuild bridges to the African-American community.

In Israel the Ethiopians served as a focus for discussion in the media and in the parliament of several of the country's most sensitive internal dilemmas. Even before the establishment of the state of Israel, Jews from many lands (e.g., Spain, Portugal, Poland, Russia, Yemen) who differed widely from each other in stature and skin color had lived side by side in Palestine. Intergroup tensions through the years in this immigrant society have involved ethnicity, class, and veteran status in the country, but prior to "Operation Moses," the issue of race had rarely, if ever, been explicitly discussed in Israel. Indeed, given heightened sensitivity to the connection between Judaism and race in the wake of the Holocaust, even to suggest a link between Jewishness and race was for years taboo. Although groups of differing complexion, on a continuum from light to dark, live together in Israel, it is only the Jews of Ethiopia who, as a group, are seen as "black." Thus, only with the arrival of this group did the notion of race become part of internal Jewish distinctions. Indeed, it is striking to note how common accusations of racism between different Jewish groups have become in the past decade and a half.

The Ethiopians' unique form of Judaism has also served as a catalyst for the reexamination of Israel's ongoing tensions over the issue of religious pluralism and the state. Israel seeks to be perceived as the unchallenged center of the Jewish people throughout the world. The fact that the Orthodox rabbinate has exclusive rights to represent Judaism in the country explicitly delegitimizes other forms of Jewishness. While modern Jewish movements such as Reform (Liberal) or Conservative Judaism can be dismissed by religious and secular Israelis alike as deviations from an ideal Orthodox model, the Ethiopians were not so easily categorized. Many Israelis saw the Chief Rabbinate's demand that the Beta Israel undergo conversion as an entrenched religious hierarchy's harassment of a "quiet" and "naive" population. The Beta Israel depict their lack of familiarity with *Halakha*—the reason for the rabbinate's special requirements—as indicative of their pure, unspoiled Judaism.

The moral and financial support given to the Ethiopians' struggle for recognition by other groups in Israel and the Diaspora testifies to their visceral identification with them and their plight. They point to the many Jewish Israelis who (unlike the Beta Israel) do not keep basic religious commandments found in the Torah, but are accepted as Jews by the rabbinate because their descent is unquestioned. Indeed, the recent immigration from the Soviet Union has brought to Israel tens of thousands of nominal Jews and their non-Jewish relatives, but their troubles with the rabbinate only sporadically elicit strong statements of concern from the general Israeli public.

During the 1980s and 1990s Israeli authorities dealt with a variety of challenges brought about by the arrival of tens of thousands of immigrants from Ethiopia. Health and housing problems were resolved, Hebrew lessons and school placements offered. While many of the most pressing problems were at least partially resolved, others remained. School results continue to be disappointing, and the community's economic situation is nothing less than dire. Although generally healthy, Ethiopian immigrants who arrived after 1991 have a high rate of HIV infection.

There is a popular perception that, regardless of the policies implemented, the process of refugee or immigrant resettlement takes at least two or even three generations. If there is even a modicum of truth in this proposition then it is clearly too early to expect the Ethiopian Jewish community to be fully assimilated into Israeli society. Yet Israel is a comparatively young country, which is only just celebrating fifty years of independence. From this perspective, two or three generations is equal to, or greater than, the history of the country to date.

Although partial solutions have been found to bridge the gap between Ethiopian Judaism and Israeli Orthodoxy, bitter tensions remain. However good the intentions of successive Israeli governments, much remains to be done. There are, moreover, areas such as religious status, racial attitudes, and social absorption in which the government can have only limited impact. As the first generation of Ethiopian Jews raised or born in Israel emerge into adulthood, they are increasingly impatient.

NOTES

1. This article is a revised and updated version of our report "Ethiopian Immigrants in Israel: Experience and Prospects," Institute for Jewish Policy Research, London, March 1998. We are grateful to the Institute for permission to reprint the information contained there.

2. This portion of the chapter is based largely on Kaplan and Rosen 1994.

3. Both one-parent families and families with more than six members are more common among those who arrived from May 1991 onward.

4. Israeli towns or cities with over 1,000 Ethiopians are: Haifa, Hadera, Netanya, Ashqelon, Rehovot, Ashdod, Ramle, Beer Sheva, Kiryat Malachi, Yavne, Afula, Kiryat Gat, and Kiryat Yam.

5. While the percentage of Ethiopians studying in boarding schools has declined (in February 1996, 4,535 of the approximately 12,000 Ethiopian students in grades 7–12 were in schools of Youth Aliyah), the resources previously invested in their education have not generally been transferred to their local community junior and senior high schools. Many parents have thus found themselves confronted with new expenses to be paid out of their usually limited resources.

6. In 1996–97, 45 percent of Jewish students and 23 percent of Arab students passed matriculation exams.

7. All statistics on HIV/AIDS are derived from the Navon Commission, 1996.

8. In considering these figures it must be remembered that Ethiopian immigrants have been tested in far greater numbers than any other group in Israel.

9. On cultural differences between Gondar and Tigtay see Rosen 1987.

10. This portion of the chapter is based largely on Salamon 1998.

11. The conclusions are based largely on Salamon 2001a and 2001b.

REFERENCES

Amir, Eli, Alex Zahavi, and Ruth Fargi. 1997. *One Root and Many Branches: The Story of the Absorption of Ethiopian Youth in Aliyat Hanoar.* Jerusalem: Magnes Press (Hebrew).

Anteby, Lisa. 1996. "Silence des ancients, enigmes de l'ecrit: les peripeties de l'alphabetisation des immigrants ethiopiens en Israel." *Revue Europeennes des Migrations Internationales* 12 (3): 77–97.

Ashkenazi, Michael, and Alex Weingrod. 1984. *Ethiopian Immigrants in Beersheba.* Highland Park, Ill.: American Association for Ethiopian Jews.

Ben-Dor, Shoshana. 1987. "The Sigd of Beta Israel: Testimony to a Community in Transition." In *Ethiopian Jews and Israel,* ed. Michael Ashkenazi and Alex Weingrod, 140–59. New Brunswick: Transaction.

———. 1990. "The Religious Background of Beta Israel." In *Saga of Aliyah,* ed. Shoshana Ben-Dor, 24–28. Jerusalem: Ministry of Education.

Benita, Esther, Gila Noam, and Ruth Levy. 1994. *Local Surveys of Ethiopian Immigrants: Findings from Afula, Netanya and Kiryat Gat.* Jerusalem: JDC–Brookdale.

Budowski, Dani, and Yosef David. 1996. *Ethiopian Jews.* Tel Aviv: Behalchin (Hebrew).

Doleve-Gandelman, Tsili. 1990. "Ethiopia as a Lost Imaginary Space: The Role of Ethiopian Jewish Women in Producing the Ethnic Identity of their Immigrant Group in Israel." In *Other Perspectives in Gender and Culture,* ed. Juliet Flower MacCannell, 242–57. New York: Columbia University Press.

Friedmann, Ya'acov. 1992. *Operation Solomon: One Year and Thirty-One Hours.* Jerusalem: AMITAI.

G'dor, Uzi. 1996. *The Absorption of Ethiopian Immigrants 1992–1995.* Jerusalem: Ministry of Absorption.

Graebner, Dieter. 1992. *Operation Solomon: die Heimkehr der Kinder der Koenigin von Saba.* Hamburg: Rasch und Röhring.

Halévy, Joseph. 1877. "Travels in Abyssinia." In *Miscellany of Hebrew Literature,* ed. A. Levy, 175–256. London: Wertheimer, Lea and Co.

Hertzog, Esther. 1998. *Bureaucrats and Immigrants in an Absorption Center.* Tel Aviv: Tcherikover.

Israel Association for Ethiopian Jews. 1995. *Step-Children of the Educational System.* Jerusalem: Israel Association for Ethiopian Jews.

Israel Journal of Medical Sciences. 1991. 27 (5).

Israel Journal of Medical Sciences. 1993. 29 (6–7).

Israel Ministry of Internal Security. 1997. "Suspects According to Country of Origin."

Israel State Comptroller. 1997. *Annual Report* 47.

Kaplan, Steven. 1987. "Leadership and Communal Organization among the Beta Israel: An Historical Study." *Encyclopaedia Judaica Yearbook 1986–87,* 154–63. Jerusalem: Keter.

———. 1988. "The Beta Israel and the Rabbinate: Law, Politics and Ritual." *Social Science Information* 27 (3): 357–70.

———. 1992. *The Beta Israel (Falasha) in Ethiopian History.* New York, N.Y.: New York University Press.

———. 1993. "Falasha Christians: A Brief History." *Midstream* 39 (1): 20–21.

———. 1999. "Can the Ethiopian Change His Skin? Racial Discourse and Ethiopian Jews in Israel." *African Affairs* 98: 535–50

Kaplan, Steven, and Shoshana Ben-Dor. 1988. *Ethiopian Jewry: An Annotated Bibliography.* Jerusalem: Ben Zvi Institute.

Kaplan, Steven, and Chaim Rosen. 1993. "Ethiopian Immigrants to Israel: Between Preservation of Culture and Invention of Tradition." *Jewish Journal of Sociology* 35 (1): 35–48.

———. 1994. Ethiopian Jews In Israel. *American Jewish Year Book 94,* 59–109.

———. 1996. Youth Aliya, unpublished paper, 2 February (Hebrew).

Kaplan, Steven and Hagar Salamon. 1998. Ethiopian Immigrants in Israel: Experience and Prospects. *JPR Report,* (Institute for Jewish Policy Research), no 1.

Karadawi, Ahmed. 1991. "The Smuggling of the Ethiopian Falasha to Israel Through Sudan." *African Affairs* 90 (358): 23–50.

Kemon, Azriel. 1996. *The First Bridge: Testimonies of Jewish Students from Ethiopia at Kfar Batya 1955–1995.* Ramat Ephal (Hebrew).

Parfitt, Tudor. 1985. *Operation Moses.* London: Weidenfeld and Nicholson.

Phillips Davids, Jennifer. 1999. "New Lives: Migration, Fertility Transition, and Life Course Change among Ethiopian Jewish Immigrants in Israel." Ph.D. dissertation, Emory University, Atlanta, Georgia.

Quirin, James. 1992. *The Evolution of the Ethiopian Jews.* Philadelphia: University of Pennsylvania Press.

Rapoport, Louis. 1986. *Redemption Song: The Story of Operation Moses.* New York: Harcourt Brace Jovanovich.

Rosen, Chaim. 1987. "Similarities and Differences between the Beta Israel of Gondar and Tigre." *Pe'amim* 33: 93–108.

Sabar Friedman, Galia. 1989. "Religion and the Marxist State of Ethiopia: The Case of the Ethiopian Jews." *Religion in Communist Lands* 17 (3): 247–56.

Salamon, Hagar. 1987. "Journeys as a Means of Communication among the Beta-Israel in Ethiopia." *Pe'amim* 33: 109–24 (Hebrew).

———. 1994. "Between Ethnicity and Religiosity—Internal Group Aspects of Conversion among the Beta Israel in Ethiopia." *Pe'amim* 58: 104–19 (Hebrew).

———. 1995. "Reflections of Ethiopian Cultural Patterns on the 'Beta Israel' Absorption in Israel: The 'Barya' Case." In *Between Africa and Zion—Proceedings of the First Conference on Ethiopian Jewry,* ed. Steven Kaplan, Tudor Parfitt, and Emanuela Trevisan Semi, 126–32. Jerusalem: Ben-Zvi Institute.

———. 1998. "Racial Consciousness in Transition: From Ethiopia to the Promised Land." *Jerusalem Studies in Jewish Folklore* 19–20: 125–46 (Hebrew).

———. 1999. *The Hyena People: Ethiopian Jews in Christian Ethiopia.* Berkeley and Los Angeles: University of California Press.

———. 2001a. "Judaism Between Race and Religion: The Case of the Ethiopian Jews." In *The Life of Judaism,* ed. Harvey Goldberg. Berkeley and Los Angeles: University of California Press.

———. 2001b. "In Search of Self and Other: A Few Remarks on Ethnicity, Race, and Ethiopian Jews." In *Jewish Locations: Traversing Racialized Landscapes,* ed. Lisa Tessman and Bat-Ami Bar On. Lanham, Md.: Rowman and Littlefield.

Salamon, Hagar, and Steven Kaplan. 1998. *Ethiopian Jewry: An Annotated Bibliography 1988–1997.* Jerusalem: Ben Zvi Institute.

Sarin, Ina Ruth. 1990. "Stories from the Ethiopian Jews: Tales Told in Israel." M.A. Thesis, University of Connecticut.

———. 1994. "Evidence of Jewish Characteristics in Tales and Legends of the 'Falashas,' The Ethiopian Jews." In *Proceedings of the Eleventh International Conference of Ethiopian Studies,* ed. Bahru Zewde, Richard Pankhurst, and Taddese Beyene, 2: 275–98. Addis Ababa.

Seeman, Don. 1997. "One People, One Blood: Religious Conversion, Public Health and Immigration as Social Experience for Ethiopian-Israelis." Ph.D. dissertation, Harvard University.

Seeman, Don. 1999. "'One People, One Blood': Public Health, Political Violence, and HIV in an Ethiopian-Israeli Setting." *Culture, Medicine and Psychiatry* 23: 159–95.

Shabtay, Malka. 1995. "The Experience of Ethiopian Jewish Soldiers in the Israeli Army: The Process of Identity Formulation within the Military Context." *Israel Social Science Research* 10 (2): 69–80.

Shelemay, Kay Kaufman. 1989. *Music, Ritual, and Falasha History.* East Lansing: Michigan State University Press.

Shwartz-Beeri, Ora. 1991. "The Material Culture of the Jews of Ethiopia." *Ariel* 85–86: 118–37.

State Comptroller. 1997. Annual Report, no. 47, 1997: 511–23.

Summerfield, Daniel P. 1997. "From Falasha to Ethiopia: The External Influences for Change 1860–1960." Ph.D. dissertation, School of Oriental and African Studies, University of London.

Trevisan Semi, Emanuela. 1985. "The Beta Israel (Falashas): From Purity to Impurity." *The Jewish Journal of Sociology* 25: 103–14.

Wagaw, Teshome. 1993. *For Our Soul: Ethiopian Jews in Israel.* Detroit: Wayne State University.

Weil, Shalva. 1995. "Representations of Leadership among Ethiopian Jews in Israel." In *Between Africa and Zion,* ed. Steven Kaplan, Tudor Parfitt, and Emanuela Trevisan Semi, 230–39. Jerusalem: Ben Zvi Institute.

Westheimer, Ruth, and Steven Kaplan. 1992. *Surviving Salvation: The Ethiopian Jewish Family in Transition.* New York: New York University Press.

PART III

Social Transformation and Political Orientation

CHAPTER SIX

The Kibbutz's Transformation
Who Leads It and Where?

∾

ELIEZER BEN-RAFAEL AND MENACHEM TOPEL

The Challenges

The kibbutz is one of the original features of Israeli society. Its inner quasi-communist egalitarianism and its dedication to development and social mobilization on behalf of national challenges have made it a symbol of the Zionist ideal. Over the years, however, the transformation of Israeli society and the development of the kibbutz itself have tarnished this privileged position. Since the mid-1980s, more particularly, the kibbutz has undergone a thorough transformation that has taken it to a new stage. The questions arising from this transformation are numerous and challenge the very identity of today's kibbutz, the extent to which it still represents a valuable experience for Israeli society, and the direction and nature of its further evolution. The answers to these questions depend, of course, on who leads the kibbutz and where. It is on these issues that this chapter focuses.

There are 270 kibbutzim in Israel, which number about 118,000 inhabitants (Pavin 2001). Typically, a kibbutz is a village of 300 to 700 inhabitants[1] and consists of a residential neighborhood with public buildings in its center (a collective dining room, children's houses, central offices), an area of services (carpentry, garage, the electrician's shop, etc.), an industrial zone, and agricultural fields.[2] The kibbutzim are dispersed all around the country but about 75 percent are settled in the periphery, at a distance from the coastal and the central regions of Israel. They are affiliated with a number of regional councils, in which they represent a major part of the population in the development of cultural, educative, economic, welfare, and physical planning activities. In several areas, the neighboring kibbutzim develop a range of regional enterprises that they own in common but that usually employ nonkibbutz manpower. The kibbutz sector as a whole constitutes about 2 percent of the national population; it contributes 38 percent of the national agriculture and 8.5 percent of the national industry. The range of agricultural interests covers all kinds of crops (the kibbutzim represent 67 percent of the national production of field crops). In industry, kibbutzim tend to concentrate in plastics, metals, and food (75 percent of the kibbutz's industrial manpower is employed in these industries). About 15 percent of the total manpower of the kibbutzim are employed in agriculture, 25 percent in industry, 12 percent in education, nearly 20 percent in financial, commercial, or reparation services, and about the same number in external jobs—with 8 percent in a diversity of nonworking situations. The wide majority of the kibbutzim (254 out of 272) belong to two federations (or kibbutz movements): the Takam, with 170 kibbutzim, and the Hakibutz Haartzi, with 84. Since the late 1990s, these two movements have been in process of unification,[3] while two small religious federations—Hakibbutz Hadati, with 16 kibbutzim, and Poalei Agudat Israel, with 2—maintain separate frameworks in the margins of the large federations.

We defined elsewhere (Ben-Rafael 1997) the three aspects that, in our eyes, best define the kibbutz in sociological terms, that is, that it constitutes, at the same time, a collective entrepreneurial enterprise and a community and is a constituent part of a status group—the "kibbutzniks." Kibbutzim are collective entrepreneurs because they are agricultural, industrial, and, in some ways, commercial enterprises that control both the human capital of their members and the material means of their welfare and development. In addition, their motivation is definitely entrepreneurial as they aspire to a permanent strengthening of their economic power and a constant improvement of their standard of living. Moreover, the many members who are employed in the outside—whether as emissaries of the kibbutz in organizations attached to the kibbutz federations and regional centers, or as academics, military officers, experts, or just employees in nonkibbutz firms—increase the kibbutz's income with their salaries. As a result, however, kibbutzim also often hire nonkibbutz, and less expensive, workers (generally about 20–30 percent of their total manpower). As an enterprise, the kibbutz tends, like any other capitalist venture, to give priority to the race for profits and expansion. This naturally pushes it to place responsibility for management and development in the most "competent hands," that is, the managers and their experts. Though, at the same time, as a collective enterprise where all members are partners, the kibbutz also constitutes a reality where the participation of everyone in decision making and the identification of everyone with the goals and purposes of the enterprise are expected. As we will see in the following, the dilemma posed by this expectation, which has existed from the very beginning of the kibbutz endeavor, is dramatically exacerbated in the process of transformation the kibbutz has gone through in the last decade.

In addition to its entrepreneurial activities, the kibbutz is also a form of community that has always considered its essence to reside in equal sharing in all major spheres of social life. Until the 1980s, institutions of direct democracy were central to the kibbutz model; that is, a sovereign General Assembly and regularly elected public committees governed the various spheres of activity.[4] Also central was a total absence of monetary rewards; individual budgets allocated by the collective were strictly egalitarian, while most living expenses were directly taken care of by kibbutz organs. The collective dining room was the symbolic center of public life, and an ambitious philosophy oriented the kibbutz's complex, collective, educational structures (children houses, class houses, regional high schools, etc.). The kibbutz's declared aim, indeed, was to shape a generation of "social humans" that accept community life as a natural milieu.[5] Yet, the basic dilemma that was essential to this aspect of the kibbutz experience resides in the fact that the individual as such was never ignored, even though the collectivist principle was considered of primary importance. It has, indeed, always been proclaimed that the kibbutz grants the individual the best opportunity for "self-realization" (*hagshama atsmit*) in a setting where, in principle, no obstacle prevented the full expression of one's social nature. This potential tension between collectivism and individualism has become a major axis of transformation in the contemporary kibbutz.

The third facet of kibbutz identity concerns its status, nay even elite, aspirations. The kibbutzniks have for long perceived themselves as conveyors of a message of wider societal significance, by embodying values like social equality and justice. Moreover, they have also been convinced that they fulfill tasks of national importance such as populating remote areas, developing agriculture, and assuming defense and military roles. For all these reasons, they should, in their own eyes, inspire the society as a whole. Hence, they used to see themselves as "first-rate" citizens and wanted to be recognized as such by nonkibbutzniks. This elitist attitude required social mobilization and a sensitivity to one's status in society, and on the other hand, it also justified segregation from the rest of society in crucial areas of social activity. In the realm of education, for instance, kibbutzniks contended that the kibbutz's capability to transfer its unique character and beliefs to the younger generation required that their educational institutions develop their own programs and methods and thus remain closed to nonkibbutz children.[6] This insistence on their "unique character" and entitlement to retain a distance from their direct environment, on the one hand, and their aspiration to achieve an influential position in society on the other, is another dilemma inherent in the kibbutzniks' self-perceived identity from the very start of the kibbutz movement. This dilemma, too, is under severe attack in the kibbutz's present-day transformation.

The roots of the crisis of the 1980s are to be found in the disruption that took place in the late 1970s when the Right rose to power (1977) for the first time ever, in a country that up to then had been traditionally dominated by social democrats. This disruption amounted to an earthquake for the kibbutz movement, which was traditionally inclined to the Left. It dislodged the kibbutzniks from longstanding governmental positions and overrepresentation in Parliament. This loss of political strongholds also caused the kibbutzim to loose a broad range of material privileges.[7] Once in power, the Right wing started systematic delegitimization of the kibbutz and raised new—ethnic and religious—groups to positions previously occupied by the kibbutz movement, positions that the latter will never be able to reconquer even when Labor comes back to power.[8] This political weakening of the kibbutz movement provided the direct context for the mid-1980s economic crisis. This crisis was national but hit the kibbutz twice as hard as the rest of the economy because of its new political vulnerability. It took place in a context where a few years of galloping inflation had brought about a drastic antiinflationary policy that threw entrepreneurs into unprecedented debts. During the 1980s the debts of numerous kibbutzim went up by tens of percents, reaching the enormous sum of 12.6 billion NIS.[9]

Many kibbutzim and kibbutz regional organizations lost their financial credibility, causing the bankruptcy of the financial groups that had been working with their money. Agreements between the kibbutz movement, the banks, and the State provided for partial solutions but the kibbutzim, in return, had to commit themselves to a whole range of measures, including selling off some of their assets and lowering their level of consumption (Sheaffer 1992). These new circumstances account partially for the fact that the kibbutz became less attractive to its sons and daughters, whose rate of departure increased dramatically, especially in the kibbutzim that experienced the most serious difficulties. While, in 1985, 400 individuals left the kibbutz, this figure jumped to 1000 in 1989; in parallel, the number of kibbutz births, which had steadily increased until 1985, has been decreasing ever since (Topel 2000). For the kibbutzniks as a whole, this crisis initiated a far-reaching, soul-searching process and set in motion an unprecedented transformation of social structures.

The Transformation

Ninety years after the first kibbutz was established, it seemed that all efforts had failed to create exemplary, viable, and prosperous egalitarian communities. The kibbutzniks reacted not only individually to the crisis but also collectively, calling for new common decisions to be made. Hectic changes were now initiated and expanded throughout the kibbutz movement, inaugurating a new era that is hardly over yet. Requestioning every well-established arrangement and sparing no area of activity, members challenged everything that had always been thought to be the quintessence of kibbutz life. No existing arrangement was taken for granted anymore, and the situation as a whole could be best described as ambiguous, precarious, and "liminal." The process of transformation now set in motion in many settlements was marked by confusion and the blurring of boundaries between what "is" and what "should be." The most daring ideas could now be raised and advocated.

Among the most popular new patterns that were now decided upon, one finds the commercialization of childrens' houses, the opening of the dining room to outside customers in return for payment, the replacement of the General Assembly and direct democracy by a restricted Council of the kibbutz, the establishment of differential monetary rewards for members on the basis of job performance and rank, the removal of restrictions on members using their private external resources outside as well as inside the kibbutz—up to the acquisition of private cars or the private enlargement of one's apartment within the kibbutz.

In a general manner, the kibbutz is moving rapidly toward a transformation that affects its most essential values. Kibbutzniks implement arrangements that legitimize their individual aspirations and protect them from collective control. The increasing formalization—and concomitant shrinking—of collective responsibility even touches on the operations of direct democracy. In the realm of consumption, individual comprehensive budgets tend to constitute a sure way of pushing ahead privatization and the centrality of the family. In its extreme form, this budget becomes a kind of family salary. In many kibbutzim, egalitarian sharing is still evident only in specific patterns, such as in the realm of education or cultural life. On the other hand, the kibbutz's entrepreneurial function is also changing drastically as the partnership principle, which has for long hindered the concentration of authority in the hands of the higher ranks, is now most often unable to withstand the growing prevalence of managers and experts, and in many factories, little room is left for rank-and-file participation in decision making. Work is now often viewed only in terms of the income it provides, which tends to make kibbutz capitalism look less different from nonkibbutz capitalism. Last but not least, the kibbutz's longstanding elitism plays now but a weak part in kibbutzniks' attitudes toward the surrounding society. These attitudes are much more pragmatic than in the past and lead kibbutzim to lower the fence that separates them from other cultural groups.

With the exception of youngsters, the crisis has fallen short of causing mass exodus from the kibbutz, which has saved it from general destabilization. Kibbutzniks chose to transform their kibbutzim rather than to leave them.[10]

In part, however, the transformations were aimed at confronting the difficulty of retaining the younger generation in the kibbutz. Hence, many a kibbutz offers the young the possibility of acquiring a higher education by paying back the community for the cost of these studies by working during vacation time. In other kibbutzim, sons and daughters may even work for a salary for a few years, as quasi-hired manpower. This is intended to offer the youngsters some freedom before they make up their minds regarding their future. Yet, kibbutzniks are not too optimistic about the prospects of retaining their offspring in large numbers.[11] Hence kibbutzim also often institute fair retirement arrangements that will make older members independent from their community's condition. Furthermore, many other kibbutzim, where members are anxious for the survival of the community, do not hesitate to set up new residential neighborhoods to attract people who are not kibbutzniks but would like to live in a rural environment. In any case, the debates about changes were, and still are, joyless and marked by a lack of enthusiasm and a loss of resolve. The sense of failure has generated feelings of guilt and endless deliberations on assumed past errors. This despair is often aggravated by personal dramas, especially among the elderly who now often feel insecure in view of the disorder they perceive all around. Many families have now started encouraging their children not to commit themselves to the kibbutz life but to look for alternative work and living situations, on the outside. Behind the apparent chaos, however, one may find a sociological thread clearly revealed by the numerous researchers who have studied the changes now implemented by kibbutzim. Our own works have tried to capture these changes at several levels. A first level concerned the events themselves that led to decisions about changes in the community.[12] We investigated, from this perspective, a stratified sample of thirty-four kibbutzim that together were representative of the Takam movement as a whole. In each of these kibbutzim, we conducted two surveys at a one-year interval about initiatives of change, discussions, decision-making processes, and patterns of implementation, carefully recorded by local informants who belonged to the research team.[13] An additional part of our research focused on members' own perceptions of the general transformation,[14] which allowed us to grasp the differential participation and attitudes of different milieus.

As a whole, this work was primarily intended to refine our questioning of "who leads the kibbutz these days, and where."

Clusters of Changes

The "change crisis" in kibbutzim clearly correlates with economic and demographic difficulties (Table 1). By no means do initiatives of change come up in kibbutzim in "regular" circumstances. Though, when demographic and/or economic difficulties do come up and members initiated changes, one can still hardly speak of a development that takes on the same forms in every kibbutz: but 31 changes (out of 118) have been found in at least eight kibbutzim, out of 34 (Table 2), which indicates the variety that one may find from one kibbutz to another in

Table 1. Change Intensity in the Context of Economic and Demographic Factors[1]

	Index of Implementation[4]		Index of Involvement[5]	
	1st Survey	2nd Survey	1st Survey	2nd Survey
Economic situation[2]	−0.408	−0.483	−0.549	0.522
Demographic situation[3]	−0.493	−0.396	−0.353	−0.450

[1]All correlations are statistically significant ($p < 0.05$; Spearman test).

[2]As calculated according to (a) "Debt capacity" defined by the bank that credits the kibbutzim; (b) the net revenue of the kibbutzim yielded by the kibbutzim to the authors; (c) an "Economic Efficiency" index (see Topel 1990).

[3]As calculated according to the evolution of the number of kibbutz members from 1985 to 1991.

[4]The relative rank of kibbutzim, within the sample, according to the number of changes recently implemented.

[5]The relative rank of kibbutzim, within the sample, according to the number of changes considered and discussed within the community and which were graded according to their specific public status (see Topel 2000).

this respect. While some changes are more popular than others, many others are less diffused and mainly characterize individual kibbutzim.

As Table 2 shows, changes that were more frequently reported concerned the transfer of direct responsibility to the individual—such as privatization of consumption budgets, increasing parents' responsibility for children's education, personal responsibility of members for finding a job, whether in the kibbutz or in the outside. Another important category concerns the restructuring of the public sphere and direct democracy—the frequency of the meetings of the General Assembly tends to be reduced from weekly to bi-annual or annual, with most of its power transferred to an elected and restricted Council or, even, to a bureaucratic Board of Directors.

More from the close and according to their contents, one may divide the 118 changes that we found, in total, in the 34 kibbutzim of the sample into three broadly defined clusters. We may call the first cluster "managerialism" on the basis of a common denominator conveying the idea of a move from existing, direct, egalitarian patterns of participation to organizational-hierarchical management. Under this heading, one finds the creation of bodies in a Board-of-Directors style and the abandonment of larger and more democratic bodies; a resort to external experts in management; a suppression of normative restrictions over the employment of hired labor; and the institution of differential financial rewards, first for extra work hours and later for any work.

A second cluster of changes is best labeled "privatism," and it indicates a trend to widen the direct responsibility of the individual member over the man-

Table 2. A List of the More Popular Changes Discussed and Adopted
by Kibbutzim

Items	Frq	Items	Frq
Liquidating local school for regional school	32	Network TV for General Assembly broadcast	13
Privatizing all consumption	29	Advertising recruitment (new members)	12
Hired nurses for kibbutz children	28	Swimming pool as "business"	11
Voting by referenda on general matters	27	Private apartment enlargements authorized	11
Children's budget joined to their parents'	26	Outside kibbutz general director	10
Encouraging members to work outside	24	Closing the dinning room at evening	10
Daycare for nonkibbutz children	22	Paying salary to kibbutz youngsters	10
Assigning a special team for changes	22	Autonomy of factories from collective	10
Boards of directors controlling factories	20	Agriculture partnership with other kibbutzim	10
Privatization of domestic energy cost	19	Agriculture partnership with private firm	9
Kindergarten for nonkibbutz children	18	Privatization of health items	9
Leasing rooms for nonkibbutz people	16	Emphasizing managers' authority	9
Social security on member's name	16	Closing the dinning room for breakfast	8
Youngster remaining in parents' house	14	Personal services as "businesses"	8
Privatization of adult higher education	13	Partnership with private industrialists	8
		Partnership in factory with other kibbutzim	8

agement of his or her life in the community, at the expense of collective responsibility. This cluster includes measures like the privatization of the budget for educational, material, or cultural needs of children, for food and energy used by families, higher education, cultural consumption, special health treatments, maintenance of the apartment, social security, etc. Under the same roof, we find transfers of responsibility from the collective to the individual regarding his or her occupation and the dismissal of normative restrictions regarding the members' uses of private resources (inheritance, gifts, or incomes from private propriety) within the kibbutz.

We call a third cluster of changes "interweaving" to describe a trend of changes sharing an emphasis on weakening the barriers that have for long warranted the kibbutz's self-segregation from the nonkibbutz population. Examples here are numerous as well: joint ventures with other kibbutzim or with private firms; licenses for individuals to work outside the kibbutz in jobs of their choosing, provided they bring in satisfactory salaries; renting rooms to nonmember residents; or making kibbutz services—dining room, children's houses, clubs, swimming pools—available to outside clients on a business basis. In turn, kibbutz members are now free to look for services in the nonkibbutz environment, including eventually sending their own children to nonkibbutz schools and using national or regional social or welfare programs.

Table 3 shows the extremely low correlation obtained between the clusters, which indicates how far the three clusters are effectively distinct from each other. These data contrast with the internal consistency of each cluster (see Table 4). Hence, the transformation of the kibbutz follows different paths that each affect differently the basic dilemmas at the heart of the kibbutzniks' identity. Organization of work and the economy becomes more and more like a regular, hierarchically managed, big business meaning that the dilemma defined as "entrepreneurship" versus "partnership" is definitively resolving to the advantage of the former. Private life expands at the same pace as the shrinking of collective life, while the principle of egalitarian sharing appears to withdraw, which means that the dilemma "individualism" versus "collectivism" is also definitively resolving to the advantage of the former. The boundaries that separate the kibbutz from the outside are less and less effective, which means that the dilemma of elitism, in which the kibbutz values its own ways over those of the rest of society and thus segregates itself, is being swallowed up in a general tendency to "de-elitize," so to speak, the kibbutz's image. The relative strength of each of these tendencies in the kibbutzim, however, varies from one kibbutz to another, and one witnesses, as an additional aspect of the kibbutz's contemporary transformation, a general process where a kibbutz may become more and more different from other kibbutzim. Whatever the reasons for this differentiation, the general outcome of these developments is that the kibbutz reality as a whole becomes more and more pluralist.

Table 3. Trends' Distinction

Inter-cluster relations	R squared	T*	Spearman
Privatism-interweaving	0.0519	1.3235	0.22781
Privatism-managerialism	3.0E−05	0.035	−0.0063
Managerialism-interweaving	0.0002	0.072	−0.0127

* $p < 0.05$

Table 4. *Internal Consistency of the Distinct Clusters of Change*
(Alpha Cronbach Test)

Managerialism		Interweaving		Privatism	
Implement	Involvement	Implement	Involvement	Implement	Involvement
0.58	0.67	0.71	0.66	0.73	0.57

Table 5 shows the forms this pluralism of kibbutz reality takes on among the various kibbutzim of the sample, by categorizing them according to how far each of them adopts changes pertaining to the different clusters. The two larger groups, as it appears, are the most radical, on the one hand, and the most conservative, on the other. Together, however, they add up to 15 kibbutzim out of 34, that is, fewer than half of the kibbutzim in the sample.

Moreover, it has also appeared, in confirmation of what has been said above regarding the movement as a whole, that the conservative kibbutzim are the strongest, demographically and economically. The other models illustrate both objective difficulties and a variety of forms of transformation. It is in this context that the questions that are at the center of this chapter take all their acuity.

The Leading Role of Kibbutz Technocrats

The question that now arises concerns, indeed, who, in actual fact, stands behind the changes. As far as our kibbutzim are concerned—and whatever path of change characterizes them—the analysis of change events clearly shows the determining role played in all communities by the men and women that function as managers, leaders, and experts in the kibbutz's major branches of activity—factories, agricultural branches, and regional cooperatives. These people, as a rule, are credentialed by a long career in positions of responsibility as well as by diplomas from institutions of higher education. In brief, they make up what we name the kibbutz's technocratic elite.

When compared to the nonelite, the data for the elite leave no doubt about their prevailing role in the process of change: these are the people who initiate the largest number of propositions of changes, get them on the public agenda, later ensure their endorsement by the public, and finally shoulder the task of their implementation (see Table 6). It is also apparent, however, that technocrats and rank-and-file do not necessarily share the same interests with the same intensity. The rank-and-file, indeed, are principally interested in the changes that we grouped under the heading of "privatism"; the technocrats are interested in changes making up the category of "managerialism"; both concur in promoting changes pertaining to the "interweaving" trend.

Table 5. Profiles of Transformational Process in Kibbutzim (N=34)[1]

Model	Frequency	Privatism	Managerialism	Interweaving
Conservative	8	−	−	−
Emphasis on managerialism	2	−	+	−
Emphasis on privatism	4	+	−	−
Emphasis on interweaving	2	−	−	+
Mixed emphases: manag. + interw.	3	−	+	+
Mixed emphases: privat. + interw.	5	+	+	−
Mixed emphases: privat. + manag.	3	+	−	+
Radical	7	+	+	+

[1]The tendency to adopt changes regarding each particular cluster is dichotomized, and the more "transformationist" kibbutzim are signaled by "+", while the less "transformationist" are signaled by "−".

Regarding some changes, to be sure, this does not come as a surprise. Technocrats are expected to, and of course actually do, support propositions that give more power and authority to managers, attach privileges to their positions, and extend the control they may exert through administrative bodies over the economy. What is less self-evident is that technocrats also tend to sustain, if not to promote, changes that concern the structure of the community itself, even when they do not directly relate to their specific interests and are raised by non-elite individuals. Most often, only local or personal circumstances may explain why technocrats oppose a suggestion of change.

The involvement and practical importance of technocrats in the kibbutz's present-day transformation attracts attention and can only be viewed in relation to the drastic change that the very appearance of technocrats in the kibbutz represented at an earlier stage—that is, in the 1970s and 1980s. Technocrats appeared in the kibbutz in the wake of the community's social and economic development. Over time, they came to include agronomists, production engineers, trained economists, and accountants. These technocrats have always contrasted with the veteran economic leaders of the kibbutz economy, as primarily illustrated by the "Merakez Meshek" (MM) or "economy director." MMs, usually self-educated people with years of practical experience as leaders of agricultural branches, used to demonstrate their total dedication to the collective economy,

Table 6. Initiators of Change Events

Initiators	Privatism	Interweaving	Managerialism	Total
Economic officials[1]	15	6	28	49
Secretary of the kibbutz[2]	4		8	12
Social officials[3]	13	2	7	22
Rank-and-file	25	7	3	35
TOTAL	57	15	46	118

[1]Including under the form of propositions of "teams of change" formally appointed to discuss and propose changes to the General Assembly—as a rule technocrats were the formal or informal leaders of these teams.

[2]In many cases, a technocrat as well.

[3]In many cases, these people in charge of committees dealing with social matters have received a higher education and tend to see themselves as professionals, identifying somehow with the technocratic culture.

in every moment of the day or the night. They definitively represented a very different type of leader from today's technocrats who ground their authority on expertise and formal qualifications. MMs saw their calling in driving the development and expansion of the kibbutz's agricultural and industrial production at nearly any cost, while the technocrats tend to exhibit a strictly businesslike approach and to evaluate the contribution of every domain of activity by a strictly cost-benefit approach. MMs insisted on the role of the kibbutz in the national economy, but the technocrat emphasizes primarily the needs of the kibbutz itself. MMs aspired to leadership in the community and intervened in most issues pending on the agenda, while technocrats want to leave social questions to specialists and focus only on their own domain of expertise. MMs saw the public and the heads of the diverse branches of activity as their reference group, while technocrats speak of their professional community beyond the boundaries of the kibbutz. While it was the Merakez Meshek that created the notion of "kibbutz economy," technocrats are the driving force behind the kibbutz's contemporary transformation and rapprochement to its environment.

Ironically enough, kibbutzniks hardly recall nowadays that because of their basic value orientations, they for long opposed the strengthening of technocrats in the kibbutz and refused to endorse professional definitions of leading functions in the kibbutz's factories and agriculture. What we are seeing now is that the contemporary changes have liberated the technocrats from all the constraints of the past. One may even suggest that every change, whatever cluster it pertains to, contributes to the removal of the kibbutz from the model that, in many ways, oppressed the technocrats in the kibbutz. This may explain in some measure the fact that technocrats are predisposed to support, *a priori,* every—or nearly every—change that reaches the public agenda and increases the departure of the kibbutz from its previous model—even when it does not directly relate to their immediate interest. Yet, interestingly enough, in spite of this strong association of technocrats with the process of transformation of the kibbutz, one would vainly look for any form of organization and coordinated political action among them, at any stage. Things take place as if these technocrats shared a sufficiently well-crystallized outlook and did not require any structure to sustain these moves that they commonly endorse. Such a structure, seemingly, would have been severely condemned by the nonelite since one sacred assumption of kibbutz life is that members belong individually to the community, and that any form of factional organization within the kibbutz is an offense to the collective.

In fact, it also seems that such a partisan action would not have been necessary anyway. From all the evidence, the sweeping delegitimization of the kibbutz model among members that occurred following the crisis of the mid-1980s has been widely channeled toward the technocratic perspective, which has been granted a new hegemony throughout the kibbutz public. Especially in this time of acute crisis, nontechnocrats appear more than ever to rely principally on technocrats to overcome their difficulties, a process that bypasses the people who used to be principal spokesmen for the kibbutz only a few years ago—ideological and community leaders whose voices have now been largely silenced. In our research, we found that these people where the principal victims, in terms of status and authority, of the overwhelming transformation of the kibbutz.

This by no means signifies, however, that some former leaders as well as the rank-and-file have no more say in the management of the community and the kibbutz enterprise. By their presence and permanent criticism of the "way things go," they remind technocrats that they do not act in a vacuum and must be accountable to the public. This is at least one explanation for the fact that, in many of the cases we investigated, the process of discussion took a very long time before a final decision was reached, let alone completely implemented. The variety of pressures exerted by the different interests involved explains why what emerges from the implementation process can be quite different from what was originally discussed and concluded.

What is more, these dynamics also explain that in different kibbutzim one may find a diversity of "change cocktails," so to speak, according to the positions of prominent individuals, the power of lobbying groups, the relative importance of different layers (youngsters, oldtimers, women, etc.), all of which make for differences of publics from one kibbutz to another. The essential trait, however, that is common to all kibbutzim is that the "sacred cows" have lost their "sacredness" and that, apart from those kibbutzim—the stronger and more wealthy ones—that refuse to undergo reform, others are evolving, to varying degrees and not necessarily consistently, toward more managerialism, privatism, and interweavering.

The Basic Positions

The analysis of fifty-two in-depth interviews that we conducted in eight kibbutzim (among our sample of thirty-four) confirms our thesis regarding the hegemony of the technocrat perspective in many of today's kibbutzim. The prevailing mood we found among both technocrats and nontechnocrats—even though couched in different styles—is characterized by a fundamentally instrumental, nonideological, view of kibbutz life. Hence, for instance, a thirty-one-year-old female member who joined the kibbutz recently and stands far away from the technocrats, told us: "What is it to be a kibbutz member? In the past, there were ideas and aspirations. Today, what matters is the quality of life, peacefulness, and a clean atmosphere. This place was already built-up when I came. What attracted me was the way of life, the education of children, and the quietness."

These are the main things that hold most subjects in the kibbutz, notwithstanding the economic and social difficulties that kibbutzim encounter. Another thirty-four-year-old female member who works in the kibbutz's factory rank-and-file could flatly state: "Here I have a house which would have cost a lot of money in the outside, and I get laundry services, education and every thing I need in daily life." The kibbutz, she insists, allows her to continue to work outside the kibbutz and to pursue a career.

Remarkably enough, in this image of kibbutz life, there is little room for elitist aspirations and most respondents do not give much attention to the affiliation of the kibbutz to the federation. Actually, they tend just to ignore its practical significance. A forty-year old female member who works in one of the kibbutz's factory as a rank-and-file confirms: "The kibbutz does not belong to the movement anymore. This is an old story. Maybe the kibbutz still belongs to the regional council. Anyway, I myself do not feel any allegiance to the kibbutz movement."

On the other hand, a typical technocrat—a manager of a kibbutz factory—was ready to say, in a more subtle manner, but with the same perspective in mind: "We have to reduce our involvement in the movement and pay more attention to what happens inside the kibbutz.... The movement has to take care only of the common interests of kibbutzim. Anything else is superfluous...."

As a rule, technocrats are more determined in their approach than nontechnocrats, but they do not exhibit positions that really contrast with the latters'. We were told by a man of forty-five, an economic leader of his kibbutz, that, "We experience today a genuine revolution! As I see it, want it and hope it!" Or another, thirty: "The solution [of the kibbutz crisis] must be radical. Flexibility here and there will not solve our problem." Most technocrats interviewed would like a fast implementation of multiple changes, especially in the realms of organization, rewarding, and resource distribution. They see the present development of the kibbutz as leading to a cooperative settlement, and many even support converting kibbutz industrial enterprises into shareholding organizations. We were told by a typical technocrat: "What matters today is the economic interest. The kibbutz is to become a cooperative settlement to survive. The kibbutz's economy will become a shareholding. If this does not succeed, all competent people will leave."

Numerous technocrats speak of the kibbutz as a community of interests grounded in the principle of equity rather than as a community implementing equal sharing: "I am for differential salaries in the kibbutz. This is the direction to go," says a twenty-nine-year-old son of the kibbutz who is manpower director in his kibbutz. He complains that the gifted one who invests more than the nongifted is discriminated against because he does not earn more. Nontechnocrats differ from the technocrats mainly by the confusion that often characterizes their position. A member of sixty, a senior worker in a kibbutz factory, told us: "There must be some relation between work and rewarding. . . . I am in favor of privatization. . . . One has to stop the waste of resources. . . . Yet, I still have an uneasy feeling about the destruction of what has been the rule for years. I cannot stand all the people from the outside who walk around, eat in our dining room, and have their children in our children's house. . . . All the changes that we carried out in the organization of our factories have not proved very useful. . . ." And a thirty-three-year-old foreman in a factory, declared: "I belong to the moderate ones. Other people want differential rewarding, but if this is accepted, this will not be a kibbutz anymore. I am anxious . . . what will happen if our factory is collapsing. . . . I think that the responsibility over the budget and work should be transferred to each individual member. But I am opposed to a differential budget."

In a general manner, nontechnocrats are less critical of kibbutz reality than technocrats, who are also more impatient for changes to take place. While all technocrats interviewed (14) were unanimously convinced that the kibbutz needs a genuine transformation, this position was shared by but one-third of nontechnocrat respondents (13 out of 38 in total). In a similar vein, 9 out of 14 technocrats complained that changes in their kibbutzim were "too slow," but this position was expressed by but 1 out of the 38 nontechnocrats. These findings bear out the idea that the contemporary transformation of the kibbutz is primarily shouldered by technocrats, in a generally nonideological climate favorable to change. In this climate, one finds little of the kibbutznik's past allegiance to the community, driven by dedication to an ambitious communist ideology and a feeling of special participation in a national project.

Creeping Changes

To complete this characterization of the process of transformation, however, we must still consider those changes—and they are numerous—that are brought about in kibbutz reality through informal channels. Such changes come from a variety of sources and consist of private initiatives on the part of individuals, work branches, or groups of members. We may call them "creeping changes" because they are generally introduced in the kibbutz gradually and "silently." They may, for instance, involve the creation of new categories of occupations within and outside the kibbutz, new forms of partnership with outside individuals or businesses, or new organizational models. A typical example found in one of the kibbutzim of the sample is new agreements contracted, without the involvement of kibbutz institutions, between the kibbutz's manager in charge of field crops and a private agriculturist, handing over kibbutz land to private hands, together with supplies of water, machinery, and professional manpower, in exchange for know-how, unskilled workers, and market contacts. Another example is the replacement of autonomous work teams in charge of diverse agricultural branches by a centralized management formed in the image of industrial management, aided by external experts, and enjoying a new independence from kibbutz institutions. In a similar vein, the regular rotation of central management personnel of the kibbutz has always been an iron rule of the community but is now tending to vanish. In many kibbutzim, technocrats pressure the community to institute a three- or four-year term for managerial positions, or even to define them as tenured jobs, instead of the two-year period that has been the norm. All these are "creeping changes" because they are instituted ad hoc without formal decisions or public debates, and, once made, remain permanent features of the kibbutz structure. At most, they are endorsed a posteriori by the restricted executive organs of the kibbutz on the basis of a tacit agreement that this "fits the general welfare." On the whole, changes that take place in a "creeping way" are most often initiated by technocrats who take the liberty to use their authority and present the communities with *faits accomplis*, in a situation where they enjoy a large measure of freedom of action. Which is not to say that in other cases, creeping changes may not also be initiated by the rank-and-file in support of the lasting influence and specific interests of non-technocrats.

The Shrinking of the Federation

In parallel to the scant attention that members pay today to the kibbutz federation, one additional major feature of the new reality is the breakdown of the authority of the kibbutz federation, and its own transformation. In the hour that numerous kibbutzim experience uncertainty and a lack of self-confidence, they imprint these feelings on the federation itself. More than ever, they are now reluctant to supply the federation with funds and manpower, and thus they do serious damage to the federation's very capability of functioning as an organ of coordination and organizational crystallization. *Volens nolens,* the federation is thus also confronted with the challenge of change.

Interestingly enough, after decades of the predominance of ideological, political, or public figures, here also one witnesses a takeover by technocrats. These new movement leaders get control of the apparatus and attach themselves to the implementation of reforms—under slogans emphasizing "efficacy" and "profitability"—in the very same spirit that transpires in the transformation of kibbutzim.[15] These technocrats' convictions are, not surprisingly, technocratic, and they are determined to thoroughly restructure the Takam. Under their rule, the federation systematically rid itself of costly functions considered to be "nonessential." Hence, for instance, the department of information (UKM)—a team of computer experts in charge of the kibbutzim's demographic statistics that was always a part of the central body—was now detached from the federation and set up to become an independent service. It was then acquired by the kibbutz of the director of the department and organized as a business to supply services, to kibbutzim as well as to the federation, on a strictly commercial basis, and in competition with other—kibbutz and nonkibbutz—firms. The same scheme was applied to the department of physical planning, which became a commercial enterprise whose shareholders are the personnel's kibbutzim.

Other units remained located within the federation but were now compelled to operate on an autonomous organizational and financial basis. The Association of the Kibbutz Industry, for instance, still belongs, formally, to the kibbutz movement (in this case all kibbutz federations), but it charges now for all its services, according to the rules of the market. The staff itself decides upon all matters of policy. Still another example, Yad Tabenkin, the Takam's center for archives and research, constitutes a completely independent body. Its budget is supplied by a fund that is its own, in addition to benevolent contributions, applied research paid by clients, and an income from the publication of books. The Takam, which used to contribute 70 percent of Yad Tabenkin's annual budget, supplies now only 10 percent. As a result, the federation has lost nearly all its former contacts with Yad Tabenkin.

All in all, about twenty-five departments and centers have been detached from the federation, in one way or another, to become completely independent financially. All this means that the movement itself is now evolving to be a care-taker of a minimal set of common interests of the affiliated kibbutzim. This, it is to be added, is the organizational model that is to prevail in the new Kibbutz Movement that is being created by the unification of the Takam and the Kibbutz Artzi. All in all, it seems that the hegemony of kibbutz technocracy has gone beyond the limits of the individual kibbutzim to invade the structures that constitute the kibbutz movement itself.

The Paradox of Technocratic Hegemony

One of the most striking features of this new technocratic regime, we would like to underline at this stage, is that technocrats—and in this they are clearly joined by nontechnocrats—support changes that not only contribute to their own power and status in the collective but also tend to restrict the scope of public control and authority. It is this process that is at the heart of the contemporary transformation of the kibbutz movement, and it is this, also, that is most central in the transformation of the kibbutz. In this latter respect, we ask how far can it go, this tendency to privatize consumption and social life, even the area of work, drastically curtailing the responsibility of collective bodies? Privatization that, in one measure or another, appears in so many kibbutzim, means that more and more areas of activity are set free from public control. This kind of development is not blindly extended to the common economic means of production, as the collective ownership of these constitutes the very basis of the power of kibbutz technocracy. Yet, on the other hand, even here one witnesses a general process of decentralization and a growing autonomy enjoyed by factories, agricultural branches, and services.

This implies, undoubtedly, an unavoidable degree of uncoordination, which, at first glance contradicts the technocrat's professional, systematic, and systemic approach. What might partially explain this apparent contradiction is the concomitant emphasis that technocrats also place on the adjustment to market requirements, which is quite alien to the bureaucratic overburdening of basic production units required by the logic of centralized control. Viewed as a whole, this development of individual kibbutzim, which parallels the evolution taking place in the kibbutz movement, is thus marked by a genuine paradox. It, indeed, means that at the moment they achieve the greatest power, technocrats may even encourage limitation and reduction of these organs that they themselves now control. In other words, the growing power of technocrats over the kibbutz is tied to a weakening of the public authority and a strengthening of the autonomy of constituent units.

This, it may then be added, might also express a convergence of the technocrats' interests with those of the rank-and-file. We indeed know that nontechnocrat individuals, who are less socially rewarded than more "important" people, are often also less committed to kibbutz control (see Ben-Rafael 1988). This conjunctive support of "liberalization" of the kibbutz situation by the technocrats, on the one hand, who do not want to bother with "superfluous worries," and by the rank-and-file, on the other, who aspire to more freedom, leaves room for an additional hypothesis according to which the new situation may also reflect, to some degree, a kind of trade-off of supports between technocrats and nontechnocrats concerning demands that are dear to each (see Ben-Rafael 1997; Topel 2000).

In Conclusion

The growth of technocratic hegemony in the kibbutz throws a new light on both the nature of the kibbutz's present-day transformation and the general meaning of the concept of "technocracy." "Technocratization" consists in the establishment of the hegemony of a technocratic perspective, and it is this process that is illustrated by the development of kibbutzim in the recent decade and a half. This happened in the kibbutz in the wake of a far-reaching political and economic crisis, under the guidance of managers, senior administrators, and experts who, in an egalitarian setting like the kibbutz, had been for years relatively deprived in comparison with their peers on the outside, and in spite of the undeniable power and prestige they had gradually gained over the veteran economic elite within their communities. What we have seen here is that conditions of crisis and the sense of liminality—of being on the edge of something not yet clarified—which they bring about, as well as the increased dependency of the community on the technocrats' know-how, were exploited by the latter to strengthen their positions and privileges. This was also possible because kibbutzniks in general had no more confidence in the beliefs that had for long cemented the collective. What eases, then, their acceptance of the leadership of the technocrats is that this leadership is inherently limited to specific areas and does not oppose, and in fact encourages, a liberalization of the social order of the kibbutz.

In brief, the contemporary kibbutz appears to be one more example of the universal contemporary experience of fractal processes (Young 1991), that is, the erosion of a group's or a community's uniqueness and particularity. This is not to say that the kibbutz's future is of no interest anymore. Illustrating how socialism joins up with capitalism, after decades of competition, the interesting question that concerns the kibbutz now is how far and to what degree is the convergence going to go. Will "something" remain that will still remind us that the kibbutz was long committed to egalitarian sharing, collective entrepreneurship, and a sense of enrollment on behalf of a national project? Will "something" remain to make this new technocratic social order carry a message of a universal significance?

The kibbutz experience was associated in the past with a completely different kind of universal message, and it is then that it achieved its greatest impact on society. Its role, however, declined slowly under the influence of capitalism, to a point where, for some time, the kibbutz still seemed to constitute a kind of "natural reserve." Yet, since the mid-1980s, the kibbutz has "caught up" with the "delay" in its decline and now has passed even the general neoliberal and technocratic development of the Israeli society, at least in some respects. This, to be sure, has taken place at the cost of a transformation of values and outlooks that were uniquely its own, and the adoption of attitudes and reference points that now stem from its cultural environment.

Yet the kibbutz still manifests a determination to look for alternate courses of collective action in hostile circumstances, rather than accepting mere disbandment. This search yields new models of kibbutz (or kibbutz-like) endeavors that diversify the kibbutz reality as a whole. Hence, today's kibbutzim constitute a multifaceted reality that is unified, if not by common "solutions" to their problems, at least by a shared confrontation of "what was once a kibbutz" with the imperatives of a new era.

NOTES

1. The kibbutz population includes inhabitants with diverse statuses. The permanent population includes members, their children, members' parents that came from the outside, and candidates. The nonpermanent population includes hired workers, students, voluntaries, new immigrants in special transitory frameworks, and, in the last years, people who rent an apartment in the kibbutz. The nonpermanent population accounts for about 15 percent in most kibbutzim, but it may reach as high as 40 percent in some settlements.

2. The agricultural area varies from a few thousand acres to ten thousand and more, depending on the geographic zone of the specific kibbutz. The land belongs to the National/Jewish Fund and is not the kibbutz's direct property.

3. In 2001, the two former large federations already existed, and, alongside them, the unified institutions of the new movement, called "the Kibbutz Movement." Most departments and funds are still separate. It is remarkable that, in the political sphere, each group of kibbutz

members remains affiliated with different parties—the Labor Party for the Takam and Meretz for the Kibbutz Artzi.

4. The kibbutz system of communal government tends to moderate the concentration of power through public nomination or election of members to rotating managerial positions. In a typical kibbutz one finds 5 to 10 rotating positions and 8 to 18 public committees with 3 to 7 members each.

5. Although, already in the 1970s, pressures from the membership—and especially from women—seriously reduced the role of the peer-group house in most kibbutzim, children's night was moved from the collective children's house to the parents' private apartments. This change confirmed, already at this stage, the strength of members' aspirations toward personal autonomy in a context where the family was achieving more and more power in the community.

6. Kibbutz education did not introduce any form of selection and refrained from examinations and grades. It is only in the terminal class of senior high school that a special and optional framework prepared students for the national graduation exams.

7. Such as in the distribution of land and water quotas by national institutions.

8. The Left's own regime depended on floating votes that came from the Right and not from the traditional Left leaning sectors whose support was taken for granted.

9. According to the State Comptroller's 1993 Annual Report.

10. Although it was not a mass exodus, the departure of youngsters dramatically changed the age structure of many kibbutzim: in 1989 the median age was 25.8; by 1999 it was of 28.9 (Pavin 2001).

11. The youth movements of today do not represent any prospect of filling up the demographic gap either. The popularity of the youth movement in Israel is now at its lowest, and they try to strengthen their impact by committing themselves to new (environmental, social, or cultural) challenges that share little with the kibbutz experience and interests.

12. At this respect, we followed the "cast-cluster" qualitative methodology (see McClintock, Brannon, and Maynard-Moody 1979; Yin 1994).

13. The informants were carefully selected and prepared for their job by the researchers. In the first steps they were instructed and accompanied in the selection of items and the work of reporting. An extended study of the informants' role and the effect of their identity has been published elsewhere (Topel 1997).

14. In the study of this dimension, we used the methodology of in-depth active interviews (see Holstein and Gubrium 1995) and encountered face-to-face tens of members of eight kibbutzim, drawn from—and representative of—the thirty-four kibbutzim of the first sample.

15. The principal figure had been successively, before his election to the function of secretary-general of the Takam, the economic director of his kibbutz, the director of his kibbutz's factory, and the general director of one of the largest regional corporations of the kibbutz movement.

REFERENCES

Ben-Rafael, Eliezer. 1988. *Status, Power and Conflict in the Kibbutz.* Aldershot, U.K.: Gower.

———. 1997. *Crisis and Transformation.* Albany, State University of New York Press.

Buber, Martin. 1983. "An Experiment That Did Not Fail." In *The Sociology of the Kibbutz,* ed. Ernest Krausz, 25–36. New Brunswick, N.J.: Transaction.

Burnham, James. 1941. *The Managerial Revolution—What Is Happening in the World.* New York: Day.

Dahrendof, Ralf S. 1965. *Class and Class Conflict in Industrial Society.* Stanford, California: Stanford University.

Dar, Yechezkel. 1992. "Changes in the Equity Basis for the Evaluation of the Work in the Kibbutz." In *Equality and Its Limits. Kibbutz: Continuity and Change,* ed. Ben-Rafael Eliezer and Zeev Soker, 37–41. Tel-Aviv: The Open University.

Djilas, Milovan. 1957. *The New Class.* New York: Praeger.

Etzioni, Amitai. 1980. *The Organizational Structure of the Kibbutz.* New York: Arno.

Helman, Amir. 1987. "The Development of the Professional Managers in the Kibbutz." *Economic Quarterly* 131 (2): 1031–39 (Hebrew).

Holstein, James A., and Jaber F. Gubrium. 1995. *The Active Interview.* Thousand Oaks, Calif.: Sage.

Maxwell, Joseph A. 1996. *Qualitative Research Design—An Interactive Approach.* Thousand Oaks, Calif.: Sage.

McClintock, Cynthia, D. Brannon, and S. Maynard-Moody. 1979. "Applying the Logic of Sample Surveys to Qualitative Case Studies: The Case Cluster Method." *Administrative Science Quarterly* 24 (4): 612–29.

Pavin, Abraham. 2001. *The Kibbutz Movement—Facts and Figures No. 6.* Ramat Efal: Yad-Tabenkin (Hebrew).

Shapira, Reuben. 1978/79. "Anatomy of Technostructure—The Case of an Inter-Kibbutz Regional Organization." *Hakibbutz,* 6–7: 276–302 (Hebrew).

Sheaffer, Zecharia. 1992. "Aspects of Organizational Decline and Crisis: The Multi-Dimensional Crisis in the United Kibbutz Movement." Ph.D. dissertation, University of Waikato, New Zealand. State Comptroller Report. 1993. Jerusalem (Hebrew).

Topel, Menachem. 1979. "To Build and Be Built—Power Elite in an Egalitarian Community." M.A. dissertation, Tel Aviv University.

———. 1985. *A Look at the Regional Cooperatives.* Ramat Efal: Yad-Tabenkin (Hebrew).

———. 1990. *Size and Economic Efficiency in Rural Cooperatives.* Ramat Efal: Yad-Tabenkin (Hebrew).

———. 1997. "Loyalty Dilemmas of Referents." *Shorashim* 10:46–58 (Hebrew).

———. 2000. *Technocrats as Agents of Change in an Egalitarian Society,* Tel-Aviv University, 2000, (Hebrew).

Trotzky, Leon. 1932. *What Next? Vital Questions for the German Proletariat.* New York: Pioneer.

Weber, Uri. 1992. *To Be Renewed—The Kibbutz in Front of His Future.* Tel Aviv: Hakibbutz Hameuchad Pub.

Weintraub, Dov, Moshe Lisak, and Yael Azmon. 1969. *Moshava, Kibbutz and Moshav.* Ithaca and London: Cornell University Press.

Yin, Robert K. 1994. *Case Study Research—Design and Methods.* Thousand Oaks, Calif.: Sage.

Young, T. R. 1991. "Chaos and Social Change: Metaphysics of the Postmodern." *The Social Sciences Journal* 28 (3): 289–305.

CHAPTER SEVEN

Elections and Voting Patterns

ও

ASHER ARIAN

The distribution of political power in Israel, as in every other democracy, is determined by the electoral rules employed, by the party system, and by the behavior of the voters.

The Electoral System

Israel adopted a parliamentary, fixed-list, proportional representation system upon gaining independence. This meant that the parliament would be selected by allocating seats to the winning political parties proportional to the number of votes they won, that the parties would construct the list of candidates, and that the prime minister would be selected by the parliament. This was a version of a familiar European form of parliamentary democracy. The entire country was a single voting district, so the size of the party delegations in the 120-seat Knesset (parliament) closely adhered to the distribution of the vote.

In 1992, the Basic Law: Government was changed to allow for the direct election of the prime minister. This was a unique and problematic Israeli invention combining aspects of the parliamentary system with presidential attributes. This method was legislated in 1992 and first employed in 1996. It was brought about by the coalition maneuvering and political conniving known as the "dirty business"—a 1990 effort by Shimon Peres, then Foreign Minister in Yitzhak Shamir's national unity government, to have himself selected prime minister by a majority of the Knesset. The effort failed, but a bizarre chapter in Israeli political history was being written and three elections were held under the new rules, the elections of 1996, 1999, and 2001.

Under the old regime, the selection of the prime minister depended on the strength of the parties in the Knesset. The president of the State, after consulting with leaders of the parties, asked a member of Knesset, usually the leader of the largest party, to attempt to form a governing coalition. The party leader was granted twenty-one days (with a possible extension of twenty-one additional days) to form a coalition, present it to the Knesset, announce its general policy outlines, and gain the Knesset's vote of confidence. If the attempt to form a coalition failed, the president appointed another candidate after consulting once again with the leaders of the parties.

Under the direct election system, both the prime minister and the Knesset were elected simultaneously. The system introduced a "balance of terror" between the Knesset and the prime minister since each could dismiss the other. The Knesset could dismiss the prime minister with a no-confidence vote of at least 61 Knesset members, or by not approving the annual budget within three months of its submission. In such cases, new elections for both prime minister and the Knesset were to be held. The Knesset could dismiss the prime minister yet remain in power if a vote of no confidence were passed by 80 or more Knesset members (at least two-thirds of the 120-member house). Were the prime minister to resign, or cease to be a Knesset member, become incapacitated, or be impeached for a criminal offense, "special elections" for the prime minister were to be held without necessitating the election of a new Knesset.

The prime minister could dissolve the Knesset with the concurrence of the president of Israel, but in that case both prime minister and Knesset would stand for election immediately. The cabinet as a collective entity could not dissolve itself and thereby dissolve the Knesset, so the term of the cabinet, and in fact its very existence, was contingent upon the prime minister.

This electoral law transformed the regime into a unique, albeit problematic, combination of a parliamentary system with presidential attributes. Both the prime minister and the Knesset were elected by the voters for a tenure of four years. A prime minister who served seven consecutive years could not run for re-election, but there was no term limit on Knesset membership.

This new constitutional order proved even less stable than the previous one and did not end the maneuvering of political parties for symbolic, political, and financial payoffs. It encouraged the candidates for prime minister to distance themselves from their parties and to ignore the will of the Knesset. Both Benjamin Netanyahu and Ehud Barak fell victim to the new system's pitfalls and neither finished their terms in office.

After the election of Ariel Sharon in the 2001 election and before his National Unity government took office, the provisions for the direct election of the prime minister were repealed and Israel returned to the previous method of selecting its prime minister. The constructive vote of confidence was introduced whereby the Knesset would have to select a replacement for the prime minister if it wanted to vote no confidence in the current prime minister and remove him from office (Arian, Nachmias, and Amir, 2001).

The Party System

The basic division of the Israeli party system, easily understood in terms of the 2001 elections, is between Likud (Ariel Sharon was its candidate for prime minister) and Labor (Ehud Barak was its candidate). These two Zionist parties represented the major divisions in the system in terms of foreign and defense policies, with Likud more militant and "Right" and Labor more conciliatory and "Left." These two parties have been the major building blocks of the system, and around them the political spectrum has been focused. Since the 1950s these parties, or portions of them that have run separately, won the most and the second most votes (see Table 1). Clustering around them are other parties of the Right and the Left, respectively; these other parties may once have been part of one of the bigger parties, or might align with one of them in the future. Add to these two clusters the group of Jewish religious parties and the Arab parties and the picture is complete except for loose odds and ends of some smaller parties (see Table 2 for election results).

Israel's political history and the development of its party system can be divided into three periods. The first period was of independence and State consolidation, dominated by Labor, from the mid 1930s, through the Six Day War of 1967, and until after the Yom Kippur war of 1973. The second period was of competition between Likud and Labor, highlighted by Likud's first ascension to power in 1977 in which the country struggled to extricate itself from the fruits of the victory of the 1967 war. The third period featured the direct election of the prime minister; both Likud and Labor shrunk in size as prime ministers tried to fashion coalitions that could deal with the consequences of the Oslo Accords of 1993, which began the process of seeking accommodation with the Palestinians.

These three periods are evident when considering the share of the two biggest parties in the 120-seat Knesset as shown in Figure 1. In the initial period Labor (Mapai) was clearly dominant without any effective competition. In the second period of competition between the two big parties they together won a large share of the total vote. In the third period the appeal of the two traditionally big parties receded, and by 1999 the combined size of the two parties was as low as it had been in the early years of statehood. This indicated the success of sectarian politics such the non-Zionist ultra-Orthodox Shas, two parties appealing to Russian immigrants, and Arab parties.

The two major policy breakthroughs (the Likud's 1978 peace with Egypt and Labor's 1993 accord with the PLO) came a year after the election in which the gap between the two parties increased. The parties in government that made the breakthroughs were big winners in the elections previous to the change in pol-

Table 1. Share of 120-Member Knesset by Two Largest Parties, 1949–96

Election Year	Biggest Winner	Second Biggest Winner	Total Seats	Competitiveness Ratio[1]
1949	Mapai: 46	Mapam: 19	65	.41
1951	Mapai: 45	Liberal: 20	65	.44
1955	Mapai: 40	Herut: 15	55	.38
1959	Mapai: 47	Herut: 17	64	.36
1961	Mapai: 42	Herut: 17	59	.40
		Liberal: 17		
1965	Alignment[2]: 45	Gahal[3]: 26	71	.58
1969	Alignment[4]: 56	Gahal[c]: 26	82	.46
1973	Alignment[d]: 51	Likud[e]: 39	90	.76
1977	Likud[5]: 43	Alignment[d]: 32	75	.74
1981	Likud[e]: 48	Alignment[d]: 47	95	.98
1984	Alignment[d]: 44	Likud[e]: 41	85	.93
1988	Likud: 40	Labor: 39	79	.98
1992	Labor: 44	Likud: 32	72	.73
1996	Labor: 34	Likud[6]: 32	66	.94
1999	One Israel[7]: 26	Likud: 19	45	.73
PM 1996	Netanyahu: 50.5%	Peres: 49.5%	100%	.98
PM 1999	Barak: 56.1%	Netanyahu: 43.9%	100%	.79
PM 2001	Sharon: 62.4%	Barak: 37.6%	100%	.60

[1]Competitiveness ratio = second biggest winner/biggest winner.
[2]Mapai and Ahdut Haavoda.
[3]Herut and Liberals.
[4]Labor and Mapam.
[5]Herut, Liberals, and others.
[6]Likud-Gesher-Tzomet.
[7]Labor-Gesher-Meimad.
[c,d,e]See notes, Table 2.

icy, but winners only in a relative sense. They were able to shift policy not because they were relatively strong, but rather because the second party was relatively weak.

Labor's uninterrupted reign ended in 1977, after which the Likud and Labor competed for power. The Likud emerged as the largest party in 1977, grew more in 1981, and then began a downward trend. Labor peaked in 1969; its reemergence in 1992 was only relative to the poor showing of Likud that year. In the period of dominance the system was one-sided; the period of competition saw a heightening of the concentration of the vote at first and then the reemergence of smaller parties.

Table 2. Knesset Election Results (120 Seats)

Election Year	1949	1951	1955	1959	1961	1965
Participation rate (%)	86.9	75.1	82.8	81.6	81.6	83.0
Labor and Left						
Mapai[a]	46	45	40	47	42	45
Ahdut Haavoda[b]	10	7	8			
Rafi[c]						10
Mapam[d]	19	15	9	9	9	8
DMC/Shinui[e]						
CRM/Meretz[f]						
Arab lists	2	1	4	5	4	4
Communist	4	5	6	3	5	4
Likud and Right						
Independent Liberals[g]	5	4	5	6	—	5
Liberals[h]	7	20	13	8	17	
Herut[i]	14	8	15	17	17	26
Tehiya/Tzomet[j]						
Moledet/Kach[k]						
Religious						
NRP		10	11	12	12	11
Aguda parties[l]	16	5	6	6	6	6
Shas						
Others	7	7	1			1

[a] Joined with Ahdut Haavoda in 1965 and the other Labor parties in 1969.

[b] See note a.

[c] Ben-Gurion's party; joined the Labor Alignment in 1969 minus the State List.

[d] Ahdut Haavoda included in Mapam in 1949 and 1951; Mapam included in Labor-Mapam Alignment between 1969 and 1988; Mapam included in Meretz in 1992 and 1996.

[e] DMC in 1977; Shinui between 1981 and 1988.

[f] Meretz in 1992 and 1996 made up of CRM, Mapam, and Shinui.

[g] Included in Liberal party in 1961 and independent again since 1965; in 1984, part of Labor-Mapam Alignment.

[h] Until 1959 known as General Zionists, joined Herut to form Gahal in 1965, and part of the Likud in 1973.

[i] Jointly with the Liberals since 1965 and part of the Likud in 1973.

1969	1973	1977	1981	1984	1988	1992	1996	1999
81.7	78.6	79.2	78.5	79.8	79.7	77.4	79.3	78.7
56	51	32	47	44	39	44	34	26
					3			
		15	2	3	2			6
	3	1	1	3	5	12	9	10
4	3	1		2	2	2	4	7
4	5	5	4	4	4	3	5	3
4	4	1	—	—	—			
26	39	43	48	41	40	32	32	19
			3	5	5	8		
				1	2	3	2	4
12	10	12	6	4	5	6	9	5
6	5	5	4	8	7	4	4	5
				4	6	6	10	17
8[m]	3	5[n]	5[o]	5[p]	—	—	11[q]	18[l]

[j] Tehiya in 1981 and 1984; in 1988, 3 seats for Tehiya, 2 for Tzomet; Tzomet in 1992; in 1996 Tzomet part of the Likud.

[k] Kach in 1984, since 1988 Moledet.

[l] Poalei Agudat Israel, Agudat Israel, and Degel Hatorah.

[m] Includes the State List (4 members), the Free Center (2 members), and Haolam Haze (2 members). The first two joined Herut and the Liberals in 1973.

[n] Includes Shlomzion (2 members), which joined the Likud after the elections, Shelli (2 members), and Flatto Sharon (1 member).

[o] Includes Tami (3 members), and Telem (2 members).

[p] Including Yahad (3 members), Tami (1 member), and Ometz (1 member).

[q] Including Israel Aliya (7 members) and the Third Way (4 members).

[l] Including Israel Aliya (6 members), Israel Beiteinu (4 members), One Nation (2 members), and the Center Party (6 members).

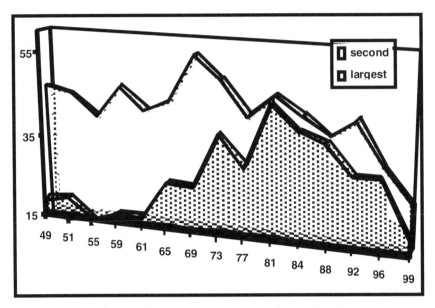

Figure 1. The Share of the Two Biggest Parties in the 120-Seat Knesset, 1949–99

Ariel Sharon won the largest victory in Israel's electoral history in the special election for prime minister in 2001 by garnering an unprecedented 62.4 percent of the ballots cast. His unprecedented achievement was somewhat lessened because never before had there been a special election for the prime minister, and never had the participation rate been as low as it was that year. In fact, Sharon received fewer votes than Ehud Barak had in his then-unprecedented victory over Benjamin Netanyahu in 1999 (see Table 3). Barak in 1999 won almost 100,000 votes more than Sharon did in 2001, even though Barak won only 56.1 percent of the vote compared to Sharon's 62.4. The obvious difference between the two elections was in the voting rate. In 1999, it was 78.7 percent compared to 62.3 percent in 2001. And most of those who did not vote in 2001 had voted for Barak in 1999. This was enough to afford Sharon his unprecedented victory.

Voting Participation

Voting turnout in Israel has always been high; about 80 percent of the eligible voters voluntarily cast ballots on voting day. Absentee balloting is not available to the public, although special arrangements are made for persons serving with the Israel Defense Forces on election day, for those in official positions abroad and their families, for persons hospitalized on election day, for sailors working on Israeli flagships, and for prisoners.

Table 3. Results of Prime Minister Elections, 1996–2001

	Valid Votes	% of Valid Votes
2001		
Ariel Sharon	1,698,077	62.4
Ehud Barak	1,023,944	37.6
1999		
Ehud Barak	1,791,020	56.1
Benjamin Netanyahu	1,402,474	43.9
1996		
Benjamin Netanyahu	1,501,023	50.5
Shimon Peres	1,471,566	49.5

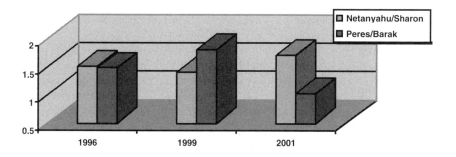

Year	Number of Eligible Voters	Total Ballots	Invalid Ballots	Valid Votes	Voter Turnout
2001	4,504,769	2,805,938	83,917	2,722,021	62.3%
1999	4,285,428	3,373,748	179,458	3,193,494	78.7%
1996	3,933,250	3,121,270	148,681	2,972,589	79.3%

The highest rate of participation in Knesset elections was in 1949, in which 86.9 percent of the eligible population voted, and the lowest rate was in 1951, with only 75.1 percent participation. The number of eligible voters between the two elections increased by 70 percent as a result of large-scale immigration; the dislocation as a result of this immigration probably explains the lower participation rate. By 1955 the rate was back up to 82.8 percent.

Non-Jews had high rates of participation in elections until the special election for prime minister in 2001. In general, their rates were high; in 1996, for example, the rate of voting among non-Jews was 77.6 percent, almost equal to the rate for Jews that year (79.3 percent). There were periods in which the non-

Jewish participation rate was slightly lower, as in the 1981 elections (69.7 percent). But the low point of 2001 was unusual: in the special election for the prime minister it was only 19 percent. Anger at the shooting deaths by the police of thirteen Israeli Arabs, alienation, disillusion with the two candidates (Barak and Sharon), distrust of the system, and the fact that no elections for the Knesset took place all contributed to bringing the rate down to this unusual low.

The motivation for nonvoting in Jewish and Arab sectors is different. Few Jews abstain for political reasons; their reasons are generally technical in nature. The most important reason among Jews has to do with the way in which the rate of voting is calculated. It is based on the population registry, and those out of the country on election day are counted among those who did not vote. The incidence of leaving the country (sometimes for years) is more common among Jews than non-Jews, and this practice deflates the rate of Jewish voting. Other technical reasons include illness, improper registration, or lack of identification.

Explaining the Vote

Patterns of support for the major political groups have been quite constant. Political change came about because the strength of support of various groups has shifted from time to time. The dominant Mapai, now Labor, found support among all groups, but especially among those who identified with the epoch in which the party rose to its peak and with the epoch's dominant values. The highlight of Mapai's (Labor's) achievements was the gaining of independence. Achieving independence accented all the projects undertaken by the Jews in Eretz Israel—immigration, building the land, security. After the founding of the State, these undertakings were continued, sometimes within different organizational settings and institutional arrangements, but with much of the same symbolism and ideological justification. One who lived through the independence epoch in Israel was more likely to identify with the dominant party. In the process of having party and movement values permeate the society, the distinction between party and state was often blurred. Achievements of state accrued to the benefit of the party. Jews who immigrated to Israel before independence and immediately thereafter continued their heavy support of Labor. The rate fell off for those who immigrated after 1955, and for Israeli-born voters.

Much of the program and appeal of the dominant Labor party at the time of independence must be seen in light of the social and political realities that the Labor leadership knew in Eastern Europe in the first decades of the twentieth century. The precarious position of the Jews, the restrictions on economic and political activity, the unbalanced nature of their occupations, the spread of rationalist feeling, the undermining of traditional religious belief and behavior—

all these things led to the creation of the socialist-Zionist experiment. The Labor leadership, almost exclusively of Eastern European origin, developed a party and an ideology that answered the needs of the nation as they saw them and experienced them.

The Likud saw the problems of the country from a different ideological perspective and consequently drew its support from different groups. Labor was notably successful among earlier immigrants and among those born in Europe and America. Likud appealed more to the native-born than to any immigrant group, and more to the Asian- or African-born than to the European- or American-born. The symbols Labor used to evoke the epoch of independence and nation building were more effective among the old than the young, more effective among those who came before independence than among those who came after independence or were born in Israel, and more effective among those born in Europe than those born in Asia or Africa.

The Likud, in opposition until 1977, gave the appearance of being broadly based in its electoral support (as was the Labor-Mapam Alignment) because it blended the appeals of its two major components, the right-wing nationalistic Herut movement and the bourgeois Liberal party. But much of this spread was an artifact of the difference between the groups that supported Herut and the Liberals. Herut was a party that appealed disproportionately to the lower-class and to lower-middle-class workers, and to Israelis born in Asia or Africa, although obviously many Ashkenazim also supported it. The Liberals, on the other hand, were a bourgeois party that received most of its support from middle-class and upper-middle-class merchants and businessmen. Since the followers of the Liberal party had higher levels of education than did supporters of Herut, the spread evident for the Likud was a balancing of two counter tendencies; thus it is misleading to read into the data that the Likud before 1977 was beginning to generate the appeal characteristic of a dominant party.

The support of the Likud came heavily from the young, from native Israelis, from Israelis of Asian or African background, and from those with lower education and income levels. Undeniably, many of these cleavages overlapped with strong differences in political opinion and religious observance. To give but one example, the same groups that tended to support the Likud tended to have hawkish opinions on foreign and defense policy. Those who were older, who had more education, who came from a European background, and who supported Labor tended to hold more conciliatory views.

The religious parties generally received about 15 percent of the vote, although in 1999 it shot up to more than 20 percent, and they were regular coalition partners in the majority of governments, whether headed by Labor or Likud. Their support came from traditional Jews from Asian or African backgrounds with low income and low education levels; from highly educated intellectuals from European origins; and from Israeli-born and educated youth imbued with religious ideals through formal schooling in the State-supported religious schools. The National Religious Party (NRP) lost votes in 1988 to the Likud for ideological reasons and to Shas for ethnic ones.

On the whole, the religious parties were relatively more successful among those with lower levels of education. The picture was more complex when support for the religious parties was considered in the light of both education and place of origin. Among the European- or American-born, support for religious parties tended to decrease with educational attainment. The Israeli-born provided the opposite picture, with religious party support increasing with additional education. In the 1980s and 1990s, Shas emerged as the major religious party. A Sephardi ultra-Orthodox party, it won its major support from traditionalists with lower incomes and lower levels of education who were from an Asian or African background. By 1999 Shas was almost as successful as Likud in competing for the votes of lower-class Sephardi voters.

Issue Voting and Demography

Issue voting grew dramatically in Israel in the 1980s and 1990s, especially regarding the divisive issue of the future of the territories, while the influence of social allegiance on voting patterns remained constant. Social and economic differences have traditionally been considered good predictors of voting behavior, although there has been a general decline in the importance of such cleavages throughout the Western world, and a simultaneous increase in issue voting (Dalton 1996; Bartolini and Mair 1990; Franklin, Mackie and Valen 1992). As the electoral importance of the territories issue grew, the role of demographic factors either remained stable or receded (Shamir 1986).

The correlations in Table 4 provide important clues as to the nature of partisanship in Israel. The correlations are between the Labor/Likud vote and various demographic and issue variables for the 1969–99 period, and the prime minister vote between 1996 and 2001 (Shamir and Arian 1999).

Sociodemographic Differences

Age has had a consistent relationship with vote, with the young somewhat more likely to vote Likud, and the old, Labor. This relationship has been generally regarded as indicating generational rather than life-cycle effects (Abramson 1989). This correlation peaked in 1973 and 1977 and reached its nadir in 1992. The 1977 reversal was led by the young: youth abandoned Labor for the promises of the

Likud or the Democratic Movement for Change (DMC). The Likud, always strongest among this group compared to other age cohorts, won 36 percent support in 1969 compared to 44 percent in 1973 and 51 percent in 1977 and 1981. The Labor-Mapam Alignment lost half its support in this youngest age group between 1973 and 1977, the same amount of support that the DMC attracted. The Alignment more clearly than ever became the party of the older, more conservative voter; the Likud, the choice of the young, even though the DMC was a party of young adults. In 1992, both the young and the old forsook the Likud; young voters were more attracted by the parties further to the right, but Labor was more successful than in the past in attracting voters across generations.

It was in the youngest voting group that the significant change came about. A tantalizing change emerged in the 1988 data, with Labor and Likud getting almost the same percentage of support among first-time voters. This hinted at a changing pattern over the last two decades in which the young chose the Likud, but Labor's optimism was only partially justified, since young voters in 1988 and 1992 tended to support parties of the extreme Left and the extreme Right as well as Labor and Likud. Labor and Rabin won in 1992 by being able to attract a substantial part of the young vote, while the Likud lost a sizable portion of it.

In 1996, first-time voters split in favor of Netanyahu at about a 3:2 rate despite the impression that the Rabin assassination had galvanized the young generation on Labor's behalf. The assassination did have the effect of mobilizing emotional support for Labor among the young, but especially among those first-time voters who would have supported Labor anyway. Although much was made of the "candles generation" of young people supporting Peres while grieving for the slain Rabin in 1996, there was no evidence that this promise materialized in the elections.

Voters under thirty split evenly between Netanyahu and Barak in 1999 but voters older than sixty preferred Barak. In the Sharon landslide of 2001, these patterns were almost reversed. Almost three in four voters under thirty supported Sharon while Sharon and Barak split the vote of those over sixty about equally.

Israeli surveys indicate that gender has never been related to electoral choice voting to a statistically significant extent.

Class differences have mattered to a degree, although correlations have been neither consistent nor strong (cf. Shalev 2002). There was usually no relationship between the Likud-Labor vote and income, but the income variable is not the best measure of class in Israel, as it is the kind of topic an Israeli is unlikely to discuss in an open manner with a stranger in an interviewer. Two other measures of class—living density (the number of persons per room) and education—tell a different story.

Class differences appeared with the 1977 reversal, with lower-class voters

Table 4. Correlations[1] Between Likud and Labor, Demographics and Issues,[2]
1969–2001

Survey[3] (N)		Demography				
	Age	Gender	Density	Education	Income	
10/69 (1017)	.17	(.05)	.07	(.00)	(−.04)	
5/73 (1062)	.27	(.01)	.15	(−.02)	(.01)	
3/77 (620)	.29	(−.03)	.18	(.01)	(.06)	
3/81 (798)	.13	(.06)	.07	.09	(.00)	
7/84 (807)	.20	(−.03)	.25	.22	.08	
10/88 (532)	.16	(.04)	.09	.15	(.01)	
6/92 (657)	.10	(.07)	.13	.24	(−.02)	
5/96 (798)	.13	(.04)	.18	.21	.12	
5/99 (599)	.11	(.07)	.19	.14	(.05)	
PM96 (1,113)	.09	(.06)	.20	.18	.12	
PM99 (898)	.07	(.04)	.21	.11	.08	
PM01 (956)	.16	(−.02)	.24	.12	(−.06)	

[1] Pearson correlations, significant above the .05 level, except for those in parentheses.
[2] The coding for these correlations was Likud = 1, Labor = 2; Netanyahu = 1, Peres/Barak = 2. Low scores for the other variables indicate young age, female, high density, low education, low income, high religiosity, Sephardi, unwillingness to concede territories for peace, favoring capitalism over socialism, and favoring public life in accordance with Jewish religious law, respectively.
[3] Preelection surveys of Jewish population used. In years for which multiple surveys were available, the one that contained the most variables used in the table was chosen.
[4] Before 1984, a question concerning the maximum amount of territory Israel should give up in order to achieve a peace

abandoning Labor in favor of the Likud. Education gained in importance after 1981, with the return to Labor of more highly educated voters who had deserted for the DMC in 1977. This process of class stratification continued in the 1980s and was still in evidence in 1992, although over time the education variable was stronger than the living density indicator. But based on the inconsistent and not too strong correlations of the vote with class indicators, combined with the pattern of correlations between the vote and socialist versus capitalistic views, the class cleavage does not seem to be the driving force behind electoral choice and change in Israel. Note that in 1996 and 1992 there is virtually no relationship between voters' preferences as to the structure of the economy and their vote, and in 1977 the correlation was of the same magnitude as throughout the 1970s.

		Issues		
Religion	Ethnicity	No terr. for peace[4]	Capitalism/ State/Socialism[5]	Religion[6]
.08	.13	.15	.23	.12
(.04)	.13	.23	.17	—[7]
.18	.32	.28	.22	.17
.19	.23	.27	.16	.20
.37	.53	.57	.32	g
.27	.27	.61	.30	.24
.40	.35	.57	(.05)	.29
.36	.30	.65	(.07)	.35
.33	.35	.67	.17	.40
.44	.28	.63	(.08)	.41
.37	.24	.67	.21	.40
.35	.25	g	.08	.35

settlement. In 1984 and after, constructed from two questions, the first asking preference between return of territories for peace, annexation, or status quo, and a follow-up question forcing a choice of those who chose the "status quo" option. In 1996 and 1999 a 7-point answer was used.

[5] The question asked about preference for the socialist or capitalist approach.

The 1973 question asked if the Histadrut labor union should both own industries and represent workers.

[6] The question asked whether the government should see to it that public life in Israel be conducted according to the Jewish religious tradition.

[7] Not asked.

Moreover, the responses to this question are to be seen more as an indicator of whether or not a voter belongs to the camp of socialism-Zionism socially, politically, or culturally, rather than from ideological commitment. And class is not the most potent correlate of the vote in Israel.

Religious and Ethnic Profiles

Religion and ethnicity were strongly correlated with the vote decision. For both of them the critical election year was 1977. Before that year, both dimensions barely distinguished Labor voters from Likud voters. Religion (measured by extent of religious observance) gained in importance over time, reaching an all-time high in the 1992 election and in the vote for prime minister in 1996. The relationship between ethnicity and the vote reached its highest point in the 1984 election, and has receded since.

The ethnic theme has changed over time as the proportions of the groups in the electorate have changed. In 1977, the majority of the electorate was Ashkenazim (53 percent), 43 percent were Sephardim, and 4 percent were Israeli-born with fathers also born in Israel. In the 1988 election, for the first time the Jews of Sephardi background outnumbered the Jews of Ashkenazi background in the electorate. In 1992, following the mostly Ashkenazi mass immigration from the former Soviet Union (FSU), the proportions were 48 percent Ashkenazim, 44 percent Sephardim, and 8 percent Israeli-born whose fathers were also born in Israel. By 1996 the Ashkenazim had grown to 50 percent, the Sephardim had gone down to 39 percent, and the Israeli-born with fathers born in Israel had grown to 11 percent. The electoral impact of the immigrants from the FSU has been enormous. They were important forces in the three turnovers in the 1990s, casting a protest vote against the incumbent in each election and bringing about the election of Rabin, Netanyahu, and Barak.

The relationship between voting and origin is not a new one in Israeli politics. In the 1948–77 period of Labor dominance, Labor regularly won support from most groups in the society. This was especially true of new immigrants, who were often in awe of the "miracle" that had returned them to the land of their fathers. These immigrants were dependent on the bureaucracies of the establishment for the whole gamut of economic, educational, health, social, and cultural needs. An increasingly large share of the electorate was of Sephardi origin, and Mapai maintained its dominant role as the largest plurality party and the leader of every government coalition. More than that, attempts to appeal to the Sephardi population at election time by lists set up by Sephardim largely failed. It was only before the mass immigration of the early 1950s that any lists manifestly linking themselves with Sephardim and Yemenites achieved representation in the Knesset.

The shift away from Labor by the Sephardim was gradual. In the 1970s the tendency became more pronounced, beyond the general trend of the Likud's growth and of Labor's decline. Ethnic voting among the Israeli public continues: ethnicity predicts the vote for both the Likud and the Alignment. In 1984 the preference ratio for the two parties among each ethnic group was about 3 to 1, with the Sephardim preferring the Likud, and the Ashkenazim the Alignment. In 1988 and 1992, the preference ratio declined, as smaller parties of the left and right extremes won more of the Ashkenazi and Sephardi votes, respectively. In 1996, both parties performed poorly, but the respective preference of the ethnic groups persisted.

The ethnic cleavage manifested itself in voting behavior dramatically in the

1977 election when many voters abandoned their long-standing practice of supporting Labor. But they shifted largely along ethnic lines. Sephardim gravitated to the Likud, and Ashkenazim to the DMC. These two defections so weakened Labor that the Likud could take over the reins of power, resulting in the beginning of the Likud era of Israeli politics. In 1981 and 1984 many of the Ashkenazim were back with Labor. The campaigns were especially bitter and focused on the feelings of having been exploited by Labor felt by many Sephardim. The ethnic vote was most pronounced in the 1984 elections, although the 1981 election campaign was most taken up with the ethnic cleavage.

The fortunes of the Likud and Labor were transferred to the second generation as well. The Likud generally retained the loyalties of the Sephardim born in Israel, while Labor did better among Ashkenazim who immigrated and among their Israeli-born children. The Likud in the 1980s gained most among the youngest and fastest-growing groups; the Alignment, losing support within all groups over time, did best in the group that was oldest and was shrinking rapidly.

In the elections of the 1980s the term "ethnic voting" was used often. It was supposed to portray the support of Jews from Asia and Africa and their children for the Likud. The fact was that the Alignment was closer to being an "ethnic party" in this sense than the Likud was. About two-thirds of Labor's voters were Ashkenazim, and a similar percentage of the Likud voters were Sephardim. This had not always been the case. In the past the bulk of both the Likud's and Labor's support came from Ashkenazim; after all, the Ashkenazim constituted a majority of the electorate. Polls going back to the late 1960s indicate that then, too, about two-thirds of the Alignment vote was from Ashkenazim, even though Sephardim also often voted for the Alignment. In the late 1960s both parties were predominantly Ashkenazi; by 1981 the Alignment had stayed that way, and the Likud had become predominantly Sephardi. The turnabout seems to have occurred in the election of 1977 when a majority of the Likud vote was Sephardi for the first time in history.

Likud in 1992 was more heavily Sephardi than in 1977, with two-thirds of its votes coming from that group in 1992 compared with about half in 1977; Labor was much more balanced, with half its voters Ashkenazim, a third Sephardim, and the rest second-generation Israelis. The Likud came close to being left only with its hard-core supporters, while Labor in 1992 was able to enlarge the circle of its voters. Labor and Peres in 1996 were unable to accelerate this trend, leading to a very close race and ultimately to defeat. In the period of the direct election of the prime minister, between 1996 and 2001, the large parties lost support from all groups. Many Sephardim found the ultra-Orthodox Shas attractive, and many Ashkenazim turned to parties of the Left such as Meretz and Shinui.

The question may also be turned around by asking how members of the two ethnic groups divided their votes between the two large parties. Again, a mirror image is provided. About 60 percent of the Ashkenazim voted Labor, about a third Likud. About 60 percent of the Sephardim voted Likud, about a third Labor. By 1984, the Ashkenazim vote was more concentrated in the Alignment than the Sephardi vote was in the Likud, about 70 percent for the former, about 60 percent for the latter. In 1988, with the relative success of Mapam and Meretz among Ashkenazim, Labor's support among that ethnic group fell to about half; Likud's support among Sephardim came close to 60 percent.

As the proportion of Sephardim grew in the electorate, it was clear that Labor would always have an uphill battle regaining power until it could increase its share of the Sephardi vote. That shift occurred in 1992. The trend was not overwhelming, but the movement of Sephardim to Labor was substantial enough to provide the bounce that Labor needed to regain power. This transformation worked only because it occurred in conjunction with two other things: the movement of other former supporters away from the Likud to parties of the Right, and the impetus given Labor by the new Soviet immigrants who supported it. In 1996, Netanyahu won two-thirds of the Sephardi vote, a third of the Ashkenazi vote, and 40 percent of the Israeli-born whose fathers were Israeli-born. Peres's support within the two ethnic groups was reversed.

Meretz did more than three times better in 1992 among Ashkenazim and second-generation Israelis than among Sephardim, and the parties of the Right were twice as popular among Sephardim as they were among Ashkenazim. Most of Meretz's support came from Ashkenazim, similar to the 3 out of 4 rate of the DMC in 1977.

Two-thirds of the voters for the parties of the Right in 1992 were Sephardim. The most notable shift was for the religious parties. They successfully adapted to the demographic shifts in Israel after 1977. From a situation in which three-quarters of their vote came from Ashkenazim, in 1992 half their vote was Sephardi, one-third Ashkenazi, and 1 in 7 was a second-generation Israeli. The religious parties drew equally from all ethnic groups in 1992, very different from their 1977 pattern, which showed strong support among Ashkenazim.

In 1996, Netanyahu's vote came primarily from Sephardim, Peres's from Ashkenazim. The surge of religious parties in 1996 was based on broad ethnic support, with different ethnic groups supporting the three religious parties. Ya-hadut Hatorah was largely Ashkenazi, Shas mostly Sephardi, and the NRP drew from both ethnic groups.

In 1999, 60 percent of the Sephardim voted Netanyahu and 60 percent of the Ashkenazim voted Barak. In 2001, even though there was a general hemorrhaging of support for Barak, he still won 60 percent of the Ashkenazi vote. By contrast, Sharon received 80 percent of the Sephardi vote.

If indeed the two major parties in the 1990s may be defined as ethnic parties, it is only in terms of their electorate. One has to keep in mind that about one-third of each ethnic group voted for the "wrong" camp. Neither party organized to further specific ethnic ends or along ethnic lines. Both Labor and the Likud were run by Ashkenazim, as has been the case with most parties in Israel. Sephardim were high on the lists, but representation was not the issue. The Likud and Labor were ethnic parties only in the sense that the vote for each of them was closely associated with ethnicity.

The important Jewish ethnic lists are Shas and the two parties of immigrants from the FSU, Israel b'Aliya and Israel Beiteinu. Shas had seen its strength grow phenomenally, from 4 seats in 1984, to 6 seats in each of the 1988 and 1992 elections, 10 seats in 1996, and 17 seats in 1999. Israel b'Aliya won 7 seats in 1996 and 6 in 1999; Israel Beiteinu 4 in 1999.

Despite the fact that since 1977 it had power only in the periods of 1984–86, 1992–96, and 1999–2001 periods, the Alignment remained identified by many as the party of the establishment. Sephardim, and especially their Israeli-born children, tended to reject Labor because of the persistent inequalities these voters perceived. Ashkenazi voters tended to reject the populism of Likud governments and longed to return to a more familiar and pragmatic past. The hawkish image of the Likud also correlated with attitudes prevalent among Sephardim. Sephardim tend to be more traditional about religion than Ashkenazim. Begin (although not the Likud party generally) was very successful in utilizing the symbols and language of religion. Many thought of Labor as antireligious, especially since it supported Meretz positions during the 1992–96 period, and because of Labor's attacks on the religious parties for what Labor termed disproportionate gains through coalition bargaining. During the races for prime minister, Labor candidates Peres and Barak pleaded with the rabbis for the support of the religious vote, but to no avail.

Issues of Concern

The twin issues of God (religion) and nationalism (the territories) were powerful predictors of the vote. On the State-religion issue, the trend of increasing correlations persists over time. The identification of Labor as an anticlerical party has strengthened, while the Likud has played to the traditional sympathies of much of its voting base, even though the origins and ideology of the Likud are very secular (Liebman and Don-Yehiya 1983).

Since 1984—the elections in which Shamir replaced Begin as the head of the Likud—the correlations of the territories issue with the vote were high. Over time, Labor has more unambiguously identified itself as the territories-for-peace party, and the platform of Labor has become less vague on this issue. The offers that Barak made to the Palestinians in the period leading up to the elections of 2001 were beyond what most Israelis were willing to contemplate at that time. The public perception of the difference between these two parties on the territories issue did not change much; almost two-thirds of the respondents in the 1981, 1984, and 1992 surveys thought these differences were big or very big. By 1996 the number jumped to 80 percent, although Netanyahu strained toward the middle in the election campaign. In 1999, the number went down to 60 percent.

Since 1996 many more voters said that the territories would be an important consideration in their voting decision. In the 1999 sample, 65 percent reported that the issue of the territories would very greatly influence their vote, compared with 71 percent in 1996. In 1992, 52 percent reported a very great influence, and fewer than a third did so in previous elections. Adding the next category of response, 92 percent in 1999, 90 percent in 1996, and 81 percent in 1992 said that it would influence them greatly or very greatly, compared with 63 percent in previous elections.

Although the territories issue may drive the vote, it does not necessarily dominate the campaign. One way of assessing the mood of the times is to consider the recurring question asking respondents to identify the major issue with which the government should deal. Breaking the answers down into foreign and security issues on the one hand (security, terror, peace, etc.) and a domestic issue on the other (housing, health, education, immigrant absorption, etc.) shows how much the public agenda varied over the years (see Figure 2.). In 1969, 1988, 1996, and 2001, foreign and security issues were mentioned by more than 70 percent of respondents. But in 1981 and 1984 fewer than 30 percent mentioned those issues, concentrating instead on domestic matters. When considered by support for the big parties (not shown), voters shift their attention in the same direction, with very small differences.

Conclusion

The chances for the continued success of a democratic regime rest in part in having social groups overlap. In Israel today we witness a lack of overlapping social cleavages, so much so as to point to a possible danger to Israeli democracy. When the political system is polarized and one group concentrates within it the religious, Sephardim, and less educated and lower-status workers voting for the Likud and religious parties, and the other group has a disproportionate share of secular, upper-class Ashkenazim voting for Labor and Meretz, the chances of intolerance, lack of communication, misunderstanding, and violence grow. These

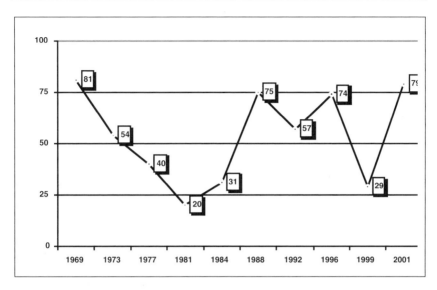

Figure 2. Security as Most Important Issue before Elections

patterns are not immutable, and it may be that with changes in the leadership of the two major parties the system will become very fluid, and new affiliations will emerge within the polity.

In many countries the amount of the vote variance explained by social structure and attitudinal variables has been reduced from the 1960s through the 1990s. This has not been the case in Israel. The difference lies in the nature of the issues that have captured the agenda. In most Western countries issues involving postbourgeois versus materialist values, gender issues, public versus private consumption, and state employment have gained ascendancy. In Israel these issues have energized only limited publics and have not become as central, critical, and engulfing as the major issue dimension in Israeli politics: the territories and the Israeli-Arab conflict. Voting in Israel became more structured, and security issues became a more important determinant of it over time.

The changing bases of electoral behavior have been attributed with causing greater individual and aggregate level volatility in the vote. And this liberation, where it occurs, means that the fortunes of political parties and leaders have become much less certain, and are dependent more on leadership skills than on organizational factors. The Israeli party system generated one electoral turnover after thirty years of Labor dominance and then four turnovers in the decade between 1992 and 2001. Given these trends, Israeli politics will be very predictable but not very stable.

REFERENCES

Abramson, Paul. 1989. "Generational Replacement, Ethnic Change, and Partisan Support in Israel." *Journal of Politics* 51.

Arian, Asher, David Nachmias, and Ruth Amir. 2001. *Executive Governance in Israel.* London: Palgrave.

Bartolini, Stefano, and Peter Mair. 1990. *Identity, Competition and Electoral Availability: The Stabilisation of European Electorates 1885–1985.* Cambridge: Cambridge University Press.

Dalton, Russell J. 1996. *Citizen Politics: Public Opinion and Political Parties in Advanced Western Democracies.* Chatham, N.J.: Chatham House.

Franklin, Mark N., Thomas T. Mackie, and Henry Valen. 1992. *Electoral Change: Responses to Evolving Social and Attitudinal Structures in Western Countries.* Cambridge: Cambridge University Press, 1992.

Liebman, Charles, and Eliezer Don-Yehiya. 1983. *Civil Religion in Israel: Traditional Judaism and Political Culture in the Jewish State.* Berkeley: University of California Press.

Shalev, Michael, with Sigal Kis. 2002. "Social Cleavages among Non-Arab Voters: A New Analysis." In *The Elections in Israel—1999,* ed. Asher Arian and Michal Shamir. Albany: State University of New York Press.

Shamir, Michal. 1986. "Realignment in the Israeli Party System." In *The Elections in Israel—1984,* ed. Asher Arian and Michal Shamir, 272–75. New Brunswick, N.J.: Transaction.

Shamir, Michal, and Asher Arian. 1999. "Collective Identity and Electoral Competition in Israel." *American Political Science Review* 93 (June) 265–77.

CHAPTER EIGHT

Women in Israeli Society

cⁿɔ

HANNA HERZOG

Why Women? Do Women Have Common Interests as a Group?

The demand for integrating women in formal politics and for their representation in it, is grounded on three types of claims: women are an interest group that must participate in the decision-making process; society will gain from the inclusion of women and their world in the formal political arena; and the underrepresentation of women negates the democratic ideas of equality and justice.

The liberal democratic discourse that prevails in Israel, as in the majority of Western democracies, assumes the universality of the system. Universality has a dual meaning: generality as opposed to particularity—that is, what citizens have in common as opposed to how they differ from each other; and universality in the sense that the law and regulations are identical for all and are implemented similarly in regard to everyone. In other words, the laws are "difference-blind," they don't differentiate between different individuals or groups. Various criticisms leveled at the liberal democratic idea indicate that this universality is a myth. In reality, different groups have different needs, distinct social histories, and diverse life experience. Moreover, equal opportunities vary according to the social structure and normative expectations. This criticism is also true concerning women. The accepted gender division of roles overlaps the distinction between two spheres of life that are perceived to be discrete—the private and the public—and creates a basic inequality between women and men in various social spheres, including women's different degree of access to positions of power. The demand to adopt the general point of view, which is actually the attitude of the dominant group (in this case, men), paralyzes or marginalizes the interests of weak groups (Young 1990). The dominance of the universal perception results in women's inability to consider themselves a group, and instills in them the idea of general citizenship and a perception of themselves as citizens possessing equal formal rights. Until feminism introduced this issue to the agenda, women did not view themselves as a group with political interests: in Israel as well, until recently, many public opinion polls elicited that strong group awareness among women was nonexistent (Yishai 1997). Women constitute one-half

195

of the electorate, but are underrepresented in the elected bodies, and in fact they constitute a weak group in the political arena.

Implicitly, the claim made for women's representation in politics contains not only the assumption that women have an interest of their own, but also that it differs from the interest of men and possesses a different, contradictory tension. This requires women themselves to be part of the decision-making process, and not to make do with the claims presented by others. Both women's perspectives and female presence must be an integral part of political debate and the decision-making process (Phillips 1994).

Has Israel's political culture enabled, and does it now enable, women to share in the political discourse and to participate in forming and shaping their lives as women and citizens?

Political Representation in the Formal Structure of Israeli Politics—A Snapshot

Israel's political system began taking shape in the final decade of the nineteenth century with the immigration of Jews to Israel (then known as Palestine). The decisive majority of the political parties were set up in Israel and they lacked a long-established tradition. One could have expected that women would share equally in the process of building a nation and founding new political institutions. Moreover, the Labor Movement, which was the leading political force in the Yishuv, the pre-State Jewish community, had adopted the idea of equality between the genders as part of its socialist ideology.

The proportional, list-based electoral method that was first implemented during the Yishuv period is considered a relatively favorable one for Jewish women, who constitute half of the Jewish voters, serve in the Israeli Defense Force, and share in what is considered, especially in a society subject to a prolonged military threat, as a primary civic duty. Over the years, Jewish women's interest in politics has heightened; women now display almost the same amount of interest as do men (Yishai 1997, p. 116).

However, despite what might be expected, Jewish women's representation in Israeli politics is low, while Arab-Palestinian women are hardly discernible in this arena (Herzog 1998a; Yishai 1997). The absence of the latter from politics is particularly salient in the light of the fact that their ratio of electoral participation is identical with that of Jewish women and men, and often exceeds it (Yishai 1997, p. 99).

The representation ratio of women in the Knesset, the Israeli parliament, has never exceeded 11 percent. Moreover, a stable growth trend in their parliamentary representation cannot be discerned. In the first three Knessets, women had a 9.1 percent representation ratio, which fell and rose alternately over the subsequent three decades, attaining 9.1 percent after the 1992 elections. However, in the 1996 elections representation dropped to 8.3 percent; only in 1999 did it rise to 11.6 percent. As a comparison, at the start of the nineties, the proportion of women in various European parliaments was as follows: Luxembourg, 50 percent; Sweden, 38 percent; Denmark, 38 percent; Germany, 36 percent; Holland, 28 percent; Belgium, 25 percent; Finland, 21 percent; Britain, 15 percent; Switzerland, 14 percent; and Portugal, 13 percent. After the 1992 elections in the United States, the ratio of women in Congress was 11 percent. All the women ever elected to the Knesset were Jewish, and no Arab-Palestinian woman has ever been elected, even on behalf of the Communist Party, most of whose representatives are Palestinian Arabs.

Israel has had one woman prime minister, Golda Meir, but even in her government, which was one of the largest Israel has ever had (24 ministers), not a single woman received a ministerial post. The majority of Israeli governments have had only one woman minister. Four governments were completely devoid of women, and two of these were among the largest Israeli governments (the tenth Knesset appointed 25 ministers, and the eleventh, 26 ministers). During the terms of office of the thirteenth and fifteenth Knesset, there were two women ministers. In the Unity Government established by Sharon in 2001, there were only three women out of thirty-two ministers, and two deputy ministers. Until then only three women had served as deputy ministers: in the twelfth, thirteenth, and in the first term of the fifteenth Knesset under the Barak government (Herzog 1996; Israel Women's Network 2001). In the Jewish municipal local authorities (governments), the proportion of women was 4.2 percent at the time of the State's establishment, but by 1965 it had fallen to a nadir of 3.1 percent. Since the 1969 elections there has been a trend of moderate but stable increase in women's representation in the Jewish local authorities, reaching 14.9 percent in the elections of 1998. The situation in the Arab local authorities is grievous: only six women have ever served on local authorities since the state's founding. In the fifty-eight Arab local authorities, only two women were elected in the 1993 elections and a similar number in 1998. Israel takes the lowest place in the list of other democratic countries. Women in Scandinavian local authorities make up a third of their representatives (in Sweden their number is over 40 percent), and in the United States their representation totals 20 percent.

Between 1950 and 1997, no more than nine women headed municipal councils; the majority were heads of the local councils in small settlements, and one of these was the head of an Arab local council. Just two of them were elected by the direct election method. The others assumed their positions after the resignation of the incumbent preceding them in the list, or as the result of a crisis that required a compromise candidate (Herzog 1999).

Among all parties, women's representation is lower than the proportion of their party membership. Women's representation is particularly low in the narrow bodies of the parties (the secretariat, offices) and larger in the broader ones (committees, centers). In the mid-90s, this pattern was broken following decisions to assure representation in the parties.

The situation elicited from the data presented so far is that women's representation is greater in those political bodies possessing less political authority. As the scale of importance and the power of political roles rises, women's representation falls proportionally. They are not found in the top positions where the decision-making process occurs, nor in powerful positions where policy is determined.

Three main factors are cited in the literature as influencing women's prospects for entering politics: the electoral method, the party structure, and the political culture (Githens, Norris, and Lovenduski 1994). This chapter attempts to engage the question of how Israeli political culture affects women's participation in politics.

A Culture of Inclusion and Exclusion

My major claim is that women's entrance or nonentrance to the Israeli political arena has been shaped by two major contradictory forces that operate simultaneously. On the one hand, they are defined as part of the collective and are recognized, treated, and organized as a social category. They are defined mainly by their social roles as wives and mothers. On the other hand, the politics of identity has been restricted by marginalizing and denouncing social identity as a basis for political action, and thus excludes women. If women try to organize within the parties and pose claims on the basis of gender, they and the issues they represent are marginalized—if not completely delegitimated. The same holds true for women's parties. On the symbolic-ideological level they are not "allowed" to make demands on behalf of women's interests. Paradoxically, the building blocks of both the inclusionary and exclusionary forces stem from the same origins.

Five basic components have produced the political culture of exclusion and inclusion of women in Israeli politics: the myth of equality, the binary gendered world perception, Jewish and Palestinian traditions, the lack of separation between State and Religion, and the Israeli-Arab conflict. These components overlap partially, interconnect partially, and may be contradictory; nevertheless, they operate simultaneously as inclusionary and exclusionary mechanisms and thus neutralize women's power in institutionalized politics.

The Myth of Gender Equality

For years Israelis grew up with an unquestioned belief that genders are equal in Israel. The myth of gender equality in Israel is nurtured by various sources. These sources are: the history of the Yishuv, which generated the myth of the pioneering woman (Bernstein 1987) and of the fighting woman; history and sociology books that have disregarded women's struggle for their right to vote, establishing the ethos of Israeli democracy and citing the right to vote and seek office that was granted women with the first establishment of the Yishuv's institutions, along with the concept of egalitarian citizenship (Fogiel-Bijaoui 1992c; Herzog 1992); women's organizations that were already an integral part of the political-party arena during the Yishuv period (Izraeli 1981); the kibbutz ideology, which propounded an egalitarian society imbued with socialist spirit and which disguised the gendered structure that actually existed in the kibbutz (Fogiel-Bijaoui 1992b); and the Declaration of Independence to which women were also signatories (Rachel Kagan, Golda Meir) and which declared the founding of a democratic state without differences of religion, race, and gender. The compulsory conscription of women to the IDF and their military service added a further stratum to the legend of equality (Izraeli 1997). Additionally, the fact that Golda Meir served as Prime Minister contributed to corroborating the fundamental belief that Israel is a society offering equal opportunities, and that the system is open to any individual who is willing and able to abide by the rules of the game.

A direct implication of this myth for the political field was that women, as a group, did not consider that the system discriminated against them, did not believe that they had another political agenda, and did not develop political behavior patterns that differed from men's.

A Binary Gendered World

The Western distinction between the public and private spheres that includes the separation between market and home, as well as consumption and production that parallel the differentiation between the genders, has deep roots in Israeli culture.

This binary perception of the world, which subordinates women to traditional female roles, is discernible in what is ostensibly the most egalitarian legislation: the Law of Defense Service (1949), and the Law of Equal Rights for Women (1951). In both these laws, it is motherhood that grants women their equal citizenship status while simultaneously distancing them to the margins of the public world. The Law of Defense Service exempts from military service Jewish women who are married and pregnant, and women with children. In a

Knesset debate on the Law, the statement made by the then prime minister, Ben-Gurion, that "the special destiny of women is the role of motherhood, than which there is no greater role" was perceived as absolutely understandable. This destiny granted women an entry ticket to citizenship, and it won them the Law of Equal Rights (1951). The Law was not justified in terms of the natural right to citizenship, but "as fulfilling the obligation and right of the Hebrew mother and her share in fostering and educating the young generation in Israel.... [I]n all of these the Hebrew woman and mother is continuing the magnificent tradition of the heroic women of Israel...." The equality that was offered was formal, and a righteous woman was described as one who "looketh well to the ways of her household" (Berkovitch 1999; Lahav 1993).

The simultaneous inclusion and exclusion of women in the public sphere is reproduced through gender segregation. Studies on the entrance of women to the labor market, including studies on the army, attest to the ongoing paradox whereby women are entering the public sphere in ever-growing numbers. Simultaneously, though, the gendered boundaries and gaps between women and men in income, prestige, and power have remained intact. Women still join the political system almost exclusively in niches designated for women, and principally by means of women's organizations that are affiliated with the parties.

Jewish and Palestinian Traditions

The gendered binary framing of the world is also nurtured by the cultural legacy of the Jews on the one hand, and of the Palestinian citizens of Israel on the other. Both societies have a strongly rooted patriarchal tradition. The economic arrangements of a market economy and of the democratic political arena, which took for granted the distinction between the two spheres, matched patriarchal perceptions perfectly.

In both cultures, women's exclusion from the public domain was supported by the substantial importance attributed to the woman in her domestic roles: "The princess's honor is best displayed in private" (*kol kvoda shel bat melech pnima*) in the Jewish version, while in the Arab (mainly Muslim) version, woman's duty is to safeguard "the family's honor." In Judaism the definition of the public mainly relates to religious-public life, and women's exclusion is achieved principally by excluding them from the world of Jewish learning: "He who teaches his daughter Torah [Bible], teaches her folly" (*Mi shemelamed et bito Torah ke-ilu melamda tiflut*). As the studies attest, the boundaries between the private and public in religious circles are open for change and for different interpretations (El-Or 1994).

Nevertheless the public/private dichotomy as a cultural frame that overlaps the division of roles between genders remains untouched. Woman's seclusion in the home is supported by a whole series of injunctions limiting woman to her home and her husband. In the Arab tradition, exclusion is based primarily on the concepts of honor and shame. The patriarchal unit (the *hamula,* the village, the religious community) constitutes a single entirety that women must abide by. They do so by obeying the behavioral code that is expected of them. At the center of this code stands sexual behavior and the demand for modesty and purity. Women must be beyond the reach of condemnation by the community; deviating from the code damages the whole community's honor. The seclusion of women within the private sphere "enables" them not only to conform with this code, but to feel respected and protected (Hasan 1994).

Lack of Separation between Religion and State

The patriarchal pattern is supported and replicated in the political and legislative arrangements in Israel, which do not separate religion and state. The traditions of religious circles' political organization, aimed at assuring the Jewish and halachic nature of Jewish society, originate in the first days of Zionist organizing throughout the world and in Eretz Yisrael, alike. The consensus on the need to preserve national unity and the State's Jewish character, compounded by the religious parties' political achievements, have enabled the institutionalization of that nonseparation of religion and state in Israel.

The decision not to separate religion and the State of Israel is embodied in what are known as the status quo agreements. An important element in the status quo agreements on matters of religion and state is the appropriation by most national authorities of the laws of personal status, and their transferal to religious bodies. Exclusive judicial authority on issues of marriage, and partial authority over matters of divorce, are in the hands of the rabbinical, Islamic, and Christian courts. The personal-religious laws of the different ethnic religious groups in Israel that apply patriarchal methods are binding on all citizens of the State, whether religious or secular. Moreover, the norms regarding personal status in the different religious affiliations are determined by male institutions, and women have no part in determining them (Raday, Shalev, and Liban-Kooby 1995). As a result, women are fettered in patriarchal frameworks and distanced from participating in public life or offering services under the aegis of state laws.

The involvement of the religious parties in political life and their influence on the status of women deviates from the laws of personal status. For example, they block women's participation in public bodies related to religious institutions, such as the religious councils. The religious councils are public bodies established under state law in which members of the public are represented. Over the years, women's participation in these bodies has been avoided by the claim that they engage in religious matters in which women must not participate. Recently, by means of the Supreme Court, women have won the right to take part in the religious councils. De facto, though, only a few settlements are implementing the Supreme Court's ruling that prohibits women's exclusion.

Attempts to anchor women's equality in basic laws were also thwarted by the religious parties. In the Basic Law—Human Dignity and Liberty, which was legislated in 1992, the right for equality is not specifically cited. This left untouched the status quo in matters of religion and state, in the framework of which women's right to equality is subject to patriarchal values in all matters concerning her personal status.

Maintaining the status quo is one of the cardinal objectives of the religious parties. Whereas, in the past, the majority of religious votes came from the Mafdal (National Religious Party), which did not exclude women from its ranks, more recently the power of ultra-Orthodox—*haredi*—parties, which openly exclude women from all public and political activities, has intensified (Herzog 1999). Religious extremism has not overlooked the Mafdal, and the tradition of several decades during which at least a symbolic number of women was represented in the Knesset, has been annulled and disappeared.

In spite of the exclusionary power of the lack of separation between state and religion, women tend to accept it as their contribution to the unity of the nation. The overriding role of religion as the social definer of the collective in Jewish society, as well as in the Arab community in Israel, includes women as an important social agent of the nation's solidarity.

The Arab-Israeli Conflict

Overshadowed by the prolonged conflict and the institutionalization of the perception of security threats as taken for granted, the binary world perception has been empowered and validated. This is mirrored in the substantial emphasis awarded to the army, militarism, and male culture, on the one hand, and to the family and family values, on the other hand (Herzog 1998b; Kimmerling 1993a; Kimmerling 1993b). Army and security form the axis of masculine identity and are perceived as male bastions, whereas the universe of women revolves around family and domesticity.

Women are perceived as representing the collective, as the nation's mothers. They are considered responsible for the nation's continuity, both in their central role of childbearers and as passing on the culture and educating the next generation. They represent the honor of the nation and symbolize its borders (Yuval-Davis 1993). In such cultural perceptions, women's place in the private sphere is not only reinforced, but also empowered. In Jewish society and in the Arab-Palestinian one as well, women are mobilized to familial roles in order to sustain identity, the boundaries of the collective, and solidarity.

Military service signifies the social boundaries between Jews and Arabs in Israel. Military service includes Jewish women in the dominant collective, but at the same time marginalizes them. The army is mainly a male institution and one of the principal institutions that reproduces the gendered structure of Israeli society (Izraeli 1997). Relations between army and society in Israel are shaped in the wider context of the security problem, creating an entire social culture. This is a culture that is diffused in all spheres of civilian life, and thus there is not only a stratifying influence, but also a cultural one. Not only do men succeed in translating their military service into better positions in the economic and political domains, they also bring their thinking patterns with them in the transition. The gendered military order is constantly reproduced in civilian society, and empowers stereotypical sexist perceptions, which already exist anyway.

Women's prospects in politics are profoundly affected by the army's centrality in Israeli society. A tendency exists to blur the demarcation lines between politics and the military, especially since some political decisions are also connected with the existence of the army and its operation. The political area tends to lose its autonomy when faced with security considerations that prioritize the representation and the interpretation of these considerations. The blurred boundaries are also reinforced by the connection between political and military elites, and by the entry of ex-military people into politics, which has achieved the utmost legitimacy. Military thinking and military considerations are considered highly appropriate for running the country, and political decisions—going to war, settlement policies, priority setting, and allocation for internal needs—are made in their light. This thinking pattern is represented by men and is identified as a male preserve. Women hardly have a foothold. A few women have reached high-ranking officer levels but, because of the army's gendered nature, they are not viewed as representing the security discourse. Identifying the army as a world of men allocates everything to men, and to the same extent, excludes women for simply being women.

The dominance of security discourse in Israeli politics is perfectly mirrored in the existing hierarchy regarding ministerial positions. The Defense Ministry is the most important; this position is given to a senior member of government and is often assumed by the prime minister himself. A similar picture is mirrored in the Knesset committees. The Foreign Affairs and Defense Committee is one of the most prestigious committees, perhaps the most prestigious of all. It is a committee where, until recent years, no woman ever set foot (Herzog 1999). While politics is one of the best developed career tracks for men who retire from military service, the same is not true for women. Not one senior woman officer has ever been "catapulted" into national politics. In local politics, there are a few such women officers, but they have never been elected as mayors nor included in leading positions in the party lists (Herzog 1999, pp. 208–209).

Subordinating various considerations to security considerations marginalizes those social issues that are generally areas of engagement with high proportions of women—health, education, and welfare. Once again, if one seeks a symbolic example in the Knesset committees, women have a higher representation rate in the committees dealing with topics considered "feminine." Such committees are considered the least prestigious of the Knesset's committees (Herzog 1996). Israel's political discourse, which focuses on questions of peace and security, splits society as a whole, and therefore women as well—and it jeopardizes every organization that seeks to promote issues related to the status of women.

The gendered world created by the dominance of the Arab-Israeli conflict is accepted as taken for granted by men and women since society as a whole is required to guard the nation's solidarity and internal cohesion. Moreover, life in the shadow of security threats has set up social barriers between Jews and Arabs. The national solidarity required of women hampers the understanding that women in both national groups possess an extensive arena for collaborating in the struggle to advance their status. Only in the past decade, with the growth of the feminist movement, has awareness grown concerning the links between the security claim and women's status.

In the Pincers of the Gendered Exclusionary and Inclusionary Mechanisms

Women have always received symbolic representation in Israeli politics. Symbolic representation enabled the myth of an open, egalitarian system to be constructed, and it reflects two opposing processes that coexist in Israel's political culture. On the one hand, awareness exists of women as a social category. Comprehensive, even advanced, legislation concerning women, such as paid maternity leave, places Israel in the vanguard of welfare states caring for their female citizens. However, much of this legislation derives not from perceptions of civil equality, but from the prevailing perception of women's traditional roles as mothers and wives, and from the importance that Israeli society ascribes to the family and to population growth.

Discrete organizing of women was encouraged and recognized, but political activity on the basis of gendered identity and as a platform for political, civil, and autonomous demands was seen as not legitimate, and induced condemnation and marginalization. The two processes—recognition of women and their marginalization—are anchored in and justified by the fundamental thinking paradigms that prevail in Israel, which were analyzed previously: the binary world, the national and religious ethos, security needs, and family values. Their role in the collective is determined mainly by their social roles as wives and mothers. These roles are considered as important to the national goals and are respected. Moreover, when entering politics, and within the party, women's participation is prescribed in gendered terms. They are channeled into "women's divisions," and into specific activities in special traditional women's roles.

The majority of parties have, either within them or in close proximity to them, women's sections, cells, or women's organizations. On the face of it, these organizations could have served as a power basis for women in politics. In fact, however, these departments became a mechanism that discriminated between women and men, channeling women toward activities in their discrete enclaves, away from ongoing party-political activity. The accepted perception was that women had a minority status that must be represented; but, as is the case with all minorities, representation was purely symbolic.

Women competed against each other to represent the party. Instead of organizing jointly in order to advance increased representation, they tended to take their marginal status for granted, as well as the assumption that women are solely designated for a few places in the general organization (which was in fact a men's organization). The statement "Women do not support other women" originates in the self-supervision and monitoring that women politicians and their women voters took upon themselves. Instead of competing with men for all the available positions, they competed with each other for the "symbolic place" allocated to them.

On more than one occasion, leaders of the women's organizations served as gatekeepers of the transition from the female enclave to the male establishment. They permitted a few women, whom they supported, to join the party's central entities. These women were the social agents who exercised supervision; they limited the entrance of many women, and at the same time acted as a fig-leaf for men against claims voiced that the system was closed to women. They were the "proof" that the system was, on the contrary, open to women who were "interested" and "suitable." For the most part, the women's departments of the different parties were also not totally autonomous, but were dependent for financing on the party, and subject to supervision by the party mechanisms.

In organizational terms, women were recognized as a social category. In their own organizations they were principally involved in those areas traditionally described as "female"—social assistance, welfare, education, and health. There was no ideological legitimacy for them to function as an interest group. They were expected to be loyal, to prefer the party's "general interest" over questions relating to advancing their status or their life conditions. The latter were defined as "particular interests," often narrow-minded and egotistical (Fogiel-Bijaoui 1992a).

Women in politics, like the representatives of other groups organizing on the basis of identity, found themselves in a constant dilemma regarding their political identity. If they chose to act as regular members, representing the party as a whole, they often found themselves categorized as "women" and directed to traditional "women's roles." If they decided to organize on a gender basis, they and the issues they handled were both marginalized.

Women's claims were phrased, in most cases, in terms of mother, wife, and secondary breadwinner, not in civil terms. Such rhetoric reinforced the binary thinking paradigm as well as their marginality in the political system. Women's organizations that were affiliated with parties thus provided means for including women in the political arena but marginalized them at one and the same time.

In the past decade, influenced by extra-institutional feminist organizations, the women's departments of the parties are undergoing change processes, while adopting feminist messages and critical attitudes toward their parties (Fogiel-Bijaoui 1992a). This phenomenon is not unique to Israel. In various parties around the world traditional women's cells have become bases for power and organizing of feminist messages (Sawer and Simms 1993).

Israel's Road to Feminism

The first wave of feminism in Israel washed over the country as early as the pre-statehood Yishuv period. It was manifested in the voices that clamored for inclusion in the public sphere. Phrased in terms rooted in socialist discourse, women from the Left sought a way to enter the male world as equals, chiefly in the *hachsharot* (pioneer training camps), in the "labor battalions," the kibbutzim, and in political activity within the workers' parties and the Histadrut (Bernstein 1987; Fogiel-Bijaoui 1992c; Izraeli 1981). Women's voices in civil circles at the same time sought to preserve their distinctiveness as women and to gain civil equality in recognition of their contribution as women and mothers (Herzog 1992).

At that period, the peak of the feminist struggle was in 1919–26, with the fight to obtain the right to vote for Yishuv institutions. As was the case across the world, women in Palestine also believed that achieving suffrage would bring equality. And like women around the world, their counterparts in Palestine would also need a few more decades to free themselves from the illusion that equality would necessarily result from the formal right of participation.

The second wave of feminism in Israel started evolving, though very slowly, around the time of the 1973 Yom Kippur War, though more emphatically after it. Only a calamity of that war's magnitude could manage to impel the issue of women's inequality into the awareness of a group of women, who started a still unfinished effort to place that issue on Israel's social and national agenda.

In the United States and Europe, the wave of feminism during the 1960s was one aspect of the waves of civil protest that flooded through the West. The liberal wave that washed over the West left Israel untouched, though not totally. Voices of social protest against ethnic discrimination were first heard in the early seventies, with the emergence of the "Black Panther" phenomenon, a movement that demanded the reallocation of economic and political resources, and of social prestige. In 1970, upon her return from the United States, Shulamit Alloni—founder of the Citizens' Rights Movement—was the first to ask, "Does Israel need a women's rights movement?" In 1972, the first radical women's movement was set up (Freedman 1990; Ram 1993).

It is noteworthy that this period marks the onset of the second feminist wave in Israel, signified by the establishment of *Nilahem* (a Hebrew acronym standing for "Women for a Renewed Society" but also meaning "we will fight,"). It is not surprising that, in a society where the dominant discourse is military, the women who challenged that dominance chose to call their movement by a name taken from the military lexicon, with the intention of transposing its meaning.

The initiative for the foundation of this movement came from two professors at the University of Haifa: Marcia Freedman, a philosopher, and Marilyn Safir, a psychologist, both originally from the United States. Their seminar engendered a radical movement that was critical of the degree to which women were suppressed in a male-dominated society. Ostensibly these changes can be viewed within the framework of the liberal social movements that flooded the West during the 1960s. In practice the Israeli story is more complicated. In the West, and especially in the United States, that decade was marked by the students' revolt, and the struggles against the Vietnam War and against discrimination suffered by blacks and women. In Israel, by contrast, a very different frame of mind prevailed. Caught up in the euphoria that followed victory in the 1967 Six Day War, the country experienced a surge of national pride and deep admiration for the armed forces. This was attended by a belief, both explicit and implicit, that brute force constituted the way to resolve international problems.

Post-1967 Israel was preoccupied with the question of borders and territories. In a society where the army, and more particularly a fighting army, is the centerpiece of social identification, civil society and civil demands are marginalized. Moreover, with the army as the fulcrum of the social ethos, the emphasis was naturally on men and on masculinity as the almost ultimate model of the "civilian" who participates in and contributes to the life of the community. The collective identification with the Six Day War encompassed men and women alike.

The appointment of Golda Meir as prime minister in 1969, together with the economic boom that followed the 1967 war, which enabled large numbers of women to enter the labor market, helped entrench the dominant myth of equality in Israeli society. Women were not aware that in practice they were channeled into "feminine" occupations and were secondary players in the work force. They did not internalize the fact that the majority of their social functions revolved around family- and home-based activity. In post-1967 Israel, women constituted less than 7 percent of the members of the Knesset, and only 4 percent of local government representatives. They were almost completely absent from the decision-making level in the economic, political, and social spheres.

In many areas of Israeli society, the Yom Kippur War of 1973 was a watershed. For women, the war served as a kind of magnifying mirror that reflected with painful clarity Israel's social structure and their place within it. The three weeks of hostilities until the cease-fire, together with the subsequent months of stepped-up mobilization of reservists, revealed the full intensity of the gendered role division that existed between men and women, and the marginality of women in the public sphere. The massive and swift mobilization of the country's males when the war erupted almost brought civilian life to a complete standstill. Factories, businesses, offices, and schools shut down. Without men the national economy virtually ground to a halt. Public transportation was sparse: there were no women bus drivers. For the first time it was disclosed that the two bus cooperatives that monopolize public transportation in Israel (*Egged* and *Dan*) neither allowed women to become members nor employed women as drivers on a contract basis.

In 1973, then, women were excluded from the three major role systems of the war effort: the military leadership, civilian administration, and war production. Many women reported a feeling of helplessness during the war. However, the feelings of anger and frustration were soon channeled into areas of activity that are considered legitimate for women: concern for the soldiers and helping to treat the wounded, the widows, and the orphans. Women baked and knitted for the men at the front, inundated the hospitals that cared for the wounded, and of course looked after family members who had remained at home. The longer the hostilities persisted, the greater became the number of caring and integration roles that were added to female tasks.

As hostilities died down, the mobilized reservists began returning home. First to be released were those who held key positions in various sectors, so that the civilian economy could be revitalized. The war had been relatively short in terms of social change. Unlike World War II, which lasted for several years and in the aftermath of which many women entered the work force, in Israel the war of 1973 only intensified the traditional role division between men and women. However, the war did have the effect of creating an awareness of what that role division meant in relation to women and their place in the society, and also in relation to the society overall. The waste of human capital that occurs in a gender-stratified society was fully manifested in the first three weeks of full hostilities, before the cease-fire took effect.

The first body to react to the situation was the Israel Defense Forces (IDF). The process of self-criticism carried out by the military high command after the war, combined with the need to bolster combat units with males and the growing recourse to advanced technologies, led the army to reassess its policy toward women. The adoption of the new technologies, whose operation required trained and high-quality personnel, opened many new military fields to women and afforded them new opportunities. Women's functions in the army became more diverse, a trend that has continued ever since.

While the IDF always makes new missions available to female soldiers on the basis of need—generally in order to offset manpower shortages—it does not pursue this policy in order to promote gender equality. A legal battle was required before the Air Force would allow women into the pilots' training courses, at least formally. The military advocate general did not oppose on grounds of principle against women pilots the attempt by the plaintiff, Ms. Alice Miller, to enter the course—that would have been too blatantly a sexist stance. Instead, he cited "defense expenditures." The military's logic was that, given Israel's security situation, the investment involved in setting up a special course for women would be incommensurate with the high costs of maintaining Air Force preparedness and combat capability. Gender equality is perceived as a luxury. That was the IDF's position after the Yom Kippur War, and it remains unchanged a quarter of a century later.

Many women were actively involved in the large number of protest movements that sprang up in the wake of the Yom Kippur War. Nevertheless, the increasing attention paid to feminist concerns after the war should not be considered a foregone conclusion. We should bear in mind that two contradictory voices made themselves heard after the Yom Kippur War. One was trenchantly critical of the government and of the social order that had consolidated itself in Israel. But another—which became increasingly dominant—demanded national mobilization and the closing of ranks. The strength of this latter call made it difficult for the protest movements, and doubly so for women, to cut their way through to the political center. Besides, feminism as a social movement was received in Israel with deep reservations. It was perceived as an American import, alien to the Israeli spirit. Worse, the demands of feminism were seen as a threat to the collective solidarity and to women's readiness to accept the dominant national agenda, which—certainly in the aftermath of the 1973 war—revolved around the security discourse and the centrality of the Arab-Israeli conflict.

It was precisely because the gendered role division had reached an unprecedented level during the war that the seeds of the feminist approach, which had been sown before the war, could thereafter flourish. The offspring, although initially small, proved sturdy. Politically, this was first seen in the success of Ratz, the Citizens' Rights Movement (CRM), in the elections to the eighth Knesset held on December 31, 1973, soon after the formal conclusion of the Yom Kippur War (the elections had originally been scheduled to take place on October 30 of that year). Ratz was the first party in Israel to be formed by a woman, Shulamit Aloni, and to espouse human rights, civil rights, and women's rights as policy guidelines. Marcia Freedman, a declared feminist, held the third place on the Ratz list.

The public protest against the blunders associated with the war, together—undoubtedly—with the frustration generated among women by the status to which they were relegated during the hostilities were translated into votes. In the event, Ratz won four seats. Ratz was the first Israeli political party to indicate the connection between the dominance of the security discourse and the inequality of women. Ratz placed the issue of women's rights and women's status in the family and in society—and not just in legislation affecting marriage and divorce—on the national agenda. In the eighth Knesset the conspiracy of silence about violence against women in the family was broken. For the first time the subject of battered women was discussed. (It was during this period that Ruth Resnick, a member of Ratz and of the feminist movement, established the first shelter for battered women.) The question of abortions was also dealt with extensively, and the feminist argument relating to a woman's right to her body was voiced. Admittedly, the Knesset did not enact legislation to legalize abortions. But the mandates of the official committees that it formed were sufficiently broad to include, for instance, the "social clause"—which defined the social conditions in which women lived as legitimate considerations in decisions about whether to permit abortions.

A perusal of the press and of the official Knesset Record from that period shows that neither the legislature nor the public was sympathetic or enthusiastic about these new themes that had been placed on the political agenda. Nevertheless, they could no longer be ignored. This was amply demonstrated in 1975, which was designated International Year of the Woman, when the then–prime minister, Yitzhak Rabin, appointed a commission to examine the status of women in Israel. It took the panel some time to get organized and to prepare its report, which in fact was not submitted until 1978—to the new prime minister, Menachem Begin. The report examined the place of women under the law and in education, the army, the labor market, the family, and in decision-making centers, and investigated the plight of women in distress. The findings revealed the scale of the inequality between the genders and constituted an eye-opener for many women (and men). Appended to the report was a pamphlet containing 241 recommendations for action that were required in order to promote the status of women and bring about equality between the genders in Israel. The marital status of women was the only issue on which the commission could not reach unanimity: this was due to the lack of separation between state and religion, and because of the dominance of Jewish tradition.

The importance of the report drawn up by the Commission on Women's Status was not only in its recommendations, but also in the opportunity it provided for women from different spheres to work together. Some one hundred women participated in the commission's efforts, and it was the first encounter between women politicians and women academics. Participating in the conferences and the sessions of the subcommittees became a means for raising consciousness. It was clear that the work invested by all those involved in preparing the commission's report was a formative experience for a new generation of leadership. One of the few resulting political achievements was the creation of the position of Advisor to the Prime Minister on the Status of Women. Only a few items in the commission's report drew attention and were dealt with. Still, the report of the Commission on Women's Status should be seen as a breakthrough. Even though some years would elapse before its implementation began—and women's organizations continue to battle for its full implementation—the report serves as a symbolic document of Israeli society's commitment to make changes in women's status.

From the late seventies onward, feminist organizing in Israel intensifies. Its features are varied, and it comprises different forms of social-feminist endeavors: feminist writing, translations of leading international feminist articles, texts written locally, and a feminist journal, *Noga*. Shelters for battered women and rape crisis centers are established. Various mutual support groups are set up by women. A women's party is founded in 1977, and although it does not attain the minimum percentage required, it is clearly another milestone in the feminist fight.

The chief characteristics of this organizing are conscious defiance, grassroots initiatives, and the absence of direct dependence on parties or institutionalized political parties. Many organizations highlight a single issue—violence against women, rape, *agunot,* injurious advertising, and so on (Fogiel-Bijaoui 1992a). Although most of them are small and marginal, one can still claim that, to a great extent, the merging of the different voices changed the public climate on the issue of women's status.

Alongside the radical feminist organizations, the Women's Network is established, defining its main mission as advocacy work with Knesset members, decision makers, and policy setters. The Women's Network was yet another inno-

vation in the community of women's organizations in Israel. Most of its founders came from the academy. Their entry to feminist activities constituted more
than crossing over the line separating the academy from politics, for it was those
women who eventually opened gender and women's studies tracks in Israel's
universities and colleges, thereby helping to expose the gendered-political aspects of the academic discourse.

Under the influence of the feminist organizations, the concept of feminism
was interpreted as less and less threatening in the institutionalized organizations
too. Increasingly, Na'amat, WIZO, and even Emunah, embarked on consciously
feminist activities, linked with consciousness-raising through training, journal-
ism, and political efforts. Greater willingness to collaborate with other organizations on specific issues was also displayed. In 1992, during the thirteenth
Knesset, the Commission on Women's Status is established. This Knesset, in
comparison with its predecessors, was more "women-friendly." The majority of
the women MKs were members of the Women's Network, that is, they defined
themselves explicitly as feminists: "When the Commission was set up, we didn't
'reinvent the wheel,' but a new engine was added to the wheel, a feminist, militant engine that crossed the lines of party, origin, age, and religion" (Committee for the Advancement of Women's Status, 1998; p. 4). It is an attempt by
women to go beyond party squabbles, and to cooperate with each other on
shared issues that have an impact on the status of women.

The commission chalked up more than a few achievements. Some are linked
to setting up frameworks dedicated to dealing with women's status (such as the
state authority to promote women's status), and to creating supervisory mechanisms for state institutions—for example, the commission's authority to request
reports from state institutions on issues concerning women. Others relate to legislative initiatives, introducing to the agenda of the Knesset and of the public
topics such as educating for gender equality, fighting injurious advertising,
single families, lesbian and homosexual rights, women in sport, preventing sexual harassment, police attitudes to victims of rape and violence, the status of
Arab women, and the Basic Law—Rights of Women. The agenda of issues that
were discussed by the commission attests to an attempt to address different
groups of women, as well as to widen public debate concerning people suffering as a result of their gender. On these issues, too, the Commission made a significant contribution in institutionalizing a feminist agenda.

It should be noted, though, that the most noticeable phenomenon in the
community of feminist organizations in Israel is that radical grassroots organizations raise new issues that are gradually adopted by the large organizations. In
consequence, the former, and their leaders, remain permanently at the margins
as a kind of eternal avant-garde, constantly initiating new ideas that a priori are

considered radical and impossible. Over time, the issues they raise are adopted by establishment women's organizations and, to some extent, they are eventually institutionalized and enter the public agenda and the Knesset. Notable examples are the issues of domestic violence, sexual harassment, and rape. Thus, the boundaries between the extra-establishment feminist discourse and the political discourse are no longer impermeable.

Since the late 1970s, but more emphatically in the past decade, there has been an outburst of voices: secular and religious women, Mizrahi women, Palestinian women living in Israel, lesbians, single mothers, mothers of soldiers, women in black, women in green, women with political views from the Right and Left, liberal, Marxist, and radical feminists, as well as women who consider gender an essentialist social category, and those who see it as constituted by social process and thus reinterpretable. All these voices are involved in the public political discourse, some loudly raised, some whispered, and others in deafening silence.

The logic of feminist thinking rules out delegitimizing any of that chorus of voices. If gender is a result of power-oriented social construction, then any idea of a single, all-inclusive gendered identity must have a coercive element. Attempts to describe this identity and to act in its name are power-driven, normalizing, and exclusionary endeavors. Feminism's attempts to speak in the name of "The Group" has been negated in light of the demand to keep feminist discourse open and constantly changing. Implementing such an idea in the political arena is highly problematic. A political movement must have a group identity in order to mobilize political power: in the absence of consensus over a common identity, it is almost impossible to mobilize politically. Hence, feminist politics in Israel, as in many other places, is divided and there are more than a few disagreements between the feminist organizations. One solution is to conduct politics of identities, attempting to bridge or, more correctly, to neutralize disagreements that extend beyond the issues that can be agreed on. For example, the modus operandi of the Women's Network, or that of Women in Black— which agreed on a single slogan, refusing to debate on other feminist issues apart from that of "End the Occupation" (Helman and Rapoport 1997)—or other attempts to set up an ad hoc coalition (like Ikar's struggle to deal with the issue of *agunot* and recalcitrant husbands who refuse to grant their wives a divorce).

The feminist voice is growing ever more diverse, preventing the formation of a uniform feminist identity that can unite women around it and crystallize them into a single political force. The multivocal, nonunified participation of feminist organizations in the formal, institutionalized political arena leaves the feminist women's organizations outside the power foci of decision makers, but they have clearly become an influential social force that must be reckoned with. Obviously, this is the achievement of a "movement," though not a movement that wins seats in the Knesset. It is a movement that aims to change the public agenda and, in this sense, in addition to being a political force, it is extending the borders of politics.

Women, Motherhood, and Politics

The dilemmas over what constitutes feminist discourse are embodied in the most dramatic way in the growing phenomenon of women who mobilize their female or maternal status to enter the political discourse. As an issue, this is not new, and it has existed ever since the feminist movement came into being. The first suffragettes were divided on the question of whether to demand electoral rights because of their unique contribution as mothers, or because of their universal civil right—a right that is blind to gender and role.

Repeated attempts by women to enter the heart of Israel's political discourse were doomed to repeated failure, as the analysis has shown so far. Israeli politics—which presents itself as gender-blind—replicated gender-based distinctions by perceiving women as being first and foremost mothers and wives. From the 1980s on, we see attempts by women to challenge this pattern, using those gendered definitions; that is, women mobilize the substantial legitimization that Israeli society grants to motherhood and femaleness, as a means of joining in the political discourse from which they are excluded.

Influenced by the dominance of the security discourse, women started to recruit mothers on the basis of their worries about their children, in order to make their political voice heard (Azmon 1997; Gilath 1991; Zuckerman-Bareli and Benski 1989). Women protested the protracted war in Lebanon under the banners of "Parents Against Silence," "Bring the Boys Home," and the "Four Mothers" organization. Calls to evacuate the Occupied Territories were accompanied by parents organizing under the slogan "Parents against Silence" and "Mothers for Peace." The "other" voice that was uttered was the female voice, which was perceived to be at variance with the dominant male voice. Though their concern was accepted with understanding, it was also disparaged—"because it's natural for women to worry"—or, as Knesset member Geula Cohen said as she observed a demonstration of Women Against Silence, "The mothers have forgotten they have a brain, and are thinking via their wombs." Often, mothers' protests were excoriated by military staff, who claimed that they should encourage the spirits of their warrior sons. Still, their voices did not die down. The Four Mothers organization played a leading role in the calls for the Israeli army to get out of Lebanon, and those calls were indeed answered. The female voice of concern was not only recruited by the Left to promote peace, but also by women from the Right, to intensify demands to settle in Judea and

Samaria. Accordingly, women from Rachelim justified a settlement outpost as a means of safeguarding their children's physical security (El-Or 1995). Like their sisters from the Left, they called to shift the maternal practices of concern and caregiving from the private sphere into the public, thus aiming to politicize the maternal voice. Terrorist attacks and the army's incursion into the territory of the Palestinian Authority in the "Defensive Shield" operation both generated other women's movements: "The Fifth Mother" and "The Seventh Day," which call for evacuating the territories and returning to the Green Line borders; as well as a new Right-wing movement, "Many Mothers" and "White and Blue Mothers," opposing the movements of women from the Left.

In contrast, with the use of mothers to claim a right of participation, and also as a means for defying the boundaries between private and public, the Women in Black, who protested against the occupation, and Women in Green and Blue and White Women, who supported continued settlements in the occupied territories, all intended to take part in the political discourse as women, and not necessarily as mothers. This attitude is particularly prominent in Women in Black, an organization that sought to relinquish women's taken-for-granted identity, in which every female is a mother or a potential mother. Through the response to Women in Black, we can see that it was easier for society to "accept" a maternal-female message than a female-feminist message. In the message of Women in Black there was a dual challenge—to the dominant security-oriented discourse and also to the gendered order, including worldviews that limit the world of women to motherhood. They sought to join the political discourse simply by virtue of being women, not by virtue of the social roles that channel them into the world of home and family. They emphasized what is common to women everywhere, and to both Palestinian and Jewish (Helman and Rapoport 1997).

Even if the women's movements that were based on being women and mothers did not attract many women, they placed fresh questions on the political-public agenda and challenged the gendered borders of Israel's political discourse. Without doubt, the most outstanding feminist achievement of those women is that they dismantled the obstacles to entering the security discourse.

Concluding Remarks

Women's politics, or alternatively, feminist politics, implies the demand to recognize women as a social category suffering discrimination and deprivation. It is a demand to recognize the gendered social world, a demand made on society to observe itself and to examine the presupposed assumptions that form the social order, and especially the sexual roles prevailing within it. Has this voice been heard in Israel? At what intensity?

To a considerable degree, the pincers of the simultaneously inclusionary and gendered culture have determined women's political prospects. As a generalization, it can be asserted that women who were elected were women in politics, but women who did not necessarily implement women's politics. True, the majority of women Knesset members and the women involved in local authorities sat on committees engaged in "female" issues, and they were without doubt among the supporters and promoters of legislation and policy influencing the world of women. However, the majority did so on an isolated basis, by virtue of their position, and to a substantial extent did so subject to the dominant agenda that is principally set by men. Without detracting from the value of their endeavors, their lack of awareness of the gendered social order made the few women who were active in political endeavors partners in reproducing the existing order.

Political culture in Israel, as outlined here, had reservations about feminist activity and marginalized it. However, since the end of the seventies, feminist organizing has grown and flourished in Israel, but women have remained mainly in the ex-parliamentary arena. The prime characteristics of this organizing are challenging awareness, grassroots growth, and the lack of direct dependence on parties or the establishment's political organizations. Many organizations focus on a single issue: combating violence against women, rape, *agunot* (women who are refused, or unable to obtain, a divorce), offensive advertising, Mizrahi women, Palestinian women, peace, and so on. Although most such organizations are still small and marginal, it can be claimed that the conjunction of this spectrum of voices is slowly penetrating the feminist organizations deserves a separate discussion; it exceeds the goal of this study, which focuses on formal politics and women's representations within it.

As the winds of feminism blew stronger, the formal sphere did not remain unaffected. Women brought about legislative changes that were aimed at enhancing equality. Among the laws that were passed were those that assured women's representation in directorships of government and public firms, stipulated equal wages for women in return for equal work, and prohibited sexual harassment. Growing awareness of the issue led to increased activity around the enforcement of laws, and greater reliance on the Law of Human Rights, in order to establish the right to equality. Some symbolic expressions of the burgeoning attempts to blur the gendered dichotomy were effected in the army by gradually admitting women to combat positions, dismantling the Women's Corps—a mechanism that had institutionalized the separation between women and men in the army—and creating frameworks for military tasks shared by men and women. This last endeavor is an interesting example of the ongoing negotiations over the social boundaries of the gendered world in Israel. Together with the attempt to blur the boundaries and to include women in the world of men, another stubborn struggle continues—that religious groups resisting such inclusion, and the allied struggle by religious men to avoid conscription and to remain in the world of the *yeshivot,* a world that remains closed to women in Israel.

Finally, the political culture of exclusion and inclusion of women in Israeli politics as analyzed here is not unique to the political sphere. It can equally be found in the army (Izraeli 1997), in the labor market (Izraeli 1999), in the literary world (Naveh 1999), and in the sphere of art and culture (Azmon 2001). In all these areas, the past decade has witnessed attempts to blur the gendered dichotomy, and to bring about the more egalitarian inclusion of women in various public domains (see data of the Israeli Women's Network 2001). However, realizing the challenge of blurring the gendered dichotomy is also strongly linked to the degree of weakening of the other mechanisms that previously reinforced the gendered boundaries. Although the myth of equality finally disintegrated a short while ago, which certainly prepared society to show greater openness to the issue of women's status, the sustainability of other mechanisms is not clear-cut. A study is required of the trajectories of development in traditional Jewish and Palestinian cultures, the intensity of the separation processes between religion and state, and the path that the Arab-Israeli conflict is taking. Even a superficial examination supports the claim that the processes occurring in each sphere are not necessarily moving along the same trajectory. Thus, for example, some changes are taking place in Palestinian and Jewish cultures that may lead to greater equality between the genders; changes in the world of religion and in the status of women in religious communities constitute only one such aspect (El-Or 1998). In contrast, at the start of the century, the Israeli-Palestinian conflict, which had seemed close to resolution, was exacerbated. Not only did the Al-Aksa intifada cut off the dialogue between Palestinians and Israelis beyond the Green Line, it also filtered into the delicate fabric of relations between Israel's Jewish and Palestinian citizens. As a result, cooperation between Palestinian and Jewish women within Israel was markedly reduced, and the feminist voices that called for change were hushed.

The simultaneous existence of inclusionary and exclusionary processes explains, to a great extent, the weakness of the feminist movement in Israel, in view of the unequal economic, cultural, and political opportunities, as well as inequalities in terms of income, power, and social prestige. At the same time, I would like to claim that, while exclusion creates subordinated social feminine enclaves, it also has the potential for social change. An ongoing segregation that exists alongside growing awareness of the need for women's inclusion in the collective has the potential for creating a new agenda, and even for crystallizing a feminine claim challenging the existing social norms and sociopolitical institutional arrangements.

REFERENCES

Azmon, Yael. 1997. "War, Mothers, and Girls with Braids: Involvement of Mothers' Peace Movements in the National Discourse in Israel." *Israel Social Science Review* 12: 109–28.

Azmon, Yael, ed. 2001. *Will You Listen to My Voice—Representation of Women in Israeli Culture*. Tel Aviv: Van Leer Jerusalem Institute and Hakibbutz Hameuchad Publishing House (Hebrew).

Berkovitch, Nitza. 1999. "Women of Valor: Women and Citizenship in Israel." *Israeli Sociology* 2: 277–317 (Hebrew).

Bernstein, Deborah. 1987. *The Struggle for Equality: Urban Women Workers in Prestate Israeli Society*. New York: Praeger.

Committee for the Advancement of Women's Status, *Report to the Knesset*. Jerusalem: 1998.

El-Or, Tamar. 1994. *Educated and Ignorant: Ultra-Orthodox Jewish Women and Their World*. Boulder and London: Lynne Rienner Publishers.

———. 1998. *New Pessach: Literary and Identity of Young Religious Zionist Women*. Tel Aviv: Am Oved Publishers Ltd (Hebrew).

El-Or, Tamar, and Gideon Aran. 1995. "Giving Birth to Settlement Maternal Thinking and Political Action of Jewish Women on the West Bank." *Gender and Society* 9: 60–78.

Fogiel-Bijaoui, Sylvie. 1992a. "Feminine Organizations in Israel—Current Situation." *International Problems, Society and Politics* 31: 65–76 (Hebrew).

———. 1992b. "From Revolution to Motherhood: The Case of Women in the Kibbutz, 1948–1910." In *Pioneers and Homemakers: Jewish Women in Prestate Israeli Society*, ed. Deborah S. Bernstein, 211–33. Albany: State University of New York Press.

———. 1992c. "The Struggle for Women's Suffrage in Israel: 1917–1926." In *Pioneers and Homemakers: Jewish Women in Prestate Israeli Society*, ed. Deborah S. Bernstein, 275–302. Albany: State University of New York Press.

Freedman, Maricia. 1990. *Exile in the Promised Land*. Ithaca, N.Y.: Firebrand Books.

Gilath, Nurit. 1991. "Women against War: 'Parents against Silence.'" In *Calling the Equality Bluff—Women in Israel*, ed. B. Swirski and M. Safir, 142–46. New York: Pergamon Press.

Githens, Marianne, Pippa Norris, and Joni Lovenduski, eds. 1994. *Different Roles, Different Voices: Women and Politics in the United States and Europe*. New York: Harper Collins.

Hasan, Manar. 1994. "Murder of Women for 'Family Honour' in Palestinian Society and the Factors Promoting its Continuation in the State of Israel." In M.A. dissertation, "Gender and Ethnic Studies," University of Greenwich, Greenwich, England.

Helman, Sara, and Tamar Rapoport. 1997. "Women in Black: Challenging Israel's Gender and Socio-Political Orders." *British Journal of Sociology* 48: 682–700.

Herzog, Hanna. 1992. "The Fringes of the Margin—Women's Organizations in the Civic Sector of the Yishuv." In *Pioneers and Homemakers: Jewish Women in Prestate Israeli Society*, ed. Deborah S. Bernstein, 283–304. Albany: State University of New York Press.

Herzog, Hanna. 1996. "Why so Few? The Political Culture of Gender in Israel." *International Review of Women and Leadership* 2: 1–18.

———. 1998a. "Double Marginality: 'Oriental' and Arab Women in Local Politics." In *Ethnic Frontiers and Peripheries: Landscapes of Development and Inequality in Israel,* ed. O. Yiftachel and A. Meir, 287–307. Boulder, Colo.: Westview Press.

———. 1998b. "Homefront and Battlefront and the Status of Jewish and Palestinian Women in Israel." *Israeli Studies* 3: 61–84.

———. 1999. *Gendering Politics—Women in Israel.* Ann Arbor: University of Michigan Press.

Israel Women's Network. 2001. *Women in Israel—Concentration of Data and Information 1999–2000.* Tel Aviv: The Israel Women's Network, The Center for Information and Research of Policy (Hebrew).

Izraeli, Dafna N. 1981. "The Zionist Women's Movement in Palestine, 1911–1927: A Sociological Analysis." *Signs* 7: 87–114.

———. 1997. "Gendering Military Service in Israeli Defense Forces." *Israel Social Science Research* 12: 129–66.

———. 1999. "Gendering the Labor World." In *Sex, Gender Politics—Women in Israel,* ed. D. N. Izraeli, Ariella Freedman, Henriette Dahan-Kalev, Slyvia Fogiel-Bijaoui, Hanna Herzog, Manar Hasan, and Hanna Naveh, 167–215. Tel Aviv: Hakibbutz Hameuchad (Hebrew).

Kimmerling, Baruch. 1993a. "Patterns of Militarism in Israel." *Archives of European Sociology* 34: 196–223.

———. 1993b. "Yes, Back to the Family." *Politika* 48: 40–45 (Hebrew).

Lahav, Penina. 1993. "'When the Palliative Simply Impairs': The Debate in the Knesset on the Law for Women's Rights." *Zmanim—A Historical Quarterly* 12: 149–59 (Hebrew).

Lovenduski, Joni, and Pippa Norris. 1993. *Gender and Party Politics.* London: Sage.

Naveh, Hannah. 1999. "*Leket, Pe-ah, Veshikha:* Life Outside the Canon." 49–106 in *Sex, Gender, Politics: Women in Israel,* ed. Dafna N. Izraeli, Ariella Friedman, Henriette Dahan-Kalev, Sylvia Fogiel-Bijaoui, Hanna Herzog, Manar Hasan, Hannah Naveh. Tel Aviv: Hakibbutz Hameauchad. (Hebrew).

Phillips, Anne. 1994. "Dealing with Difference: A Politics of Ideas or a Politics of Presence?" *Constellations* 1: 74–91.

Raday, Fransis, Carmel Shalev, and Michal Liban-Kooby, eds. 1995. *Women's Status in Israeli Law and Society.* Jerusalem and Tel Aviv: Schocken Publishing House (Hebrew).

Ram, Uri. 1993. "Emerging Modalities of Feminist Sociology in Israel." *Israel Social Science Research* 8: 51–76.

Sawer, Marian, and Marian Simms. 1993. *A Woman's Place: Women and Politics in Australia.* Sydney: Allen and Unwin.

Uday, Mehta S. 1990. "Liberal Strategies of Exclusion." *Politics and Society* 18: 427–57.

Yishai, Yael. 1997. *Between the Flag and the Banner: Women in Israeli Politics.* Albany: State University of New York Press.

Young, Iris Marion. 1990. "Polity and Group Difference: A Critique of the Ideal of Universal Citizenship." In *Feminism and Political Theory,* ed. C. R. Sunstein, 117–41. Chicago, London: University of Chicago Press.

Yuval-Davis, Nira. 1993. "Gender and Nation." *Ethnic and Racial Studies* 16: 621–32.

Zuckerman-Bareli, Chaya, and Tova Benski. 1989. "Parents Against Silence." *Megamot* 32: 27–42 (Hebrew).

CHAPTER NINE

Religion in the Israeli Public Square

ᘿᔓ

CHAIM I. WAXMAN

Background

Most students of Israeli society agree that although Israel is not as secular as are most modern societies, it is not a theocracy.[1] And yet religion plays a much greater role within the Israeli polity than it does, for example, within the American polity. Israel was established as a Jewish State, and the vast majority of Israel's Jews—secular as well as religious—agree that Judaism is a basic and necessary component of being Jewish and, therefore, of Israeli society and its political culture. As a consequence, the nature of religious conflict in Israel is much different than it is in other modern societies (Liebman and Don-Yehiya 1983, 1984). It is not simply a conflict between religious and secular Jews. Indeed, the division of Israel into these two camps is a major oversimplification. The ideologically secular are actually a relatively small minority in Israel, though they are a vocal minority and are prominent in the academy and the media. The largest sector is the traditionalist sector, that is, those who are religiously traditional but not observant according to Orthodox standards. The Orthodox Jews themselves may be subdivided into *haredi,* or ultra-Orthodox, and modern Orthodox. The different religious perspectives of these groups has long served as a source of tension, even in the pre-State era. It is not unique to Israel and is in fact characteristic of many Jewish communities in the modern era. The basic conflict in Israel is over the limits of religion within the political sphere, and the basic tensions are those that emerge from the power struggles between religious and secular parties. But the impact and consequences of these conflicts are not then limited to specific Israeli political parties. They have had a major impact on relations between Israel and the Diaspora at various times in recent years.

The Israeli elections of 1996 resulted in significant gains for the religious parties. For the first time, the religious parties garnered more than twenty Knesset seats. These gains are not, as might be assumed, owing to the higher birth rate among religious Jews than among secular Jews. Nor are the gains the product of a massive *ba'al teshuva,* or "religious return" movement, or the result of a mass exodus of the secular from Israel or its political system. Rather, the gains appear

221

to be the product of the religious parties' pursuit of ideological and ethnic politics. As Eliezer Don-Yehiya has indicated, although the political relevance of class divisions in Israel declined after the Six Day War, ideological and ethnic divisions did not. Since the 1980s, two of the largest religious parties have responded to the ideological and ethnic rifts, with Shas playing the ethnic card and attracting traditional, nonreligious Sephardim, and the National Religious Party (NRP) playing the ideological card (Don-Yehiya 1997). Moreover, with Labor's victory in 1992 and the prominence of Meretz in the Labor coalition, many of the Sephardim and the religious felt they had no alternative but to return to the religious parties. From 1977 to 1992, many felt that the Jewish character of Israel and the interests of the religious communities were in good hands under the Likud. With Labor's victory in 1992 and especially with its partnership with Meretz, which projected an anti-religious stance, many among the religious returned to the religious parties. There is no question that the rift is very deep. However, the rhetoric of protagonists on both sides should be avoided. The fact is that the religious-secular rift is not new in Israel. Indeed, it preceded the establishment of the State of Israel by decades. There were clashes at the early Zionist congresses, and they were not limited to verbal assaults; the antagonists came to physical blows on more than one occasion (Luz 1988). Despite the rhetoric by extremists on both sides, the empirical evidence indicates the persistence of a basic unity among Israeli Jews that is much stronger than any differences between them with respect to the issue of religion in Israeli society (Liebman and Katz 1997). This is not to suggest that the issue is not a serious one. On the contrary, it is one of the most serious domestic issues in Israel and it raises the question of whether the recent patterns of Israeli religio-politics will further exacerbate and even threaten that underlying social unity.

The Religious Parties: Power and Influence

The religious parties in Israel cannot be analyzed, particularly by a sociologist, without considering how Israelis perceive those parties and the impact they have on "the religious situation" there. Three religious parties in the 1996 elections won sufficient votes for seating in the Knesset: Shas, the National Religious Party (NRP), and United Torah Judaism (UTJ). Those elections presented them with the greatest electoral gain in Israel's political history. Together, they won almost 20 percent of the votes and gained twenty-three Knesset seats. The previous high was eighteen seats, and, perhaps even more significant, the religious parties suffered an aggregate decline in 1992 from eighteen to sixteen seats. In other words, their 1996 feat was an increase of 50 percent in their number of seats (Table 1).

Table 1. Number of Knesset Seats of Religious Parties, 1949–99

	'49	'51	'55	'59	'61	'65	'69	'73	'77	'81[3]	'84[4]	'88	'92	'96	'99
Aguda group[1]		5	6	6	6	6	6	5	5	4	4	7	4	4	5
NRP[2]	16	10	11	12	12	11	12	10	12	6	4	5	6	9	5
Shas											4	6	6	10	17
Total	16	15	17	18	18	17	18	15	17	10	12	18	16	23	27

[1]Includes Poalei Agudat Israel and/or Degel Hatorah.

[2]In 1949, there were four religious parties, Aguda, Poalei Aguda, Mizrachi and Poalei Mizrachi, and they ran on a joint religious list. Mizrachi and Hapoel Hamizrachi were separate parties until 1956, when they merged into the NRP.

[3]These figures do not include Tami, a Sephardi party which was not explicitly a religious one although, in effect, it was. It received three seats in 1981 and one in 1984.

[4]In 1984, Poalei Aguda joined with Matzad to form the Morasha list which won two seats. The figure for the Aguda Group includes the two seats won by Agudat Israel and the two of Morasha.

The 1996 electoral gains were actually experienced by only two of the three religious parties, Shas and the NRP. UTJ succeeded solely in retaining the four seats it had previously held. Shas, by contrast, increased its parliamentary power from six to ten seats, and the NRP increased from six to nine seats. How one views these gains depends on the background against which they are measured. On the obvious level, the gains of Shas were the greatest. Shas, an acronym for the Hebrew of Sephardi Torah Guardians, was founded in 1984 when its leaders seceded from Agudat Israel, which is headed by Ashkenazim. But Shas's origins go back even further and are, in part, an ironic consequence of an action by the NRP in the previous year.

In 1983, a rift between the NRP and the Ashkenazi chief rabbi, Shlomo Goren, led to the NRP's pushing through legislation that limited the tenure of the chief rabbis to ten years, with the consequence that Goren and his Sephardi counterpart, Rabbi Ovadia Yosef, would soon be forced to leave office. Simultaneously, Yosef and his colleagues felt that Agudat Israel had been oblivious to the needs of Sephardim both within the party itself and within the world of higher *yeshivot,* academies of Torah learning. Local elections in Israel's cities were taking place that year, and Rabbi Yosef and his colleagues decided to run their own slates in Jerusalem and Bnai Brak, very probably as a trial balloon for subsequent national elections. The party was originally to be called Sach, an acronym for Sephardi Haredim, but that name was rejected by the electoral council. The name Shas was chosen instead (Horovitz 1989, pp. 134–43). The party, although officially *haredi,* made its focus the ethnic rather than the religious issue, and it appealed to all Sephardim, regardless of the affiliate's religious conduct. It also differed from the Ashkenazi *haredi* Agudat Israel in that it did not demur from Zionism. Rather, it referred to itself as a *haredi,* rather than secular, Zionist party (Dayan 1999, p. 7).

Shas's achievements in the local elections in Jerusalem and Bnai Brak took everyone by surprise, and it decided to run a slate in the 1984 national elections. For that campaign, Shas attained the support of Rabbi Eliezer Shach of Bnai Brak (1894–2001), the spiritual leader of the Lithuanian sector of the *haredim,* who had long feuded with Rabbi Simcha Bunim Alter, the spiritual leader of Gur hasidim and the head of Agudat Israel. In its initial election, Shas achieved four Knesset seats. Its record, thus, is one of growth from an initial four, to six in 1988, to ten in 1996, and to seventeen in 1999.

The impressive success Shas has had in such a brief time may be attributed to its appeal to the large Sephardi population, many of whom felt alienated from and neglected by the traditional parties, which are Ashkenazi-dominated. In addition, because of different historical circumstances than those of the Ashkenazim, Sephardim do not have the kind of religious-secular polarization that is present in Ashkenazi communities, and Shas, especially through its dynamic political leader Arye Deri, was able to appeal to and attract traditional, though not *haredi* nor even religiously observant, Sephardim. The traditional Sephardi masses are willing to have rabbinic leaders, such as Rabbi Yosef, and do not find this troublesome. On the contrary, they readily accept it. Thus, despite Deri's conviction, in March 1999, on numerous counts of fraud and obstruction of justice, he remained the political leader of Shas and had the backing of both Rabbi Yosef and the masses of Shas voters, who viewed his years-long trial as an Ashkenazi campaign against Sephardi political leaders. Indeed, Deri produced and widely distributed a sophisticated videocassette and CD-ROM entitled "*Ani Ma-ashim*" (I Accuse), in which he presented his case for an Ashkenazi-elitist conspiracy not only against him but against Sephardim as a group. In one segment, after relating the prosecution charges concerning his affluent lifestyle, Deri showed his own modest apartment in the Har Nof section of Jerusalem and contrasted it with the luxurious private homes of the very judges who found him guilty.

Despite the predictions of some that his conviction would harm Shas in the election, Deri's campaign was actually highly successful. The fact that Meretz and, especially, Shinui ran vitriolic anti-*haredi* campaigns probably also contributed some votes to Shas, in reaction to what was viewed by some traditional Israeli Jews as unjustified and unprecedented hostility toward religion in general. Be that as it may, Shas's Knesset representation grew from ten to seventeen seats, a much greater growth than that of any other party, and it became the third largest party, in terms of Knesset representation. Deri himself, however, was forced to resign from the party's leadership when Ehud Barak made it clear that he would not enter into any coalition negotiations with Shas as long as Deri, a convicted criminal, remained at its helm. His successor, Minister of Labor and Social Affairs Eli Yishai, initially received a lukewarm to hostile reception by many Shas members who were Deri loyalists. Although he managed to overcome challenges and continued as party spokesman in both the Barak and Sharon governments, many of Deri's loyalists remained embittered by what they viewed as the Yishai's double-crossing of Deri. Assuming that Deri remains out of the Shas political limelight, it remains to be seen whether the party will be able to retain its Knesset representation after the next election. Indeed, retaining their seventeen members of Knesset will be an even bigger challenge, in that there will no longer be independent elections for prime minister. As a result, it is probable that a significant number of those who voted for Shas in 1999 will vote for Labor or, more likely, Likud in the next election.

As for the NRP, it has had a much more erratic experience in recent years. The history of the NRP goes back to the early days of the World Zionist Organization (WZO). When the Fifth Zionist Congress in 1901 resolved to enter the educational sphere, many religious members of the WZO, who believed that secular nationalism was antithetical to Judaism, refused to acquiesce to a program of secular Zionist education. Under the leadership of Rabbi Isaac Jacob Reines, the Mizrachi movement was founded in Vilna in 1902 as the religious Zionist organization within the WZO. It was the first recognized separate federation within the World Zionist Organization. The name is an acronym for *mercaz ruhani* (spiritual center), and its banner was, "The Land of Israel for the people of Israel according to the Torah of Israel." In 1904, a world conference of Mizrachi was convened in Bratislava, Czechoslovakia (then Pressburg, Hungary), and the Mizrachi World Organization was founded with the objective of educating and promoting religious Zionism in all religious Jewish circles. The first convention of the American Mizrachi Organization was convened in 1914, under the influence of Rabbi Meir Bar-Ilan (Berlin), who was then general secretary of the world Mizrachi organization, in Hamburg (Altona), and who had toured the United States extensively during the previous months.

After World War I, a group that, in addition to being sympathetic to the goals of Mizrachi, believed in settlement and labor, formed the Hapoel Hamizrachi (Mizrachi Labor) Organization, which went on to found a series of religious kibbutz and moshav settlements. Although Hapoel Hamizrachi worked very closely with Mizrachi, the two were separate, autonomous organizations and initially remained so when they were transformed into political parties in the Knesset. They merged in 1956 and became the National Religious Party (NRP). From 1951 to 1977, they jointly occupied ten to twelve seats in the Knesset.

After the Six Day War, as Don-Yehiya has elucidated (1994, p. 60), activist messianism in the religious Zionist community emerged and spread as a result of developments within Yeshivat Mercaz Harav, the yeshiva founded by Rabbi Abraham Isaac Kook and then headed by his son, Rabbi Zvi Yehuda Kook. Under the latter's influence, the yeshiva became the spiritual center of activist messianism, and it produced the core leaders and activists of Gush Emunim. This activist and radical group incorporated notions that legitimated "any means necessary" (to borrow a phrase from American black nationalists of the 1960s) in the pursuit of its goals. This meant that not only the interests of other countries but also those within Israel, even if instituted by the government of Israel, could be blatantly ignored if they hindered the realization of the messianic goals. Mercaz Harav also took on a central role in the educational system of religious Zionism, especially in the systems of yeshiva high schools and nationalist, "*hesder,*" yeshivas, which developed during the late 1950s and 1960s, largely in reaction to a growing secularism within the public religious educational network. As a result, the ideology of radical religious Zionism was propounded as religious dogma in the increasing number of schools to which religious Zionist parents sent their children, and it increasingly gained adherents within the religious Zionist community (Sprinzak 1991, pp. 107–66).

During the early 1970s, a bitter dispute between the radicals and moderates erupted within the national religious ranks, and the victory of the territorial maximalists abruptly ended the tradition of a separation between religion and politics in the religious Zionist community. Since then, despite the forebodings of senior members of the party, the NRP has changed from a democratic party led by a religiously conscious and politically astute laity to a party in which the religio-political rulings of rabbis determine policies and action.

Although the NRP gained three seats in 1996, that increase was the first that the party had experienced in a decade and a half. In 1981, the party had lost half of its twelve seats, and it declined from its representation of two-thirds of the combined religious parties to less than half. It had lost even further in 1984 and 1988 and declined to less than a third of the combined religious parties votes. The 1992 elections gave the NRP a modest gain of one seat, but that only brought it back to what its number of seats had been in 1981. The increase to nine seats and about 40 percent of the combined religious parties' votes in 1996 appeared to suggest a major change in the party's electoral fortunes.

However, the NRP suffered a major setback in 1999, with the loss of four Knesset seats as the result of a combination of factors. Most significantly, the formation of the "National Unity" (*ihud hale-umi*) coalition, consisting of Rehavam Zeevi's Moledet, Benny Begin's Herut, and Hanan Porat's Tekuma parties, drew significant numbers of highly nationalistic religious Zionists from the

NRP because, prior to his defection, Porat had long been an activist within the NRP and, ironically, he had sworn his allegiance to the NRP when he returned to the fold after the collapse of his earlier attempt at establishing a strong joint religious-secular nationalist party.

In addition, the NRP was not able to attract more moderate religious nationalists because of its maneuverings, which placed a number of strongly nationalistic candidates at the top of the list despite the wishes of the party's membership for a more moderate list, as manifested in its primary elections. In addition, in the 1999 election campaign, the *haredi* party, UTJ, projected itself as a nationalist party. Deputy housing minister Meir Porush, son of Aguda leader Menachem Porush, claimed to have delivered more Jewish housing to the territories than any of his predecessors, and the slogan for the party was, "We will go on believing and building." The significantly increased presence of *haredim* in the territories is due less to their ideological commitments to Judea and Samaria than to their high birth rate and relatively low economic status, which makes housing within the "Green Line" less affordable for them. That new presence as well as the increasingly strident nationalism of UTJ drew those in the national religious camp who viewed the NRP as too weak either in its religious or national commitments (Keinon 1999).

In addition, 1981 witnessed the onset of a trend that has not reversed itself, namely, the departure of Sephardim from the NRP in favor of Tami, initially, Likud, and, most significantly, since 1984, of Shas. Indeed, according to Eliezer Don-Yehiya, the ethnic factor has been central in the religio-political arena since 1981, and it delivered the "knockout" blow to the NRP (Don-Yehiya 2001). Contrary to popular impression, he suggests, Sephardim and *haredim* have much in common from a sociological perspective. They are both characterized by the centrality of the traditional community, including the strong roles of family and local community, as well as admiration for charismatic leaders and involvement in holy rituals, among others, all of which are alien to modern society. In addition, the memberships of both Shas and the *haredi* parties identify with spiritual leaders, rather than professional politicians. The NRP, on the other hand, despite its being a religious party, was always integrated within the modern world and was always led by professional politicians.

Probably also related to the NRP's dramatic decline, 1981 also marked a significant change in the nature of the relationship between the Zionist NRP and the non-Zionist *haredi* parties, the most significant of which, Agudat Israel and Degel Hatorah, combined to form UTJ in 1992. In contrast to the acrimony that traditionally marked their relationship, they now functioned as partners in a coalition, the factions of which had similar goals and values. This change was a product of three basic developments. There were religious changes in the national religious camp, as mentioned previously, with the emergence of rabbis as determiners of political positions. There were also political changes within the *haredi* camp. If, as I have argued elsewhere, there has been a "haredization" of American Orthodox Judaism (Waxman 1998), it seems appropriate to characterize the developments in Israel as "the *hardalization* of Israeli Orthodoxy," "*hardal*" being a play on the Hebrew term for mustard and an acronym for "*haredi-leumi*," or "ultra-Orthodox-nationalist." The nationalism of the *haredi* sector should actually not be all that surprising. The masses were probably always highly nationalistic. Indeed, it appears that there is, in many countries, a correlation between political conservatism and religious conservatism. The *haredi* leadership has, until recently,[2] officially been nonnationalistic because of the opposition to secular Zionism, but that did not prevent the masses from being nationalistic. Their increasing nationalism appears to be rooted in their greater sense of security within Israeli society. By security, I do not mean security from external challenges but, rather, from internal ones. In the pre-State and early-State periods, the *haredi* sector felt threatened from the secular majority and was, thus, somewhat ambivalent about the entire notion of Israeli sovereignty. In recent decades, however, almost the entire Orthodox sector of Israel, *haredi* and modern Orthodox (Liebman 1998), has grown and developed a sense of self-confidence. *Haredim,* in particular, not only do not feel threatened by the secular, they are confident to the point of triumphalism and, if anything, believe that the days of secularism in Israel are numbered. They are also reacting to challenges to the "status quo" by non-Orthodox segments of Israeli society by aligning themselves with the more nationalistic parties that have typically been more open to religious traditionalism, as will be discussed below.

Judaism in the Public Sphere

The term *status quo* in this context dates back to a letter, signed by David Ben-Gurion, Rabbi Judah Leib Fishman (Maimon), and Yizhak Gruenbaum, in the name of the Jewish Agency, that was sent to leaders of Agudat Israel in June 1947, wherein it was agreed that, in the State of Israel, the religious situation would continue as it had previously been, with freedom of religion in the private sphere and with traditional Judaism in the public sphere. As outlined in the letter, the Jewish Sabbath, Saturday, would be a national day of rest; all kitchens in government-run buildings would adhere to the kosher dietary laws; marriage and divorce would remain in the realm of the rabbinic courts; and the various educational streams—religious, secular, and independent—would be institutionalized within the State (Warhaftig 1988, pp. 34–36).

Almost since the beginning, the Orthodox and the secular have each alleged that the other side has abrogated the "status quo agreement" (Liebman and Don-Yehiya 1984, pp. 31–40). For example, throughout the years, one of the most persistent issues of strife has been that of Sabbath observance, which has become both a national issue and a local one. On the national level, the NRP has consistently sought to have the government enact and enforce a Sabbath Law, under which all nonessential public facilities, and especially buses, trains, and El Al, Israel's national airline, would cease operation from sundown Friday to sunset Saturday. Some of the parties, especially Mapam, were opposed to any such restrictions. A compromise was worked out to the effect that the Sabbath was accepted as an official day of rest, but the specifics of the law, what was and what was not forbidden, were left to the local municipalities. The result was that, except in Haifa and several other areas, public buses did not run on the Sabbath. To the Orthodox Jew, the observance of the Sabbath is one of the most basic precepts of Judaism; it is the fulfillment of a Commandment, and it serves as a testimony to the very act of Creation. To many non-Orthodox, even if the Sabbath does have some religious significance, the Sabbath Law is a great inconvenience, if for no other reason than the fact that Saturday is the only day that one might spend shopping or at leisure with family and friends. The unavailability of public transportation, especially if one cannot afford a car or a private taxi, may be viewed as an unjustifiable restriction of a basic freedom.

Even more serious is the open conflict that has persistently erupted on the local level, most notably in a growing number of sections of Jerusalem that have amassed large numbers of *haredim.* In these neighborhoods, many of the residents attempt to bar all traffic on the Sabbath on the grounds that it disturbs the Sabbath peace. The *haredim* and their secular counterparts hold frequent demonstrations and counterdemonstrations, which frequently become violent confrontations between the demonstrators and the police, with neither side being noted for its restraint. Although the modern Orthodox have tended to eschew such demonstrations, many of them are sympathetic to the overall attempt to maintain the religious significance of the Sabbath. Indeed, it was over the issue of an alleged violation of the Sabbath by the state that the NRP legitimated its secession from the ruling coalition, which led to the fall of the first Rabin government in 1977.[3]

The other major issue has been that of "who is a Jew?" This issue is, on the one hand, much more basic than that of the Sabbath but, until recently, except for a few cases, it was viewed as a somewhat esoteric question. The question derives from the founding of the state as the "Jewish State" and the variety of interpretations given to the significance and raison d'être of that state, with the answers ranging from those who conceived of it in completely secular terms to those who perceived it from a specifically religious perspective. The issue burst forth as a real question in 1958, with the immigration of Jews from countries behind the Iron Curtain, where there had been considerable intermarriage and many of the new immigrants had non-Jewish wives. The question arose as to whether these wives and their children could be registered as Jewish on their identity cards. To the Orthodox, this was not merely a particular problem insofar as these wives and children were concerned; it was a much broader problem because when these children grew up and married, they might involve many others (their spouses) in the problem of intermarriage. After a bitter debate and the resignation of Mizrachi from the government, Prime Minister Ben-Gurion took the unique step of writing to some fifty intellectuals and "Sages of Israel" throughout the world, asking them to give their opinion on the question of Jewish identity and how to register Israelis of mixed marriages. The majority responded in accordance with the Orthodox view (Ben-Raphael 2001; Litvin and Hoenig 1965). The issue abated with the decision of the government to leave registration to the Ministry of the Interior, which in 1960 returned to NRP control.

In 1962, the question of "Who is a Jew?" erupted once again, but this time on a much more isolated level, with the case of "Brother Daniel," a Jewish-born Catholic monk who applied for Israeli citizenship under the Law of Return, which grants the right to automatic citizenship to any Jew upon immigration. Brother Daniel (Oswald Rufeisen) requested citizenship and Jewish nationality on the grounds that he was born Jewish and that he still regarded himself as ethnically Jewish. The case came to the Supreme Court, which ruled (not unanimously) that, by being an apostate, he had broken his historic link with Judaism and thus was not eligible to enter under the Law of Return. As to his nationality, that space on his identity card was left blank.

The issue arose once more as a national question with the arrival of a large group of Bene Israel, Jews from India who had, for centuries, been isolated from world Jewry, and among whom, it was suspected, intermarriage was commonplace. With its sweeping ruling, which in effect gave all of the Bene Israel full legitimate status as Jews, the Chief Rabbinate itself became embroiled in a bitter conflict with many other rabbis, especially those of Agudat Israel, which has never accepted the authority of the Chief Rabbinate. The latter began to hedge and apply qualifying conditions to its original liberal decision. These qualifications, in turn, incurred the wrath of the non-Orthodox community. Even with these qualifications, there were some rabbis who refused to abide with the decision of the Chief Rabbinate, which resulted in the Knesset's demanding that legal charges be brought against all resisting rabbis. A not atypical ad hoc arrangement between the Ministry of Religious Affairs and the rabbis quieted the situation temporarily, to the dissatisfaction of many of the Bene Israel. In mid-1964, the Knesset (including the NRP) strongly condemned the Chief Rabbinate and ordered it to satisfactorily resolve the plight of the Bene Israel immediately. In the end, the Chief Rabbinate accepted a compromise and rescinded the decrees that singled out the Bene Israel, substituting a general order to investigate all cases that involved questions about the legitimacy of the parents.

Again, the issue quieted down for a while, but not without far-reaching consequences. First of all, the Chief Rabbinate had now come to be perceived as an insensitive and heartless obstacle to the ingathering of downtrodden Jews from the Diaspora, even in the eyes of many who had previously given tacit support to its functioning. Moreover, the stature and authority of the Chief Rabbinate were significantly diminished as a result of the disparaging and defamatory character of the public arguments and debates between many rabbis of differing opinions.

The next major episode in the "Who is a Jew?" issue involved the Shalit and Helen Seidman cases. The former involved the non-Jewish wife of an Israeli Navy lieutenant who wanted to have her children registered as Jewish nationals; the Seidman case involved a woman who had been converted by a Reform rabbi (and who had subsequently married a Kohen, a member of the priestly tribe who, according to traditional Judaism, are forbidden to marry converts), a conversion that is not legitimate according to traditional Jewish law (Liebman 1970). To these cases was then added the issue of intermarriage among the recent arrivals from countries behind the Iron Curtain. A number of rabbis raised serious questions about the validity of a number of conversions performed in those countries, and the rabbi of the Lubavitch *hasidim,* Rabbi Menachem Mendel Schneerson, alleged that Israeli officials were counseling Soviet-Jewish émigrés with non-Jewish spouses to claim Jewish parentage for their spouses upon their arrival in Israel, so as to avoid any problems. The fear among some of those in the non-Orthodox community was that if Russian-Jewish émigrés encountered difficulties upon their arrival in Israel, those Jews still in Russia might be discouraged from attempting to emigrate. On the other hand, the Orthodox, while cognizant of and sympathetic to the plight of Russian Jewry, opposed risking what it viewed as the future of Judaism through evasive detours of this dilemma.

With the emergence of Shas as a significant component of the ruling coalition, the entire issue of "Who is a Jew?" has become much more politicized because Shas has sought to enact legislation that would recognize only conversions performed according to the mandates of *halakha,* Jewish religious law, as defined by the Orthodox rabbinic elite. This would, in effect, delegitimate conversions by Reform and Conservative rabbis in Israel and abroad, and it has thus become a major matter affecting relations between Israel and Western Jewish communities, especially the American Jewish community.

Although the "Status Quo Agreement" has endured for more than half a century, it appears that both the religious and the secular are increasingly unhappy with it, and its endurance highly questionable. As Aviezer Ravitzky points out, both sides perceive that conditions now are radically different from when the agreement was reached. One secular argument, for example, is that in the past there were relatively few *haredim* who were exempted from military service but that today the numbers are much too high to justify the religious exemption. One religious argument is that private transportation on the Sabbath was exempted from the law prohibiting the operation of buses because there were very few private cars. Today, however, the proliferation of private cars traveling on the Sabbath makes a mockery of the law establishing the Jewish Sabbath as an official day of rest (Ravitzky 1999, pp. 267–69).

Cultural and Sociopolitical Variations

Above and beyond these changes, there have developed a number of basic "culture shifts"[4] in Israel, among both the secular and religious nationalists, with the result that there is today, particularly among the secular, much less emphasis on the corporate character of Israel and a much greater emphasis on the individual. The importance of the state is increasingly perceived in terms of the extent to which it guarantees individual rights. By contrast, among the religious nationalists, there has been a dramatic increase in the significance of the philosophy of Rabbi A. I. Kook, which focuses on the inherent corporate character of the Jewish people and the inevitable expansion of holiness among the people and within the Holy Land, Eretz Israel. Thus, both the secularists and the religious nationalists are increasingly unhappy with the "status quo agreement," which was a pragmatic compromise (Ravitzky 1999, pp. 269–70).

That the pattern of "antagonistic cooperation,"[5] which has prevailed for the past half-century, may no longer be tenable is further suggested by the fact that both the *haredi* and modern Orthodox sectors have a greater sense of self-confidence, and they now feel much less threatened by each other and increasingly view themselves as having a common antagonist, secularism. They are, thus, less concerned with challenging each other and are more ready to cooperate with each other. The cooperation is still limited and only de facto at times, but it is no longer inconceivable to envision explicit mutual cooperation between their respective rabbinic leaders.

Some religious Zionists viewed the post-1967 developments, including what they perceive to be a growth of religious fundamentalism within mainstream religious Zionism, as antithetical to Jewish tradition and the historic principles of religious Zionism. Accordingly, in 1975, they founded Oz Veshalom and Netivot Shalom, two religious Zionist peace movements that ultimately merged.

Meimad is another reaction to Mizrachi's moves to the nationalist and religious Right. Broader in scope than Oz Veshalom-Netivot Shalom, it initially formed as a political party with a more moderate approach to the territories than that of the NRP. However, when it failed to gain sufficient votes for a Knesset seat in the 1988 elections, it reorganized as a public action movement that deals with a range of important social and political issues in Israel from a religious-ethical perspective. Primary among its objectives have been the prevention of a Kulturkampf, or culture war, in Israel and a bridging of the growing gap between the religious and secular communities. Its spiritual leader is Rabbi Yehuda Amital, who is also the cofounder and cohead of Yeshivat Har Etzion, a higher yeshiva in the Gush Etzion region that incorporates army service in its program. After the assassination of Yitzhak Rabin, his successor, Shimon Peres, appointed Amital a minister in his cabinet. Amital's main efforts were devoted to fostering moderate religious Zionism and bridging the gap between the religious and secular communities. If subsequent developments are any indication, his efforts did not bear much fruit.

Meimad returned to active politics in the 1999 campaign and joined with Labor and others to form the One Israel slate, headed by Ehud Barak. Although Barak won decisively, it is an open question whether Meimad helped attract a significant number of One Israel votes. It may well be that Meimad lost in stature because it changed from a social movement to a political organization.

The involvement of the *haredi* sector in the Israeli political system has increased since the ascension of the Likud to political leadership in 1977. The initial and, perhaps, clearest manifestation was their joining the government. In 1988, there were numerous rifts in Agudat Israel, and Habad *hasidim* promised that the widely revered Lubavitcher Rebbi, Rabbi Menachem Mendel Schneerson, would give a blessing to all those who voted for Aguda. Two years later, in 1990, the Rebbe devoted much of his energy to an all-out effort to prevent Shimon Peres from forming a coalition. By 1996, *haredi* political activity was not limited to Habad and a handful of others. Then, many *haredim* played very active roles in the Netanyahu campaign. The fact that he was also the clear choice of the NRP fostered an alliance between the *haredi* parties and the religious Zionist ones and resulted in Netanyahu's winning of approximately 90 percent of the votes of Orthodox voters (Don-Yehiya 1997).

As was mentioned previously, the *haredi* masses are today among the most nationalistic in Israeli society, and they appear to be even more nationalistic than the religious Zionist sector, previously viewed as a stronghold of the political Right (Sprinzak 1998). Surveys consistently reveal that the overwhelming majority of *haredi* respondents hold strong nationalistic views. Contrary to the widely circulated notion that the Sephardim of Shas and the Ashkenazi *haredim* represented by the Degel Hatorah party are, in principle, amenable to territorial compromise on the basis of *pikuah nefesh,* that is the primacy of life and saving life,[6] the evidence indicates otherwise. Although the respective leaders of Shas and Degel Hatorah, Rabbi Ovadia Yosef and Rabbi Eliezer Schach, might consider territorial compromise on that basis, their followers staunchly oppose such compromise. It is, therefore, no surprise that a very small percentage of *haredim* supported the Oslo peace accords. One survey found that "only 9 percent of the Haredi respondents were in favor of the peace process, as opposed to 24 percent among the national-religious and 56 percent among the secular" (Ilan 1998). Indeed, already in 1994, only 4 percent of the *haredim* supported the Oslo negotiations, whereas among religious Zionists four times as many, 16 percent, supported them (Ilan 1998). And, in 1998, when Netanyahu signed the Wye Accords, Habad cut all ties with him and indicated that he was no better than Ehud Barak.

With respect to the alleged dovishness of Shas, Ephraim Yuchtman-Yaar and Tamar Hermann argue that the sole basis for the perception is a rabbinic ruling by Rabbi Ovadia Yosef, issued in 1979 and published in the mid-1980s. Their reading of his ruling suggests that "Rav Yosef's attitude toward the question of territorial concessions is also saturated with fear and even revulsion toward the Arab world. Moreover, it is also clear from the passage that his readiness to concede territories is only of limited duration, in the hope and faith that eventually conditions will change and all of the Land of Israel will come under Jewish control as promised in the Book of Books" (Yuchtman-Yaar and Hermann 2000, p. 36). Be that as it may,

> in the late 1980s, Rav Yosef turned down a request from Labor Party figures to publicly support an idea they had formulated of holding an international peace conference. Furthermore, when Shimon Peres asked him in 1989 to reiterate his ruling about the Sinai also with respect to the territories in dispute in negotiations with the Palestinians, he refused on the grounds that when he compared the claims of the experts on the left, who recommended a territorial compromise, and the claims of the security experts from the right, who opposed it, he was not persuaded by the former that this was really a case of *pikuach nefesh,* and hence was not prepared to place his *halachic* authority at the service of the return of territories. (Ibid.)

Given the widespread perception that the *haredim* do not serve in the army, there was resentment in some quarters over their Right-wing politics because their votes may move the country to a war in which they will not fight. Indeed, the issue of military service was among the most divisive in the religious-secular rift, possibly even more so than that of religious coercion.

In all probability, however, this issue will wane in the foreseeable future, as a result of several factors. In the 1999 coalition agreements, an agreement was reached according to which the *haredi* parties agreed to the notion of military service for its males after a deferment of five years for those engaged in study in a yeshiva. Also, there has been an increase in the number of *haredim* who present themselves for military service, and a special unit of the army, the "*nahal haredi,*" has been created to enable *haredim* to train and become active members of the Israel Defense Force (IDF). (Noam Demsky directed an award-winning documentary film on the *nahal haredi,* entitled "*Peyot Yerukot*" ["Green Sideburns"].) Much more important than both of these is the fact that the Israeli army is becoming increasingly professional and is less dependent on mass conscription. Indeed, top army officials have conceded that they would not know what to do with the *haredim* if, indeed, they did present themselves for service in significant numbers. There are indications that there will be radical changes in the role of the military in Israeli society. Among these changes will be an end to universal service as it exists today and, thus, an end to the military service issue in the religious-secular rift.

On the other hand, the religious-secular rift, especially as it relates to military service, may be exacerbated as a result of the dissolution, in July 2001, of the special women's division of the IDF, *He'l Nashim,* and its replacement with almost complete sexual equality there. The heads of the *hesder yeshivot,* who have been, heretofore, committed to military service by their students, threatened to prohibit their students from serving in the IDF if there are women in the units in which the students serve. Chief of General Staff, Shaul Mofaz, has been trying to placate the concerns of those rabbis; the degree to which mutual agreement can be reached remains to be seen (see, e.g., Shapiro and Gilbert 2001; Sheleg 2001; Prince-Gibson 2001).

The increasing participation of *haredim* in the political process is strikingly apparent in their rates of voting. Some estimates suggest that their rate of voter participation in elections for the prime minister and Knesset significantly exceeds that of any other segment of the Israeli population, and that it does so in municipal elections by as much as 20 to 50 percent. To some extent, the high rate of *haredi* voter participation stems from some of the same sociological characteristics that have resulted in the growth of that community. As I have discussed elsewhere (Waxman 1998), as contrasted with the modern Orthodox, the *haredi* community is characterized by a clear sense of authority. This is so because the notion of submission to the authority of the tradition as espoused by the experts of the tradition is one of the most basic characteristics of all religious orthodoxies. Authority and tradition are prerequisites for religious orthodoxy. Within an orthodoxy the individual is expected to internalize tradition so as to perceive himself as not having any choice but to conform to all of its dictates. The notion that the individual has the ability to choose is heretical, as Peter Berger elucidates. As he points out, "the English word 'heresy' comes from the Greek verb *hairein,* which means to choose. A *hairesis* originally meant, quite simply, the taking of choice" (Berger 1979, p. 27). From the perspective of religious orthodoxy, one has no choice,[7] and from the perspective of traditional Jewish Orthodoxy, the absence of choice included the inevitable submission to the ultimate authority of the rabbinic-scholarly elite.

The submission of the *haredi* masses to the authority of the rabbinic elite renders the potential for organization and mobilization much greater within that community. This is especially so since the realm of the authority of the rabbinic elite is much broader than that of religious leaders in more modern communities. Within the framework of haredism, the authority of the rabbinic leadership is not limited to that which in modern society is defined as the strictly religious realm. To the *haredi,* there is no distinction, because every aspect of life is within the purview of *halakha,* Jewish religious law, and therefore every decision of the rabbinic leader is halakhic, Jewishly religious, and as binding as his decisions on such matters as what is kosher.

There is also, within the *haredi* community, a great concern with acceptance, that is, with being accepted as part of the community and behaving according to the standards set down by the community's leadership. This makes for a high degree of conformity in such matters as dress and general patterns of behavior.

In addition, communication within the Orthodox community is greatly facilitated by the fact that members, *haredi* and modern Orthodox, can be found in synagogues and *yeshivot,* schools of Jewish religious education. They are, therefore, highly "reachable." The relative ease of communication enhances the potential for organization within that community.

As a result of the greater potential for communication and organization, as well as the submission to central authority figures, the *haredi* leadership are able to get out the vote when they decide to. Their sense of affinity for the political parties of the Right and their partnership with those parties have resulted in their having an increasingly vested interest in maintaining and extending those ties. They are therefore much more likely to call upon their followers to support those parties. As a result, the *haredi* masses typically follow their leaders' calls and deliver their votes in large numbers to the Likud and its allies. Even in the 1999 elections, when there were no unambiguous calls from *haredi* leaders to support a specific candidate, *haredim* and, indeed, most Orthodox voters overwhelmingly voted for the parties of the Right.

In contrast to the increasing voter participation of the *haredim,* the secular sector appears to be experiencing a pattern not dissimilar from that found in the

United States, namely, a decrease in the rate of voter participation. Thus, while the rate of voting in religious Bnai Brak increased from 79 percent in 1973 to 84 percent, as compared to the national rate of about 78 percent, it decreased in the largely secular area of Givatayim, from 89 percent in 1973 to about 82 percent in 1996 (Ilan 1998).

A Final Remark

The recent challenges to Orthodox control of the rabbinate and, concomitantly, the Personal Status Law, which governs such matters as marriage and divorce, have strengthened the Orthodox determination to maintain its control over these areas by increasing their alignment with those parties prepared to cede that control to them. This was a major factor in a massive *haredi* demonstration against Israel's Supreme Court in February 1999, because the *haredim* believed the court was insensitive to its perspective and what it has viewed as the agreed-upon status quo, ever since the government of Ben-Gurion. Invariably, it has been the political Right that the *haredim* view as their ally in this battle, and that relationship will probably continue, despite the fact that all of the religious parties joined the Barak coalition. They joined the coalition for pragmatic reasons even as they are ideologically and emotionally closer to Likud and other parties on the Right. The question that remains is whether the increased power of the *haredi* parties will lead to their greater acceptance as a legitimate and integral part of Israeli society or whether those religio-politics will, in turn, lead to a real *kulturkampf* in the Holy Land.

By mid-2000, it appeared that, indeed, Israeli society was on the verge of splitting along religious-secular, as well as ethnic, lines. Since then, however, what has come to be called "Intifida Al Aksa" has defused much of the internal strife within Israel. As Georg Simmel (1955) and Lewis Coser (1956) pointed out, external conflict typically results in greater internal cohesion. For the foreseeable future, it may be predicted that the prospects for significant internal conflict are minimal to nonexistent.

NOTES

1. An earlier version of this chapter appeared under the title "Religio-Politics and Social Unity in Israel: Israel's Religious Parties," in Robert O. Freedman, ed., *Israel's First Fifty Years* (Gainesville: University Press of Florida, 2000).

2. At least until the 1999 election campaign when, as indicated previously, UTJ projected itself as a nationalist party.

3. The case involved an Israeli plane that landed after the onset of the Sabbath. At any rate, it seems certain that the NRP would have left Labor and allied itself with the Likud.

4. The term *culture shifts* is from the work of Inglehart (1990, 1997).

5. The term is adapted from Sumner (1954).

6. Kopelowitz and Diamond (1998), for example, argue that, in contrast to the "messianic ideology" of the NRP, which weakens democracy, Shas's religious approach strengthens democracy, including making it more amenable to territorial compromise.

7. This is one interpretation of the verse "*Lo tukhal lehit'alem*" ("You will not be able to avoid it") (Deuteronomy 22:3).

REFERENCES

Ben-Raphael, Eliezer. 2001. *Jewish Identities: Fifty Intellectuals Answer Ben-Gurion.* Beer Sheva: BenGurion University Press (Hebrew).

Berger, Peter L. 1979. *The Heretical Imperative: Contemporary Possibilities of Religious Affirmation.* Garden City, N.Y.: Doubleday.

Coser, Lewis A. 1956. *The Functions of Social Conflict.* Glencoe, Ill.: Free Press.

Don-Yehiya, Eliezer. 1994. "Does the Place Make a Difference?: Jewish Orthodoxy in Israel and the Diaspora." In Chaim I. Waxman, ed., *Israel as a Religious Reality,* ed. Chaim I. Waxman, 43–74. Northvale, N.J.: Jason Aronson.

———. 1997. "Religion, Ethnicity and Electoral Reform." *Israel Affairs* 4(1) (Autumn): 73–102.

———. 2001. "Knockout to Religious Zionism." *Meimad* 22 (July): 30–33.

Dayan, Arye. 1999. *The Story of Shas.* Jerusalem: Keter (Hebrew).

Horovitz, Moshe. 1989. *Rabbi Schach.* Jerusalem: Keter (Hebrew).

Ilan, Shahar. 1998. "They Believe in the Booth." *Ha'aretz,* March 31.

Inglehart, Ronald. 1990. *Culture Shift in Advanced Industrial Society.* Princeton: Princeton University Press.

———. 1997. *Modernization and Postmodernization: Cultural, Economic, and Political Change in 43 Societies.* Princeton: Princeton University Press.

Keinon, Herb. 1999. "A Most Uncommon Marriage." *Jerusalem Post,* April 30, B1.

Kopelowitz, Ezra, and Matthew Diamond. 1998. "Religion That Strengthens Democracy: An Analysis of Religious Political Strategies in Israel." *Theory and Society* 27: 671–708.

Liebman, Charles S. 1970. "Who Is Jewish in Israel?" *American Zionist* (December) 27–31.

———. 1998. "Modern Orthodoxy in Israel." *Judaism* 47 (4) (Fall): 405–10.

Liebman, Charles S., and Eliezer Don-Yehiya, 1983. *Civil Religion in Israel: Traditional Judaism and Political Culture in the Jewish State.* Berkeley: University of California Press.

Liebman, Charles S., and Eliezer Don-Yehiya. 1984. *Religion and Politics in Israel.* Bloomington: Indiana University Press.

Liebman, Charles S., and Elihu Katz, eds. 1997. *The Jewishness of Israelis.* Albany: State University of New York Press.

Litvin, Baruch, and Sidney B. Hoenig, eds. 1965. *Jewish Identity: Modern Response and Opinions.* New York: Feldheim.

Luz, Ehud. 1988. *Parallels Meet: Religion and Nationalism in the Early Zionist Movement, 1882–1904.* Philadelphia: Jewish Publication Society.

Prince-Gibson, Naomi. 2001. "A Problem with Women." *Jerusalem Post,* August 17.

Ravitzky, Aviezer. 1999. *Freedom Inscribed: Diverse Voices of Jewish Religious Thought.* Tel Aviv: Am Oved (Hebrew).

Shapiro, Haim, and Nina Gilbert. 2001. "Mofaz Tells Chief Rabbis Religious Soldiers' Problems Exaggerated." *Jerusalem Post,* August 9.

Sheleg, Yair. 2001. "Mofaz Listened as Rabbis Spoke of Women." *Ha'aretz,* August 9.

Simmel, Georg. 1955. *Conflict,* trans. Kurt H. Wolff. Glencoe, Ill.: Free Press.

———. *The Web of Group-Affiliations,* trans. Reinhard Bendix. Glencoe, Ill.: Free Press.

Sprinzak, Ehud. 1991. *The Ascendence of Israel's Radical Right.* New York: Oxford University Press.

———. 1998. "Netanyahu's Safety Belt." *Foreign Affairs* 77 (4) (July/August): 18–28.

Sumner, William Graham. 1954. *What the Social Classes Owe to Each Other.* Caldwell, Idaho: Caxton.

Warhaftig, Zerah. 1988. *A Constitution for Israel: Religion and State* (*Hukah le-israel: dat umedina*). Jerusalem: Mesilot (Hebrew).

Waxman, Chaim I. 1998. "The Haredization of American Orthodoxy." *Jerusalem Letter/Viewpoints,* no. 376. Jerusalem Center for Public Affairs, February 15.

Yuchtman-Ya'ar, Ephraim and Yochanan Peres. 2000. *Between Consent and Dissent: Democracy and Peace in the Israeli Mind.* Lanham, Md.: Rowman & Littlefield.

PART IV

Manifestations of Jewish Identity

CHAPTER TEN

Judaism in Israeli Culture

ev

ELIEZER SCHWEID

Background

The substitution, following the creation of the State of Israel, of the term "Israeli Culture" for that of "Hebrew Culture," which had been the accepted one during the pre-State Yishuv period, expresses a transformation in the culture itself.[1] Not only did the political and social institutions of cultural life change, but also the way of life and patterns of human relationships, which find their expression in creativity. As a result, the understanding of the nature and function of culture, of spiritual life and of spiritual creation as a uniting and identifying process, likewise changed: these are no longer perceived as the central factor identifying one national society or people, while the society or the nation as a whole no longer seeks to satisfy all its spiritual needs or to express all of the selves of its component individuals within the framework of nationality.

Thus, the totality of creation as constituted by the expressions of all the individuals and groups is no longer understood within the monistic framework of national culture, but is perceived as composed of many different compartments, including the national, the religious, and the national-religious, which are not necessarily open to one another, and do not even necessarily connect all of their component individuals to a single national society or to one people. In place of the national society and culture that seek to mix and to connect, there are manifested, in retrospect, a broad gamut of partial identities and belongings. Not only various communities, ethnic groups, or movements, but even each individual can identify partially with several of these, taking from each one his own "piece" (how much our young people love the expression "this piece," *ha-keta ha-zeh* as a form of expression typifying their way of thinking!) as he wishes.

In other words, the individual no longer entirely defines his identity within the realm of nationalism, or even that of religiosity. Where then is such wholeness to be identified? As mentioned, this definition has been removed to the instrumental and organizational framework of the material culture, described in the universal political terms of the state. This is in fact the significance of Israeliness, which for the majority of those who identify themselves as Israelis connotes civil political-linguistic-territorial belonging. This usually incorporates a certain measure of Hebraism as well as of Judaism, in the religious, traditional, or national sense, but generally in a partial and fragmented way. Even when these are to be found at the center of personal identity, they are not inclusive, but are liable to be limited, marginalized, or externalized in relation—friendly or hostile—to the identity of others in the nation, or even to disappear entirely, leaving in their wake, like the smile of the Cheshire cat, a hazy memory of origin.

This reality, which may be seen today with great clarity, was the dialectic result of the establishment of the State. I said "dialectical result," as it is quite clear that such was not the intention of the founders, who "after two thousand years of Exile" created a Jewish State to be based upon Hebrew culture. The state was called Israel after the ancient name of the people, for whom in turn the land was named, to indicate a distinct cultural and national identity. According to the Declaration of Independence, Israel was intended to be, not only "the state of the Jews," but also "a Jewish State," a center that would symbolize unity and from whence the spiritual heritage would flow to the people as a whole. Based on this approach, laws were introduced shaping a policy of ingathering of exiles and their social-cultural integration, of Jewish national education, and of the shaping of a Jewish public realm. Moreover, in its early years the State functioned as the melting pot it hoped to be, whose purpose was to forge an inclusive cultural-national identity on the basis of the tradition of Hebrew Culture from the period of the Yishuv.

However, the result of this process, which in practice focused upon the establishment and grounding of a modern Israeli statehood (*mamlakhtiut*), in which priority was given to the factors of national security and economic and organizational-instrumental creativity, and with the emphatic desire to shape a civil society based upon a consciousness of statehood, was just the opposite. The unifying national message focused upon the immediate work at hand: the establishment of state institutions and their economic, technological, administrative, socio-professional, legal-professional, and political functioning—areas whose development and perfection predominantly required the internalization of knowledge and expertise drawn from external, Western sources, and not specifically from the values of the tradition.

Against the background of these emphases within the formal education frameworks, a process of voluntary rehabilitation of the cultural, religious, traditional, ethnic, or modern-national heritages brought by the immigrants from different backgrounds also began. Simultaneously, the quest for identity on the part of young people who had been born and educated in the State began to occur at a growing distance from their parents' old-fashioned cultural sources, and closer to the contemporary outside sources from which originated the scientific and technological tools and contents vital for the defense, building, and grounding of the State as a prosperous Western civilization. Thus, the effort to integrate and to unite the people within the melting pot of a national state culture led to the forgetting and decline of the Yishuv culture, and to the emergence of the multicompartmentalized and fragmented Israeli culture described above.

Reconstructing Culture

As mentioned, the initial factor leading to this change was the establishment of the State as an institutional-governmental system on a suitable basis of modern civilization. However, in the broader sense one may speak of an historical process of consolidation that continued over a generation and was affected by two more factors alluded to above: the demographic transformation, caused by a series of waves of mass immigration from several different countries of origin, and the cultural transformation that took place in the sources of influence of Western civilization following the Second World War. I refer here primarily to the spread of modern and postmodern American civilization, together with its scientific-technological, socioeconomic, institutional-governmental, legal, social-ethical, and spiritual characteristics.

The mass *aliya* rejected the Hebrew culture of the Yishuv as being for the most part alien to it, as well as inadequate and irrelevant, and in the final analysis brought about its destruction. The main cause of this was the vast size of this *aliya:* not only in the sense that within a few years Israel's Jewish population doubled in size, thereafter continuing to grow at a similar rate to this very day. More important, upon its arrival each *aliya* created a sociocultural milieu of up-rooted masses of people whose cultural memories were suppressed and denied expression during the traumatic process of absorption, and who were equally unable to internalize or creatively confront the cultural influences of the absorbing society, beyond absorbing certain material elements and passively accepting the secular values that accompanied them.

This, together with the fact that the Yishuv culture was intended to act as an absorbing and integrating force—namely one that dominated the immigrants, who were alien to it, and forcibly changed their culture while guiding them toward itself—led to the emergence of destructive and decadent features of mass culture. Such features included social, linguistic, behavioral, and spiritual "gaps" and "breaks," coupled with material manifestations typical, on the one hand, of a culture of poverty and, on the other, of a culture of exaggerated wealth (relative to the poorer class). It would seem that, only after a period of time—once the socioeconomic consolidation of the new *aliya* had allowed suppressed cultural memories to begin their rehabilitation—did the long-term structural effect of the mass *aliya* became clear: to wit, the emergence of a wide range of cultural heritages, different and alienated from one another in nearly all their ways of expression, language, manners, and values.

If truth be told, the sense of alienation, whose source lay in the strong assimilating influences of the cultures of the various different countries of origin, was already manifest in the initial social encounter between the *aliyot* and the veteran Yishuv, characterized in practice by a rejection that was clearly opposed to the ideology of absorbing the *aliya* in the Israeli the melting pot. This sense was expressed in the image of the "Second Israel"—a comprehensive term used to refer to the *ma'abarot* (absorption camps), development towns, *moshavim,* and poor urban neighborhoods into which the *olim* were absorbed. The assimilatory power of the various different countries upon the new *olim* was clearly stronger than the common Jewish denominator, which was anchored on the one hand to tradition and religion, and on the other to awareness of origin and destiny and to weak and confused memories of fragments of tradition. Since we are concerned with the issue of the Judaism of Israeli culture, it is important to emphasize the sense of alienation that was aroused within each new wave of immigration: the new *olim* came to the country on the basis of their own Jewishness, a fact that isolated them in their country of origin and generally caused their rejection by it. However, during their initial encounter in Israel they stood out specifically for their "non-Jewish" foreignness, to the extent that it completely hid the signs of their common cultural code. The *olim* who came to the State of Israel were thus viewed by the veteran, absorbing society—including those immigrants who had preceded them by only a few years—as Iraqis, Moroccans, Yemenites, Romanians, Russians, Americans, Ethiopians, etc.

This fact could not but delay the process of their acceptance and cultural reconstruction for a long time, leading to the harsh and painful struggles that are documented in the literary and artistic creations of the first years of the State, and which still echo in contemporary Israeli literature. In any event, there is no cause for surprise that the earliest phase of the process of cultural and Jewish reconstruction of the various *aliyot,* which took place following the acquisition of education and expertise and the internalization of the social norms of the general absorbing culture, did not lead to dialogic meetings in the social-cultural realm. On the contrary, it increased the walls of hostility and alienation, particularly with regard to those values expressing the unique Jewish identity of all those of a particular ethnic origin. So much so, that at times it seemed as if the only common Jewish characteristic of Israeli culture was the confrontation, friction, and debate among the different forms of Jewish identity—various kinds of religious Jews, traditionalists, ethnics, or alternatively modern religionists or humanists—struggling for their place within a growing sense of alienation both on the public street and within literary and artistic creation.

In the long run, thus, a process of acceptance took place, through self-reha-bilitation and painful adjustment to the framework of statehood and its mod-ern framework of education and civilization. But, at least for the present, the de-velopment of common material values and external forms of behavior has not led to the development of a mutually fructifying dialogue or to the consequent creation of a shared culture with a clear distinctiveness of its own, based on the positive "codes" of a Jewish cultural heritage.

One might pose the question: What is it that prevents mutual opening and fructification on the level of social ethic and spiritual creation? The most obvi-ous answer is the dominating force of the sociological process that levels down different societies in terms of their underlying culture, and that, in retrospect, expresses the overpowering sweeping influence of a third factor: contemporary Western culture, in its American form, carried by the economic and sociologi-cal taking root of the "society of abundance," marked by external and showy materialism, extreme competitiveness, and self-centred individualism. On this level, cultural socialization challenges the very value of cultural traditions as such. It denies the importance of historic group identities, placing at the center the value of individual self-realization, drawing upon the present alone, and cre-ating an impregnable barrier between an ironic high culture, that tends toward cosmopolitan universalism and is alienated not only from its own tradition and people, but from the majority of society. It would appear that only Orthodox-religious or fundamentalist-religious identities are able to succeed (at the price of extreme closedness) in withstanding this sweeping influence with even par-tial success, at least for the moment.

The Role of Zionism

One should mention at this point that the Hebrew culture of the Yishuv period was developed by the main streams within Zionism (socialist-pioneering Zion-ism, general spiritual Zionism, romantic-nationalistic Zionism, and religious Zionism) under the influence of European nationalism, humanism, and social-ism of the first half of the twentieth century. The theoretical models, the ideo-logical messages that guided its realization and ways of life, the educational pro-cess in the schools, as well as the literary and artistic creations of the Yishuv period—all embodied varied and original means of emulating and applying the patterns, contents, educational processes, and movements of cultural creativity of Europe, expressed in the revived Hebrew language and against the background of layers of literary heritage and Jewish tradition, particularly the consciousness of Jewish history.

The transformation effected by the shift in the source of influence from Europe to the United States, against the background of the ahistoric, asocial, a-ideological, and anational postmodernism that characterized the period following World War II was immediate and sweeping. For nearly a generation, however, Zionism remained the ideology that shaped the official identity of the State of Israel, despite the fact that during that period it had actually changed from a controversial minority ideology to a general Jewish consensus.

Against the backdrop of the traumatic memories of the Holocaust, Zionism, as realized within the State, became the central symbol of Jewish unity and identity. It became the accepted ideology among all those Jews who related positively to their Jewishness, whoever they might have been and whatever might have been their relation to the culture of their people or its religion. One could therefore point with pride to the fact that, among all the ideologies that led mass movements in Europe between the two world wars, Zionism remained the only one that after the war demonstrated its correctness and its possibility of realization. On the other hand, immediately after the War of Independence there were also to be heard harsh statements to the effect that Zionism had "gone into parentheses"—that is, that it had ceased to guide actual actions or to be realized in the individual way of life, and had instead become a kind of credo.

After the creation of the State of Israel, Zionism in effect became the official ideology of the general state education system. From a concrete program involving elements of settlement, the establishment of an ideal society, and the creation of Hebrew culture, Zionism became an ideological-emotional declaration of faith, realized through means of conscription into the compulsory state framework of Israel Defence Forces (IDF) service (including extended reserve duty), expression of solidarity with the Jewish people, acceptance of emotional responsibility for the lot of the people after the Holocaust, loyal citizenship to the State and the country (that is, overcoming the temptations of emigration), and a sympathetic attitude to the social absorption of the *aliya*. Thus a broad range of everyday social and cultural life was left open for the absorption of new ideals deriving from that same source from which Israel derived its much-needed economic, political, and defense support, and upon which it also drew the scientific education, technology, and expertise vital to its development and prosperity. There was, it is true, a certain delay in the process of absorbing the American sociological models and cultural ethos, owing to the economic need of most of the Israeli population during the early years of the State and the socialist-centralized policy followed in confronting this need. However, from the beginning of the 1960s there began a gradual improvement and change in the socioeconomic policy, while the results of the Six Day War led to the breaking down of all barriers. The socialist policy withdrew, and together with it collapsed the institutions of its realization (the Histadrut) and the social frameworks it had created (the collective settlement). In its place was created the economic-social foundation required for the individualistic competitive ethos and other characteristics of American mass culture, and particularly of its youth culture. In terms of the Jewish characteristic of Israeli culture, the value syndrome that developed against this background may be described as a type of assimilation that strives to obscure all unique characteristics of modern national identity, conveying legitimacy only to self-enclosed, sectarian religious units, which are limited to their compartment without influencing the cultural periphery within which they are mixed in an external and alienated manner.

Developments in Israeli literature can also manifest some distinct redefinition of Jewish identity from the earlier period of contemporary Israel. Before the establishment of the State of Israel and during its initial development, Zionism and Israeli Jewishness were viewed by Hebrew writers as aspects of Jewish identity, not substitutes for it. In the perspectives of Gordon, Mapu, Bialik, Mendele, and Agnon, among many others, Zionism and Israel were understood as necessary tools for the preservation of Jewish identity. It was not until the late 1950s that Israeli literature manifested a radical transformation in the definition of Jewishness, with Israeli identity now replacing Jewish identity. Beginning with Yizhar, Shamir, and Megged, and then in Oz and Yehoshua, Israeli identity becomes a modern substitute for the Jewishness of the past, and when it does not live up to the hopes and aspirations of those who view it as such, they become ambivalent and increasingly perceive the failings and "original sins" of Zionism.

In the Realm of Education

In its most crystallized form, the result of the above discussed processes, on both the theoretical and practical levels, was fashioned in the realm of education. I would refer to three levels of messages: the message of the learned curriculum, the message of the instructional framework, and the direct ideological messages, both overt and covert, of the "general school" system. The greatest change in the educational philosophy of the "general State" school is expressed in its abdication of the functions of cultural-value socialization of its students—what is known as the passing down of heritage, in the sense of the creation of a cultural-historic perspective, the conveying of a feeling of belonging and rootedness of the individual in the culture of his origin: his family, his community, and his people; and its encouraging of the formulation of an overall personal-social worldview that presents the individual with binding and meaningful ideals of human life.

During the early years of education, in kindergarten and the lower elementary grades, such educational messages still stand out; however, as one approaches the high school years, these are gradually neglected and pushed to the margins. In their stead come messages of "instruction" (not "education"!), of "knowledge" and "expertise," whose main purpose is professional socialization within a broad range of specialized areas, acquired on the basis of individual choice. Greatly diminished is the general, compulsory learning framework that is intended to pass on the heritage, to crystallize a value-oriented worldview, and to create a circle of culture-based, identity-forming dialogue shared by all students.

The educational philosophy of the high school and university is thus primarily directed to "preparation for life" in the narrow sense of professional socialization: individualistic, contemporary minded, and pragmatic-functional. The main goal is to prepare students for the competitive race that awaits them in their adult life after their years of schooling, in accordance with their specific talents and choices, and of course within the framework of the expectations of the marketplace. This being so, greatest encouragement is given during the course of studies in school to the personal competitive motivation, rather than to that of solidarity and belonging: the entire system of educational tracking and testing (particularly the baccalaureate exams, which symbolize the guiding myth and goals of education) is directed toward outstanding egoistic attainment. (In this it is diametrically opposed to the original humanistic sense of "outstandingness," which demands prior commitment of the individual to the other and to the group, and the desire to excel in giving to them.)

Against such a background, it is self-evident that there inevitably emerges a serious problem in the realms of social values, of the consciousness of personal spiritual identity, and of orientation toward a life of meaning. It is true that this problem, known in professional jargon as "the problem of education for values," is being sincerely confronted by the educational leadership. However, precisely that formulation, and the manner in which attempts are made to answer it, indicates the nature of those values: the school curriculum itself, and its manner of instruction, including the teaching of humanistic and Judaic subjects, are themselves understood as collections of information and as professional disciplines, rather than as identifying sources of value education that shape and fashion a worldview. For that reason, the need is felt to add alongside them "education for values," as yet another subject with its own tools of instruction and specialized professional training for its teachers, as if values were a kind of knowledge or skill like all the others. There likewise follows from this an institutionalized consensus: in order to develop education for values, one requires special systems, whether within or outside the school framework (generally speaking, outside the school framework, because the school curriculum already seems excessively full), that need to be presented as a kind of informal, additional enrichment; in other words—study that does not demand any effort, but is absorbed pleasurably, like a kind of entertainment, and certainly not as something that requires exams and marks, like those other kinds of instructional matter that are taken seriously.

The practical implication of this is that even the humanistic and Judaic subjects taught by the school, such as Bible, history, Hebrew language and literature, and even Oral Torah and Jewish thought, as well as the declarative messages of the school vis-à-vis identification with Zionism and the Jewish people, and the various supplements to education for values (for example, values of proper behavior and civic political values, such as education for democracy) are not perceived as being connected with the main function of the school, which is its instructional activity, and certainly have no connection with the motivations encouraged in order to strengthen the learning process.

There is thus no real connection between the messages of Zionism, Judaism, humanism, and democracy and the central instructional task of the school, which is in itself defined by and conveys messages of competitive achievement and the desire for private and present-oriented success and happiness. Any relation to the society and the people, to history and to cultural heritage, or to the vision of some historical future of the people and of mankind, is likewise exclusively understood from the utilitarian-functional viewpoint of the individual, and is therefore seen as at most of secondary importance.

Obviously, the issue of the Jewish identity of the student of the general school also arises within the framework of education for values, at least in its political context. The leadership of the general educational system seems to have become concerned about it at least once every decade, with a kind of compulsive cyclicity. One hears public criticism by spiritual leaders concerning the fact that the general school does not properly meet the Jewish and Zionist expectations that Israeli society wishes to convey to the younger generation to assure its ongoing identification with it. The claim is articulated that the degree of humanistic education, and particularly of Jewish education, received by the students in the school is too weak and that ignorance reigns. They complain that the identification of the students with the Jewish People and with Zionism is superficial, and in particular that it does not enable them to withstand the temptation of *yerida* (emigration from Israel), or that it is insufficient to create a basis for understanding and connecting with Jews of the Diaspora and with new immigrants. Nor does it provide youth with a sufficiently convincing answer to the existential questions: Why do I need to carry the burden of responsibility for the realization of Zionism, and particularly, why do I need to sacrifice precious years of my life in military service and to endanger my life for the sake of the People and the State, when the message of the school is consistently directed toward the ideal of individual self-realization?

The first cycle of public confrontation with these questions occurred at the beginning of the 1960s at the initiative of Education Minister Zalman Aran. At the time, a program was launched known as "Jewish consciousness," whose success began and ended with a tempestuous public debate, hardly reaching the students in their classrooms at all. The Six Day War and the Yom Kippur War led to a spiritual crisis in Israeli culture, two of whose outstanding expressions were the movement of "return" to religion (*hazara bi-tshuva*) and the "quest for roots." The Education Ministry responded to this challenge with extracurricular programs carried out in a network of special institutions—the Zionist Institutes, Gesher, and Shorashim. But again the results were not satisfactory; at the beginning of the 1990s a new warning was issued concerning the widespread ignorance, superficiality of Zionist identification, and increased *yerida* among those born in the country who had served in the IDF. A new public commission of inquiry, the Shenhar Commission, was appointed, which sat for three years until it proposed a program for general reform in the teaching of Judaic and humanistic subjects, suitable to the general nonreligious public, under the title People and World (*Am Ve-Olam*), based upon the perception of Judaism as an open, humanistic culture.

In light of the regularity with which this problem resurfaces, it is difficult to deny the existence of a general wish on the part of the general public in the State of Israel to convey to its children messages of Jewish identity suitable to the cultural reality of our postmodern age. It is nevertheless difficult to deny that most of the families belonging to the public who send their children to the general school system do not wish or do not know how to do so themselves within the framework of their familial and communal milieu. They expect the school to do it for them. But it turns out that neither does the general school wish, or know how, to do this with its own tools. The answer is that the school is unable to stand up to the pressure of its commitment to other educational and instructional messages, which reflect prior economic, social, security, and political pressures.

The educational system is thus hard pressed to find an educational substitute based upon a clear, pan-Jewish consensus acceptable to all that does not increase the burden of an already overloaded program of study, but that will work primarily on the emotional-existential level. An appropriate substitute is found in memories of the Holocaust and the establishment of the State and in the consciousness of a pan-Jewish "covenant of destiny" that took shape within the people following the World War II. The members of the generation who witnessed the Holocaust and were saved from it—the remnants of a genocidal act directed against the entire people, including future generations—and who then experienced the establishment of the State of Israel as a miracle of redemption, were united in accepting their identity as Jews against the background of the apocalyptic events they saw with their own eyes and experienced upon their own flesh. It was incumbent upon them to rebuild the Jewish People and to protect it from the threat of a future Holocaust, whether this was one of physical or of spiritual destruction (that is, assimilation). The State of Israel is the fortress. The younger generations, against whom the Holocaust was also directed, are obligated to know and remember and take upon themselves the same oath and obligation toward their people and their State. This, then, was the answer found to the questions "Why be a Jew?" "Why live in the State of Israel?" and "Why serve in the IDF and absorb *aliya?*" Over and beyond teaching the cultural heritage of the people, and over and beyond systematic instruction in its textual sources and history, the educational system was called upon to give this inclusive and definitive answer. How so? By experiential, traumatic education in the apocalyptic, mythic memory that connected the Holocaust and the establishment of the State of Israel as a contemporary saga of exodus from enslavement to freedom and from subjugation to redemption. The teaching of the history of the Jewish People in the modern period focused primarily upon the Holocaust and upon Zionism, but emphasis was given to it by means of experiences and rituals: visits to Yad Va-shem, the visit to Auschwitz, participation in the March of the Living, and ceremonies for the Day of Remembrance for the Holocaust, Memorial Day for the Fallen of the IDF, Independence Day, and Jerusalem Liberation Day. One should also emphasize in this context that literature, art, theater, and the communications media all contributed to underscore these messages to the general public, and particularly its young people.

It is not the intention of this chapter to describe in detail the development in Israel and the Diaspora of the memorialization of the Holocaust and the establishment of the State, and its institutionalization and transformation into the central ecumenical force uniting the Jewish People in our time and leaving its impression upon all levels of Jewish cultural creativity—literature, art, scholarship, theory, and religious and national ritual. In the context of this discussion, one may emphasize the centrality of education in crystallizing this memory as the primary message of identification with the Jewish People and with Judaism, passed down as a sacred "oath" from parents to children in a chain of three generations. One should also note that this was a deliberate and planned development, intended to provide an answer to the danger of a "holocaust of assimilation," of obscuration of the national cultural image, and of the loss of will to identify with the people, with Zionism, and with the State as a Jewish State.

The capture of Adolf Eichmann in 1960 and his bringing to trial in Israel was done with this intention. Indeed, the trial succeeded in raising the identifying and unifying message of the Holocaust to the level of national ecumenical consciousness (see also Dalia Ofer's article, chapter 17 in this volume). It gave the first push to the inculcation of the awareness of "Holocaust and Rebirth" to all of the educational systems in Israel and the Diaspora; however, the process of crystallization and conveyance of this idea reached its full realization and acceptance in the Six Day War (also in the consciousness of the Western countries in relation to the Jewish People and Israel). It is easily demonstrated that, alongside the power of the actual experiences that caused the return of the memory, and the impression of this memory upon the second and third generations after the Holocaust, a deliberate decision was made on the part of the political and educational elites to propose a convincing and unquestioned existential substitute for the messages of identity that had been conveyed in the past by systematic study and transmission of the shared tradition: study of the sources of Judaism, study of Jewish history, crystallization of a humanistic-Jewish and national-Zionist worldview, and education for realization of Zionism in the project of settlement and in social ways of life. The instructional-spiritual training in the themes of Holocaust and Heroism and Independence and Rebirth came, therefore, as a substitute for, and not necessarily as a complement to, the earlier educational messages.

The message conveyed by the religious school system is, of course, different, in that it stresses the transmission of the religious heritage as a central body of knowledge, as faith, and as a way of life, and it imposes absolute commitment in its definitions of the religious and national-religious identity of the people. However, it is also worth emphasizing that, with regard to all other areas of cultural creation, there is no difference between the State-religious and general educational streams in Israel. As a result, the teaching of religious values is seen in the State-religious schools as the only and exclusive message of cultural identity, because whatever does not come under the realm of religion is not seen as belonging within Judaism. This clearly demands a considerable degree of separation, in terms of outlook and in way of life, from nonreligious, or even from non-Orthodox-religious, Jews. As a result, an unresolved tension exists in State-religious education between two opposing value orientations: one absolute in terms of Jewish identification, and the second relative but attractive in terms of appealing to the desire for personal success in the various realms of general cultural activity, understood, not as part of Jewish culture, but as a kind of external, neutral area from the viewpoint of values.

The larger question pertaining to the overall Jewish image of Israeli culture is: What shared identifying cultural denominator is created between the students of the State-religious system and those of the general State schools? What unites them as members of a distinct culture? Do they have a common Jewish language? Do they have any unifying cultural content, apart from the myth of Holocaust and the Rebirth, conscription to the Army, and citizenship in the State? There is no convincing positive answer to these questions. The significance of this fact will be clarified further if we turn our attention to the ongoing debate in the State of Israel from the time of its founding until today surrounding the question of Jewish identity, in two areas: the Jewish identity of the State itself (especially in contrast to its identity as a democratic state), and the Jewish identity of the individual, namely, "Who is and what is a Jew?" One might say that the polemic discussion in these two realms encompasses the programmatic thinking that has been created to date concerning the significance of Jewish culture in the State of Israel.

Jewish Identity: The Perspective of the State and the Individuals

In the political and legal realms, the question of the Jewish identity of the State of Israel has been primarily discussed in the context of the status of established religion in a secular democracy and the status of non-Orthodox Jewish religious movements in the State of Israel (Jewish pluralism). However, the level of personal and public concern and involvement displayed during the course of what has been a stormy and prolonged debate changed the discourse into a *Kulturkampf* that had significant impact on the social milieu and on everyday life, and that in practice shaped the nature of Israeli Jewish society. This polemic is in fact reflected on all levels of social-cultural creativity, including literature and art.

From the cultural and spiritual viewpoint, the subject of controversy is, on the one hand, the degree and manner of the presence of traditional Jewish symbols in the Jewish "public street" in the State of Israel and, on the other, the legitimacy of halachic norms shaping individual Jewish identity and the Jewish way of life in the family and the community. Because of Knesset legislation, the following cultural characteristics are to be found in the public domain of Israel:

- Hebrew as the official national language, whose acquisition is the act of national-cultural absorption most emphatically demanded of new immigrants (on this point there is general consensus);
- respect for the Hebrew calendar, its sabbaths, holidays, and other dates, through their recognition as official days of rest and by refraining from their profanation by State institutions, the army, the municipalities, and public corporations, as well as their commemoration in various other degrees and manners within the public street;

- respect for the demands of kashrut by institutions of the State, the army and the municipalities;
- commitment of the State to meeting religious needs in a manner that fully affirms the presence of religious institutions and activities in the public realm— particularly synagogues, study houses, and other institutions of religious instruction, which exert considerable effort to influence public life as much as possible.

By virtue of Knesset legislation, halachic norms shape the definition of individual Jewish identity, with regard to acceptance, conversion, and registration as Jews, as well as family laws pertaining to marriage and divorce. As a result of this legislation, for the majority of the Jewish residents of the State of Israel, the ecumenical presence of symbols of Jewish identity and belonging is impressed upon the course of personal life. One should take particular note of the acceptance of central symbolic ceremonies expressing the belonging of the individual to the people: circumcision, bar/bat mitzvah, marriage, and burial and mourning. One might add to these other symbolic customs, such as the placing of a *mezuza* upon the door of one's home. All these together join into a cultural web that may be defined as a civic religion or secular tradition.

The legally sanctioned presence of symbols of Jewish belonging in the public domain therefore penetrates into the private realm as well. It shapes the symbolic status of the Orthodox-Zionist and ultra-Orthodox (*haredi*) religious public, defining it as that community that accepts upon itself the *halacha* (Jewish religious law) to the full extent, and that provides necessary religious services to the general public. One might say that Orthodox Jewry in all its streams (perceived by the non-Orthodox public as one Jewry) functions as a central symbol representing the Jewish identity of the people in the Jewish State, and it is this fact that causes Judaism as a general concept to be understood even by the nonreligious public as one whose significance is defined in terms of religion alone, rather than in terms of a general national culture. The almost inevitable result that follows from this is that, for the majority of the nonreligious public, the personal relation to Judaism, and ipso facto one's self-definition as a Jew, are not felt as an expression of contents coming from within and expressed in a spontaneous manner in everyday life, but as an external expression, emerging only at certain times, of a voluntary or coerced relation to certain cultural features fixed by the religious public. The secular Israeli adopts these for himself at the appropriate times in order to signify his belonging in principle to his public, which as such is Jewish, and to indicate his awareness of this. But to this end he requires the mediacy and help of "professional Jews," because he himself doesn't know the culture that they represent in a substantive way, nor does he participate in it in an active manner as an expression of his own feelings and thoughts.

This statement is a far-reaching one that demands explanation. The ceremonies of civil religion shape the course of personal life at the points of birth, maturity, establishing a family, giving birth to children, and the conclusion of life—indeed, they echo within the way of life of the family and affect the everyday consciousness of belonging to a people and state. Moreover, together with the ceremonies of civic religion, nonreligious Jewish family life typically draws upon further signs of tradition, particularly folkloristic elements and those of sabbaths and festivals, which in varying degrees become part of the cultural milieu. This is demonstrated in the extensive study conducted by the Guttman Institute and Keren Avihai (see Levy et al., chapter 11, in this volume). Moreover, that same study observes two additional phenomena characterizing the dynamics of the processes of Jewish cultural identification in Israel: the ceremonies of civic religion are increasingly understood as an external, coercive presence; at best, this presence is conformed to without a feeling of being forced, but in many cases compliance comes with open unwillingness and a feeling of having no alternative. In either case, most of the nonreligious public perceive the ceremonies to be external rather than an organic part of the continuity of the milieu of personal, family, and communal life. Second, the choice of those signs that are willingly adopted to mark the sabbath and festivals is made largely on the basis of their suitability to a secular, present-oriented cultural milieu and way of life. These signs bear little relation to a tradition that is rooted in religion, but rather evoke a certain positive and pleasurable relation to folklore. It is hence clear that the secular milieu created through the use of traditional "materials" removes itself progressively from religious meanings, even to the point of becoming unaware of such meanings. And the context in which this takes place is that of a present-oriented mass folk culture that derives from external sources and has almost completely lost its unique character. The feeling of coercion, of rebellion against the imposed nature of religious symbols and norms, and in particular the growing feeling of contradiction between the halachic norms imposed upon the general public by means of the institutions of the Rabbinate, and the liberal-universal values and norms advocated by the secular public—all these sustain the stormy legal and political polemic and has give it the coloration of a cultural war.

Thus far, acquiescence in religious norms as an obligation imposed upon both the public street and an individual's private life in Israel has been bolstered by three factors:

- a sense of responsibility toward preserving the unity of the people, particularly so long as the feeling of a security threat against the State of Israel originating in external enemies continued;
- political considerations rooted in the party structure of the government of the State;
- the fact that most members of the first and second generations of those who immigrated after the establishment of the State remained traditional—even when they joined the general (that is, nonreligious) sector of the Jewish public—and hence related positively to at least some of the religious impositions and did not find it unduly difficult to make their peace with the rest, accepting their importance for purposes of national unity.

Increasing Cultural Conflict: Secularization and Post-Zionism

During the past decade a dramatic change has come about regarding at least the first and third of those three factors. With the passing of the first generations, a new generation of young Israelis educated in the general school system came of age imbued with attitudes to the contents of traditional Judaism that differed substantially from those of its parents. At the same time, the mass immigration from the states of the former Soviet Union flooded Israel with people who had neither knowledge of nor connection to Jewish contents of any sort. And finally, the peace process, insofar as it dispelled the sense of an external threat hanging over the State of Israel, released its people from feeling an urgent, existential need to assure pan-Jewish unity at any cost.

In this context, a highly polarized debate has flared up concerning the issue of peace and the "whole Land of Israel." This debate tends to accentuate the rifts that have developed between the religious-Zionist public and the secular public, further weakening any drive toward pan-Jewish agreement. At the same time, protest and opposition in the name of democratic values and individual freedom have become stronger, while public support for "religious legislation" comes exclusively from the religious public and an interested segment of the political leadership, but not from the majority of spiritual leaders and nonreligious educators.

Two facts illustrate the transformation that has taken place in the way of life and culture of Israel. First, despite the fact that religious legislation remains largely unchanged (status quo), obedience to it is progressively weakening. The Jewish and Israeli public domain has become increasingly secularized and "general," a situation felt particularly on the sabbath and festivals, as we have seen. Religious legistation has become an irksome legal fiction, generating dispute and conflict. Its psychological and sociological impact is tangible enough, but largely negative in terms of the attitude of the general public to Jewish symbols:

rather than eliciting identification and contributing to knowledge and under-standing, these symbols, and the legislation that requires them, provoke a hos-tile attitude and a debate almost entirely lacking in intellectual content, which tends to slide into verbal and physical violence.

Second, opposition to religious legislation has become a central tenet of the new ideology that has come to displace Zionism in defining secular Israeli iden-tity. Whereas Zionism was understood as a form of Jewish national identity, the new ideology styles itself as "post-Zionist"—apathetic toward national and re-ligious values as such, but intensely opposed to them if they seek to shape the image of the state and supersede the values of democracy and freedom of the individual. In the new ideology, individual dignity and happiness have become the universal values meant to shape, not only the government, but also the so-cial and cultural ethos. Post Zionism is presented to the Israeli Jewish public, not simply as an option for a new cultural identity beyond Judaism and Zion-ism, but as an exclusive and all-encompassing identity staunchly opposed to the continued definition of Israel as a Jewish-Zionist State. Since post-Zionism is concerned with the interests of all citizens as private individuals, it opposes giv-ing preferential political or constitutional expression to any of the national or religious groups within it as well as to any perspective involving biographical or historical past and future.

The demand for separation of religion and state arose in the very earliest stages of the debate between the religious and the secularists, even before the es-tablishment of the State (one must remember that Herzl's political vision in-cluded this demand as a prerequisite of the State of the Jews, even though as a practical statesman he himself laid the groundwork for the later compromise be-tween religious and secular Zionism known as the status quo). But in the past this demand was raised as a legal and political limitation demanding satisfactory solutions to the issues of personal identity, conversion, and family life, to which the nonreligious public was particularly sensitive and to which religious *halacha* did not give adequate consideration. The assumption was that it would be pos-sible to find appropriate solutions to such problems without damaging the Jew-ish and Zionist identity of Israel per se, and without denying the status of the Jewish religion as an influential factor in society and culture.

For that reason, even those who sought changes in the *halacha* did not de-scribe the authoritative status granted to religious institutions in Israel in certain areas as expressing a substantive contradiction between Jewish identity and democratic identity. Such has not been the case in recent years. Today this con-frontation makes the claim that there is a substantive contradiction between the terms "Jewish State" and "democratic state" and that one needs to choose be-tween them without compromise. Democracy is hence presented, not only as a form of government based upon the decisions of the majority and respect for the freedoms of all its citizens, but as a universal, all-embracing worldview intended to shape all aspects of social and cultural life in the state. That is to say, it is also meant to provide the universal identity of its citizens as individuals, whereas the particularistic values and norms of religions, and of national and social movements, must be subordinated to the values of liberal democracy and exist beneath them as private, partial relations. It is thus self-evident, according to this view, that the Jewish or Zionist component must be removed from Israeli identity. From now on, these values will be at best a particular, partial compartment within the identity of those wishing it for themselves alone, but not for the whole.

The Israeliness-Jewishness Dichotomy

We now turn to the confrontation on the second plane, that of personal identity, beginning with the debate surrounding the question "Who is a Jew?" This question arose on the legal-political plane against the backdrop of the implementation of the Law of Return, which was unanimously accepted in the Knesset as an expression of Israel's Jewish-Zionist identity. However, the debate rapidly expanded to include the spiritual level along the axis of the question "Who is a Jew?"

The reason for this expansion is self-evident: if the State accepts the ruling that individual Jewish identity is defined by *halacha* and therefore based upon religious authority, and not upon secular national law and authority (notwithstanding the fact that the religious definition as such is ethnic and does not in substance contradict the national definition), it conveys to its citizens the clear message that Judaism as the contents of personal identity is defined as a religious worldview and way of life rather than as a cultural-national one, and specifically in exclusive accord with Orthodox faith and *halacha*. This results in a strange paradox: the Jewishness of the secularist, even if he is nationalist and Zionist, and even if he is traditional, is recognized both by the religious establishment and the State, not on the basis of his own criteria and his own cultural characteristics, but on the basis of criteria imposed by religious Jews with whose worldview he disagrees and whose way of life he does not share. That is, one's formally recognized Jewish existence (defined as birth to a Jewish mother) is perceived by the nonreligious Jew as an existence empty of any authentic Jewish content, yet filled with content that is not authentically Jewish, or not Jewish at all. Such a nonreligious Jew is likely to become hostilely alienated from religion and to externalize his Jewish identity as something irrelevant to his own perception of himself as a Jew. Another response is possible: One may be a Jew by "identity" but not a Jew in "essence." This person is likely to be asked repeatedly by religious Jews, in tones of rebuke and accusation, "In what sense are you Jewish?" or "In what sense are we Jewish?"

The change from the reality that existed during the Yishuv is striking and of great significance. During that period, the Jewish national community defining itself as secular (*hiloni*) or free-thinking attached importance to the religious definition of Judaism only in one respect: members of that community could relate to their religious brothers and sisters as members of their people, seeing them as Jews based upon the secularists' own nationalist criteria without needing to accept any specific definition of Jewishness. It was the secularists' clear feeling that Jewish values, ways of life, and cultural creativity consisted of all the values, folkways, and creations of those people who were born as Jews, married as Jews in their own culture, and wished to live within their own Jewish national framework. Thus, whatever they did and created, including those elements they borrowed from other cultures, was seen as Judaism, and the challenging of their Jewishness by religious people did not particularly impress them. On the contrary; they launched a countercriticism, preferring their own Jewishness to any other kind of Judaism.

It seems reasonable to assume that, had a similar approach been taken with the Jewish public street in the State of Israel, the dichotomy between the "Israeli" and the Jew within him, or between "Israelis" as a group and "religious Jews" as a group, would not have come about. Everything that the "Israeli" created and made for himself and his society would have been considered by himself and by those of his group as Jewish, while everything that the "Jew" did for his own sake and that of his society would be considered Israeli—and each group would have found its own way toward the sources and history of Jewishness. But once a reality was created in which Israeliness came to be considered as something apart from Jewishness, while Jewishness was viewed as being apart from Israeliness, this dichotomy became unavoidable for both religionists and secularists of various types. Israeliness now became a thing unto itself, and Judaism a thing unto itself. The two may indeed make peace with and complement one another (in the case of religious Zionists), or may exist parallel to one another as two adjacent compartments (in the case of national-Zionists or traditionalist-secularists), but they may also entirely contradict one another (as in the case of non-Zionist religionists or secularists holding a negative attitude to religion or to Zionism).

In terms of the sociology of culture, the significance of this phenomenon is that, instead of the syndrome characterized during the Yishuv period as a process of acculturation and cultural renaissance, the State of Israel witnessed the development of a syndrome that may best be described as, on the one hand, assimilation, and on the other, a split between identity-preserving Jews and assimilating Israelis. Thus, in the State of Israel, created by the Zionist movement in order to serve as a dyke against assimilation, there has gradually come about a cultural syndrome of assimilation and schism comparable to that which developed in the Diaspora.

Regarding those Jews who assimilate to their Diaspora or Israeli culture, Jewish identity is understood, at best, as a marginal compartment within a multistoried culture and personality, most of whose compartments are non-Jewish and are instead anchored and domesticated within the surrounding cultural environment, Western or Eastern. Hence, they identify as Americans, Frenchmen, or Israelis, more than they do as Jews. In the less favorable case (from the viewpoint of Judaism), their Jewish identity is expressed in alienation from the form of external identity that other Jews attempt to impose upon them, which they reject with all their strength. They thereby remain Jewish in a certain sense, their rejection of Jewishness itself being a form of involvement.

For those Jews who separate themselves from their environment and define themselves as Jews alone, Judaism is an absolutely obligatory cultural identity, although the range of its applicability is narrow. Their attitude toward the surrounding culture, whether "goyish" or "Israeli" (that is, "goyish-Jewish") vacillates between openness to a beneficial external environment and withdrawal from one that is seen as threatening and dangerous.

In the middle, among the religious-Zionist, traditional, and secular-national public, there still exist substantial bridging elites that wish the State of Israel to preserve both its Jewish and its democratic identity, its heritage and its relation to modernity, and who wish Israeli culture to renew the processes of adaptation and renaissance that created the Hebrew and Jewish-Zionist cultures within the Land of Israel. These elites wish to renew a multifaceted Israeli culture that conducts an ongoing creative dialogue within itself on the basis of traditional values and cultural language shared by all Jews in Israel and the Diaspora.

Discussion

Is there any possibility for realizing such a vision? One cannot ignore the great difficulty: postmodern Western culture, which developed following World War II (and is the source of "post-Zionist" and "post-Jewish" thinking in Israel), expresses a universal syndrome in modern Western culture, whose dominant cultural ideology is assimilation in the form of the "global village." The elites representing this tendency on the highest social levels in the West do not ascribe any importance to national and religious traditions, notwithstanding the fact that these traditions are once more struggling for their existence with great vitality on the folk levels of many countries, and even within Western culture. In any event, the academic elites, particularly the technocratic and communication elites, are abandoning these traditions and striding toward a vision of a cosmopolitan secular culture, that is always contemporary and always prepared for futuristic changes, and that inevitably transforms all forms of cultural identity into something transient, external, and exchangeable. This postmodern syndrome clearly negates any possibility of halting the process of sweeping assimilation discernible today among Diaspora Jewry, as not only does this process not encounter opposition within its environment, it even receives great encouragement from it. It is worth remembering in this context that the Jews of the Diaspora belong by and large to the middle and upper sociocultural classes in the West. Against this backdrop, it seems as if the only way for the Diaspora Jews to preserve their particularistic-partial identity is that of religious Orthodoxy. It alone is capable of creating a workable, effective, and particularistic compartment, combined with effective cultural integration within the open secular environment.

By contrast, the Jewish State that preserves its national and cultural identity may provide effective protection against the sweep of an assimilating culture, thereby allowing a creative process of adaptation and revival of elements of its own heritage, dialogic pluralism, and openness to the higher values of neighboring cultures—both Western and Eastern. One must recognize, however, that this is no easy task. It requires "swimming against the stream" of that which is fashionable and contemporary in the West, and socioeconomic inertia tends to lead to failure.

Thus, if the tendency to be swept along by the materialistic and individualistic/selfish values of the culture of a society of abundance ceaselessly imported from the United States continues, and there is no reorientation in Israeli education in the direction of transmitting the cultural heritage and expression of our own cultural identity, this possibility will be nullified and the split between an encapsulated Orthodox Jewish religious culture and a secular Israeli culture alienated from its Jewish sources will become a conclusive fact.

NOTE

1. A previous version of this article appeared in Urian and Karsh 1999, pp. 9–28.

REFERENCES AND FURTHER READING

Budick, Emily M., ed. 2001. *Ideology and Jewish Identity in Israeli and American Literature.* Albany: State University of New York Press.

Etzioni-Halevy, Eva. 2002. *The Divided People: Can Israel's Breakup Be Stopped.* Lenham, Md.: Lexington Books.

Schwied, Eliezer. 1996a. *Zionism in a Post-Modernistic Era.* Jerusalem: Hassifria Haziyonit, Publishing House of the World Zionist Organization (Hebrew).

———. 1996b. "'Beyond' All That: Modernism, Zionism, Judaism." *Israel Studies* 1: 224–46.

———. 2000. "The Multifrontal Cultural War in Israel." *Democratic Culture* 3: 187–98.

Urian, Dan, and Efraim Karsh, eds. 1999. *In Search of Identity: Jewish Aspects of Israeli Culture.* London: Frank Cass.

CHAPTER ELEVEN

The Many Faces of Jewishness in Israel

❧

SHLOMIT LEVY, HANNA LEVINSOHN, AND ELIHU KATZ

Introduction

The most severe of the several intergroup conflicts within the Israeli Jewish society is that between religious and nonreligious Jews. The highly problematic nature of this relationship has been reflected for many years in studies and surveys of the perceived quality of intergroup relations and of attitudes toward the "status quo" between state and religion. In spite of these negative assessments, Israeli Jews are committed to Jewish continuity on both the individual and the state levels. This commitment is expressed in a variety of sometimes contradictory self-definitions and behaviors. The many faces of Jewishness in Israel is the focus of this chapter. In 1991, a sociological study entitled "Beliefs, Observances and Social Interaction Among Israeli Jews" was conducted by the Guttman Institute (Levy, Levinsohn, and Katz 1993). The results of this study triggered intense public discussion (Liebman and Katz 1997). A decade later, the Guttman team undertook to replicate this study, taking advantage of the existence of a "baseline" against which to measure change (Levy, Levinsohn, and Katz, 2002).[1] While the study takes no explicit account of politics, it is evident that religion (and ethnicity) made major inroads into the political system, such that one prime minister was hailed as "good for the Jews," and another threatened to form a coalition of "secular" parties. There was talk about a wave of *hazara beteshuva* (religious returning), while others conjectured that the society was moving away from tradition. If the number of religious parliament (Knesset) members is an indicator of the society's religiosity, Israel must be judged to be more religious than at the start of the decade, but if the number of cafes open on shabbat is an indicator, the society must be judged less religious. Changes in beliefs, attitudes, and actions provide yet another, perhaps better, view of the situation, and that is what the present study attempts to do.

Substantively, this study, like its predecessor, seeks to characterize the Jewishness of Israelis in terms of the nature of their self-defined religiosity, their observances, their identities as Jews and Israelis, their beliefs and values, their attitudes toward differences amongst them, and their stand on the role of the State

265

in matters of religion and tradition. That these matters occupy public opinion is evident in the increased concern expressed by respondents in the studies. In 1991, 61 percent of respondents said they were "interested" or "very interested" in "questions relating to the place of religion in Israel"; this proportion rose to 69 percent in 1999.

Methodologically, the study follows its predecessor exactly, making room only for the arrival of almost a million immigrants from the former Soviet Union (FSU). Similar to the 1991 study, the current one is a nationwide research on the adult Jewish population (twenty years of age and over) residing in all types of communities in Israel (excluding *kibbutzim*). A sample comprising 2,466 respondents was selected representing this population. In addition a special national representative sample of the adult FSU immigrants who arrived in Israel since 1989 was grafted onto the original sample design, making it possible to portray the society in 1999 as a whole with the inclusion of its new immigrants ("the combined sample"), while also making it possible (by excluding the special FSU sample) to compare the identically designed 1999 sample with the 1991 sample of veteran Israelis. Thus, the research population includes 2,466 veteran Israelis sampled as in the 1991 study, plus the special sample of 406 FSU immigrants of whom 373 are Jews.[2] The combined sample comprises 2,839 respondents. Interviewing was conducted in the second half of 1999, concluding at the end of January 2000, a few months before the outbreak of violence that began in October 2000.

Like its predecessor, this study employs a structured questionnaire in which all questions—about 150 in number—are "closed." Each question was read to respondents face-to-face, at home, by a trained interviewer. The bulk of the questions focused on the identities (Jewish, Israeli, religious) of the respondents, his/her beliefs, values, and observances, attitudes toward the place of religion in public life, and an assessment of the goodness of intergroup relationships among Israeli Jews.

This chapter presents the highlights of the study.[3] The findings are presented for the population as a whole, and are further analyzed in terms of two major typologies: (1) a scale of eight types of religious identity that combines a measure of self-defined religiosity together with self-reports of respondents about the extent of their observance of traditional religious behaviors; and (2) a typology of ethnic origin, as defined by the birthplace of the respondent and his/her father. These two typologies are closely related, in that respondents of Eastern origin (Mizrahi, Sephardi, Asian-African) are much more likely to define themselves as religious, and to observe many more traditions, than are those of Western origin (Ashkenazi, European), and certainly more than the FSU immigrants.

Religious Identity

RELIGIOSITY Over the course of the decade, there has been no change in the self-reported level of observance of religious tradition: 16 percent are strict observers, 20 percent observe to a great extent or "mostly," 43 percent observe somewhat, and 20 percent do not observe at all. There has been some change, however, in the self-definition of religiosity. Thus, the present study finds an increase (from 38 percent to 43 percent) in the proportion who say they are "not religious" and a corresponding decline in the proportion representing themselves as "traditional."[4] There is a hint of an increase in the proportion of the ultra-Orthodox (*haredim*)—about which more will be said below—but the size of this religious community (16 percent) remains essentially unchanged (Table 1). The distributions of response to these two questions (self-reported level of observance, and self-defined religiosity) make plain that there is a much higher reported level of observance than of religiosity; about 50 percent describe themselves as not religious, but only about 20 percent describe themselves as not at all observant.

"NOT RELIGIOUS/OBSERVE SOMEWHAT" The scale (Guttman 1944) that combines these two questions (self-reported level of observance and self-defined religiosity) yields a step-wise typology that ranges from *haredi* (ultra-Orthodox who observe strictly) to antireligious/not at all observant. The scale enables us to distinguish between different types of "religious," "traditional," and "nonreligious" individuals according to the degree of their observance (Table 2). Actually,

Table 1. Religious Identity, 1991 and 1999 (Percentage)

	1991	1999
Religious Observance		
Strictly observant	14	16
Observe to a great extent	24	20
Observe somewhat	41	43
Do not observe at all	21	21
TOTAL	100	100
Self-Defined Religiosity		
Ultra-Orthodox (*Haredi*)	3	5
Religious	12	12
Traditional (*Massorti*)	42	35
Not Religious	38	43
Anti Religious	5	5
TOTAL	100	100

Table 2. Religious Identity Scale

Scale-type	% in Combined sample*
1 *Haredi*	5
2 Religious, observe strictly	7
3 Religious, observe to a great extent	4
4 Traditional, observe to a great extent	16
5 Traditional, observe somewhat	17
6 Not religious, observe somewhat	29
7 Not religious, totally nonobservant	18
8 Antireligious, totally nonobservant	4
TOTAL (N = 2,717)	100

*Combined sample refers to the aggregate of respondents including immigrants from the FSU.

each kind of religious self-definition is divided according to level of observance with the exception of the two extreme scale types: (1) *haredi,* and (8) antireligious. This distinction is not only helpful in gaining better understanding of the meaning of being "religious," "traditional," or "not religious," but it also shows the complexity of Israelis' "Jewish" behavior. Of the eight steps on this scale, the predominant type, by far, is "not religious/observe somewhat" (scale-type 6).

Some 30 percent of Israeli Jews may be characterized in this way, while none of the other scale-types is more than half as large. Runners-up are "not religious/not observant" (18 percent), "traditional/somewhat observant" (17 percent), and "traditional/mostly observant" (16 percent). Since the three "religious" scale-types also add to 16 percent, the model type (not religious/observe somewhat) stands out even more prominently.[5] This scale is of very high predictive value; it correlates extremely well with almost all of the attitudes, beliefs, values, and practices included in this study.

"TRADITIONAL" The scale helps dispel some of the confusion surrounding the term *masorti* (traditional). Table 2 makes clear that this group splits into two when it comes to self-described observance, and the study shows throughout that this distinction is most meaningful. The traditionals who observe to a great extent are much closer to the religious who observe similarly, while the traditionals who observe "somewhat" lean, in observance and belief, toward the nonreligious who observe somewhat. By the same token, the two groups who share the same great extent of observance (scale-types 3 and 4) differ from each other markedly according to whether they call themselves "religious" or "traditional." In approval of the opening of cinema and coffee houses on Shabbat, for example, scale types 4, 5, and 6 differ from each other—in spite of their similarities—by increments of 30 percent points (23 percent to 52 percent to 85 percent). This progression holds true in almost all other matters. Stated otherwise, the scale makes clear that both aspects (religiosity and observance) are needed to explain the variety of attitudes and behaviors observed in this study.

RELIGIOUS IDENTITY AND AGE As in 1991, religious identity does not vary much among different age groups. Younger and older persons are distributed similarly on the religious identity scale. The same pattern is observed among American Jews; Cohen (1998) indicates that despite the high rate of intermarriage in the younger age groups, young Jews are characterized by levels of religious commitment and practice similar to those of their elders. Moreover, this pattern holds even when discounting intermarried respondents.

ETHNIC DIFFERENCES IN RELIGIOUS IDENTITY There is a continuing ethnic divide between Ashkenazim and Mizrahim, that is, between those of Western and Eastern origin, both in self-defined religiosity and in self-reported observance. The Mizrahim are considerably more religious, and more observant, than the Ashkenazim. The *haredi* group is predominantly Ashkenazi in origin, while the other religious and the more observant traditional groups have Mizrahi majorities. The nonreligious are mainly of Western origin (Table 3).

Thus, the three Western groups—those born abroad, their children, and FSU immigrants—all congregate in the two nonreligious scale-types, those who observe somewhat and those who do not observe at all. Israeli-born to Israeli parents who are of mixed ethnic origin (i.e., one parent is Ashkenazi and the other is Mizrahi) behave like the Ashkenazim.

GENERATIONAL DIFFERENCES IN RELIGIOUS IDENTITY As was the case in 1991, the second generation of Mizrahim are less religious and less observant than their parents. Unlike 1991, however, when second-generation Ashkenazim were no different from their Western-born parents, in 1999 we find that the second generation Ashkenazim are also moving away from their parents: some are becoming more religious, others—a larger group—are becoming less religious. While the changes, to date, are small, they suggest that a polarizing process may be at work. Thus, among Ashkenazim, the proportion of *haredim* is higher in the Israeli-born generation than in the foreign-born generation (7 percent and 4 percent respectively), while the percentage of not religious/not observant is also higher in the second generation than the first (31 percent and 22 percent respectively).

SPECIFIC OBSERVANCES Just as the extent of self-reported levels of observance far exceeds the self-defined levels of religiosity, so does the proportion who actually observe specific rituals and ceremonies exceed the number who describe themselves as at least somewhat observant. Thus, well over half of Israeli Jews attend the Passover Seder (85 percent), fast on Yom Kippur (67 percent), and light Shabbat candles (51 percent). Almost every home has a mezuzah affixed to

Table 3. Ethnic Composition of the Levels of Religious Identity (Percentage)

| | Ethnic Origin of Respondent and His/Her Father | | | | | |
Religious Identity	East-East	Israel-East	Israel-Israel	Israel-West	West-West	Total
Haredi (N = 113)	18	19	31	21	11	100
Religious, strictly observant (N = 179)	26	31	16	12	17	100
Religious, observe to a great extent (N = 113)	24	37	17	9	13	100
Traditional, observe to a great extent (N = 423)	25	39	12	9	15	100
Traditional, observe somewhat (N = 443)	16	38	14	5	27	100
Not religious, observe somewhat (N = 761)	7	21	16	14	42	100
Not religious, totally nonobservant (N = 458)	3	12	20	22	43	100
Anti-religious, totally nonobservant (N = 107)	1	11	28	16	44	100
Total in sample %	13	26	17	13	31	100
N	339	684	437	337	800	2,597

the door. Two-thirds attach high importance to the traditional life-cycle ceremonies that mark the passage from birth (circumcision), puberty (bar mitzvah, bat mitzvah), marriage, and death (burial, kaddish, and shiv'a). Ethnic differences apply to all these rites and ceremonies, in the sense that the proportion of Mizrahim who hold them in high esteem is greater than the proportion of Ashkenazim who do likewise.

These data illuminate the seeming paradox of "not religious/observe somewhat." The simplest explanation for the ostensible disparity between self-defined religiosity, self-reported level of observance, and actual observance has to do, apparently, with subjectively disconnecting traditional observance from its religious roots. While the more religious are performing *mitzvot* that have halakhic force, the nonreligious are choosing to perform traditional behaviors from the repertoire of the Jewish cultural heritage.

Patterns of Observance

Some 70 percent of Israeli Jews consider that their lives are being lived "in the spirit of Jewish values." Only the "totally non-observant" (whether they consider themselves nonreligious or antireligious) do not think so, suggesting that it takes at least "some" observance, however minor, to think of oneself as living in the spirit of Jewish values. It is evident from these data that though Jewish living is by no means equated with orthodoxy, the term "Jewishness" cannot be completely disconnected from traditional behavior, even if the bond is weak and cultural behavior varies widely.

Apart from the 15 to 20 percent who are "Orthodox" in both religiosity and practice, and the 20 percent who are neither religious nor observant, the remaining 60 percent represent a variety of combinations as evidenced by the intermediate scale types, but especially by the predominant "not religious / somewhat observant." The pattern of observance of a majority of this group includes the traditional Passover Seder, the Yom Kippur fast, Hanukkah candles, avoiding *hametz* on Passover, and according high importance to the traditional rites of birth and death.

Searching further for the behavioral meaning of "observe somewhat" leads to the self-defined "traditionals who observe somewhat" (scale-type 5). In addition to the practices of the "not religious / observe somewhat," this group also marks the Shabbat eve by candlelighting, kiddush, and a festive meal; attends synagogue on Yom Kippur; keeps separate dishes for Passover; eats dairy foods on Shavuot; and attributes high importance to all the life-cycle ceremonies.

In other words, it can be said that the predominant pattern of Israeli Jewishness, behaviorally speaking, consists of (1) ceremonial observance of Shabbat eve, (2) partial observance of kashrut, (3) holiday observances, especially of the Passover Seder, Yom Kippur fast and synagogue, and Hanukkah candles, and (4) holding the life-cycle ceremonies in high regard. The decade has seen some decline in each of these observances, but they remain at a very high level. We now consider each of the observances in more detail.

(1) SHABBAT Approximately eight in ten Israelis think it is "important" or "very important" to mark the Shabbat in some way, although only half (52 percent) attribute the same degree of importance to marking the Shabbat in accordance with religious tradition. Indeed, this half of the population "regularly"

observes the ceremonies of Shabbat eve—candles, kiddush, festive meal. A quarter of the population "never" observe these practices.

These Shabbat ceremonies are augmented by spending time with children and family, and resting. But that is the limit, more or less, of halakhic observance by the majority. All but the most religious use electricity, watch television, travel, and engage in other leisure activities involving money. However, many refrain from work on Shabbat, especially in public.

Regular synagogue attendance on Shabbat is limited to the three religious scale-types, who are joined by about 40 percent of the "traditionals/observe to a great extent."

(2) KASHRUT Kashrut observance is more widespread than observance of Shabbat eve, and certainly more than observance of the Shabbat proscriptions. Over half of Israeli Jews "always" eat kosher food and refrain from eating unkosher food. Over 40 percent maintain separate utensils for meat and dairy.

Some three-quarters of Mizrahim are strict about kosher food, compared with fewer than half of the Ashkenazim. The percentage of those who observe the separation of utensils is twice as high among the Mizrahim (60 percent and 30 percent, respectively). All groups have experienced small drops in kashrut observance over the decade.

(3) FESTIVALS AND HOLIDAYS Although there has been a slight drop in festival observance as well, it is still the case that most Israeli Jews—two-thirds and more—observe ceremonies and customs relating to the major holidays, for reasons (which were not investigated in this study) that seem appropriate to him/her. It is easy to imagine the attractiveness of Passover or Hanukkah to the non-religious, and perhaps somewhat more difficult to explain the high observance of the Yom Kippur fast and the liturgy of the High Holidays. The Passover Seder outranks all other holidays for each of the religious scale-types and for all of the ethnic groups—except for new immigrants from the FSU.

With respect to holiday observances, taking part in some form of Passover Seder, lighting Hanukkah candles, marking Purim, and building a Sukka are about 10 percent more frequent in the second generation of Ashkenazim than the first. It is a good guess that the socialization of children to Jewish tradition is at the heart of this phenomenon.[6]

There are some other customs, such as Mezuzah, which, as has been noted, is pervasive—at least on the front door. When asked whether the mezuzah serves to protect the home, a majority of the more religious groups (scale-types 1–4) are "certain" that this is the case, while only a minority of the other groups are equally "certain."

Visiting the graves of *Tsadikkim* (righteous ones) periodically is also characteristic of most religious groups, especially the *haredim* (83 percent). It is a behavior altogether overlooked by the nonreligious and antireligious. Comparing the ethnic groups, this is clearly a Mizrahi phenomenon.

These behaviors, together with head covering, daily prayer, and belief in the protective power of the mezuzah are far more characteristic of Mizrahim than of the Ashkenazim of either generation. Only a small percentage of the FSU immigrants observe these traditions.

(4) LIFE-CYCLE RITES Respondents were asked how much importance they attribute to family observance of the various rites that usher in changes of status in life. Most respondents (some 60–65 percent) consider the traditional celebration of birth, barmitzvah, marriage, and death to be "very important." Batmitzvah still lingers behind (43 percent). Only a negligible proportion (4 percent to 9 percent) believe that it is "not" or "not at all" important that their families observe these traditional rites.

The less religious groups tend to value the ceremonies of birth and death rather more highly than traditional barmitzvah and marriage ceremonies. Birth and death rites—more than other rites—may symbolize one's belonging to the Jewish people, entering and leaving life as Jews. Again, the Mizrahim value these ceremonies much more highly than the Ashkenazim (80–90 percent and 50–60 percent respectively), and the FSU immigrants are far behind (around 30 percent).

Jewish and Israeli Identity

JEWISH AND ISRAELI: MUTUAL IDENTITIES Two-thirds of Israeli Jews feel "strongly" about their identity as both Jews and Israelis. More than half "would very much want" to be reborn as a Jew and as Israeli, if this were possible. Only a small minority of 5 percent do not identify themselves as Jews or Israelis, replying "not" or "definitely not."

Jewish identification—"feeling part of the Jewish people"—increases in strength with each step up the scale of religiosity. So does feeling Israeli; except for the *haredim,* Israeli identity also increases with religiosity. Among the more religious groups, the strength of Jewish identity outweighs that of Israeli identity (although, as has just been said, both are high). Among those lower on the scale of religiosity, Israeli identity outweighs Jewish identity.

In general, the Eastern groups—first and second generation—are more strongly identified as both Jews and Israelis than the Western groups. Among the first generation—those born abroad—these two identities are equally high. In the second generation, however, Israeli identity somewhat exceeds Jewish identity. On the other hand, the FSU immigrants, in spite of their lesser religiosity, feel more Jewish than Israeli, at least so far.

COMPONENTS OF JEWISH IDENTITY An ethnic group's identity is determined by a variety of components. Three main types are: national-historical, religious-cultural, and biological (which was not examined in this context). Accordingly, seventeen identity components were constructed. The strong relationship between Jewish and Israeli identities is further revealed in the respondents' choices from the list of seventeen components contributing to their feeling of being part of the Jewish people (for an exposition of this approach, see Levy 1985). The *haredim* choose religion and tradition as the most important influences on their identity as Jews, and place the Zionist experience—living in Israel, Israel's wars, establishment of the State, etc.—last. The Holocaust appears in the lower half of their list.[7] The other religious groups give equal high ranking to the religious and the national/Zionist experiences. In the remaining groups on the religiosity scale, namely, the traditional and the nonobservant, as well as in all ethnic groups—that is, among the large majority of the population—the Zionist/Israeli components rank as the most influential on Jewish identification. The influence of the Holocaust comes next. However, the Holocaust ranks equally high as the Israeli experience among the first generation of Ashkenazim (born in the West). A similar pattern was observed by Herman (1977). Herman reports that when the youth were asked to indicate what historical events most influenced them, the majority mentioned the Israeli experience components, such as the establishment of the State and the wars of Israel, together with the Holocaust.

Among the FSU immigrants, the Holocaust ranks at the top.[8] This finding to some extent confirms the growing stand taken by historians that the Holocaust has become a central, if not the primary, Jewish identity component of Diaspora Jews (Novick 1999; Wolffsohn 1994, 1997). The growing salience of the Holocaust among Israeli youth was also reported by Farago (1989). The Holocaust was the first event spontaneously mentioned by Israeli youth in 1985 as influencing their Jewish identity. Greater influence is attributed to the Holocaust as an overall concept than to any of its two aspects that were investigated: the aspect of annihilation (Auschwitz), and the aspect of heroism (Warsaw Ghetto revolt). However, a systematic difference was found between these two aspects. In most of the religious identity scale-types, somewhat more influence is attributed to Auschwitz than to the Warsaw Ghetto revolt, with the greatest gap being among the *haredim* (61 percent and 36 percent, respectively). It appears, then, that the annihilation aspect has a somewhat stronger effect on Jewish identification than the heroism aspect. It should be noted that social-cultural components such as the Hebrew language and literature and the struggle for social justice, precede the Jewish heritage components in shaping the Jewish identity of the "nonreligious." However, only a minority of the nonreligious attribute high influence to social-cultural components.

An objective analysis correlating the influence attributed to each identity component with the respondents' Jewish identification (feeling of belonging to the Jewish people) indicates that components relating to religious tradition and Jewish heritage outweigh the influence of Zionist/Israeli, cultural-social components and the Holocaust. Hence, the subjective ranking differs from the objective one in that it lays greater emphasis on the influence of contemporary history compared to the influence of Jewish tradition and heritage, which correlate the highest with Jewish identification. In other words, Jewish identification in Israel cannot be disconnected from Jewish heritage, even if subjectively it is perceived to have less influence.

ONENESS OF THE JEWISH PEOPLE Israeli Jews feel that they are part of world Jewry. In spite of this expression of solidarity, and almost irrespective of their own level of Jewish identity, Israeli Jews sense that there is a difference between themselves and the Jews of the Diaspora. This feeling has sharpened during the past decade. While 57 percent responded positively in 1991 to the question whether Jews in Israel and Jews in the Diaspora are different people, in 1999 already 69 percent agreed with this statement (the main change occurring in the affirmative answer—"definitely agree"). However, the majority of respondents continue to believe that Israeli Jews and Diaspora Jews share a common fate.

Kurt Lewin (1952) emphasized the centrality of interdependence to group identification, compared to similarity or difference among group members. The findings of our study, like those of earlier studies, support this stance. While interdependence ("common fate") is highly correlated with personal Jewish identification, there is hardly any correlation between Jewish identification and the perception that Jews in Israel constitute a different people from Diaspora Jews.

Beliefs and Values

UNIVERSAL AND PARTICULAR BELIEFS Belief in God, in a supreme power governing the universe,[9] and reward and punishment—the most universalistic of religious beliefs—are widespread in Israel, and, like traditional behaviors, vary in strength by religiosity and by ethnicity. Thus, belief in God ranges from about 80 percent among the Mizrahim of both generations, to about 50 percent of the Western groups, and about 30 percent among FSU *olim*. Belief in life after death drops from 58 percent to 13 percent along the ethnicity scale. The third generation—Israelis born to Israeli parents—falls in between East and West as far as beliefs are concerned; it will be recalled that they resemble the Western groups in traditional behaviors.

More specific Jewish beliefs—in the divine origin of Torah, in the coming of the Messiah, for example—are strongly held by the more religious and more

Eastern groups. On the whole, it would not be far wrong to conclude that Israelis are a more "believing" people than might have been thought. Similarly
high levels of belief are also characteristic of American Jews: 56 percent believe
that there is "definitely" a God, and 27 percent say "probably." That "God
watches over you" and that "God has a special relationship with the Jewish
people" are beliefs held either "definitely" or "probably" by majorities. Belief in
God is considered to be essential for a person to be a good Jew, according to over
half of American Jews (Cohen 1998). Israelis are not far behind (45 percent):
"belief in God" contributes far more to the feeling of Jewish belongingness than
the value of "being religious." Altogether, belief and observance are more characteristic of Israeli Jews than "being religious," which strengthens the inference
that religiosity is associated with the acceptance of halakhic authority.

VALUES Family values such as honoring one's parents and founding a family
head the value hierarchies of all groups in the population. "Personal integrity"
is almost as high. Hedonistic values such as "having a good time," "making
money," and "enjoying beauty" rank lowest.

In between is a set of collectivistic and altruistic values such as contributing
to society, being a good friend, being a good citizen, and the like. These are far
more likely to be affirmed by the more religious groups (Levy 1986; Maslovaty
and Dor-Shav 1988; Rokeach 1973). "Contributing to society" ranks lowest
among FSU immigrants.

Public Policy and Jewishness

JEWISHNESS IN THE PUBLIC SQUARE A large majority (78 percent) believe
that the State should have a Jewish character, but not necessarily a religious one.
An even stronger question—one without a caveat—asks respondents whether
the "State should see to it that public life be conducted according to the Jewish
religious tradition?" This question comes close to polarizing the society: the religious groups say yes, the nonreligious groups say no; the Mizrahim say yes, the
Ashkenazim say no; the FSU immigrants are strongly opposed. Thus, there is
clear sympathy for the idea of a "Jewish" State, an understanding that the expression of this Jewishness will not necessarily be "religious," and a sharp division over whether it is the job of the State to see to it that (religious) tradition
be given a place in public life.

KASHRUT IN PUBLIC PLACES There is some confusion here, which may or
may not be clarified by delving into particulars. Thus, a large majority (around
80 percent) support the observance of kashrut in public establishments, for example, although there is a reduction of support over the decade. A strong minority of the nonreligious/not observant (45 percent) also give support. Only

the antireligious (31 percent) and the FSU immigrants withhold support. This support, however, does not extend to making kosher licenses conditional on other forms of observance; only the most religious groups (scale-types 1–4) agree, while the other groups oppose this restriction. Among the ethnic groups, only the first generation of Mizrahim accept it.

CIVIL MARRIAGE Support has increased over the decade for the introduction of civil marriage in Israel. Some 60 percent of the population agree. The most religious groups do not. Among the ethnic groups, 75 percent of first-generation Mizrahim oppose the institution of civil marriage, compared with a drop to 58 percent among their children, the second generation. Sixty percent of the Western groups, and 77 percent of FSU immigrants are in favor.

In practice, however, a majority of all groups by religiosity and by ethnicity would not themselves opt for civil marriage if it were instituted. Only about half of those who favor the availability of civil marriage would make use of that availability; the Israeli-born ashkenazim and the FSU olim are most strongly attracted (38 percent and 45 percent respectively), although many of these stipulate that they would combine religious and civil ceremonies.

JEWISH DENOMINATIONS Six in ten Israelis think that status of the Conservative and Reform Movements should be equal to that of the Orthodox. Once more, there is the expected difference between the more and less religious scale-types, and between mizrahim (who are divided over this issue) and Ashkenazim. This time, however, the FSU sides with the mizrahim, being far more doubtful than the other Western groups about granting full equality to non-orthodox movements in Judaism. As with civil marriage, only a small proportion favoring this liberal policy consider themselves candidates for affiliation with the Conservative or Reform movements.

EDUCATIONAL STREAMING Most Israeli Jews are satisfied that the educational system—with its several streams—continue to be organized as at present. Unrelated to religious identity or ethnic background, about one in every five support the introduction of another educational stream that would teach in the spirit of Jewish tradition without actually offering religious education. Most Israeli Jews (60 percent) would like to see more teaching of Jewish subjects in the general school system, and more attention to Jewishness in television programs.

UNIVERSAL CONSCRIPTION An overwhelming majority (90 percent), including some of the most religious respondents, are in favor of drafting yeshiva students into the Israeli army (IDF), with two-thirds agreeing further that religious women also serve, whether in the army (65 percent) or in alternate national service (13 percent).

PUBLIC OBSERVANCE OF SHABBAT A large majority of respondents (70 percent) believe "that consideration should be given to preserving the character of the shabbat in public." Yet there is unclarity to determine how this principle is to be reconciled with the rather widespread permissiveness—including that of many religious persons—toward the operation of public transportation on Shabbat, the opening of eating places and places of entertainment, and—to a somewhat lesser extent—urban shopping malls. A majority of all ethnic groups support the Shabbat opening of these services, except for the first-generation of Mizrahim, who are divided on this subject.

In sum, with respect to most of the issues having to do with public life, there is strong support for giving expression to Jewishness in public life, and, at the same time, a liberal permissiveness that wishes for (1) a greater openness to activities that have heretofore been restricted, such as civil marriage and "status quo" concerning the Shabbat, (2) a desire to keep government at arm's length in these matters, and (3) an implied message of "trust us."

INTERGROUP RELATIONS A similar sort of "contradiction" applies to the assessment of the goodness of interpersonal and intergroup relations among Israeli Jews. On the one hand, an increased number of respondents report that they are making an effort to understand others who are different from themselves. At the same time, these same respondents report a serious worsening of intergroup relations, both ethnic relations and relations between religious and nonreligious groups, the latter being judged by 82 percent to be "bad" (Table 4). A well-known social phenomenon is that social solidarity increases in times of crises, while intergroup conflicts may intensify under relatively peaceful and prosperous conditions. It should be borne in mind that the interview stage of the study was completed a few months before the outbreak of the violence in September after the collapse of the peace talks.

Table 4. Quality of Intergroup Relations: 1991 and 1999 (Percentage)

	Quality of Relations				
	Very Good	Pretty Good	Not So Good	Not Good at All	Total
Group interethnic relations					
1991	9	59	28	4	100
1999	7	42	39	12	100
Religious/nonreligious relations					
1991	2	26	53	19	100
1999	2	16	46	36	100

With respect to religious / nonreligious relations, the 1999 study further found that publicly displayed separation in dress and religious behavior creates antagonism between religious and nonreligious groups, while blatant nonreligious behavior, such as permissive hippy appearance, eating *hametz* in public during Passover, etc. is not positively accepted by respondents irrespective of their religious or ethnic identity.

Social and Religious Change Over the Decade

CHANGES OVER TIME The last decade has witnessed a small, yet noticeable, trend toward less religiosity—in identity and observance, although not in belief, and in attitudes toward public life. Part of this change is due to the arrival of hundreds of thousands of immigrants from the FSU. Subtracting the special sample of these respondents makes it possible to examine changes between 1991 and 1999 that are attributable to the internal dynamics of the veteran population alone. Many of these changes have already been noted above.

Jewish identity remains strong and unchanged. There is a marked rise, however, in the proportion who feel that the Jews of Israel and the Jews abroad are "different peoples."

In terms of religious identity, a small polarizing tendency has become evident: in 1999, there are more persons who identify themselves as "nonreligious" and slightly more who identify as "*haredim*." This change is at the expense of the response "*masorti*" (traditional), which has declined. This trend reflects generational change in both ethnic groups, but particularly among the Ashkenazim, whose second generation appears to be moving (somewhat) toward both poles.

In terms of observance, there are small drops (5–6 percent) in the ceremonial observance of Shabbat eve candlelighting (but not other observances), in refraining from nonkosher food, and in the importance attributed to religious marriage—three of the most important indicators of religious behavior among the otherwise nonobservant. On the other hand, there is reported increase in attendance at a Passover Seder. There is some increase of belief in a supreme power in the world, and in reward and punishment for behavior. On the whole, however, there is little or no change reported in most religious behaviors, including synagogue attendance on Shabbat and holidays.

With respect to public life, there has been an increase in the percentage who believe that the State should ensure that public life be conducted in accordance with tradition, while, in apparent contradiction, support for liberalization of Shabbat restrictions on transportation and on recreational and even shopping facilities continues to grow. There is a corresponding relaxation in the popular support for the kashrut of public institutions, and an increase in support for the establishment of civil marriage. Curiously, there has been some falling off in the widespread support for conscripting yeshiva students.

With regard to intergroup relations, a sharp decline has taken place in assessing the quality of relations between ethnic groups and between religious and nonreligious groups. The latter being judged as the worst. It is a well-known that social solidarity increases in times of crisis while intergroup conflicts may intensify under relatively peaceful and prosperous conditions. It should be borne in mind that the interview stage of this study was completed a few months before the outbreak of violence that began in October 2000, after the peace talks collapsed.

As far as values are concerned, family values head the list, even slightly more strongly; care and empathy for others has increased, while hedonism and materialistic values have declined somewhat. It should be borne in mind, however, that most of these changes are rather small, and sometimes inconsistent.

FSU IMMIGRANTS Apart from the dynamics at work internally in the veteran Jewish community, social and religious change—mostly in the same directions—has been affected, externally, by the massive migration from the FSU. Their influence can be measured by comparing the 1999 sample with and without the FSU *olim*. While there are certain large differences between the FSU group and the rest, the overall imprint of this *aliya* is in the neighborhood of about 5 percent.

The large majority (90 percent) of FSU immigrants identify as Jews, albeit less "certainly" than veteran Israelis (35 percent and 70 percent, respectively). Previous studies revealed that only those who replied affirmatively ("definitely yes") to being part of the Jewish people have a positive Jewish identification, while the others do not (Levy 1985). The identity of FSU immigrants as Jews is more widespread than their identity as Israelis. While the establishment of the State and the Holocaust rank highest among the components contributing to Jewish identity for all Israeli Jews, the Holocaust heads the FSU list (see discussion above on Jewish identity). Ritual observances are far less important for the FSU immigrants than for veteran Israelis as influences on their Jewish identity.[10]

Altogether, the FSU immigrants are less religious, less observant, and less believing than even the second-generation of veteran Ashkenazim whom they most closely resemble. Seventy percent concentrate in the two nonreligious scale-types (not religious/observe somewhat, and not religious/observe not at all) compared with 46 percent of veteran Israelis. The predominant category for the *olim,* as for the population as a whole, is "not religious/observe somewhat." Some 40 percent of *olim* fast on Yom Kippur (41 percent "always"), light Hanukkah candles (40 percent "always"), and mark the festivals with appropriate foods (dairy on Shavuot, refraining from *hametz* on Passover). What is striking is the low participation in any form of Seder on Passover, which leads one to wonder whether they might be waiting to be invited. Only one-quarter of FSU immigrants, compared with 85 percent of veteran respondents, partake of this most central of Jewish ceremonies; in fact, more *olim* avoid *hametz* than join at a seder table. One-quarter light Shabbat candles.

FSU immigrants and veterans differ in the importance attributed to life-cycle ceremonies. Circumcision and marriage show the largest differences (around 25 percent); bar mitzvah and rituals surrounding death show smaller differences (10 percent).

The FSU immigrants also fall behind the veteran population in religious beliefs, especially in specific Jewish beliefs such as the chosenness of the Jews, the divine origin of the Torah, and so on.

The FSU immigrants are even more unsympathetic to state-initiated religious restrictions on public behavior. They are sympathetic to enforcing kashrut rules in public establishments; they strongly favor civil marriage; they do not approve of the official standing of the Chief Rabbinate; they are much less concerned than the veterans that the public character of Shabbat deserves being taken into consideration (48 percent and 72 percent respectively).

In short, the FSU immigrants are attached to Judaism, though far less committed to Jewish religiosity, practices, and beliefs, and seemingly much more skeptical about the role of tradition in public policy. Their identity as Israelis is still unsure, largely coinciding with the "social-distance" indicated by Al-Haj and Leshem (2000).

Conclusions

At both the individual level and the level of the State, as we have seen, there is strong Jewish identification, and in both cases there is also the caveat, "but not necessarily religious." The data do suggest, however, that—at the individual level—one needs to be at least somewhat observant to identify oneself (and to be considered by others) as "Jewish." Observance and religiosity overlap perfectly only among the most "Orthodox" groups, who are both religious (*dati* or *haredi*) and strictly observant. For the rest, observance and self-defined religiosity do not completely coincide. Indeed, as has been noted repeatedly, the modal Israeli Jew is "not religious/observe somewhat."

Certain other expressions of Jewishness—such as speaking the Hebrew Language, studying the Tanach, giving charity, or exploring the country—characterize some of the not religious/nonobservant; superficially, at least, they do not stand out prominently, although they deserve further investigation. Apart from these, it seems likely that dissonance at the individual level—between self-described observance and self-defined religiosity—is resolved by separating traditional observance from its religious moorings. The word *dati,* applies only to those who accept *halakha* as their source of authority and apply *halakha* to all their behavior. Others who are observant but not *dati* are actively selective in their traditional behaviors. Not only do they reject *halakha* as authority, they choose to perform observances or traditional behaviors from the repertoire of the cultural heritage, and probably they do not treat observance as central to their lives. It would be a mistake, however, to see this behavior as random; in fact, patterns of observance, while selective, have a "lawful" structure, as we have shown in the 1991 study.

The dilemma at the level of the State—wanting the State to be Jewish but resisting State imposition of traditional Jewish behavior in the civic sphere—appears to be resolved in a different way. Here, the collectivity "volunteers" to substitute—at least in part—for what it wishes the State not to do. Just as *halakha* is rejected as authority at the individual level, the State is rejected as authority in the public sphere. A majority of Israeli Jews wish the society to have a Jewish character but they wish to see to it themselves, apparently. Admittedly, as in the case of the individual, the study did not explore the possibility that people have alternative ideas about how the Shabbat, say, should be observed in public; perhaps they are alluding to a desire for different cultural expressions as a way of expressing the Jewishness of the Shabbat. This deserves much more research.

And reminders of things to worry about: (1) the deteriorating quality of intergroup relations, worst of all between religious and nonreligious; (2) the exacerbation of these relations by virtue of the sizeable overlap between religiosity and ethnicity; (3) the gradual drop in the strength of Jewish identification on the part of the nonreligious (i.e., the better-educated Ashkenazim); (4) the confusion over the meanings of "Jewish" and the role of the "State" in the consensual "Jewish State"; and (5) the growing sense that the Jews of Israel and of the Diaspora are two different peoples.

Finally, we need to be much more careful with concepts, as we have seen, in that words like *dati, shomer* (observe), *mitzvot* (precepts), and *belief* all have overtones—including political overtones—that deserve much deeper investigation from the point of view of the people, not just academicians and researchers.

NOTES

1. Both studies were conducted at the initiative of the Avi Chai Philanthropic Foundation.

2. Only the 373 Jews are included in our analysis.

3. The detailed results are available in Levy, Levinsohn, and Katz 2002.

4. While the question concerning self-reports of observance was asked in both studies, the religious question was asked only in the present study. The comparison presented here is based on data from the Guttman Institute's study on "Leisure, Culture and Communication in Israel," conducted in 1990, and using the same sampling methods as the 1991 study. The leisure study has been published by the Open University Press in Israel.

5. If the anti-religious/not observant are added to the nonreligious/not observant, the total for this combined group is 22 percent. However, these two scale-types behave rather differently and are therefore separated in the analysis.

6. In 1991, there was no difference between the Ashkenazi generations in holiday observance, except in building a Sukka. The two studies find both Mizrahi generations more observant than Ashkenazim, where the first Mizrahi generation observes more than the second.

7. In terms of percentage, the *haredim* attribute somewhat more importance to the Holocaust than do the other groups. In rank order, however, the Holocaust falls below the religious components.

8. The FSU immigrants attribute less influence to each component compared to the veteran respondents. See note 10.

9. The belief in God, and in a supreme power governing the universe, continues to head the beliefs ranking, as it has for many years (Ben-Meir and Kedem 1979).

10. Analysis of the responses of the FSU immigrants suggests that a "response bias" may be at work, which is expressed in a reluctance to choose the extreme positive category ("very important") in replying to scaled questions. Thus, the responses of immigrants and veterans often coincide in rank order, in spite of percentage differences.

REFERENCES

Al-Haj, Magid, and Elazar Leshem. 2000. *Immigrants from the Former Soviet Union in the Nineties: A Decade Later* (*Highlights*). Haifa: Haifa University, The Center for Multiculturalism and Educational Research (In Hebrew).

Ben-Meir, Yehuda, and Perry Kedem. 1979. "A Measure of Religiosity for the Jewish Population of Israel." *Megamot* 24 (3): 353–62 (Hebrew).

Cohen, Steven M. 1998. *Religious Stability and Ethnic Decline: Emerging Patterns of Jewish Identity in the United States.* New York: Jewish Community Centers Association.

Farago, Uri. 1989. "The Jewish Identity of Israeli Youth, 1965–1985." *Yahadut Zemanenu* (Contemporary Jewry: A Research Manual) 5: 259–85. Jerusalem: Institute of Contemporary Jewry, Hebrew University of Jerusalem (Hebrew).

Guttman Louis. 1944. "A Basis for Scaling Qualitative Data." *American Sociological Review* 9: 139–50.

Herman, Simon N. 1977. *Jewish Identity: A Social Psychological Perspective.* Beverly Hills, Calif.: Sage.

Levy, Shlomit. 1985. "Jewish Identity Components as Motivators for Jewish Identification among Jewish Youth and Adults in Israel in the 1967–1982 Period." Ph.D. dissertation, Hebrew University of Jerusalem (Hebrew).

———. 1986. *The Structure of Social Values.* Jerusalem: Israel Institute of Applied Social Research.

Levy, Shlomit, Hanna Levinsohn, and Elihu Katz. 1993. *Beliefs, Observances and Social Interaction among Israeli Jews.* Jerusalem: Louis Guttman Israel Institute of Applied Social Research.

———. 1997. "Beliefs, Observances and Social Interaction among Israeli Jews: Guttman Institute Report." In *The Jewishness of Israelis,* ed. Charles S. Liebman and Elihu Katz, 1–37. Albany: State University of New York Press.

———. 2002. *A Portrait of Israeli Jewry: Beliefs, Observances and Values among Israeli Jews 2000.* Jerusalem: The Guttman Center of the Israel Democracy Institute and AVI CHAI Foundation (Hebrew); (main findings in English).

Lewin, Kurt. 1952. *Field Theory in Social Science.* London: Tavistock.

Liebman, Charles S., and Elihu Katz, eds. 1997. *The Jewishness of Israelis.* Albany: State University of New York Press.

Maslovaty, Nava, and Zecharia Dor-Shav. 1988. "The Connection between Observing Religious Tradition and Values Domains in Value Structure of Adolescents Studying in a Large City in Israel." *Bisde Hemed* 32 (1–2): 90–96.

Novick, Peter. 1999. *The Holocaust in American Life.* Boston and New York: Houghton Mifflin.

Rokeach, Milton. 1973. *The Nature of Human Values.* New York: Free Press.

Wolffsohn, Michael. 1994. *Eternal Guilt? Forty Years of German-Jewish-Israeli Relations.* New York and London: Columbia University Press.

———. 1997. *Meine Juden—Eure Juden (My Jews—Your Jews).* Munich and Zurich: Piper.

CHAPTER TWELVE

The Israel Reform and Conservative Movements and the Market for Liberal Judaism

❧

Ephraim Tabory

It is a paradox of religious life in Israel that nonobservant Jews appear to have greater respect for Orthodox Judaism, a denomination whose precepts they reject on a personal level, than they do for the Reform and Conservative movements that try to cater to their needs. While the majority of Israel's Jews are non-Orthodox, Orthodox Judaism is the denomination that many Israelis perceive to be most religiously legitimate. Only 20 to 25 percent of Israel's Jews say they are "religious," which in Israeli terminology translates as Orthodox. The rest identify themselves as either "traditional" or "nonreligious" (Ben Meir and Kedem 1979; Kedem 1991). Efforts undertaken by the Israel Reform and Conservative movements to attract "traditional" and "nonreligious" Jews have met with limited success. The movements provide a combined estimate of fifteen thousand persons who they say take part in their congregational activities on a regular basis in 2002. Even if the figure were double this number, it would indicate that the movements are serving less than 1 percent of the Jewish population in Israel. At the same time, there are indications, which I present later, that suggest greater acceptance of the movements. I present here a profile of the Israeli movements that will enable us to examine how the movements have been affected by their location in Israeli society, and, in turn, to evaluate the impact of Reform and Conservative Judaism on Jewish life in Israel.

The Movements in Israel

The Reform movement in Israel had its "modern" (post-statehood) beginnings in 1958, with the founding of the Harel synagogue in Jerusalem, followed by five additional congregations in the early 1960s. Following a conference for those interested in a religious alternative to Orthodox Judaism in 1965, the six basically independent congregations incorporated themselves as the Israel Movement for Progressive Judaism in 1971. The movement has grown to include two kibbutz settlements, a communal settlement, a group within one other kibbutz, and some twenty-eight urban congregations that hold regular services. Many of the

weekly services are sparsely attended, unless there is a bar or bat mitzvah celebration. Without downplaying the importance of the congregations for the
members and those who attend services, using religious participation as a criterion of success indicates that the movement has not yet made strong inroads in
Israeli society (Tabory 1983, 1998). There are additional data, however, that suggest that the Israeli public may be more receptive to programs outside of the traditional congregational setting.

Conservative congregations have fared somewhat better. The Conservative
movement was formally established as the Masorti [Traditional] Movement in
1979, following the uniting of the Rabbinical Assembly in Israel and congregations previously under the auspices of the United Synagogue of Israel. The
name of the movement is intended to project to Israel's traditional Jews that *this*
is the movement for them. The Conservative movement lists fifty-two congregations on its rolls in 2001, but some of them do not hold regular services. The
Conservative movement has also established a kibbutz settlement and it has a
moshav affiliated with it as well. The settlements established by both movements have had limited impact on their respective movements on a macro level.
They have not contributed as much to an increase in the perceived legitimacy
of the denominations in urban Israeli society as some people had hoped from
having such an Israeli establishment as one of their institutions (Meirovich
1999). Of course there has been a general decline in the prestige of the entire
kibbutz movement over the years. The non-Orthodox settlements have been
affected by this change in a variety of ways, including their ability to attract
members dedicated to the banner of liberal Judaism.

The Reform movement says that about five thousand persons are involved in
its congregational activities on a regular basis, and the Conservative movement
provides a figure of ten thousand people. These estimates do not include those
persons who take part in other activities, or who are otherwise exposed to the
movements in the course of the year. The number of people who participate in
some liberal movement activity outside of the congregational services does appear to be growing.

A substantial number of the people involved in the movements on a regular
basis were already affiliated with them prior to their immigration to Israel or, in
the case of native Israeli members, came into contact with them while on a prolonged stay abroad. An overrepresentation of people born in English-speaking
countries, relative to their proportion in the Israeli Jewish population, characterizes the Conservative movement more than it does the Reform movement.
Given the religious-ideological nature of immigration from North America, it
is not surprising that those who move to Israel are more religiously identified,
thus benefiting Conservative more than Reform, Judaism in Israel.

The Conservative movement also has a substantial number of members who migrated from South America. Both movements are now seeking to attract migrants from the former Soviet Union, and to that end issue some of their publications in Russian as well as in Hebrew (and English and Spanish, in the case of the Conservative movement). The Conservative movement has developed special programs, such as Midreshet Yerushalayim (under the auspices of the Schechter Institute, to be discussed below) and Shorashim (Project Roots, under the aegis of the Masorti Movement), to help immigrants from the former Soviet Union discover their Jewish roots. These programs are also aimed at migrants from other countries as well, such as Ethiopia and Cuba, to rediscover their Jewish roots. The Reform movement has established congregations and study groups for Russian speakers. The movements cannot count on immigration from Western countries as a source of continuous growth, since migration from those countries, especially non-Orthodox migration from the United States, had considerably abated even prior to Intifada Al Aksa (2000–). The upshot of this is that new members have to be converted to Reform or Conservative Judaism in order for the Israel movements to grow. To some extent, some of the synagogues of the movements, especially those with a large concentration of persons with the same native language, serve an ethnic function for some of their members (Tabory and Lazerwitz 1995).

Twelve Reform and eighteen Conservative synagogues employed at least a part-time rabbi in 2001. Many of the Conservative congregations are too small or do not have the financial means of employing a rabbi. The Reform movement underwrites most of the expenses involved in hiring congregational rabbis. Both movements are trying to produce more Israeli rabbis. The Reform movement trains its local rabbis at Hebrew Union College in Jerusalem. Conservative rabbis are trained at the Schechter Institute of Jewish Studies, the Masorti (Conservative) Movement's graduate and rabbinical school in Jerusalem, which is affiliated with the Jewish Theological Seminary of America. In 2001, there were sixteen matriculated students registered in Hebrew Union College's rabbinical program for Israelis and twenty-two students in the Schechter Institute's program. In both movements, the Israeli program includes native Israelis as well as immigrants from a variety of countries. Both men and women are trained in these facilities— the Conservative movement in Israel was slower in adopting a more egalitarian role for women than its counterpart institutions in the United States, but women now can be ordained as rabbis. Hebrew Union College has ordained twenty-four rabbis in Israel since it began its program twenty-three years ago, and forty rabbis have been ordained by the Schechter Institute in Israel.

The movements do not find it easy to recruit denomination members with strong backgrounds in Jewish studies for their rabbinical programs. The lack of a sufficient number of knowledgeable and committed Jews who might be interested in serving as non-Orthodox rabbi is compounded by the question (which also affects the supply of rabbis in other countries) regarding the ability to earn enough to justify this as a vocation.

Each movement has a rabbinical association that includes those rabbis currently living in Israel. The Conservative movement numbers 150 persons who belong to the Rabbinical Assembly (about 10 percent of all Conservative rabbis worldwide), but many of these persons are not active in movement activities (Steinberg 2000). The Reform movement has about 45 members in its Council of Progressive Rabbis (Maram, or Moetzet Rabbanim Mitkadmim). Each of the rabbinical associations has subcommittees that deal with specific subjects. The *halakha* subcommittee of the Conservative movement's Rabbinical Assembly, for example, has dealt with a wide range of religious questions regarding Jewish life in Israeli society. That subcommittee, through 2001, has issued six volumes of Responsa. Each of the movements has its own *Beit Din* that deals with conversion to Judaism. The Reform movement has issued several "certificates of supervision" to food establishments stating that, "All of the food sold in the restaurant and its divisions are suitable for observers of tradition (*shomrei masoret*) according to the principles of the Shulkhan Aruch and other determiners of *halacha*," even though the institution may operate on Shabbat, or have non-Jewish decorations, such as a Christmas tree. The certificate does not mention the word "kosher" because only the Chief Rabbinate is empowered by civil law to issue a certificate of Kashrut. The Conservative movement has rejected the idea of its providing some type of supervision because of halakhic and legal considerations.

Youth Activities

The future of religious movements depends heavily on the continued affiliation of future generations of current members. The movements have a problem in this regard. The Reform movement has no national youth movement of which to speak. (There are about 120 youngsters involved in its youth programs, and it has a summer program that enrolled about 300 campers in 2000.) The movement was fortunate, in the late 1990s, to have an individual who volunteered to initiate a young adult program. He created a Young Forum (*Forum tzeirim*) for men and women ages 20 to 35. The Young Forum, which had about 100 members in 2001, is listed as a sponsor on many of the movement's publications, especially those dealing with religious equality and civil rights. Most of the members are native Israelis with little background in established religion. These youth exerted much effort to formulate the movement's platform, adopted in 2000, and they are active on university campuses. Many of the Young Forum members do not attend synagogue services on a regular basis, but more participate in study groups. A few of the members have entered the movement's rabbinical program. It will be interesting to see what these youngsters do, vis à vis the movement, when they stop being students and become more established in their careers and lifestyles.

The Conservative movement has had some success in involving their youth in movement activities. There are some 23 Noam (Noar Masorti, or Conservative youth) groups in Israel, with about 1,300 members. These groups are generally, but not always, affiliated with local congregations. A national director coordinates their activities. Regional activities are held periodically. The director of the youth program says that Noam attracts Conservative youth, as well as nonaffiliated others, including modern Orthodox youngsters. The high percentage of children in the youth movement who speak English, Spanish, and other languages led to a campaign to speak Hebrew because "we are in Israel, and this is a state that speaks Hebrew." (*Itonoam* December 1999). In 2000, between 350 and 500 youngsters attended Ramah Noam, a summer camp with programs ranging from several days, for the youngest groups, to several weeks for high school youth. The head of the youth program estimates that 85 percent of the camp children are from families affiliated with the Conservative movement, although the children themselves do not necessarily attend the congregations regularly. The movement is proud of its bar and bat mitzvah program in twenty-five of the fifty schools for disabled children in Israel. The program is not necessarily geared to attracting the youngsters or their parents as ongoing movement members.

The Conservative movement also has a young adult program, Marom (Mercaz Ruchani Masorti, or Conservative Spiritual Center), established in 1995, to provide a study and social framework for, inter alia, graduates of the youth movement Noam, and of the Tali school program (discussed below). The program, which has about 70 active members (mostly university students) among the 230 people on its mailing list, published its first newsletter in 2000. There is a debate in the movement about whether the program should place emphasis on expanding and increasing its roll of active members (outreach) or on strengthening the commitment of current members (inreach). The movement also has several military—*Nachal* programs for its high school graduates, and Conservative youth are also involved in the *garinim* (i.e., groups), serving a voluntary year in a development town before enlisting together in the army. A *garin,* in 2000, comprised about fifteen people.

Educational Programs

If only minimal attention is given to the institutions of the movements, it is because a primary purpose of this chapter is to discuss the denominations within the framework of Israeli society, rather than focus only on their internal developments. Some of the congregations and groups are indeed thriving, and there are many persons who find the prayer services and congregational meetings to be extremely significant on a personal level. These people simply do not represent the non-Orthodox population at large at this time. Indeed, they may not even represent many of those who have a more tenuous affiliation with the movements. One area of activity that appears to be resonating better among non-Orthodox Israelis is Jewish education.

The educational system provided for non-Orthodox children in Israel is concentrated in Israel's public school system, known as the "State educational system." (There is a parallel State-religious school system for Orthodox children, and also various other systems geared to different ultra-Orthodox groups in Israel.) A group of parents, in 1974, wished to provide their children with a greater level of Jewish education than that offered by their State school in Jerusalem. These persons, mostly of American Conservative background, utilized a provision of the National Education Act of 1953 that allowed them to determine part of the school's curriculum, if they could get 75 percent of the parents to submit a specific proposal. In retrospect, these parents were the pioneers in establishing the Tali (Tigbur Limudei Yahadut, or Enriched Jewish Studies) program in the general (i.e., non-Orthodox) school system (Zisenwine 1999; Tali 1995). The basic idea is that children can receive enhanced Jewish education in a pluralistic, noncoercive environment that emphasizes tolerance and democratic values. In 2000–2001 the Tali network encompassed more than 64 schools and 42 kindergartens reaching 20,000 children. The connection between the Conservative movement and the school program was considerably downplayed—even denied—in the early days of this development. The fear was that any institutional connection with a non-Orthodox denomination would spell political doom for the program. The program receives support from the Tali Education Fund (founded in 1983), which is located in the Conservative movement's Schechter Institute of Jewish Studies in Jerusalem. It is there that curriculum for the program is prepared, and teachers are trained. Indeed, the Schechter Institute has four hundred students enrolled in its graduate programs, which are geared to help them become more knowledgeable teachers actively involved in the school system. Teacher training facilities have also been established in other regional areas. The Schechter Institute considers the Tali program as constituting a Conservative school system in Israel, although the program is officially under the supervision of the Ministry of Education and the Ministry insists that the program is entirely nondenominational.

The Reform movement has also entered the educational field by opening fifteen nursery schools, forty-two kindergarten classes, and two first-grade classes. Some of the kindergartens are under the private auspices of the movement, and some are part of the municipal education system in the various cities. The Reform movement is responsible for one Tali school in Jerusalem, and also the Leo Baeck Education Center in Haifa. The movement would like to be more involved in the Tali program, and was trying to figure out how to accomplish this in 2001. The educational division of the organization was one of the more active arms of the Reform movement in the late 1990s, but many of the people involved in it were let go at the end of 2000, because of economic considerations. The division is very close to being closed down in 2001. The acting head of the educational division is hoping to reevaluate the relationship with the Tali system, if the division continues to function. It is her (quite accurate) perception that parents in at least some of the Tali schools do not know about the involvement of liberal religious movements in the Tali program, or they do not want any such involvement. In fact, the Tali schools have not yet contributed much to the growth of either movement, and the level of Jewish identification of *Tali* school graduates appears to be very uneven. A study of the Tali program is warranted to understand the organizational relationships among the Ministry of Education, the local schools that may seek affiliation with the program as long as they receive additional funds with no educational requirements being made of them, the Tali Fund, and the two movements.

Research is also needed to understand the motivation of the parents who send their children to the Tali programs, the private nurseries (in the synagogues) and to the kindergartens. Some Israeli families who send their children to the special educational programs may do so because of their perception that these programs are generally on a higher level than regular public school programs. A certain amount of religious knowledge (but not indoctrination) may be acceptable to them as an additional cost of such quality education. Other parents, of course, specifically seek out this type of education. Better understanding of the motivation of the parents involved in the educational activities is important, because the educational field seems to be a sphere of activity that may promise even greater success for the movements in the future. Furthermore, as a component of Jewish identity, interest in Jewish learning seems to be on the rise even as it is unrelated to traditional practice.

Some of the congregations conduct adult education classes. Both the Conservative and Reform movements have a Yeshiva or Bet Midrash (House of Learning)—terms generally used for Orthodox institutions—in Jerusalem. The Conservative movement also has Midrashiyot Iyun, or Study Centers, in five additional cities. There is developing interest in Israel for programs that focus on Jewish sources and texts among some groups in the non-Orthodox population in Israel, but that interest is more on an academic level than it is on a practical level that might benefit the liberal movements at this time. The Conservative movement has conducted two study days for women. Over four hundred women attended these sessions.

The Social Environment of the Movements

The size of a social movement is not necessarily a criterion for its success. Robert Merton (1976) points out that even a small movement may be considered successful if it attracts a substantial proportion of its potential members. However, movements that purport to be geared to the majority of a country's population but fail to attract those people may have a problem with regard to the perceived legitimacy and authenticity of their values. Given that Reform and Conservative Judaism are religious movements, why have they achieved less success in Jewish Israel than in non-Jewish countries?

It is no surprise that Orthodox Judaism totally denigrates Reform and Conservative Judaism. Orthodox Judaism views itself as the true representative of Torah Judaism. Those who do not follow its precepts are considered to be sinners (Who Are You Reformers 1997). The demand for recognition by the non-Orthodox movements is made in the name of pluralism. Orthodox Judaism by definition rejects pluralism. Minority status in Israel, relative to other denominations, would have two major implications for Orthodox Judaism. One relates to simple interests. The Orthodox establishment is able to ensure the provision of important resources, including money, because of its strong hold on Israeli religious life. Relegating Orthodox Judaism to a minority status relative to other religious denominations in Israel would considerably loosen the grip that it has on political and state life. Beyond that, recognition of Reform and Conservative Judaism in Israel would challenge the religious message of Orthodox Judaism as it has been challenged before.

For the most part, Israeli Jews refer to Orthodox Judaism as the measure by which they define their own level of religiosity. Non-Orthodox Jews generally identify themselves as traditional or as nonreligious because they do not fulfill the requirements of Orthodox ritual, not because they necessarily maintain a secularist ideology. It is much easier for Orthodox Judaism to countenance Jews who do not practice the religious commandments than to face movements that question the legitimacy of their authority. Indeed, "normal" religious laws can even be suspended when talking about Reform Judaism, leading to the following answer about whether it is permitted to speak ill (*lashon hara*) of Reform Jews:

> The Response of Rabbi Avraham Naamad (2000):
> The Chafetz Chaim wrote … "the proscription against *Lashon Hara* refers to a person who according to the law of the Torah is still your colleague" … in torah and commandments, but [for] those people who are recognized as … those who deny the torah and prophets of Israel, it is a positive commandment to denounce them and shame them … [A]s King David said "I will hate those who hate God," and the Reform and those like them deny the torah and it is the mitzvah of mitzvot to speak evil of them, and even though it says in the torah "your way is a way of tranquility" nevertheless here it is a mitzvah to speak evil of them and to shame them and to insult them since these people are no longer part of your people.

At least some non-Orthodox Israelis seem to share perceptions of Reform and Conservative Judaism similar to those espoused by Orthodox leaders. Matti Golan (1992; back cover), for example, a non-Orthodox journalist who wrote a book in the form of a dialogue between an American and an Israeli Jew, has his Israeli state that Conservative Judaism is the first step out of Judaism, and Reform Judaism is the first step into Christianity. Hebrew University professor of political science and former director general of Israel's Ministry of Foreign Affairs, Shlomo Avineri, was credited with reflecting the attitude of many non-observant Israelis when he said that "I won't go to a synagogue, but the synagogue I won't go to is an Orthodox one."

The fact that the Reform and Conservative movements have not made strong inroads into the non-Orthodox population on the congregational level raises some question about the nature of Reform and Conservative Judaism as religious movements. This was put forth early on by the executive director of the World Union for Progressive Judaism, Rabbi Richard Hirsch (1972: 15–16), who wrote that, in the United States, "many Reform members belong to our synagogues because we offer the most palatable, the most aesthetic, and the easiest way to be a Jew. In other words, I suspect that the most influential factor in building American Reform Judaism has not been theology, but sociology" He added that:

> Israel offers a real test of our authenticity. For in Israel, there is no societal pressure or inner compulsion to join a synagogue in order to identify as a Jew. No Israeli Jew is subconsciously moved by the question "What will the gentiles say?" … The liberal Jew in America will never have a full and proper relationship to Israel until there is a liberal movement in Israel. Until then we shall always be considered as outsiders and therefore shall consider ourselves

creations of the diaspora ... an American sect practicing a way of life which can flourish only in a gentile soil, aliens and oddities foreign to the authentic Judaism of Eretz Yisrael. (Hirsch 1972, p. 19)

Not every non-Orthodox leader will agree with this opinion, but there are those for whom it remained current in 2001. In a speech to the international convention of the World Union for Progressive Judaism in March 2001, Rabbi Ammiel Hirsch, head of Arza/World Union, North America, said that:

> We remind our people that a strong Progressive movement in Israel is in their direct self-interest. If we can be dominant only in America and nowhere else in the Jewish world; if we can succeed only in the United States and not in the Jewish state, then our critics are right - we are nothing but a diaspora phenomenon, largely American, good for a certain moment and place in time, but not rooted in the soil and the soul of our people, and not anchored against the winds and vicissitudes of history.

Many of the persons interviewed in the course of my research indicated their belief that expansion and growth would indeed increase the perceived legitimacy of their movements. The lack of rapid growth thus far is often attributed to the impediments placed before the movements in Israel. The movements have had to work hard, indeed, to overcome negative perceptions, and the acts of discrimination perpetrated against them. Some congregations have had difficulty in obtaining land for the construction of a synagogue or even just renting premises for prayer services. While the construction of Orthodox synagogues and salaries of congregational rabbis in Israel are not routinely funded by the government, it is still easier for Orthodox institutions to obtain civic funds for their needs. The liberal movements have inevitably had to petition the High Court of Justice to obtain the funds that they thought they should receive. Congregational dues taken for granted in countries such as the United States serve as an impediment to synagogue affiliation in Israel. Many Israelis assume that the Conservative and Reform movements are well funded by their counterpart movements abroad but the amount actually rendered to the Israeli movement is not so generous as to allow them to develop and expand without consideration of financial restraints.

An additional factor that affects the movements is the limited official status granted to them. Marriages and conversions performed by the rabbis are not recognized by the State. Reform and Conservative Jews have been prevented from taking their seat on local Religious Councils, which are only administrative bodies for the provision of religious services at the local level (as opposed to law-making bodies). Some people would rather disband the Councils than

allow non-Orthodox Jews to take part in them. The movements have also suffered vigilante-type violence, including physical assaults on the participants at
Reform and Conservative services at the Western Wall in Jerusalem, and arson
attacks on a Reform kindergarten near Jerusalem in 1999 and on a Conservative
synagogue in Jerusalem in June 2000. While these attacks are scurrilous, and
while many paragraphs could be filled detailing additional incidents and acts of
discrimination against the liberal denominations, it is questionable whether the
absence of such acts would have led the denominations to grow at a greater pace.
Discrimination does contribute to the perception of the environment in which
the movements have found themselves in Israel as hostile, and to a feeling of
persecution that leads the rabbis and movement leaders to place the fight against
hostility and discrimination high on their public agenda. Public denigration of
the liberal denominations, such as newspaper advertisements placed by the
Chief Rabbinate of Jerusalem stating that the commandment to hear the blow-
ing of the *shofar* (rams horn) is not fulfilled if it is heard in a liberal synagogue
(*Jerusalem Post,* Sept. 5, 1980), contribute to a general atmosphere of illegiti-
macy. Furthermore, withholding financial resources from the movements makes
it harder for them to offer the educational and cultural programs that the Israeli
public might be more interested in pursuing than their desire to participate in
a congregational based prayer service.

The Reaction by the Movements

The movements have worked hard to refute the charge that they are imported
and religiously inauthentic organizations. They have tried to make minimum
use of English in their prayer books. They routinely claim that their contemporary membership includes a higher percentage of native-born Israelis than in the
past. The movements have also formulated platforms and issued publications
depicting themselves in a positive manner to counter the charge that they are
just less observant movements.

Legal Reactions to Unequal Treatment

The most concerted reaction by the movements has been on the political and
legal levels. Political parties in Israel are routinely lobbied and politicians and
media persons have been sent to the United States to learn more about liberal
Judaism. Legal action against discrimination has included an unsuccessful petition to the Supreme Court to recognize marriages performed by Reform rabbis
in the 1980s (High Court of Justice 1982). In general, the movements were loath
in their early years in Israel to undertake substantial political and legal action

against the government. The best explanation for this reluctance was the American background of many of the leaders that led them to refrain from involving politics with religion.

A fundamental change took place with the formation of the Reform movement's Israel Religious Action Center (IRAC) in 1987. While legal cases regarding the definition of who is a Jew, such as those involving Brother Daniel and Binyamin Shalit constituted significant challenges to the religious and political establishment in the past, their effect was limited in altering the overall balance of religion and state (Abramov 1976). IRAC, directed by Uri Regev, a lawyer and one of the first native Israelis to be ordained a Reform rabbi in Israel, undertakes a multifaceted legal attack in a systematic, organized, and concerted manner. In addition to petitioning for the recognition of Reform conversions, it challenges the rejection of Reform members in local religious councils and the nonallocation of funds to the liberal denominations in Israel. It has also protested the allocation of funds to ultra-Orthodox institutions and established a watchdog function to oversee the money given to them. In 2001 it recruited lawyers in the United States with civil rights expertise to join its organization, Attorneys for Religious Freedom in Israel.

Occasionally, IRAC represents the Conservative movement as well. That movement has become more willing to challenge the Israeli establishment, especially after the appointment of Ehud Bandel, the first native Israeli to be ordained a Conservative rabbi in Israel, as its president. The Conservative movement has also formed its own legal department and submitted its own petitions to the High Court of Justice, particularly with regard to the funding of its educational projects, and the recognition of children converted by Conservative rabbis. Still, the constraints of the Conservative membership, as well as economic considerations, have had an impact on the readiness of that movement to be more involved in an expanded legal and political struggle. It is the Reform movement and IRAC that lead the legal challenge against discrimination and constitute the primary challengers of the religious status quo in Israel. Two issues the center has dealt with in recent years, a Conversion Bill and appointments to religious councils, especially manifest this.

The Conversion Bill

Israeli policy, since 1989, has been to recognize foreign non-Orthodox conversions but not those that are performed in Israel. A Conversion Bill was proposed in reaction to a 1995 decision by the Supreme Court sitting as the High Court of Justice (The Rabbinical Court Jurisdiction Act 1997). In this case, a woman converted by a Reform *Beit Din* in Israel petitioned to receive an immigrant's visa as a Jew. The Court ruled that recognition of a conversion performed in Israel regarding the Population Registry Law and the Law of Return is not subject to the requirements of the Mandatory Religious Community (Change) Act. The requirement for the confirmation of a conversion by the (Orthodox) Rabbinate relates only to issues of personal status (High Court of Justice 1993). The Court also indicated that the Knesset should determine which conversions conducted in Israel should be recognized for purposes of the Law of Return.

The reaction by Orthodox political parties was to demand legislation declaring that the state recognizes only Orthodox conversions. The Conversion Bill, which passed the First Reading in 1997, states that "the conversion of a person in Israel will be in accordance with *Din Torah*," and that no conversion will be recognized without the approval of the Chief Rabbi of Israel. Knesset member Moshe Gafni (United Torah Judaism) said he would submit an additional bill that would also include the rejection of non-Orthodox conversions performed abroad (*Yated Ne'eman* April 1, 1997). Rabbi Eric Yoffe, President of the Union of American Hebrew Congregations, called the proposed bill a declaration of war on American Jews. "If Reform Rabbis in Israel are not Rabbis and the conversions are not conversions, that means that our Judaism is not Judaism and we are second rate Jews" (*Jerusalem Post* April 1, 1997).

In order to prevent a rift between American Jewry and Israel, an agreement was reached with the heads of the American non-Orthodox movements to establish a committee to try and resolve the issue. The committee was chaired by Yaakov Ne'eman, an Orthodox Jew who was soon to be appointed Minister of Finance. For the first time in Israeli history, representatives from the Israel Reform and Conservative movements were officially included as members of a committee formed to deal with non-Orthodox conversions to Judaism. After long deliberations, a proposal was formulated to establish a joint conversion institute that would include Reform and Conservative representatives on its board. The board would determine the curriculum, and the teachers would include Reform and Conservative Jews. This would provide the movements with a degree of recognition that would enable them to accept the second part of the proposal—that an Orthodox *beit din* (religious court) would conduct the actual conversion procedure.

The Council of the Chief Rabbinate issued a response to this proposal on February 9, 1998, stating:

> [that it] received the unambiguous communication from the Finance Minister that there are not, and would never be again non-halachic conversions in Israel and that he accepted a clear commitment to prevent all actions called "conversions" but are only fake conversions. The Chief Rabbinical Council demands that exclusivity of conversion in accordance with halakha be enacted in law and receive legal force.... The ... Council calls upon all who are

able to prevent the actions of others who do not believe in Torah from Heaven, who try to shake the foundations of the Jewish religion and by this separate the nation in an attempt to implant in the heart of the nation deviation from the accepted tradition passed down from generation to generation. They have already brought about the disastrous results of assimilation among Diaspora Jewry. The Sages of Israel have forbidden any cooperation with them and their methods. One cannot consider establishing a joint institute with them.... The Rabbinical Council calls for a unified recognition of one conversion done according to the Law of Moses and Israel and carried out by the rabbinical courts of the Chief Rabbinate of Israel. And this after the converts learn the foundations of Judaism according to the tradition passed down from generation to generation and to halakha.

Because of this rejection, the Ne'eman Committee members never signed the recommendations and no formal agreement was ever reached by the committee. Eighty of Israel's 120 member Knesset voted their symbolic support for the Committee's intended recommendations in February 1998. That vote encouraged the parties to go ahead, anyway, and the Government of Israel and the Jewish Agency formally established a Joint Institute of Jewish Studies. The Reform and Conservative movements agreed to participate subject to the stipulation that this would not be used against them in their legal petitions or be interpreted as an agreement to cease their own independent conversion procedures. The first group of 40 students was converted in 2000. The approach of the Orthodox establishment, thus far, has been that the test of the *beit din* is the graduate, and not where he or she studied. This is a major joint initiative of Orthodox and non-Orthodox denominations that brings the Reform and Conservative movements one step closer to acceptance and recognition in Israel. The real test will occur when a conversion candidate openly declares to the *beit din* that he or she intends to be a Reform or Conservative Jew.

Religious Councils

Reform and Conservative challenges have also had a significant impact on who can serve on religious councils. Conflicts over membership in religious councils have related to the appointment of nonreligious Jews and women. A 1964 court decision determined that the members on this administrative body must not have an antireligious orientation although they need not be Orthodox Jews. Furthermore, members should have a positive interest (as opposed to a neutral orientation) in the provision of religious services (Elbaz 1964). In line with this, the Court has also ruled that non-Orthodox men and women not be disqualified from serving on the councils (High Court of Justice 1987).

Despite judicial rulings, the Orthodox establishment has continued to oppose the seating of Reform and Conservative members. Knesset Member Moshe Gafni (United Torah Judaism) compared the participation of Reform Jews in religious councils to a terrorist's penetration of military headquarters. The State Chief Rabbis convened Orthodox functionaries in 1994 to protest the inclusion of non-Orthodox people on religious councils. Jerusalem Chief Rabbi Izhak Kolitz stated that it is inconceivable that judges in civil legal courts who know nothing about Torah should be allowed to determine halachic matters (*Ha'aretz* February 23, 1997: p. a7). In a statement to the High Court of Justice, Netanya Sephardi Chief Rabbi David Chelouche proposed that the Reform movement should establish its own council, just as other religions do in Israel, explaining that:

> Their Sabbath is no Sabbath, their *kashrut* is not *kashrut*, family purity is unknown to them, carcasses and unclean animals are their regular food, and they despise marriage ceremonies according to the religion of Moses and Israel, performing instead marriages which are contrary to *Halakha* and the tradition handed down from generation to generation, and in addition, many of them are intermarried. (Jerusalem Post, July 7, 1997: 12)

In this case, the Supreme Court (sitting as the High Court of Justice) went further than repeating its rulings supporting the appointment of a Reform woman to a religious council; the Court actually ordered the Minister of Religious Affairs to sign the requisite documents of appointment. The Shas party minister adhered to an order by Shas leader, Rabbi Ovadia Yosef, not to sign the document. A rotation agreement to transfer the Ministry from Shas to the National Religious Party allowed Prime Minister Netanyahu to sign the papers in an interim period when he himself headed the office.

Even orders by the High Court of Justice and pressure by the Minister of Religious Affairs calling upon the religious councils with non-Orthodox members to actually convene were met with opposition. Orthodox council members simply refused to attend the meetings. Orthodox authorities feared that nonattendance at religious council meetings might lead to a situation in which the attending Reform and Conservative members would be able to run the council. The Minister of Religious Affairs therefore amended the Administrative Regulations to require a minimum quorum for the council to convene. This ensured that even religious council sessions convened by court order would have no legal validity.

The challenges of the Reform and Conservative movements and the decisions by the High Court of Justice led to a tremor, if not upheaval, in state-religion relations in 2001. A quarter of a million *haredi* Jews demonstrated against the court's activism in February 1999. The Haredi community was demanding that religious issues be removed from the jurisdiction of civil courts.

Indeed, a bill relegating consideration of constitutional issues to a more "representative" court, rather than to the Supreme Court passed its first reading in Israel's Knesset in 2001. The purpose of the bill was to undermine the liberal, civil rights orientation of the Supreme Court.

While the non-Orthodox movements have yet to win over the conservative, right of center, nonreligious public in Israel, the legal battles pitting the conception of Israel as a democratic and a Jewish state against one another continue. Support for the Reform and Conservative movements comes, inter alia, from nonreligious Jews who are against religious involvement in the state, and who view these movements, particularly the Reform movement, as their ally. Leading Israeli, nonreligious authors, for example, published an advertisement in the Israeli press in 1999 following the *haredi* demonstration described above, calling upon Israelis to support the movements in the struggle against the Orthodox establishment. In this regard the movements face a possible dilemma. Inasmuch as many nonreligious people in Israel express support for the non-Orthodox position, it is possible that the denominations will be identified as antireligious movements, rather than as religious movements. In the short run the liberal movements may be more supported by those who oppose the Orthodox establishment than by those who seek a positive, liberal religious alternative (Tabory 1992). A public opinion survey conducted for the Reform movement put the following question forth before respondents in May 2000: "There are three primary denominations in Judaism: Orthodox, Reform and Conservative. With which of these denominations do you most identify?" Thirty-five percent of the respondents said Reform, and this included 51 percent of those who identified themselves as "secular" and 27 percent of those who identified themselves as "traditional" when asked about their own religious identity. Thirteen percent of the respondents said Conservative, including 14 percent of those who identified themselves as "secular" and 17 percent of those who identified themselves as "traditional" (Machon Dachaf 2000). A survey in 1999 that asked a similar question found that 29 percent of the respondents most identify with the Reform, 24 percent with the Orthodox, and 10 percent with the Conservative denominations (Shiluv 1999). People may "most identify" with these denominations for a variety of reasons, ranging from a quest for more religious spirituality to identification with those who oppose the Orthodox establishment. (One Conservative leader used both interpretations to explain the results: the larger number of persons who indicate the Reform movement, he said, do so because of that movement's opposition to the Orthodox establishment. The smaller number of people who indicate the Conservative movement do so because they "are really interested in us.")

Joint Activities and the Market for Religious Alternatives in Israel

While there has been some cooperation between the movements on the political and legal levels, the denominations have been careful to maintain some distance between themselves in order to retain separate identities. This is more important for the Conservative movement, because if it could persuade the general public that it is a halakhic movement, only somewhat removed from modern Orthodox Judaism, it might become more accepted. A publicity campaign jointly conducted by the movements between August 1999 and June 2000 illuminated to the movements themselves that they had different target audiences. The campaign utilized a slogan that "there is more than one way to be Jewish" to inform the Israeli public about the liberal denominations. The movements also emphasized that women were accorded equality in the liberal synagogues in the yearlong advertising campaign. The specific advertisements were created by an advertising agency together with representatives of the movements and the San Francisco–based Richard and Rhoda Goldman Fund that financed the campaign. As these joint meetings evolved throughout the year, the Reform movement came to identify the nonreligious population (as well as traditional Jews) as their potential audience. The Conservative leaders became further convinced of what was apparently their initial view—that liberal Orthodox Jews disillusioned with Orthodoxy constitute an important potential audience (Sheleg 2000). The Conservative movement, in fact, tried to publish an advertisement in the National Religious Party's newspaper, *Hatzofe,* in 2000, under the banner of "we all wear the same *kippa* [skullcap]," basically inviting Orthodox Jews to try out a Conservative synagogue. (The Orthodox newspaper rejected the ad.) The movement's inclusion of liberal Orthodox Jews as a target group does not contradict the movements' attempt to also attract other groups. The joint public relations venture serves as the framework for our discussion of the potential market for liberal Judaism in Israel.

We earlier noted that the movements' main problem in Israel is the apathy of the Jewish public. The special aspect of religious observance that characterizes Israeli Jews is that they have no need to justify what they do—they just do it. The level of Jewish ritual observance of the average Israeli Jew falls between that of Reform synagogue members and Conservative Jews who are not members of a synagogue in the United States (Tabory 1983; Levy, Levinsohn, and Katz 1993; Lazerwitz et al. 1998). Many non-Orthodox Israeli Jews observe some aspect of Shabbat and holidays, such as lighting candles in the home (even without a blessing), or conducting some form of Passover Seder. Many fast on Yom Kippur and observe some degree of kashrut in the home. The motivation for the practices performed may be more cultural than religious (cf. Deshen 1997).

As in countries such as the United States (Sklare and Greenblum 1967), rites of passage in Israel, including circumcisions, bar mitzvahs, weddings, and funerals are observed to a greater degree, and generally in a Jewish—Orthodox—manner. At the same time, the persons involved generally follow a non-Orthodox daily lifestyle. For example, 87 percent of the population feel that a wedding ceremony performed by a rabbi is important (Levy, Levinsohn, and Katz 1993), and most people have no ideological difficulty coping with a ceremony conducted by Orthodox rabbis. Feminism in Israeli society is still rather limited (Izraeli and Tabory 1993; Yishai 1997). A wedding ceremony in which the woman plays a subordinate role and is "bought" by her partner does not bother many women sufficiently to demand large-scale change at this time (especially since they treat the wedding merely as a formal ceremony and do not take the texts seriously). Equal roles for men and women in prayer services, emphasized as a principle by the movements, especially in their 1999–2000 advertising campaign, is not yet important for most Israelis, and thus not an attractive feature leading to large scale expansion at this time. In fact, many women, even within the movements, are not anxious to utilize their rights for greater roles in the services. The prayer books of the Reform and the Conservative movements include the matriarchs alongside the patriarchs in the *Amidah* prayer as an option to the traditional text that only lists the patriarchs. As far as many non-Orthodox Israeli Jews go, though, the patriarchs are as irrelevant to their religious life as are the matriarchs. Most Israelis have simply rejected the synagogue, which, for them, is the establishment in which institutionalized prayers are to be said.

There are, however, some indications of fissures in the non-Orthodox population's willingness to tolerate Orthodox practices. There is less readiness to celebrate rites of passage in an Orthodox manner, on the one hand, and more willingness to celebrate bar and bat mitzvah celebrations and weddings under Conservative and Reform auspices, on the other. This change warrants further clarification.

The Celebration of Rites of Passage

Formal legitimacy from the authorities in Israel aside, there are indications regarding the emergence of a "normative dignity" (Berger and Luckman 1967), that is, a process of informal acceptance among a population that is increasingly viewing a former deviant object as acceptable. A substantial number of Israeli families are now willing to hold a bar or bat mitzvah service in a non-Orthodox congregation. A 1999 survey asked "If you had to use the services of a rabbi for a bar mitzvah (or other ceremonies), which of the following rabbis would you prefer to utilize?" Twenty-three percent of the sample indicated a Reform rabbi, 7% a Conservative, and 39% an Orthodox rabbi (Shiluv 1999). These numbers do not indicate that the respondents will actually use (or actually used) a Reform or Conservative rabbi, but they do indicate potential willingness on the attitudinal level.

Some of the congregations conduct bar mitzvah services almost every week. The Tel Aviv Reform congregation, for example, conducts a morning and an afternoon (*mincha*) mitzvah celebration every week, and the synagogue is booked for the next two years. It is noteworthy that while one might have thought that bat mitzvah celebrations would be especially popular in non-Orthodox congregations, since there is no parallel celebration in Orthodox synagogues, that is not the case. Estimates of the ratio of bat to bar mitzvah celebrations range from one in ten to one in four. Since there is no established tradition of girls reading from the Torah, non-observant Israelis do not feel compelled to arrange a religious rite of passage for their daughters, though they do for their sons. Feminist actions by these teenagers would also set them apart from their peers, and there is special reluctance to make a double statement of dissimilarity by undertaking an act that is perceived to be religious.

In the past, many families (aside from members of Reform congregations) would not agree to a celebration in a non-Orthodox synagogue for two reasons. First, the non-Orthodox congregations were quite simply beyond the pale. Second, even if the family itself was willing, consideration had to be given to friends and relatives who might be reticent about attending a Reform or Conservative ceremony. That consideration had not been completely overcome in 2001. Still, the older generation of more traditional Jews is dying off, and the negative stigma of the denominations is dissipating. In this context, it is relevant to differentiate between first- and second-generation non religious Jews (Tabory 2003).

First-generation nonreligious Jews identify themselves as secular on a cognitive level, but still maintain an affective orientation that is colored or determined by traditional Judaism. Some of these people reject the regular practice of religion for themselves, but they want to do it "the traditional way" when they do choose to take part in a religious service. There seems to be an increasing number of second-generation nonreligious Jews, who were themselves raised in nonreligious homes and environments, and who identify themselves as secular on a cognitive level, but who have an affective orientation that prevents them from celebrating a rite of passage in anything but an Orthodox manner.

There is also a "push" factor at work: there are Orthodox congregations that are actively propelling potential celebrants away from their synagogues. Some Orthodox congregations do not allow bar mitzvah families to invite guests to the Shabbat service so that they will not drive to the synagogue. One Orthodox Tel Aviv synagogue does not allow a bar mitzvah family to bring its own candy to throw following the boy's torah service, fearing that the candy might not be kosher. These practices might be understandable from an Orthodox perspective, but they also tend to repel the non-Orthodox families from the Orthodox synagogue. The Reform and Conservative congregations—especially those located in dignified buildings—now provide a tenable, and increasingly acceptable, alternative.

Attendance at bar and bat mitzvah celebrations in non-Orthodox synagogues has given more exposure to the movements among the non-Orthodox Israeli population. Five percent of the general Jewish Israeli population say they have attended a Reform bar/bat mitzvah, and 2 percent say they have attended such a ceremony in a Conservative synagogue. Eight percent of those who identify themselves as "secular" attended a Reform ceremony, and 4 percent attended a Conservative ceremony (Teleseker 2000). Occasionally, guests who are impressed by these celebrations decide to observe their own child's rite in a Reform or Conservative synagogue. This happens even though the overwhelming majority of the participants and guests continue to reject regular synagogue attendance as an option for themselves. At this stage, one could expect the movements to be at least somewhat satisfied if the non-Orthodox Israeli Jew would declare that "I still do not go to a synagogue," and add "but the synagogue I do not attend (at least regularly) is Reform or Conservative." The movements would be even happier if the Israeli public, having in general rejected all synagogues, would be attracted to and interested in their other activities, particularly in the field of Jewish education.

Non-Orthodox weddings are an even more interesting phenomenon than bar and bat mitzvah celebrations because a wedding performed in Israel by a non-Orthodox rabbi is not recognized by state authorities. (A child is bar or bat mitzvah, of course, regardless of whether he or she takes part in any formal ceremony.) The Conservative movement says that its rabbis perform 200 weddings a year in Israel. The number provided by the Reform movement for 2000 is 800. According to the Director General of the Orthodox Rabbinical Courts, about 32,000 couples wed in Israel in 2000; 4,894 couples wed in civil proceedings abroad; and several hundred couples wed in alternative proceedings in Israel (Chazot 2001). The Reform movement requires the married couple to undergo a civil wedding procedure abroad since the civil authorities in Israel (but not the Chief Rabbinate) recognizes that ceremony and will then register the couple as married. The Conservative movement encourages, but does not require an additional ceremony at this time (the topic is under discussion in the movement), since it maintains that its own ceremonies are in accordance with Jewish law. The movement's intention is that Orthodox *halakha* should accept this claim, but this is really impossible since the Conservative movement, in contravention of Orthodox law, allows women to serve as witnesses at the marriage ceremony.

The movement does notify government authorities (the Ministry of Interior and the Chief Rabbinate) about the weddings they conduct, in order to prevent the individuals who wed through them to marry someone else without first obtaining a proper divorce.

Only a handful of non-Orthodox marriage ceremonies were conducted in Israel in the early 1990s, and inevitably the few couples who chose this alternative did so because of an Orthodox impediment against their marrying (such as the injunction against a Cohen, of Priestly descent, marrying a divorcee). The number has increased considerably since then (Jacobsen 1999). Most of the couples choosing a non-Orthodox rabbi in 2000 could have had an Orthodox rabbi conduct their service if they so chose. The exact motivation of the couples is unknown. Only in a few cases are the persons marrying identified as Reform or Conservative Jews. Some of the couples want a decorous ceremony that they fear they will not experience in the state Rabbinate, or they are disturbed by the pre-marriage encounters with the Orthodox authorities. Some couples want a more egalitarian service (in which the bride can give the groom a ring, or in which the marriage document does not refer to the bride as having been bought by the groom). In many cases, though, part of the motivation appears to be pure antipathy toward the Orthodox establishment. While some couples specifically request a woman rabbi to perform their wedding ceremony, the overwhelming number of wedding couples indicate their preference for a male rabbi. Their willingness to undertake an innovative ceremony has its limitations. In a few cases, couples who registered with a female rabbi even backed out of the agreement, citing family reservations as their consideration.

Reform and Conservative rabbis perform many more bar and bat mitzvah celebrations than weddings. A wedding, unlike a bar or bat mitzvah celebration, involves questions about the legal status of the celebrants. Discussions with couples who have attended "wedding fairs" conducted by the Reform movement to promote non-Orthodox weddings suggest that the greatest hesitation about a non-Orthodox ceremony relates to the validity of the ceremony and the legal status of their future children. They are also concerned about what would happen if they divorce. Some of the fears are misguided. For example, some people are afraid that a child born to parents married by a non-Orthodox rabbi will be considered a *mamzer* under Jewish (Orthodox) law. A *mamzer*, though, is a child born from people involved in an adulterous or an incestuous relationship. One of the purposes of the wedding fairs is to reduce the non-Orthodox wedding fears, but it is hard to ease anxieties when the couples know that the ceremony is not recognized by the State. It is very likely that the number of couples who would choose a Reform or Conservative rabbi for their wedding ceremony would increase substantially if such weddings were officially recognized in Israel. The 1999 survey cited above regarding bar mitzvahs also asked respondents about the rabbi that they would most prefer inviting for a wedding (Shiluv 1999). Twenty-one percent of the respondents indicated a Reform rabbi, 7 percent a Conservative, and 42 percent an Orthodox rabbi. A 2000 survey further asked respondents which ceremony they would prefer if alternative services were considered legal. About a third of the sample (34 percent) said they would prefer an alternative service (civil wedding, or a Reform or Conservative ceremony). This included 52 percent of those who identify themselves as "secular" and 22 percent of those who identify themselves as religiously "traditional." Thirty-six percent of the "secular" and 73 percent of the "traditional" groups said they would prefer the Orthodox ceremony that is currently common today (Teleseker 2000). Fifty-nine percent of those who would prefer some alternative ceremony indicated that they would primarily prefer a civil ceremony; 21 percent would primarily prefer a Reform service, while 6 percent would prefer one that is Conservative.

The Religious Market

It is difficult for religious movements to thrive when their major feature attracting participants are one-time celebrations of rites of passage. There is no indication at the present that those Israelis who are non-Orthodox, and yet selective in their religious practice, are searching for a religious movement that would legitimize any belief they might or might not have, or that would justify, in religious terms, their chosen degree of observance. While Jewish Israelis may be disturbed by religious based laws and requirements that impinge on their personal lifestyles, there is little desire to fundamentally rebel against the system in a manner that would lead to the formation of an alternate religious movement (Levy, Levinsohn, Katz 1993; Liebman and Katz 1997). Liebman and Don-Yehiya (1983) noted close to twenty years ago that most nonreligious Jews in Israel have a positive orientation toward Jewish tradition; they simply draw the line at observing the religious commandments, and issues of religious conscience do not arouse them. Even though a small (and growing) number of Jewish Israelis now do *not* have a positive orientation toward Orthodox Judaism, they are still not interested in a liberal religious movement any more than they are inclined to join an Orthodox one.

Consideration of the interface between the liberal denominations, which are Western religious movements, and the Sephardi population in Israel is warranted, for that group numbers about half of Israeli Jews. Many Jews from an Oriental background accept Orthodox assumptions about the nature and requirements of Judaism. The highest percentage of respondents in the Levy,

Levinsohn, and Katz (1993) study who are at least mostly observant, are from an Asian/North African background. Sixty-nine percent of those people are at least "mostly observant." The style of prayer in Reform synagogue is somewhat alien to Jews from such a background. (Conservative services are much more similar to Israeli Orthodox Ashkenazic services.) These persons also tend (at least for the present) to have a more traditional orientation toward sex roles. The idea of men and women sitting together in a prayer service, or of a woman wearing a prayer shawl or receiving a torah honor is quite alien to them. They thus have the least incentive for joining a religious movement that emphasizes gender equality. This situation might change in the future with increasing secularization, and merging, or blurring, of ethnic lifestyles. Only 42 percent of persons born in Israel and of Asian/North African descent say they are "mostly" or "totally" observant. Still, as Leslau and Bar-Lev (1994) note, there is a large disparity, among Oriental youth, between their self-identification as "very nonreligious" and the substantial amount of tradition they nevertheless observe. These researchers suggest that the adoption of religious patterns of behavior among Asian/North African youth may signify an identification with a collective that behaves in a like manner, whether it is made up of the Jewish people, Israeli Judaism, or a restricted group made up of the surrounding community. The implication for the liberal movements at present is that they would appear to be at least somewhat inappropriate alternatives for Jews of Asian/North African background. This considerably narrows the potential market of the movements.

In sum, a problem that non-Orthodox denominations have in attracting those who identify as nonreligious or secular persons is that they are asking people who negate a religious identity to join a religious movement. Many Israeli Jews take their Jewish identity for granted, or ignore it as an important element in defining who they are. There is less need for most people to express Jewish identity in Israel through affiliation with any religious movement than there might be in other countries. The small size of the country and the strong social control exerted in the Orthodox community make it unlikely (but not impossible) for disgruntled Jews to join a synagogue that is publicly identified as non-Orthodox without suffering social pressure. It may be easier for the disillusioned Orthodox to cease or privately alter their religious practice, but remain in the Orthodox community, than it is for them to join a different denominational synagogue and cut themselves off from their social community. The term *kippa'im* has come to signify those who practice little religion, other than wearing their *kippa* or skullcap.

The movements realize that synagogue programs in themselves will not attract large numbers of Israeli Jews. The Reform movement emphasizes its community and cultural centers, as opposed to its houses of worship, and the Conservative movement emphasizes its educational institutions. Some leaders in the latter movement, however, feel that education can only be a step on the road to synagogue affiliation, because Conservative Judaism does emphasize its halakhic approach, and the importance of synagogue worship. Still, the programs planned in both movements can provide a sense of community that Israelis, and especially new immigrants, may find attractive, especially as they are organized in a manner that emphasizes social and cultural (but not Orthodox religious) tradition.

The Future for Liberal Judaism in Israel

A key feature of Reform and Conservative Judaism is that it facilitates the "privatization" of religion, the isolation of religious life from public practice. It enables Jews to take part in secular social life without undue restrictions. The practices retained by Reform and Conservative Judaism in the United States are those that are compatible with the American social environment (Sklare and Greenblum 1967). Many American Jews who want to be part of the general society and yet retain a degree of Jewish identification affiliate with the non-Orthodox branches of Judaism.

Nonaffiliation with a religious denomination in America appears to lead to (as well as to indicate) marginality in the Jewish ethnic community. Thus, even individuals who are religiously lax may be motivated to affiliate with an institutionalized form of Judaism in order to retain and manifest an ethnic Jewish identity. There is little question of one's Jewish identity in Israel, however. One need not join a synagogue to ensure that one's children receive some Jewish education or meet other Jews. The use of Hebrew as the vernacular and the incorporation of Jewish symbols into Israel's "civic" religion negate or, at least, moderate the function that a liberal religious movement might play in strengthening Jewish identity. Adherence to Orthodox halakha is also less of an impediment to active participation in Israeli society than it is abroad. Israel is geared to the observance of Jewish holidays; *kashrut* is observed in most public institutions and many other places as well. There is less social pressure in Israel pushing Jews away from punctilious religious observance or drawing them to affiliate with a more liberal denomination, even if they choose not to be Orthodox. There may be some motivation abroad for affiliating with Reform or Conservative synagogues because of their perception as higher-class movements (especially in the past). This does not seem to be a factor that could attract members to the movements in Israel.

Some secular Israelis identify and sympathize with the non-Orthodox movements because of their struggle against the religious establishment. The civil rights oriented party, Meretz, for example, supports the Reform and Conservative movements as part of its civil rights agenda. But these movements want more than to serve as a channel for people who protest against the Orthodox establishment—they strive to offer a form of Judaism to meet a spiritual need of the Israeli public. As Ezra Spicehandler (1968), then Dean of the Hebrew Union College in Jerusalem, wrote:

> Frustrated by the slow growth of liberal Judaism in Israel, some of us prefer to think that the fault lies in the disabilities imposed upon the Reform Rabbis of Israel. We delude ourselves that if only we were permitted to perform marriages and receive State funds ... we would be free to rally thousands of Jews to the banner of Reform. This is a gross and pathetic fallacy. We will grow in Israel, not by gaining these privileges, but by offering a meaningful answer to the spiritual problems of modern man.

The pioneering spirit of early Israel has dissipated (Eisenstadt 1992; Shapira 1999). Orthodoxy is becoming more extreme—it is distancing itself from the people. Over two hundred thousand non-Jews have immigrated since 1989. Orthodox Judaism does not readily welcome these persons. In turn, these people reject a fundamentalist religious orientation that makes it difficult for them to convert. And yet, these non-Jews and their children are living in a Jewish society in which they internalize a Jewish identity by virtue of their educational experiences and daily life. Some of these persons might find a spiritual home in the Reform or Conservative movement if the movements identify the nature of their spiritual needs and cater to them, and can convert them. The fact that Russian-speaking Jews have little experience with Orthodox Judaism and the liberal orientation that characterizes many of these migrants makes it easier to attract them to liberal religious movements.

It is interesting that while the Conservative movement reports being larger than the Reform movement, more Israelis indicate a willingness to employ a Reform rabbi rather than a Conservative rabbi. It seems that non-Orthodox Israelis who want to celebrate events in a Jewish manner, want a movement that caters to nonreligious Jews. The Conservative movement is perceived to be more similar to Orthodox Judaism. Indeed, a suggestion has been raised in the Reform movement to allow nonreligious people to join the movement while retaining their secular identity (Pratt 2000). This has not yet happened, but it reflects a perception that may be more common among non-religious Jews concerning the nature of the identity of Reform Judaism. A magazine article described how one of the Reform rabbis had turned the Reform movement into a real hit. The article noted that celebrities and yuppies flock to the rabbi, and that he performs hundreds of wedding ceremonies and bar and bat mitzvah celebrations. It went on to say that he travels on Shabbat, eats in non-kosher restaurants, wears a *kippa* only in special circumstances; and does not reject same-sex unions. The title of the article was "Chief Rabbi of the Secular" (*Anashim,* January 25, 2000). It is possible that people who identify themselves as nonreligious would feel relatively less comfortable in the Conservative movement which defines itself as halakhic.

Conclusion

In the long term, the movements are having an impact on the relation between state and religion. Legal challenges in Israel reveal the precarious commitment of Orthodox political parties to the consideration of minority rights as part of their orientation to democracy. Orthodox political parties have suggested that legislation be used to circumvent rulings by the High Court of Justice in favor of non-Orthodox religious practices. The question for some people in Israel is not religion and state, but religion or state. Some Orthodox Jews say it is better to separate religion from state, if the lack of such separation means having to grant recognition to non-Orthodox Judaism. Data from hundreds of interviews with non-Orthodox Jewish Israelis (conducted by my seminar students between 1998 and 2000) indicate that many persons are opposed to specific manifestations of "religious coercion," but they nevertheless want to live in a society that is characterized by a Jewish nature. At the same time, many of these people find it difficult to formulate what the character of such a state should entail. "The single Israeli is no longer capable of finding his 'Israeliness'," writes Shaked (1999; p. 85), "for it has disappeared while he was trying to flee from it. What remains is a people with a blurred image, living a secular life, smitten by guilt feelings for a lost 'Yiddishkeit' which it does not know how to define for itself."

The political and legal activism of the movements may reduce their stigmatization in time and lead to incorporation of their ideas in the identification of Israel as a Jewish society. The potential long-term impact of the educational programs undertaken by the movements should not be underestimated in this regard. Official recognition of the rabbis can lead to a large number of people being willing to turn to the movements for alternative religious services, especially with regard to the celebration of rites of passage and life cycle events. (The Reform movement is now involved in a program to train [male and female] medical doctors to perform circumcisions [*brit mila*].) Male circumcision is almost a universal phenomenon in Jewish Israel, but some families have begun to oppose this act (Tabory and Erez 2003). A Reform procedure undertaken by a doctor might be better accepted among less traditional Israelis. The people who seek these "alternative" services may be expressing a religious need, but they may also be looking for a way to manifest their cultural, national, or some other form of expression of Jewish, or Israeli, identity. The movements have to face the question of whether this is enough to sustain religious organizations in the long run.

The legal activities and the educational programs of the movements do not necessarily lead people to join the synagogues in the short run. The legal and political challenges exerted by the movements, however, may level the playing field and enable the denominations to compete on an equal footing with a longer-term impact. Finke and Stark (1988) claim that the abolition of state religions leads to greater religious participation because of the ability of religious movements to evolve and provide for the unmet needs of the population. Those needs have gone wanting because the monopoly status of the reigning church led it to turn "lazy" and unresponsive to the needs of the members. The theory has not gone unchallenged (cf. Olson 1999), but the basic idea is thought provoking. What might be the impact of true, unfettered religious competition on Israel as a Jewish state and as a democratic society, and on the vitality of Judaism in general, in Israel and abroad? This is a question that the liberal denominations in Israel would truly like to test, and that the Orthodox establishment clearly wishes to avoid.

ACKNOWLEDGEMENTS

I am grateful to the rabbis and the lay and professional leaders and staff of the Israel Movement for Progressive Judaism and the Masorti (Conservative) Movement for their cooperation in my research and for their willingness to share with me their observations and opinions in such a forthright manner. My special thanks are extended to the following persons who were kind enough to read a preliminary version of this article and provide me with constructive comments: Rabbi David Ariel-Yoel, Executive director, Israel Movement for Progressive Judaism Ms. Chaya Baker, coordinator of Marom; Rabbi Ehud Bandel, president, Masorti (Conservative) Movement; Ms. Bonnie Boxer, Israel representative of the Richard and Rhoda Goldman fund; Rabbi Professor David Golinkin, president and rector, Schechter Institute of Jewish Studies; Rabbi Reuven Hammer, vice-president, International Rabbinical Assembly; Rabbi Michael A. Marmur, dean, Hebrew Union College (Jerusalem); Rabbi Yoram Mazor, executive secretary, the Council of Progressive Rabbis (Maram); Professor Michael A. Meyer, Hebrew Union College-Jewish Institute of Religion, Cincinnati; Rabbi Andrew M. Sacks, director, Israel Rabbinical Assembly; Rabbi Uri Regev, director, Israel Religious Action Center. The Israel Movement for Progressive Judaism has also been extremely gracious in providing me complete copies of all the survey research that it has commissioned, and the information center of the Israel Religious Action Center has helped me search for various articles and documents.

REFERENCES

Abramov, S. Zalman. 1976. *Perpetual Dilemma: Jewish Religion in the Jewish State.* London: Associated University Presses.

Anashim [People]. Israeli community weekly (Hebrew).

Ben-Meir, Yehuda and Peri Kedem. 1979. "Index of Religiosity of the Jewish Population of Israel." *Megamot 24:* 353–62 (Hebrew).

Berger Peter L., and Thomas Luckmann. 1967. *The Social Construction of Reality.* London: Allen Pane.

Chazot, Rami. 2001. "About 30 percent of Couples Marrying in Israel Divorce." *Yediot Acharonot* [Israel daily], January 11, p. 19 (Hebrew).

Deshen, Shlomo. 1997. "The Passover Celebrations of Secular Israelis." *Megamot 38* (4): 528–46 (Hebrew).

Eisenstadt, S. N. 1992. *Jewish Civilization: The Jewish Historical Experience in a Comparative Perspective.* Albany: State University of New York Press.

Elbaz, Shimon. 1964. "Shimon Elbaz et al. vs. The Minister of Religious Affairs, and others." *Piskei Din* 18 (part 4): 603–13 (Hebrew).

Finke, Roger and Ronald Stark. 1988. Religious Economies and Sacred Canopies: Religious Mobilization in American Cities. *American Sociological Review* 53: 41–49.

Golan, Matti. 1992. *With Friends Like You.* Israel: Kinneret Publishing House (Hebrew).

Ha'aretz. Israel Daily Newspaper (Hebrew).

High Court of Justice. 1982. HCJ 47/82, The Foundation of the Israel Movement for Progressive Judaism, Rabbi Moshe Zemer, Rabbi Mordechai Rotem vs. Minister of Religion, Chief Rabbinical Council of Israel, *Piskei Din,* 43 (2) 661–722 (Hebrew).

High Court of Justice. 1987. HCJ 153/87, Shakdiel vs. Minister of Religious Affairs et al., *Piskei Din* 42 (2): 221–77 (Hebrew).

High Court of Justice. 1993. HCJ 1031/93, Alian (Hava) Pessaro (Goldstein) and The Movement for Progressive Judaism in Israel vs. The Minister of the Interior and The Director of the Population Registry, *Piskei Din* 49 (4): 661 (Hebrew).

Hirsch, Richard G. 1972. *Reform Judaism and Israel.* New York: Commission on Israel, World Union for Progressive Judaism.

Itonoam. Periodical of the Masorti Youth Movement (Hebrew).

Izraeli, Dafna N., and Ephraim Tabory. 1993. "The Political Context of Feminist Attitudes in Israel." In *Women in Israel,* ed. Yael Azmon and Dafna N. Izraeli, 269–86. Volume 6, Studies of Israeli Society. New Brunswick: Transaction.

Jacobsen, Chanoch. 1999. "The Informal Legitimization of Reform Weddings in Israel." *CCAR Journal: A Reform Jewish Quarterly* (Summer): 54–63.

Jerusalem Post. Israel Daily Newspaper.

Kedem, Peri 1991. "Dimensions of Jewish Religiosity in Israel." In *Tradition, Innovation, Conflict: Jewishness and Judaism in Contemporary Israel,* ed. Zvi Sobel and Benjamin Beit-Hallahmi, 252–77, Albany: State University Press of New York.

Lazerwitz, Bernard, J., Alan Winter, Arnold Dashefsky, and Ephraim Tabory. 1998. *Jewish Choices: American Jewish Denominationalism.* Albany: State University of New York Press.

Leslau, Avraham, and Mordechai Bar-Lev. 1994 "Religiosity among Oriental Youth in Israel." *Sociological Papers* (Sociological Institute for Community Studies, Bar Ilan University) 3 (5): 1–57.

Levy, Shlomit, Hanna Levinsohn, and Elihu Katz. 1993. *Beliefs, Observances and Social Interaction among Israeli Jews.* Jerusalem: The Louis Guttman Israel Institute of Applied Social Research.

Liebman, Charles S., and Eliezer Don-Yehiya. 1983. *Civil Religion in Israel: Traditional Judaism and the Political Culture in the Jewish State.* Berkeley: University of California Press.

Liebman Charles S., and Elihu Katz. 1997. *The Jewishness of Israelis: Responses to the Guttman Report.* Albany: State University of New York Press.

Machon Dachaf. 2000. *Attitudes of the Israeli Public on Topics Related to Religion-State.* May (Hebrew).

Meirovich, Harvey. 1999. *The Shaping of Masorti Judaism in Israel.* New York and Ramat Gan: The Institute on American Jewish-Israeli Relations of the American Jewish Committee and the Argov Center of Bar-Ilan University.

Merton, Robert K. 1976. *Sociological Ambivalence and Other Essays.* New York: The Free Press.

Naamad, Avraham. 2000. "Speaking Evil of the Wicked." *Yom LeYom,* November 16 (Hebrew).

Olson, Daniel V. A. 1999. "Religious Pluralism and US Church Membership: A Reassessment." *Sociology of Religion* 60: 149–73.

Pratt, Dan. 2000. "Religious or Non-religious, That is the Question: A Suggestion for Beginning a Discussion on Relations between Reform-Secular." *Betelem* 3:11 (Hebrew).

Shaked, Gershon. 1999. "Shall We Find Sufficient Strength? On Behalf of Israeli Secularism." In *In Search of Identity: Jewish Aspects in Israeli Culture,* ed. Dan Urian and Efraim Karsh, 73–85. London and Portland, Or.: Frank Cass.

Shapira, Avraham. 1999. "Spiritual Rootlessness and Circumscription to the 'Here and Now' in the Sabra World View." In *In Search of Identity: Jewish Aspects in Israeli Culture,* ed. Dan Urian and Efraim Karsh, 103–31. London and Portland, Or: Frank Cass.

Sheleg, Yair. 2000. *The New Religious Jews: Recent Developments among Observant Jews in Israel.* Jerusalem: Keter Publishing House Ltd. (Hebrew).

Shiluv Market Research and Strategic Planning. 1999. *Findings and Conclusions of a Survey on: Denominations in Judaism—The Effectiveness of the Publicity [Campaign] of the Reform and Conservative Movements.* Submitted to the Movement for Progressive Judaism, the Masorti Movement, and the Goldman Foundation. October (Hebrew).

Sklare, Marshall, and Joseph Greenblum. 1967. *Jewish Identity on the Suburban Frontier.* New York: Basic Books.

Spicehandler, Ezra. 1968. What Can We Say to Israel? *Yearbook Central Conference of American Rabbis* 78: 227–36.

Steinberg, Theodore. 2000. "A Brief History of the Rabbinical Assembly in Israel." In *A Century of Commitment: One Hundred Years of the Rabbinical Assembly,* ed. Robert E. Fierstein. New York: The Rabbinical Assembly.

Tabory, Ephraim. 1983. "Reform and Conservative Judaism in Israel: A Social and Religious Profile." *American Jewish Year Book 1983.* 83: 41–61.

———. 1992. "The Identity Dilemma of Non-Orthodox Religious Movements: Reform and Conservative Judaism in Israel." In *Tradition, Innovation, Conflict: Jewishness and Judaism in Contemporary Israel,* ed. Zvi Sobel and Benjamin Beit-Hallahmi, 135–52. Albany: State University of New York Press.

———. 1998. *Reform Judaism in Israel: Progress and Prospects.* New York and Ramat Gan: The Institute on American Jewish-Israeli Relations of the American Jewish Committee and the Argov Center of Bar-Ilan University.

———. 2003. "'A nation that dwells alone': Judaism as an Integrating and Divisive Factor in Israeli Society." In *Traditions and Transitions in Israel Studies (Books on Israel 6),* ed. Laura Zittrain Eisenberg, Neil Caplan, Naomi B. Sokolofl, Mohammed Abu-Nimer, 89–112. Albany: State University of New York Press.

Tabory, Ephraim, and Sharon Erez. 2003. "Circumscribed Circumcision: Motivations and Identities of Israeli Families Who Choose Not to Circumcise Their Sons." In *The Covenant of Circumcision: New Perspective on an Ancient Jewish Rite,* ed. Elizabeth Wyner Mark. Hanover, N.H.: Brandeis University Press, University Press of New England.

Tabory, Ephraim, and Bernard Lazerwitz. 1995. "Americans in the Israeli Reform and Conservative denominations." In *Israeli Judaism,* ed. Shlomo Deshen, Charles S. Liebman, and Moshe Shokeid, 335–45. Volume 7 of the Publication Series of the Israel Sociological Society. New Brunswick, N.J.: Transaction.

Tali. 1995. *Tochnit Limudim: Tigbur Limudei Yahadut BeVet Hasefer Hamamlachti* [Educational Curriculum: Enriched Jewish Studies Program in the State School]. Jerusalem: The Ministry for Education and Sport (Hebrew).

Teleseker, 2000. "Public Attitudes Toward Alternative Marriages. Survey Undertaken for the Forum for Free Choice in Marriage." January (Hebrew).

The Rabbinical Courts Jurisdiction Act. 1997. (Marriage and Divorce) (Amendment) *Yated Ne'eman,* Israel Daily Newspaper (Hebrew).

Who Are You Reformers Jerusalem: Man of Information Center (Hebrew).

Yated Ne'eman, Israel Daily Newspaper (Hebrew).

Yishai, Yael. 1997. *Between the Flag and the Banner: Women in Israeli Politics.* New York: State University of New York Press.

Zisenwine, David. 1999. "Jewish Education in the Jewish State." In *In Search of Identity: Jewish Aspects in Israeli Culture,* ed. Dan Urian and Efraim Karsh, 146–55. London and Portland, Or: Frank Cass.

CHAPTER THIRTEEN

The Quest for Spirituality among Secular Israelis

೭

Elan Ezrachi

Introduction

The "Jewishness" of secular Israelis has long been regarded as a subject of intense debate in the Israeli public discourse. Zionist educators began questioning the notion of continuity of Zionist ideology when successive generations of native-born (Sabra) Israelis began moving away from the legacy of the founders. Urgently, the issue of Jewish identity was raised. In a community that based its ethos on the rejection of traditional Judaism, the Jewishness of the next generation was, at best, an ambiguous matter. Put on the agenda were questions such as: To what extent would native Israelis regard themselves as Jews? How would they relate to the Jewish heritage and culture of their ancestors? What would be their attachment to world Jewry? Would they continue sustaining the State of Israel as a *Jewish* State?

Such questions were extensively deliberated within the educational community (which in the pre-State days was also considered the intellectual elite of the emerging community). Rosenstein describes the discussions regarding the place of Judaism in the General School system under the British Mandate. This system, which later on became the Israeli Public School system, promoted ambivalent attitudes toward Judaism within the educational process, reflecting the internal conflict of secular Zionist ideology (Rosenstein 1988).

In the 1950s, when Israeli public education was forming, the question was raised again. The same ambiguity that was evident in the pre-State days was carried over to the public education system consolidated through legislation in 1953 (Eden 1976). In the mid 1950s there was a public crisis in response to a challenge that came from a group of young Israelis, who were known as the Canaanites. The Canaanites (or, with their real name: the New Hebrews), a small fringe group of young intellectuals and artists, presented an identity option that stepped out of the boundaries of normative Judaism. Land and language supplanted history and Jewish peoplehood. The leadership of Israel's secular community was flabbergasted. The idea of young Israelis—just a few years into the independent State, with the Holocaust still a fresh and painful memory—discarding a positive self-definition as Jews was unacceptable (Shavit 1984).

This served as a rallying cry for what would turn out to be a series of educational initiatives and interventions over the next forty years. Then, the formal response was a national campaign called the "The Jewish Consciousness Program," designed to "cure" the problem and "instill" a Jewish awareness among young Israelis through a variety of cognitive means. Similar programs have taken place over the years with much fanfare and limited success. Most famous and recent was the Shenhar Commission Report. The Shenhar Report, chaired by a noted Haifa University Professor, Aliza Shenhar, examined the state of Jewish Studies in the secular public school system. Her commission made sweeping and far-reaching recommendations that were the basis for many programs in the 1990s: teacher training, formal and informal programs, intensive seminars for faculty and students, and curriculum development.

All these point to a fundamental duality in the Israeli secular identity. Secular discourse seems to be caught in an unresolved tension between forces of rebellious breakaway and continuity from mainstream Jewish culture and religion. Secular Israeli identity means to some a total rejection of Jewish expression and even hostility toward Jewish symbols and rituals, and to others, a mild version of a nonobservant life style with some respect toward traditional Judaism. The strong presence of Orthodox Judaism added a negative sociopolitical base line, keeping many secular Israelis away from any type of religious activity associated with the Orthodox. This duality can be found also on the level of the individual identity of Israelis who at times express great hostility toward Judaism and at times rush to traditional modalities that they normally reject. This is particularly true regarding life-cycle events such as circumcision, bar mitzvah ceremonies, and funerals. The political arrangement known as the "status quo" kept this ambivalence in check, while public discourse was focusing on nation building and national security.

Bekerman and Silverman (1999) presented an analysis of Israeli society from a social-constructivist perspective. They argued that Israeli society is strongly divided between traditionalists and liberals and each side is defined by both its own positive views and negative images of the other: "members of the liberal camp assume that western culture is superior to other cultures, in general, and to the traditional Jewish culture in particular" (p. 95).

As to the values of Western culture, which Israeli liberals ascribe to, Bekerman and Silverman describe them as follows:

1. Western culture places emphasis on the philosophical, scientific and spiritual aspects of human life, while Jewish traditional culture emphasizes the latter's functional, material, ritualistic, and concrete aspects. 2. It is universal and humanistic, while Jewish traditional culture is particularistic, tribal, and ethnocentric. 3. It is present to future oriented and forward looking, while

Jewish traditional culture is oriented from present to the past and backward looking. 4. It encourages the development of an autonomous, free, and rational individual, while the Jewish traditional culture develops a heteronymous, bonded and irrational individual. (Bekerman and Silverman, p. 95)

This "either-or" dichotomy is a basic structural feature in Israeli culture and identity. Any development in Israeli secular expression has to take this internal tension into account.

Signs of Discontent

In the 1960s and '70s there were initial signs that certain secular Israelis might be discontented with the "rejectionist" nature of secular Jewish identity. This discontent marked the beginning of a discourse that was aimed at changing the condition of secular Jewish identity and was oriented toward action. Two journals dedicated to cultural and identity issues were the main platforms for a new discussion of Israeli Jewish identity.

The first was *Shdemot,* a meeting place for young Kibbutz intellectuals who were questioning their Jewish identities in the context of Kibbutz life. *Shdemot,* under the leadership of a young Kibbutz member, Avraham Shapira, became an important tool for young Israelis who sought a new understanding of their Jewishness. The writings in *Shdemot* emphasized the need for personal Jewish fulfillment, with a strong influence of Martin Buber's existentialist philosophy.

The *Shdemot* circle was a generational group that came together because of spiritual malaise, in search of something that was missing from contemporary Kibbutz life. Gad Ufaz describes how "they felt that the Kibbutz needed renewal, both in the realm of ideas and in the way responsibility was passed on to the next generation. . . . They sought to substitute a new social ethos for the prevailing collective, activist approach" (Ufaz 1999; p. 136). A large portion of the *Shdemot* activity could be labeled as a return to Jewish sources. This was a second generation's response on the part of those who felt they had been cut off and denied "access to the depth and the spiritual wealth nourished within Jewish tradition and history" (ibid.).

The other platform was a journal named *Petahim,* which strongly emphasized a pluralistic critical approach to Jewish culture in Israel. The editor and the leader of the group was Joseph Bentwich, a veteran educator, who already in the 1950s argued that Israeli education lacked a Jewish spiritual element. The *Petahim* group included active members who were founding members of Jerusalem Congregation Mevakshei Derech (the seekers of the path), associated with the American Reconstructionist ideology. That journal no longer exists.

Suffice it to say that both initiatives were confined to a small group of active thinkers and educators far removed from mainstream Israeli discourse.

Secular Israelis were faced with another alternative in the 1970s: a small, albeit vocal movement toward strict Orthodox observance, known as Hazara Beteshuva (return with repentance). Stories of young, educated, secular Israelis who found their way to Orthodox Judaism were becoming a common feature in the media. This trend peaked with the dramatic move of popular Israeli entertainer Uri Zohar in the 1980s (Urian 1999). The sudden appeal of ultra-Orthodoxy to elite Israelis (including senior military personnel) was another factor that contributed to the discourse.

The mid 1970s gave rise to a new educational intervention. A group of Israeli educators founded the Zionists Institutes (which later on became Melitz: Centers for Jewish Zionist Education). This was a network of programs that offered Israeli high schools one-shot retreat-style seminars on Jewish identity. Such seminars reached a large proportion of the youth cohort. The idea behind these "Jewish Identity Seminars" was to provide an environment in which young Israelis can connect with their own personal Jewish Israeli narratives. It was thought that the school system and the prevailing political climate were hindrances to the development of a positive Israeli Jewish identity. The seminars, which utilized a liberal educational method called "Values Clarification," provided a safe environment to reflect on personal identity narratives.

In the mid 1990s a new body of data came into the discussion: The Guttman Institute Report. The report was based on a massive, large-scale survey of Jewish beliefs, behaviors, and social relations among Israelis. The survey discovered that there are certain positions, values, and customs that are shared by the vast majority of Jews in Israel. These shared values included: commitment to Jewish continuity, celebration of Jewish holidays and life-cycle events, etc. The sponsors of the report could say that (secular) Israelis are actually much more Jewish than is commonly perceived (Levy, Levinsohn, and Katz 1993). The report received a barrage of mixed reviews. Critics charged that the survey may have reflected quantitative data in regard to observance of Jewish holidays and life-cycle events, but the actual meaning of this observance was unexplored. Many regarded the data as indicating observance of cultural norms, rather than distinct Jewish behavior (Liebman and Katz 1997).

In summary, secular Jewish identity in Israel up until the 1990s was pulled between three poles: the classical Zionist rejection of traditional Judaism, which at times can be quite hostile to any form of spiritual Jewish expression; The "return" of select secular Israelis to a strict ultra-Orthodox lifestyle; and the realization that the masses of Israeli Jews never really abandoned the Jewish tradition and are, in effect, "quite traditional."

The 1990s: From Alienation to Reclamation

The 1990s set the stage for many changes in Israeli society and culture. Several momentous political and cultural events, as well as social and economic trends, dramatically altered Israel, particularly during the second half of the decade. The arrival of Jews from the former Soviet Union and Ethiopia, and of foreign laborers from all over the globe, created more diversity in civil society. Sepharadic Jews, long invisible and underrepresented in the political sphere, gained visibility and a stronger voice. Signs of American culture were suddenly everywhere. Israel celebrated its fiftieth anniversary, and embarked on a robust debate about the State's future character and national identity.[1] In addition, the peace process encouraged Israelis to imagine stability and prosperity into the future.

No one event, however, shook Israel so much as the tragic assassination of Prime Minister Yitzhak Rabin on November 4, 1995. It brought the polarization between Orthodox and secular Jews into greater focus and crystallized the need for change. In particular, many Israelis began to question the exclusively Orthodox definition of Israeli Judaism and the Orthodox establishment's political and legal control over Jewish identity. Although the assassination was a political act, it represented a war of ideology and symbols reaching far beyond the political nature of the act itself. In an essay called "Jewish Identities in Post-Rabin Israel," journalist Yossi Klein Halevi wrote: "The nightmare scenario for the state of Jewish identity in Israel is of a schizophrenic people divided into two irreconcilable camps: one secular and democratic, perceiving little value in Judaism; the other traditionalist and xenophobic, perceiving little value outside Judaism" (Klein Halevi 1998).

This period of rapid and dramatic change was conducive to certain developments in Israeli Jewish life. Up until now the entire trend of secular Israelis seeking a deeper connection to Jewish sources was based on two centers: one in Jerusalem primarily around the Shalom Hartman Institute, Melitz, and the budding Conservative and Reform movements; the other in the North of Israel, at the Oranim Kibbutz college.

In 1989, two young educators, Ruth Calderon, a secular woman who studied at the Shalom Hartman Institute, and Motti Bar-Or, a modern Orthodox rabbi, founded Elul. Elul marked a new trend, which later on was labeled "the Jewish Books Movement."[2]

Elul attracted young adults who were searching for a meaningful intellectual experience, through the study of Jewish texts. Elul managed to expand beyond the handful of Israelis previously engaged in similar activities (Sheleg 2000). Soon afterward, toward the mid-1990s, the Jewish Books movement became well known when elite and celebrated groups in Israeli society began to engage in text study. One such exclusive group, called Shaharit, consisted of media and cultural icons in Israeli public life: Orthodox and secular. The members of Shaharit met regularly to study and reflect on Jewish texts. One of the leading figures in the group was the journalist and critic Yaron London. In an interview in the newspaper *Ma'ariv* in September 1996, he offered these reasons for joining the group: "I joined Shaharit because I have a feeling that the result of overlooking two thousand years of Jewish culture is the next generation's alienation from language, culture and Jewish literature. I feel that soon my own children and grandchildren will not understand what I myself write" (Sheleg, p. 304).

The concern for the identity of the next generation is a recurring motif in the Jewish Books movement. Many Israelis mostly from Ashkenazi backgrounds who were educated in the (secular) Israeli school system came to study only in midlife. They were concerned that the "true" Zionist spirit of Israel was fading and, with it, the natural connection to Jewish sources that was part and parcel of the Labor Zionist orientation.[3]

Their emotional reaction can also be seen as a response to the Westernization and rapid economic development of the 1990s, which enhanced the allure and influence of consumerist material values. Without a solid basis of Jewish culture as its anchor, they feared that Israeli culture would become indistinguishable from Western materialist culture.

Toward the end of the 1990s, the Jewish Books movement saw a significant growth in the numbers of participants and in its geographic spread. *Batei midrash* (the plural of *beit midrash,* house of study) opened all over the country under a wide range of sponsorships. New players entered the field: the Reform and the Conservative movements, the Israeli Association of Community Centers, the Ministry of Education, local municipalities, and independent initiatives. The media, on occasion, reported about special programs, festivals, and cultural events and gave this trend a visibility that was lacking.

In response to the massive growth in the scope of the Jewish Books movement and adult Jewish learning, the Ministry of Education appointed a professional to oversee the activity. Orly Kennet, who served in this capacity, has written about this phenomenon. She argues that there is indeed a movement of secular Israelis who are building a new infrastructure for a fresh and vibrant Israeli Judaism. She described this trend as a "positive social cultural activity, which does not seek confrontation with the Orthodox and holds no political agenda. It focuses on infusion of meaningful and relevant Jewish content into lifecycle events and the yearly calendar" (Kennet 2000, p. 88). She defines this trend as a quiet grassroots revolution that will produce a diverse and vibrant Jewish secular culture. She saw it happening in the education system, in the community, in intimate learning opportunities, in large-scale events and festivals, in art and culture, and in leadership development.

As the Jewish Books movement was gaining public recognition, several other developments emerged in Israel that pointed toward a larger movement of Jewish renewal. After years of being marginalized, the Conservative and Reform movements managed finally to penetrate the Israeli scene with a set of programs and services aimed mostly at the secular population (Tabory 2000). The two liberal movements established their presence in Israel in a variety of ways: synagogues, educational initiatives, advocacy, and alternative religious services for life-cycle events (Ezrachi 2001).

At the same time, there has been a growth in "new age" trends among Israelis looking for spiritual expression, such as meditation, healing, and alternative lifestyles. While this trend had little Jewish content at the outset, it was open to the inclusion of Jewish components as it became more popular.[4]

In 1998, a new umbrella organization was created by the name of Panim. Panim sought to increase the awareness of the Israeli public at large to the existence of a network of organizations and services that offer Israelis a variety of positive Jewish expressions. This organizational development reflects the dynamism of a new grassroots movement of Israelis who are prepared to make a focused effort to express their Jewishness.

Critique and New Directions

This review of institutions, initiatives, and directions is significant in that it reveals a picture that did not exist before, one that indicates a shift in Israeli secular sensibilities. Yet, one must ask the hard questions concerning the overall impact of these new developments. Critiques of the Jewish Books movement come from both the religious and secular ends of the spectrum. Some point out that the Jewish Books movement is only a marginal cultural fad for the (Ashkenazi) yuppie elite that is bound to fade when the next fad comes along. Some define the movement as reductionist and apologetic, ultimately lacking any real basis for ongoing community. It is true that almost none of the books groups have included any form of ritual or community involvement, with participation limited to weekly study sessions of some sort. Still, in reality many of these groups relate to the regular study of Jewish texts as a ritual in its own right, creating a sense of community. Nonetheless, despite the enthusiastic accounts, the sheer numbers of non-Orthodox Israelis who are engaged in significant Jewish exploration is quite limited.

Similar critique is voiced regarding the Reform and Conservative movements from both Orthodox and secular directions, arguing that there is no room for religious alternatives in Israel. Liberal Judaism is a product of the Western Diaspora, while Israel has room for one only form of (authentic) religion, and for its diametrically opposed twin: secularism. This critique reflects a number of issues as well. First, there is a consistent resistance on the part of intellectual elites to include Jewish expressions in the mainstream of Israeli culture. Jewish expressions are seen as anywhere between folklore and missionary work and not taken seriously. Second, these so-called secular critics, as well as Orthodox, continue to view Jewish expression as the sole property of Orthodoxy. This "unholy" alliance has served to undermine secular initiatives, and secular critics fail to see this. Finally, the political climate in Israel contaminates any attempt to have a serious discussion on issues of identity and culture.

Discussion: Israeli Jewish Identity Reconstructed

The issue at the heart of this discussion is the nature of Israeli non-Orthodox Jewish identity and spirituality. Does the mainstream Israeli non-Orthodox community need a spiritual expression(s)? And if so, what kind? And what are the historical and cultural ingredients that make up the new Israeli Jewish identity?

Clearly, Zionist discourse did not take into account an existential condition in which Jewish identity would not be a given, but rather an option. According to Zionist ideology, it was always assumed that only in the Diaspora would Jews need to affirm their Jewishness against the backdrop of the (non-Jewish) open society. Israel, with a majority Jewish society and a strong collective ethos, was spared the fundamental diasporic identity dilemma. Thus, terms like assimilation, intermarriage, Jewish continuity, Jewish neighborhood, and voluntary Jewish associations are absent from the Israeli lexicon.

Israel in the 1990s became a place where Jewishness was not as obvious as before. Intellectually, it was argued that Israel is moving away from the collective period into a post-Zionist era. The move would make Israel a country for all its citizens rather than a Jewish State.[5] In addition, sociologically, Israel was in fact becoming more diverse, open, exposed to global trends and less ideological (Ezrachi 1997).

Thus, before one discusses the possible venues for renewed Jewish expression among non-Orthodox Israelis, there is a need to establish the fact that at the basis of contemporary Israeli society there is an emerging Israeli (and not necessarily Jewish) identity. This Israeli identity is shared by a large group of people living in Israel, speaking Hebrew, and taking part in the Israeli polity. Most Israelis are of Jewish descent, and a substantial minority comes from other traditions (and nationalities). Unlike the Diaspora, it is unclear how Israelis can express the choice of being Jewish since the demarcation lines between the Jewish and Israeli domains are blurry. Unlike the Diaspora, which provides a set of formal expressions for Jewish identification, that are normally based on education and organizational affiliation, the Israeli framework lacks clearly defined parameters for non-Orthodox Jewishness.

David Hartman, a well-known philosopher and educational activist, published a book on Israelis and the Jewish tradition (Hartman 2000). Hartman, himself an American-born, American-trained, modern Orthodox rabbi, credits secular Israeli culture for its ability to sustain a secular Jewish identity, unlike the American Diaspora, which has failed to do this. Israel, he argues, "is the most viable option for Jews who wish to place their identities within a secular frame of reference" (Hartman, p. 16). However, Hartman recognizes that "Israeli identity has become more ambiguous and complicated because of a confident, thriving Diaspora" (Hartman, p. 23).

Hartman concludes that many secular Israelis "now realize the great mistake they made in relinquishing their spiritual heritage to the Orthodox practitioners of Judaism." He asserts that an effort has to be made to change this trend: "If we fail to help these Israelis become intellectually adequate to reconnect with their tradition, we will further aggravate the religious-secular polarization that poisons the political climate of Israeli society" (Hartman, p. 149).

Anita Shapira adds another important historical perspective in her analysis of Labor Zionist leaders and their attitudes toward the Jewish tradition. In reviewing this complex relationship, she demonstrates where the tradition energized these pioneers and where it paralyzed them. Shapira contends that messianic passion stirred these pioneers who transformed traditional symbols and even rituals into a new, emerging Israeli identity (Shapira 1997).

The same might be said for Oz Almog's work 2001 on native-born Israelis (*Sabras*) of the Palmach (a pre-State paramilitary group). Almog tells the story of this generation, which is considered to be the generation of the Israeli political and cultural elite of the early State years. In telling their story, Almog makes no reference to their celebrations of the Jewish holidays or life-cycle rituals. He examines certain cultural expressions such as folk dancing and group singing: "The 'hora' celebrated unity, the joy of youth, the vitality of a new emergent nation." The same is said of folk singing, where traditional devotional singing in the synagogues was replaced with a form of public singing of secular Zionist songs. The native Israelis used singing and dancing as a vehicle for shaping individual identity within the collective experience. Such expressions of collective identity under the secular Zionist narrative have been dramatically reduced since that time.[6]

Charles Liebman (1999) discusses the prospects of Israeli secular Judaism. He admits at the start that, as an observant Jew, he has a particular interest in the revitalization of Israeli secular Judaism in order to prevent the possibility of Israel's losing its overall Jewish character, something that some post-Zionist intellectuals would like to see. Liebman describes the cultural developments in Israeli non-Orthodox society in recent years. He brings in some very useful historical and sociological insights that go beyond the understanding of the secular Zionist narrative.

Historically, Liebman argues that the attempt to create a humanistic (European), intellectually oriented secular Jewish culture has failed. Aside from the revival of the Hebrew language, the Israeli secular elites turned away from the intellectual Jewish tradition and chose a liberal, Western option without a distinct Jewish character (Bekerman and Silverman 1999). In other words, the efforts to create a comprehensive Jewish culture with no relation to the Jewish religion have proven wrong and unsuccessful. Liebman concludes that, "removing all traces of religion might leave one with a vestige of culture. . . . Perhaps," he says, "this is what some people once meant by the term 'Hebrew culture'" (1999, p. 33).

Liebman identifies two other possibilities for secular expression. One is the venue of Jewish ethnicity, which means minimal association with (intellectual) Jewish culture but strong ethnic ties to family traditions, folklore, and community. Ethnic identity is based on the lowest common denominator of Jewishness and therefore is superficial and limited.

A second option, and the preferable one in Liebman's view, retains the religious component but affirms religion as culture rather than religion as mandating a relationship to God. In others words, secular Judaism of this kind retains a religious component and recognizes that religion constituted the major if not the exclusive content of the Jewish culture of the past.

By conflating the theoretical approach of "religion as culture" with the sociological reality of Israeli Jews, Liebman finds a solid basis for the creation of a vibrant secular Judaism in Israel. The Guttman Report indicated that the vast majority of Israelis are not "religious" in the conventional meaning of that term, but they do observe many traditional customs and rituals, and while their observance is partial and selective, it is not random, individual, or unsystematic. These observances are not without intent and they are motivated by a conscious commitment to the continuity of the Jewish people. In other words, Liebman summarizes, "Contrary to what is sometimes said, most Israeli Jews observe the tradition in part but do not believe that their pattern stems from laziness, laxity or negligence. They are participating in a patterned form of observance which is not Halacha, but which they have transformed into the folkways of secular Judaism. . . . [T]heir secularism is neither rebellious nor anti-religious" (1999, p. 35).

Liebman admits that it is hard to predict the future of Israeli secular Judaism. The decline of the collective ethos and the fact that the elites are not taking an active role in revitalizing and redefining Judaism are hindrances to the possibility of secular Jewish continuity. Perhaps we would serve this discussion by looking at larger Western trends. Is Israel unique in its current situation, or is this part of some greater picture of the global village?

Most Western scholars of sociology and culture have recorded the breakdown of communal structures and allegiances. Some note, with concern, the dangers of rampant material consumerism and its effects on communal life. However, there are leading sociologists of religion who are trying to understand these trends by looking at different models of affiliation and allegiance. Two leading scholars, Wade Clark Roof and Robert Wuthnow, have shifted their focus to following the spiritual narratives of individuals (Roof 1999; Wuthnow 1999). They contend that, while many indicators show significant decline in institutional and religious affiliation for Americans, there remains a serious and deep attachment to familial and religious traditions, which have been revisited and reclaimed throughout their life journey, extending into adulthood. This perspective has already shaped the discussion among Jewish researchers attempting to describe current trends in American Jewish life. Here, too, scholars such as Arnold Eisen, Steven M. Cohen, and Bethamie Horowitz are using new terminology to explain where the majority of American Jews place themselves. Terms like the "sovereign self" and "journeys and connections" are helpful concepts affirming that Jewish commitments are not necessarily in decline but rather are being transformed. These changes may be happening more in the comfort of home and with friends than in institutions or denominations (Eisen and Cohen 2000; Horowitz 2000).

Similar things might be happening in Israel. It seems that the future of Israeli discourse on non-Orthodox Judaism in Israel needs to shift to observing individual(s) and the ways they construct meaning in Jewish and Israeli life. The collective narrative, while useful for explaining yesterday's trends, has proven to be insufficient for reading the present and imagining the future.

Conclusion

Zionism succeeded in creating a cultural and political platform for public Jewish life. The reality in which there is a large sovereign community with over five million Jews who speak Hebrew, live the Jewish calendar, and honor, the historical symbols of the land of Israel provides a solid baseline for Jewish identity. However, the conditions for individual identity development and personal Jewish expression have shifted in many ways. Young Israeli Jews of today are not socialized into the collective Zionist narrative, as Israel is moving along with the rest of postmodern Western cultures toward further individuality and more fluid identity categories.

This reality highlights the role of the individual and the family in constructing a meaningful Jewish life (or opting out of a Jewish option). David Hartman suggests an approach that is less authoritative in bringing Israelis into the Jewish fold. Theologians and religious leaders need to relate more seriously to secular Israelis who are looking for meaningful ways to reconcile tradition and modernity. Hartman adds: "in establishing the state within the biblical homeland, secular Zionists made a decision against assimilation and against breaking their ties with Jewish history. . . . [S]ecular Israelis continue to participate in the body of politics of the Jewish people" (Hartman 2000, p. 153). It is therefore imperative, Hartman argues, to invite Israelis to enter Jewish life without an a priori assumption of a religious doctrine.

It might be urged that we look at Israelis through the prism of their needs and quests. As individuals, Israelis need a set of spiritual outlets to nurture them in times of happiness and distress, through sickness and success, in private and collective moments. Israeli parents are concerned with the knowledge and value base of their children. Citizens are sensitive to the plight of the poor and the hungry. An entire society is concerned about the environment, the judicial system, issues of war and peace. All these challenges can be addressed within a Jewish framework and with Jewish sensibilities.

In order for Israelis to find Jewish answers to their universal concerns, there needs to be a radical transformation of programs and services available to them. To date, there is a shortage of appropriate options for Israelis (or, say, a default situation that forces Israelis to consume inappropriate Orthodox services). For interested Israelis there is a lack of spiritual leadership, limited places to go to for meaningful egalitarian and esthetic worship, scarce tools for home-based rituals, not enough books, theater, music, and media programming to infuse the public with new ideas and options. It is clear that there is a growing thirst for Jewish answers to the Israeli spiritual quest. There is also, increasingly, a range of offerings of creative programs for the new marketplace of Jewish spirituality. Only if these dynamic energies meet and interact, fuel each other, and stretch the boundaries will a meaningful and mainstream Israeli Jewish life emerge.[7]

NOTES

1. This debate is commonly known as the issue of Post-Zionism. It was introduced by Israeli intellectuals known as the "new historians." For a summary of the debate on Post-Zionism, see Furstenberg 1997.

2. It is believed that the Israeli novelist Chaim Be'er coined the term. In Hebrew it translates as "the Jewish Bookcase/Library Movement."

3. Oz Almog, a sociologist at the Jezrael College, calls this group the Veteran Zionist Bourgeoisie (in an interview). See also Almog's book on the Israeli *sabra* (Almog 1997).

4. Outside of the scope of this article, the 1990s have witnessed significant developments in the Modern Orthodox community in Israel, known also as Religious Zionists. These developments included moderation in personal Jewish practice, demand for more significant roles for women, greater personal meaning in prayer and ritual, and openness to dialogue and sharing with the secular world (Sheleg 2000).

5. This is a mixture of descriptive and prescriptive statements that are part of the public debate around Post-Zionism (Furstenberg 1997).

6. Yaron Ezrahi provides a personal and intellectual description of the transition from collective identity to individual expression that has occurred in recent years (Ezrahi 2001).

7. This is the place to mention the important work of Rabbi Naamah Kelman who is writing a dissertation on new forms of Jewish weddings in Israel. This is an example of a new "market" for Jewish activity that would not have happened unless a critical mass of young couples and a handful of creative spiritual leaders had found each other and created a new form of Israeli Jewish expression.

REFERENCES

Almog, Oz. 2000. *The Sabra: The creation of the New Jew. A Portrait* Berkeley: University of California Press.

Bekerman, Zvi, and Marc Silverman. 1999. "Israeli Traditionalists and Liberals: A Social Constructivist's Perspective." *Israel Studies* 4 (2). 90–120.

Eden, Shevach. 1976. *The Goals of Education in Israel.* Tel Aviv: Maalot (Hebrew).

Eisen, Arnold M., and Steven M. Cohen. 2000. *The Jew Within: Self, Family, and Community in America.* Bloomington: Indiana University Press.

Ezrachi, Elan. 2001. *Jewish Renaissance and Renewal in Israel: A report of the Dorot and Nathan Cummings Foundations.* New York: The New Israel Fund.

Ezrahi, Yaron. 1997. *Rubber Bullets: Power and Conscience in Modern Israel.* New York: Farrar, Strauss, Giroux.

Furstenberg, Rochelle. 1997. *Post Zionism: The Challenge to Israel.* Ramat Gan: The American Jewish Committee and the Argov Center of the Study of Israel and the Jewish People, Bar Ilan University.

Hartman, David. 2000. *Israelis and the Jewish Traditions: An Ancient People Debating Its Future*. New Haven: Yale University Press.

Horowitz, Bethamie. 2000. *Connections and Journeys: Assessing Critical Opportunities for Enhancing Jewish Identity*. A Report to UJA Federation, New York, June.

Kennet, Orly. 2000. "The Filling Carriages: The Trend toward Jewish Studies among Secular Israelis and its Critique." *Panim—Quarterly for Society, Culture and Education* (Summer). Tel Aviv (Hebrew).

Klein Halevi, Yossi. 1998. *Jewish Identity in Post Rabin Israel*. New York and Jerusalem: American Jewish Committee, Institute of American Jewish Israeli Relations.

Levy, Shlomit, Hanna Levinsohn, and Elihu Katz. 1993. *Beliefs, Religious Observance and Social Relations among Jews in Israel*. Jerusalem: The Guttman Institute for Applied Social Research.

Liebman, Charles S. 1999. "Secular Judaism and Its Prospect." In *In Search of Identity: Jewish Aspects of Israeli Culture,* ed. Dan Urian and Ephraim Karsh. London: Frank Cass.

Liebman, Charles, and Elihu Katz, eds. 1997. *The Jewishness of Israelis: Responses to the Guttman Report*. Albany: State University of New York Press.

Roof, Wade C. 1999. *Spiritual Marketplace: Baby Boomers and the Remaking of American Religion*. Princeton, N.J.: Princeton University Press.

Rosenstein, Marc. 1988. "The New Jew: The Idea of the Zionist Educational System in Palestine Up to the Establishment of the State of Israel." *Studies in Jewish Education*. Hebrew University, vol. 3 (Hebrew).

Shapira, Anita. 1997. *New Israelis Old Israelis*. Tel Aviv: Am Oved (Hebrew).

Shavit, Yaakov. 1984. *Melvri Ad Knaani (from Hebrew to Canaanite)*. Tel Aviv: Domino (Hebrew).

Sheleg, Yair. 2000. *The New Religious Jews: Recent Development among Observant Jews in Israel*. Jerusalem: Keter (Hebrew).

Tabory, Ephraim. Spring 2000. "The Influence of Liberal Judaism on Israeli Religious Life." *Israel Studies* 5 (1) (Spring). 183–203.

Ufaz, Gad. 1999. "The *Shdemot* Circle Members in Search of Jewish Sources." In *In Search of Identity: Jewish Aspects of Israeli Culture,* ed. Dan Urian and Ephraim Karsh. London: Frank Cass.

Urian, Dan. 1999. "*Baalei Teshuva* (Returnees to the Religious Fold) in Israeli Theatre." 230–252 In *In Search of Identity: Jewish Aspects of Israeli Culture,* ed. Dan Urian and Ephraim Karsh. London: Frank Cass.

Wuthnow, Robert. 1999. *Growing Up Religious*. Boston: Beacon Press.

PART V

Civil Commitment and Collective Memory

CHAPTER FOURTEEN

Civil-Military Relations in Israel at the Outset of the Twenty-First Century

ᐁᔓ

GABRIEL BEN-DOR AND AMI PEDAHZUR

Introduction

Civil-military relations in Israel have been one of the most crucial aspects of Israeli society since the establishment of the State in 1948. One of Israel's principal features is the maintenance of a large military establishment, larger than in any other Western democracy under peacetime conditions. The country also allocates a greater share of its national resources to defense than any other democracy in recent times. Above all, perhaps, the nation has seen some of its best citizens devote the major part of their lives to military service over many years. However, despite the great importance of the military in the life of the state, civilians still continue to control it, a fact that has never been seriously challenged or endangered. Israel has never been even close to joining the club of praetorian states where military coups and juntas dictate the course of political events and processes (Ben-Eliezer 1997; Peri 1996). Its democratic character has been an integral part of the life of its society, with full concurrence of the military in the ethos and value system involved (Akzin 1955; Fein 1967; Gutmann 1969; Lissak 1996). On the other hand, civil-military relations in the country have not been free of stress and tension (Peri 1999). These have been a fact of life for a long time, are still very much felt, after a half-century of statehood, and are likely to persist for a long time to come, as problems continue to be unresolved.

One of the main features of civil-military relations in the country, and perhaps the single most important thing that there is to know about the military establishment in Israel, concerns political culture. This is particularly important because Israel still lacks a formal constitution, and its structural features are fluid and in the process of crystallizing into some degree of permanence. On the other hand, cultural features of values, beliefs, and habits related to politics have been persistent and more or less consistent over time.

Characteristics of Civil-Military Relations in Israel

Officers in the IDF

Unlike the situation in other countries with rich military traditions, Israel has no formal officer training schools for its young people. There are no military academies as such, although there have been one or two high schools that prepare their students for military service during their (regular) studies. In order to reach officer status, Israeli soldiers have to pass a battery of tests evaluating their fitness for officer rank, and to undergo various intensive training courses lasting several months, normally first for Non-Commissioned Officers, and then for junior officers. The system is competitive and allows virtually anyone of ability to become an officer, whereas those who are unable to compete successfully will not reach officer status, regardless of their social or educational background.

Relations between officers and other ranks in the Israeli military are notoriously informal and relaxed compared with most other nations, so that the usual social distance between officers and others is virtually nonexistent. All this has been instrumental in preventing the country from developing an officer corps separate from the rest of society that would hold a set of norms and values that might differ from, and threaten, the ongoing democratic political process in the country.

In addition to all this, the Israeli Defense Forces (IDF) have developed a doctrine of quick rotation of senior manpower. The practical meaning of this doctrine was historically that the most senior officers were discharged from the military some time in their forties, or early fifties at the very latest. The less senior officers, once their prospects of further promotion were ended, were discharged after about twenty years of service and normally not later than their early forties. The result of this policy was that officers were able to develop a second career at a stage in their lives when this was still possible and not too difficult. Another advantage was the avoidance of the frustration associated with lengthy service by relatively older officers who had no chance of further promotion (Lissak and Guttman 1971).

Of course, the reasons for quick rotation were not necessarily always those cited above. Sometimes it was simply the ambition to inject fresh manpower into the service to avoid the staleness and conservatism associated with an old and established officer corps, as happens in many countries with large military establishments. This effort has been largely successful, although much criticism has been heard over the years about the willingness of the military to release outstanding people during the prime of their lives, at the top of their professional abilities, but this has been considered a price well worth paying.

Officers in Politics

One of the many consequences of the quick rotation in the military is that many officers find a second career in politics. Although, there are fewer of them now than there used to be, they are still very much present, and at some critical points in time they are again all-important. In the wake of the wave of suicide bombings in early 1996, both major parties scrambled to fill the top slots of their lists with former officers, projecting an image of toughness and determination in the face of a deteriorating internal security situation. In the case of the Likud bloc, people like Sharon, a former general and minister of defense, and Raful, a former chief of staff, appeared prominently, whether by the choice of the party members in primaries, or owing to interparty agreements among the three parties making up the Likud-Gesher-Tzomet bloc. In the case of Labor, things were that much more acute, with the assassination of Rabin, himself a former chief of staff. However, his place was filled to some extent by foreign minister Ehud Barak, the recently retired chief of staff, as well as brigadier-generals Benjamin Ben-Eliezer, the minister of housing, and Efraim Sneh, the minister of health, all three among the top ten candidates on the list. Nevertheless, the top echelons were not heavily dominated by ex-Generals as in the case of previous governments or candidate lists in previous elections. The same scenario repeated itself prior to the 1999 elections when the newly retired chief of staff Amnon Lipkin Shahak joined the new Center Party while the former generals Matan Vilnaei joined the Labor Party. in 2001 the Likud prime ministerial candidate, Ariel Sharon, asked the former chief of staff Dan Shomron, as well as former generals Amiram Levin and Yossi Peled, to join him.

The Involvement of Military Officers in the Peace Process

It should be noted that many of the officers find themselves involved in politics prior to their retirement. The top military brass have been extremely involved in the negotiations with the Palestinians in recent years, to the point where at times they positively seemed to dominate them. This is not entirely new. One may recall that after the Yom Kippur War it was the military that negotiated initially with the Egyptians, way before the Sadat initiative. However, the two situations are not entirely comparable. The case of Egypt was quite simple. There had been a war, with indecisive results. Consequently, there was a need for various military arrangements to institutionalize ceasefire and other agreements, and the Egyptians had no trouble with that, while they objected for quite a while to more politically oriented talks; hence they were more comfortable with military negotiations than with ones between civilians. In the light of that, the willingness of Israel to send its top officers to these talks made sense; in fact it may have been the only natural and sensible thing to do. On the other hand, with the Palestinians things were entirely different. The diplomatic breakthrough was a matter of political decisions and had nothing to do with the military situation between the parties; hence there was no apparent reason to let the military dominate the talks. Nevertheless, the military was called upon heavily to represent Israel in the various talks between Oslo I and Oslo II, and following also on issues that were perceived as quite partisan and divisive with the Israeli body politic.

Things were, in fact, even more blatant in the negotiations with Syria. Here there is a sense of similarity, in some ways, with the Egyptian situation of some twenty-five years ago. The Syrians like to have a lot of military representatives at the talks, in order to deemphasize the direct political contacts between the parties. Still, the Israeli leadership at times goes overboard in its dependence on the military, by positively inviting the top military echelons to say what they need for Israeli security and whether or not the possible withdrawal from the Golan Heights is tolerable.

This seems to deposit in the hands of the army something approaching a veto, at a time when it is obvious that there is a political decision at stake, so that the military may be important in an advisory capacity, but clearly they are not entitled to a veto on a matter that is not within their sphere. To be fair to them, they do not want this veto, nor are they eager to be dominant in any of the negotiations, but they are drawn into the vacuum created by the hesitations and weakness of the some of the civilian leadership involved.

The Citizen's Army

After describing the officer strata we now turn to describe the larger part of the military, that is, stratum of enlisted men. Israel, shortly after its War of Independence (1948–49), made a conscious decision to build and maintain a "citizen's army." In practice this meant compulsory service for each citizen, with collective and individual exemptions allowed by the minister of Defense. However, the norm has been that citizens serve for a given period (in recent years this has been around three years for men and two for women), after completing high school or on reaching the age of eighteen. They only enter the labor market or go on to higher education after military service. Such service has become an important component of personal and collective identity in the country and is still considered a crucial part of growing up and of merging the diverse groups and elements making up Israeli society within a fruitful and constructive framework. In particular, the military is considered to have played a key role in the Israeli melting pot—the absorption of large-scale immigration.

The Professional Army

However, a small country like Israel always has difficulties in maintaining a military establishment of a size commensurate with the threat from its large and numerous enemies. Hence the doctrine has been to maintain, in addition to the conscripted army, a professional force of several tens of thousands of career people, as the core that would train others and prepare the infrastructure for predicted eventualities in cases of war and emergency (Cohen 1997a; Linn, 1997). In particular, professional services such as the Air Force and the navy have relied heavily on career officers although they, too, have used other forms of human resources as well.

The Reserve Forces

The bulk of the force of the Israeli military, at least in terms of numbers, has always been the reserves. Ever since 1949, the norm has been that each individual, after discharge from compulsory service, is deployed in an appropriate reserve unit. (It should be noted that the IDF's reserve units are still primarily male units, and were all-male throughout most of Israel's military history.) Be that as it may, an annual training period keeps him or her up-to-date on the latest military knowledge and skills in his/her particular field. The reservist also serves a number of days per year to help in the army's daily running. In the case of emergency or war, total mobilization of hundreds of thousands of reservists is supposed to enable the Israeli military to gain the strength needed to face an Arab onslaught. For this operation a period of time is needed. So the doctrine has been that the regular army—the conscripts and the professionals—keep the enemy at bay for the time needed, which is defined in various ways, at times forty-eight hours and at other times longer.

Reserve service is quite a burden, historically speaking. At various times, it has been extended for men up to the age of fifty-one, and at times, depending on strategic as well as budgetary considerations, the number of days served per year can reach sixty, in times of routine security. When the situation worsens, mobilization is in practice virtually unlimited. This was the case during the Yom Kippur War and its aftermath, when in 1974 large numbers of reserve soldiers served six months or more. This fact influenced Israeli society in many aspects. Soldiers experienced enormous difficulties in their family lives, academic training, and especially their careers. The absence of so many men from their working places for such long periods had a severe effect on the strength of the Israeli economy (Linn 1997, 31; Leshem and Lissak 1999). The long service of many Israeli civilians during the Yom Kippur War motivated the Knesset to pass a special law entitling those serving over this period to special benefits. Accusations

335

were heard at the time that the military sometimes discharged soldiers serving five months or more, only to recall them later, hence disrupting the uninterrupted sequence of service and denying them the benefits.

Universal Service?

In practice, universal service has never been applied. The very question of who should serve has been one of the ways to define political identity and belonging in the country. While the service of new immigrants who, upon arrival in Israel, were enlisted in the reserve forces—as well as the service of women,[1] a unique feature of Israeli society—has emphasized the universal nature of service, there have been many contradictory trends. Large groups of citizens have been exempt: the law of security service allows the minister of defense to use his discretion, virtually without limit, in permitting exemptions (Cohen 1997b).

Minorities, that is, Arabs, have been and still are exempt, both from military service as such and from any other form of compulsory national service (an alternative idea that has come up numerous times but has always been found impracticable for one reason or another). In the mid-1950s compulsory conscription was applied to Druze and Circassian men, and there are considerable numbers of Beduin, as well as a small number of Christian volunteers, but that is all. The Arab population as such is simply outside the reality of compulsory service. It is defined as untrustworthy when there is a strong likelihood of service leading to confrontation with Arabs from outside the borders. The Arab leadership in the country has been all too willing to concur in this policy. There are some expectations that an Israeli-Palestinian peace will change this drastically, but so far nothing along these lines has taken place.

Therefore, in effect, there is no universal conscription, and there never has been. On the contrary, conscription has served to delineate and sharpen lines of division between the majority and the minority, between those who have been considered to be the owners of the State, so to speak, on the one hand, and those who are suspected of not being totally loyal to it on the other (Landau 1969). It is noteworthy that these lines of demarcation have been accepted with relatively little protest by both the majority and the minority, testifying to the devastating effect of the Arab-Israeli conflict on the delicate and complex web of Israeli society.

Moreover, even within the Jewish majority, the idea of universal conscription has been implemented only partially. From the very beginning of the system of conscription, certain groups of religious Jews have been exempt. Among the national religious Zionists, men have been subject to conscription, but religious women who undergo an examination by an exemption board do not serve in the military as such. Some are totally exempt, while others participate in a form of "national service," during which they fulfill certain social and educational functions, most of which bear no resemblance to the functions and norms of military service whatsoever (Heymount 1967).

An entire sector of Jewish society, that of yeshiva (religious academies) students, is also exempt, either totally or else for a period of several years—during their advanced religious studies—after which they serve for a short training period and then in the reserves. Many of them are already married and well into their late twenties. Their numbers run into the tens of thousands, and this collective exemption, which has been the focus of much traditional debate in Israeli society, has been justified by the traditional commitment of Jews to Torah learning as a vital contribution to the survival of the Jewish people. However, very large numbers of Jews consider this a poor excuse and argue that the ultra-Orthodox (*haredim*) have merely found a way to escape the difficulties of lengthy military service altogether. Indeed, the frustration of many secular Jews was manipulated by political parties, such as Tsomet in 1992 and Shinui in 1999. Public pressure on this issue in the late 1990s caused the formation of a committee headed by a former Supreme Court judge. This was the Tal Committee, which was supposed to find the way to integrate the ultra-Orthodox community into the army. However, the Committee's recommendations indicated no real deviance from the status quo.

Commitment to the Army

Generally, in the past, within the mainstream of Israeli society, there was a very high degree of commitment to military service as ideological proof of belonging to the core of society. In addition, there was a practical consideration as well: Jews who had not served in the army would find it difficult, if not impossible, to be accepted in the various strata of Israeli society, particularly when it came to employment, in both the public and the private sectors. Because of this, various groups of people who, for diverse reasons, found it difficult to be accepted for military service, positively insisted on being conscripted. The military authorities themselves were less than thrilled with the prospect of having to deal with various sectors of the population deficient in education and skills considered important for service in the various military forces. Thus, socially disadvantaged groups of Oriental Jews, at times associated with protest movements such as the Black Panthers, insisted with various degrees of success on their members being drafted into the army, most of the time against the will and judgment of the military authorities (Hurewitz 1963; Perlmutter 1968; Roumani 1979).

The country has never been able to agree on a coherent policy on this difficult issue. In fact, the decisions made were haphazard, and many times simply depended on the convictions and values of the individual leaders involved. For instance, when Rafael Eitan (Raful) was chief of staff in the late 1970s and early 1980s, there was an active policy of recruiting disadvantaged youths and trying to upgrade their education and skills while they served in the military. However, during most other periods, there was reluctance on the part of the top military echelons to engage in activities of this kind, which were considered costly and not really within the proper realm of the chores and duties of the IDF (Cohen 1993).

In recent years, many changes have taken place in relation to conscription. These changes have become more and more noticeable, and by the mid-1990s the mass communications media started extensive discussions on the difficulties associated with them (Cohen 1995; Ha'aretz September 9, 1996; Ma'ariv, January 1, 2000; Ha'aretz, September 12, 2000). Today, the gist of the change has been that Israeli society as such no longer considers military service to be a central and absolutely indispensable role of all citizens in the country. In practice, this has meant that more and more people have attempted to escape military service either totally, or else by evading reserve service duty during the years following the basic three-year period in the military.

A survey conducted for the purpose of this study confirmed the assumption that large numbers of reserve soldiers are dropping out of service. The survey included 501 Jewish men at the age of military service (25–50). The analysis of the data reveals that 13.8 percent of the respondents had never served in the reserves, 17.8 percent had been discharged from the army, and 8.2 percent of those registered had not served even one day during the past year. Thus, with regard to the total sample, the percentage of Israeli men who do not serve in the reserve army is 43.7 percent. An interesting trend that emerges from the survey, congruent with existing evaluations, is that most of those who managed to get discharged from the reserve forces did so in recent years (93 percent in the past ten years). It appears that this is an increasing trend: 60 percent of those discharged in the past decade left in the past five years. Among those who still serve, 60 percent serve in combat units and forty percent serve in rear units.

In practice, there are many different ways of evasion. The laws of compulsory service are clearly registered, and State authorities have considerable means at their disposal of imposing and enforcing them. However, it is obviously impossible to compel hundreds of thousands of mature citizens to serve when they are not absolutely convinced that the service is necessary, particularly when these citizens have all kinds of medical and military forms of assistance at their disposal. Also, the authorities have always been willing to take into consideration economic factors and considerations. Many people have postulated that their livelihood as business entrepreneurs and employees in sensitive positions was in jeopardy because of reserve service. Once the system is flooded with requests of this kind, it is impossible to maintain a minimal degree of order along with fairness. Indeed, by using a logistic regression procedure, we found out that the chances of an Israeli-born bachelor who is an employee (not an independent businessman) serving in the reserve forces are 85.6 percent, four times higher than those of a non-Israeli-born married person who is a father of two children or more and owns his own business (21.6 percent).[2]

In the past, not serving because of medical causes in general, and for reasons having to do with mental health in particular, used to be a stigma of such a severe nature that it was almost impossible to overcome it in later life in Israeli society. This was tragic enough for young people who simply could not serve owing to the objective limitations of their health situation. In recent years, this tendency has changed dramatically and even drastically, not because of anything directly military, but because of changing norms and perspectives in Israeli society at large. Actually our survey revealed that 27.5 percent of the respondents said that they would not hesitate to apply to the mental health officer and be labeled as exempt from reserve duty on the basis of mental incompetence.

Israel, by the beginning of the new millennium, became a society in search of normality, however defined by the various sectors in the society (Peri 1999). One reason for this was the peace process, which encouraged the impression that Israel's continued existence is no longer in question, and that there is no direct existential threat. In the past, of course, the slogan of "no alternative"—the conviction that whatever was done was inevitable—was one of the most important motives for service in the military. Once that conviction was badly shaken by the Peace Process, the voluntary basis for service was also undermined. However, that is only one part of the problem.

The other part is that Israeli society in general has changed enormously. The rising standards of living are obvious, but they are not necessarily the most important elements in this change. Indeed, the most important part may be that which has resulted from the revolution of mass communications in the country. Israelis have become more and more part and parcel of the Western world, which has preached the gospel of self-fulfillment, individual freedom, the pursuit of material well-being, and a critical attitude to governments and the ideological considerations that they give for justifying the sacrifices demanded of their citizens (Schiff 1992). Indeed, the survey indicates a significant positive correlation between both economic individualism, as well as low levels of social capital, and lack of motivation to serve.[3]

The third part of the tendency to try to evade military service has been dissension in Israeli society about the basic objectives and norms of the country (Barzilai and Inbar 1992). Ever since the Six Day War in 1967, there have been increasingly sharp arguments about war and peace, settlements and territory, and above all the necessity for military action. After the Yom Kippur War of 1973, there were organized protests of discharged reserve units and formations, but these did not challenge the notion of universal service as a vital necessity (Ben-Dor 1977). There had been some forms of protest during the War of Attrition in 1969–70, when high school students just before conscription wrote letters to the prime minister and asked critical questions about government policy, questioning its wisdom and raising questions about whether they could serve with good conscience under a government that did not appear to pursue peace with sufficient vigor (Lenir 1985).

However, this kind of protest activity gained real momentum after the war in Lebanon in 1982, the first war since 1956 to be considered a "war of choice," that is to say, a war that was not absolutely necessary and justified by threat (Linn 1986). In contrast to the 1956 war, that of 1982 was lengthy, with hundreds of casualties, heatedly debated in public, and above all, an all too obvious failure. One unhappy result of this was the increasing unwillingness of young people to risk the best years of their lives, and even their health and life, for goals that many of them disagreed with and even abhorred. This became even more pronounced during the Intifada, when the need to risk lives to put down an insurrection, in a way that seemed beyond repression, deterred many people in the military from identifying with the needs of the military as officially defined. Of course, this discontent grew even further when the then chief of staff argued that the Intifada in any case could not be solved via military means, and that only a political solution was viable (Inbar 1991).

Curiously enough, the phenomenon of massive social dissension—which has split Israeli society sharply since the 1970s—has been paralleled by practical considerations of the military establishment itself. Budgetary restrictions have become an increasingly dominant fact of life in the military, which now has to define its priorities sharply and with care. Of course, contrary to some public myths, budgetary considerations have always played an important role in policies and strategies adopted by the military. In recent years, however, this consideration has become ever more important, owing to the manifold conflicting demands on the government budget, as well as the increasing unwillingness of the public to sustain the defense budget at its traditional high level. After all, the world is talking of making money, not war; and the leaders of Israel speak more and more of peace as a way of ensuring existence and securing interests. In practice, during the discussions about the State's budget for 2001, the government initiated a cut of 800 million shekels (200 million U.S. dollars) in defense allocations. This fact was severely criticized by the chief of staff, Shaul Mofaz, who argued that this cut would endanger the ability of the IDF to confront security hazards (*Yediot Achronot,* Sept. 5, 2000).

Civil-Military Relations in the new Millennium

In the light of these circumstances, many planners in the IDF are now willing to contemplate taking on some of the "sacred cows" of the system. They feel that the army of the future will demand more and more professional training and skills, hence a three-year period of initial service will be too short and will not justify the necessary investment of time, energy, and money. It is better to reserve that investment, in their view, for people who will serve five years or more, so that they can apply their knowledge to the practical problems of the military for at least a minimal period, and preferably for several more years thereafter (Moskos and Woods 1988). The model is that of the air force, where the backbone of the crucial manpower, particularly the pilots, is lengthy training, further service of several years, and the added incentive of acquiring a prestigious and employable profession, promising a civilian career later on.

If that kind of model were to be adopted in the rest of the IDF, a veritable revolution would be likely to ensue, in more ways than one. Compulsory conscription may be shortened or even completely eliminated or extended, an action that is compatible with various pressures and demands of the population. This would allow the military to offer more attractive financial incentives to the professional officer corps, at a time when prevailing conditions do not permit this. Indeed, many of the existing incentives are under attack from both the public and officials of the Treasury. The army would become more professional, and also more free of the pressures created by shifting public moods. However, needless to say, it would still depend not only on widespread public support, and it would be many years before it could dispense with the need to use reservists and draftees, a fact that was reinforced during the El-Aktza Intifada events.

On the other hand, the most important melting pot in Israeli society would almost disappear, or at least drastically decline in its impact (Roumani 1979). This most salient and popular national institution would change its character from one that has been uniquely Israeli to one that can now be seen in the advanced industrial countries of the West, where the problems of security are incomparably less pressing and visible. Israel has undergone many difficult periods since the establishment of the State half a century ago. Radical changes in civil-military relations could alter the whole structure of Israeli society, politically and socially. The country would have to find a new web of civil-military relations, with different norms and regulations.

Should such an eventuality occur, which is something that Israeli society definitely needs to prepare for, it is also likely that the old modes of civilian control over the military would have to be replaced by new and quite different methods. The old modes, as mentioned before, were based on the coherence and universality of political culture in the country, when the military were not sufficiently distinct from the rest of society. It may be more accurate to say that the military elite were not sufficiently distinct from the civilian ones to create a different political culture and constitute a threat to the supremacy of the civilians over the military, a trend that was reinforced by the nature of the "civilian army," as well as by the rapid turnover in the officer corps itself.

In the future, all this may well change, because a smaller but more professional army, which would exclude from service large strata of the population, and in which there would be more career officers, might just create the sort of distinct political subculture (Rapaport 1962) that has never existed in Israeli society and that would no longer guarantee acknowledgment of the supremacy of the civilian level over the military establishment. There may be also a feeling of alienation developing between the military and the rest of society, and this is likely to grow in a more professional era; but the fact is that it is already very discernible at the beginning of the new millennium.

NOTES

1. For some of the women, military service does not end after two years. Women used to be part of the reserve forces until the age of twenty-four or until they got married. Following the Palestinian riots in late 2000 the IDF initiated a new program according to which single women under the age of thirty will be recruited for reserve service. In the future they will have the opportunity to serve either as warriors, drivers, medics, or in other positions that support the combative forces. Eitan Rabin, "Success in the First Initiative to Recruit Women to Reserve Service," *Ma'ariv,* January 7, 2001.

2. In order to evaluate the respondents' prospects for serving we used the following equation: Log of Odds = log $(p)/(p-1)$ = $a + b_1x_1 + b_2x_2 + \ldots + b_kx_k + e$. In order to create the profiles we used the following procedures: $P = 1/1 + e^{-z}$; $Z = a + b_1{}^*$ (variable value); e = 2.7182.

3. Lack of motivation to serve in the reserve army was measured using a seven-item measure. The questions were tested by a factor analysis in order to see if the variables fit into one category, as well as to ensure that their combination into one variable is appropriate statistically as well as theoretically. The results showed that the variables fit into one category. The combined measure showed a high level of reliability.

Economic individualism was measured by two items and social capital by one. In order to look into the correlation between these variables and the lack of motivation to serve we used the Pearson test. Both findings were significant and strong; however, economic individualism was found a little bit stronger ($r = .25{}^{**}$) than low levels of social capital ($r = .20{}^{**}$).

REFERENCES

Akzin, Benjamin. 1955. "The Role of Parties in Israeli Democracy." *Journal of Politics* 17 (4): 507–45.

Barzilai, Gad and Efraim Inbar. 1992. "Do Wars Have an Impact?: Israeli Public Opinion After the Gulf War," *Jerusalem Journal of International Relations* 14 (1): 48–64.

Ben-Dor, Gabriel. 1977. "The Military and Politics in Israel," pp. 411–432 in Moshe Lissak and Emanuel Guttman eds., *The Israeli Political System*. Tel Aviv: Am Oved., (Hebrew).

Ben-Eliezer, Uri. 1998. *The Making of Israeli Militarism*. Bloomington, In: Indiana University Press.

Cohen, Stuart A. 1993. "Israel and Her Army: Towards a Posture of Military Role Contraction?" *Journal of Political and Military Sociology* 22.

———. 1995. *Studying the Israeli Defense Forces: A Changing Contract with Israeli Society*. Ramat Gan: The Besa Center, Bar-Ilan University.

———. 1997a. "Portrait of the New Israeli Soldier." *Meira—Middle East Review of International Affairs* 1 (4): 1–16.

———. 1997b. "Military Service in Israel: No Longer a Cohesive Force." *The Jewish Journal of Sociology* 39 (1–2): 5–23.

Fein, Leonard. 1967. *Politics in Israel*. Boston: Little, Brown.

Frish, Felix. "The Chief of Stuff: The Cut Down in the IDF Budget Will Cause Severe Consequences." <http://www.ynet.co.il.5.9.00>.

Gutmann, Emanuel E. 1969. "Some Observations on Politics and Parties in Israel." *India Quarterly* 17 (January–March).

Heymount, I. 1967. "The Israeli Nahal Program." *Middle East Journal* 21 (3).

Hurewitz, Jacob C. 1963. "The Role of the Military in Israel." In *The Military in the Middle East,* ed. Fisher Sydney Nettleton. Columbus Ohio: Ohio University Press.

Landau, Jacob M. 1969. *The Arabs in Israel: A Political Study*. London: Oxford University Press.

Leshem, Eli and Moshe Lissak. 1999. "Development and Consolidation of the Russian Community in Israel," pp. 135–174 in Shalva Weil ed., *Roots and Routes: Ethnicity and Migration in Global Perspective*. Jerusalem: Magnes Press.

Limor, Yoav, and Ofer Shelach. "The Army of Peace." *Ma'ariv*. January 7, 2000.

Linn, Ruth. 1986. "Conscientious Objection in Israel During the War in Lebanon." *Armed Forces and Society* 12: 489–511.

———. 1997. "Patterns of Crisis among Israeli Reserve Soldiers." *Jewish Journal of Sociology* 39 (1–2): 24–45.

Lissak, Moshe. 1996. "Uniqueness and Normalization in Military Government Relations in Israel." In *Basic Issues in Israeli Democracy,* ed. Raphael Cohen-Almagor, 227–45. Tel-Aviv: Sifriat Poalim (Hebrew).

Lissak, Moshe, and Emanuel Guttman, eds. 1971. *Political Institutions and Processes in Israel*. Jerusalem: Academon (Hebrew).

Moskos, Charles. S, and Frank. R. Woods, eds. 1988. *The Military: More Than Just a Job?* Washington D.C.: Pergamon Brassey's International Defense Publishers.

Peri, Yoram. 1996. "Is Israel a Militaristic Society?" *Zmanim* 56: 94–112 (Hebrew).

———. 1999. "Civil-Military Relations in Israel in Crisis." *Megamot* 39 (4): 375–99.

Perlmutter, Amos. 1968. "The Israeli Army in Politics: The Persistence of Civilian over Military." *World Politics* 21 (4).

Rabin, Eita. "The IDF: The Numbers of Those who Drop Out of the Reserve Force is Much Bigger than the Numbers of Those Who Join It." *Ha'aretz,* September 9, 1996.

Rapoport, D. C. 1962. "A Comparative Theory of Military and Political Types." In *Changing Pattern of Military Politics,* ed. Samuel P. Huntington. New York: Free Press.

Roumani, Maurice M. 1979. *From Immigrant to Citizen: The Contribution of the Army to National Integration in Israel: The Case of Oriental Jews.* The Hague: Foundation for Study of Plural Societies.

Schiff, Rebecca L. 1992. "Israel as an 'Uncivil' State: A Reconsideration of Civil-Military Relations." *Security Studies* 1: 636–58.

Sinai, Ruthi. "The Motivation Starts at Home." *Ha'aretz,* September 12, 1996.

CHAPTER FIFTEEN

The Cleavage between Jewish and Arab Israeli Citizens

ભ/ર

Ephraim Yuchtman-Yaar and Ze'ev Shavit

There should not be one law for the Jew and another for the Arab.
—Chaim Weizmann, *Massa VaMa'as*

Introduction

In recent years, the term "sectarian society" has been increasingly used to describe Israeli society and the direction in which it is heading. Experts and laymen agree that Israel is a fragmented society composed of many competing groups based on national, ethnic, religious, cultural, political, and socioeconomic factors. The conflicting interests between various sectors generate fierce pressure and tensions that undermine the very foundations of Israel's social integration, collective identity, and the legitimacy of its institutions. These processes can potentially put an end to the era of Zionist ideology, by replacing Zionism with alternative ideologies, either particularistic in nature (such as Jewish-religious) or more universal in nature (such as post-Zionism or anti-Zionism).

The fragmentation of Israeli society is not a new phenomenon. From the beginning of the Zionist enterprise, the Jewish[1] society that had been established in Palestine during the pre-State era was formed from a mosaic of divergent groups. This is what prominent students of that period, such as Horowitz and Lissak (1978), referred to when they characterized the Jewish community at that period as a sectarian society. The "Old Yishuv" and the "New Yishuv," religious and secular, Zionists and anti-Zionists, Sephardim and Ashkenazim, liberals and socialists, Left and Right—all these were stones in the mosaic of Jewish society in British Mandate Palestine.

However, For the most part, the political center of power that emerged at that time succeeded in deflating the tensions between the various Jewish sectors and in fostering identification with the collective goals they shared. Therefore, the Jewish community managed to function relatively effectively, even though it lacked the formal governing authority that was in the hands of the British

Mandate. This is because the Yishuv's internal authority was based on a wide consensus about the Jewish national goals that crossed the borders of most sectarian interests and ideological rivalries (with the exception of a small number of marginal Jewish groups and, most importantly, the Palestinians). The fact that the Declaration of Independence on the eve of the founding of the State was signed by representatives of the entire political spectrum, including anti-Zionist parties such as the ultra-Orthodox Agudat Yisrael and the Communists, is one of the most palpable expressions of this wall-to-wall consensus.

The establishment of the State of Israel was the high point of the Yishuv leadership's power and legitimacy. During the period of the first two or three decades of the state, the main developmental trend in Israel was aimed at the "Israelization" of the Jewish populace, according to the model of the "good society," as envisioned by the leadership of the Zionist movement. The efforts for social integration were intended to consolidate "One Israel," which meant actually "One Jewish Israel," and were nurtured by ideas and catchphrases such as "nation building" and "melting pot" (Eisenstadt 1967). Scholars such as Eisenstadt (1985), Horowitz and Lissak (1989), Peres (1971), Swirski (1981), and Smooha (1978) have already pointed to the structural and cultural cleavages, as well as the failures of the government's policies in the social, economic, and educational fields, which hampered the integrative processes needed to alleviate the socioeconomic and cultural gaps. The potency of these cleavages was manifested in the formation of new social movements and political forces, which grew continually stronger during the 1980s and 1990s. These changes led to a new social reality fragmented by competing groups, all chipping away at the society's integrative forces—particularly the collective identity that the veteran Zionist elite formulated and nurtured since the time of the Yishuv.

We subscribe to the view that a number of rifts in Israeli society were matured in recent decades to the extent that they pose a threat to its unity and integration. However, even the rifts that are generally thought of as particularly problematic in Israeli society today—those between the Jewish and Arab citizens of Israel, religious and secular Jews, Ashkenazim and Sephardim, and political Right and Left[2]—vary considerably in terms of their levels of intensity. Indeed, the most severe and perhaps insolvable is the conflict between the Arab and Jewish communities.

As a prelude, it should be noted that even though all four of these rifts are generally depicted as dichotomies, this description applies in fact only to the cleavage between Arabs and Jews. For example, when speaking of the rift between religious and secular Jews, the differing degrees of religiosity and secularism cannot be ignored. Not all secularists are atheist, antireligious or antitradition—just as not all religious people devoutly keep all the commandments or reject out-of-hand anything that represents the modern, secular, and democratic world. The difference between a dichotomous division and differentiation based on divergent points on a continuum is not just a technical matter. There is a much greater potential for attaining flexibility and bridging between divergent groups if they are situated at differing gradations on the same ladder or plane of argumentation.

Another factor to be taken into consideration is the level of overlapping that exists across the various issues of contention between rival groups. The more they find themselves on opposite sides of the fence regarding different issues, the less the chance of reaching compromise or bridging between them. Hence, when these two conditions merge (that is, a dichotomous division between groups that overlaps across many issues), the potential for a deep, protracted conflict becomes greater. Considering the cleavages prevailing in Israeli society, what makes the rift between the Arab and Jewish communities in Israel so unique is that the merger of these two conditions applies only in this case. In other words, the Jewish and Arab citizens of Israel represent two distinct and mutually exclusive groups that are separated from each other on the basis of a number of highly significant characteristics, including their national, ethnic, religious, and cultural identities. These considerations should be borne in mind as we proceed to analyze the evolution of the relations between the two communities.

The Pre-State Era

Jewish-Zionist immigration and settlement in Palestine, which began toward the end of the nineteenth century, was critical for the implementation of the ultimate goal of the Zionist movement to establish in Palestine a national-Jewish entity. However, with the relentless progression of the Zionist enterprise, the relations between the growing Jewish community and the native Palestinian community were destined to develop into a bitter conflict. This deterministic assessment, according to which the Israeli-Palestinian conflict was unavoidable, is based on the observation that both peoples intended to implement their national aspirations on the same territory, with each claiming that it is theirs. In other words, the existential interests of the two sides were inherently contradictory. From the Palestinian viewpoint, therefore, the differences between the various ideological camps within the Zionist movement during the period of the Yishuv, including, on the one hand, the ultra-nationalist Revisionists and, on the other hand, moderates like "Brit Shalom" (Peace Covenant), which envisioned binationalism, were only minor. Such a compromise implied that the local Palestinian community, which was at that time much larger than the Jewish community, would have to bear the price of giving up at least parts of its own land to foreign colonizers and settlers who had no legitimate rights in Palestine. Similarly, from the Zionist viewpoint, denying the rights of Jewish immigration and Jewish settlement in Palestine—the historical homeland of the Jewish people—was unthinkable since the vision of renewing Jewish national independence could have been achieved only in that land.[3]

During the period of the British Mandate the antagonism between the Jewish and Palestinian populations resulted in the emergence of a "dual society," with the two communities developing apart (Horowitz and Lissak 1977; Metzer 1998) while striving to achieve their colliding national goals. This conflict culminated in the war of 1948, when the Palestinians (and the Arab world as a whole) refused to accept the partition plan that was adopted by the United Nations in order to satisfy the national aspirations of both sides. However, the outcomes of the 1948 war have not resolved the conflict between the two nations. On the contrary, the problem has become more difficult and complex. On the one hand, about 750,000 Palestinians either escaped from their country or were forced to leave it by the Israeli armed forces, seeking refuge in neighboring Arab countries (Morris 1987; Shapira 1995).[4] On the other hand, about 150,000 Palestinians who remained within the boundaries of the new Jewish State became a dominated minority that experienced extensive and systematic discrimination, despite their entitlement to equal status as Israeli citizens.[5] In order to explain the predicament of this minority, it is necessary to take into consideration the impact of two major, mutually related factors: the characteristic of Israel as a Jewish and Democratic State,[6] and the enduring conflict with the Palestinian people and the Arab world.

The definition of Israel as a Jewish and democratic state contained within it potential tension between the particularistic commitment to maintain the Jewish character of the State and the universalistic obligation to maintain its democratic values. We are dealing here with a condition of structured incompatibility that was compounded by the inherent contradiction that exists, as noted earlier, between the identities of the Arab minority and the Jewish Majority. These contradictions had profound and mostly negative implications for the relations that have evolved between the two communities from the early days of the State of Israel until present times. In order to deal with these contradictions, Israel has made a distinction between the collective and individual rights of the two communities. On the collective level, only the Jewish community was entitled to special legal rights, as manifested in the Law of Return. The Arab community was recognized as a religious and cultural minority but not as a political entity. It is true that at the individual level of civil rights, the State's laws made no distinction between Arabs and Jews. But in practice the Arab citizens were subjected to a systematic policy of discrimination in most domains, including a lesser share for Arab municipalities in the State's annual budget and the experience of unequal opportunities in the labor market.

However, it is very difficult to separate the internal division between the Jewish and Arab citizens of Israel from the external conflict that exists between Israel and the Arab world, in particular the Palestinians. As will be discussed below, the influence of this conflict varied in intensity and direction over the years. Nevertheless, it has always been at the background, and occasionally at the foreground, of the internal dynamics of Israeli State and society, including the relations between the Jewish majority and Arab minority. In particular, Israeli Arabs could not have escaped the consequence of being stigmatized as part of a nation that threatened Israel's very existence and with whom Israel has been in an ongoing war. Accordingly, they have often been perceived and treated as a potential fifth column by the political elite as well as by the larger Jewish public.

Yet, while both the internal and external factors have persistently impeded the potential for harmonious coexistence, based on equality and mutual empathy, the interrelations between the two communities have undergone substantive changes over time. These changes can be delineated according to three major phases of development, as discussed below.

The Period of the Military Rule: 1949–66

As noted, the outcomes of the 1948 war have established a new reality in the structure of demographic and power relations between the two communities, based on Arab subjugation to Jewish supremacy. Thus, the "War of Independence" for the Jews was the "Nakba" (catastrophe) for the Arabs. Most of the Palestinian population living in areas that became the State of Israel were either expelled or fled from the country[7] and dispersed, for the most part, among the Arab countries of the region as refugees. Most of the Palestinian villages were destroyed (Kabha and Barzilay 1996; Khalidi 1992), and only about 150,000 Palestinians remained within Israel's borders after the establishment of the state.[8] They have become a small and defeated community, amounting to only 12 percent of the Arab population that had lived in Palestine before the war. The large majority is composed of villagers with only a small urban middle class and a thin layer of leadership able to be represented in the Jewish government.

As a result of the Arabs fleeing Israel and the influx of Jewish immigrants, the demographic ratio between the two populations that existed during the British Mandate period was reversed, so that the Jews became the overwhelming majority within the State of Israel. As noted, Israel was declared a Jewish state in the Declaration of Independence. Yet, although that declaration had also granted equal rights to the Arabs as Israeli citizens, the Israeli government's policy toward the Arab minority was in fact ambivalent—benevolent in some respects and highly discriminatory in others. Perhaps a good expression of the government's ambivalent attitude in the first days of statehood was the fact that two authorities with opposing approaches were in charge of the Arab population's affairs. The Civilian Authority—the government's Minorities Office—had adopted a political-humanitarian attitude and attempted to maintain good relationships with the Arab population and to secure its rights. The Military Authority—an administration of military rule that was instituted in the areas populated by Palestinian Arabs—had embraced a harsh policy and acted so as to control the Arab population's life under conditions of stiff regulations. Only a year after the establishment of the State (and four months after the signing of the armistice agreements with the neighboring Arab states), the second approach had won: the Minorities' Ministry was abolished, and the military administration remained the only authority to deal with the Arab population.[9] The official reason given to justify the military rule was based on considerations of national security. The argument was that the loyalty of the Arab citizens to the newly established Jewish State was questionable and that they might collaborate with hostile parties outside Israel, particularly the Palestinians living in the West Bank and the Gaza Strip, to undermine Israel's security (Amitai 1998). In this context, it should be noted that the period following the 1948 war was characterized by widespread infiltration of Palestinian refugees across the Israeli borders for various purposes. Some returned in order to resettle in their previous villages or to harvest the crops that had been left behind during the war, while others penetrated the border for the purpose of theft, robbery, or even murder. Given this reality, the military rule was intended to facilitate the supervision of the Arab population and cut its ties with the outside Palestinian and Arab populations.

But by imposing a military rule upon the Arab citizens of the state, the Israeli government had institutionalized and legitimized an important characteristic of Israeli society, regime, and collective identity—a characteristic that lasts in some respects until today, long after the military rule was abolished: a dual standard in conducting a democracy. This dual standard implied the curtailment of some of the basic democratic rights of Israel's Arab citizens, rights guaranteed by the Declaration of Independence. Under the conditions of the military rule, this was done mainly through two practices. The first practice was restrictions on the freedom of movement. The military rule had put severe restrictions on the freedom of movement of the Arab citizens, in two ways. One was on the personal level: the military governor could prohibit any person from staying in a certain place under his jurisdiction, or he could put any citizen under police supervision. The military rule had also put restrictions on the freedom of movement from the Arab residential areas to other parts of the country.

Anyone who wanted to move "out" had to ask for a special moving permit, which was given only to those who were considered loyal and trustworthy by the officers in charge, or were ready to cooperate with the authorities. The second way movement was restricted was on the collective level: the military governor could close a road or an area and prohibit anyone from moving through it. Permits were given here, too, under the same conditions. Consequently the Arab population had found itself in practical segregation from the Jewish population, including the Jewish labor market, which was crucial to it's economic welfare and development.

Another practice curtailing the democratic rights of the Arab citizens was security and political control. Movement restrictions and the ability to give movement permits were used not only as a means of control, but to mobilize informants and cooperators among the population, threatening potential suspects and even putting them in detention. The Military Rule had a vast authority considering security matters and could put in detention, sentence, and convict anyone suspected of committing hostile acts or spreading hostile propaganda. The legal rules that prevailed under this system were based on martial law and not civil law, and the courts were martial as well.[10] The officers of the military rule efficiently controlled the populace through deep involvement in its daily life. They gathered considerable information about what was going on within the Arab localities and often made decisions concerning people's material welfare, jobs, and personal freedom. In other words, they regulated the lives of the Arab citizens of Israel on all levels—from the collective to the very personal—and this situation gave the military rule a powerful mechanism of control.

Politically, control over Israel's Arab population was secured through massive voting for the dominant party, Mapai. This was achieved mainly through two modes of cooptation: by establishing Arab satellite parties, known as "minority lists," that were connected to the dominant party; and by using "notables"— typically heads of big and powerful families—as voters' mobilizing agents in exchange for various forms of gratification.[11] The Knesset members from the satellite parties were totally loyal to the regime's interests and voted accordingly, as opposed to Arab Knesset members from the leftist opposition parties.[12] Thus, beginning with the first general elections of 1949 through the elections of 1969, these lists enjoyed the support of about 40 percent to 60 percent of the Arab electorate, constituting the largest block of Arab parties. Furthermore, about one-third of the Arab public gave its votes to Jewish-Zionist parties. A small minority of less than 30 percent, and in some years less than 20 percent, voted for the Communist Party. The latter was an anti-Zionist party, representing at that time both Jewish and Arab voters and waging a consistent political struggle against military rule and discrimination against Israel's Arab citizens.[13]

One cannot understand the functioning of the military rule and the whole situation of the Arab Minority in the Jewish State in the two decades following the establishment of the State without taking into account the segregation of the Arab minority, its economic dependence, and the sociological impacts of both. Since the 1948 war most of the Arab population has concentrated in three geographic areas: the Galilee in the northern part of Israel, the Negev in the southern part, and an area known as "The Triangle" in the central part of the country. Small numbers of Arab citizens have lived in a few mixed cities, mostly in neighborhoods of their own. This situation of ecological separation made it easier for the government to use the Military Rule as a mechanism of control, and both helped to develop the reality of segregation, which was strengthened by the restriction of the Arabs' free movement. On the whole, the political elite and the public at least tacitly supported the government's policy toward the Arab minority at large, since the latter were viewed as a potential enemy.[14] The only political parties that had consistently protested against this reality during the fifties and the sixties were the small and outcast (for being anti-Zionist) Communist Party, and the bigger and "legitimate" (Zionist) Social-Democratic party of Mapam.

But discrimination was not political only. As we have already noted, most of the Arab population that remained in Israel was rural since most of the urban middle class left the country during the 1948 war. This population had been suffering from economic deterioration already before 1948 owing to the decline of traditional agriculture as the main base of the Palestinian economy. The essence of that change was the transformation of many providers from agriculture to daily work within the urban economy. Thus they became the lowest urban proletariats while still living in the village (Rosenfeld 1964, 1968). The breaking up of the Arab urban economy as a result of the 1948 war, and the loss of land, forced many Arabs to seek their living in the Jewish sector. But the restrictions on geographic mobility under the Military Rule prevented Arab Israelis them from competing with the Jewish labor force under conditions of severe shortage in employment opportunities caused by the massive Jewish immigration after 1948. The main consequence of this situation was a high rate of unemployment within the Arab sector.[15] Furthermore, much of the available work was temporary or seasonal and was mediated by local contractors who had good relations with the military rule officers and who took a high percentage of the workers' fees for themselves as a commission. Employment bureaus were few and discriminative in their policy. In general, getting work in the Jewish sector depended on acquiring a movement permit from the military rule administration, on good relations with the middlemen, or on good luck in getting a job through the employment bureau.

The other employment alternative was developing jobs and small businesses inside the Arab sector. But this direction of economic development was limited, too, by lack of governmental assistance, while at the same time Jewish entrepreneurs who wanted to start a business in the Jewish economic sector got such assistance. Those businesses that were owned by Arab entrepreneurs had suffered from various obstacles and difficulties.[16]

In general, during the military rule era the government's investments in material and human infrastructure in the Arab sector for the purpose of economic development and personal and community welfare had been minimal. For example, at the beginning of the sixties many of the Arab villages still were not wired to electricity. The Arabic education system had suffered since the establishment of the State from discrimination in the allocation of resources, both material and academic, thus creating unequal opportunity structures for Arabs and Jews. Although this differential structure persists into present times, it was especially evident during the period of the military rule (Al-Haj 1995; Swirski 1990). The same policies have applied in the domains of welfare and other public services (Haidar 1987a; Al-Haj and Rosenfeld, 1988; Rosenhek, 1996).

Another important aspect that helps to understand the Arab status in the Jewish State during the era of the military rule was the expropriation of land and real estate property (Amitai 1998; Benziman and Mansour 1992; Lustick 1980). From the beginning of the Zionist project, the acquisition of land was the main Zionist strategy for implementing the national vision, bearing the name "redemption of the land" (Kimmerling, 1983). Before the establishment of the State the Jews were able to acquire Arab land by purchasing it. The establishment of political sovereignty in Palestine and the total victory over the Palestinian Arabs created the further opportunity to acquire land through confiscation of large portions that had belonged to those who left during the war. In the first two years the expropriation was formally sanctioned by various emergency regulations issued during the war, which were judicially questionable. In 1950 and 1952 the Knesset adopted two laws to regulate the practice of land expropriation and made it formally legal. During the first four years of independence, massive expropriations took place, including large shares of land that had been owned by Arab citizens of Israel and continuing after the first years on a smaller scale. Much of the expropriated land and real estate was transferred to Jewish settlers, mainly new immigrants, and used to establish new Jewish towns and villages. Some was expropriated for military needs.

There are no exact data about the amount of Arab land confiscated, but it is estimated that it amounted to some 40 to 60 percent of the total amount of land that had been under Arab ownership before 1948.[17] What is important for our discussion is the fact that the government conducted and legitimized massive expropriation of previously Arab land. By so doing, it reinforced the effects of military rule, tight control, segregation, discrimination, and economic dependence in bringing about the inferior status of the Arab citizens of Israel during the first years of statehood.

Without belittling the importance of security considerations, it appears that military rule was also a means of securing Jewish dominance for the future. It institutionalized Arab dependence on the State's apparatus and institutions and on the Jewish economy, and it legitimized discrimination in the allocation of resources for economic, municipal, and educational development.[18] The military rule and its policy of restricting freedom of movement increased the social distance between Jews and Arabs, their mutual negative images, lack of knowledge about each other, and even mutual fear. Practically, the military rule caused Jews and Arabs to be isolated from each other in almost every domain of everyday life. A critical determinant as well as an expression of this isolation was the decision to exempt the Arab population from compulsory military service, which had been instituted by the State in its early days. While this practice served the interests of both sides, there is little doubt that it also enhanced the sense of estrangement between the two communities. One of its major consequences was that the Jewish population, preoccupied with its own difficulties, was hardly aware of, let alone cared about, the predicament of the Arab citizens. With a few exceptions, the same may be said of Israeli social scientists, whose members paid hardly any attention to the State's Arab citizens; and when they did so, they presented a stereotypical and one-dimensional view (Haidar 1987b; Zureik 1979).

The tight control and economic and political dependency weakened the Arabs' ability to organize to protect their civil rights and develop their own identity.[19] Thus it signified, in Pappe's words, "non-confidence of the state in its Arab citizens" (Pappe 1995, p. 626), that is, an institutional expression of a basic conviction concerning Arab citizens in a Jewish state. This in turn created a collective memory of oppression and left a heavy sediment for the future of Jewish-Arab relations.

Military rule was established and maintained within a wide consensus of the Jewish public and leadership, but it had its opponents. At first they came mostly from the opposition parties on the Left and the radical Right,[20] and from the former minister for minorities' affairs Bechor Shitreet. But as the years went by, especially after the killing of forty-nine Arabs near the village of Kafr Kasim on the first day of war in 1956, more and more politicians (even within the government) and public figures joined in criticism of the government's policy. The military rule was finally abolished at the end of 1966, after a series of relief measures, instituted gradually and after a long public debate and political negotiations and consultations.[21] But as we have said, it remained an important element of the Arab collective memory in Israel.

From the Late 1960s through the Late 1990s:
Israelization and Palestinization

The abolition of the military rule in 1966 and the outcomes of the Six Day War in 1967 have contributed to the development of two major processes among the Arab citizens of Israel: Israelization and Palestinization. As we shall see, these processes have evolved in some respects independently, but they have consistently interacted with each other. This interaction resulted in the formation of a unique minority group that it is neither fully Israeli nor purely Palestinian, since its members have not been fully integrated within the collective boundaries of either community. Al-Haj used the concept of "double peripherality" to capture the unique condition of this group (Al-Haj 1997).

The process of Israelization had already begun during the era of the military rule, the result mainly of two complementary factors: On the one hand, the Israeli Arabs had been isolated from the Palestinian communities outside Israel, including those in the West Bank and the Gaza Strip. On the other hand, they had been exposed, despite the constraints imposed by military rule, to the influence of the Israeli-Jewish society. Thus, they took part in large numbers in Israeli politics by participating in general and local elections, with voting rates that lagged just a little behind the national average. In fact, in some years, the rates of participation among the Arab voters were higher than among the Jewish voters (Neuberger 1998). Through such participation the Arab citizens gained an important experience in learning and using the democratic rules of the political game, despite the negative implications of the military rule. Furthermore, the school system in the Arab community was formally integrated within the larger Israeli educational system. This was expressed in two major respects: First, when the law of compulsory and free education was adopted by the Israeli government, it was also enacted in the Arab community. Second, the curriculum in the Arab schools included the learning of Hebrew as a second language as well as other subjects related to Israeli history, literature, and culture.

However, the process of Israelization has intensified in the post–military rule era, owing mainly to the opening of the Israeli labor market to Palestinian workers and growing ties between the economic sectors of the two communities. For example, Lewin-Epstein and Semyonov (1993) report that nearly one-half of Arab working men and women were employed outside the Arab labor market. Furthermore, with the continued growth of the educational level in the Arab population, its occupational structure has become more like that of the Jewish population. This process resulted primarily from the decline in farming and the rise in white-collar occupations within the Arab labor force. Thus, between 1972 and 1983, the percentage of farm workers declined from 30.6 percent to 11.8 percent, while that of white-collar workers grew from 19.9 percent to 24.4 percent. The parallel figures for the Jewish labor force were 5.7 percent and 3.5 percent for agricultural workers, and 36.4 percent and 37.0 percent for white-collar workers.[22] At the same time, the Arab population experienced a significant rise in its educational level—a process that had begun, as noted above, already during the 1950s and 1960s. Thus, while the median number of years of schooling in 1961 was 1.2, by 1990 it went up to 9.0 (CBS 1991). Note that the figure for 1961 mostly reflects the schooling level of the Arab population that prevailed during the period of the British Mandate. In any event, as a result of the rising levels of schooling and the increase in the amount of interaction with the Jewish community, the recent generations of Israeli Arabs have become fluent in Hebrew and quite familiar with Israeli culture and lifestyle. In fact, some Arab writers (like Anton Shammas) have made significant contributions to Hebrew literature and poetry. Hand in hand with this processes went a decline in fertility rates among Arab women, from 9.2 births in 1960 to 4.7 in 1996; the equivalent figure among the Jewish population in these years was 3.5 and 2.6 births (Kopp 1998, p. 165).

Another critical aspect of the Israelization of the Arab citizens of Israel has been manifested in their electoral behavior. As noted, their rates of participation in the national elections had usually been quite high. However, the 1960s through the 1980s witnessed a gradual decline in the electoral power of the Satellite lists, (i.e., smaller parties that align with a large party to form a bloc) until their final demise in the elections of 1984. The votes that had previously been given to those parties went either to Zionist parties or to the Communist Party and the newly formed Arab national parties. It should be noted that the division between the Zionist and non-Zionist parties did not necessarily imply a distinction between an Israeli and an anti-Israeli orientation. That is, the debate was between those who believed that the interests of the Arab minority could best be served by increasing its influence within the Jewish parties, and those who thought that these interests could be better served through an increase in the electoral power of Arab parties. In both cases, the focus of Arab electoral behavior was a concern for Arab interests, which testifies to the Arab commitment to the Israeli political arena. At the same time, it cannot be ignored that the relative share of the Zionist and non-Zionist parties among the Arab voters was affected by the policies of the Israeli authorities toward the Palestinians in the Occupied Territories. Thus, the Zionist parties received fewer Arab votes in 1988 (40 percent) than in 1984 (49 percent), while the Arab national parties, including the communists, went up at the same time from 51 percent to 60 percent. This change can be attributed to the dismay of the Arab voters at the government's policy in the wake of the first Palestinian Intifada that began in

December 1987. Furthermore, the electoral behavior of the Arabs was reversed in the following elections of 1992, when the Zionist parties received 52 percent of the Arab votes, as opposed to 48 percent given to the Arab parties. These results can probably be attributed to the hopes that prevailed among the Arab citizens of Israel that the Labor government, under the leadership of Yitzhak Rabin, would advance the peace process between Israel and the Palestinians. The same logic applied to the outcomes of subsequent elections in Israel. Thus, in 1996, following the assassination of prime minister Rabin and the crisis of the peace process, the voting trend was again reversed, with the Arab national parties receiving 62 percent of the Arab electorate compared with 38 percent given to the Zionist parties. This pattern was more pronounced in the elections of 1999, when the Arab and Jewish parties obtained 77 percent and 23 percent of the Arab vote, respectively. Moreover, the two most nationalistic Arab parties, Balad (National Democratic Covenant) and Ra'am (United Arab List) won seven Knesset seats, while the Communist Party (Hadash), which includes a few Jewish members and supporters, received only three seats.[23]

The electoral behavior of Israeli Arabs reflects a broader and more complex process of Israelization that had characterized this community over time. As noted by Smooha (1998), while their Palestinian identity and solidarity is deeply rooted, Israeli Arabs have gradually accepted the reality of being a minority within a Jewish state. To be sure, this reality has never been their cherished dream. Nevertheless, they have adopted a realistic approach based on the assumption that their future is ultimately tied with this state and, accordingly, they should struggle to advance their individual and collective goals on the basis of their rights as Israeli citizens. This approach was reflected in the results of a public opinion survey conducted by Smooha in 1995 (Smooha 1998). Thus, almost 80 percent of the Arab community believed that its goals could be achieved through the democratic procedures provided by the state's political system. This figure was considerably higher than the percentage of Israeli Arabs who had held this view—about 61 percent—in 1988. Going beyond the political realm, Smooha reports that in the survey of 1995 nearly 70 percent of the respondents said that they were more similar in lifestyle and daily behavior to Israeli Jews than to the Palestinians in the Occupied Territories. The comparable figure obtained in the survey of 1988 was 55.5 percent. A similar trend was found in regard to the importance of the Israeli component in the personal identity of the Arabs. In 1976, 51.2 percent agreed that the term "Israeli" appropriately describes their personal identity. This response declined to 45.7 percent in 1988 and went up to 63.2 percent in 1995. Note the correspondence between these patterns of change and the fluctuations in the Arabs' vote for Jewish versus Arab parties. Finally, in all the surveys conducted by Smooha between 1976 and 1995, it was found that only a small minority of Israeli Arabs was ready to move to a Palestinian state, were such a state to be established. The percentage expressing such readiness has declined over time from 14.4 percent in 1976 to 4.2 percent in 1995 (Smooha 1998). Furthermore, a vast majority of Israeli Arabs is unwilling to forego their Israeli citizenship in favor of Palestinian citizenship, even if it would not involve having to change their place of residence.[24] It should be noted in this context that Israeli Arabs criticize the Palestinian Authority as being undemocratic and as offending civil rights, and they cherish Israeli democracy and freedom of speech (Gha'nem 2001, p. 13; Rekhess 2002).

Notwithstanding their process of Israelization, the Arab citizens of Israel have at the same time undergone a consistent process of Palestinization. This process has developed along two different though related paths: enhanced affinity to and solidarity with the Palestinian people, and an increased consciousness of their own predicament as a deprived national minority in a Jewish state.

As noted by Neuberger (1998), the Palestinization of Israeli Arabs in terms of identification with the Palestinian (and Arab) people was nourished by a series of events and developments. First, the results of the Six Day War, particularly the occupation of the West Bank and the Gaza Strip as well as other Arab land and the humiliation of Arab armies, deepened their hostility toward Israel and their empathy with their own people. These sentiments were reinforced by the fact that the Israeli occupation put an end to the prolonged isolation of the Israeli Arabs from the Palestinian population in the Occupied Territories and facilitated the renewal of close contacts between the two Arab/Palestinian communities.

The solidarity with their Palestinian compatriots has increased over the years with the growing of the Palestinian resistance to Israeli occupation and the strengthening of the PLO during the 1970s, when it was recognized by the Arab world and most of the world's nations as the only legitimate body representing the Palestinian people. Correspondingly, The PLO has initiated different avenues of contact with the Palestinian Arab community in Israel, following a long period of disregard for, and even some distrust of, the Israeli Palestinians by the PLO and the Arab world as a whole. The PLO symbolized for the members of that community the viability of the Palestinians as a people and served as a source of pride and identification. The impact of these sentiments was dramatically manifested during the first Palestinian Intifada, which began at the end of 1987 and lasted until early 1991, with the beginning of the Gulf War.

In addition to unequivocal declarations of support by its intellectual and political leadership, the Arab community expressed its solidarity with the Palestinian uprising in different ways: financial help, shipment of food and medical products, street demonstrations, and strikes. In fact, while most of these activities were kept within the framework of the law, there were a few instances of sporadic violence, such as throwing stones and Molotov cocktails. Nevertheless, as noted by Gha'nem and Ozacky-Lazar (1990), these acts of sympathy with the Palestinian uprising and of protest against the Israeli government didn't cross the Green Line. That is, the Arab citizens of Israel were careful to prevent the penetration of the Intifada from the Occupied Territories into Israel. At the same time, the majority of Israeli Arabs didn't embrace the PLO's plan of establishing in the whole of Palestine (the entire territory west of the Jordan River) a Palestinian state that would replace the State of Israel. Instead, as shown consistently in the polls conducted by Smooha from 1976 through 1995, most of them supported the establishment of an independent Palestinian State in the West Bank and the Gaza Strip alongside the State of Israel.[25] This attitude probably reflects the simultaneous influence of both Israelization and Palestinization of the Arab citizens of Israel.

The interaction between the two processes, Palestinization and Israelization, that have occurred through the years resulted in a trend that may be described as "collective introversion," within which the Arabs in Israel have developed an agenda of their own.[26] The essence of that agenda has been manifested in the intensification of the demand that the Israeli authorities would respect both their individual rights as Israeli citizens and their collective rights as a national minority.[27] However, one cannot capture the full meaning of this trend of collective introversion without taking into account the fact that the Arab citizens of Israel have been suffering from blatant discrimination and deprivation even after the abolition of the military rule. These discriminatory practices and the resulting feelings of deprivation are perhaps the two most prominent characteristics of the Arabs' status in Israel, encompassing various domains of life on both the institutional and the personal level, including laws and regulations, attitudes of decisionmakers at different levels and of the Jewish public, allocation of state resources to Arab municipalities and institutions, municipal regional planning, housing policy, the educational system, the labor market, and the criminal system (Alterman and Stav 2001; Haidar 1995; Kimmerling 1999; Lewin-Epstein and Semyonov 1993; Rattner and Fishman 1998; Rosenhek 1996; Shavit 1992; Smooha 2001a; Tessler and Grant 1998; Yiftachel 1998)[28]—all of this despite Israel's declared commitment to social and civil equality.

Generally speaking, as we have already noted, the processes of Israelization and Palestinization experienced by Israeli Arabs has enhanced both the awareness of their marginal status in the Israeli and Palestinian societies and the self-confidence needed to voice their feelings. The resulting trend of collective introversion has been nourished by a series of converging processes.

From the viewpoint of the Israelization process, the Israeli Arabs have become more familiar with the Israeli democratic system and more effective in using it for their own purposes. As noted before, this familiarity led them to become disaffected from the Palestinian Authority for its lack of democratic norms. Perhaps more important, with the passage of time, the Arabs in Israel have been gradually convinced that the solution to their problems in Israel should come from "within" and not from "outside"—that is, from the Palestinian Authority.[29] At the same time, Israeli society has become more open and tolerant, particularly since the Labor Party lost its hegemony in the late 1970s—a process that facilitated the ability of the Arab citizens to get organized politically in the struggle to improve their conditions. Furthermore, the expansion of education and rising standards of living among Arab citizens, coupled with their closer contacts with the Jewish community, enhanced among them the sense of relative deprivation and the demand to have the same size piece of the pie as the Jewish citizens.

From the viewpoint of the Palestinization process, the Arabs in Israel could have afforded to concentrate on their own needs, following the beginning of the peace process between Israel and the PLO in 1993. In other words, as Palestinian national aspirations for political independence seemed more realistic than ever, the Palestinians in Israel concentrated their efforts to realize their own aspirations as a national minority.[30]

The trend of collective introversion has been manifested in different ways. One of them, already mentioned, has been the growing tendency to vote for Arab parties, which reflects the concern for Israeli Arabs' interests as a Palestinian national-cultural minority within the state of Israel. Another political expression of collective introversion is the rise in public protest actions that have been organized by purely Arab associations and have given expression to Israeli Arabs' reactions to political events related to the Palestinian cause as well as to their own complaints and concerns.[31] These activities took form in different ways: general strikes, parades, demonstrations, and rallies. Occasionally, they included acts of violence and clashes with police forces. The most prominent protest action is known as the "Day of the Land" (Yom Ha'adama), which took place for the first time in March 1976 and has continued yearly since then. From the seventies onward many voluntary Arab associations and organizations have been established on the local and the national levels. These enterprises have dealt with many issues concerning the Arab citizens of Israel, including welfare, education, national and cultural rights, land confiscation, inequality (mainly in the allocation of state resources), and issues concerning specific groups such as students, teachers, etc.[32] The last two decades have seen a significant rise in Islamic activism among Israeli Arabs. Many Islamic organizations have been founded, dealing with religious, welfare, family, and educational issues. The Islamic movement started to be involved in local politics in 1983 and since then has enjoyed significant successes. In 1996 it took part in the national elections within the United Arab List and sent two Knesset members.[33] A very significant expression of collective introversion is what Rekhess called "opening the 1948 files" (Rekhess 2002). This includes a struggle for compensation for confiscated lands; a struggle to let the "inner refugees" rebuild their villages and resettle there; reviving the collective memory of the "Nakba" and inserting it into the public agenda of the Arab and Jewish sectors alike; and restoring the Palestinian pre-1948 history.

Postscript: October 2000 and Onward

The apparent collapse of the Oslo Process, particularly following the second Camp David summit, which was held in July 2000, greatly frustrated the Arab citizens of Israel. They gave vent to their feelings of frustration in October 2000, when, soon after the outbreak of the second Palestinian Intifada following the bloody events at the Al-Aqsa Mosque in Jerusalem, many of them took to the streets in a violent protest, unprecedented in its scope and severity.[34] The protest was probably triggered by the Al-Aqsa events but behind it stood deeper and more complex reasons, which encompass Israeli Arabs' feelings of social exclusion and frustration, probably triggered the protests (Reiter 2001; Ozacky-Lazar and Gha'nem 2001). On the one hand, their hopes for the achievement of the Palestinians' national goals, namely, the establishment of an independent Palestinian state were not realized. On the contrary—it has contributed to the "opening of the 1948 files" and, through this, to the increase of old tensions between Arabs and Jews in Israel. On the other hand, because of the collapse of the peace process, their particularistic expectations that a peace treaty between Israel and the Palestinians would improve their collective status in Israeli society have remained unfulfilled. After a short period of grace during the Rabin government, they were again discriminated against in the allocation of state resources, and the socioeconomic disparities between Arabs and Jews have remained unchanged. Again and again they have been regarded by most of the Jewish public and political parties (including Rabin's Labor Party) as unfaithful citizens, and hostility toward them within the Jewish community has become widespread. The Arab frustration was especially great considering the fact that in the 1999 elections they had supported Ehud Barak almost unanimously, yet his government did little to improve their status and opportunities, despite prior promises, and ignored their political leadership. Thus, Israeli Arabs felt socially excluded and politically blocked, without any ability to influence the political process through the democratic procedure. Hence the violent protests of in October 2000.

Notwithstanding, according to a public opinion poll covering a representative sample of both the Jewish and Arab populations of Israel conducted just a few days after the riots (Yuchtman-Yaar 2000), both groups attributed the protest demonstrations to the same causes. Eighty percent of the Arab respondents said the riots were a response to the events at the Al-Aqsa Mosque in Jerusalem and a show of solidarity with the Palestinian people in the territories, while only 16 percent attributed them to Israel's policies of discrimination against Israeli Arabs. Similar results were taken from the Jewish respondents—72 percent and 22 percent respectively. But the two groups saw the reasons for the demonstrations' having spiraled into violent clashes, resulting in loss of mostly Arab life and property, somewhat differently. The Arab respondents placed the blame primarily on the police (42 percent) and the government (33 percent), while the Jewish respondents attributed it to the leadership of the Israeli Arabs (62 percent) and the Arab demonstrators themselves (25 percent). These statistics testify to the huge chasm that exists between the two communities—in effect creating two different narratives of what happened in the October events. Furthermore, it is clear that the rift between them extends much further than this specific episode. Thus, for 70 percent of the Jews and 58 percent of the Arabs in the sample, the term "Israeli" applies only to Jews, while only 29 percent of the Jews and 40 percent of the Arabs think that the term applies to both Jews and Arabs.

It should be noted that the survey had been conducted a few days after the October events took place and it was then still premature to decide whether they signified a real turning point in the process of Israelization or an emotional turbulence caused by the bloody events. But today it can be argued that those events did reflect a turning point in the relations between Arabs and Jews in Israeli society, at least for the near future. Even today, the Jewish public is still largely reluctant to visit Arab villages, accommodations, and restaurants as it had done in the past. In general, it appears that this avoidance stems from a combination of fear (even if it is mostly unfounded) and hostility. At the same time, no serious effort by the interested parties on either side has yet been made to change this atmosphere. Thus there have been no changes in the discriminatory policy toward the Arab minority, and no public campaign intended to lower the levels of tensions and hostility has been launched among either the Jewish or Arab communities.[35] It seems almost obvious to note that the continuation of the second Palestinian Intifada and the growing amount of bloodshed associated with it on both sides make it politically and psychologically very difficult to change the current trend of mutual hostility between the Arab and Jewish communities in Israel.

As the results of the survey cited earlier indicate, the Jewish public tends to relate to the Israeli Arab population as a single entity, perceiving it as inseparable branch of the Palestinian population in the Occupied Territories. The Jewish public finds it difficult to believe that Israeli Arabs can maintain a dual loyalty—to their people on the one hand and their state on the other. Nevertheless, we don't necessarily see an inherent contradiction between the two allegiances. It cannot be overlooked that the growing demand for recognition as a political minority group with special rights, let alone the demand to nullify the Jewish-Zionist character of the state, testifies to the fact that at least some Arab citizens are beginning to realize that holding on to two ends of the stick (Palestinian and Israeli) is problematic. Nevertheless, we believe that although a complete solution to the conflict between the Jewish majority and Arab minority is unattainable in the foreseeable future, it is still possible to achieve a situation of coexistence—with much less animosity and perhaps even a reasonable level of mutual acceptance.

In order to reach that situation, at least three conditions must be met: First, the signing of a peace treaty and an end to the historic conflict between Israel and the Palestinians. Such a reality would more or less remove the thorn of suspicion and antagonism from the way the Jewish public relates to Israeli Arabs. It would at the same time meet the national needs of the Arab minority, provided that the end of the conflict would bring about the establishment of an independent Palestinian state. Second, Israel must eliminate discrimination against the Arab minority and implement a policy of "affirmative action," at least for a period of a few years, in order to reduce as much as possible the cumulative effects remaining from its long-term policy of discrimination. Keeping in mind that Israel considers itself as a Jewish and democratic state, it goes without saying that Israel owes it not only to its Arab population but also to itself to grant its Arab citizens full equality and civil rights. Third, Israeli Arabs must abandon the idea of transforming Israel into a "state of all its citizens," as well as the demand for recognition as a national minority with special political rights (as opposed, for example, to the demand for recognition as a cultural and religious minority). Without dwelling on the ideological aspect of this demand, the reality is that the vast majority of the Jewish public is unwilling to compromise on Israel's character as a Jewish state. Therefore, its sees the concept of "a state of all its citizens" as a threat to Israel's very existence, in both the concrete and spiritual meanings of the concept. We believe that if the State of Israel truly adopts the principle of an egalitarian policy as a national strategic objective and not just a tactical move, it will be possible to attain a pattern of relationships between the two communities built upon mutual recognition and understanding.

However, it would be naive to think that, by doing so, the strife between the Jewish and Arab populations in Israel would necessarily disappear as long as the Jewish majority continues to view preserving the Jewish character of the state as one of its most cherished goals (and all indications point to a broad-based consensus among the Jewish public on the Zionist principle that Israel should be a Jewish and democratic state), it is more likely that the Arab minority will not be accepted as a full partner in the society.[36] In the best of scenarios, even if Israel would grant its Arab citizens full and equal rights, they might be able to enjoy their status as equal citizens under the law, but they would still be considered as outsiders vis-à-vis the Jewish community.

NOTES

1. The Jewish population in the British Mandate era expanded and developed alongside the Arab-Palestinian population as a separate community. Most of the contact between the two populations was economic in nature, and even these contacts were cut off almost entirely in the wake of the Arab rebellion of the 1930s. Regarding this subject see: Metzer 1998; Kimmerling 1983.

2. Some researchers would add to the list of rifts the relationship between new immigrants from the former Soviet Union and the veteran Israelis. There is no doubt that this group of new immigrants has tendencies toward isolation, accompanied on the one hand by feelings of cultural superiority compared to Israeli society, and, on the other hand, by complaints that the Israeli public are hostile to them and insensitive to their problems of absorption. Nevertheless, one should not undervalue the importance of the speedy integration into the economic and political systems, which is unparalleled by any group of immigrants in other countries, particularly when considering that we are referring to a very short span of time. We are also not convinced that the cultural and social isolation of the Russian immigrant community will last for two or three generations. In this context, it would be interesting to compare their conditions with those of the wave of immigrants that arrived from Germany in the 1930s. As we know, they too tried to maintain the cultural heritage they brought with them, and many of them continued to hold onto the German language, literature, and culture. Not only that, the German immigrants also felt alienated from the absorbing society, had difficulty integrating into the existing political system, and, therefore, established their own political party. However, the differences between them and the veteran population at that time disappeared already in the second generation. It is true, though, that the wave of immigration from Russia is much larger than that which came from Germany, so the potential for maintaining the cultural heritage and social isolation is greater. In addition, it is much easier nowadays to maintain an affinity to one's original country, either by visiting there often or through the mass media, such as television. Yet despite these factors, we believe that even under these conditions it is only a matter of time until they will fully integrate into Israeli society.

3. Actually, the decision to choose Palestine (Eretz Israel) as the only territory where the Zionist project can be implemented was adopted by the 7th Zionist Congress in 1905, following bitter debates about alternative territorial solutions such as the "Uganda Plan."

4. The figure of 750,000 is based on official estimates of the United Nations.

5. At the end of the 1948 War, the Jewish population of Israel numbered about 650,000, while the total size of the Israeli population stood at 800,000. At the beginning of 2002, the total size of the Israeli population was about 6.5 million, divided between 5.3 million Jews and 1.2 million Arabs (Palestinians). Note that the proportion of the Arab minority in 2002 was

nearly the same as in 1948 (a little over 18 percent). However, whereas the growth of the Arab population was due mostly to higher fertility rates, compared to the rates within the Jewish population, the growth of the latter resulted mainly from mass immigration, particularly during the 1950s and 1990s.

6. The characterization of Israel as a Jewish and democratic state was constitutionally codified in two major pieces of legislation known as: Basic Law: Human Dignity and Freedom, and Basic Law: Freedom of Vocation, passed by the Israeli Parliament in 1992. These two laws explicitly refer to the Declaration of Independence as the source defining Israel as a Jewish and Democratic State.

7. Some were forces to leave as a result of expulsions and threats by the IDF forces, while others left as a result of the call by Arab leaders suggesting, and even encouraging, temporary flight, until "the danger passes." Regarding the argument on this issue see: Morris 1987; Shapira 1995.

8. As a result of the armistice agreements signed between Israel and the neighboring Arab states, Israel expanded its area by about one-third compared to the area allotted to it by the UN. These areas included a substantial number of local Arab populations. The armistice agreement between Israel and Jordan gave Israel another area (that was not conquered by the IDF) with 30,000 more Arabs who lived in it.

9. The legal base of the military rule was formed by the Mandatory Defense (Emergency) Regulations, 1945. See: Amitai 1998; Benziman and Mansour 1992; Pappe 1995.

10. Official statistics show a high rate of security offenses. They also show a high rate of criminal offenses compared with the Jewish population. In addition to "objective" sociological explanations, such as marginalization, alienation, unemployment, and material hardships, Korn suggests that, once reported to the police, criminal offenses by Arab citizens were "over-processed" compared with those of the Jewish population. That is, the police tended to prosecute criminal offenses in the Arab sector more than it did the same type of offenses in the Jewish sector. Korn sees this tendency as an effect of the general atmosphere of control over the Arab population; see Korn 1995.

11. For a discussion of cooptation as a method of control, see Lustick 1980.

12. One of the greatest paradoxes was in 1963 when the three Knesset members from the satellite Arab parties voted against ending the military rule! The other five Arab members from the opposition parties had voted for it. For a detailed discussion on Arab leftist activity in Israel, see Kaufman 1997; Neuberger 1993

13. In 1965 the Communist Party was split, mainly according to the Jewish-Arab divide. The Jewish Communist Party disappeared over the years, while the other (Rakach), though remaining nominally a Jewish-Arab party, actually became a party that represented the civil and national interests of Israel's Arab citizens; the vast majority of its supporters have been Israeli Arabs.

14. Polls that were conducted a short period after the military rule was removed (1966) and shortly after the Six Day War (1967) pointed to the existence of a significant amount of social distance between the two communities and lack of readiness for close relationships (es-

pecially on the Jewish side). In addition, they differed considerably in regard to attitudes and opinions concerning the Arab-Israeli conflict (Peres 1971).

15. In 1961 Arabs constituted 17.7 percent of the unemployed (Benziman and Mansour 1992, p. 177)—higher than their proportion of the total population.

16. For further analysis of the economic situation of the Arab sector during the military rule era, see Haidar 1995; Lustick 1980; Benziman and Mansour 1992.

17. For data about land expropriations in the fifties and sixties, see Jiryis 1976; Amitai 1998; Benziman and Mansour 1992.

18. For a detailed discussion of the centrality of the term "dependency" as used to understand the Arab minority's position within the Jewish state, see Lustick 1980.

19. For discussions of the Arab collective identity in the first two decades of statehood, see Peres and Yuval-Davies 1969; Peres 1970; Hofman, and Debbiney 1970.

20. The radical Right opposed the military rule mainly because of its political utility for the ruling party, Mapai.

21. For further details, see Pappe 1995; Benziman and Mansour 1992.

22. Adopted from Lewin-Epstein and Semyonov 1993, p. 53, table 3.3. For more figures, see Haidar 1995, p. 121, table 5.10.

23. For figures through the 1996 elections, see Neuberger 1998, p. 123; for the 1999 election figures, see the Knesset website: <www.Knesset.gov.il/elections/index.html>.

24. This was demonstrated, for example, in a survey conducted by the Tami Steinmetz Center in 1999, within the framework of the "Peace index" project. According to this survey, about 66 percent of the Arab respondents would be unwilling to exchange their Israeli citizenship for Palestinian citizenship within the framework of a peace treaty that would involve handing over regions with high concentrations of Arab population, such as the "Large Triangle," to the Palestinian state.

25. As cited in Neuberger 1998, p. 74.

26. Rekhess uses the term "localization" to describe the Israeli Arabs' concentration on solving their own problems and improving their own status within the Israeli state and society after the Oslo agreements and the establishment of the Palestinian authority. But we maintain that this term associates intuitively with a geographical location and does not catch the full sociological meaning of this trend. This meaning encompasses a social collective that uses most of its resources for its own needs and for its collective future as a self-defining social group. See Rekhess, 2002.

27. In recent years the Arab demand has been to get full recognition as a political-national minority. More and more Arab circles, led by Knesset member Azmi Bishara, have raised the demand to nullify the Jewish-Zionist character of Israel and instead declare it as "a state of all it's citizens."

28. See also various reports of Sikkuy—the Association for the Advancement of Civic Equality—edited by Shalom Dichter.

29. Rekhess 2002. This statement is reminiscent of a somewhat similar situation when the

young Palestinian national movement had decided in the 1920s to stand on its own when its leaders became disappointed with the Syrian national movement.

30. For further analysis, see Rekhess 2002.

31. During the fifties and the sixties there were protest actions organized by the Jewish leftist parties.

32. Neuberger presents a list of the main bodies; see Neuberger 1998, p. 67.

33. For more details, see Rekhess 2000; Haidar 2000.

34. Thirteen Israeli Arab demonstrators were killed in clashes with the police. One Jew was also killed, apparently by Arabs. The government established a national commission of inquiry as a result of these events to investigate their causes, including the behavior of the police. The commission had not yet completed its deliberations at the time of this writing.

35. For further discussion of the October 2000 events' implications, see Smooha 2001b.

36. A number of scholars claim that because Israel defined itself as a Jewish and democratic state, as expressed in the Declaration of Independence, it should not be seen as a democracy in every respect, but rather as a special kind of democracy, such as an "ethnic democracy." Others go even further and claim that Israel doesn't even represent a democratic regime, but rather other kinds of models, such as "Ethnocracy," "National Democracy," and others. On this subject, see Gha'nem, Rouhana, and Yiftachel 1999; Rouhana 1998; Smooha 1999; Yiftachel 1999.

REFERENCES

Al Haj, Majid. 1995. *Education, Empowerment and Control: The Case of the Arabs in Israel.* Albany: State University of New York Press.

Al-Haj, Majid. 1997. "Identity and Orientation Among the Arabs in Israel: A State of Double Peripherality." *Medinah, Mimshal Ve'Yehasim Beinle'umyim* 41–42: 97–117 (Hebrew).

Al Haj, Majid, and Henry Rosenfeld. 1988. *Arab Local Government in Israel.* Tel-Aviv: International Center for Peace in the Middle East.

Alterman, Rachel, and Tami Stav. 2001. *Confrontation and Agreement Through Language: How Urban and Regional Plans in Israel Relate to the Arab Sector.* Tel Aviv: Tel Aviv University, The Tami Steinmetz Center for Peace Research (Hebrew).

Amitai, Yossi. 1998. "The Arab Minority in Israel: The Years of Military Rule, 1948–1966." In *Independence—the First Fifty Years,* ed. Anita Shapira, 129–48. Jerusalem: Zalman Shazar Center (Hebrew).

Benziman, Uzi, and Atallah Mansour. 1992. *Subtenants.* Jerusalem: Keter Publishing House (Hebrew).

Central Bureau of Statistics (CBS). 1991. *Statistical Abstract of Israel.*

Eisenstadt, S. N. 1967. *Israeli Society.* New York, N.Y.: Basic Books.

———. 1985. *The Transformation of Israeli Society.* London: Weidenfeld and Nicolson.

Gha'nem, As'ad. 2001. "Why Did the Events Break Up and What Was Their Influence?" *I'yunim Babitahon Hale'umi* 1 (Hebrew).

Gha'nem, As'ad, and Sarah Ozacky-Lazar. 1990. "Green Line, Red Line: The Arabs in Israel and the Intifada." *Surveys of Arabs in Israel* 3.

Gha'nem, As'ad, Nadim Rouhana, and Oren Yiftachel. 1999. "Questioning 'Ethnic Democracy.'" *Israel Studies* 3: 253–67.

Haidar, Aziz. 1987a. *Social Welfare Services for Israel's Arab Population.* Tel Aviv: International Center for Peace in the Middle East.

———. 1987b. *The Palestinians in Israeli Social Science Writings.* Washington, D.C., and Kingston, Ont.: International Center for Research and Public Policy, Near East Cultural and Educational Foundation of Canada.

———. 1995. *On the Margins: The Arab Population in the Israeli Economy.* London: Hurst and Company.

———. 2000. "The Islamic Current—Politics and Religion." Paper presented at the Congress of the Program for the Research of Arab Politics in Israel (Hebrew).

Hofman, John, and S. Debbiney. 1970. "Religious Affiliation and Ethnic Identity." *Psychological Reports* 26: 1014.

Horowitz, Dan, and Moshe Lissak. 1977. *Origins of Israeli Polity—Palestine under Mandate.* Chicago Ill.: University of Chicago Press.

———. 1989. *Trouble in Utopia—The Overburdened Polity of Israel.* Albany, N.Y.: State University of New York Press.

Jiryis, Sabri. 1976. *The Arabs in Israel.* New York: Monthly Review Press.

Kaufman, Ilana. 1997. *Arab National Communism in the Jewish State.* Gainesville: University Press of Florida.

Kimmerling, Baruch. 1982. *Zionism and Economy.* Cambridge, Mass.: Schenkman Publishing.

———. 1983b. *Zionism and Territory.* Berkeley: Institute of International Studies, University of California.

———. 1999. "Religion, Nationalism and Democracy in Israel." *Constellations* 6 (3): 339–63.

Kopp, Ya'akov, ed. 1998. *Allocation of Resources to Social Services 1998.* Jerusalem: The Center for the Research of Social Policy in Israel.

Korn, Alina. 1995. "Crime and Law Enforcement in the Israeli Arab Population under the Military Government, 1948–1966." In *Israel—The First Decade of Independence,* ed. Ilan Troen and Noah Lucas, 659–79. Albany, N.Y.: State University of New York Press.

Lewin-Epstein, Noah, and Moshe Semyonov. 1993. *The Arab Minority in Israel's Economy: Patterns of Ethnic Inequality.* Boulder Colo.: Westview Press.

Lustick, Ian. 1980. *Arabs in the Jewish State, Israel's Control of a National Minority.* Austin and London: University of Texas Press.

Metzer, Jacob. 1998. *The Divided Economy of Mandatory Palestine.* Cambridge: Cambridge University Press.

Morris, Benny. 1987. *The Birth of the Palestinian Refugee Problem.* Cambridge: Cambridge University Press.

Neuberger, Benyamin. 1993. "The Arab Minority in Israeli Politics 1948–1992—From Marginality to Influence." *Asian and African Studies* 27 (1–2): 149–69.

———. 1998. *The Arab Minority: National Alienation and Political Integration.* Tel Aviv: The Open University (Hebrew).

Ozacky-Lazar, Sarah, and As'ad Gha'nem. 2001. "Intifadat Al-Aqsa among the Palestinian Citizens in Israel: Reasons and Consequences," *Skirot Al Ha'aravim Be'yisrael* 27 (Hebrew).

Pappe, Ilan. 1995. "An Uneasy Coexistence: Arabs and Jews in the First Decades of Statehood." In *Israel—The First Decade of Independence,* ed. Ilan Troen and Noah Lucas, 617–58. Albany, N.Y.: State University of New York Press.

Peres, Yochanan. 1970. "Modernization and Nationalism in the Identity of the Israeli Arab," *Middle East Journal* 24: 479–92.

———. 1971. "Ethnic Relations in Israel." *American Journal of Sociology* 76 (6): 1021–47.

Peres, Yochanan, and Nira Yuval-Davies. 1969. "Some Observations on the National Identity of the Israeli Arabs." *Human Relations* 22 (3): 219–33.

Rattner, Arye, and Gideon Fishman. 1998. *Justice for All? Jews and Arabs in the Israeli Criminal System,* Westport, Conn.: Praeger.

Reiter, Yitzhak. 2001. "Between Two Intifadas: From Identification to Violence." Paper presented at a Conference on "The Arabs in Israel: A New National Agenda," Tel-Aviv University Dec. 20, (Hebrew).

Rekhess, Elie. 2000. "The Islamic Movement in Israel and its Linkage to Political Islam in the Occupied Territories." In *The Jewish-Arab Rift in Israel: A Reader,* ed. Ruth Gavison and Dafna Hacker, 172–209. Jerusalem: The Israel Democracy Institute (Hebrew).

———. 2002. "The Arabs in Israel after the Oslo Process: Localization of the National Struggle." *Hamizrah Hehadash* 43: 275–304 (Hebrew).

Rosenfeld, Henry. 1964. "From Peasantry to Wage Labor and Residual Peasantry: The Transformation of an Arab Village." In *Process and Pattern in Culture: Essays in Honor of Julian H. Steward,* ed. Robert Manners, 211–34. Chicago: Aldine Publishing Company.

———. 1968. "Change, Barriers to Change and Contradictions in the Arab Village Family." *American Anthropologist* 70 (4): 732–52.

Rosenhek, Zeev. 1996. *The Housing Policy Toward the Arabs in Israel in the 1950's–1970's.* Jerusalem: The Floersheimer Institute for Policy Studies.

Rouhana, Nadim. 1998. "Israel and Its Arab Citizens: Predicaments in the Relationship between Ethnic States and Ethno-National Minorities." *Third World Quarterly* 19: 277–96.

Shapira, Anita. 1995. "Politics and Collective Memory: Israeli society." *History and Memory* 7 (1): 9–40.

Shavit, Yossi. 1992. "Arabs in the Israeli Economy: A Study in the Enclave Hypothesis." *Israel Social Science Research* 7 (1): 45–66.

Smooha, Sammy. 1978. *Israel: Pluralism and Conflict.* Berkeley and Los Angeles: University of California Press.

———. 1998. "The Israelization of the Collective Identity and the Political Orientation of the Palestinian Citizens of Israel—a Reassessment." In *The Arabs in Israeli Politics: Dilemmas of Identification,* ed. Elie Rekhess, 41–53. Tel Aviv: Dayan Center.

———. 1999. "The Viability of Ethnic Democracy as a Model of Conflict-Management: Comparing Israel and Northern Ireland." In *Comparing Jewish Societies,* ed. Todd Endelmann, 267–312. Ann Arbor: University of Michigan Press.

———. 2001a. "Arab-Jewish Relations in Israel as a Jewish Democratic State." In *Megamot Bahevra Ha'yisraelit,* ed. Ephraim Ya'ar and Ze'ev Shavit, 292–313. Tel Aviv: The Open university of Israel (Hebrew).

———. 2001b. "Attitudes toward Arab-Jewish Relationships in Israel and the October 2000 Riots." *I'yunim Babitahon Hale'umi* 1: 17–32 (Hebrew).

Swirski, Shlomo. 1981. *Sephardim and Ashkenazim in Israel: The Ethnic Division of Labor.* Haifa: Machbarot Lemechkar Ulebikoret (Hebrew).

———. 1990. *Education in Israel—The Area of Separate Realms.* Tel Aviv: Breirot (Hebrew).

Tessler, Mark, and Audra Grant. 1998. "Israel's Arab Citizens: The Continuing Struggle." *The Annals of the American Academy of Political and Social Science* 555: 97–113.

Yiftachel, Oren. 1998. "Planning and Social Control—Exploring the Dark Side." *Journal of Planning Literature* 12 (4): 395–406.

———. 1999. "'Ethnocracy': The Politics of Judaizing Israel/Palestine," *Constellations* 6 (3): 364–90.

Yuchtman-Yaar, Ephraim. 2000. "Attitudes Towards the Relationships between Arab and Jewish Citizens of Israel." Paper presented at a symposium on "Basha'ar," Tel Aviv, October 26.

Zureik, Elia T. 1979. *The Palestinians in Israel—A Study in Internal Colonialism.* London: Routledge and Kegan Paul.

CHAPTER SIXTEEN

The Sanctification of Space in Israel Civil Religion and Folk Judaism

❦

Yoram Bilu

Introduction

The terrain in Israel, as befitting the Holy Land, is densely dotted with *lieux de memoire* (Nora 1989), sites and places charged with transcendental significance. Lacking in practical and instrumental uses yet replete with symbolism, these places derive their cognitive and emotional salience from the wider meaning-giving systems—religious tenets, folk-mystical doctrines, national ideologies—in which they are embedded. As spatial emblems of historical and metahistorical narratives that represent highly mythologized events and characters, they are supposed to inspire awe and invoke exaltation in those who embrace the symbols and values that these commemorative narratives convey. It is impossible to chart the historical vicissitudes and political transformations that the Holy Land has undergone without taking into account the constitutive role of its sacred geography. Common to all these "sites of memory" is the fact that they cross over the ontological hiatus between the leaving and the dead. This attribute links together Elijah's Cave in Mount Carmel with the Cave of Abayeh and Rabba near Biria; Joseph's Tomb in Shechem-Nablus with the Statue of the Roaring Lion in Tel-Hai; the Fire Scroll Monument in the Forest of the Holy Martyrs with the Paratroopers' Monument near Rehovot; the Tomb of Rachel, wife of Rabbi Akivah, with the Tomb of Baruch Goldstein in Kiriat Arba; and the Mount of Olives Cemetery with the Military Cemetery and the National Holocaust Commemoration Center (Yad Va-Shem) in Mount Herzl.

These selected examples deliberately bring together two analytically distinct avenues of spatial sanctification related, on the one hand, to civil religion, political myths, and state cults and, on the other hand, to folk religion, mystical traditions, and the cult of the saints. The sites in both avenues—multitudinous and widely dispersed in the landscape—are hierarchically organized: civil monuments and saints' shrines alike span the whole range between sites that are local—with low visibility and circumscribed popularity—and sites that are of national significance. Together they constitute an elaborate complex of Jewish and Israeli "sacred geography." In what follows I seek to chart a preliminary map of this geography, delineating the major processes and patterns of sanctification in the two avenues and situating them historically. Although the crux of the work is more descriptive then analytic, I believe that the very juxtaposition of the two systems will serve to promote the idea that processes of sanctification in traditional and civil religion are comparable and interconnected. I touch upon this similitude and points of linkage in my concluding remarks.

The Holy Place in Judaism

The sanctification of space in Israel's civil religion and folk religion has been informed by the idea of the holy in classical Judaism; but in both systems this association was ridden with tensions and inconsistencies. The holiness of the land was a major tenet in Jewish theology from time immemorial (Eliade 1959; Kunin 1994). At the same time, however, the notion that the holy could be physically grounded has been a perennial source of ambivalence in a religion where one of the designations of a boundless, immaterial god is *Ha-Makom* ("the Place").

Gurevitch and Aran (1991) suggest that this ambivalence may reflect an immanent gap in Judaism between the abstract tenor of "The Place"—a transcendental idea, out of place, above and beyond it—and "a place"—one that is a concrete and unself-conscious part of a local landscape. Noting the value-laden differentiation between the highly appreciated "people of the book" and the near-pejorative "people of the land" (*Am Ha-aretz*), Gurevitch and Aran conclude that Jews found it hard "to go native," to be conveniently and continuously settled in a bounded place. This pattern was augmented, if not constituted, by a long history in exile, away from the chosen land. Living in widely dispersed communities, politically powerless and without control over territory, and wandering from place to place as a result of persecutions and economic exigencies—these experiences generated a special dependency on time rather than on space as the major cosmological vehicle for religious sanctification (Heschel 1951; Zerubavel 1981). Against the background of historical traumas, a peculiar Jewish temporal rhythm has emerged that pulsates from "low" to "high," from disaster to redemption. This cultural code was resorted to and elaborated following the destruction of the Second Temple and the loss of the territory, which transformed the spatial matrix in Jewish cosmology into a metaphoric wish encapsulated in the ritual calendar (holidays), the life-cycle ceremonies, and the holy text. The provinces of holiness were reduced (or magnified) to memories, and the realization of the promise embodied in "the Promised Land" was relegated to an unspecified future.

Needless to say, this "temporal bias" was far from absolute. Even though Judaism was constituted as a religion of commemoration (Yerushalmi 1982)—all the more so after the destruction of the Temple and the loss of the Holy Land— the idea of the holy could hardly be maintained without spatial manifestations. In diasporic Judaism the synagogue and the cemetery, though manifold, replaceable, and devoid of predetermined sanctity, became the twin abodes of holiness in each and every community, universal markers of Jewish life. The cemetery has been the setting for various practices of folk veneration, which took place around the tombs of sainted figures. These popular practices were hardly mentioned in the biblical and talmudic literature. But it is an open question whether this silence reflects a genuine absence of saint worship and folk pilgrimages in ancient and rabbinical Judaism or, more probably, the elitist views of the promulgators of this literature who opposed these popular practices. This hostility was possibly nurtured by the potential threats that local cults could pose for the monotheistic notion of the Divine (associated with the built-in ambivalence about place-bound holiness in Judaism) and, before the destruction of the Temple, for its exclusively hegemonic status as *axis mundi.*

Despite this ambivalence, popular cultic activities related to saint worship were viably maintained throughout the centuries. The first systematic documentation of holy sites and itineraries associated with saint worship in the Holy Land comes from the eleventh century C.E., when Jewish travelers from Europe visited these places following the First Crusade. But there are indications that the institutionalization of cultic activities around the sanctuaries had started several hundred years earlier (Reiner 1988). As against the paucity of allusions to saint worship in classical Judaism, popular traditions of visits to saints' sanctuaries ebb and flow throughout the second millennium.

The Sanctification of Space in the Zionist Ideology

The sanctification of space in Zionism was based on a dual heritage. First, it emerged in the historical context of the national liberation movements in Europe that gave rise to the modern nation-state and its ideological ethos, sanctifying national territory and deeming holy martyrs the soldier-citizens who died defending its borders. Second, it was nurtured by the renewed association to the Jewish traditional *lieux de memoire* (Azaryahu 1995). From the outset, the revolutionary-utopian vision of the Zionist movement was articulated and amplified through the deployment of a wide array of Jewish traditional symbols. The religious vocabulary and spiritual symbolism gave the Zionist project an eschatological significance. Note, for example, the appropriation of the word "ascent" (*aliya*), with its spiritual connotations, originally associated with the pilgrimage to the temple (*aliya la-regel*) and the reading of the Torah (*aliya la-Torah*), to designate immigration to Israel and the conquest of the land (*aliya al ha-qarqah*) respectively. These traditional sediments were laid down primarily in the pre-State heyday of socialist-collectivist Zionism. They were evident in the mystification of the biblical landscape, in the national and agricultural reframing of religious festivals, in the literature devoted to commemorating the victims in the struggle for the land, and in the tombs and monuments of exemplary pioneers that became loci of cultic and pilgrimage activities (Almog 2000; Liebman and Don-Yehiya 1983; Zerubavel 1995).

The symbolic structures of political sovereignty, shaped in Israel in the formative years after independence, were grounded in the national shrines of commemoration and in state rituals. As shown by Azaryahu (1995), the political elite of the young country devoted much effort to shaping Israel's civil culture by integrating the establishment of the State into the Jewish collective memory as articulated by the narrative of secular Zionism (Azaryahu 1995; Zerubavel 1995). The foundation myth of Israel was linked to two new, interrelated national cults: the rites of independence and the cult of the fallen soldiers. Independence Day, the major national holiday, was incorporated into the ritual calendar of traditional festivals and woven into the thematic matrix of liberation and heroism evident in Passover, Hanukkah, and other festivals. It was declared a national sabbatical and accorded a special prayer by the Chief Rabbinate. In addition, attempts were made to cast Independence Day in the traditional mold of Passover, with special blessings, *Haggadah*-like text, and a festive meal. This semi-religious molding, together with the national military themes of the holiday, have diminished throughout the years, while the popular recreational activities such as picnicking and barbecuing have become the center of the festival. The second constituent of the state cults revolves around the commemoration of the fallen soldiers. The cult of the fallen soldiers is grounded, on the one hand, in the ethos of patriotic sacrifice exalted in all modern nation-states and, on the other hand, in the Jewish heritage of sacrifice, martyrdom, and national heroism. The major arenas of spatial commemoration here are the military cemeteries and war monuments. In 1989 no fewer than 866 war monuments were documented in Israel (Shamir 1989). Until 1957, 121 monuments had been erected for the fallen soldiers of the War of Independence alone. Three hundred new war monuments were added in the ominous eight-year period between 1967 and 1974, which gave rise to the Six Day War, the War of Attrition, and the Day of Atonement War. The mythologization of the wars is reflected in a new heroic topography, which includes a wide array of commemorative representations varying in their degree of inclusiveness or specificity. Private, municipal, and national war monuments abound side by side with memorials commemorating fallen soldiers of specific units, corpuses, or the army as a whole. There are monuments devoted to one particular battle, to one war, or to the whole series of wars. Monuments also differ in terms of grandeur and complexity, and span a wide range of signification, from metaphoric and abstract depiction of the soldiers' heroic spirit to iconic representations of the myth of combat-related locales. Most visible among the sacred relics of famous battles that figure in the latter category are the armored trucks on the road to Jerusalem, the water towers of Negba and Yad Mordechi, two kibbutzim in the northern Negev, and the Syrian tank in Degania. All of these relics date back to the War of Independence.

Here, too, as in other domains of spatial commemoration, a trend toward growing institutionalization and centralization is evident over the years. This trend appears as a State-initiated response to the uncontrolled flourishing of war monuments in the first decades after independence. In 1982 a special chapter on commemorative monuments, designated "national sites," was formally added to the Law of National Parks and Nature Reserves. The plan to build the IDF Museum and Israel National Memorial in Mount Eitan, west of Jerusalem, constitutes the culmination of the attempts to regulate, control, and centralize the commemoration of military death in Israel. If this ambitious project is realized, the new commemorative complex will become, together with Mount Herzl, the national shrine for the cult of the fallen soldiers in the country.

The cult of the fallen soldiers is extended to the "family of bereavement," the close kin of the dead viewed as "living monuments" (Volkan 1990). The normative behavioral patterns of mourning and loss expected from them have been changed throughout the years. Private bereavement does not seamlessly resonate any more with the collective patterns of commemoration (Rosental 2001). Subdued and introverted in the formative years of the State, it later became more personal, individualized, and emotional. Following the gradual corrosion in the IDF's glorification since the 1970s, particularly following the Day of Atonement, Lebanon Wars, and the Palestinian popular uprisings (Intifadah), a more critical and subversive tenor has been added to the manifestations of bereavement. This strengthening of the personal aspects of bereavement has a spatial dimension too, as in recent years the military system has become more tolerant of slight deviations from the standard design and epitaph typical of soldiers' tombs (Malkinson, Tubin, and Eliezer 1993).

The Zionist ethos viably persists in the temporal *lieux de memoire* constituted by the national ritual calendar. The uniquely Israeli two-day sequence in which Independence Day immediately follows Remembrance Day reinforces the sublime significance of death in war as a sacrifice indispensable for independence. The two-day juxtaposition brings to a closure a highly ritualized period starting with Passover, the commemoration of the paradigmatic transformation from bondage to freedom, and thus the traditional harbinger of independence. Just five days after the end of Passover, on the 26th of Nisan, Holocaust Day commemorates the most horrible catastrophe that befell the Jewish people in modern history. The seven-day gap between Holocaust Day and Remembrance Day, which resonates with the Jewish traditional week of mourning (*shiva'a*), constitutes a linkage of "distant proximity" between the two commemorative events. No such temporal buffer is required between Remembrance Day and Independence Day, since the national ethos that views death in battle as the ultimate sacrifice without which sovereignty could not be achieved renders the juxtaposition of the two days understandable and "natural."

The historical national succession from Holocaust to Independence resonates with Jewish cultural time, which pulsates from darkness to light (Heschel 1951; Yerushalmi 1982; Zerubavel 1981). Note that the opening act of creation in the Book of Genesis is the transformation from darkness to light. This cosmological move recurs in the Jewish day, which starts in the preceding evening; in the Jewish week, which flows from the "lowliness" of mundane weekdays to the spiritual altitudes of the sacred Sabbath; and in the narrative plot of festivals like Passover, Hanukkah, and Purim.

This rhythm resonates also with the spatial organization of the national pantheon in Har Herzl. One could ascend from the Holocaust Memorial, nestled hidden and distant on the southwestern slope of the mount, to the military cemetery, the embodiment of the struggle for independence. Adjacent to and above the military cemetery lies the Plot of the Great of the Nation, with Herzl's tomb as a symbolic *axis mundi* at the peak (Handelman and Shamgar-Handelman 1997). This temporal rhythm grants surplus meaning to the contrasting state ceremonies that open Remembrance Day and Independence Day (Handelman and Katz 1990). As against the opening ceremony of Holocaust Day in Yad Va-Shem, which represents a primordial chaos, the Jewish traumatic experience of cosmic annihilation, the Remembrance Day ceremony appears as the uncompromising negation of chaos. A semiotic reading of the ritual reveals that all its constituent elements convey the monolithic unity of the nation-state cemented and vivified by the self-sacrifice of the soldiers. The themes of the ritual, unequivocally collectivist, are articulated through traditional Jewish idioms. Jewish religious liturgy is dominant in the ritual, the setting of it is the Western Wall, metonymically representing the Temple, and metaphorically, the Jewish people. The encompassing presence of this ritual zone may be taken as symbolic of the idea that the Jewish people "contain" and precede the Zionist nation-state.

Following the assertion of national sacrifice and the Zionist cosmos, the monolithic austerity of the Remembrance Day ceremony can be replaced by civil and more relaxed themes of pluralism and ethnocultural variability that come to the fore in the Independence Day ceremony. Here the symbols of the nation-state, with Herzl's tomb in the center, constitute the decor, and the main orator is the speaker of the Knesset. His speech, which reviews the ebbs and flows of last year's major events, accentuates the significance of the parliament as the bastion of democracy and equality. The framework of this ceremony is more "open," the symbols more heterogeneous, and the audience more varied then the inner-oriented "family of bereavement" in the Remembrance Day ceremony. The vision of egalitarian pluralism within the State is particularly manifest in the lighting of twelve torches, standing for the twelve biblical tribes of Israel. The individuals granted the honor of lighting the torches are representatives of Israel's rich ethnocultural and religious mosaic, and may include non-Jews. Selected for their contributions to the collective, their brief self-presentations give voice to their divergent biographies and backgrounds. Thus the core value that the ceremony conveys is that of social integration and commitment to common goals without foregoing ethnocultural diversity.

The two wings of the precinct of Har Herzl, the military cemetery and the Holocaust memorial, together with war monuments in the cemetery and in other locales, constitute cultic arenas for national death in Israel. But the differential presence of the dead in these sites leads to divergent modes of signification and sacredness (Handelman and Shamgar-Handelman 1997). The fact that the tombs in the military cemetery contain the body of the fallen substantially decreases the need for elaborate metaphoric representation of the dead. Modest gravestones with a terse standard epitaph cover the soldiers lying in the land for which they fought and died. Contingent with the dead, the gravestone is metonymically rather then metaphorically related to him. The tomb and the cemetery at large are part of the territory of the nation-state.

In terms of the presence of absence, war monuments are located between the military cemetery and the Holocaust Memorial. The fallen soldiers it commemorates are not lying underneath it, and their absence is compensated for by some symbolic elaboration. Monuments are often situated in the scene of the battle they commemorate and may include authentic relics from the fighting (e.g., destroyed military vehicles or weapons). This contiguity may soften the absence of the dead but it cannot entirely compensate for it. Therefore in war monuments the degree of the visual metaphoric representation is higher than in the military cemetery.

The dead of the Holocaust, designated "victims," were also nationalized by the State and granted a symbolic citizenship. But since they had lived and died in remote territories, it is difficult to link them to the local Israeli landscape. As against the widespread deployment of military commemoration, The Holocaust is memorialized in specialized centers, such as Yad Va-Shem and the Museum of the Ghettos' Fighters. The linkage between these sites and the areas in which they are located appears arbitrary and contrived. Yad Va-Shem is the presence of absence, and the salience and pervasiveness of the absence is correlated with the high elaboration of metaphoric representation. The visit to Yad Va-Shem is the voyage to otherness. In the enclosed edifices—the Hall of Remembrance, the Children's Memorial, the Holocaust Museum, and the Valley of the Destroyed Communities—the contrast between in and out is striking. Replete with ingenious modes of representation, they remain quite invisible to the outside observer. In sheer contrast, the visible, open-air representations in Yad Va-Shem are monuments and statues commemorating heroism and valor during World War II. Apparently, the latter representations are more easily tolerated by the local landscape.

Despite the inconvenient incorporation of the commemorative representations of the Holocaust into the local scene, its impact on Israel's civil religion appears to be growing. A traumatic landscape of memory, which had been partially repressed during the formative years of the State, is becoming a significant matrix for bolstering the national identity of young Israelis. Of the three festive days commemorating genocide, heroic sacrifice, and sovereignty, the national contents of Independence Day seem to become more routinized. This kind of attrition is typical of successful civil religions that lost their revolutionary zeal following the realization of their political goals. Holocaust Day and Remembrance Day appear less affected by routinization, despite recent claims that the collective sentiments of bereavement are corroded too, as national death is undergoing "privatization" (Rosental 2001). The awe-inspiring, transcendental connotations of incomprehensible death in the case of the Holocaust, and of recurring death in an unending military conflict, serve to preserve the significance and emotional intensity of these commemorative events.

Moving from the temporal to the spatial, the Mount Herzl complex appears as the most impressive geographical representation of Israel's civil religion (Yarden 1998). Historically, the emergence of the Zionist pantheon in Mount Herzl occurred in an auspicious period. In the first two decades spanning the 1948 and the 1967 wars (1948–67), the planners of the shrines and cults of the young State could pursue their projects unperturbed by the magnetic power of the traditional holy sites in Eastern Jerusalem and the West Bank that remained under Jordanian rule. This fresh course of action could not be taken had the traditional centers remained accessible after the 1948 War. Since Israel's civil religion draws many of its idioms from the Jewish traditional religion, it is hardly conceivable that the new sites could compete with the old ones for hegemony as the sacred abodes of the State. It is not far-fetched to assume that Herzl's remains would have been reinterred on the top of the Mount of Olives facing the place of the temple. Ironically, it was the failure of the military offensive in Eastern Jerusalem at the end of the 1948 War that paved the way for establishing the new national centers in western Jerusalem without the burden of Jewish religious symbolism.

The director of the Ministry of Religious Affairs in the 1950s, S. Z. Kahana, concerned by the loss of the traditional sacred topography, invested a lot of effort in transforming Mount Zion, the only traditional center that remained in Jewish hands, into a world spiritual center for the Jewish people. Aside from the restoration of the Tomb of King David, an old-time pilgrimage site, he densely populated the Mount with *lieux de memoire* that included the Holocaust Crypt, the Temple Mount Observation Point, and the designated place for the annual lighting of the Torch of the Maccabees in Hanukkah. He even sought to erect there the ritual center for Remembrance Day. Despite Kahana's creativity and stamina, however, Mount Zion alone could not compete with the civil national pantheon that emerged in Mount Herzl. The degree to which the first nineteen years of "smaller Israel" were crucial for the development of the Israeli civil religion became evident following the 1967 War, when the mythical sites of memory in Jerusalem, Bethlehem, Hebron, and Nablus fell under Israel's rule. Following that war and through the 1970s, with the fateful 1973 War and the political shift of the 1977 election that brought to power the right-wing Likud, Jewish traditional symbols have become more prominent while the socialist-collectivist ethos has lost its hegemony. These changes had spatial implications. The major Zionist myths of Masada, Bar-Kokhba, and Tel-Hai became contested and gradually lost their attraction as national pilgrimages sites (Ben-Yehuda 1995; Liebman and Don-Yehiya 1983; Zerubavel 1995). The Western Wall has become the most popular shrine in the country, frequented by Israeli Jews from the whole gamut of religious affiliations and convictions. The activities that take place at the Wall are most variegated, combining the individual with the collective, and the religious with the political. State ceremonies, military pledges of allegiance (some of which where moved to the Wall from Masada), and political rallies coexist with a plethora of religious activities. These activities, which include daily prayers, personal petitions, life-cycle rituals, and pilgrimages on the main Jewish festivals, culminate in the 9th of Av ceremonial fast that commemorates the destruction of the Temple (Stopper-Perez and Goldberg 1994).

It is interesting to explore the major "desertions" from the Zionist pantheon in Har Herzl against the changes in the civil religion since the 1970s. The founding father of the state, David Ben-Gurion, chose to be buried in the desert frontier that had been his abode during his last years, thus propagating in life and death the Zionist message of inhabiting the arid and vacant Negev. Menachem

Begin's choice of burial place, in contrast, conveys the magnetic attraction of the traditional Jewish centers. By preferring a "simple Jewish funeral" over a state funeral, and a "plain tomb in the Mount of Olives Cemetery" over the Plot of the Great on Har Herzl, Begin gave voice to the interplay of Jewish traditional and nationalistic values that inspired him politically. This interplay characterized the shift in contents that Israel's civil religion underwent under his rule. The contrasting cosmologies of Mount Herzl in Western Jerusalem, with its national-Zionist accent, and the Jewish traditional Mount of Olives in Eastern Jerusalem, are lucidly reflected in the respective "landscapes of memory" in which the tombs of prime ministers Rabin and Begin are situated. Rabin's burial site, located in the vicinity of Herzl's tomb, overviews the military cemetery, where many of the soldiers who fought under him in the War of Independence and in later battles are buried. Begin's tomb is located in the cemetery, emblematic of the Jewish uncompromising yearning for Zion. Moreover, Begin specifically requested to be buried near the tombs of two underground (pre-State) fighters—one of whom was a member of the Military National Organization headed by Begin—who committed suicide together just before being sent to the gallows.

The outpour of emotions during Begin's funeral and the cultic manifestations that occurred spontaneously during following visits to his tomb gave rise to the expectation that Begin's glorification is imminent. But these sentiments of veneration attenuated rapidly, after a short, highly contrived climax during the 1992 election campaign, when Begin was "revived" by various political parties (Bilu and Levy 1993). Rabin's tomb, in contrast, still continues to attract visitors, and an elaborate system of commemoration has been erected to retain and propagate his "legacy" (Grinberg 2000). While we lack the historical perspective to evaluate Rabin's place in Israel's fluid and highly contested collective memory, it appears that an efficacious machinery, propelled by Rabin's family, is operating to lengthen the "shelf life" of his memory. Begin's family, in sheer contrast, actively resisted the cultic expressions that appeared on Begin's tomb after his death.

Generally speaking, popular sentiments and spontaneous acts of devotion by themselves cannot sustain for long any *lieu de memoire*. The charisma of holy places of all sorts has to be repeatedly "manufactured" and "marketed" (Bilu and Ben-Ari 1992). Without an effective indoctrination system and a logistic infrastructure to make such places visible and accessible, their salience and popularity will rapidly dwindle. In short, holy places require agents, "saint impresarios," to nourish them (Bilu 1990). In Israel, these agents of commemoration span the whole spectrum from state authorities to concerned individuals. The Department for the Commemoration of Fallen Soldiers in the Ministry of Defense and the Center for Holy Places associated with the Ministry of Religious Affairs are two such powerful government agencies in the civil and traditional domains of commemoration respectively. But in the field of military sanctification, pressure groups such as the Association of Bereaved Families, and even individual bereaved parents may leave their marks too. Similarly, religious groups and individuals may affect the "holy geography" of popular saint tombs, as we shall soon see. The power of the state as hegemonic agent of memory should not be underestimated despite the gradual corrosion in the collectivist dimensions of commemoration. Even in a "post-Zionist era," Mount Herzl is still a functioning national monument, given the awe invoked by death nationalized by the State: the victims of the Holocaust in Yad Va-Shem, the fallen soldiers in the military cemetery, and more recently, the prime minister turned martyr for peace. One may look for the prospects of Har Herzl and the planned project of the IDF Museum and Israel National Memorial on Mount Eitan, west of Jerusalem, to augur the future ideological face of Israel. Will the two civil-Israeli pantheons overpower the mystique of the traditional sites of memory in the east? Will the projected attempt to transfer the national ceremony opening Remembrance Day from the Western Wall to Mount Eitan be the first salvo in a future *kulturkampf*?

The efforts of the "Bloc of the Faithful" (Gush Emunim, the radical religious-nationalistic movement that spawned many of the ideological settlements in the West Bank) to "sanctify" the Occupied Territories are based on the ardent espousal of old symbols and myths compromised or abandoned by civil-collectivist Zionism. This neo-Zionist rejuvenation is embedded in an eschatological matrix. In this vein, Jerusalem Day, celebrated on the 28th of the Jewish month of Iyar, has become the temporal marker of the miraculous victory in the 1967 War, which brought back the Jews to their sacred centers. This celebration resonates with the Jewish cultural rhythm that pulsates from crisis to deliverance, and its location in the ritual calendar *after* Independence Day challenges the civic notion that views the establishment of the State in 1948 as the peak event on the ritual calendar. Gush Emunim's new sites of memories are metahistorically constructed of condensed layers of memory that overlay biblical narratives with contemporary political events.

This multilayered commemoration is particularly evident in Hebron. Here past events are selectively aligned to form a coherent narrative, tying together the Cave of the Patriarchs and the first kingdom of David with the 1929 Pogrom, which put an end to the Jewish community in Hebron, and the restoration of that community following the 1967 War. Another impressive site of memory is the Yamit religious academy in the Gaza Strip, built as a huge Star of David with one angle buried in the sand, to commemorate the destruction of the town of Yamit in the Sinai following the peace accord with Egypt (Feige 1995). The old Zionist strategy of building new settlements to commemorate pioneers killed by Arabs was amply appropriated by the Gush (El-Or and Aran 1995), together with other means designed to strengthen attachment to the territory. These means included the restoration of biblical geography by conferring old Hebrew names on new settlements, active involvement in archaeological excavations designed to expose the Jewish past, and consecration of the land through ritualized hiking and trekking.

In places like Jerusalem and Hebron, the metaphysical and historical past heavily sedimented in a bounded symbolic space may create mystical sentiments capable of unleashing violent energies. Such eruptions have occurred in remote and recent history. In the past the violent conflicts of the First Crusade and the Crimean War were precipitated by hostilities in local holy places. In the last two decades contested precincts, primarily the Temple Mount (Haram el-Sherif), the Cave of the Patriarchs, and Joseph's Tomb in Nablus were triggers of violence.

The Sanctification of Place in Contemporary Folk Judaism

In sheer contrast to naive melting-pot notions of ethnic amalgamation and secular progress, folk religious practices related to holy figures and their shrines are thriving in Israel at the turn of the millennium. Too varied to be exhausted within narrow ethnic boundaries, these cultic phenomena nevertheless attract more Mizrahi (of Middle Eastern and North African extraction) than Ashkenazi Jews. Among Mizrahim, Israelis of Moroccan extraction are clearly overrepresented in the cult of the saints.

It would be erroneous to view these cultic phenomena as fossilized traditions from a remote past. Rather, they partake of a dynamic system of beliefs that is flexible enough to accommodate to the current Israeli reality. The popularity of these phenomena is a measure of their viability: It is estimated that the major 120 holy sites in Israel are frequented annually by 6 to 7 million visitors. The major *hillulot* (death commemoration celebrations) at Meron (Rabbi Shimon Bar-Yohai), Tiberias (Rabbi Meir Ba'al Ha-Ness), and more recently, Netivot (Rabbi Israel Abu-Hatsera) attract dozens of thousands of pilgrims, apparently constituting the largest annual gatherings in the country.

The development of the holy sites is bilateral: top-down, from the political and religious centers to the rank and file, but also bottom-up. At the institutional level, the principal agent of sanctification has been the Ministry of Religious Affair. The pioneer attempt to revive folk tradition related to holy sites was made by the first director of the Ministry, S. Z. Kahana, who in the early 1950s founded the Association for Holy Places in the Land of Israel. Aside from granting formal recognition to sites with long-established traditions, the ministry took care of the renovation and maintenance of many of the sites and added new ones to the official list. Ambitious plans are being prepared to transform the pilgrimage tourism of the third millennium into a major industry, with centrally designed remodeling, sale booths and toilets, and computerized audiovisual information centers. In many a case, massive sanctification from above starts as a response to grassroots local initiatives. As Deshen (1994) has asserted, the over-representation of Mizrahim in many of these cults reflects the selective erosion in their adherence to religious practices in Israel: while many of them have become less observant, their basic religious perspective has remained intact. Hence they are more amenable to novel religious activities that are not highly demanding in terms of daily observance yet are saturated with strong mystical and magical meanings. The central role of Moroccan Jews in the cult of the saints in Israel is historically based. Shaped by the confluence of Maghrebi saint worship (Eickelman 1976; Geertz 1968; Gellner 1969) and Jewish mysticism (Stillman 1982), the folk veneration of saints played a major role in the lives of the Jews in traditional Morocco. The mass immigration of Moroccan Jews to Israel during the 1950s and 1960s confronted the newcomers with a major challenge of maintaining cultural traditions rejected by the Israeli mainstream. Saint worship appeared particularly vulnerable in the new country, since it was linked to specific places now remote and inaccessible. Immigration to Israel meant, among other things, a painful dissociation from the *tsaddiqim,* and this loss exacerbated "the predicament of homecoming" (Deshen and Shokeid 1974). Facing enormous difficulties after immigration, the support of the *tsaddiqim* was a cultural resource that the immigrants could not easily forgo. Yet the pressures exerted on them to shed their ethnocultural heritage and to embrace the reigning ideology of secular-collectivist Zionism, together with the disengagement from the Maghrebi sites, contributed to the general diminution and decentralization of the *hillulot.* They had been reduced to domestic affairs, modestly celebrated at home or in the neighborhood synagogue (Stillman 1995; Weingrod 1990). Once the immediate difficulties of absorption were mitigated, however, Moroccan Jews responded to the separation from the saints by embracing various substitutes for the tombs that had been left behind. In what follows I present the major avenues for renewing the alliance with the saints.

I. "APPROPRIATING" OLD-TIME NATIVE PILGRIMAGE SITES Most accessible among the compensatory alternatives were the tombs of local *tsaddiqim,* mainly from the biblical and the Talmudic eras. The "Moroccanization" of these old-time pilgrimage traditions has been particularly noted in the popular, all-Israeli *hillulot* of Rabbi Shimon Bar-Yohai (acronym: Rashby) in Meron near Safed, and of Rabbi Meir Ba'al Ha-Ness in Tiberias (Bilu and Abramovitch 1985; Shokeid 1977). For the mystically oriented Jewish communities in Morocco, the fact that Rabbi Shimon was the alleged author of the sacred *Zohar* (the Book of

Splendor), the canonical text of kabbalah mysticism, granted him a particularly elevated stance among the *tsaddiqim*. Rabbi Shimon's *hillula* in Israel brings together up to 200.000 celebrants—4 percent of the State's entire Jewish population. North African Jews and their descendants form the majority of the pilgrims in Meron and Tiberias and they imbue the pilgrimage with a distinctive Maghrebi style.

2. "ANNEXING" LOCAL, COMMUNITY-BASED PILGRIMAGE SITES Maghrebi Jews living in development towns throughout the country have adopted burial sites of native *tsaddiqim* in their vicinity. Although most of the pilgrimages thus created did not exceed local or regional boundaries, the resultant pattern of devotion appears closer than the "national *hillulot*" to the traditional Maghrebi pattern of a community with its own patron saint.

The creation of the *hillula* of Honi Ha-Me'agel ("the circle-maker"), a legendary talmudic sage, in the northern town of Hatsor Haglilit, is perhaps the most well-known among the regional *hillulot*. An old-time tradition located the tomb of Honi in an ancient burial cave some fifteen miles east of Safed. The site was frequented only sporadically, in times of drought (the termination of which was considered Honi's specialty). Honi's fine hour came about after the development town of Hatsor Haglilit had been founded near the cave. His popularity mounted after the 1967 and 1973 wars, in which the town, situated not far from the border with Syria, did not suffer the slightest damage, ostensibly owing to the *tsaddiq*'s miraculous intercession. Consequently, Honi's *hillula* was scheduled on Israel's Day of Independence. The celebration in Hatsor is a medium-size pilgrimage attracting several thousands of celebrants from the town and its environs.

The same Maghrebi pattern of a community with its own patron saint could be seen evolving in other new towns, like Yavneh, Carmiel, and Beit-Shemesh. In Yavneh, for example, a local cult emerged around the tomb of Rabban Gamliel, located in a Muslim shrine in the center of the town. The *hillula* was dated to the 18th of Sivan, the death anniversary of a venerated scion of the Abu-Hatsera family, Rabbi Israel, buried in Colombe-Bashar, Algeria, simply because the son-in-low of the late *tsaddiq* was the head of the local municipality. In some places, a reappropriation of sites connected with the forebears of the tribes of Israel (Jacob's sons) but associated for years with Muslim saint worship has been taking place (Sasson 2001). Examples are the sanctuaries of Dan (near the town of Beit-Shemesh), Benjamin (near Kefar Saba), and more recently Reuben (near Ashdod and Yavneh).

3. CREATING NEW CONTEMPORARY SAINTS Given the dynamic nature of saint veneration in Morocco, it is not surprising that in Israel, too, new cult centers have been established around the tombs of contemporary rabbis. The most impressive example is that of Rabbi Israel Abu-Hatsera, nicknamed Baba Sali, a

descendant of the most revered Jewish family in southern Morocco. Since his death in 1984, Baba Sali's tomb in the southern development town of Netivot has become a popular pilgrimage center, second only to Rabbi Shimon's sanctuary. On regular days, the site is probably the most "active" holy location in Israel after the Wailing Wall (Bilu and Ben-Ari 1992). The growing popularity of the shrine in Netivot has been informed by the meteoric rise of Baba Sali to the status of a national *tsaddiq,* the saint of Israel of the 1980s and 1990s.

In contrast to other *hillulot,* the festival in Netivot is the object of intense "promotion campaigns," complete with media coverage, official invitations, special bus lines, organized markets, and an elaborate "holy industry" in which the saint's portrait adorns a wide variety of artifacts, from prayer books and bottles of arak to key chains and holograms. Moreover, the *hillula* also draws organized political interests and personages such as the prime minister and cabinet ministers, party leaders, and local officials, as well as representatives of the Chief Rabbinate. The conscious planning evident in the effective system for selling the saint that Baba Baruch, Baba Sali's controversial son and successor, set into motion is an ample manifestation of the extent to which charisma can be "manufactured" or "synthesized." Baba Baruch's entrepreneurial endeavor is impressively inscribed in the land of Netivot. The *tsaddiq's* tomb was enclosed in a spacious whitewashed sanctuary, and an opulently decorated synagogue was erected next to it. This impressive edifice, visible from a distance (Weingrod 1993), is now part of a larger, walled enclosure that includes a parking lot, a picnic area, vendors booths, and other facilities. In addition, the father's (now Baruch's) residence was enlarged and the foundations for Kiriat Baba Sali, a big religious campus, were laid. Today the campus includes several buildings housing the headquarters of Baba Baruch's organization, a yeshiva (religious academy), a Talmud Torah (religious school), and a kindergarten. These were built in a distinctively Moorish style, sharply at odds with the plebeian neighborhood surrounding them. In 1996 the Ministry of Religious Affairs officially declared the sanctuary a holy site. Following the declaration, the Jewish National Fund started to transform the empty space between Kiriat Baba Sali and the shrine into Baba Sali's Park, in the shape of a huge *hamsah* (hand-shaped amulet).

Another contemporary case concerns Rabbi Hayim Houri, a Tunisian Rabbi who died in 1957 in the southern town of Beer-Sheva. The limited accessibility of the tomb, inconveniently located in the midst of a densely populated municipal cemetery, does not stop the crowds from transforming the cemetery into a scene of joy and ecstasy during the *hillula.* At the same time, it points to the spontaneous, unplanned nature of Houri's emergence as a sainted figure, "the saint of Beer-Sheva" (Weingrod 1990). The sanctuaries of Baba Sali and Rabbi Hayim Houri are preeminent among the many other cases of present-day enshrinement, even among Ashkenazi Hasidim. Among the Maghrebi cases, the development of the shrine of Rabbi Moshe Pinto in Ashdod bears resemblance to the glorification of Baba Sali in Netivot. The Pinto family also boasts a noble genealogy, replete with *tsaddiqim,* and like the Abu Hateseras, they too seek to stake a claim in the local map of holy sites (see below).

4. TRANSFERRING JEWISH MOROCCAN SAINTS TO ISRAEL THROUGH DREAMS Although the "Moroccanization" of local *hillulot* and the creation of new saints contributed to the preservation of hagiolatric practices under changing circumstances, their function should be seen as *compensatory* rather than *restorative.* To cope with the painful loss of the Maghrebi saints, a more direct and daring accommodation had to be called for, namely, the "symbolic translocation" of saints from Morocco to Israel (Bilu 1987, 1990). Here we deal with the spontaneous initiative by people who were inspired by a series of visitational dreams in which they were urged by a Maghrebi *tsaddiq* to erect a site for him in their home. The initiators, whom I designate "saint impresarios," were men and women around midlife, typically coming from the rank and file.

The most well known Jewish Moroccan *tsaddiq* to be transferred to Israel via dreams is Rabbi David u-Moshe, with sites in Safed, Ashkelon, and Ofakim. The "House of Rabbi David u-Moshe" in Shikun Canaan, Safed, erected immediately after the 1973 War, became a sweeping success, with thousands of devotees flocking to the domestic shrine on the *hillula* day (the first day of Heshvan). The founder, an afforestation worker (now retired), has become an inspiring model for several other impresarios. Shrines of other translocated Maghrebi saints were erected in Beit Shean (Rabbi Avraham Aouriwar), Kiryat Gat (Rabbi Machluf Ben Yosef Abu-Hatsera), Ramle (Slat L'ktar, a Tunisian female saint), and recently Or-Akiva (Rabbi David Ben Baruch) and Beer-Sheva (Rabbi Ya'aqov Wazana).

5. SITUATING LOCAL SAINTED FIGURES IN NEW SHRINES THROUGH DREAMS A variant of the previous pattern is a dream-based shrine referring to a local rather than imported tradition. According to a legendary tradition mentioned in the Babylonian Talmud (Eruvin 19a), the entrance to the Garden of Eden in its terrestrial form is located in the town of Beit Shean in the Jordan Valley. In 1979 a Beit-She'ani inhabitant announced that he had discovered this entrance in the backyard of his house. Elijah the Prophet, the gatekeeper of the Garden of Eden and the protagonist of the dreams that precipitated the discovery, is the patron saint of the site (Bilu 1990). Other dream-based shrines, reviving or inventing local traditions, have been added in recent years to Israel's sacred geography, from Yeruham in the Negev (where a domestic shrine for Rabbi Shimon Bar-Yohai was established by a female impresario) to a moshav in the upper Galilee (where the tomb of Isaiah the Prophet was recently discovered).

6. REINTERRING THE REMAINS OF JEWISH MOROCCAN SAINTS IN ISRAEL

A more palpable restorative method has been the digging of the remains of *tsaddiqim* buried in Morocco—until recently a clandestine affair—and reinterring them in Israel. The most famous case was that of Rabbi Hayim Pinto from Ashdod. Rabbi Pinto, the chief rabbi of Kiriat Mallachi, entombed there the remains of four holy ancestors of his, which he managed to smuggle from Morocco in a suitcase. An impressive shrine covers the quadripartite tomb and draws a fairly large following. In recent years, the remains of other cherished rabbis from Morocco have been reinterred in Israel by their descendants.

Following the peace treaty with Egypt, Moroccan-born Israelis have been allowed to visit their country of origin. As a result, the shrines there have become accessible once more. Indeed, judging from their itineraries, many of the tours from Israel to Morocco are pilgrimages no less than touristic ventures (Levy 1997). But the number of visitors is still too small to render the Israeli alternatives redundant. In addition, the notion of a patron saint bespeaks of intimacy and easy availability associated with a strong sense of localism that remote shrines cannot provide.

Needless to say, the sites associated with North African saint worship do not exhaust the holy geography in Israel. The visitors to the popular shrines clearly exceed narrow ethnic and regional boundaries. As healing shrines, they attract supplicants with a wide range of life problems, although specialized centers also exist. Most popular among the specialized shrines are Rachel's tomb (for fertility problems) and Rabbi Yonatan Ben-Uziel in Amuka near Safed (known for matchmaking). Given the many agencies vying for hegemony in the domain of sanctification, it is not surprising that some of the sites are hotly contested. In recent years the tombs of Dan (near Beit Shemesh), Samuel (in Nebi Samuel, northwest of Jerusalem), and Havakuk (northwest of the Sea of Gallilee), among others, have become targets for competing initiatives to win media coverage. Hasidic sects, mystical associations, *yeshivot* (religious academies) of "born again" Jews (*hozrim bitshuva*), local municipalities, and private entrepreneurs are involved in these conflicts. These conflicts can be easily escalated if Muslim claims to some of the sites, now dormant or low-keyed, were to be raised more vociferously. The bloodshed in the contested sites in Hebron, Nablus, and Bethlehem during *Intifada al-Aksa* is a grim reminder of that possibility.

The appeal of holy places and spiritual centers in Israeli society does not stop at the borders of the country. This appeal has both centrifugal and centripetal manifestations. The former is evident in the involvement of many Israelis of varied backgrounds in pilgrimages and spiritual quests that encompass a wide territory outside the country. Examples include Israelis of Maghrebi extraction frequenting the major Jewish shrines in Morocco; Hasidim prostrating themselves on tombs of Hasidic masters in Poland, Boleros, and Ukraine; high school students surveying the concentration camps in Poland; and young backpackers wandering between spiritual centers and ashrams in South Asia. This search for roots and elective centers (spiritual centers outside of one's own society to which one is committed), in the Diaspora or among the "Others" may be associated with the weakening of the centripetal Zionist ethos. But research on the tourist-pilgrims to Morocco (Levy 1997) and the students visiting the heart of darkness on Polish soil (Feldman 2000) indicates that the respective tours augment their Israeli identity. As Feldman has shown, the high school tours to Poland are carefully designed as an initiation rite, seeking to imprint in Israeli teenagers the memory of the Holocaust as a constitutive ingredient of their identity. The import of Jewish sites of memory from the Diaspora and their deployment in the land of Israel reflects the opposite, centripetal orientation. Examples include the Baba Sali complex in Netivot distinguished by its ornate Moorish style; the replica in Kfar Habad of the late Lubavitcher Rebbi's stronghold on 770 Eastern Parkway in Brooklyn; and famous synagogues from Libya and Tunisia rebuilt in Zeitan and Ofakin respectively (Weingrod 1993). To these foreign markers, incongruously planted in the native landscape, one can add the aforementioned translocated Jewish Moroccan *tsaddiqim* and the ethnic festivals imported to and publicly celebrated in Israel. These include the Moroccan *Mimuna* (Goldberg 1978; Maman 1991), integrated into the local calendar as a state-sponsored all-Israeli event, the Kurdish *Seherrana* (Halper and Abramovitch 1984), the Persian *Ruz-e-begh* (Weingrod 1990), and recently, the Ethiopian *Sigd* (Ben-Dor 1987). Certainly this process, in which personified and nonpersonified markers of space and time from other cosmologies are gouged in the Israeli terrain, reflects the growing ethnocultural pluralism characteristic of present-day Israeli society. But the deep meanings of this process are open to opposite interpretations. On the one hand, it might be viewed as part of a process of "symbolic diasporization" that reflects and hastens the downfall of the Zionist hegemony (Cohen 1983). On the other hand, the transfer of Maghrebi sites of memory to the local landscape, while accentuating ethnic distinctiveness, bespeaks an ethnicity that is altogether Israeli-oriented. The painful immigration process is brought to closure when the Jewish Moroccan saints eventually follow their ex-followers to Israel. A dialectic process typical of emerging ethnic identities all over the world is at work here. Only after the newcomers had become more secure in their Israeli identity could they assert their ethnic roots and distinctiveness by proudly engaging in the ceremonies, pilgrimages, festivals, and cults that constitute their ethnocultural heritage. The emergence of the cult of the saints in Israel's urban periphery reflects an authentic sense of belonging. Beyond the fact that through this revival of folk traditions the immigrants retrieve part of their past heritage lost upon *aliya,* the return of the saints also bespeaks a growing attachment to the locality, despite the difficulties of absorption (or, rather, because of them). This patriotic sense of localism can be discerned in many of the current manifestations of the cult of the saints. Note the role ascribed to Honi Ha-Me'agel in defending the town of Hatsor from the Syrian army during the wars of 1967 and 1973. The fact that Baba Sali was buried in Netivot rather than in a predesignated lot in the Mount of Olives Cemetery is less impressive than the discovery of the Gate to Paradise in Beit She'an; but the outcome was similar in both cases: the emergence of a new, magnificent shrine in remote, unattractive development towns. (In retrospect, the Beit She'ani shrine collapsed after a few years while the center in Netivot has maintained its popularity.)

In this context, it is significant that the same event—a firm decision to change the place of living by moving to a less peripheral town or neighborhood—precipitated the dream apparitions of most of the "saint impresarios" who erected domestic shrines to Jewish Moroccan *tsaddiqim* (Bilu 1990; Bilu and Hasan-Rokem 1989). The recurrent pattern may have reflected the ambivalence that the protagonists felt toward their communities as well as the resolution of that ambivalence. The ongoing presence of the saint who came to stay has inextricably bound the initiators to their places of living; the initial plan to "desert" the town was countervailed by a solemn vow to stay forever in the old houses now turned into shrines. In Eliade's terms (1959), the manifestations of the holy in the urban periphery of Israel may be viewed as a resort to a traditional pattern of "sanctifying" the locale in order to render mundane living more meaningful and gratifying. The symbol system employed, embodied in the cult of the saint, is a far cry from the Zionist ideology that gave rise to the kibbutz and the moshav, but is no less conducive perhaps to expressing and further bolstering a genuine attachment to the locale. For many local denizens the saints represent an urban transformation that is congenial and welcome. Evaluating the changes in Netivot following the death and rapid sanctification of Baba Sali, one local inhabitant said with a modicum of pride: "A town that was 'outside' of Israel's map, is now not only 'on' the map, thanks to Baba Sali it is also 'above' it." Indeed, places like Baba Sali's sanctuary in Netivot and Rabbi David u-Moshe's House in Safed have been swiftly integrated into Israel's sacred geography.

In summary, this essay should be viewed as a preliminary attempt to chart a comprehensive map of Israel's sacred geography that includes folk-religious as well as civil-national traditions. Given the religious-like aspects of nationalism (Anderson 1983; Mosse 1990), exploring the ways in which these two sets of traditions often intermingle in present-day Israel appears as a timely project. I mentioned the cultic manifestations associated with the commemoration of late prime ministers Begin and Rabin, but the meeting of the religious with the political by far exceeds these cases. One amazing example is the sanctification of the tombs of Yeoshuah and Olga Hankin in the northern slopes of Mount Gilboa by Jewish Kurdish immigrants from nearby *moshavim* (Shenhar-Alroy 2000). The transformation of the resting place of the renowned Zionist activist and his wife into a shrine of a biblical figure, a prophet, or even King Saul (who lost his life on Mount Gilboa) again reveals the genuine need of the newcomers to associate themselves with a patron saint. But in exploring the traditional pattern that gave rise to this creative transformation, we should not ignore the semi-hagiographic articulation of Hankin's achievements in Zionist historiography. After all, he was deemed "the *redeemer* of the Valley" (of Jezre'el).

As I have tried to show, attachment to one's place of residence has been a key element in the renewal of saint worship in Israel. This local patriotic aspect endows the cult of the saint with a clear national flavor. We discussed the heyday of Honi the Circle-Maker as the saint of Hatsor following the wars of 1967 and 1973, and the selection of Israel's Independence Day as the day of his *hillula*. But issues of security and military protection have been voiced in the cult of many other *tsaddiqim,* local as well as imported. The association between religious beliefs and nationalism is all the more manifest in regard to old-time holy sites. The list of Jewish holy places prepared by Yitzhak Ben-Zvi during the British Mandate was politically motivated as a testimony to the antiquity of the Jewish presence in the Holy Land. Later, in the fifties, when the director of the Ministry of Religious Affairs initiated a project for identifying saints' tombs in northern Israel, he designated it "Judaizing the Gallilee." The blood-stained conflict over holy sites in the Occupied Territories indicates how difficult it is to separate between popular and national (or nationalistic) sentiments in present-day Israel. The fact that the Jewish National Fund has established public parks around the popular shrines of Rabbi Yonatan Ben-Uziel and Baba Sali is another point of juncture between the two avenues of sanctification.

It would be erroneous to deem the map of the sacred geography charted here a fixed representation of old-time traditions sustained by the extraordinary qualities of the sites and the spontaneously erupting emotional fervor of the believers. The cults of the holy sites are dynamic, multilayered phenomena that are retained, modified, or discarded as a result of intricate power struggles between individuals, groups, and institutions propelled by a host of personal, religious, economic, and political interests. Since in the Holy Land the territories of the sacred are densely populated and heatedly contested, holy places critically ask for saint agents to tend and maintain them. These agents span the whole gamut from the individual level to the state level. Some of them are individual entrepreneurs motivated by a mystical vision or economic opportunity (or both), like the Jewish Moroccan saint impresarios aforementioned. On the collective level, there are associations of various sorts, from groups of bereaved parents and military veterans seeking to commemorate fallen soldiers and military heroism, to folk-religious associations for perpetuating old and new traditions related to holy shrines. Finally the State itself, through executive agencies such as the Department for the Commemoration of Fallen Soldiers and the Center for Holy Places, is a powerful agent of sanctification. Apparently the avenues of sanctification within civil religion represent more institutionalized, "top-down" processes than those in traditional religion. But this distinction, stemming from gaps in political and economic resources, seems to be blurred in recent years, with the growing involvement of governmental and municipal agencies in places involved in folk traditions.

REFERENCES

Almog, Oz. 2000. *The Sabra: The Creation of the New Jew.* Berkeley: University of California Press.

Anderson, Benedict. 1983. *Imagined Communities: Reflections on the Origin and Spread of Nationalism.* London: Verso.

Azaryahu, Maoz. 1995. *State Cults* Sede Boker: Ben-Gurion University Press (Hebrew).

Ben-Dor, Shoshana. 1987. "The Sigd of Beta Israel: Testimony to a Community in Transition." In *Ethiopian Jews and Israel,* ed. M. Ashkenazi and A. Weingrod. New Brunswick, N.J.: Transaction Books.

Ben-Yehuda, Nachman. 1995. *The Masada Myth: Collective Memory and Myth Making in Israel.* Madison: University of Wisconsin Press.

Bilu, Yoram. 1987. "Dreams and Wishes of the Saint." In *Judaism Viewed from Within and from Without: Anthropological Studies,* ed. H. E. Goldberg, 285–313. Albany, N.Y.: State University of New York Press.

———. 1990. "Jewish Moroccan 'Saint Impresarios' in Israel: A Stage-Developmental Perspective." *Psychoanalytic Study of Society* 15: 247–69.

Bilu, Yoram, and Henry Abramovitch. 1985. "In Search of the Saddiq: Visitational Dreams Among Moroccan Jews in Israel." *Psychiatry* 48 (1): 83–92.

Bilu, Yoram, and Eyal Ben-Ari. 1992. "The Making of Modern Saints: Manufactured Charisma and the Abu-Hatseiras of Israel." *American Ethnologist* 19 (4): 672–87.

Bilu, Yoram, and Galit Hasan-Rokem. 1989. "Cinderella and the Saint." *Psychoanalytic Study of Society* 14: 227–59.

Bilu, Yoram, and André Levy. 1993. "The Elusive Sanctification of Menachem Begin." *International Journal of Politics, Culture, and Society* 7 (2): 297–328.

Cohen, Erik. 1983. "Ethnicity and Legitimation in Contemporary Israel." *The Jerusalem Quarterly* 28: 111–24.

Deshen, Shlomo. 1994. "The Religiosity of the Mizrahim." *Alpaim* 9: 44–58.

Deshen, Shlomo, and Moshe Shokeid. 1974. *The Predicament of Homecoming: Cultural and Social Life of North African Immigrants in Israel.* Ithaca, N.Y.: Cornell University Press.

Eickelman, Dale F. 1976. *Moroccan Islam: Tradition and Society in a Pilgrimage Center.* Austin: University of Texas Press.

Eliade, Mircae. 1959. *The Sacred and the Profane.* New York: Harcourt.

El-Or, Tamar, and Gideon Aran. 1995. "Giving Birth to a Settlement." *Gender and Society* 9: 60–78.

Feige, Michael. 1995. "Social Movements, Hegemony, and Political Myth: A Comparative Analysis of the Ideologies of the Bloc of the Faithful and Peace Now Movements." Ph.D. Dissertation, The Hebrew University (Hebrew).

Feldman, Jackie. 2000. "'It Is My Brother Whom I am Seeking': Israeli Youth Voyages to Holocaust Poland." Ph.D. dissertation, The Hebrew University.

Geertz, Clifford. 1968. *Islam Observed: Religious Development in Morocco and Indonesia.* Chicago: University of Chicago Press.

Gellner, Ernest. 1969. *Saints of the Atlas.* Chicago: University of Chicago Press.

Goldberg, Harvey E. 1978. "The Mimuna and the Minority Status of Moroccan Jews." *Ethnology* 17 (1): 75–87.

Grinberg, Lev. 2000. *Contested Memory—Myth, Nation, and Democracy.* Beer-Sheva: Ben-Gurion University Press (Hebrew).

Gurevitch, Zali, and Gideon Aran. 1991. "On the Place: Israeli Anthropology." *Alpa'im* 4: 9–44 (Hebrew).

Halper, Jeff, and Henry Abramovitch. 1984. "The Saharanei Celebration in Kurdistan and Israel." In *Jews of the Middle East,* ed. S. Deshen and M. Shokeid. Tel-Aviv: Shocken Books (Hebrew).

Handelman, Don, and Elihu Katz. 1990. "State Ceremonies in Israel: Remembrance Day and Independence Day." In *Models and Mirrors: Towards an Anthropology of Public Events,* D. Handelman, 191–235. Cambridge: Cambridge University Press.

Handelman, Don, and Leah Shamgar-Handelman. 1997. "The Presence of Absence: Memorialization of National Death in Israel." In *Grasping Land: Space and Place in Contemporary Israeli Discourse and Experience,* ed. E. Ben-Ari and Y. Bilu, 85–128. Albany: State University of New York Press.

Heschel, Abraham J. 1951. *The Sabbath: Its Meaning for Modern Man.* New York: Farrar, Strauss and Young.

Kunin, Seth. 1994. "Judaism." In *Sacred Place,* ed. J. Holm. London: Pinter.

Levy, André. 1997. "To Morocco and Back: Tourism and Pilgrimage among Moroccan-Born Israelis." In *Grasping Land: Space and Place in Contemporary Israeli Discourse and Experience,* ed. E. Ben-Ari and Y. Bilu, 25–46. Albany: State University of New York Press.

Liebman, Charles S., and Eliezer Don-Yehiya. 1983. *Civil Religion in Israel.* Berkeley: University of California Press.

Malkinson, Ruth, Shimshon S. Tubin, and Witztum Eliezer. 1993. *Loss and Bereavement in the Jewish Sciety in Israel.* Jerusalem: Cana and the Ministry of Defense Publishing Houses.

Maman, Aharon. 1991. "La fete de la Mimouna: etude etymologique du term et coutumes." In *Recherches sur la culture des juifs d'Afrique de nord,* ed. I. Ben-Ami, 85–95. Jerusalem: Communaute Israelite Nord-Africaine (Hebrew).

Mosse, George L. 1990. *Fallen Soldiers: Reshaping the Memory of the World Wars.* New York: Oxford University Press.

Nora, Pierre. 1989. "Between Memory and History." *Representations* 26: 7–25.

Reiner, Elchanan. 1988. "Pilgrims and Pilgrimage to the Land of Israel: 1099–1517." Ph.D. Dissertation, The Hebrew University (Hebrew).

Rosental, Ruvik. 2001. *Is Bereavement Dead?* Jerusalem: Keter (Hebrew).

Sasson, Avraham. 2001. "Folk-Sanctification of Tombs in Israel." *New Directions* 4: 153–70 (Hebrew).

Shamir, Esther. 1989. *Gal-Ed: Monuments for the Fallen in Israel's War.* Tel-Aviv: The Ministry of Defense Publishing Houses (Hebrew).

Shenhar-Alroy, Aliza. 2000. *Jewish and Israeli Folklore.* New York: International Academic Publishers.

Shokeid, Moshe. 1977. "Sanctity and Profanity in Pilgrimage to Meiron." In *The Generation of Transition,* ed. M. Shokeid and S. Deshen, 93–109. Jerusalem: Yad Ben-Zvi Press (Hebrew).

Stillman, Norman A. 1982. "Saddiq and Marabut in Morocco." In *The Sephardi and Oriental Jewish Heritage,* ed. I. Ben-Ami, 489–500. Jerusalem: The Magnes Press.

———. 1995. *Sephardi Religious Responses to Modernity.* Luxemburg: Harwood Academic Press.

Stopper-Perez, Danielle, and Harvey E. Goldberg. 1994. "The Kotel: Toward an Ethnographic Portrait." *Religion* 4: 309–22.

Volkan, Vamik D. 1990. "'Living Statues' and Political Decision-making." *Mind and Human Interaction* 2 (2): 46–50.

Weingrod, Alex. 1990. *The Saint of Beersheba.* Albany, N.Y.: State University of New York Press.

———. 1993. "Changing Israeli Landscapes: Buildings and Uses of the Past." *Cultural Anthropology* 8 (3): 370–87.

Yarden, Ophir. 1998. "The Sanctity of Mount Herzl and Independence Day in Israel's Civil Religion." In *Sanctity of Time and Space in Tradition and Modernity,* ed. A. Houtman, M.J.H.M. Poorthuis, and J. Schwartz, 317–48. Leiden: Brill.

Yerushalmi, Yosef H. 1982. *Zakhor: Jewish History and Jewish Memory.* Seattle: University of Washington Press.

Zerubavel, Eviatar. 1981. *Hidden Rhythms: Schedules and Calendars in Social Life.* Chicago: The University of Chicago Press.

Zerubavel, Yael. 1995. *Recovered Roots: Collective Memory and the Making of Israeli National Tradition.* Chicago and London: The University of Chicago Press.

CHAPTER SEVENTEEN

History, Memory, and Identity
Perceptions of the Holocaust in Israel

လာ

DALIA OFER

Introduction

The memory of the Holocaust is negotiated in Israel in an unmediated way through the survivors and their families, who represent a significant subgroup within the population. Voices of survivors are not homogeneous as they represent both an individual and, despite their differing experiences during the war, a group voice. Sever Plotzker, writing in the Hebrew daily *Yediot Aharonot*, presented an extreme example of such diversity in the title of his article "Everyone and His Auschwitz." He is broadening the process of interpretation beyond the survivors to every Jew and his/her effort to give meaning to the destruction (Plotzker 1993).

In the last two decades, children of survivors have negotiated their memories as transformed from their parents' stories or silence, through their studies in school, and in the public discourse. Many who are classified as "second generation" feel very ambivalent in their approach to the legacy of the Holocaust. On the one hand, they feel obligated to carry the messages of their parents and transmit their stories and thus keep the memory of the Holocaust (Vardi 1990). On the other hand, they resent being stigmatized as a group *obligated* to carry the memory of their parents (Lentil 1998, p. 178; Lentil 2000, pp. 157–76). An important element in the narrative of children of survivors is their expressed desire not to be different from their friends, but to have fathers and mothers who fought in the War of Independence like their peers. They wanted to be "normal" and recalled their parents' efforts to raise them as "healthy and brave" Israeli children. In addition, their parents' silence about their past could be both disturbing and comforting at the same time (Semel 2000).

The imperative to remember is embodied in Jewish tradition and is a fundamental characteristic of Jewish culture (Yerushalmi 1989), whose relation to the Holocaust was expressed as a command such as the one included in a postwar edition of the Passover *Haggada:* "In each generation should a Jew see himself as if he himself experienced the Nazi Hell" (Gutman 1960). Remembering and searching for meaning was viewed as a national commitment and as a means to avoid future catastrophes for Jews and for humanity in general. Still, but along with the wish to connect the Holocaust to "here and now" as an identity of fate that connected the Jewish people ran a contrary will to define it as an experience that belonged to "there"—the Diaspora, an alien political and social space (Herman 1970, pp. 36–37, 75–80; Herman 1977, pp. 87–101; Brug 1997, pp. 19–23).

Thus the process of thinking and rethinking about the destruction of European Jewry, writing and rewriting the history of the Jews in occupied Europe, demonstrated the tension between the personal and the national, between "here" and "there." The personal narrative belonged to both "here" and "there" and it formed the foundation for the knowledge about the Holocaust as well as for the collective awareness. However, historians, writers, and political leaders feared that the history of the Holocaust would become merely a chronicle of atrocities and suffering, while the national meaning of the callous intent and policy of annihilation of all the Jews would become secondary. They feared that it would contribute to a relativization and banalization of the Holocaust. Moreover, if the history of the Holocaust were to end up as nothing more than a list of pogroms and murders, it would reinforce the alienation experienced by some Israelis toward Jewish life in the Diaspora (Ofer 2000, pp. 29–31).

Despite the diverse approaches of Israelis toward the Holocaust, an important common denominator is found in the commitment to ensure the future of the Jewish people. Many associated this commitment with their perceptions of, and efforts toward, the realization of Jewish life in the State of Israel. The term "Jewish life" ranges from a strictly religious perspective to an atheistic and secular one. Beyond this basic commitment to the Jewish future, opinions of Israelis on the meaning of the Holocaust vary considerably.

I am concerned here with two major issues: (1) How were patterns of commemoration developed? (2) The public fashioning of Holocaust memory and the search of individuals and particular communities for their own way of commemoration. These issues necessarily lead to the question of identity and how history and memory agree or disagree in constructing the narrative of the Holocaust. They refer us also to the impact of understanding the Holocaust on the life of Israelis, on the mentality of Israel as a collective entity, and on the self-understanding of individuals in Israel as survivors, heirs, and kin to the victims. This understanding is imprinted in Israeli culture—in literature, theater, the arts, the social milieu—and in the attitude of Israelis toward others as enemies or friends, and toward the nations of the world. Inevitably our attention is drawn also to the political dimension, in which the memory and lessons of the Holocaust have been both used and abused (Ofer 1996, pp. 836–39; Lentil 1998, pp. 174–75; Ofir 1986, pp. 2–7).

Thus the rhetoric, commemorative ceremonies, and monuments, in what one may call the pattern or design of commemoration, reflect the transformation in Israel's self-understanding. Of course, the form that commemoration took was related to the historical facts of the Holocaust, and to both its universal and particular national meaning. It also demonstrates the gradual, painful, and nonlinear process of the dissemination of destruction.

My discussion relates to two themes: the formulation of the patterns of remembrance that emerged through the efforts of individuals, institutions, and political bodies, and the pluralistic character of those patterns. I conclude by reviewing the teaching concerning the Holocaust and tours for youth to Poland. In my analysis I employ the concept of collective memory and the agency of memory as presented by Jay Winter and Emmanuel Sivan in *War and Remembrance* (1999). I also follow the concept formulated by Barry Schwartz (1982, pp. 347–402) and Yael Zerubavel (1995) relating to the social context of memory and the negotiation between past and present among different social agencies in constructing collective memory. On the issue of identity, I review here the research of Shimon Herman (1970a), Uri Farago (1983), and Yair Auron (1993). These writers view the Holocaust and Jewish identity as they relate to major events and experiences both in Jewish history and in contemporary events. The historical memory of Exodus, a more contemporary event such as the Six Day War, the ongoing struggle with the Palestinians, and the transitions in the identity of East European Jews following the dismemberment of the Soviet Union all contribute to the formation of identity. Eviatar Zerubavel (1996, pp. 283–99) suggests a way to connect identity and the memories of individuals and families and the larger society.

Commemoration and Remembrance

Ambivalence toward the Holocaust is manifested in various ways. From the linguistic perspective, it is expressed in the contrasting elements found within the phrases *Shoah U'tekumah* (Holocaust and Rebirth) and *Hurban U'geulah* (Destruction and Redemption). Although these phrases are rooted in the fundamental understanding of the relation of present to future in Jewish tradition, the concepts form a dialectic that is hard to accept (Ofer 1996a). Such a message places a burden on individuals and the society, calling for great responsibility, and demanding a meaningful way of connecting oneself to the fate of the Jews during those frightful days.

This self-consciousness is also reflected in the search for modes of remembrance. Individuals who wanted to follow the conventional way of remembering a deceased relative were unable to observe the *yahrzeit* (the annual anniversary on the date of death), since, in so many cases, neither the date nor a gravesite was known. Naming a child after a deceased relative was common, but even this left a sense of unease, since many still hoped to be reunited with family members, and in fact this sometimes happened, even decades later, when almost all hope had been lost.

In the public sphere, there was a tension between modern, mostly European, commemorative patterns—such as creating a tomb for the "unknown soldier" or other monuments, and the traditional Jewish commemoration involving the recitation of *Tehilim* (the Book of Psalms), the study of *mishnayot,* and writing *kinoth.* Aaron Barth of the Jewish National Fund and a member of Mizrahi (the religious Zionist organization), at a meeting of the Yad Vashem Committee established in the fall of 1946, complained that commemoration plans that centered on monuments resembled a ritual for the dead and were therefore alien to Jewish tradition. Instead, he proposed that centers of higher Jewish learning— *yeshivot*—be established (Barth 1946).

Nonreligious members of the committee agreed that learning and research were central to any commemoration project. However, they had in mind historical and sociological research projects that would further an understanding of the circumstances that had led to the Holocaust and would explore the mechanism of destruction and the responses to the Holocaust of the Jewish leadership and ordinary Jews in the ghettos and camps. Individuals and members of Yad Vashem Committee proposed a number of ideas for commemoration sites. Ideologically, all the proposals stressed a firm commitment to assure the future of Jewish life and the conviction that the Land of Israel should be the central place in the Jewish world for a national remembrance of the Holocaust and that a site should be erected in that country. Many agreed that a physical monument, in establishing a sacred space, could reflect the dimensions of the tragedy.

I shall not elaborate the history of public commemoration from 1942, when the first ideas emerged; through the March 1950 Israeli Knesset decision to establish Yom Hashoah as an annual day of commemoration; the establishment of Yad Vashem in 1953; the endorsement in 1959 of regulations for public conduct on Yom Hashoah—a brief period of silence; to the closure of restaurants and places of entertainment. My detailed analysis of the subject appears in David Wyman's book *The World Reacts to the Holocaust* (1996). I will identify here only some general aspects of the public state commemoration.

It was formalized, as with many other public ceremonies in Israel, in a blend of modern and traditional patterns, and was greatly influenced by the memorial ceremonies for Israeli soldiers who lost their lives in the War of Independence (Rein 1994). The date was set according to the Jewish calendar, to take place in the period between Passover and Shavuoth, a traditional period of mourning for the students of Rabbi Akiva. Rituals included a special *yizkor* prayer, lighting of memorial candles, and reading the Book of Psalms. However, the inherent tension between the traditional and the secular, as mentioned above, did not dissipate. It manifested with the setting of a second date by the Chief Rabbinate already in 1946 for reciting Kaddish for those whose dates of death and gravesites were unknown. This alternate day was the tenth of the Hebrew month Tevet, a minor fast day that recalls the breaking of the walls of Jerusalem after a long siege by the ancient Babylonians, which led to the capture of the city and destruction of the Temple on the ninth of Av (Ofer 1996b, pp. 860–61; Stauber 2000, pp. 48–58).

In smaller circles of Israeli society, such as *landsmannschaften,* survivors led the activities; in kibbutzim and moshavim and in a number of synagogues, particular types of commemoration were developed. *Yizkor* books were published in which the names of the dead were listed, and community books (*pinkasei kehiloth*) were made as well. Survivors to commemorate a town, a ghetto, a region, or an assembly center for deportation erected monuments. In some cemeteries, gravestones were erected at the side, although no one was buried there. In synagogues, special corners were dedicated to destroyed communities or families. These efforts testified to the need for a physical place and a prescribed space for remembrance (Ofer 1996b, pp. 854–61; Ofer 2000, pp. 26, 50 nn. 13, 14; Baumel n.d., pp. 146–70).

Such alternatives were not in contrast to the state law but rather served to supplement the official national activities. They were initiated by voluntary associations, seeking to establish a particular form of commemoration and to tell a story that was at once personal, individual, and collective. The most important examples are the museum and study center established in 1950 at Kibbutz Lohamei Hagetaot by survivors who committed themselves to rebuild their lives while telling the story of the Holocaust and stressing the meaning of Jewish resistance to Nazism. Another example is Kibbutz Yad Mordechai, established in 1943, and named after the leader of the Warsaw Ghetto uprising. There, too, a museum was erected as well as a monument to Mordechai Anielewicz. From the museum one is led to another memorial, which recalls the heroic defense against the Egyptian army during the War of Independence. In this place, the heroism of the ghetto days is directly connected to the heroism of the IDF soldiers at Yad Mordechai.

To this category one should add the particular ways in which schools and educational institutions, especially teachers in individual classes, observe Yom Hashoah. The personal stories of survivors were presented in these alternative forms of commemoration, and a public legitimacy was acknowledged for individual testimony in the wake of the Eichmann Trial in 1961.

On May 23, 1960, Prime Minister David Ben-Gurion announced in the Knesset that Adolf Eichmann, the chief executor of the "Final Solution," was in Israel and would be tried according to the 1950 Law for the Punishment of Nazis and Nazi Collaborators.[1] Almost a year later, on April 11, 1961, Eichmann's trial began in Jerusalem. The verdict condemned him to death, and he was executed on May 31, 1962.

The Eichmann trial was a turning point in shaping the attitude of Israelis to the Holocaust. During the two years between Eichmann's arrival in Israel and his execution, Israelis began confronting the recent past with some humility and with greater sincerity than ever before. Moreover, in the wake of the trial, Israelis reflected on their self-images, their Zionist tenets, and their bonds with diaspora Jewry. "No one would leave this court hall the same person as he was when he entered," wrote Haim Gouri, a well-known poet who reported on the trial (Gouri 1963, p. 73; Yablonka 2001).

During the first months after the capture of Eichmann, the survivors were the subjects of pride, as expressed in Alterman's phrase "get on your feet Jewish Woman" (Alterman 1962, p. 497). During the trial itself they emerged as heroes who embodied in their rehabilitation the meaning of Jewish rebirth. By the end of the trial, survivors were seen as "living memorials"—a crucial role in a society in which the formation of the collective memory was so important. Survivors as a group (rather than historians or employees of Yad Vashem) became even more essential in this new stage in the dialogue and negotiation of the Holocaust. Many more survivors now felt impelled to employ their personal testimony for the education of the future generation. They were asked to tell their stories to young students and soldiers. Education became a central stage in the heritage of the Holocaust; on this I elaborate later.

As a result of the Eichmann trial, the first step had been taken in ensuring that survivors would no longer be an anonymous group of people—now they had become individuals with names and biographies. Israelis had not appreciated the individual survivors of the Holocaust with whom they worked, sat in the theater, and walked together on the streets (Doron May 16, 1961, p. 4; Tavor, 1961, p.). The sense of solidarity that derived from this realization called for deeper contemplation of the Holocaust and its meaning, and a stronger effort to empathize with memories that impinged on survivors' daily lives in Israel. A greater appreciation was expressed for their personal achievements. The artist Yehuda Bacon, the writer "Ka-Tzetnik" 1961 (Yechiel Dinur), and poet Abba Kovner were appreciated as spiritual giants who were to construct and preserve Israel's memory (Moshe Tavor, May 3, 1961, p. 5; Ya'akov Even Hen, 1961, p. 1; 1961, pp. 1, 3; Nahum Pundak, July 7 1961, pp. 3–4).

Public legitimization and a new willingness on the part of survivors to tell and of others to listen continued over the following decade and created a new public discourse. The process of listening carefully to diverse voices of the Holocaust became normative and, in a sense, there began a competition to promote one's memory and to redefine heroism and survival in a way that allowed individuals a public space for personal memory and commemoration.

Interesting examples can be drawn from the history of commemoration in different kibbutzim in Israel. In a pioneering study, Micha Balf (1998) pointed to similarities and differences in the development of memorialization in two kibbutzim, Ma'agan Michael, and Ma'ayan Zvi.

The social structure of these two kibbutzim is quite different, as they belong to two different streams of the kibbutz movement. Ma'agan Michael of the more Left-wing Kibbutz Meuhad movement, was founded by two youth groups—a Zofim group from Haifa, whose families were of German origin and had immigrated to Palestine in the 1920s and 1930s; and a Youth Aliyah (`Aliyat hano`ar)[2] group from Germany who arrived in Palestine in the mid-1930s. The Youth Aliyah members had previously lived in Jerusalem at an educational institute and then went to Kibbutz Ein Gev. Kibbutz Ma'agan Michael also absorbed a very small number of Holocaust survivors.

Ma'ayan Zvi had been established almost ten years earlier as part of the Homah u'migdal settlement of Hever Hakvutzot movement. Membership comprised two youth groups from Germany and a number of Holocaust survivors who joined the kibbutz after the war. The members were older and had taken up permanent residence there since 1941. They had been aware of their own parents' difficult situation in Germany before the war and had tried in vain to get immigration certificates for them (Balf 1998, pp. 44–46). Information about the fate of the Jews in occupied Europe and about the deportation of German Jews was made known to those in Palestine through the press and in kibbutz journals. In the early 1940s, a Youth Aliyah group from Germany who had completed their education in Jerusalem joined the kibbutz. A few individuals who had managed to leave Germany just before war broke out also joined. Among them was a sixty-year-old woman whom the younger members called "Granny Yacob." She became the "great mother figure" for the youngsters who missed their parents and siblings, especially the Youth Aliyah girls.

Most members of Ma'ayan Zvi lost their extended families during the war, and some were the only ones that remained of their families. Kibbutz members received a substantial sum of reparation money from Germany that proved to be very important for the investments and economic growth of the kibbutz.

The two kibbutzim developed different patterns of commemoration, and at a different pace. The similarity between the two communities was in the move toward the personal and individual narrative in commemoration ceremonies and, eventually, in the increased role of the high-school students who visited Poland in shaping the commemoration.

While in Ma'agan Michael the commemorative ceremony became more important as it gained a more personal, emotional, and individual nature following the deaths of parents and the creation of the community's cemetery, in Ma'ayan Zvi the founding members of the kibbutz preferred a formal and quite unemotional ceremony.

In Ma'agan Michael during the 1950s, those who wished to attend the ceremony at Kibbutz Lohamei Hagetaot were able to go. It is not clear what may have taken place in the kibbutz itself, since the guidelines given in kibbutz journals for the ceremony were not remembered by the veterans as ever being practiced.

The few references found in the kibbutz journal about Yom Hashoah, are couched in the typical rhetoric of the period. Most entries allude to the Warsaw Ghetto Uprising (noting that it was "three years from the Uprising," "five years from the Uprising," "eleven years from the Uprising," etc.). Along with this, one finds the conventional view of anti-Jewish discrimination throughout history from Haman to Hitler; and the unimaginative comparison between the political isolation of Israel and that of the Jews in the ghettos.

In the 1960s, the kibbutz began to display more individual ways to commemorate the Holocaust. In 1962, the organizers of the Yom Hashoah ceremonies suggested ways of commemoration within the family framework, to include parents and children of all ages. In the following years, modifications continued. The initiative and living spirit behind this change came from two of the four survivors who had joined the kibbutz almost twenty years earlier. They had never told their personal stories in any kibbutz forum and had not expressed their own views about the commemoration of the Holocaust. In the early 1960s, however, they became active. Was this a sign of the general change in Israel following the Eichmann trial, and the legitimization of the stories and testimonies of the "simple Jew" next to the heroes of the uprisings and the partisans? Two new elements appeared in the ceremonies: it was open to school children, and it contained personal testimony and the letters of a survivor. It was directed toward the centrality of the individual Jew and his fate during the Holocaust, with a decreased focus on the national aspect and more attention given to the solemn atmosphere and aesthetics. Participants were thereby enabled to meditate on their own feelings and memories.

The establishment of the community cemetery led to another phase in the remembrance of the Holocaust dead. Members whose parents had been murdered in the Holocaust expressed a need for a physical site and monument in the cemetery for their loved ones, and this was erected in 1987. On Yom Hashoah of that year, Zilah Telem read aloud publicly the only postcard she had received from her father in the summer of 1942. It was a standard note from the Drancy concentration camp a few days before he was deported to Auschwitz to his death. He wrote "Don't worry, I am fine, I need nothing. I am going to a labor camp" (Balf 1998, supp. 17). She explained her personal feelings and the meaning of the monument for her personally, her family, and the kibbutz in general. Despite the fact that she had regularly joined other French survivors and their relatives in a memorial ceremony at Moshav Roglith, she really wanted a monument in the same place where she herself would ultimately be buried. Although a monument is no more than a name on a stone, she admitted, it is very meaningful for her. She now had a place to put a flower or a stone; she could sit and meditate. Her children and grandchildren, she added, will also be able to do the same.

It is significant that in the same issue of the kibbutz journal, one of the members, Eli Nezer, published a poem "Teudat Zehut" (Identity card). His "identity card" included the dead of his family, their voices, their last breath, and their words, which inspired him not to lose hope. Their words were "*lech lechah*" ("go forth" as G-d said to Abraham), and these words followed him to Palestine. The last part of the poem is a silent dialogue between the poet and his family. The eyes of the dead stare at him and in their silence they deliver their voices of *kinoth* (mourning poems), which in turn become his hymns (Balf 1998, supp. 18). From this time not only was the individual Jew represented in the ceremony but also the personal stories and images of kibbutz members and their relatives.

What made the personal dimension of the commemoration even more evident were the pictures of family members exhibited in the kibbutz dining hall during Yom Hashoah, together with a short text recounting their lives and ultimate fate. The ceremony now took place at the burial ground, where the members of Ma`agan Michael could "close the circle." After many years, when they were themselves parents and had faced from a different angle the danger of war and the experience of death, they chose to commemorate their loved ones in the traditional way of mourning, yet in a mode appropriate to their own life.

A decade later, another meaningful change occurred: the high-school youth, who had visited Poland as part of their own maturation, took over the ceremony of Yom Hashoah. They did not alter the ceremony at the cemetery that had been fashioned in the previous decade, but they introduced their own point of view and understanding of the Holocaust. They added readings of their own poems and selections from their journals recorded during their trip to Poland. They gave their own personal testimonies on the tour in Poland and spoke of their personal confrontation with the past and present. An intergenerational dialogue emerged that became a central theme in the remembrance and commemoration of the Holocaust.

The process in Kibbutz Ma'ayan Zvi was very different, although it, too, showed the move from the general to the specific—from the point of view of the kibbutz community to the very personal perspective taken when the second generation visited Poland and took over the leadership in formulating the ceremony of Yom Hashoah.

In Ma'ayan Zvi, the ceremony for Yom Hashoah was initially formulated in the late 1950s. It included an opening with classical music, the reading of *yizkor* that Yad Vashem published for the victims of the Holocaust, and poems. Music alternated with the readings, providing intervals for personal reflection. The performance was rehearsed and participants were given specific directions. The form was preserved from year to year, using the same texts and order. The literary selections were those common in other ceremonies held throughout Israel, including works of poets such as Alterman and Shlonski, as well as selections from the collection of children's poems written in Theresienstadt, published as *I Never Saw Another Butterfly*. Chapters from the Bible were read as well as descriptions and commentary on major events of the Holocaust. The commentaries were general and oriented to the national consensus. Judging only from the selection of texts, it is clear that the ceremony was typical of those in any labor community in the country, with nothing specific to the residents of Ma'ayan Zvi.

The setting was very formal. The same four people read the texts from a table separated from the listeners, who sat passively in rows in front of them. For the founding members of the kibbutz, the ceremony provided a framework for their own personal meditation. The content was secondary to the atmosphere of respect, with space for silence to enable each individual to remember, think, and experience longing (Balf 1998, pp. 56–59). Some of the younger people considered the atmosphere to be cold and detached; they found the silence difficult, and when they began to be more involved in organizing the ceremony they introduced some changes.

The form of the commemoration seems at first quite puzzling when one remembers that, of 140 kibbutz founding members, no fewer than 70 had lost both father and mother in the Holocaust. Another fourteen members had lost one parent, and a further eleven members were survivors of the camps and ghettoes who joined the kibbutz after the war. It seems that the kibbutz members were at that time unable to expose their emotions openly and needed a mediating ritual. The normative and "public" character of the ceremony, along with the familiar texts, served as an anchor to meditate on their personal pain, and allowed space for reflection (Balf 1998, pp. 59–61).

It is important to note that in Ma'ayan Zvi, a remembrance hall was established in 1988, when the kibbutz celebrated its fiftieth anniversary. Mounted on one of the walls are small copper plaques on which are engraved the names of two hundred of the kibbutznikim's family members who were murdered by the Nazis. Among the names are also members of the Maccabi movement who perished during the Holocaust. (Members of this movement had established this kibbutz). Next to some of the plaques are photographs of the dead. The three remaining walls contain the names and pictures of fallen soldiers from the kibbutz, other members, and children who have died. The fourth wall remained empty to allow for the future inclusion of the parents of kibbutz members who live with the children at Ma'ayan Zvi in their old age (Angress 1988).

This room in which the remembrance of the victims of the Holocaust is central is the place where, each Yom Kippur, the kibbutz members perform a ceremony of repentance and meditate on the meaning of life and death. It is beyond the scope of this essay to develop this theme here; however, it bears upon the meaning of the destruction to the kibbutz members.

In the 1990s, the conventional pattern of commemoration was changed when the youth of the kibbutz who had visited Poland contributed to the ceremony, based on their own experience. They chose different music, changed the setting of the room, and read some of the writings from their travel journals. Some of the older members felt embarrassed, and one even left the room in anger. While the older generation viewed the ceremony as an opportunity for self-reflection and an expression of inward emotions, the youth who took over expected the ceremony to alleviate emotion and create identification.

The following year a greater number of younger members and families with children participated in the ceremony. The older members, who either had been hesitant to accept the changes or had opposed them, admitted that the modified ceremony appealed to the kibbutz members and should be accepted.

We learned from the experience of these two kibbutzim that the process they developed was based on their own group background and subculture. Ma'agan Michael was more open to changes and frequently attempted new patterns of commemoration. The national formula of commemoration provided the symbols, literature, and images, which were central in setting the general stage and provoking a search for the particular. But only the self-searching of the members of these communities and the integration of their own life experiences through self-reflection could provide the form and content of their local commemoration and create ways to keep their memories alive through the generations.

It is interesting to note that some of the stormiest events in Israel related to the memory of the Holocaust, such as the reparations debate and the Kasztner affair, passed without comment in the official kibbutz journals in both kibbutzim. Commemorating the Holocaust turned out to be for their members a meaningful journey to the past and a way of negotiating between past, present, and future.

In the national framework of commemoration one can view a similar process in which the tone changed from a general, nonpersonal voice to the individual voice. In 1989, Yad Vashem began the *Lekol ish yesh shem* (Each person has a name) project, in which individuals read aloud the names of family members murdered during the Holocaust. The personal experience is also visible now in the main ceremony at Yad Vashem, in which survivor testimonies are screened while survivors light memorial candles.

Another interesting phenomenon of the last few years is "alternative commemoration." Young people are seeking their own way to commemorate the Holocaust and express their unease about the established state commemoration at Yad Vashem and other institutions. The movement began within the educational framework at the Mizrahi Kedmah school, which offers an alternative curriculum aimed at promoting pride in the Mizrahi cultural heritage. The conventional commemorations expressed a Eurocentric approach to the Holocaust, and Kedmah's idea was to add to the ceremony an awareness of other genocides, and thus give a more universal meaning to the event. Therefore a seventh candle was lit next to the six representing the Jewish six million. This flame stood both for the Armenian genocide that took place during World War I and for other persecuted minorities such as Native Americans, African Americans, etc. Such a different approach amounts to a protest, signifying the discontent felt by this political and social group with the Israeli identity. It aims to promote a multicultural approach to the established rituals.

The search for different forms of commemoration extends to a number of different groups, mostly made up of young people, some of them descendents of Holocaust survivors who resent the use of the word "holy" and "holiness" in reference to the Jews murdered by the Nazis. They find another way to express their feelings toward the victims of the Holocaust, mostly with irony. They criticize the conventional conceptualization of the Holocaust with its emphasis on victimhood in political and social issues. They offer a look at both perpetrators and victims as human beings, finding merit and fault in both groups and tying the Holocaust directly to the Israeli-Palestinian conflict. They use different music and avoid the usual symbols such as the Israeli flag, the kaddish prayer, etc. This provocative approach is yet another facet of the dialogue and proves that it is a lively discourse. Its scholarly and political manifestations can be seen in Ronit Lentil's book (2000) and in the writings of Adi Ofir (1986).

In recent years, the mass media have shown many documentaries on survivors and their families. Filmmakers—often children of survivors—have produced films of their family history and opened up conversations with their parents who had previously remained silent about their pasts.

The sense of identity of children of survivors and their children's self-understanding in relation to the Holocaust was the topic of a recent documentary entitled *Ararat* (produced and directed by Avivah Zuckerman for Israeli Educational Television in 2001). Three generations of artists—painters, sculptors, writers, dancers, and musicians—were interviewed and their works presented. At issue was the motivation for the artist's creativity and the role of the Holocaust as a direct or indirect inspiration. Was the act of writing, painting, etc., therapeutic, or was their major motivation the wish to commemorate? Artists who were children and grandchildren of Holocaust survivors were ambivalent about the feelings that had motivated them to create on a topic connected to the Holocaust. Next to the resentment that some expressed clearly and the wish to free themselves from the memory of the Holocaust, they realized that what pushed them to create art on Holocaust-related topics was stronger then ideologies or simple wishes. At the same time, they accepted that they were unable to ignore their inner need to work with Holocaust material and take note of the experiences of their families and other survivors. One of the interviewees compared her relationship to the Holocaust to a marriage in which one is attracted to one's partner yet also needs to maintain one's own self, and fight with him / her. Such expressions connect strongly to Nava Semel's sense of identity as the daughter of survivors (Semel 2000). She is able to pinpoint the impact of her mother's experience on her own motherhood, her anxieties, and her general attitude toward life.

In this context Steven Spielberg's great effort to document the stories of all survivors brought forth not only people who wanted to interview survivors, but also survivors who wanted to be interviewed. In Israel, this effort, in cooperation with Yad Vashem, has produced a very large number of new interviews. Participants in the project feared that with the aging and dying off of Holocaust survivors, their stories would be lost forever. The interviewers were interested in the history of the Holocaust, and their intensive exposure to the testimonies reinforced in them the sense of the centrality of the Holocaust as an epoch-making event. The role of live testimony in shaping the social agencies of memory—such as the educational framework, including not only the classroom but also and especially the trips to Poland—is also central.

The Educational Framework

Teaching the Holocaust

Ever since the late 1940s, Israeli intellectuals and educators have expressed concern that the memory of the Holocaust would fade and that knowledge of European Jewry and its social and spiritual world would disappear. This, they feared, would fulfill Hitler's wish to obliterate the Jews (Keren 1985, pp. 24–30, 71–85).

It seemed obvious at first that the Holocaust should be taught within the discipline of history. However, a sense of unease was expressed in discussions about the teaching of the Holocaust and the ability to transmit to later generations an understanding of it. One concern derived from an anxiety that the terrible stories of the Holocaust might cause "emotional damage" to youngsters. In addition, Israeli teachers tended to denigrate diaspora Jewish history in general, and that related to the Holocaust in particular.

Many young students held negative stereotypes of diaspora Jewry, which derived in part from the critique of diaspora life depicted in the Hebrew literature they studied. The poverty and humiliation of the Eastern European Jews were stressed, and, among the modern Hebrew writers, one could even find the use of antisemitic stereotypes.

Jewish history after the destruction of the Second Temple was perceived mostly as a series of persecutions and pogroms under the outdated reign of religious and rabbinical law. Many nonreligious youngsters felt very detached from Jewish religious reality and were encouraged to maintain such feelings through direct or hidden messages from their parents. The other side of the coin was admiration for the free, proud, brave, straightforward, "native"-born sabra, who displayed a remarkable sense of solidarity with the peer group and dedication to national causes (Rubinstein 1977, pp. 100–101; Shapira 1990; Almog 2000, pp. 124–36; Ben Amos and Bet-El 1999).

Until the early 1970s, most of the information students gained about the Holocaust was through attendance at various commemoration ceremonies, but even these were not introduced into the mandatory school curriculum until 1985. Thus, the knowledge the young student acquired was neither systematic nor coherent, and was completely divorced from any historical context. It was loaded with phrases suitable for commemoration ceremonies and aimed at engaging the participants emotionally. Thus, the difficulty young students and youth had in relating to the events of the Holocaust was intensified by the lack of information and any real intellectual challenge. Issues such as the passivity of the Jews and the Psalmist's phrase "as sheep to the slaughter" were often referred to by youth as a sole explanation for the large number of Jews murdered in Europe. In this respect the collective memory rather than history was dominant in the minds of many youngsters.

In the early 1960s, one outcome of the Eichmann Trial was a greater effort to introduce the study of the Holocaust into high school history textbooks. An analysis of these books still reveals a strong emotional and ideological bias. Ruth Firer, who researched Israeli textbooks, defined this period in the teaching of the Holocaust as the "Zionist" stage (Firer 1987).

During the 1970s, a considerable change occurred in the interest of the educational system in teaching the Holocaust. This was the outcome of various political and social developments after the wars of 1967 and 1973. The public reaction to these two quite different experiences that had caused deep anxiety and fear, and the analogies to the Holocaust that had been made in public discourse, led educators and historians to realize how inadequate was the knowledge about the Holocaust (Ofer 1996b). In the face of increasing criticism of the Ministry of Education's curriculum planning, the development of a structured Holocaust curriculum could no longer be put off.

The expansion of Holocaust research had provided more suitable books for teachers and made more general knowledge available. Graduates of the universities who had studied the Holocaust in an academic framework became part of a new generation of teachers who were able to introduce and lead changes in the teaching of the Holocaust. Many of these teachers had been high school students in the late 1950s and 1960s and concurred with the criticism voiced by a number of historians and educators concerning the absence of a historical approach to the study of the Holocaust. Thus a new tension between history and memory emerged in the sphere of education.

Haim Schatzker, a historian and educator, published a provocative article entitled "Trends in the Understanding of the Holocaust in Israeli Society" (Schatzker 1970, p. 22, 1992). The teaching of the Holocaust, he wrote, lacked a conceptual framework. It provided no intellectual stimulation, lacked historical context, and led to no understanding of its universal meaning. The outcome was mythologizing the Holocaust and it left the students with a sense of great unease, and the wish to withdraw the memory of the Holocaust from their life. They demonized the perpetrators and felt no empathy with the victims. Thus, irrational statements regarding the Jews, the Germans, and the other nations of the world were used as explanations of the horrible events.

Schatzker called upon Israeli teachers to liberate their minds from the commemoration framework and set regular study goals for the Holocaust, applying the same standards employed for any other study unit. Knowledge, information, and historical analysis were essential elements that all teachers should demand (Schatzker 1973).

He also opposed the presentation of the Holocaust as a uniquely Jewish event and demanded that its universal context and meanings be introduced. The attempted annihilation of the Jews extended the limits of Jewish history, and its meaning could be understood only if both the Jewish and universal contexts complemented one other (Simon 1963).

Three major opinions prevailed in clarifying the educational goals in Holocaust teaching. The first approach emphasized the need to strengthen Zionist identity through the Holocaust. The lesson transmitted through this approach was that the Jews had not seen the "writing on the wall" because of their false hopes concerning Jewish emancipation. The events of the Holocaust destroyed these illusions forever, and thus the return to Israel embodied the "lesson" learned from the Holocaust. The establishment of the State of Israel was the miraculous manifestation of both the Holocaust and Zionism (Firer 1987).

The second approach, promoted by Arie Carmon (1988), a historian and educator at the Institute of Democracy, offered "education toward values as the main goal of teaching the Holocaust." The student was to search for meaning in the events of the Holocaust in order to shape his personality as a human being and a Jew. It should be an intellectual and emotional challenge that would serve the individual in both searching for his identity and reflecting on his role in society.

The third approach regarded the primacy of historical knowledge from a positivist point of view. Acquisition of knowledge as the prime goal for the teaching of the Holocaust was essential in formulating the identity of young Israelis. Schatzker, Yisrael Gutman, and other historians have promoted this approach since the late 1970s. The Holocaust, as "an epoch-making event," had to be studied in depth. The goal, as Schatzker and Gutman stated it, was knowledge for the sake of knowledge, and the methodology to be used was a systematic historical analysis that would raise the major issues through readings of primary documents and a comprehensive comparative study. A textbook following these guidelines was provided for the students (Gutman and Schatzker 1990), and it became the most popular textbook on the Holocaust. However, in spite of the claim that knowledge of the events of the Holocaust was the primary goal, the textbook emphasized the meaning of the Holocaust from a broad Jewish and human perspective. The Zionist message was clearly presented as one of the options open to Jews, but the universal human message was also clearly stated in the book.

In 1999, two new textbooks for high school students, Yisrael Gutman's *Holocaust and Memory* and Nili Keren's *The Holocaust—a Journey to Memory,* were published in Israel. Both books put the word *memory* in the title to demonstrate the authors' attempts to consider the mind of an Israeli high school student immersed in the multivocal representations of the Holocaust of the last decade in rituals and the mass media. The two books considered the role of the Holocaust in the self-understanding of Israelis, but in addition stressed the importance of knowledge and a critical reading of memoirs and documents. Despite considerable differences between them, the two books placed the Holocaust in the context of Jewish history and modernity, and integrated the research of the last two decades. They presented the perspective of the individual who had lived during the Holocaust period, his relation to the family, the community, and his own wish to live and survive the Nazi onslaught. Keren's book mentioned the genocide committed by the Nazis on other nations and both discussed the mass murder of Poles committed by the Nazis during the occupation of Poland.

The question that emerges is what role both the study of history and collective memory played in shaping the images of the Holocaust and the self-understanding of Israelis. A look at the trips to Poland may offer a possible direction.

Trips to Poland

The first group visits to Poland were arranged in the period following the Eichmann trial and were initiated by Sara Nishmit, a survivor from Kibbutz Lohamei Hagetaot, who was involved in educational programs and wrote extensively on her Holocaust experience and on children during the Holocaust.

Following the 1967 War, however, Poland cut its political relations with Israel, and Israelis were no longer allowed to enter the country. In 1987, the initiative reemerged, and again it was the kibbutz movement that began to organize trips. The first ones took place in the 1980s when Poland was still under communist rule and martial law. The atmosphere in the country was very bleak: the streets were quite dark in the evenings, and the popular mood was gloomy. The Israeli students stayed at Janusz Korchak institutions, which were not very comfortable. The organizers considered the combination of a gloomy external space and a thoughtful internal milieu to be appropriate, corresponding to the kind of pilgrimage the trips were offering. Despite the fact that kibbutz educators had not held in-depth deliberations on the educational goals of these trips, outlining what they wished the students to carry away with them at the conclusion of the visit, they felt that the overall emotional impact of the trip was satisfying (Keren 1998, pp. 93–100; Keren 2000).

Why was it the kibbutz movement that initiated the trips to Poland? It may have been a result of the initiative of members who were committed to the commemoration of the Holocaust, possibly survivors (as was the case in the years 1965–66). Yet there were a number of auxiliary conditions in the kibbutzim that made the project feasible. Youth could earn the money to pay for the trip by contributing days of work to the collective; another motivation stemmed simply from the opportunity to go abroad. Yet in a number of kibbutzim, students were offered the choice of a trip to Greece or Poland, and it was Poland that they selected. Thus the trips carried a character of both pilgrimage and tourism. Unlike a merely tourist excursion, there was little consultation with the students about the program. Thus, the pilgrimage quality was more evident in the first groups, comprised of motivated individuals, students, and teachers. They advocated a preparatory program of a few months before departure for Poland. The students learned the history of the Holocaust, listened to survivors stories and conversed with them, read literature, and became well-informed about the history of the destruction in Poland.

The experiences of the first groups were greatly appreciated by educators as an additional stage in the study of the Holocaust—a peak or even a catharsis of meaningful emotional and intellectual experience. Pioneering with an experience that was both challenging and awakening produced a process of deliberation for both educators and students that impressed many. It was expressed in small internal publications of the groups after their return, in which they submitted poems, drawings, and thoughts noted while there and after their return. An analysis of these materials reveals diverse reactions. All students are grappling with the meaning of Jewish history and the role of Israel and Zionism in assuring the future of the Jewish people. However, no less apparent are the universal human messages. Students were clearly asking themselves a number of questions about the role of good and evil in human societies, about human nature, and about the capability of political leaders and a political order to shape individuals. They concluded by demanding of themselves that they become active citizens with a concern for social justice. All expressions are very personal and sincere (Ofer 2003; Balf 1998, supp).

Such heartfelt pondering of these disturbing issues should not be viewed as a "natural outcome" of the visit to the destroyed Jewish communities in Poland. It emerged from an educational process before, during, and after the trip. The intimacy of the experience (a small group, and the familiar social structure within it) and its encouragement of openness toward the Polish surroundings (which were quite gloomy during the late 1980s and early 1990s) contributed greatly to the sense of tolerance and the broad perspective.

One of the problems that the teachers and guides encountered was the emptiness of the Jewish landscape in Poland. The remains of Jewish culture are mostly concentrated in cemeteries and a small number of monuments and synagogues. The gap between students' expectations and what they actually saw in a city such as Warsaw was quite shocking. And thus, educators found themselves seeking a means to soften the frustration felt by the participating students, leading them on a guided independent walk through the main landscapes of the past, providing maps and texts for each section of the city (Atzili 1992).

Beginning in early 1988, the Ministry of Education decided to expand the project for high schools in general. Small scholarships were offered so that students from the disadvantaged sectors of society could also participate. The program is voluntary, and only a small number of students in each year's tenth to twelfth grades take part. But altogether some 1500 students go each year, aiming to be in Poland during Yom Hashoah. The climax of the visit is the commemorative ceremony at Auschwitz. Here Israeli students are not alone: they are

411

joined by Jewish students from the Diaspora, Israeli officials such as the IDF Chief of Staff, the president, minister of education, and leaders of Jewish organizations and Jewish communities. They march together the few kilometers from Auschwitz to Birkenau. This is called the "March of the Living" despite the traces of death that the participants see around them. Thus, the march forms a connection with those who marched before them, the living Jewish youth walking the path of the doomed Jews.

The March of the Living demonstrates Jewish resurrection with all its symbolic icons—an Israeli flag, the lighting of candles, the recitation of Kaddish for the dead, and reading out the names of victims. Survivors join these trips and take a central role in telling their own personal stories to the youth. Their life stories are heard while traveling by bus from one site of destruction to another, as well as in a more formal way in front of the death installations in Auschwitz. In many respects this is the climax of the trip.

Later trips have developed very differently from the first ones. As the numbers of participants grew dramatically, logistical problems emerged. Strict security measures had to be taken, and the program was carefully scrutinized and controlled. The students stayed in hotels, which brought out the tourist-like character of the trip, unlike the earlier journeys. Students were isolated from the Polish social and cultural environment, not only because they could not speak Polish, but because the program was tightly scheduled from early morning to late at night, with no encounters with contemporary Poland, or even with Polish youth. Students, teachers, and guides were enclosed in the buses and hotels, moving toward the places of destruction and breathing in the atmosphere and time of destruction. Little time was left in which the group members could discuss their daily experiences among themselves. And thus, despite the extensive preparatory sessions previous to the trip, there was actually very little encounter with Poland. Much of the broad Jewish and human message was lost; the event became an emotional happening that conveyed an immediate, almost instant, Jewish national lesson. Many students expressed a stronger Israeli and Zionist identity after they came back or while still in Poland. Thoughts such as "now we know why we are Israelis," or "only here we realized the meaning of the Jewish State," are often expressed, as if the physical and cultural space of Poland without Jewish life served to underline the meaning of being an Israeli Jew. The alien surrounding of Poland that is strongly emphasized in the bare landscape of the destruction sites, and the strong social feeling of togetherness, built an emotional inner storm that left little space for reflective criticism (Feldman, 2000, pp. 103–48, 324–36). In this respect the trip to Poland may contradict the intellectual and historical goals set for teaching the Holocaust in the classroom. The question of how these adolescents would integrate the two conflicting experiences in the future would speak to their development as grown-up persons and would require an independent research.

Conclusion

As we have seen, the memory of the Holocaust in Israel is multifaceted. It reflects people of different generations and backgrounds who grapple with the meaning of the Holocaust and its significance both in their private experience and in their relation to the collective. On the other hand, there is an institutionalized effort to establish a "meta-memory" of the Holocaust. We learned that all these voices—the individual, the group, and the national—are speaking to each other and thus creating a conversation. This conversation is taking place in a specific social and cultural context that is evolving and changing constantly.

In a country that has experienced several wars, and where national identity is either denied or contested by another people with whom Israel shares territory, the Holocaust often appears as an antithetical reality. However, a majority perceives it as a central event in Jewish history that calls for a reflective approach. Certain Israelis fear that, if the Holocaust were a focus, militarism would become a tolerated ideology in Israel, and that the lesson of the Holocaust—framed as never again being a victim unable to fight against its enemy—would come to dominate Israel's worldview (Dubi Helman 1983; Uri Brener 1983; Schweid 1983; Aloni, April 24: 1996). In their eyes the transition from being perceived as a victim to becoming a perpetrator was an alarming possibility. More recently, a provocative post- or anti-Zionist approach has done just that: viewed Holocaust commemoration as a means to promote nationalistic identity, militarism, and a particularistic historical memory that denies any universal meaning of the Holocaust. However, the critique relating to the manipulation of the Holocaust by various political forces, voiced strongly after 1977 (Ofir 1986, pp. 2–7; 1995) seems one-sided in view of the multiple individual and group efforts to shape commemoration patterns.

Therefore, beyond the historical fact of the Holocaust, its central meaning lies in the ongoing dialogue between the individual, the community, the society, and the events of the past as reflected by those who write, study, think, and present it in an artistic form. This dialogue represents an endless effort to understand the meaning of the Holocaust, and a permanent search for ways to incorporate its lessons into the collective memory. On the other hand, it was apparent in the study that collective memory itself became a central factor in constructing the memory of the Holocaust—in particular for those who never experienced it. The tension between collective memory and its symbolism and myth and the study of the history of the Holocaust is visible in teaching the subject in the schools and is strongly represented in the visit to Poland.

NOTES

1. The law concerning Nazi collaborators, which was ratified by the Israeli Knesset in August 1950, was initiated by lawmakers under great pressure from Holocaust survivors. Some survivors met in Israel people who they thought were collaborating with the Nazis as Kapos, or through the Jewish police, or in any other manner. They wanted to bring them to court; however, the legal system did not allow this owing to the lack of any legislation. The first discussion in the Knesset took place on March 27 (*Divrei Haknesset* vol. 5, n.d.: 1142–62), the final discussion on August 10 (*ibid.*, vol. 6: 2397.)

2. Youth Aliya was established in 1932 to assist youth from Germany find new opportunities in Palestine. The movement was supported by the Zionist Movement of America and was headed for many years by Henrietta Sold. As the Nazi policy of persecution spread in Germany and other European countries, and during the war years, Youth Aliyah was an important institution helping to rescue youth and children. After the war, it was crucial in reconstructing the life of orphans and youth who survived the Holocaust.

REFERENCES

Almog, Oz. 2000. *The Sabra: The Creation of the New Jew.* Berkely, Calif: University of California Press.

Aloni, Shulamit. 1996. Speech on the occasion of the Israel Prize ceremony, April 24. Israel Information Service.

Alterman, Nathan. 1962. "Mozenei Mishpat" (The Scales of the Trail). In *Hatur Hashviyi,* vol. 3. Tel Aviv: Hakibbutz Hameuhad. 497–500.

Angress, Judith. 1988. "Remembrance Hall in Ma'ayan Zvi." Ma'ayan Zvi Archive (MZA).

Atzili, Avraham. 1992. *Madrich Lametayel Bevarsha* (A guide to the traveler in Warsaw) (Tel Aviv: Moreshet).

Auron Yair. 1993. *Jewish and Israeli Identity.* Tel Aviv: Sifriat Hapoa'lim (Hebrew).

Balf, Micha. 1998. *Bein Yam Vecarmel* (Between Mt. Carmel and the Mediterranean: the development of public commemoration of the Holocaust in Kibbutz Ma'agan Michael and Ma'ayan Tzvi). Master's thesis, Hebrew niversity of Jerusalem.

Barth, Aaron. 1946. Meeting of Yad Vashem Committee, Central Zionist Archive (CZA), S53/1671, September 16.

Baumel, Judy. 1995. "In Everlasting Memory: Individual and Communal Holocaust Commemoration in Israel." *Israel Affairs* 1(3): 146–70.

Ben Amos, Avner, and Ilanah Bet-El. 1999. "Tekasim Hinuch vehistorya: yom hashoah veyom hzikaron bevatei hasefer beyisrael" (Ceremonies, education, and history: Holocaust Day and the memorial day in schools in Israel). In *Education and History,* ed. Rivka, Peldhai and Immanuel Etkes, 457–80. Jerusalem: Shazar. (Hebrew).

Ben Gurion, David. 1960. *Divrei Haknesset* 29: 1286.

Brener, Uri. 1983. "Al mashmauth hashoah beyamenu" (On the meaning of the Holocaust in our days). *Mibifnim* 45 (1–4): 254–56.

Brug, Muli. 1997. *Nes hagevurah: Haavnayah hamamlackhtit shel zickhron hashoah* (The flag of heroism: the state construction of the memory of heroism in the Holocaust). Master's Thesis, Hebrew University of Jerusalem (Hebrew).

Carmon, Arie. 1979. "Teaching the Holocaust as a Means of Fostering Values." *Curriculum Inquiry* 9 (3): 209–28.

———. 1988. "Teaching the Holocaust in Israel." In *Methodology in the Academic Teaching of the Holocaust,* ed. Zev Garber, 75–91. Lanham, N.J., New York, and London: University Press of America.

Ettinger, Shmuel, and Michael Ziv. 1960. *Divrei Hayamim* (History) 4(2): Jerusalem: Yuval.

Even Hen Ya'akov. 1961a. "Trial Diary." *Hazofeh,* May 2, p. 1.

———. 1961b. "Trial Diary." *Hazofeh,* June 4, pp. 1, 3.

Farago, Uri. 1983. "The Awareness of the Holocaust among Israeli Studying Youth." *Dapim Leheker Hashoah* 3: 159–78.

Fay, Doron. 1961. "But for the Grace of God." *The Jerusalem Post,* May 26, p. 4.

Feldman, Jackie. 2000. *It Is My Brother Whom I Am Seeking: Israeli Youth Voyages to Holocaust Poland,* Ph.D. dissertation, Hebrew University of Jerusalem.

Firer, Ruth. 1987. "The Holocaust in Textbooks in Israel." In *The Treatment of the Holocaust in Textbooks,* ed. Randolph L. Braham, 178–88. New York: Columbia University Press.

Gouri, Haim. 1963. *Mul Ta Hazkhukhit: Mishpat Yerushalayim* (The Glass Cage: The Jerusalem Trial). Tel Aviv: Hakibbutz Hameuhad (Hebrew).

Gutman, Yisrael. 1960. "Yom Hashoah" (Holocaust Day). *Hashsavua Bakibutz Haartzi* (This Week in the Kibbutz Haartzi), April 22, p. 1.

———. 1999. *Holocaust and Memory.* Jerusalem: Shazar Center and Yad Vashem.

Gutman, Yisrael, and Haim Schatzker. 1990. *The Holocaust and Its Meaning.* Jerusalem: Shazar Center.

Helman, Dubi. 1983. "Al mashmauth hashoah beyamenu" (On the meaning of the Holocaust in our days). *Mibifnim* 45 (1–4): 246–48.

Herman, N. Simon. 1977. *Jewish Identity: A Social Psychological Perspective.* Beverly Hills, Calif.: Sage Publications.

———. 1970. *Israelis and Jews: The Continuity of an Identity.* Philadelphia: Jewish Publication Society.

Ka-Tzetnik. 1961. "I Was on Another Planet." *Davar,* June 8, 1961, p. 3.

Keren, Nili. 1985. *Hashpaot me`azvei da`at hakahal umehkar hashoah `al hadiun hakhinukhi beyisrael 1948–1981* (The impact of public opinion and historical research on the development of educational thought and educational programs concerning the Holocaust in Israel 1948–1981). Ph.D. dissertation, Hebrew University, Jerusalem (Hebrew).

———. 1998. "Masa leyizuv hazickron" (Student trips to Poland—a memory forming journey).

In *Memory and Awareness of the Holocaust in Israel,* ed. Yoel Rappel. Tel-Aviv: Mod-Publishing House (Hebrew).

———. 1999. *The Holocaust: A Journey to Memory.* Tel Aviv: Tel Aviv Books.

———. 2000. "Holocaust Education Towards the 21st Century." *Studia Judaica* 9: 159–74.

Lentil, Ronit. 1998. "To Reoccupy the Territory of Silence: Israeli Writers and Film Makers as daughters of Survivors." In *Memory and Awareness of the Holocaust in Israel,* ed. Joel Rappel. Tel Aviv: Mod Publishing House (Hebrew).

———. 2000. *Israel and the Daughters of the Shoah: Reoccupying the Territories of Silence.* New York, Oxford: Berghahn Books.

Ofer, Dalia. 1996a. "Linguistic conceptualization of the Holocaust in Palestine and Israel, 1942–1953." *Journal of Contemporary History* 31: 567–95.

———.1996b. "Israel." In *The World Reacts to the Holocaust,* ed. David Wyman. 836–922. Baltimore, London; Johns Hopkins University Press.

———. 2000. "The Strength of Remembrance: Commemoration of the Holocaust during the First Decade of Israel." *Jewish Social Studies* 6 (2) (Winter): 24–55.

———. 2001. "The Israeli Discourse on the Holocaust." In *The Holocaust in Jewish History,* Jerusalem: Yad Vashem.

Ofir, Adi. 1986. "On the Renewal of the Name." *Politika* 8 (June–July): 2–7 (Hebrew).

Ofir, B. 1958. "Al Limud Hashoah Beveit Hasefer Beyisrael" (On the teaching of the Holocaust in Israeli Schools). *Yediyot Yad Vashem* 15–16 (April): 19–20.

Oron, Yair. *Jewish and Israeli Identity.* Tel Aviv: Sifriyat Hapoalim (Hebrew).

Plozker, Sever. 1993. *Yediot Aharonot,* 22 April, p. 19.

Pundak, Nahum. 1961. "The Man with the Black Robe." *Dvar Hashavu'a,* July 7.

Rein, Esti. 1994. "Mehantzaha collelet lehantzhaha individualit: andartaot lezeckher hashoah, beyisrael" (From general to individual commemoration: Holocaust monuments in Israel). *Gesher* 126 (Winter): 70–81.

Rubinstein, Amnon. 1977. *Liheyot 'Am Hofshi* (To be a free nation). Tel Aviv: Schocken.

Schatzker, Haim. 1970. *Ha'aretz,* May 1, p. 22.

———. 1973. "Ba'ayot didaktiot Behoraat Hashoah" (Didactic issues in the teaching of the Holocaust). *Masuah* 1: 18–26.

———. 1992. "Teaching the Holocaust in Changing Times." *Moreshet* 52 (April), pp. 165–71 (Hebrew).

Schwartz, Barry. 1982. "The Social Context of Commemoration: A Study in Collective Memory." *Social Forces* 61: 374–402.

Schweid, Eli. 1983. "Al mashmauth hashoah beyamenu" (On the meaning of the Holocaust in our days). *Mibifnim* 45 (1–4): 257–59.

Semel, Nava. 2000. "How Did You Survive?" *Studia Judaica* 9: 113–21.

Shapira, Anita. 1990. "Dor Baaretz" (A generation in the land). *Alpayim* 2: 178–203.

Shelav, Jacob. 1958. "Hashoah Betoda'at Dorenu" (The Holocaust in the awareness of our generation). *Yediyot Yad Vashem* 15–16: 2–3.

Shmueli, Ephraim. 1961. *Toldot 'Amenu* (History of our People), vol. 7. Tel Aviv: Yavneh.

Simon, Arie. 1963. "Hearot leba'ayat hashoah behinukhenu" (Comments on the Holocaust in our education). *Da'at Uma'as Behinukh: Sefer Arnon* (Arnon book: study and practice in education), ed. Yohanan Tverski, 360–65. Tel Aviv: Public Committee.

Stauber, Roni. 2000. *Halekah Lador: Shoaha ugvurah bamahshavah Hatziburith Baaretz Bishnot hahamishim* (Lesson for This Generation: Holocaust and Heroism in Israeli Public Discourse in the 1950s). Jerusalem: Yad Ben Zvi Press, Ben Gurion Research Center Sede Boker, Ben Gurion University.

Tavor, Moshe. 1961a. "Trial Diary." *Davar,* May 2, p. 2.

———. 1961b. "Trial Diary." *Davar,* May 3, p. 5.

Wardi, Dina. 1992. *Memorial Candles: Children of the Holocaust.* London: Routledge.

Winter, Jay, and Emanuel Sivan. 1999. *War and Remembrance in the 20th Century.* Cambridge: Cambridge University Press.

Wyman, David S., ed. 1996. *The World Reacts to the Holocaust.* Baltimore, Md.: Johns Hopkins University Press.

Yablonka, Hannah. 2001. *The Eichmann Trial.* Jerusalem: Yad Ben Zvi (Hebrew).

Yerushalmi, Yosef Hayim. 1989. *Zakor: Jewish History and Jewish memory.* New York: Schocken Books.

Zerubavel, Eviatar. 1996. "Social Memories: Steps to a Sociology of the Past." *Qualitative Sociology* 19 (3). 283–99.

Zerubavel, Yael. 1995. *Recovered Roots: Collective Memory and the Making of Israeli National Tradition.* Chicago and London: The University Press of Chicago.

PART VI

Israel and Diaspora Jews

CHAPTER EIGHTEEN

The Israelis and the Jewish Diaspora

അ

Gabriel Sheffer

During the course of the last decade, most dispersed nations, including World Jewry, have experienced profound ideological, structural, and behavioral changes. Such changes have occurred both on the collective, national level and within each of the Diaspora communities of these dispersed nations. Consequently, both the peoples in their homelands as well as those in diasporas, including the Israelis and the Jewish Diaspora, have become engaged in an agonizing reexamination of the trends determining their new situation. These trends are of a circular nature: they are influenced by reorientation in homeland-Diaspora mutual perceptions, attitudes, and activities, while these restructurings have in turn influenced the behavior of the people in the homelands and the diasporas. In this context the involved actors, including, of course, Israeli-Diaspora relations, have begun to reconsider, among other issues, homeland-diaspora relations. Since this aspect has not been adequately studied, it merits serious reexamination.

In this vein, this chapter has two purposes: first, to reconsider the specific case of Israeli-Diaspora relations, primarily from the homeland's perspective; second, to use the insights to be gained from the analysis of this case to shed light on some general theoretical aspects of modern Diasporism.

From the former point of view—that of the specific case of Israeli-Diaspora relations—the focus in this chapter is on a number of issues: the attitudes of the Israeli public toward the Diaspora, the current ideologies and agendas of the main Israeli political camps and parties, the formal positions of the various Israeli governments that were formed during the last decade, and the debatable issue of interdependence between the two parts of the nation. As to the theoretical perspective, there is a need for a few more elaborate preliminary comments, which follow in the next section.

Preliminary Theoretical Remarks

It is almost superfluous to mention that, far from disappearing, the number and size of ethno-national diasporas has recently been growing. Partly owing to their number and size, and partly because of the new global political setting, such diasporas have become significant actors in the trans-state, regional, and intrastate arenas. To mention only a few: the Armenian, Jewish, and Chinese "historical diasporas"; the Irish and Italian "modern diasporas"; and the Moroccan, Tamil, Sri-Lankan, and Vietnamese "incipient diasporas," are all alive and active (concerning these three categories of ethno-national diasporas, see Sheffer 2002). Despite assimilatory and integrative trends, as well as return movements, membership in these and many other ethno-national diasporas is in fact expanding, their geographical dispersal is increasing, and their activities are intensifying.

In many cases, members of such diasporas serve as determined agents for spreading their respective homelands' cultures and for promoting their interests. Thus, the existence of efficient diasporic lobbies acting to protect and enhance the political and diplomatic interests of their homelands in host countries, regional unions, and global systems is well known and documented (e.g., Shain 1999). The same applies to diasporas' financial support of their homelands—the current rough estimate of total annual remittances by these diasporas to their homelands is about $90 billion (*Economist,* August 19, 2000). Similarly, such diasporas as the Turkish in Germany, the Irish in the United States, and the Armenian in the United States invest in their homelands. Most important, members of such ethno-national diasporas are inclined to keep continuous contact with and to extend help to their homelands.

These facts are not surprising, as the most essential features of these diasporas' common profile are their continuous connections with their homelands and the loyalty that they demonstrate toward them, based on their primordial cum-psychological/symbolic ethno-national identities. This profile of ethno-national diasporas contains some additional features: These entities are created by both voluntary and forced migration to host countries, usually not adjacent to the homelands; the members of these entities remain minorities in their host countries; and, based on their primordial and psychological/symbolic ethno-national identity, Diaspora members develop a strong sense of solidarity that in turn serves as a significant backdrop factor for their various activities. Once formed, most of these entities organize and establish elaborate cultural, social, and political bodies and networks involved in contacts and relations with a multitude of trans-state, international, and host country actors (for the full definitional profile of the diasporas, see Sheffer 1986b, 1994, 2002).

It should be noted, however, that at the very core of the Diaspora phenomenon are three sets of reciprocal relations—Diaspora-homeland, Diaspora–host country, and relations with other communities of the same Diaspora (Sheffer 1986b). There is abundant quantitative and qualitative evidence to indicate that diasporas are engaged in intensive reciprocal exchanges with these actors that result in substantial multilateral flows of cultural, political, and economic resources. Some of these exchanges have been analyzed and documented in academic and nonacademic publications. However, most of these studies have focused on diasporas' relations with their host societies and governments. Thus, in the rapidly proliferating literature on ethno-national diasporas, the most frequently discussed issues are the following: Migration to host countries; permanent settlement in these host countries; identity and identification after the establishment of the diasporic communities in their host countries; assimilation and integration vs. separation and autonomy; language, culture, folklore, solidarity, and loyalty; and cooperative vs. conflictual relations with host societies and governments (Cohen 1997; Vertovec and Cohen 1999).

Similarly, the relations between homeland and host country against the backdrop of diaspora existence and activities on behalf of the homeland have reasonably been explored. Here, however, it should be noted that, while the demographic, sociological, cultural, collective psychological, and ideological aspects of Diasporism have been examined, the political angle has been almost utterly neglected. Similarly, various empirical questions pertaining to homeland-Diaspora relations and their theoretical implications have been less explored. The general gist of the few available studies on this aspect, except for some of my own publications (Sheffer 1993a, 1994), is that homeland-Diaspora relations are pretty idyllic. It has been maintained that homelands generally maintain close contacts with their diasporas, that they are concerned about assimilatory and integrative processes occurring in their diasporas, that they are committed to the protection and promotion of these diasporas, that they would come to the rescue of their diasporas if these were to find themselves in distress and be persecuted, that they consider their diasporas' well-being to be an important national issue, that they are attuned to the needs and wishes of their diasporas, and that they always welcome the return of members of their diasporas. A closer look at these relations reveals a different situation.

Admittedly, it is difficult, and sometimes even biased, to infer general theoretical conclusions from a single case study. Yet the theoretical and methodological justification for the adequacy of the application of insights that will be gained from the analysis of Israeli–Jewish Diaspora experience is based on the view that, because of its similarities to other diasporas, rather than its uniqueness or peculiarity, the Jewish Diaspora and its relations with the homeland indeed constitute a proper representative case (Sheffer 2002).

The Case of Israeli-Jewish Diaspora Relations

In light of these preliminary observations, we may now briefly introduce the case of Israeli–Jewish Diaspora relations. A realistic analysis of this case is especially important as, even more emphatically than in other similar cases, Israeli, Jewish, and Gentile observers share a certain myopic view of the nature of Israeli-Diaspora relations. Thus most observers are inclined to think that the fundamental attitude of the Israelis and the policies pursued by successive Israeli governments have always been intended to strengthen their relations with the Diaspora, to come to its rescue during periods of persecution and stress, and to ensure its existential and practical interests.

This idealized perception, which not surprisingly is also held by some hostile observers and anti-Semites, deserves critical analysis. Quite a different picture emerges when Israeli attitudes and governmental policies toward the Diaspora are attentively and critically examined. Rather than the above idyllic picture, a critical scrutiny of these relations reveals ambiguity, fickleness, a strong emphasis on Israeli interests, and duplicity. Even the relatively few studies that focus on this perspective show that, at the very least, this issue has always been more complex, multifaceted, and not so innocent in comparison to the depictions with which most bystanders are usually acquainted (Liebman 1977; Vital 1990; Don Yehiya 1990; Sandler 1993). These aspects will be elaborated further on in this chapter.

As has been said above, the analysis here pertains to a recent period, that is, the period since the collapse of the Soviet Union in the late twentieth century. This starting point has been chosen because that major international development, along with certain related processes on both the global and regional (Mid-Eastern) levels, has altered Israeli and Diaspora positions. Among other things, the collapse of the Soviet Union enhanced the Jewish exodus from Russia and the former Soviet republics, and compelled Israel to deal with an unexpected, enormous influx of Russian Jews and non-Jews. Thus some of World Jewry's perennial worries and problems were solved, while other new problems emerged. Though this time perspective is short, it is evident that the migration of about a million and a half persons from the former Soviet Union to Israel, the United States and other host countries during such a short period has major implications for Israel and the Diaspora. These implications reinforce the need for a thorough reexamination of Israeli-Diaspora relations and justify the focus on the occurrences during the last decade and a half.

Though the following aspects are not at the epicenter of the discussion in this chapter, there is also a need to remember the aggregate impacts of recent developments that have occurred on the global level and inside most host countries regarding Israel and its relation with the Diaspora. Globalization, liberalization, democratization, and regionalization have influenced Israeli societal and governmental attitudes and policies toward their brethren in the Diaspora. For example, Israeli perceptions and positions concerning foreign relations in general and those with the Diaspora in particular have been influenced by reactions to

Israeli policies and actions vis-à-vis the Palestinians as reported in the global media. Similarly, Israeli attitudes toward the Diaspora are influenced by criticisms of Israel expressed by liberal segments in the Diaspora, on the one hand, and by rightist and religious Gentiles who sympathize with Israel, on the other.

Furthermore, not only have there recently been perceptual and attitudinal changes, but certain concrete economic and political developments have also affected these relations. These include the major decline in Diaspora allocation of financial resources for Israel, and in changed Diaspora positions vis-à-vis the World Zionist Organization, the Jewish Agency, and other "national" bodies and enterprises.

Moreover, the need for a comprehensive reexamination of these relations is enhanced by a perennial problem that exists in the realm of homelands-diasporas relations, including the Israeli–Jewish Diaspora case. This pertains to homelands' persistent declarations concerning their "total and continuous sympathy towards and support of 'their' diasporas" and the "existential importance of intimate reciprocal connections" with these entities. Yet when actual homeland policies are examined, it soon becomes clear that there is a discernable gap between such declarations and the actual positions and policies pursued by these governments and other agencies. In the case of Israeli-Diaspora relations, it is sufficient to peruse the attitudes and policies of the five Israeli prime ministers who served during the late twentieth century—Shamir, the late Rabin, Peres, Netanyahu, and Barak—to note the substantial gap between declarations and actions.

Israeli Attitudes and Contacts with the Diaspora

As a first step in the analysis of Israeli attitudes toward the Diaspora, a distinction should be made between four groupings within the Israeli society. The first group consists of those Israelis who have close relatives in the Diaspora. This category may in turn be divided into two subgroups: The former consists of Israelis who have relatives among the *yordim* (Israelis who permanently or for longer periods reside abroad), and the latter includes Israelis who have relatives whose grandparents, parents, or themselves have not been born in Israel or resided there. The chances are greater that members of the first subgroup will maintain more persistent connections with their relatives and also obtain from them greater support. Similarly, these Israelis will conduct more regular and intensive communications and host more visits of Diaspora Jews than members of the second subgroup. Nevertheless, in comparison with other Israelis, members of both subgroups have more intimate knowledge of Diaspora life, show greater concern about developments in the Diaspora, and are ready to espouse clearer positions in this sphere.

The second group is that of the general "interested public"—namely, those Israelis who have no familial connections with the Diaspora, but have traveled abroad, observed Diaspora Jews, visited Diaspora communities, hosted Diaspora Jews visiting Israel, demonstrated interest in the Diaspora, and studied it in a more systematic manner. These Israelis tend to show sympathy toward the Diaspora in general, and particularly toward specific communities that they happen to know better. These Israelis would also be ready to participate in meetings with Diaspora Jews visiting Israel, attend lectures about the Diaspora and other related functions, serve on committees and as delegates to Zionist congresses, and act in Israel and abroad on behalf of the Diaspora.

However, the largest group is that of apathetic Israelis. Although, as will be shown below, these Israelis may express their general identification with and concern for the Diaspora, they are in fact neither knowledgeable about nor interested in Diaspora realities, and therefore care only marginally about its development and problems. Their occasional expressions of affinity with their brethren abroad, though not entirely cynical lip service, are culturally and politically almost meaningless. Moreover, they would not go out of their way to act on behalf of the Diaspora.

The fourth group is the smallest, but most vociferous and active in this sphere. This is composed of "professional Zionists" and other Israelis who are either employed or voluntarily active in the various institutions and bodies dealing with Israeli-Diaspora relations. Their involvement in Diaspora affairs is motivated by a combination of real concern for the Diaspora and the fact that this is their main professional occupation or social-political activity.

These qualitative observations are buttressed by a few less impressionistic assessments of the Israeli public attitudes toward the Diaspora. These are the results of public opinion polls conducted from the late 1960s until the 1990s, especially by the Louis Guttman Israel Institute of Applied Social Research. The Institute conducted periodic surveys during the late 1960s, 1970s, 1980s, and early 1990s, and produced over-time analyses of the results of these polls.

In a note prefacing the analysis of these polls, the pollsters draw attention to the important fact that, generally speaking, only those Israelis who answer that they are "extremely positive" about their "belongingness" and affinities with the Diaspora can indeed be regarded as having genuine positive feelings in this respect. Those Israelis who answer only "yes" or "positive" to such questions tend to behave more like those who deny having any feelings of belonging (Levy and Guttman 1987; Levy, Levinsohn, and Katz 1993).

At the outset of the discussion of the Israelis' attitudes toward the Diaspora, it should be noted that the surveys clearly indicate a marked change in the general attitude of the Israelis toward the Diaspora since the late 1960s. While, during the pre-State period and immediately following its establishment, the negation of the Diaspora in the sense of Galut (exile) was a strong "negative myth," today it does not play a prominent role in the minds and sentiments of most Israelis (Levy and Guttman 1975; Smith 1984; Tzemach 1986; Don Yehiya 1990).

Furthermore, according to these and more recent surveys, during the 1973 War 66 percent of Israeli Jews answered that they definitely felt themselves to be "part of the Jewish People throughout the world." A clear change occurred after that war, which elicited strong reactions. Thus, in April 1974 only 46 percent stated that they had that definite sense of belonging. Seven years later, in January 1981, 58 percent said that that they felt very positively about being part of the Jewish people; in 1986, 67 percent said they did so; and in 1992, 65 percent said that they felt this to be the case (Levy and Guttman 1987, Levy, Levensohn, and Katz 1993). According to these surveys, then, except for the fluctuations that occurred after the traumatic 1973 War, two-thirds of Israeli Jews feel that they are an integral part of the Jewish People. A breakdown of the figures in the 1993 survey has shown that this sense of belongingness depends to a great extent upon religious observance. Thus, among the "totally nonobservant Israelis" only 46 percent feel that they are a part of the Jewish People, whereas among the "strictly" and "mostly" observant Jews the percentages are definitely higher— 83 percent and 80 percent respectively (Levi 1993).

Here it is worth noting that there was a noticeable difference between the sense of belonging expressed by Diaspora Jews, especially by American Jews, and by the Israelis. Thus, in the 1980s about 70 percent of American Jews said that their concern for Israel is a very significant factor in their Jewishness. This implies that more American Jews identified with the entire nation than did Israelis (Cohen 1983).

More important in the context of the present analysis: according to the pollsters of the Guttman Institute, the feeling of belonging to World Jewry did not necessarily imply that one saw no difference between Israeli Jews and other Jews around the world. Thus, in June 1967, 55 percent of the Israelis said that they "definitely agree" or "agree" that there is such difference; in 1973, 62 percent said that they felt that there was such difference; in 1981, 43 percent said so; in 1986, 44 percent; and in 1993 about 50 percent expressed that sense.

The surveys also reflected the fact that feelings of belonging to the Jewish People correlate with other aspects of identity and identification. One of these aspects is that of mutual dependence between Israel and the Diaspora. In the early 1990s, about three-quarters of the Israelis believed that Jews in Israel and in the Diaspora share a common fate, 68 percent agreed with the proposition that Israel would not be able to survive without a strong relationship with the Diaspora, but a larger majority (77 percent) agreed with the proposition that the Jewish Diaspora would not be able to survive without Israel. Again, this means that the Israelis thought that the Jewish State was the main anchor of Jewish persistence, whereas the surveys from the 1970s and 1980s showed that only 32 percent to 41 percent of Israelis thought so.

Similar attitudes were expressed regarding the right of Diaspora Jews to intervene in Israeli affairs (Levy and Guttman 1987): A majority was for parallel autonomy of Israel and the Diaspora. It is unfortunate that the surveys of the early 1990s did not examine Israelis' attitudes in regard to their right to intervene in the affairs of Diaspora Jews. Nevertheless, the assumption here is that, since the time those surveys were published, and as a result of cumulative changes on the global, regional, and local levels, the opposition to mutual intervention has only grown. Also important in the context of this chapter are the findings that about 68 percent (i.e., between 63 percent and 72 percent) of the Israelis felt that when deciding on foreign policy the Israeli government should consider the implications for Diaspora Jews (Levy and Guttman 1987; and cf. Smith 1984 and Tzemach 1986,).

Though these studies did not distinguish between the grassroots and political elites, actually there is an evident gap between these two groups—generally speaking, the politicians tend to disregard the attitude of their followers and show greater cynicism in this sphere.

The Formal Positions of the Israeli Political Camps and Parties

In contradistinction to the well-known claims about the "end of ideology" and "the end of history," ideology and memories about historical events still play an important role in Israel in the processes of aggregation of voters' wishes, in the articulation of their goals, and in the mobilization of party members, supporters, and voters. These perceptions and attitudes consequently influence the formulation of political policies. In this vein, and despite the shift of the entire system to the religious-nationalist "right" that has occurred since the 1973 War (which in turn resulted in voters' movement across bloc lines and in the 1977 critical elections), the Israeli party system still essentially consists of three loosely organized ideological camps. These are the center-left, center-right, and religious camps (Arian 1997; Dowty 1998; Shamir and Arian 1999). Thus, in order to simplify the discussion of positions of various parties in this highly complex system, the following discussion focuses on the main political parties in each of these three camps.

The Center-Left Bloc

THE LABOR PARTY Although the Labor Party's power was severely decimated during the 1990s and especially in the opening years of the twenty-first century (most notably in the wake of Prime Minister Barak's devastating defeat in the 2001 elections), it is still the largest party in the Knesset and hence in this bloc. While attitudes and policies pertaining to security and foreign policy constituted the first chapter in the Labor platform for the 12th Knesset (elected in 1988), the Jewish Diaspora was only discussed in chapter 12 of this platform, entitled "Zionism, The Jewish People, Immigration and Absorption." This chapter opens with a statement about the principles of socialist Zionism and the necessity for their implementation. According to the Labor Party's platform, these principles expressed the moral and social values of Judaism and constituted the precondition for ensuring Israel's centrality in World Jewry. Most of that chapter dealt in great detail with the need to ensure Jewish *aliyah* (return immigration) and the integration of the immigrants into Israeli society. Yet only one subsection of that chapter (12.5) discussed Israeli-Diaspora relations.

Maintaining its traditional explicitly Israel-centric position, the party unequivocally stated that Israel is *the* national center. The Labor platform rejected "all theories about dual-centrality" (meaning the centrality of Israel and the American Jewish community in World Jewry). The platform asserted that Israeli-Diaspora relations should be based on Israeli-Diaspora cooperation in building the homeland and ensuring Jewish continuity in Israel and abroad, as well as in strengthening Jewish identity and emphasizing that the situation in Israel influenced the entire Jewish People. Yet it said that Israeli-Diaspora cooperation was mainly intended to ensure Jewish immigration to Israel. The platform maintained that Labor would encourage full cooperation, an open dialogue, and direct contacts with groups and organizations in Israel and the Diaspora. Another subsection (12.6) in that platform dealt with the World Zionist Organization (WZO) and pledged the party's support of that movement. The party was determined to put the ultimate Zionist mission (that is, encouraging immigration to Israel) high on the order of priorities of the WZO (the Labor Party's platform for the 12th Knesset).

The party's platform for the 13th Knesset (elected in 1992) did not include any specific chapter or clause concerning the Diaspora or Israeli-Diaspora relations. The Labor Party's platform, published on the eve of the 1996 general elections, included some sections on Israeli-Diaspora relations that did not add much to what had been said in the 1988 program. However, in the chapter on "Religion and State" in the 1996 platform, the party stated that it would examine the establishment of a national educational authority responsible for promoting "Jewish consciousness and tradition" in both Israel and the Diaspora. This authority "would deal with all questions pertaining to relations among the Jewish People and to Israeli-Diaspora relations, and find suitable solutions for the continuity of Jewish identity." Immediately following this chapter, the platform presented a chapter on "Immigration and Integration." Probably under the influence of Knesset member Yossi Beilin, who has been a determined proponent of reforms in this sphere and of the introduction of new cooperative endeavors (Beilin 1999), this chapter of the platform suggested a project resembling Project Birthright, which Beilin had initiated and sponsored (Labor Party platform for the 14th Knesset).

Here is the place to somewhat elaborate on Beilin's challenging proposals for reforms in Israeli-Diaspora relations. Beilin argues that the current revolutionary changes in World Jewry dictate urgent action based on a profound dialogue between Israel and the Jewish communities, especially with the American-Israeli community. According to Beilin, such dialogue should be conducted within a new world Jewish organization (which he calls "Beit Israel"—the House of Israel), which would function as a Jewish parliament, and which should replace all old Jewish and Zionist organizations. The new national organization's tasks should include efforts to unite the entire nation, including all those who regard themselves as Jews; it should direct all Jewish activities, especially in the Third World; it should deal with Jewish education; it should be responsible for project "Birthright"; among its tasks will also be mobilizing and training young leaders; and it should tackle antisemitism, racism, neo-Nazism and neo-Fascism. Beilin also suggests that funds raised by Jewish communities should primarily be directed to finance intracommunal rather than Israeli needs (Beilin 1999).

The Labor Party did not publish a new platform on the eve of the 1999 elections, and instead used its previous platform.

MERETZ This party was formed as a result of a union between three center and center-left parties. One of the parties that formed Meretz was the Ratz Party, formerly a liberal dovish center party. The section on Israeli-Diaspora relations in the party's platform for the 1988 elections was short. It stated that the party would act to promote the renewal of Zionism and of Jewish life in Israel and the diasporas; the main goal was the concentration of the Jewish people in the homeland. The party asserted that renewal of Zionism would assist Jewish communities in maintaining Jewish life in the Diaspora, encourage Jews to immigrate, and facilitate the integration of these immigrants (Ratz platform for the 12th Knesset). Mapam, formerly the only socialist party in the center-left bloc, did not mention Israeli-Diaspora relations in its platform for the 1988 elections.

On the eve of the 1992 general elections, Ratz and Mapam were joined by Shinui (also a liberal and moderate party) and together formed the center-left

Meretz party. The united party's platform for the 1996 elections mentioned the Jewish Diaspora in the chapter that dealt with the status of religion in Israel. It stated in this context that Israel should implement the ideals of "humanist Zionism"—i.e., a separation of state and church aimed at avoiding religious pressures and constraints. It continued with a statement about the right of all Jews to immigrate to Israel and become Israeli citizens without any religious limitations. Thus, citizenship should be granted to every person who declares him/herself to being bona-fide Jewish. This statement referred to the debates about conversion and "Who is a Jew?" then raging in Israel. Like the platforms of most other Zionist parties, this one included a detailed chapter on the integration of Jewish immigrants, advocating substantial investment in this sphere rather than in the settlements in the Occupied Territories. Immigrants' integration should be implemented while Israeli authorities respect the principles of pluralism. This statement reflected the new global liberal views, but clearly contradicted the melting-pot conceptions that had influenced Israeli policies from 1948 until the 1980s.

The chapter on "Religion and State" in the 1999 Meretz Party's platform was somewhat more explicit on Israeli-Diaspora relations. It included the following statement: "Israel's strong bonds with Jewish history and tradition are manifested by its ties with Diaspora Jews, the Law of Return, the commitment to immigrants' integration and the Hebrew language." Essentially, the chapter on the encouragement of Jewish immigration and their integration was very similar to the relevant chapters in previous platforms.

THE ISRAELI-PALESTINIAN PARTIES Though some Jews are members of the Hadash party, it has predominantly been an Israeli-Palestinian party. In view of the growing Palestinian nationalist and Moslem religious sentiments in this community, it is not surprising that neither Hadash nor other Israeli-Palestinian parties address Israeli-Diaspora relations. In this regard the only exception is the Balad party, which indirectly deals with this issue. This party advocates that Israel should become a "state of all its citizens," which means the rejection of the fundamental principle that Israel is "a Jewish and Democratic state." In this framework the party demands the annulment of the Law of Return, which serves as an essential link between Israel and World Jewry (Balad Party platform for the 1999 elections).

The Center-Right and Right

LIKUD Since the 1990s this Jewish liberal (in regard to social and economic issues) and nationalist party has modified some of its social, political, and economic positions, but not its views about the solution of the Arab-Israeli and Palestinian-Israeli conflicts. Consequently it may be regarded as a center-right party. In chapters A and B of its 1988 platform the party stated that Israel is the sole instrument for implementing Zionism. The party also emphasized the "undisputed and unalienable" eternal right of the entire Jewish People over the Land of Israel. Next the party vowed to implement the main Zionist ideals—Jewish return, settlement, building (or rather, rebuilding) the homeland, and fostering close Diaspora ties with Israel. The party asserted that the encouragement of immigration to Israel and prevention of emigration from it (*yerida*) were essential for the survival of Israel and of the Jewish nation (in that order). The most significant factor in facilitating the achievement of these goals was the promotion of ties with the Diaspora. That is, the Likud's approach toward the Israeli-Diaspora bond has been essentially instrumental. Thus, it was only in this context that Likud advocated the investment of substantial resources in Jewish education in the Diaspora (Likud platform, 1988).

The Likud platform for the 1992 elections repeated these ideals, ideas, and policy guidelines. Most notably when dealing with strategies for strengthening Israeli-Diaspora affinities and connections, the platform emphasized Israel's centrality in the Jewish nation. The next platform, published on the eve of the 1996 elections, included a separate chapter that dealt with the Jewish People (chapter 5). Generally speaking, there were no major deviations from or additions to what had been said in the party's previous documents. However, it should be mentioned here that, in line with the concept of Israel's centrality in the Jewish nation, in this platform the Likud argued that Israel should undertake the task of preventing Jewish assimilation in the Diaspora. Like the Labor Party, the Likud stated that this should be accomplished through the promotion of Jewish education in cooperation and coordination with the leaders of the Jewish communities abroad. This was a further example of the changed positions vis-à-vis the legitimacy of diasporic existence and abandonment of the "negation of the diaspora" attitude.

Yet, it is not clear whether that reference indicated readiness to recognize the Jewish Diaspora's autonomy and equality with Israel. In any case, the Likud views Israel as the most essential center of the entire Jewish nation. This is in line with the traditional Israeli-centric view of Israeli nationalist/rightist elites as well as of rank and file. Generally speaking, with but few changes and few additions, such as the inclusion of a call for the release of Jonathan Pollard and action concerning compensations to Holocaust victims, the party's 1999 platform was almost identical to the previous ones.

YISRAEL BA-ALIYAH Until the 1999 elections this was the only so-called "Russian party" in Israel. On the eve of those elections the party split and a new, more rightist and nationalist party, was established—Yisrael Beitenu (on the eve of the

1999 elections this party did not present a well-developed platform). Though the establishment of Yisrael Beitenu affected Yisrael ba-Aliyah's political power, the latter remained the larger among the two Russian parties. Through a mix of ideological and pragmatic considerations, this party made a concerted effort to promote connections with and show care for the Jewish community in Russia and in the former Soviet republics.

Yisrael ba-Aliyah dealt more explicitly with the issue of "Israeli-Diaspora Relations," which was the title of the last chapter in the party's platform for the 1996 elections. In a nuanced fashion, but basically similar to most other Israeli parties, the attitudinal starting point of this party was that "Israel belongs to all Jews and strives to become central to their existence, culture and tradition." The difference between this and other Zionist parties' positions becomes clear in the first operational clause, which stated that the ingathering (or, to use a more neutral term—the return) of all Jews to Israel was and still is the main Zionist goal. Yet the party made it clear that "this does not mean the negation of the Galut (Diaspora) as an equal and legitimate element in Jewish society." The platform further elaborated this particular position by stating that granting support to Jewish communities in order to ensure continuity and Jewish life in the Diaspora should be accomplished through adequate coordination among Jewish and Israeli trans-state and local organizations. Moreover, the party asserted that Diaspora Jews should be able to participate in the development of the homeland, but this should not be done through the mediation of Israeli and Diaspora bureaucratic organizations. In the same vein, the platform stated that proper conditions should be created to enable Diaspora Jews to feel that they are regarded as an integral part of Israeli society (sic!) and equal partners in decision making with regard to Israeli-Diaspora affairs. This part of the platform also called for minimal impact of narrow political and party interests on Israeli-Diaspora relations.

As may have been expected, the party's platform included an elaborate section on immigrants' integration that specified its position vis-à-vis some of the main issues that influence Israeli-Diaspora relations: Most important, it called for maintaining intact the Law of Return and warned against its dilution by its application to non-Jews. Similarly, the section on Religion and State calls for reforms in the right of civil marriage for those who cannot be married according to the rabbinical rules in Israel. It also calls for the establishment of civilian cemeteries and the removal of all constraints on the way to conversion (the platform as it was adopted by the party's convention, March 17, 1996). All in all, because of its membership and their connections to the Russian Jewish community, this party presented the most elaborate platform concerning the Diaspora and its relations with Israel.

The Right

A number of parties constituted this segment of the Israeli party system. Some of these, such as the Tehiya-Tzomet Party, existed for only relatively short periods, while others, such as Moledet, exhibited greater persistence and survived the changes in Israeli collective mood and voting patterns. The main interest of these parties was to maintain Israel's hold over the Occupied Territories and "ensure Israel's security." Otherwise these parties have espoused neo-conservative positions in regard to Israeli economy and society. To facilitate the attainment of their overriding nationalist goals, these parties have strongly advocated the encouragement of Jewish immigration to Israel, immigrants' integration, and prevention of emigration out of Israel (Tehiah and Tzomet platforms for the 12th, 13th, 14th, and 15th Knessets).

MOLEDET Only in Moledet's platform for the 1996 elections was there a specific reference to Israeli-Diaspora relations. Thus the last chapter (chapter 39) of this party's platform outlined its positions in this sphere. The party maintained that Israel is the epicenter of the entire Jewish nation and that it had been established to ensure the ultimate concentration of all Jews in Eretz Israel. Therefore common action is essential for attaining this joint Israeli and Diaspora goal. The platform envisioned a particular division of labor between Israel and the Diaspora—the Diaspora should be responsible for encouraging and organizing the immigration of Jews to Israel, Israel and the Diaspora should combat assimilation together, and Israel should ensure the security of the Jews all over the world and promote Jewish education. The party called for at least one visit to Israel by every Diaspora Jew.

The Religious and Ultra-Religious Camp

A preliminary note of clarification is in place here: the main distinctions between the National Religious Party and the ultra-Orthodox (*haredi*) parties lie in their attitudes toward the Zionist ideology, the role of the state in national life, the status of religion in the Israeli political system, and the attitude toward modernism and modernity. While the National Religious Party was and still is a Zionist party (that is, maintains that the state has a major role in maintaining and enhancing the national welfare as well as that the status quo in regard to the role of religion should not be altered; by no means does it oppose modernism), the *haredi* parties are non-Zionist, religious fundamentalist, and extremely anti-modernist parties. These different attitudes toward Zionism have influenced their positions toward the Jewish Diaspora.

THE NATIONAL RELIGIOUS PARTY (THE NRP) The party's platform is based on a call for inseparable trilateral loyalties—to the Torah, to the Jewish People, and to Eretz Israel. As indicated, their declared loyalty to the Jewish People colors their attitude toward the Diaspora. Thus, in the chapter on Beliefs and the State in its platform for the 12th Knesset (1988), the NRP declared its full support for cooperation of all Jews all over the world in the struggle to implement the Zionist project. Like the attitudes of other Jewish parties, the NRP advocated the energetic encouragement of Jewish immigration to Israel and immigrants' integration. Yet, as might have been expected, this party demanded the amendment of the Law of Return so that it should explicitly apply only to Jews according to the matrilineal principle, and to those who have been converted to Judaism only according to the Orthodox tradition. Like other Zionist parties, the NRP also expressed great concern about the massive assimilation, intermarriages, and resultant demographic losses in the Diaspora. According to the party's platform, this could be rectified only through Jewish nationalist and Zionist (presumably religious) education in the Diaspora (NRP platform of 1988).

The main thrust of the party's statements concerning Israel and the Diaspora in the platform for the 1992 elections was similar to that of the previous platform. However, the 1992 platform introduced some variations on the national theme—maintaining a Jewish majority in Israel was regarded as a prime national mission, and therefore Jewish immigration should be explicitly and urgently encouraged. To accomplish this goal and ensure Jewish continuity in the Diaspora, the Israeli government should launch comprehensive educational projects in the Diaspora. No major changes were introduced in the platform for the 1996 and 1999 elections.

YAHADUT HATORAH HAMEUCHEDET (UNITED TORAH JEWRY) This is the joint list of the two ultra-Orthodox non-Zionist Ashkenazic *haredi* parties— Agudath Israel and Degel Hatorah. Ideologically these parties are quite distant from the Zionist parties, including the NRP. Though they have been deeply involved in Israeli politics since the late 1940s, their main interest is in promoting ultra-Orthodox religion and religiosity in Israel. The contents of their platforms well demonstrate this fact—they deal with such issues as religious education, Sabbath observance, supply of Kosher food, opposition to military service of young *haredi* men and women, negation of the Reform and Conservative movements, staunch opposition to abortions, etc. Nevertheless, these parties joined the other Jewish parties in arguing the urgent need for immigration to Israel, immigrants' integration (presumably within the *haredi* sector in Israel), and prevention of emigration from Israel (*yerida*), especially of ultra-Orthodox and Orthodox persons. The party also advocated the allocation of resources for ultra-Orthodox Jewish education in the Diaspora (Yahadut Hatorah Hameuchedet platform for the 1996 elections). As could have been expected, these platforms also dealt with some central issues pertaining to the Diaspora and its relations with Israel. These issues pertain to the debate concerning the "Who is a Jew?"

issue and the controversy over conversion to Judaism. On these issues the party's position was clear—"the concept 'Jew' has been the same since Israel became a nation in antiquity, and must be defined only according to *halakha*." According to this party, the biased use of the concept "Who is a Jew?" in the Law of Return "serves as a threat to national unity and its existence on the one hand, and encourages assimilation and intermarriage, on the other."

In sum, the description and analysis of these formal positions of the various Israeli parties shows that, except for Yisra'el be-Aliyah, both the Zionist and non-Zionist parties continued to adhere to the basic Israel-centric orientation toward the Diaspora. That is, Israel is perceived as the main national center, and therefore, thus all these parties argue, its security and well-being should come first in the national order of priorities.

Generally, the common attitude of these parties toward the Diaspora has been instrumental. Though most parties have abandoned the basic traditional tenet of the "negation of the Galut," they continue to emphasize the overriding importance of Jewish immigration to Israel and immigrants' integration. Basically this means that they have mainly regarded the Diaspora as a source for human resources and for political and financial support for Israel. If at all, some parties mentioned in their platforms the need to ensure Jewish continuity in the Diaspora through launching educational projects there. Yet, only a few parties mentioned the need for Israeli financial investment in such projects or that these projects should be a result of cooperation on equal footing between Israel and the Diaspora.

Israeli Governments' Positions

There is always a considerable gap between the formal positions, on the one hand, and the actual policies and actions of most democratic governments, on the other. This has also been the case regarding Israeli governments' positions and actions vis-à-vis the Jewish Diaspora. Furthermore, there has been only a limited correlation, but by no means full correspondence, between the platforms of separate coalition parties and the formal positions of the various governments headed by Labor and Likud in the 1990s and early years of the twenty-first century. Though in the final analysis what really matters are governments' actions rather than their formal pronouncements, in the context of the present chapter it is rather more pertinent to examine the formal positions of the various Israeli governments vis-à-vis the Diaspora. This is necessary because, regardless of the diminished significance of ideology and pronounced goals and positions, such formal positions reflect actual attitudes and to a certain extent influence policies.

Thus, the very first clause in the 1988 National Unity Government Guidelines (approved by the Knesset on December 22, 1988) dealt with the Jewish People. It stated that the government "acknowledges [Israel's and the Diaspora's] common fate and struggle for the survival of the entire Jewish nation both in the homeland and the Diaspora." The 1988 government repeated the traditional pledge to continue with determined endeavors to create the social, economic, and spiritual infrastructures for the achievement of what it regarded as Israel's main raison d'être—the encouragement of Jewish immigration from all countries and their ingathering in Israel. However, it is worth noting here that, although the Soviet Union was on the verge of collapse, the emphasis was on immigration from Western countries rather than from the Soviet Union or its empire. The government further declared that it would launch a determined struggle to save persecuted Jews and to facilitate their immigration to Israel (this was the reference to Soviet Jews). Unlike various statements about specific policies intended to attain other goals that were mentioned in the operational parts of those guidelines, no specific policy guidelines were mentioned in the context of the Jewish Diaspora (*Israel Government Yearbook* 1988). At several points in his inaugural speech presenting the National Unity Government to the Knesset on December 22, 1988, Prime Minister Shamir referred to the Diaspora—but again most of these references were general and of a very distinct Israel-centric flavor. Thus, for example, Shamir mentioned that, in view of the menacing international conditions that might affect the entire nation, societal and political unity in Israel was a sine qua non for strengthening Diaspora connections with the homeland. Yet the prime minister did not mention the need for strengthening Israel's ties with the Diaspora. He added that Diaspora Jews were expecting national consensus in Israel concerning vital issues, and therefore it was incumbent on Israel to do its utmost to demonstrate unity that in turn would ensure unity in World Jewry. He mentioned the fact that the American Jewish community had been instrumental in maintaining good relations with the American government, and called for the continuation of these relations, which would benefit Israel. He said that, due to the American Jewish community's significant role in securing Israeli interests, the government would do its utmost to maintain close ties with this community. He then referred to Soviet Jewry and called for their freedom to emigrate. He added that Israel expected the Soviet government to permit Jewish education and active religious and cultural life there, thus implicitly recognizing the legitimacy of Diaspora life outside the homeland. He pledged that Israel would neither forget nor abandon any Jew who might find himself in distress, and that the government would continue to do its utmost to assist them, especially to immigrate to Israel. Finally, in this context he referred to the issue of conversion that had been widely debated in the Diaspora, and stated that the government would maintain the status quo in this sphere (*Divrei Ha-Knesset,* December 22, 1988). The guidelines of Shamir's 1990 government regarding Israeli-Diaspora relations were virtually identical to those of his previous government (*Israel Government Yearbook* 1990).

A marked change in the importance, focus, and tone of the statement about Israeli-Diaspora relations was evident in the formal position adopted by the 1992 Rabin government. The relations with the Diaspora were upgraded and mentioned at the beginning of the Government Guidelines (approved by the Knesset on July 13, 1992; *Government Yearbook* 1992). Clause 5 of those guidelines was titled "Immigration Absorption." From an even more pronounced Israel-centric standpoint, it focused on the ultimate necessity of supporting Jewish immigration from the former Soviet Union and Ethiopia. It strongly deplored emigration out of Israel (*yerida*), vowed to facilitate immigrants' integration, and only vaguely pledged help for the immigration of Jews in distress. In other words, this was a more markedly Israel-centric approach. Except for mentioning the need to encourage the immigration of Russian Jews, Rabin made no explicit reference in his inaugural speech in the Knesset (*Divrei Ha'Knesset,* July 13, 1992) to the Jewish Diaspora or to Israeli-Diaspora relations.

The Netanyahu government, established on June 17, 1996, repeated the statements made by the 1988 and 1990 Shamir governments almost verbatim. This meant that there was a marked degree of inertia and continuity in the instrumental and Israel-centric positions of the Israeli government. Thus, in the preamble to the Netanyahu Government Guidelines it was stated that it would act to "increase immigration to Israel and integrate new immigrants in all walks of life." In the section on "Peace, Security and Foreign Relations," the government stated that it would act against any manifestation of antisemitism throughout the world. Only then and in that context did it mention that the government "will act to enhance the ties and mutual responsibility between Israel and Jewish communities in the Diaspora." These guidelines repeated the commitment to change the Law of Conversion "so that conversions to Judaism in Israel will be recognized only if approved by the [Orthodox] Chief Rabbinate." Section IV of the guidelines dealt with Jewish immigration and integration, which was actually a verbatim repetition of the relevant passages in the 1988 Shamir Government Guidelines. This implies that this issue was again dealt with from a clearly instrumental and Israel-centric point of view (*Israel Government Yearbook* 1996).

Only clause 15 in the preamble to the guidelines of the Barak government (established in 1999) dealt with the Jewish Diaspora. Like all previous Israeli governments, it stated that the government would strengthen Israel's relations with Diaspora Jews. It should be noted that, in comparison with the statements made by previous governments reviewed in this section, these guidelines contained a new element—a reference to the notion that these relations should be based on a continuous Israeli-Diaspora dialogue. One of the purposes of this dialogue should be to find the most suitable means for strengthening the identity of Diaspora Jews. It also stated that the government would help Jews struggle against assimilation as well as against antisemitism and racism. These emphases may have been made under the influence of the minister of legal affairs, Yossi Beilin. In comparison with previous guidelines, the Barak government's guidelines included what probably was the longest and most detailed section on immigrants' integration, yet there were no significant new features in this section (section 8, *Israel Government Yearbook,* July 6, 1999). Prime Minister Barak dedicated most of his inaugural speech in the Knesset to the peace process and domestic issues, without mentioning at all relations with the Diaspora.

Mutual Dependence?

The above analysis indicates that the Israeli society is far from being homogenous in its concern and attitudes regarding the Diaspora. Public opinion surveys have shown that most Israelis feel that there is a difference between them and Diaspora Jews. Furthermore, except for the "professional Zionists," many Israelis show a degree of indifference and apathy toward the Diaspora. It should be noted, however, that, far more than secular Jews, religious persons in Israel feel that they are close to Diaspora Jews.

The reason for these sentiments might be that, as shown by those surveys, the Israelis, their parties, and successive governments have essentially assimilated the fact that the Jewish Diaspora will not disappear, that core diasporic communities will continue to exist in the foreseeable future, and that there is a great deal of vitality in these communities. In other words, there has been a major change in the Israelis' view concerning the "negation of the *Galut.*"

Nevertheless, many Israelis still regard the Jewish Diaspora as dependent on the homeland rather than the other way around. Though most Israelis, including Israeli politicians and governments, pay lip service to the notion of mutual dependence, to the need for an open and candid dialogue with the Diaspora, and to Israel's reliance on the Diaspora's social, financial, political, and diplomatic support, they actually regard Israel as the predominant national center that has the "historical right" and capability to influence the "Diasporic periphery's" behavior.

More important, despite a greater degree of tolerance toward Jewish existence outside Israel and fewer references to "the negation of the Galut (exile)"—that is, the negation of Jewish "abnormal" existence outside the homeland—there has not occurred any major change in the fundamental Zionist tenets implicitly held by many Israelis, their parties, and their governments. This inertia and persistence in adhering to those Zionist tenets determines the position that "the sooner the Jews immigrate to Israel the better for them and for Israel." This inherent attitude explains the strong, persistent emphasis on immigration to Israel and integration there. This is in line with the notion that Israel exists as a haven and refuge for all Jews who need or wish to escape life in the Diaspora, especially in view of the recent recurrent outbursts of racism and antisemitism.

Though there are no clear references to Israel's integration in the global economy, its economic growth, its relations with democratic states, and its direct contacts with most leaders of the powerful and developed states, many Israelis and certainly their governments realize that Israel can manage on her own, that it needs fewer resources than the Diaspora can and is willing to supply (which in any case have dwindled), and that it therefore can and should abandon any notion of dependence on the Diaspora.

These changes in Israeli attitudes are enhanced by the evident tendencies in the Diaspora to foster its own continuity. Basically, this has been a reaction to accelerating demographic changes caused by increasing rates of intermarriage, assimilation, and apathy, and in view of the shortage in available resources. Now, many Israelis, albeit not the "professional Zionists and activists," would accept the argument advanced, for example, by Yossi Beilin, that Israel should lower its expectations and demands for financial and political support by the Diaspora.

Concluding Theoretical Observations

These new realizations and attitudes in Israel and the Jewish Diaspora lead to the emergence of "normal" homeland-Diaspora relations in the sense of their similarity to the relations between other homelands and their diasporas. This observation has been elaborated in some of my articles (Sheffer 1993a, 1993b, 1996, 1999) and is further summarized in the next section.

Like many other dispersed ethnic nations, World Jewry should be viewed as a trans-state social-political coalition or federation transcending the borders of homeland and host countries. Furthermore, it should be viewed as comprising autonomous communities that maintain complex contacts but develop separately. The Israelis deal with the complex security, political, and economic issues confronting them, and Diaspora Jews deal with the specific conditions in their host countries. This tendency toward "autonomous coexistence" is strongly influenced by recent globalization and by internal dynamics in the various communities. Hence, more Israelis have realized that both the actual conditions and the normative considerations concerning the prevailing hierarchical order of the various communities in World Jewry should finally be recognized and internal-

ized, and consequently openly legitimized. This means that some Israelis begin
to internalize that full recognition should be granted to the emerging order of a
number of equal Jewish centers, rather than to the problematic adherence to the
questionable traditional Israeli-centric approach.

Practitioners and observers alike also realize that, more than ever before, the
relations between Israel and the Diaspora, and especially between Israel and the
richer and more prosperous communities (which, as mentioned, nevertheless
face some grave dilemmas concerning their future), resemble the relations between other diasporas and their homelands. In all these cases, the principle of
autonomy is becoming the norm. This is becoming widely accepted by both
homelands and host countries out of pragmatic considerations—for autonomous coexistence increases the loyalty of diaspora communities to their host
countries, and thus ameliorates the perennial dilemma of loyalty that has created so many difficulties for diasporas everywhere, including the Jewish Diaspora. Ultimately, such recognition will also "normalize" relations between Israel
and the Jewish Diaspora, to the benefit of all parties involved.

The last few comments about the "normalization" of the Jewish Diaspora
and of its relations with its homeland mean that it now has similar features to
many other ethno-national diasporas, making it possible to infer from the particular study of the Israeli-Diaspora relations to the general phenomenon.
Hence it is only proper to conclude this chapter by briefly suggesting some general theoretical conclusions pertaining to homelands, to ethno-national diasporas and to their mutual relations.

The recent large waves of migrants of various national origins have resulted
in their permanent settlement in host countries, and consequently in a growing
number of ethno-national diasporas and in increased membership in both established and incipient ethno-national diasporas. These trends have in turn
greatly enhanced the cultural, social, political, and economic significance of these
entities. Consequently, their new political position in the global, regional, and
internal systems has drawn attention to various aspects of their existence and especially to the reciprocal relations with their homelands. Nevertheless, as noted
at the beginning of this chapter, we still lack general insights into the way in
which homelands regard and treat "their" diasporas.

The analysis of the Israeli case, as presented in this chapter from the homeland's point of view, corroborates some of my assumptions concerning this aspect of modern Diasporism that had been neglected by scholars. The Israeli case
shows that, first and foremost, homelands strive to maintain the traditional perception of idyllic relations between themselves and "their" diasporas. But while,
in the past, core members of diasporas who had not been assimilated or fully integrated into their host societies were regarded as in a kind of exile, more recently

most homelands are realizing that members of these entities have made explicit decisions to permanently settle in their host countries, and to view these host countries as their home, but to maintain close ties with their old homelands.

Despite the growing acceptance of the normalcy of diasporic existence, and despite the enhanced societal legitimacy granted to members of diasporas who feel at home abroad, both homeland leaders and their rank and file still regard the homelands as the essential national centers, responsible for maintaining the nation intact.

This view, which is held partly out of national (and one might probably say nationalist) inertia, partly because of an unfounded sense of superiority, and partly because of profound suspicions and uncertainty about Diaspora loyalty, creates gaps between the two parts of these dispersed nations—that is, between homelands and diasporas. Again, as seen from the homelands' point of view, there is a considerable gap between the official statements about the national importance of the Diaspora, its security and well-being, on the one hand, and the actual policies pursued by homeland governments, on the other.

Homeland governments have their own agendas and order of priorities, which they usually pursue to the best of their capabilities. Under these circumstances they often disregard their diasporas' urgent needs or delay diplomatic and political efforts on their behalf. Generally, homelands would be ready to actively support their diasporas on a quid pro quo basis. Thus, homeland governments invest in their diasporas only if they assume that the latter invest their own resources in the homeland and are ready to act on their behalf when these homelands deem it necessary. For example, as shown by the Israeli-Diaspora, homelands invest in educational projects in the Diaspora in order to maintain contact with and, one may add, also a certain degree of control over their diasporas.

Smaller and poorer homelands, in particular, also hope for the return of the more successful members of their diasporas. This has been the case with Ireland, Israel, Armenia, Turkey, and some of the republics in the Balkans (it should be noted here that larger and richer homelands, such as Germany, have shown greater reluctance to encourage the return of certain diasporic groups and to deal with their absorption). Such homelands are ready to invest some resources in persuading diasporans to return, as well as in their reintegration in the homeland, with the hope that the returnees would import the needed resources.

Yet with the further development of globalism, liberalism, democracy, pluralism, and, in some cases, multiculturalism, it seems that homeland governments and rank and file increasingly begin to accept the permanency of the Diaspora phenomenon and appreciate the various cultural, political, and economic benefits to both homelands and diasporas that can be gained from maintaining intimate relations with the diasporas.

In sum, although the actual relations between most homelands and their diasporas are still far from being idyllic, a change is occurring also in this sphere. The greater legitimacy and respect shown by homelands toward their diasporas may lead to a more balanced set of loyalties and relations. In this vein, a shift may happen in these relations: from self-proclaimed predominance of the homelands to homelands-diasporas coexistence in sort of trans-state federations. Such initial changes are already noticeable in World Jewry (Sheffer 1999), which, like some other well-established diasporas, serves as a precursor to future global trans-state political arrangements.

REFERENCES

Arian, Asher. 1997. *The Second Republic: Politics in Israel.* Tel Aviv: Zmorah Bitan (Hebrew).

Beilin, Yossi. 1999. *The Death of the American Uncle.* Tel Aviv: Yediot Ahronot (Hebrew).

Cohen, Steven. 1983. "Attitudes of American Jews Towards Israel and Israelis." New York: American Jewish Committee.

Cohen, Robin. 1997. *Global Diasporas: An Introduction.* London: UCL Press. *Economist,* August 19, 2000.

Don-Yehiya, Eliezer. 1990. "'Galut' in Zionist Ideology and in Israeli Society." In *Israel and Diaspora Jews,* ed. Eliezer Don-Yehiya. Ramat Gan: Bar Ilan University Press.

Dowty, Alan. 1998. *The Jewish State.* Berkeley: University of California Press.

Levy, Shlomit, and Louis Guttman, 1975. *The Israeli Public's Attitudes towards the Jewish People and Zionism.* Jerusalem: Hebrew University of Jerusalem.

———. 1987. *The Israeli Public's Attitudes towards the Jewish People and Zionism.* Jerusalem: Israel Institute of Applied Social Research.

Levy, Shlomit, Hanna Levinsohn, and Elihu Katz. 1993. *Beliefs, Observations and Social Interaction Among Israeli Jews.* Jerusalem: Louis Guttman Institute.

Liebman, Charles. 1977. *Pressure without Sanctions.* Rutherford, N.J.: Fairleigh Dickinson University Press.

Sandler, Shmuel. 1993. *State of Israel, Land of Israel: The Statist and Ethno-national Dimensions of Foreign Policy.* London: Greenwood.

Shain, Yossi. 1999. *Marketing the American Creed Abroad: Diasporas in the US and their Homelands.* New York: Cambridge University Press.

Shamir, Michal, and Alan Arian. 1999. "Collective Identity and Electoral Competition in Israel." *American Political Science Review* 93 (2): 265–77.

Sheffer, Gabriel. 1986a, ed. *Modern Diasporas in International Politics.* London: Croom Helm.

———. 1986b. "A New Field of Study: Modern Diasporas in International Politics." In *Modern Diasporas in International Politics,* ed. Gabriel Sheffer, 1–15. London: Croom Helm.

————. 1988. "The Illusive Question: Jews and Jewry in Israeli Foreign Policy." *The Jerusalem Quarterly* 46: 104–14.

————. 1993a. "Jewry, Jews and Israeli Foreign Policy: A Critical Perspective." In *Diasporas in World Politics: The Greeks in Comparative Perspective,* ed. Dimitry Constas and Athanassios Platias, 203–209. London: Macmillan.

————. 1993b. "Ethnic Diasporas: A Threat to their Hosts?" In *International Migration and Security,* ed. Myron Weiner, 283–86. Boulder, Colo.: Westview Press.

————. 1994. "Ethno-national Diasporas and Security." *Survival* 36 (1) (Spring): 60–79.

————. 1996. "Israel Diaspora Relations in Comparative Perspective." In *Israel in Comparative Perspective,* ed. Michael Barnett, 53–84. Albany: State University of New York Press.

————. 1999. "From Israeli Hegemony to Diaspora Full Autonomy: The Current State of Ethno-National Diasporism and the Alternatives Facing World Jewry." In *Jewish Centers and Peripheries. European Jewry between America and Israel Fifty Years after World War II,* ed. Ilan Troen, 29–40. New Brunswick: Transactions.

————. 2002. *At Home Abroad: Diaspora Politics.* New York: Cambridge University Press.

Smith, Hanoch. 1984. "Israeli Attitudes toward America and American Jews." *Tefuzut Israel* 22 (2): 29–62.

Tzemach, Mina. 1986. "Israeli Attitudes toward Judaism, American Jewry, Zionism and the Israeli-Arab Conflict." Unpublished report on public opinion survey.

Vertovec, Philip, and Robin Cohen. 1999, eds. *Migration, Diasporas and Transnationalism.* Cheltenham: Edward Elgar.

Vital, David. 1990. *The Future of the Jews.* Cambridge, Mass.: Harvard University Press.

CHAPTER NINETEEN

The Emigration of Jewish Israelis

ℰↃ

STEVEN GOLD

Introduction

As reported in the *Israel Bulletin of Statistics,* between 1948 and the end of 1992 438,900 Israelis were living overseas on a long-term basis (Yisrael Shelanu 1995). This group includes persons born abroad as well as native Israeli Jews (*sabras*). The largest fraction resides in major North American Jewish communities, including New York, Los Angeles, and Toronto. Others live in Paris, London, and Sydney. According to demographic analysis, this flow is the predictable outcome of prior migration. Further, because of Israel's recent record of economic growth and the arrival of almost a million new immigrants from the former Soviet Union, it is of little consequence to Israel's viability. Calvin Goldscheider (1996, p. 59) writes that rates of emigration "from Israel are relatively unimportant at the societal level and do not threaten the longer-term social demographic consequences of immigration."

Yet, from the Israeli point of view, migration is a weighty problem. It threatens the Zionist assertion that Israel is the best place for Jews to live. And practically, Jews are needed to populate the Jewish State and to ensure its military, economic, and demographic viability in a hostile world region. While the Hebrew term *aliya* celebrates Jews' movement from the Diaspora to Israel, *yerida* describes the stigmatized path of Israelis who descend from the promised land into the Diaspora. Emigrants are the *yordim.* During the 1970s, Israeli politicians such as Prime Minister Yitzhak Rabin were especially vitriolic on this issue, calling Israeli emigrants "moral lepers," "the fallen among the weaklings," and "the dregs of the earth" (cited in Ritterband 1986, p. 113; Kimhi 1990). However, by 1992, Rabin had recanted these statements (Rosen 1993, p. 3). Since that time, Israel has substantially transformed its treatment of emigrants, now providing them with outreach programs and inducements to return.

If Israel has, until recently, been antagonistic to the emigration of its citizens, Jewish communities outside of Israel have also been ambivalent about these newcomers. Following the lead of the Israeli government (which wanted to discourage settlement), Diaspora Jewish communities initially offered little of the support that they have customarily extended to immigrant Jews. However, since the late 1980s, in accordance with evolving Israeli policy toward expatriates, and realizing the value of this energetic, Jewishly-conscious, and Hebrew-speaking population in their midst, Jewish communities in settlement countries have established various communal services for recently arrived Israelis.

Recent Jewish population studies in New York (1991), Los Angeles (1998), England (1998), and South Africa (1993) all enumerate Israelis, their presence one of the few positive tendencies in a general trend of aging and shrinking Jewish demographics. Moreover, regardless of the policies of their communal agencies, Diaspora Jews (and Israeli émigrés as well) discern that the arrival of former Israelis bears a marked similarity to earlier Jewish migrations to Western Europe, North America, and other "lands of opportunity" in order to acquire education, affluence, individual freedom, family unification, and security (Goldscheider 1996; DellaPergola 1992).

To a considerable extent, Israel and Jewish communities beyond its borders are mutually involved, interdependent, and maintain good relations. However, the two settings uphold distinct assumptions about where Jewish people, especially Israelis, belong. Having been socialized in Israel, but living in the Diaspora, Israeli emigrants confront this paradox of membership and belonging as individuals and within the communities they create in places of settlement. Gabriel Sheffer (1998) makes this point in his provocatively titled article in *The Jewish Year Book* (of England), "*Yordim* (Emigrants) Are the Authentic Diaspora." As French sociologist Reginé Azria intimates, emigration (in both temporary and permanent forms) is now an accepted feature of Israeli reality: "Thus, today, some Jews are simultaneously Israeli Jews and diaspora Jews without being concerned about either this or which passport they carry. They travel around the world simply because they feel like it, or because they need to for professional, academic, family or vacation purposes" (Azria 1998, p. 24). This chapter discusses the motives and experiences of Israeli emigrants and how their presence outside the Jewish State affects their identities as Jews and Israelis.

Data for this essay were collected by American and Israeli researchers through in-depth interviews and participant observation fieldwork with Israeli migrants in several settings. A major source was 194 interviews (conducted in both Hebrew and English) with a socially diverse sample of Israeli migrants and others knowledgeable about their community in Los Angeles between 1991 and 1996. In addition, we interviewed 50 Israelis in London between 1998 and 2000, and 14 in Paris in 1999. Finally, interviews with 30 returned migrants were conducted in Israel in 1996, 1997, and 2000. Most interviews were tape recorded, translated into English (if conducted in Hebrew), and transcribed. All names of respondents in this report are pseudonyms. Additional data were obtained through census analysis and communal surveys collected in several points of settlement.

Motives for Migration

When asked why they went abroad, most Israelis offered one of three overlapping responses—economic opportunities (including education), family factors, and a need for broader horizons (Gold 1997; Rosen 1993; Sobel 1986; Herman 1988; Sabar 2000). For example, Yossi, a Los Angeles building contractor, alludes to both "broadening his horizons" and increasing economic opportunities as he describes his desire to come to the United States.

> I came here in February '78 as a student. Back in Israel, I see and hear so much about America and I figure America is somehow the final place in the progression of the world. Whatever happens in the world, somehow, America has a good hand in it. And so I decide that maybe it is the main source and I want to learn about America and open up my mind. And also, back home, there was not adequate opportunities.

A fairly large number, generally women and children, came to accompany their husbands and fathers who sought economic betterment and educational opportunity (Kimhi 1990; Lipner 1987). In 1986, marriage to an American citizen accounted for a third of all Israelis who received immigrant status to the United States (Herman 1994, p. 92). Further, in fieldwork interviews, Israelis often mentioned coming to host societies to join relatives. And reflecting the other side of the same process, émigrés in hostlands described bringing Israeli relatives and friends to join them.

While the Israeli economy has recently witnessed a meteoric rate of growth, a fraction of Israelis who were self-employed prior to migration and retain their entrepreneurial pursuits in points of settlement continue to assert that Diaspora settings are better for capitalistic endeavors than Israel (Uriely 1994; Gold 1994a; Gardner 2000; Hiltzik 2000). This is reflected in the following exchange with an émigré in the garment business in Los Angeles:

> For the people who were in business in Israel, you don't even have to ask why they came here. We just know that they came to do business. America is a better country for business. Less regulations, taxes and controls. They want you to do some business. Israel, it's too much socialism.

As is the case with most migrant populations, Israelis are involved in chain migration. The presence of established coethnics in the host society is a valuable resource for later migrants. It lowers the social and economic costs associated with migration and plays a major role in both organizing receiving communities and retaining ties to the country of origin. Israelis also ease their resettlement by residing in the Jewish neighborhoods of major cities (Herman and LaFontaine 1983; Schmool and Cohen 1998; R. Cohen 1999).

While most Israelis travel abroad with the specific goals of education, economic advancement, or family unification, another group may go as part of a "Secular Pilgrimage" of world travel—a common rite of passage among Israelis following their military service, which is compulsory for men and women alike (Ben-Ami 1992). Israelis interviewed in Paris, London, Los Angeles, and New York described how they had arrived as part of their travels, picked up a job to earn some cash, and then had "gotten stuck"—because of economic opportunities, relationships, or other factors—for a period longer than they had initially planned. Issac described this:

> Israel is a country that is not easy to live in. Everybody finishes the army after three or four years. After the army, you understand life differently. So you are ready to try something else. I came to Los Angeles, and then I met my wife and that's how I started. We had kids. I got into the clothing business and I stayed.

An additional explanation for Israeli emigration is the desire to be outside the confines of the Jewish State. For supporters of Israel, direct criticism of the Jewish State by those living beyond its boarders is seen as disloyal and, as such, is relatively infrequent among émigrés. However, in explaining why they left Israel, certain migrants described feelings of disillusionment or a general attitude of not being able fit into the social order. Israelis who are from stigmatized ethnic backgrounds sometimes claim they left because of discrimination (Sobel 1986; Uriely 1995). Similarly, some members of Israel's Ashkenazi elite complain about the growing influence of the Orthodox and Mizrahi[1] portions of the Jewish State (Kafra and Shelach 1998). Finally, Israelis occasionally describe their exit as an effort to avoid military duty and the ever-present violence associated with life in the Middle East (Sobel 1986). According to an Israeli government estimate, about 5 percent of all permanent emigrants exit because of ideological reasons (Yisrael Shelanu 1995).

Demographics of Israeli Emigration

In any study of migration, questions regarding the numbers and characteristics of the populations involved always arise. However, because migrants are difficult to locate, contact, and interview, their enumeration is a problematic task (Heer 1968; Anderson and Fienberg 1999). As a consequence, scholars of migration are accustomed to studying migrant populations with imperfect data. That being said, debates about the size of Israeli emigrant populations tend to be more pervasive and heated than those linked with most other groups. Academics, journalists, and communal activists affiliated with Israel, host societies, and émigré communities continue to dispute whatever estimates are presented. Claims that the local population is three to four times as large as indicated by census or survey-based tabulations surface in nearly every place of settlement (Herman and LaFontaine 1983; Herman 1988, 1994; Gold and Phillips 1996; Cohen and Haberfeld 1997; R. Cohen 1999). Despite the manifold ideological and religious controversies associated with Israeli emigration, by far the most contentious issue surrounding this group involves estimates of their numbers in diaspora communities.

Population Estimates

In the following discussion, I attempt to use the best data available from respected demographers, while also acknowledging the limitations in existing demographic information about Israeli émigré populations. The 1990 U.S. Census enumerated 90,000 Israeli-born persons and 144,000 people living in Hebrew-speaking homes "almost all of which can be assumed to be Israeli" (Fishkoff 1994; Gold and Phillips 1996). According to the British Census, there were 12,195 Israeli-born persons in the United Kingdom in 1991. However, because Israel's population includes many persons who were not born there, the number born in Israel accounts for only a fraction of all Israeli Jews in England. Using the ratio of Israeli-born to all Hebrew speakers determined in the U.S. Census, Schmool and Cohen (1998, p. 30) estimate that approximately 27,000 Israelis live in England. Drawing from South African census data, Dubb (1994, p. 17) estimated that the legal-resident Israeli population of South Africa in 1991 was 9,634. Many of France's Israeli emigrants trace their ancestry to former French colonies in North Africa. Because of their possession of French citizenship or their birth outside Israel, only a small fraction of these are enumerated as Israelis in the French Census. Based on official national population censuses, the figures for Israeli citizens permanently living in France were 3,500 in 1981 and 2,900 in 1990 (Council of Europe 1998; DellaPergola 2000). According to the 1996 Canadian Census, 21,965 Canadian residents indicated that they possessed Israeli Citizenship. Finally, the 1996 Australian Census enumerated 5,923 Hebrew-speaking persons.

It would be incorrect to assume that Israelis in these points of settlement will remain permanently. Rather, data suggest that a significant fraction of Israeli emigrants eventually return (Cohen 1996; "For Those Returning Home" 1995; Chabin 1997). In fact, the "failure to consider Israelis' high rates of return migration may be one of the reasons for the popular perception that the number of Israelis" overseas is as high as assumed (Cohen and Haberfeld 1997, p. 200). During the mid-1990s, approximately 12,000 Israeli emigrants returned home yearly (Chabin 1997; Yisrael Shelanu 1995).

Family Composition, Ethnicity, and Occupational Characteristics
According to data collected in the United States, United Kingdom, and Canada, Israeli emigrants are a young population. They are likely to be married and living with children, and have larger families and a lower divorce rate than native-born Jews in points of settlement (Gold and Phillips 1996; Schmool and Cohen 1998; R. Cohen 1999; Horowitz 1993).

Drawing from 1980 census data, Paul Ritterband (1986, p. 121) reported that in New York City, 16 percent of Israeli-born immigrants were Oriental Jews. Forty-five percent of Rosenthal's (1989, p. 64) respondents from Brooklyn and Queens reported themselves as Ashkenazi, 42 percent as Sephardic/Oriental, and 13 percent as a mixture of both. Herman and Lafontaine (1983, p. 102) found that 58 percent of naturalized Israelis in Los Angeles were of Ashkenazi origins while 37 percent were Sephardic/Oriental, and 2 percent were mixed.

Journalistic reports sometimes depict Israeli emigrants as employed in menial occupations, such as cab drivers or furniture movers (Ben-Ami 1992; Sabar 1996). However, every study based on systematic analysis of census or survey data demonstrates that emigrants are far more educated and skilled than Israelis generally, and among the most very highly educated of all arrivals in countries of settlement. Yinon Cohen (1996, p. 78) found that "regardless of the data and methodology used, Israeli Jewish immigrants in the US were found to be more educated and to hold higher status occupations than both US and Israeli populations." Fifty-four percent of Israelis in New York and 58 percent in Los Angeles have at least some college, while fewer than 15 percent in either city are not high school graduates. While Israeli emigrants are already a highly educated group, they tend to further improve their educational credentials while abroad (Toren 1980; Rosenthal and Auerbach 1992; Schmool and Cohen 1998).

In New York, Los Angeles, and the United Kingdom, approximately half of the Israeli emigrant population are employed as managers, administrators, professionals, or technical specialists (Gold and Phillips 1996; Schmool and Cohen 1998). According to the 1990 U.S. Census, their rate of self-employment—22 percent—is the second highest of all nationality groups in the United States, exceeded only by Koreans. This high rate of self-employment is achieved by extensive economic cooperation—involving coethnic hiring, subcontracting—and by the concentration of Israelis in a number of areas of economic specialization. Entrepreneurship has long been a viable economic strategy for Jewish migrants, who, as a group, are party to an extensive tradition of self-employment prior to their arrival in this country. Israelis are notably active in the real estate, construction, jewelry and diamond, retail sales, security, garments, engineering, information technology, and media industries (Gold and Phillips 1996; Waldinger and Bozorgmehr 1996).

As their generally lucrative occupations might indicate, the earnings of Israelis in the United States are considerable. In fact, persons tracing their ancestry to Israel rank fifth in family income out of 99 ancestry groups tabulated in the 1990 Census (Yoon 1997). Employed Israeli men residing in New York City were making on average approximately $35,000 annually in 1989, while their counterparts in Los Angeles were making an average of almost $49,000. These figures exceed those of all foreign-born men in either city, and best the earnings of even native-born whites in Los Angeles. Employed Israeli women in New York and Los Angeles also earn more than the average for all foreign-born women, but make less annually than native-born white women in these cities. As native speakers of Hebrew who are often trained as educators, Israeli women frequently find employment as instructors in Jewish institutions, including synagogues and schools.

While Israeli emigrant men have very high rates of labor force participation, a considerable fraction of Israeli women in the United States, United Kingdom, Canada, and Australia are not in the labor market. For example, a survey of Israelis in New York found that only 4 percent of the women indicated "housewife" as their occupation in Israel, while 36 percent did so in the United States (Rosenthal and Auerbach 1992, p. 985). In the United Kingdom, a higher rate of male labor force participation was also evident, with 76 percent of Israeli men and 48 percent of Israeli women over age sixteen economically active (Schmool and Cohen 1998, p. 30). As discussed below, Israeli emigrant women often devote their time and effort to domestic and communal activities intended to enhance the quality of family life in points of settlement (Lipner 1987; Gold 1995a). This makes Israelis distinct from many other contemporary migrant groups, who maintain higher labor force participation rates for women in the host society than in their countries of origin (Pedraza 1991).

Experience of Adaptation

Reflecting the controversy about Israeli migration, existing literature on the group offers very different images of their adaptation. One body of studies argues that because emigration violates the basic tenets of Zionism, Israeli emigrants' experience is one of alienation, isolation, and guilt regarding their presence in the Diaspora (Shokeid 1988; Linn and Barkan-Ascher 1996). Seen as "Jewish communal deviants" both by their countrymen and by host country Jews, they are said to occupy a "liminal" (temporary/outsider) status in host societies and as a result, suffer a guilty identity crisis that prevents community unification, integration with host Jews, and the development of realistic, long-term plans regarding settlement (S. Cohen 1986; Shokeid 1988, 1993; Mittelberg and Waters 1992; Uriely 1995).

In contrast, a second body of work emphasizes their positive adjustment. Writing in *The Harvard Encyclopedia of American Ethnic Groups,* Arthur Goren (1980, p. 597) states that Israelis "have successfully established themselves in the professional life of the greater society and have contributed to the Jewish community as teachers and communal functionaries." Reports from South Africa, the United Kingdom, the United States, and Canada characterize Israelis as having done quite well. They are highly educated, entrepreneurial, prosperous, fluent in English, have high rates of naturalization, make important contributions to economic and cultural life, and are likely to reside in comfortable neighborhoods, near other Jews (Frankental n.d.; Waterman 1997; Cohen and Gold 1996; Bozorgmehr et al. 1996). Generally white, they encounter little racial discrimination and have easy access to the local Jewish community, within which they often live and work (Gold and Phillips 1996). While the two images seem diametrically opposed, both reveal an element of truth. Despite their impressive earnings and occupational prestige, after residing abroad for decades, Israelis often express feelings of nostalgia for the Jewish State (Shokeid 1988).

Israelis' ambivalence about being abroad may be partially explained by the fact that they are voluntary immigrants, a relatively unique status among Jews. Most Jews who have entered Western countries during the last three hundred years have been de jure or de facto refugees, with few opportunities for returning to their countries of origin. By contrast, Israelis retain the real possibility of going back to Israel; indeed, host country Jews, the Jewish State, and even the migrants themselves generally agree that they should return. As voluntary emigrants, Israelis describe their sojourn as temporary, and many make frequent trips back to the Jewish State, sometimes culminating in permanent repatriation (Lipset 1990; Kadish 1998; R. Cohen 1999; Shokeid 1988). In the words of a community leader in Los Angeles:

> Israelis would always suffer a certain touch of nostalgia because they are missing the things that they grew up with. Psychologically, most Israelis did not come here to be Americans. They did not come here to swear to the flag; to sing the national anthem and to go to Dodgers games. They came here to have the house and the swimming pool and the two cars and the job and the money.

Communal Patterns

Several scholars have argued that Israelis' ambivalence about emigration discourages their formation of ethnic communities (Shokeid 1998; Mittelberg and Waters 1992; Uriely 1995). However, a growing body of evidence collected in Los Angeles, New York, Chicago, London, Toronto, and other cities reveals that Israeli migrants have developed many activities and organizations in order to address their misgivings about being outside of the Jewish State (Gold 1994a; Shor 1998; R. Cohen 1999). Community activities include socializing with other Israelis; living near coethnics (and within Jewish communities); consuming Hebrew-language media (produced locally and in Israel); frequenting Israeli restaurants and nightclubs; attending coethnic social events and celebrations; joining Israeli associations; working with other Israelis; consuming goods and services provided by Israeli professionals and entrepreneurs; keeping funds in Israeli banks; participating in Israeli-oriented religious, language, recreational, day-care, and cultural/national activities; raising money for Israeli causes; calling Israel on the phone; and hosting Israeli visitors. While some communal settings are the product of migrants' own efforts, others are maintained in cooperation with local Jewish communities or with the Israeli government.

In the course of field work in Los Angeles, one research team identified some 27 Israeli organizations—ranging from synagogues, Hebrew schools, and political groups to scouting programs, sports teams, business associations, and even a recreational flying club (Gold 1994b). This number of organizations exceeds that created by other middle-class immigrant groups in Los Angeles, including Iranians and Soviet Jews (Gold 1995b; Kelley and Friedlander 1993). Such a multiplicity of organizations allows émigrés to maintain various Israeli practices and outlooks in host society settings. A similar set of organizations exists in New York, Toronto, London, and other points of settlement (Shor 1998; R. Cohen 1999; Rosen 1993).

Gender and Family Adaptation

In nearly every study of Israeli emigration, we find that while migration was a "family decision" and the family as a whole enjoys economic benefits as a result of it, the decision to migrate was made by the men for the expanded educational and occupational opportunities available abroad (Gold 1995b; Rosenthal and Auerbach 1992; Sabar 2000). Dafna describes how moving to London disrupted the egalitarian relationship that she and her husband, Zeev, had maintained in Israel:

> Zeev and I were always equals, both in our way of life and our careers, and here that balance changed. Here, his career was more central and more important than mine. So he was the one who determined our future in terms of our stay here. So my career became a job that I did not have to do. I could choose to stay at home or go out to work. It was not an important consideration in our lives.

Once in the host society, men often enjoy the benefits of such expanded opportunities, and accordingly, feel more comfortable with the new nation. Women, however, especially those with children and established careers, have more negative views of migration. Survey research interviews reveal that Israeli women are less satisfied with host societies and retain a stronger sense of Israeli and Jewish identity than men. Even when Israeli women work in host societies, they often have less of a professional identity than men and would prefer to return home (Kimhi 1990, p. 95).

Our own interviews as well as the literature indicate that a large fraction of Israeli women go abroad, not of their own volition, but only to accompany their husbands who seek economic and educational improvement. In the words of Rachael:

> For most of the people that came here, the men came and the women came after them. Like when I came, my husband came for a job. I had to leave my job and I had to find a new job and it was very painful. I think more and more now there are women coming on their own, but if you look at most cases, it is the men coming after jobs and it means that the women are the ones that have to take care of finding apartment, finding schools for kids and they get depressed, very badly depressed.

Once in the point of settlement, through their immersion in education and work, men develop a social network and a positive sense of self. Women, however, often remain isolated in the home—saddled with the task of caring for children in a strange new country and lacking access to social networks. Further, because they are responsible for child rearing and many of the family's domestic and social activities, Israeli women are the family members who most directly confront alien social norms and cultural practices. However, separated from the resources and knowledge to which they had access at home, Israeli immigrant women find their domestic and communal tasks—such as building social networks, finding appropriate schools and recreational activities, dealing with teachers and doctors, obtaining day care and the like—to be quite difficult. This increase in difficulty in women's tasks is contrasted to the various advantages life abroad yields for husbands involved in the economic sphere.

It is important to note that, while many of the economic advantages of the overseas stay can benefit Israeli women as well as men, owing to the gender-based division of labor these advantages most commonly go to men alone. Lipner's research indicates that an Israeli woman's family status and involvement have much to do with her opinion of life outside of Israel. Younger women who had few social attachments prior to migration (i.e., no children or established careers) looked forward to migrating and often enjoyed being abroad. However, women who had children and who were forced to give up good positions in Israel to come to the host society had a much harder time, experiencing their exit as "devastating" (Lipner 1987, pp. 144–145).

In reflecting on their experience outside the Jewish State, Israelis contrast the nation's positive economic and occupational environment to its communal and cultural liabilities: Immigrants almost universally regard Israel as a better place for kids. It is safer, has fewer social problems and does not impose the manifold generational conflicts Israelis confront when raising children overseas. Further, in Israel, Jews are the culturally and religiously dominant group. The institutions of the larger society teach children Hebrew and instruct them in basic national, ethnic, and religious identity as well as Jewish history. However, in going abroad, Israelis become a minority group and lose government-provided resources as well as communal networks based upon family, friendship, and neighborhood, which provided a social life and assistance in raising children.

A major source of family conflict occurs when various family members disagree regarding their chosen country of residence. These problems are most dramatic when one spouse is born in the country of origin or has many native-born relatives, while the other's family resides in Israel. Similarly, children who have spent much of their lives overseas often prefer to remain while their parents wish to return to Israel. Finally, parents may wish to remain abroad for career opportunities, while children wish to return to Israel.

In general, we found that Israeli families were relatively resilient and provided valuable assistance and support to their members. At the same time, Israeli families sometimes suffered from financial problems, separation from relatives, and generational conflicts in communication and identity. The presence of children appears to be a major incentive that motivates immigrant families to reevaluate their collective identity at the point of settlement, and often to take steps—including returning to Israel—so that children will experience some form of Jewish and/or Israeli training.

Jewish Identity and Involvement in Jewish Life

Israeli and Diaspora-Jewish notions of group membership contrast because the basic group identities associated with being Israeli, on the one hand, and Diaspora Jewish, on the other, are rooted in particular cultural/national contexts. For many Israelis, ethnic identity is secular and nationalistic. In fact, émigrés universally referred to themselves in national terms as "Israelis," while calling local coreligionists "Jews." While Israelis are knowledgeable about Jewish holidays and speak Hebrew, they most directly connect these behaviors to "Israeliness" rather than Jewishness. Reform and Conservative Judaism, with which many Western Jews affiliate, are all but unknown in the Jewish State. Rituals, including marriages and conversions, performed by these denominations' rabbis in Israel have no legal standing there. Finally, while Diaspora Jews are accus-

455

tomed to life as a self-supporting subcommunity in a religiously pluralistic society, Israelis grew up in an environment where religion and nationality were one and the same, and religious activities were subsidized by the State.

Because of Israelis' lack of familiarity with Diaspora forms of Jewish identification and involvement, some pundits decry their assimilation into non-Jewish cultural patterns. They assert that Israelis' very exit from the Holy Land signifies a move away from the Jewish ideal, and that their participation in and contribution to Jewish activities is limited and oriented toward secular pursuits with little religious content—meals, parties, Israeli folk dancing, and sports (Shokeid 1988).

In contrast, other observers argue that Israelis actively participate in host country Jewish life while simultaneously maintaining their links to Israel by noting that the Israelis speak Hebrew, live in Jewish neighborhoods, are involved in a variety of Jewish institutions, and visit Israel frequently. While survey data on Israelis' Jewish behaviors are relatively scarce, and available only in the United States, those that exist indicate that established immigrants engage in many Jewish behaviors at rates equivalent to or sometimes higher than is the case among native-born Jews. Based upon data collected for the 1997 Los Angeles Jewish Population Survey, Israeli-by-birth households are more likely than all Los Angeles Jews to send their children to day school, belong to Jewish organizations, give to the United Jewish Federation, and identify as Orthodox (Herman 2000). Moreover, Israeli migrants' synagogue membership, at 27 percent, is quite close to that of Americans. Further, 80 percent of Israeli parents provide their kids with some form of Jewish education at some point during their lives—50 percent of Israeli kids in Los Angeles and 35 percent in New York attend Jewish day schools. The figure for children age 5–17 from Israeli-by-birth households in Los Angeles is twice as great as that of all Jewish households in Los Angeles (Herman 2000). Israelis' rate of intermarriage to non-Jews, at only 8 percent, is 40 percent less than the recent average for American Jews (Gold and Phillips 1996).

When comparing Israeli immigrants' observance of Jewish religious practices—lighting candles on Shabbat and Hannukah, attending synagogue on the High Holy Days and Shabbat, and fasting on Yom Kippur—with their patterns in Israel, we find that among naturalized Israelis in New York and Los Angeles, ritual behaviors have actually increased. Increased rates of ritual practice reflect the efforts of these Jewish migrants to retain their religious identity within a predominantly non-Jewish country (see Table 1). (Gold and Phillips 1996). Finally, a growing number of Israeli-emigrant parents are acting to reestablish connections with Israeli and/or Jewish behaviors through special family activities of their own creation or involvement in various Israeli migrant programs such as after-school Israeli Hebrew courses and Hebrew language scouting activities.

Table 1. Israeli Immigrants' Observance of Jewish Customs in Israel and the U.S. *

Author	U.S.			U.S. Jews	Israel		
	Herman	Rosenthal	Sachal-S.	NJPS	Herman	Rosenthal	Sachal-S.
Location of study	LA	NY	LA	US	LA	NY	LA
Practice							
Light Shabbat candles	88	87	61	43	73	68	67
Light Channukah candles	100	91	—	83	95	85	—
Attend synagogue on holy days	83	87	58	59	81	78	69
Attend synagogue on Shabbat	45	70	55	—	44	53	55
Fast on Yom Kippur	84	79	73	58	71	66	78

*Always, usually or sometimes.

Sources: Herman: data collected from 40 randomly selected Israelis naturalized between 1976 and 1982 in Los Angeles County (Herman and LaFontaine 1983).
Rosenthal: data collected from 205 Israelis in Brooklyn and Queens, 1984–86, consisting of subsamples of 155 randomly selected naturalized Israelis and 50 snowball-sampled nonnaturalized Israelis. From the 205 questionnaires, data on 870 individuals were collected (Rosenthal 1989).
Sachal-S: data collected from 100 Israeli immigrants in Los Angeles in 1991–92. (Sachal-Staier 1992).
NJPS: National Jewish Population Survey, 1990.

Transnational Israelis

Transnationalism, a new approach in the field of migration studies, has been created precisely to understand a growing number of international migrant communities, who, like Israeli emigrants, maintain social, cultural, and economic links to multiple nation states on a more or less permanent basis (Schiller et al. 1992; Portes et al. 1999). A central point of transnationalism is its view of migration as a multilevel process that involves various links between two or more settings rather than a discrete event constituted by a permanent move from one nation to another. The concept of transnationalism suggests that by retaining social, cultural, and economic ties with two or more countries, people can avoid the impediments traditionally associated with long distances and international borders. At the same time, transnationalism reminds us that people often remain intensely involved in the life of their country of origin even though they no longer permanently reside there.

A whole series of factors concerning Israelis makes their movement from the Jewish State to Western host societies relatively easy. They are well educated and often possess occupational and cultural skills that are useful in both nation-states. They generally have access to networks in both countries that can provide a broad variety of resources ranging from pretravel information to job opportunities, child care, housing, and a social life. While some Israelis in points of settlement lack legal resident status, as a group, they are very likely to become naturalized and are among a select few allowed to have dual citizenship (Jasso and Rosenzweig 1990). Even prior to migration, Israelis often feel extremely familiar with host society cultures as a result of their exposure to popular culture, reports from other visitors, and intergovernment relations. As Israeli social scientist Zvi Sobel put it, "America, it might be posited, has become the alter ego of Israel in political, economic and cultural terms" (Sobel 1986, pp. 192–93).

A great proportion of the Israeli population has resided within the Jewish State for fewer than two or perhaps three generations. Accordingly, their family lore and cultural baggage are rich with both expectations and skills associated with life in other settings. Many émigrés we interviewed had lived in other nations, ranging from Japan and Hong Kong to Switzerland, England, South Africa, Italy, and Latin America, prior to their settlement in the United States, Canada, France, Australia, or the United Kingdom. And these included not only professionals and high-level entrepreneurs but also less skilled and less educated migrants such as carpenters and restaurant workers.

Further facilitating Israel transnationalism are the extensive political and economic relations and numerous links shared by the host societies and Israel. We have already noted the variety of Israeli-oriented activities that allow migrants to maintain a semblance of the Israeli life in the Diaspora. Because travel between the two nations is easily arranged, Israeli migrants often report making frequent trips to Israel, and it is not uncommon for children to return to spend holidays, summer vacations, and to complete their military service (Burston 1990). London resident Batya takes pride in preserving her contacts with Israel.

> I managed to maintain the relationship with my Israeli family and friends like they were before. I talk with them often, I meet them whenever I come or they visit here. I always meet with everybody when I come. I had organised two meetings of my Kibbutz and my high school mates. These were very exciting. We are still very good friends. We write to each other—mainly e-mail, and we meet. Some of my friends visit my parents and sisters regularly, and it's like another family to them.
>
> I want to be together. They are an important part of my life even if I live in London. I still have relationships with the trainees I trained during my army service, and I meet with them as well. I invest a lot in these relationships in order to keep them as they were before. Some of my friends here—their

relationships in Israel gradually disintegrated simply because they put very little into the maintenance of these friendships. Mine didn't. I don't forget my life in Israel.

In these ways, the Israeli context, history, and culture have prepared members of this group for transnationalism. It would appear that the whole notion of being an Israeli versus a member of a Western host society is not nearly as clear-cut a distinction as the literature on international migration would generally suggest. Instead, such factors as flexible notions of ethnic and national identity, access to and participation in social and occupational networks, and the ability of people to sustain cultural competence and legal status in more than a single society allow Israelis to maintain meaningful forms of involvement in multiple national settings at one time. In fact, we interviewed several Israelis who lived in the Jewish State while traveling to Europe, the United States, or even Australia to maintain jobs and levels of income they desired.

Despite these many factors permitting Israelis to maintain a transnational existence, nevertheless, many remain troubled by the distance—physical as well as cultural—between nations. As suggested in the following quotes, even some Israelis who accomplished a great deal abroad were so concerned with the communal and cultural liabilities of Diaspora life that they decided to return for the good of their children.

> Gilda: The considerations were around the kids entirely. We knew we would be going back to something which has less to offer us from many aspects and we knew we had to do this for the kids' sake.

> Sharon: My husband and I both felt very deeply that a child needs to have an identity. We felt that our children were loosing that identity. We felt that if we are not going back, then we are depriving them from that identity and they are helpless in that respect. They would not even understand that they missed out on something. We knew what they would miss out on, though. And that's why we decided to go back.

Hence, for many Israelis, transnationalism is a reality. This does not mean, however, that it is an easy way of life. While these migrants build communities and networks that help them cope with the social and cultural dimensions of ties to two nations, and while they enjoy economic benefits from migration, most are not quite comfortable with this status. In the words of a Los Angeles accountant: "Israel is my mother and America is my wife, so you can imagine the way I must feel."

In conclusion, regardless of emigrants' reactions to life overseas, the number of Israelis who travel, live, and work abroad is likely to increase. Israel's growing social, economic, and cultural integration with other countries means that national boundaries will impose ever fewer restrictions on connections with external entities. At the same time, these tendencies will be advanced by the enhanced accessibility of low cost and highly efficient forms of communication and transportation, as well as further reductions in official and informal sanctions on Israeli emigration. As a consequence, Israeli emigrants (and their associates abroad) are likely to follow multiform lines of action—including settlement, sojourning, commuting, and return—to adapt to the myriad circumstances, opportunities, and obstacles that they confront.

NOTES

1. Respondents used the terms Sephardic, Oriental, Eastern, and Mizrahi interchangeably to describe Jews with origins in Asia, the Middle East, and North Africa.

REFERENCES

Anderson, Margo J., and Stephen Fienberg. 1999. *Who Counts? The Politics of Census-Taking in Contemporary America.* New York: Russell Sage Foundation.

Australian Bureau of Statistics. 2000. Unpublished 1996 Census of Population and Housing data. Custom Tabulation.

Azria, Régine. 1998. "The Diaspora-Community-Tradition Paradigms of Jewish Identity: A Reappraisal." In *Jewish Survival: The Identity Problem at the Close of the Twentieth Century.* ed. Ernest Krausz and Gitta Tulea, pp. 21–32. New Brunswick, N.J.: Transaction.

Basch, Linda, Nina Glick Schiller, and Cristina Blanc-Szanton. 1994. *Nations Unbound: Transnational Projects, Postcolonial Predicaments, and Deterritorialized Nation States.* Basel, Switzerland: Gordon and Breach Publishers.

Ben-Ami, Ilan. 1992. "Schlepers and Car Washers: Young Israelis in the New York Labor Market." *Migration World* 20 (1): 18–20.

Bhachu, Parminder. 1985. *Twice Migrants: East African Sikh Settlers in Britain.* London: Tavistock.

Blumberg, Rae L. 1991. "Introduction: The Triple Overlap of Gender Stratification, Economy, and the Family." In *Gender, Family, and Economy: The Triple Overlap,* ed. Rae L. Blumberg, 7–32. Newbury Park: Sage.

Bozorgmehr, Mehdi, Claudia Der-Martirosian, and Georges Sabagh. 1996. "Middle Easterners: A New Kind of Immigrant." In *Ethnic Los Angeles,* ed. Roger Waldinger and Mehdi Bozorgmehr 345–78. New York: Russell Sage Foundation.

Burston, Bradley. 1990. "Consulate General in LA Reports: Over 400 Israelis in LA Return for Army Service." *Jerusalem Post,* December 28.

Cohen, Rina. 1999. "From Ethnonational Enclave to Diasporic Community: The Mainstreaming of Israeli Jewish Migrants in Toronto." *Diaspora* 8 (2): 121–36.

Cohen, Rina and Gerald Gold. 1996. "Israelis in Toronto: The Myth of Return and the Development of a Distinct Ethnic Community." *Jewish Journal of Sociology* 38 (1): 17–26.

Cohen, Steven M. 1986. "Israeli Émigrés and the New York Federation: A Case Study in Ambivalent Policymaking for 'Jewish Communal Deviants.'" *Contemporary Jewry* 7: 155–65.

Cohen, Yinon. 1996. "Economic Assimilation in the United States of Arab and Jewish Immigrants from Israel and the Territories." *Israel Studies* 1 (2): 75–97.

Cohen, Yinon, and Yitchak Haberfeld. 1997. "The Number of Israeli Immigrants in the United States in 1990." *Demography* 34 (2): 199–212.

Council of Europe. 1998. Recent Demographic Developments in Europe. Strasbourg: Council of Europe.

DeJong, Gordon F., and James T. Fawcett. 1981. "Motivations for Migration: An Assessment and Value-Expectancy Research Model." In *Migration Decision Making: Multidisciplinary Approaches to Microlevel Studies in Developed and Developing Countries,* ed. Gordon F. De Jong and Robert W. Gardner, 13–58. New York: Pergamon.

DellaPergola, Sergio. 1992. "Israel and World Jewish Population: A Core-Periphery Perspective." In *Population and Social Change in Israel,* ed. Calvin Goldscheider, 39–63. Boulder: Westview.

———. 1994. "World Jewish Migration System in Historical Perspective." Paper presented at International Conference on Human Migration in a Global Framework, University of Calgary, Alberta, Canada, June 9–12.

———. 2000. Personal Communication, March 12.

Dubb, Allie A. 1994. *The Jewish Population of South Africa: The 1991 Sociodemographic Survey.* Cape Town: Kaplan Centre for Jewish Studies and Research, University of Cape Town.

Eisenbach, Zvi. 1989. "Jewish Emigrants from Israel in the United States." In *Papers in Jewish Demography 1985,* ed. U. O. Schmelz and S. DellaPergola, 251–67. Jerusalem: The Institute of Contemporary Jewry, The Hebrew University of Jerusalem.

Elizur, Dov. 1980. "Israelis in the U.S." *American Jewish Yearbook* 80: 53–67.

Fishkoff, Sue. 1994. "Don't Call Us Yordim." *Jerusalem Post,* March 4.

Frankental, Salley. N.d. "Israelis Encounter Diaspora." Paper for Conference "Jewries at the Frontier," University of Cape Town.

Gardner, Gregg Shai. 2000. "Nobel Prize Winner Sees Israel as a 'Locomotive Power.'" *Jerusalem Post* Internet Edition, Monday June 12.

Gold, Steven. 1992. *Refugee Communities: A Comparative Field Study.* Newbury Park, Calif.: Sage.

———. 1994a. "Patterns of Economic Cooperation among Israeli Immigrants in Los Angeles." *International Migration Review* 28 (105): 114–35.

———. 1994b. "Israeli Immigrants in the U.S.: The Question of Community." *Qualitative Sociology* 17 (4): 325–63.

———. 1995a. *From the Workers' State to the Golden State: Jews from the former Soviet Union in California.* Boston: Allyn and Bacon.

———. 1995b. "Gender and Social Capital Among Israeli Immigrants in Los Angeles." *Diaspora* 4 (3): 267–301.

———. 1997. "Transnationalism and Vocabularies of Motive in International Migration: The Case of Israelis in the U.S." *Sociological Perspectives* 40 (3): 409–26.

Gold, Steven J., and Bruce A. Phillips. 1996. "Israelis in the United States." *American Jewish Yearbook,* 51–101.

Goldscheider, Calvin. 1996. *Israel's Changing Society: Population, Ethnicity and Development.* Boulder: Westview Press.

Goren, Arthur A. 1980. "Jews." Pp. 571–98 in Stephen Thernstrom (ed.) *Harvard Encyclopedia of American Ethnic Groups.* Cambridge, Ma.: Harvard-Belknap Press.

Heer, David, ed. 1968. *Social Statistics and the City.* Cambridge, Mass.: Harvard University Press.

Herman, Pini. 1988. "Jewish-Israeli Migration to the United States Since 1948." Paper presented at the Annual Meeting of the Association of Israel Studies, New York, June 7.

———. 1994. "A Technique for Estimating a Small Immigrant Population in Small Areas: The Case of Jewish Israelis in the United States." In *Studies in Applied Demography,* ed. K. Vaninadha Rao and Jerry W. Wicks, 81–99. Bowling Green, Ohio: Population and Society Research Center.

———. 2000. "The Jews of the Jews: Characteristics of Los Angeles Households of Israelis by Birth and Israelis not by Birth." Paper submitted for Division E Contemporary Jewish Society, The Thirteenth World Congress of Jewish Studies, December.

Herman, Pini, and David LaFontaine. 1983. "In Our Footsteps: Israeli Migration to the U.S. and Los Angeles." MSW thesis, Hebrew Union College.

Hiltzik, Michael A. 2000. "Israel's High Tech Shifts into High Gear." *Los Angeles Times,* August 13.

Horowitz, Bethamie. 1993. *The 1991 New York Jewish Population Study.* New York: United Jewish Appeal—Federation of Jewish Philanthropies of New York.

Jasso, Guillermina, and Mark R. Rosenzweig. 1990. *The New Chosen People: Immigrants in the United States.* New York: Russell Sage.

Kadish, Sharman. 1998. "'A Good Jew or a Good Englishman?': The Jewish Lads' Brigade and Anglo-Jewish Identity." In *A Question of Identity,* ed. Anne J. Kershen, 77–93. Aldershot: Ashgate.

Kafra, Michal, and Offer Shelach. 1998. "Yordim '98." *Ma'ariv,* August 7 (Hebrew).

Kelley, Ron, and Jonathan Friedlander, eds. 1993. *Irangeles: Iranians in Los Angeles.* Berkeley: University of California Press.

Kimhi, Shaul. 1990. "Perceived Change of Self-Concept, Values, Well-Being and Intention to Return among Kibbutz People Who Migrated from Israel to America." Ph.D. dissertation, Pacific Graduate School of Psychology, Palo Alto, California.

Linn, Ruth, and Nurit Barkan-Ascher. 1996. "Permanent Impermanence: Israeli Expatriates in Non-Event Transition." *Jewish Journal of Sociology* 38 (1): 5–16.

Lipner, Nira H. 1987. "The Subjective Experience of Israeli Immigrant Women: An Interpretive Approach." Ph.D. dissertation, Washington, D.C.: George Washington University.

Lipset, Seymour Martin. 1990. "A Unique People in an Exceptional Country." In *American Pluralism and the Jewish Community,* ed. Seymour Martin Lipset, 3–29. New Brunswick, N.J.: Transaction.

Mittelberg, David, and Mary C. Waters. 1992. "The Process of Ethnogenesis among Haitian and Israeli Immigrants in the United States." *Ethnic and Racial Studies* 15 (3): 412–35.

Pedraza, Silvia. 1991. "Women and Migration: The Social Consequences of Gender." *Annual Review of Sociology* 17: 303–25.

Portes, Alejandro, Luis E. Guarnizo, and Patricia Landolt. 1999. "Introduction: Pitfalls and Promise of an Emergent Research Field." *Ethnic and Racial Studies* 22 (2): 217–327.

Ritterband, Paul. 1986. "Israelis in New York." *Contemporary Jewry* 7: 113–26.

Rosen, Sherry. 1993. "The Israeli Corner of the American Jewish Community." Issue Series #3. New York: Institute on American Jewish-Israeli Relations, The American Jewish Committee.

Rosenthal, Mira. 1989. "Assimilation of Israeli Immigrants." Ph.D. dissertation, Fordham University, New York.

Rosenthal, Mira, and Charles Auerbach. 1992. "Cultural and Social Assimilation of Israeli Immigrants in the United States." *International Migration Review* 99 (26): 982–91.

Sabar, Naama. 1996. *Kibbutz L. A.* Tel Aviv: Am Oved Publishers (Hebrew).

———. 2000. *Kibbutznicks in the Diaspora.* Albany: State University of New York Press.

Sachal-Staier, Michal. 1993. "Israelis in Los Angeles: Interrelations and Relations with the American Jewish Community." MBA thesis, University of Judaism, Los Angeles.

Schiller, Nina Glick, Linda Basch, and Cristina Blanc-Szanton. 1992. "Transnationalism: A New Analytic Framework for Understanding Migration." In *Towards a Transnational Perspective on Migration: Race, Class, Ethnicity and Nationalism Reconsidered,* ed. Nina Glick Schiller, Linda Basch, and Cristina Blanc-Szanton, 1–24. New York: New York Academy of Sciences.

Schmool, Marlena, and Frances Cohen. 1998. *A Profile of British Jewry: Patterns and Trends at the Turn of a Century.* London: Board of Deputies of British Jews.

Sheffer, Gabriel. 1998. "'The Israeli Diaspora' Yordim (Emigrants) Are the Authentic Diaspora." In *The Jewish Year Book,* ed. S. Massil, xix–xxxi. London: Valentine Mitchell.

Shokeid, Moshe. 1988. *Children of Circumstances: Israeli Immigrants in New York.* Ithaca: Cornell University Press.

———. 1993. "One Night Stand Ethnicity: The Malaise of Israeli-Americans." *Israel Social Science Journal* 8 (2): 23–50.

Shor, Gil. 1998. "Israelis in L.A.: Present and Absent." *Israel L.A.,* September 16, p. 5 (Hebrew).

Smooha, Sammy. 1978. *Israel: Pluralism and Conflict.* Berkeley: University of California Press.

Sobel, Zvi. 1986. *Migrants from the Promised Land.* New Brunswick, N.J.: Transaction.

Statistics Canada. 2000. Custom Tabulation from 1996 Census.

Toren, Nina. 1980. "Return to Zion: Characteristics and Motivations of Returning Emigrants." pp. 39–50 in Ernest Krausz (ed.), *Migration, Ethnicity and Community* (Studies of Israeli Society VI). New Brunswick, N.J.: Transaction.

Uriely, Natan. 1994. "Rhetorical Ethnicity of Permanent Sojourners: The Case of Israeli Immigrants in the Chicago Area." *International Sociology* 9 (4): 431–45.

———. 1995. "Patterns of Identification and Integration with Jewish Americans Among Israeli Immigrants in Chicago: Variations Across Status and Generation." *Contemporary Jewry* 16: 27–49.

Waldinger, Roger and Mehdi Bozorgmehr. 1996. *Ethnic Los Angeles.* New York: Russell Sage Foundation.

Waterman, Stanley. 1997. "The 'Return' of the Jews into London," pp. 143–60 in Anne J. Kershen (ed.) London: *The Promised Land? The Migrant Experience in a Capital City.* Aldershot: Avebury.

Yoon, In-Jin. 1997. *On My Own: Korean Businesses and Race Relations in America.* Chicago: University of Chicago Press.

PART VII

Conclusion

CHAPTER TWENTY

Challenges for the Twenty-First Century

❧

UZI REBHUN AND CHAIM I. WAXMAN

The articles in this volume have focused on and delineated social and cultural developments that characterized Jews in Israel in the closing decades of the twentieth century. As in every society, challenges are rarely fully met and, if they are, their very resolutions create new directions for action and policy consideration. Within this context, we indicate here four major areas of social challenge that Israeli Jews face as we enter the first decade of the twenty-first century.

Internal Challenges: The Social Dimension

In the transition from models of socialist economy to those of capitalism and free economy, coupled with technological progress, the level of inequality in Israeli society has progressively deepened. The demand for skilled workers with a high educational level has grown, and the salaries offered them have shot up. By contrast, traditional industries have been hurt and their workers have been forced to accept wage decreases. In contemporary Israel there is a tremendous gap in income (both salary and capital) between the top decile and the bottom decile (Audenheimer 2001). This gap has increased especially during the last twenty years and is one of the largest in the Western world (Kopp 2001; Strasler 2001). This social gap largely overlaps with group belonging—between Jews and Arabs, and among the former in relation to ethnic origin. It derives in large part from differences in professional qualifications, in which a high proportion of Jews of European-American origin are employed in academic and administrative professions. This proportion decreases significantly among Jews of Asian or African origin, and even more among the non-Jewish population. It is also affected by the growing differential in economic reward for different kinds of economic activities (Kopp 2001).

Not only has the gap in distribution of income grown, but the dimensions of poverty are also becoming more serious. Were it not for the state's welfare policy, providing social security payments for guaranteed income, for unemployment, and stipends for the elderly and for children, the number of impoverished in Israel would be far higher than it is at present (Sheref 2001). It should be noted that the designation of any given individual as being below the poverty line does not necessarily match the popular image of this state. A large portion of the poor in Israel are not literally starving; they do not live in a density of more than two people per room; and they enjoy most modern consumer goods, including refrigerator, television, and cellular phones. However, these families do not have sufficient free income to enable them to enjoy various kinds of leisure activities and vacations (Plotzker 2001).

A principal cause of large income gaps is educational level. The higher the level of education, the better the employment status and the greater the opportunities for economic mobility and advancement in terms of positions and salary (Strasler 2001). Similarly, families with two wage-earners generally enjoy an income level sufficient to lift them above the poverty level (Kopp 2001). It therefore seems reasonable to assume that social policy needs to turn increased attention over the coming years to improving the overall educational level and to introducing general and technological studies into different sectors of Israeli society, particularly in the peripheral districts of the country, in the *haredi* sector, and in the Arab sector (Strasler 2001). Simultaneously there is a need for a change in both values and culture that will emphasize the social and economic importance of professional training for women and their participation in the civilian work force.

Education and cultural-value characteristics are important determinants of the individual's economic situation, and changing them may assist to a certain extent in reducing the present income gaps. Such a tendency in the direction of greater equality will also reduce tensions and feelings of frustration among the more deprived groups in Israeli society. This will in turn engender a greater similarity in positions, and decrease the need for political organization in order to achieve particularistic social and economic goals. Income level thus serves as a mediating factor between models of personal behavior and characteristics of society on the macro level.

Another social framework that is experiencing an increase in inequality is the division of the burden of reserve military duty—an important military reservoir for Israel in times of emergency—between the different sectors of the population. While the non-Jews, specifically Israel's Arab population, as well as the majority of the *haredi* population, have never served in the army, the phenomenon of evading reserve duty has recently increased within the mainstream of Israeli society as well. But even among those who are called up to annual reserve duty, only a small proportion of those fulfilling vital functions are called for prolonged periods, up to the maximum allowed by law, owing to budgetary constraints (Shelach 2001). This inequality creates a strong feeling of injustice and reduces the sense of motivation. As it seems reasonable to assume that security matters will continue to occupy a central place in the national agenda, the possibility of change in the model of reserve duty has recently begun to receive increased attention. The approach of a people's army, according to which everybody serves in the IDF and carries a more or less equal share of the nation's security needs, will need to undergo a certain transformation. Reserve duty will continue to be obligatory for all, but for those who serve extended periods of time, there will be a need to treat it as a type of second job within which framework the soldier will enjoy salary and other social benefits (Shelach 2001). This model, practiced in one form or another in many Western countries, will greatly moderate the rhetoric about the unfair division of the burden. This change will need to be accompanied by a general value-oriented approach toward those who serve, which will view them as a social elite of great importance.

Israel as a Jewish and Democratic State

The definition of Israel as a Jewish state did not begin with Israel's Knesset or with its Declaration of Independence. Even before that, the United Nations Partition Plan called for the establishment of "Independent Arab and Jewish states." In its description of the intended state as a Jewish state, reference was, obviously, to the national composition and character of the state. The United Nations certainly did not intend that Israel should be a theocratic state. At the same time, there is no denying that religion is an integral part of Jewish culture. Judaism is a religo-ethnicity and an ethno-religion. Religion and ethnicity are integrally interrelated in ways that are perhaps even more idiosyncratic than is the norm even in the Middle East, let alone the West.

In the modern West, religion and ethnicity are two fairly distinct categories. For example, one can be French or German and one can be Protestant, Catholic, Jew, Muslim, or any other religion. Western European states have long been ethnically homogeneous and religiously heterogeneous. In the Middle East, there is a much deeper relationship between religion and ethnicity. But even there, one can be a Muslim Arab or a Christian Arab; one can be an Arab Muslim or a non-Arab Muslim. But there are no recognized Muslim Jews, Christian Jews, etc. Judaism is inherently connected with Jewish ethnicity. Thus, a Jewish state, in the sense of the national homeland of the Jewish people, is, therefore, a state in which Judaism is part of the national culture, at the same time that the state is definitely not a theocracy.

Nor is the notion that Judaism is part of Israeli national culture entirely unique. Religion as a part of the larger national culture is characteristic of many countries in the modern West. Despite the separation of church and state in the

United States, every banknote and coin bears the words "In God We Trust," and the oaths of office taken by elected national government officials, from the president to members of Congress conclude with the phrase, "So help me God." Every United States president, in his inaugural address, has made reference to God's will and a mission. Christmas is a national holiday in the United States, as well as in most if not all Western countries. Indeed, there seems no denying that America's "civil religion" has a definite Christian character to it.

The establishment of Christmas as a national holiday in the United States is not undemocratic because the overwhelming majority of America's citizens are Christian and the country was established in the Christian cultural tradition. Sunday is the day of rest in the United States just as Friday is in Muslim countries. Moreover, in the United States, there are counties, such as Bergen County in New Jersey, in which department stores are forbidden to open on Sunday. This, despite the fact that there are significant numbers of non-Christians in those counties, some of whom may close their businesses on other days, such as Shabbat, because of their personal religious commitments. The constitutionality of such "blue laws" has been upheld by the highest courts.

Of course, there are those in Israel, as there are elsewhere, who very much wish that it were a theocracy. There has been a struggle between the religious and the secular at least since the very beginnings of the Zionist Organization (Luz 1988), and that is one of the major internal Jewish struggles to this day. Nevertheless, the sides have, from the beginning, willy nilly agreed to compromises that have enabled them to work out the differences between them and to carry on in their work together. As one scholar put it some years ago, the religious wish that there were no secular Israelis, and the secular wish that there were no religious Israelis, but they each realize that they cannot go it alone, that they are dependent on the other, and they arrive at what often appears to be irrational compromises that nevertheless enable them to carry on (Avineri circa 1986). Their relations are somewhat reminiscent of a distinction the German sociologist Ferdinand Tönnies drew between the *Gemeinschaft* and the *Gesellschaft* (translated into English as "community" and "society"). In the *Gemeinschaft*, he says, they are essentially united despite all of the things dividing them; in the *Gesellschaft*, they are essentially divided despite all of the things uniting them (Tönnies [1887] 1957). Within that context, as the evidence provided by Levy, Levinsohn, and Katz in chapter 11 of this volume indicates, the majority of Israel's Jews appear to still have *Gemeinschaft*-like relations with each other.

Nevertheless, there is a growing number of Israelis, particularly in the secular media and academia, who view the notion of Israel as a democratic and Jewish society as an oxymoron. Thus, Shlomo Zand argues that Israel's national anthem, "Hatikva,"[1] discriminates against Arabs and other non-Jewish Israelis: "the very designation of the state as a Jewish state contains within it an anti-equalitarian element" (Zand 2000). Similarly, Baruch Kimmerling argues that since Israel's Declaration of Independence only "refers to equality of religion, race, and sex, but not to nationality," it is inherently undemocratic. As he puts it, "There are no rights for the Arabs as Arabs according to the Declaration of Independence, while for the Jews there are. And it is precisely here that the basic inequality lies, not only in the Declaration but in the entire Israeli regime, because in the absence of collective rights people's individual civil rights are also harmed" (Kimmerling 2001).

However, as was indicated previously, this type of situation is not unusual in democracies, many of whose national anthems speak of roots and a past that are alien to some of its citizens. This is especially the case in countries that have experienced waves of immigration and many immigrant groups. As Daniel Friedmann avers,

> Many democratic countries zealously guard their national-cultural foundation. At the end of WWI, portions of Alsace-Lorraine were taken from Germany and annexed to France. The latter immediately introduced there its educational system, including the French language. When the British Empire crumbled, after WWII, a massive wave of immigrants from its former colonies threatened its character. Within a short time, England changed its laws and put a brake on the flow of immigrants. (Friedmann, 2000)

The Law of Return is another issue frequently cited as discriminating against non-Jews, especially Arabs, in Israel because it grants automatic and almost immediate citizenship to Jewish immigrants but not to non-Jews. However, the fact is that many democratic countries, indeed most countries, have selective immigration laws, and there is nothing unique in a country's giving special status to its nationals and their families. This is what Israel, as a Jewish national democracy, does for its nationals; Israel was established as the national home for the Jewish people. In addition, it may be argued that the Law of Return is an affirmative action–type law that gives special privileges to Jews because of the history of persecution and discrimination against them in Diaspora countries. Other countries give special status to their nationals.

The absence of a constitution is sometimes cited as a major flaw in Israel's democracy. On the one hand, it is also true that England does not have a constitution. On the other hand, as Asher Arian points out, "Great Britain has a tradition of hundreds of years of guarding civil liberties and developing their meaning" (Arian 1989, p. 195). The relatively short political life of Israel, by contrast, has been marked by more than a decade of military rule, in which civil liberties were highly restricted; and several more decades of the (Emergency) Defense Regulations of 1945 continue to place serious limits on those liberties as they are known in the United States.

As for why Israel does not have a constitution, it is typically alleged and accepted as a given that it is the religious parties who have consistently prevented Israel from framing a constitution because they assert the dominance of religious law, *halakha*. However, the late Yonathan Shapiro, whom no one ever even suspected of being sympathetic to the religious parties, asserts that the reason Israel has no constitution is that Ben-Gurion did not know how to deal with the issue of minorities, especially Israeli Arabs. He campaigned against a constitution despite the arguments in favor of it presented by the majority in Mapai, including a number of its senior officials, and, in the end, he was able to persuade the Political Committee to adopt his position despite some staunch opposition (Shapiro 1996, pp. 30–33). In essence, it appears from Shapiro's account, Ben-Gurion used the religious parties as scapegoats by claiming that he had to bow to their opposition to a constitution in order to save the coalition; in reality, he himself was opposed, but because of his fears of the Israeli Arab issue, not because of his fears of either Heaven or the religious parties.

This leads to the last point, namely, that Israel's character as a national Jewish democracy is weakened, in the final analysis, not by the debate between religious and secular Zionists nor by its retaining both the Law of Return and "Hatikva," but by the limitations it places on the rights of its non-Jewish population. The call for equality of rights to all Israeli citizens is not the exclusive possession of any political and/or ideological faction. None other than Moshe Arens, a leading figure in Likud and one whose Zionist credentials have never been challenged, has frequently criticized Israel for its lack of attention to the needs of its Arab population. For example, he asserted:

> Successive governments of Israel have, throughout the existence of the state, essentially ignored the country's non-Jewish population. Israel has been governed as a Jewish state that has paid little heed to the minorities in its midst. With few exceptions, the full privileges of citizenship have not been extended to them and they have not been required to shoulder the full obligations of citizenship.

In its treatment of its Arab citizens, Israel's democracy is flawed, just as racism is a blight on America's democracy. But the fact that Israel does not yet fully live up to its ideals does not render those ideals unattainable. Indeed, for many, Zionism has not yet fully achieved its mission and will not do so until Israel becomes a fully developed Jewish national democracy.

Overall Jewish Challenges: Israel and the Diaspora

With the massive exodus during the last decade from the territory of the former Soviet Union, few Jews remain in places where they suffer oppression and official anti-Jewish discrimination. A look at the geographic map of the Jewish people at the beginning of the twenty-first century reveals that most Jews live in Western countries, in the more advanced of which they enjoy complete political freedom and socioeconomic opportunities. The United States constitutes the largest Jewish concentration in the world with 43.2 percent of World Jewry; 37 percent live in Israel; 9.4 percent in Western Europe, South Africa, and Oceania; 4 percent in Eastern Europe; 2.7 percent in Canada, and another 3.2 percent in Central and South America. The rest of World Jewry is dispersed in a variety of places, each of which constitutes a very small Jewish presence (Della-Pergola 2000). It stands to reason that the strong position of Diaspora Jewry in their places of residence will continue to exist in the foreseeable future, a factor that is likely to largely stabilize the system of international Jewish immigration at relatively low levels.

During the first five decades of its independence, the State of Israel was the main country absorbing Jews, most of them refugees from oppression and hardship. A central component of the Zionist idea, which manifests itself in the constant desire to bring Jews to immigrate to Israel, will now need to find suitable ways to attract Western Jewry. For most Diaspora Jews, *aliya* is not a viable response to the challenges of Jewish continuity. Unlike the push factors that motivated the bulk of immigration to Israel thus far, the material socioeconomic balance in favor of the lands where the majority of Diaspora Jewry lives today requires the strengthening of Israel's unique attractive powers—ideological and religious—while assuring a high level of modernization and technological development. In fact, the period of *aliya* of distressed Jewry to Israel having ended, the central element in relations between Israel and Diaspora Jewry must now be redirected toward deepening the connections and common values shared between them, which only in a few isolated cases will lead to a total identification expressed in *aliya* and settlement in the Jewish state. We are likely to witness a switch in roles, whereby the material and moral support that have thus far been directed from the Diaspora to Israel will change to an encouraging function in which Israel will provide moral support for Diaspora Jewry.

Recently, significant changes have occurred in the degree of identification of Diaspora Jewry. It is well documented that the level of religious observance has declined, and the degree of involvement in organized activities and of communal solidarity has similarly weakened (Waxman 2001). The most explicit expression of this is the growth in the degree of intermarriage between Jews and non-

Jews, which has reached the level of more than 50 percent among young people. While this indicates the involvement and acceptance of Jews by the general American society, it also constitutes a factor eroding the vital power of the community and of dynamic vibrant Jewish life. Under these circumstances, the group identification of a growing number of Jews assumes a purely symbolic value, primarily on the major holidays and at certain points along the life cycle, but without any commitment to an ongoing ethno-religious behavior or organizational involvement (Rebhun forthcoming). The distancing from particularistic Jewish models of behavior is also expected to reduce the function of Israel as a source of Jewish identity, and certainly the chances for widespread *aliya*. Not only does the American Jewish community need to confront these tendencies; the State of Israel with its various institutions also needs to play a role in strengthening Jewish education and the connection to Israel among the younger generations, through extending both financial and technical resources to establishing programs of study for the Jewish schools in the Diaspora and visits to Israel. Another important means of exposing Israel to the Jewish public in the Diaspora would be to provide more opportunities for extended stays in Israel in the framework of sabbatical years, professional courses, and other work connections.

Local developments within Israeli society, particularly the strengthening of cultural pluralism and a wider recognition of non-Orthodox religious expressions and identity will also contribute to mutual closeness between Diaspora Jewry, particularly that of the United States, and Israeli society. While in many areas Israeli society is undergoing accelerated processes of Americanization that reduce cultural and even linguistic differences with American Jewry, the religious movements reflecting the tendencies of the majority of U.S. Jewry have yet to enjoy full recognition on the part of the Israeli establishment. Even more, repeated attempts to amend the Law of Return so as to challenge the legitimacy of conversion conducted abroad by Conservative and Reform rabbis deepen the split between American Jewry and Israel. On the other hand, on the secular fringes of Israeli society there are those who attempt to abolish the Law of Return, which perhaps more than anything else symbolizes the innate connection between the State of Israel and World Jewry. This comes on top of post-Zionist voices in Israel calling for a focus upon the here and now, at the expense of, among other things, Diaspora Jewry. An emphasis on as many common factors as possible between Israel and the Diaspora will contribute to greater pride on the part of the latter in the land of the fathers, and will likewise influence other facets of ethnic-religious identification.

The above-mentioned two dimensions represent inner processes within Israeli society, and between it and the broader circle of the Jewish people, and as such are dependent upon the balance of power among different portions of the Jewish population. On the other hand, an external factor that will surely have great impact upon the nature of Israel-Diaspora relations is the political and security situation of Israel in the Middle Eastern front. This dimension involves a certain paradox. Past experience indicates that times of crisis and of external threat are also times of internal strengthening and Jewish unity. True, continued instability in the region will delay certain important social and cultural decisions concerning the Jewish nature of the Israeli society, but it will harness Diaspora Jewry as a political and economic lobby for Israel, thus strengthening Diaspora Jewish identity. But it seems reasonable to assume that such political circumstances may also repel some of those who might have planned to immigrate to Israel. On the other hand, a situation of secure calm and a continuation of the peace process will again leave Diaspora Jewry free to turn their attention to what is happening in their own communities; insofar as they will renew the attempts to strengthen cultural pluralism here, this may also lead to a certain increase in immigration rates. This being so, each of the alternatives concerning the political situation in Israel, that is, both danger and stability, will have far-reaching and nonuniform implications for Israel-Diaspora relations and the likelihood of *aliya*.

Taking into account the differences in the components of demographic dynamics between Israel and the Diaspora, and particularly natural growth and changes of identity, by the beginning of the second decade of the present century Israel is expected to be the largest Jewish community in the world; and, by the middle of the century, the home of an absolute majority of World Jewry (i.e., of more than half the Jews in the world) (DellaPergola, Rebhun, and Tolts, 2000). In fact, already today more than half the Jewish children aged fifteen and under live in Israel. Hence, the prime responsibility for Jewish education and cultural continuity among the future generations will gradually pass from the Diaspora to Israel. This is in addition to the leading role of support of Israel in relation to the tendencies of aging and shrinkage of Jewish communities in other parts of the world.

The Challenges of Globalization

There has emerged, in the second half of the twentieth century, as Roger Inglehart analyzes it, a major "culture shift" in modern societies. Inglehart's comprehensive cross-cultural surveys and analyses reveal broad international patterns. In his analysis of survey data gathered in twenty-five industrial societies, primarily in Western Europe and the United States, between 1970 and 1986, Inglehart argues that "economic, technological, and sociopolitical changes have been transforming the cultures of advanced industrial societies in profoundly important ways" (Inglehart 1990, p. 3) Following Maslow's need hierarchy, according to which the need for food, shelter, and sex are on the lowest rung and must be satisfied before a person can move up the pyramid to its apex, self-actualization, Inglehart maintains that individuals are most concerned with the satisfaction of material needs and threats to their physical security. "Materialist" values, which are characteristic of less secure societies, economically and otherwise, Inglehart avers, are values that emphasize material security. In the area of politics, these would focus on such needs as strong leaders and order. In the realm of economics, the values emphasize economic growth and strong individual achievement motivation. In the area of sexuality and family norms, the emphasis would be on the maximization of reproduction within the two-parent family. And within the realm of religion, the emphasis is on a higher power and absolute rules. However, once the basic material needs are satisfied and physical safety is assured, they strive for "postmaterialist" values that entail the satisfaction of more remote needs, many of which are in the spiritual, aesthetic, and interpersonal realms. Their focus becomes self-fulfillment and personal autonomy, rather than identifying themselves with their families, localities, ethnic groups, or even nations. The "culture shift" is manifested in a declining respect for authority and decreased mass participation; an increasing emphasis on subjective well-being and quality of life concerns; an increasing emphasis on meaningful work; greater choice in the area of sexual norms; declining confidence in established religious institutions and declining rates of church attendance; and an increasing contemplation of the purpose and meaning of life. This shift, which entails a shift from central authority to individual autonomy, has taken place in "postmaterialist" society, that is, the West in the late-twentieth century.

It should be pointed out that greater focus on individual concerns, such as autonomy and self-fulfillment, among "postmaterialists" does not mean that they are more selfish or egotistical than materialists; those are normative terms. It does, however, mean that postmaterialists are less bound by group affiliations. Indeed, that should not be so surprising, since one of the basic distinguishing features of modernity, as compared to traditional society, is the greater emphasis on the individual (Bellah et al. 1996; Putnam 2000).

As the data from the studies by Levy, Levinsohn, and Katz in this volume indicate, Israel does not yet qualify, in this sense, as a highly developed postmodern society. Relatively few Israeli Jews wish to detach themselves from World Jewry, and only a minority agree that nationality should be separated from religion. Nevertheless, there is a segment—which is probably growing—of the society and culture that can characterized as postmodern. According to Charles Liebman (1997), Jewish society in Israel is composed of three distinct subcultures: the "religio-political," the "consumerist-postmodernist," and the "secular-Jewish." The "consumerist-postmodernist" subculture represents a small percentage of Israeli society (Waxman 1997) but a highly influential one. It is perhaps most pronounced in academia, especially among social scientists, as well as among those in the news media—reporters, journalists, and commentators—and among political and business elites.

Whether or not the "consumerist-postmodernist" culture will continue to grow cannot be predicted at this point in time. Since the onset of "Intifida Al Aqsa," there has been a sharp decrease in the sense of physical security within Israel and an increasing sense of fatalism vis-à-vis the Israeli-Palestinian conflict. These are not conditions that are likely to promote "consumerist-postmodernist" culture. In addition, the bombing of the World Trade Center in New York City, on Sept. 11, 2001, apparently by a group of Muslim-Arabs, appears to have shaken the sense of complacency that characterized much of the West in recent years. There is now a heightened sense of fear and anxiety concerning the future of global terrorism. The WTC bombing had unpredictable consequences in the United States where, for several decades, social scientists had been writing of a decreasing sense of community and civic involvement and increasing individualization and atomization in American society (Bellah et al. 1996; Putnam 2000). Few if any would have predicted the tremendous outpouring of civic involvement that manifested itself after the bombing. Whether this is indicative of a long-term shift remains to be seen. If it is, and it manifests in Israel as well, it will clearly have impact on many of the social issues discussed in this volume. The Israeli elections of 2003 appear to have diminished the power of sectarian cultural and religious parties, but the votes may be a reflection of fear and desperation. As such, they may indecisive for the long run social and cultural character of Israeli society.

On the other hand, especially in the event of a rapprochement between Israel and the Palestinian Authority, there may be reason to assume that the "consumerist-postmodernist" culture will grow, because of the strong influence of the United States and all of Western society on Israel. As the West becomes increasingly consumerist, there is every reason to assume that Israeli society will be influenced by these patterns and they will increasingly manifest themselves there. Consumerist-postmodernist culture is clearly a challenge to the norms and values that have prevailed in Israel during the twentieth century.

NOTES

1. The song, written by the Hebrew poet Naftali Herz Imber Imber, circa 1880, subsequently was adopted as the anthem of the Zionist Organization, and then as the national anthem of Israel. It reads,

> As long as deep in the heart
> The soul of a Jew yearns,
> And towards the East
> An eye looks to Zion,
> Our hope is not yet lost:
> The hope of two thousand years
> To be a free people in our land,
> The land of Zion and Jerusalem.

REFERENCES

Arens, Moshe. 2001. "Ignorance is Not Bliss." *Ha'aretz,* April 3.

Arian, Asher. 1989. *Politics in Israel: The Second Generation,* rev. ed. Chatham, N.J.: Chatham House.

Audenheimer, Alisa. 2001. "Income in the Upper Decile 31 Thousand Shekels; in the Lowest—711 Shekels." *Ha'aretz,* June 27.

Avineri, Shlomo. ca. 1986. Unpublished address on religious-secular relations in Israel.

Bellah, Robert N., Richard Madsen, William M. Sullivan, Ann Swidler, and Steven M. Tipton. 1996. *Habits of the Heart: Individualism and Commitment in American Life,* updated ed. Berkeley: University of California Press.

DellaPergola, Sergio. 2000. "World Jewish Population, 2000." *American Jewish Year Book* 100: 484–95.

DellaPergola, Sergio, Uzi Rebhun, and Mark Tolts. 2000. "Prospecting the Jewish Future: Population Projections 2000–2080." In *American Jewish Year Book 2000,* 103–46.

Friedmann, Daniel. 2000. "Either Conflict or Integration." *Ha'aretz,* October 17 (Hebrew).

Inglehart, Ronald. 1990. *Culture Shift in Advanced Industrial Society.* Princeton: Princeton University Press.

———. 1997. *Modernization and Postmodernization: Cultural, Economic, and Political Change in 43 Societies.* Princeton: Princeton University Press.

Kimmerling, Baruch. 2001. "Discrimination in the Declaration." *Ha'aretz Weekend Magazine,* Letters, August 10, p. 4 (Hebrew).

Kopp, Yaacov. 2001. "Economic Policy Should Aspire to Social Justice." *Ha'aretz,* June 28.

Liebman, Charles S. 1997. "Reconceptualizing the Culture Conflict among Israeli Jews." *Israel Studies* 2 (2) (Fall): 172–89.

Luz, Ehud. 1988. *Parallels Meet: Religion and Nationalism in the Early Zionist Movement 1882–1904*. Philadelphia: Jewish Publication Society.

Plotzker, Sever. 2001. "Poor with a Cellular Phone." *Yediot Achronot,* June 15.

Putnam, Robert D. 2000. *Bowling Alone: The Collapse and Revival of American Community.* New York: Simon and Schuster.

Rebhun, Uzi. (Forthcoming). "Jewish Identification in Contemporary America: Gans's Symbolic Ethnicity and Religiosity Theory Revisited." *Social Compass.*

Shapiro, Yonathan. 1996. *Politicians as a Hegemonic Class: The Case of Israel.* Tel Aviv: Sifriat Poalim (Hebrew).

Shelach, Ofer. 2001. "The Mythodology of Reserve Duty." *Yidiot Achronot,* July 13.

Sheref, Uri. 2001. "Banks for the Recovery of the Community." *Ha'aretz,* July 3.

Shtrasler, Nehemia. 2001. "This Deserves the Education Prize." *Ha'aretz,* June 29.

Tönnies, Ferdinand. [1887] 1957. *Community and Society,* trans. Charles. P. Loomis. New York: Harper Torchbooks.

Waxman, Chaim I. 1997. "Critical Sociology and the End of Ideology in Israel." *Israel Studies* 2 (1) (Spring): 194–210.

———. 2001. *Jewish Baby Boomers: A Communal Perspective.* Albany: State University of New York Press.

Zand, Shlomo. 2000. "To Whom Does the State Belong?" *Ha'aretz,* October 10 (Hebrew).

Contributors

Asher Arian is a Senior Fellow at the Israel Democracy Institute and Professor of Political Science at the University of Haifa. He is Distinguished Professor at the Graduate School of the City University of New York.

Gabriel Ben-Dor is Professor of Political Science and Director of the Center for National Security Studies at the University of Haifa in Israel. A former Rector of the university and a former President of the Israel Political Science Association, he has written widely on Middle East politics, the political role of the military, ethnic politics, national security, and strategic studies.

Eliezer Ben-Rafael is Professor of Sociology at Tel-Aviv University where he holds the Weinberg Chair of Political Sociology and is the President of the International Institute of Sociology. His books include *Jewish Identities: The Answers of the Sages of Israel to Ben-Gurion* (2001, Hebrew and French); *Crisis and Transformation: The Kibbutz at Century's End* (1997, Hebrew and English); *Language, Identity and Social Division: The Case of Israel* (1994); *Ethnicity, Religion and Class in Israel* (1991).

Yoram Bilu is a Professor at the Hebrew University of Jerusalem and has a joint appointment in the Department of Psychology, where he holds the Sylvia Bauman Chair, and the Department of Sociology and Anthropology. His research interests lie in the areas of psychological and psychiatric anthropology, anthropology of religion, and Israeli society. His recent publications include: *Grasping Land: Space and Place in Contemporary Israeli Discourse and Experience* (Albany: State University of New York Press, 1997, coedited with Eyal Ben-Ari) and *Without Bounds: The Life and Death of Rabbi Ya'aqov Wazana* (Detroit: Wayne State University Press, 2000).

Sergio DellaPergola is Professor and former Chair of the Avraham Harman Institute of Contemporary Jewry. A leading Israeli demographer, his work has largely dealt with social and cultural aspects of population across the Jewish Diaspora and in Israel.

Elan Ezrachi is the Director of the "Jewish Experience of Israel" at the Jewish Agency's Education Department and the lay chair of "Panim," an umbrella organization for Jewish Renaissance and Renewal in Israel.

Steven J. Gold is Professor and Associate Chair in the Department of Sociology at Michigan State University. He is the author of several books on the sociology of migration and ethnicity, and numerous articles on immigrant families, ethnic self-employment, qualitative methods, and community development. His first book, *Refugee Communities: A Comparative Field Study,* was a finalist for the Robert Park Award in 1993. His most recent book, *The Israeli Diaspora,* was published by the University of Washington Press and Routledge in 2001.

Hanna Herzog, Professor in the Department of Sociology and Anthropology, Tel Aviv University, specializes in political sociology, political communication, and sociology of gender. She is the author of *Gendering Politics—Women in Israel* (Ann Arbor: University of Michigan Press, 1999).

Steven Kaplan is Professor of Comparative Religion and African Studies at the Hebrew University of Jerusalem. He is the author of several books and numerous articles on the religious history of Ethiopia and on Ethiopian immigrants to Israel.

Elihu Katz is currently Professor of Communication at the University of Pennsylvania, Emeritus Professor of Sociology and Communication at the Hebrew University, and former Research Director of the Guttman Institute.

Elazar Leshem is Adjunct Professor at the Paul Baerwald School of Social Work of the Hebrew University of Jerusalem. He serves as the Chair of its Joseph J. Schwartz M.A. Program in the Management of Community Organizations, Non-Profit Organizations and Public Policy.

Hanna Levinsohn is a Senior Researcher and Coordinator of the Continuing Survey of the Guttman Institute of Applied Social Research. Her special field of interest is public opinion on current political issues, including the "peace process" and Israeli broadcasts.

Shlomit Levy has been a Senior Research Associate at the Louis Guttman Israel Institute of Applied Social Research since 1965, and is a Visiting Researcher at the Institute of Contemporary Jewry of the Hebrew University of Jerusalem. Her major interest is in the integration of theory construction with data analysis, and she has written extensively on Jewish identity and identification, Zionism, values, well-being, and social problem indicators.

Dalia Ofer is a Max and Rita Haber Professor of Holocaust and East European Studies and the Academic Head of the Vidal Sassoon International Center for the Study of Antisemitism of the Hebrew University of Jerusalem. A winner of the Jewish Book Award, she is the author and editor of numerous books in Hebrew and English and has published over fifty articles on the history of the Holocaust, immigration to Palestine and Israel, gender, and the memory of the Holocaust in Israel.

Ami Pedahzur is a Lecturer at the Department of Political Science, University of Haifa. He is the author of a work in Hebrew about extreme right-wing political parties in Israel (Ramot, Tel-Aviv University, 2000), as well as numerous articles on the subjects of political extremism, political violence, and political parties.

Uzi Rebhun is Lecturer at the A. Harman Institute of Contemporary Jewry, the Hebrew University of Jerusalem. He is the author of *Migration, Community and Identification: Jews in Late 20th Century America* (Hebrew, 2001).

Hagar Salamon is a Senior Lecturer in Jewish and Comparative Folklore at the Hebrew University of Jerusalem, and a Senior Research Fellow at the Harry S. Truman Institute for the Advancement of Peace. Her publications include *The Hyena People: Ethiopian Jews in Christian Ethiopia* (1999); *Ethiopian Jews: An Annotated Bibliography* (1998, with Steven Kaplan), as well as many articles on the culture of Ethiopian Jews both in Ethiopia and Israel.

Eliezer Schweid is Professor Emeritus of Jewish Thought at the Hebrew University of Jerusalem. He is a very prolific scholar specializing in Judaism and modern Jewish philosophy, and was awarded the Israel Prize in 1994.

Ze'ev Shavit teaches sociology at the Open University, Tel Aviv.

Gabriel Sheffer is a Professor of Political Science at the Hebrew University of Jerusalem and has written extensively on ethno-national diasporas. His forthcoming book *Diaspora Politics: At Home Abroad,* was published by Cambridge University Press in 2003.

Moshe Sicron is a Professor Emeritus at the Department of Population Studies, the Hebrew University of Jerusalem, and former Director of the Israel Central Bureau of Statistics.

Sammy Smooha is Professor of Sociology at the University of Haifa. A specialist in comparative ethnic relations, he has published widely on the internal divisions in Israeli society and on Israel in a comparative perspective. His books include *Israel: Pluralism and Conflict* and *Arabs and Jews in Israel*, vol. 1 and vol. 2.

Ephraim Tabory is Senior Lecturer in the Department of Sociology at Bar Ilan University and is Deputy Director of that university's Interdisciplinary Graduate Program on Conflict Management and Resolution. He has written widely on Conservative and Reform Judaism in Israel.

Menachem Topel is a sociologist and a member of Kibbutz Mefalsim (since 1963). He is a kibbutz researcher, and Head of the Desk of Social Studies Research at Yad Tabenkin, Israel. He lectures on sociology, technocracy, and the kibbutz at the Academic Colleges of Ashkelon and Sapir. His studies include *Power Elite in an Egalitarian Community* (Hebrew); *Organization, Power, and Leadership in the Kibbutz Community* (Hebrew); and *Technocrats as Agents of Change in an Egalitarian Society* (Hebrew).

Chaim I. Waxman is Professor of Sociology and Jewish Studies at Rutgers University. He co-edited *Jews in America* (1997), and co-authored the *Historical Dictionary of Zionism* (2000). His most recent book is *Jewish Baby Boomers: A Communal Perspective* (2001).

Ephraim Yaar-Yuchtman is a professor of sociology and social psychology and the holder of the Rappaport Chair of Sociology of Labor. He previously served as Dean of the Faculty of Social Sciences and chaired the Israeli Committee for Research Funds (The Israeli Ford Foundation). He has published several books and numerous articles in scholarly journals in the areas of Israeli society, public opinion, the Israeli-Arab conflict, social inequality, work and organizations. Since 1994 he has written a monthly column, known as the "Peace Index" for the Israeli daily, *Haaretz*.

Index

Abortion, 210, 435

Absorption centers, 100, 123, 246

Abu-Hatsera, Israel (Baba Sali), 382, 384–85, 388, 389, 390

Advisor to the Prime Minister on the Status of Women, 211

Affirmative action, 62, 65, 139, 363

Africa: foreign workers from, 21. *See also* North Africa; South Africa

African Jews. *See* Asian and African Jews; Ethiopian Jews; Mizrahim; Oriental Jews

Agricultural settlements, 5, 8, 54

Agudat Israel: Ashkenazi ultra-Orthodox supporting, 71; and Bene Israel, 230; in coalition government, 10; Declaration of Independence signed by, 346; in elections, 1949–2001, 178, 223; Schneerson supporting, 233; Shas and, 223, 224; and status quo agreement, 228; in United Torah Jewry, 227, 435

Agunot, 211, 213, 216

AIDS, 122, 130–31, 144

Al-Haj, Majid, 107, 108, 111, 281, 355

Alignment, 177, 188, 189, 190

(Aliya). See Jewish immigration to Israel; Jewish settlers in Palestine

Almog, Oz, 323, 327n.3

Aloni, Shulamit, 207, 210

Alter, Simcha Bunin, 224

Alterman, Nathan, 399, 403

American Jews: belief in God among, 276; concern for Israel among, 427; Conservative and Reform Judaism compatible with social environment, 308; and the Conversion Bill, 297; of Eastern European origin, 25; and Ethiopian Jews, 142–43; as failing to sustain a secular Jewish identity, 323; "haredization" of Orthodoxy of, 228; Israeli emigrants, 449, 450–51, 452, 456–57; as percentage of World Jewry, 473; Soviet Jewish immigration, 81; as transforming Jewish commitment, 325; in "Who is a Jew" debate, 15

American Mizrachi Organization, 225

Amharic language, 138

Amital, Yehuda, 233

Amuka, 387

Am Ve-Olam (People and World) program, 252

Anielewicz, Mordechai, 398

Antisemitism, 4, 139, 430, 438, 439, 440

Arab-Palestinian women: in Arab patriarchal tradition, 200, 201; cooperation with Jewish women, 217; familial roles for women, 203; political representation of, 196, 197

Arab parties, 176, 356, 357, 360, 431

Arabs: Muslims and Christians among, 469. *See also* Arab-Palestinian women; Israel-Arab conflict; Israeli Arabs; Palestinian Arabs

Arafat, Yasser, 67

Aran, Gideon, 372

Aran, Zalman, 252

Ararat (television documentary), 406

Arens, Moshe, 472

Arian, Asher, 471

Army, the. *See* Israeli Defense Forces

Ashdod, 386, 387

Ashkenazim: both major parties run by, 191; as charter group in Israeli society, 56, 70; class status of, 60; collective memory of, 55; cultural differences from Oriental Jews, 12–16, 49, 52–69; cultural hegemony of, 56–57; economic gap with Oriental Jews, 467; emigration from Israel, 448, 450; formation of, 68; as fully assimilated, 69; globalization and, 66; in Jewish population of Palestine in 1948, 8; on Judaism in public sphere, 276, 277; kosher kept among, 272; Labor Party supported by, 58, 183, 189, 190, 192; life-cycle ceremonies observed among, 270; marriage within, 68; middle-class housing for, 57; and multiculturalism, 72; Oriental Jews matching population of, 12; patterns of observance among, 273; political agenda set by, 59; political differences among, 17, 183, 189; in the professions, 60; religious identity among, 269; Soviet Jews' attitude toward, 103, 104; ultra-Orthodox as predominantly, 269